The Nikon Way

The Nikon Way

including the Nikkormat

HERBERT KEPPLER

Focal Press
London & Boston

Focal press
is an imprint of the Butterworth Group
which has principal offices in
London, Boston, Durban, Singapore, Sydney, Toronto, Wellington

First published 1977
Second edition 1978
Third edition 1982

British Library Cataloguing in Publication Data

Keppler, H.
The Nikon way. – 3rd ed.
1. Nikon camera 2. Nikkormat camera
I. Title
771.3′1 TR263.N5

ISBN 0-240-51185-9

Photoset by Butterworths Litho Preparation Department
Printed in England by Page Bros. Ltd., Norwich, Norfolk
Bound by the Dorstel Press Ltd., Harlow, Essex

Contents

SLR principles

The Nikon and Nikkormat cameras are 35 mm single-lens reflexes. Generally, they are used at eye-level, but some Nikons may be used with waist-level finders. With a single-lens reflex, you view the world through your lens in a sharply delineated picture frame. You look neither up nor down. You see the image straight ahead of you. The camera is an extension of your eye. Turn the focusing ring, and the image suddenly becomes crisp. However, not all parts of the subject are equally crisp. If you need to, you can either refocus on the important parts, or close down the iris of your lens sufficiently to render both subject and additional areas in adequate sharpness. By changing lenses you can adjust the picture area to see far greater angles than your eye can see, or you can narrow your view with telephoto lenses to see incredible detail at distances. And all this is clearly visible on your viewfinder screen.

The first time a photographer looks through a single-lens reflex, he can hardly stop himself from exploring his immediate surroundings through the eye of his new-found instrument. The bright large viewfinder shows him close-ups, wide angle and telescopic views. Suddenly, his equipment really shows him the pictures he can get. I have never known a single-lens-reflex owner to lose his awe of the magic view through the finder. The Nikon-Nikkormat cameras and lenses are excellently made examples of the single-lens-reflex design. To make sure nothing can be lost, the camera and normal lenses are backed up with an enormous array of accessory lenses and equipment.

Interchangeability

Much of this equipment is interchangeable. The original Nikon F remained unchanged for 15 years. By fitting the appropriate viewfinder, the owner of a 1959 F can update his camera to any of the range up to the final 1974 Photomic FTn model. The lenses remain interchangeable to date. Within this basic compatibility, Nippon Kogaku have introduced improvements in design and operation. These include improved motorised transports and

How the Nikon and Nikkormat work

When you are viewing and focusing, light enters fully-opened lens iris diaphragm, is reflected upwards by mirror to focusing screen where condensing lens brightens image. The pentaprism above turns the image round for eye-level viewing and reverses it to be correct right to left.

So you see a correctly oriented image through the magnifying eyepiece.

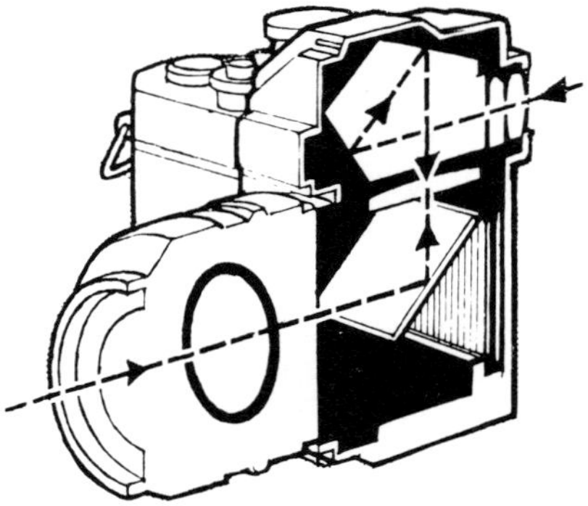

When you press shutter release to take a picture, the iris diaphragm of the lens closes to the aperture you have predetermined, the mirror swings upwards allowing the light from the lens to strike the film which is exposed through the travelling focal plane shutter opening.

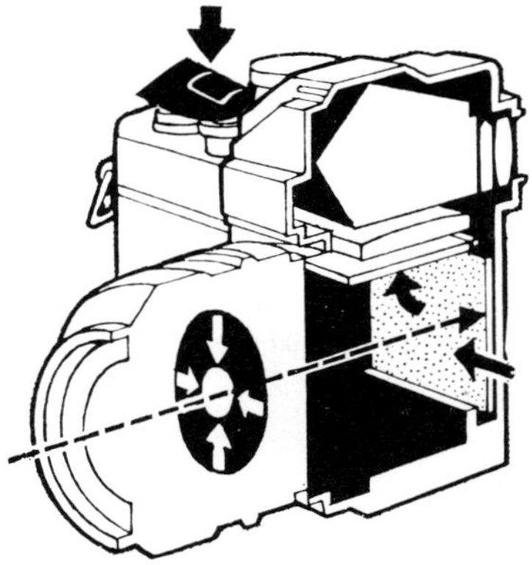

At exposure end, the lens iris diaphragm re-opens instantly, the mirror swings down again in place, the shutter closes and you again see the viewing and focusing image through the finder. At fast shutter speeds, these actions take place so swiftly you will notice only a brief blink through the finder.

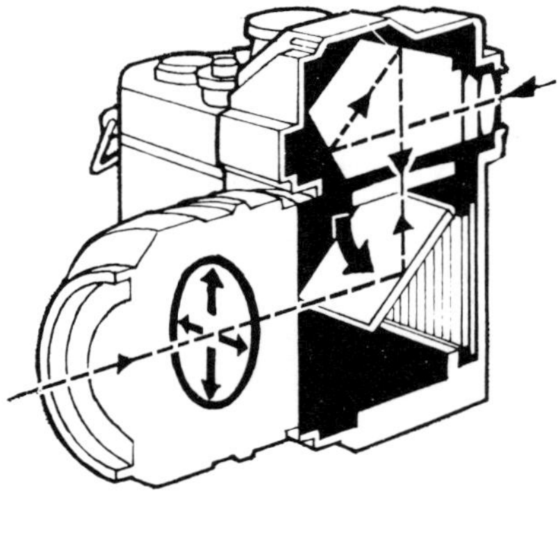

Shutter and aperture

The focal plane shutter on most Nikons consists of two travelling metal foil curtains. The width of the gap between the two determines the shutter speed. High shutter speeds: 1/500 to 1/2000 s have narrow slits, moderate shutter speeds such as 1/125 and 1/250 s have a medium slit while long shutter speeds of 1/60 or slower allow the entire film to be exposed at once. Nikkormats operate in much the same manner except the shutter is composed of metal blades that travel vertically. With Nikkormats the shutter is open completely even at speeds of 1/125 s.

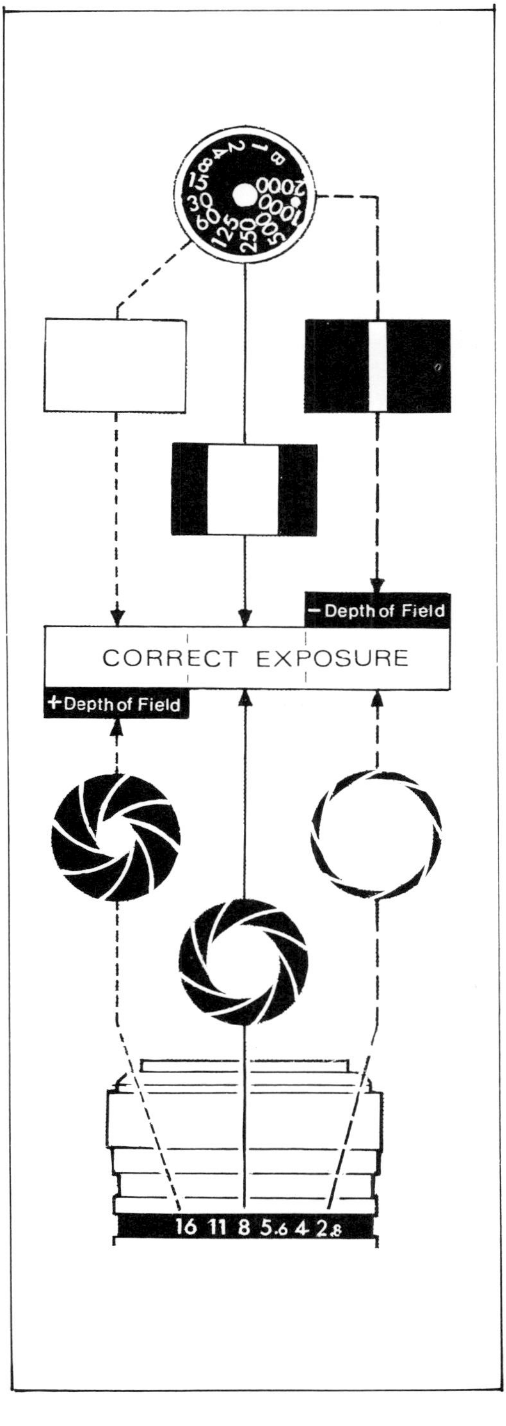

A multi-blade metal leaf iris within each Nikkor or Nikon lens varies the size of the lens aperture. The larger the *f*/number, the smaller the aperture.

These two controls: shutter speed and lens aperture, vary your exposure.

A fast speed and wide aperture, such as 1/2000 at *f*/2.8; a moderate speed and aperture, such as 1/250 at *f*/8; and a slow speed and small aperture, such as 1/60 at *f*/16 all give the same exposure.

Your choice depends on whether you wish to a high shutter speed to stop subject action (and also possible camera shake) or you would rather have increased depth of field (depth of sharpness) which you will obtain with the smaller lens apertures.

automated exposure systems. We will go into great detail to differentiate the new models from the old and explain just how they differ and what they can do that the earlier models cannot.

On the Nikkormat with its built-in metering system no viewfinder updating is possible, of course; but in terms of accessories such as lenses, the same timelessness is true.

Modern viewing

A five-sided prism (a pentaprism) is set on the tiny ground glass of the waist-level 35 mm single-lens reflex. This produces a right-way-up, right-way-round image. (In fact, the prism on your camera has eight sides. This is because three unused corners have been cut off to reduce its size.) A magnifying eyepiece at the back of the prism enlarges the image so it can be clearly seen for both viewing and focusing. A condenser built into the focusing screen evens out the brightness of the image. This is almost invariably of the collapsed (fresnel) type, consisting of a series of concentric ridges.

Today's focusing screens, such as those used in the Nikons and Nikkormats, produce amazingly crisp viewing images corner to corner and edge to edge.

Even with a pentaprism, some photographers find it difficult to see the precise point of exact focus on a ground-glass screen. Unlike separate coincident or split-image rangefinders, the screen image of an SLR requires judgement of when the image is at its sharpest. The smaller the maximum aperture of the lens, the more difficult the focusing becomes (since the image is darker and the depth of field greater). Wide-angle lenses with their vast depth of field often seem almost impossible to focus accurately.

The solution is found in cementing, inserting or moulding two angled prism halves below the central portion of the focusing screen. Looking at the centre of the screen, the photographer sees a small bisected circle. When the image is not in focus on the screen, the image appears split and misaligned. Focusing the lens lines up the split image within the circle.

Many photographers find it a great help. It works well with both moderately wide-angle and long lenses in addition to the normal lens. However, it does need a line (usually vertical) to bisect when out of focus and to line up when in focus. When there is no straight line in the picture at the focused plane, the split-image rangefinder is less useful. The photographer once again has to depend on his judgement. To help, the manufacturers normally surround the rangefinder with a microprism collar, so that the fresnel rings do not add extra confusion.

The second focusing aid is the microprism. The prism collar is broken up into an area of tiny three- or four-sided pyramids, essentially forming a whole field of tiny split-image rangefinders operating in many directions. When the

Focusing systems

A. Plain screen shows fuzzy subject image when out of focus. Image becomes clear when the focus is sharp.

B. Microprism area shatters out of focus image but snaps into crispness when focus is correct.

C. Split-image rangefinder image splits and is displaced laterally when out of focus. Image parts line up when in proper focus.

D. When image is in focus, left, light strikes rangefinder centre thus transmitting unsplit image. Out of focus light, right, causes wedges to deflect light in opposite directions, separating image.

E. Correctly chosen split-image rangefinder, left, allows both halves of circle to be seen easily. Steep split-image wedges, right, such as you might want for wide angle lens, transmit too large a light ray bundle with tele lenses causing darkening of one prism circle. Focal length of lens and wedge angle must match for best results.

F. Large lens aperture, left, provides sufficiently small light ray bundle to be seen easily. Too small an aperture produces larger light ray bundle, right, impossible for eye to see completely. Hence, one semi-circle will darken when focusing at too small a lens opening.

G. With cross hairs in clear spot scientific focusing screen, image is in focus when subject remains stationary in respect to cross hairs if eye is moved from side to side as illustrated. This is known as parallax focusing.

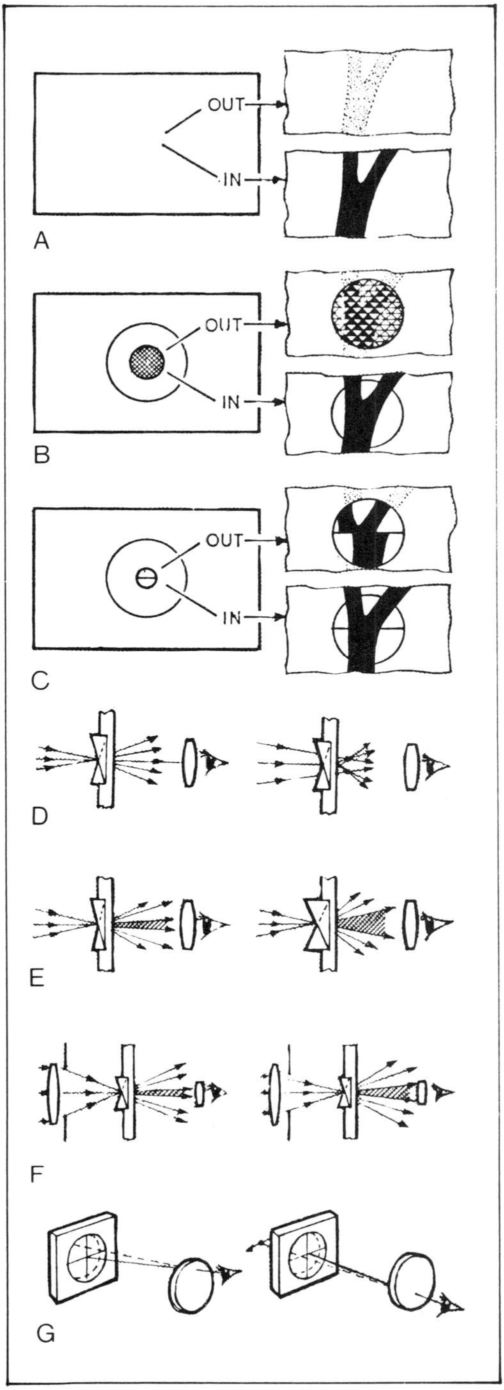

image is out of focus, the microprism collar area tends to shimmer and appear blurred. At the precise point of focus, the microprism area steadies. Both types of focusing aids have their enthusiastic users, and a combination is now the standard Nikkormat screen while the Nikon F2 offers you a choice. There are other focusing devices for special purposes that we'll take up later.

Another essential feature for a modern 35 mm SLR is the automatic diaphragm mechanism. The focusing screen of any view or reflex camera is at its brightest when the lens aperture is wide open. In addition, the lens is easier to focus at full aperture because the depth of field (zone of adequately sharp focus) is then very shallow. Although there is really only one plane of sharpest focus, no matter the aperture, sharpness falls off gradually in front of and behind the main plane – more swiftly at large apertures than at small. Therefore the exact focus of a lens is easier to find at a large aperture than at a small aperture.

However, most photographs are not taken at full aperture. The lens must be closed down to the smaller aperture after viewing and focusing, but before taking the picture. Today, 35 mm single-lens reflexes have built-in mechanisms which automatically close the lens to any predetermined aperture and then reopen it again directly after exposure.

Coupled with the rapid-return mirror (which flips upward during exposure and swiftly returns to the down viewing position afterwards), the automatic diaphragm gives the user the impression of almost continuous bright viewing, even though in reality the finder is blacked-out during the instant of exposure. If you are looking through the finder of your SLR, you see everything but the instant of exposure. This short black-out doesn't seem to have much effect in practice.

These particular features, then – pentaprism, split-image rangefinder or microprism, automatic diaphragm and rapid-return mirror – are the essential ingredients of a 35 mm SLR, and make it different from any other camera.

Nikons and Nikkormats

Since entering the field in 1959, Nippon Kogaku have supplied various ranges of SLR cameras.

The original Nikon F continued virtually unchanged for 15 years. It was superseded in 1972 by the modernised F2 model. The newer model has provision for an increased range of accessories including automatic exposure control. The various Nikon F and Nikon F2 model designations over the years have to do basically with changes in the interchangeable metering system prism. The basic camera remained the same.

During 1977 Nippon Kogaku introduced a smaller, lighter Nikon camera body of new design starting with the Nikon FM. Additionally, the Nikkormat EL and ELW were replaced by the Nikon EL2 (rather than Nikkormat). The FE of 1978 represented the EL2 type of automation in the FM body. The EM of 1979 is a comparably new departure in design – a simplified SLR. In 1981 Nikon introduced a much-advanced EM-type model, the FG, with program automation, manual speeds and TTL flash metering; and an advanced FM2.

A completely new, smaller and lighter F model was finally created in 1980, the Nikon F3, with built-in auto-exposure capability, a liquid-crystal display of shutter speeds within the finder and much more.

The Nikkorex, introduced in 1960, was very different to the Nikon F. It had a diaphragm shutter and a built-in coupled meter. Attachments converted the fixed-mount *f*/2.5 50 mm lens to *f*/4 35 or 90 mm lenses. Right-way-round eye-level viewing was through an ingenious mirror system instead of a pentaprism. This was not removable. In 1962, this camera was restyled to become the Nikkorex II.

As an alternative to the 50 mm lens, the Nikkorex 35 Zoom mounted a 43–86 mm *f*/4 lens. This, too, was permanently fixed to the body.

The Nikkorex F, introduced in 1961, was more conventional. It used a vertical-run metal focal plane shutter, and mounted Nikon F lenses (from 28 mm to 1000 mm) in the normal Nikon bayonet. It could be fitted with an accessory exposure meter coupled to the shutter speed and lens aperture.

Nikon cameras

1959 Nikon F although improved constantly remained basically same in body until discontinued in 1975.

1962 Nikon F Photomic was Nikon F but prism had built-in meter with cell at front of prism.

1964 F Photomic T was first through-the-lens meter Nikon.

1967 F Photomic TN featured centre-weighted metering.

1969 Nikon Photomic FTN featured shutter speed visible in viewfinder, semi-auto indexing of lenses.

1972 Nikon F2 has new body, speeds 10 to 1/2000 second, aperture and shutter speeds visible in finder.

1972 Nikon F2S prism, features light emitting diodes and contacts for EE exposure control unit.

1977 Nikon F2A, similar to F2 but with automatic aperture indexing.

1977 Nikon F2AS, extended metering range and diode readout.

1977 Nikon FM is a lighter, compact camera design with LED finder readout,provision for 3.5 fps motor.

1977 Nikon EL2 is similar to Nikkormat ELW but has silicon photo diode metering system, autoexposure compensator, automatic aperture indexing.

1978 Nikon FE is based on FM body but has aperture-priority auto exposure, shutter-speed needle indicator in finder, manual speeds.

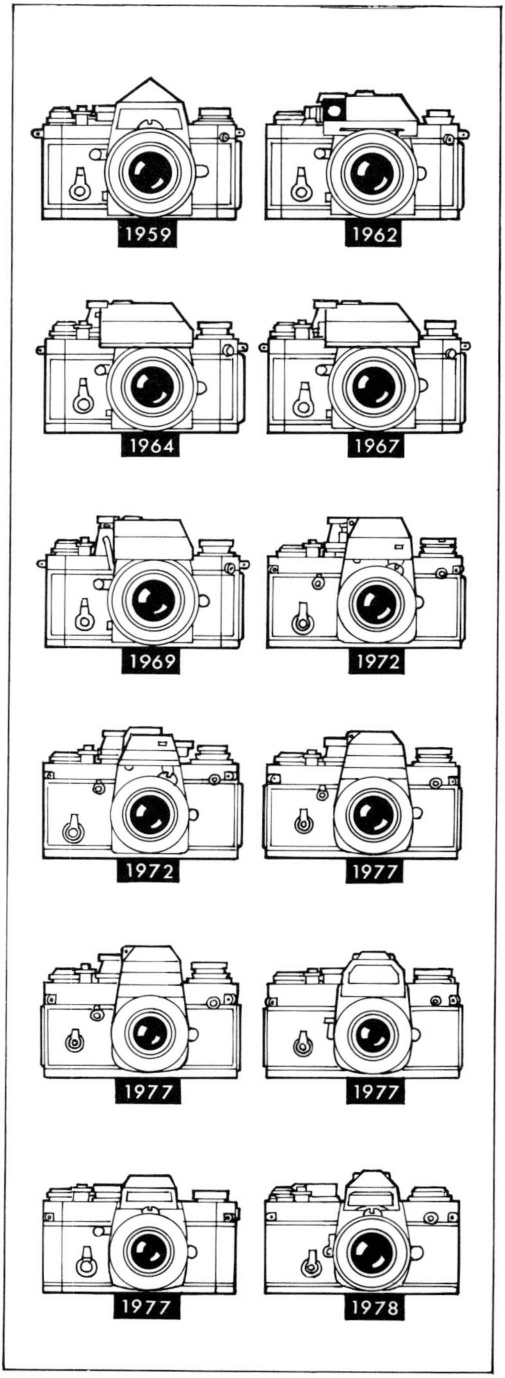

1979 Nikon EM ultra compact has aperture-priority auto exposure only, audible signals, special accessory flash, auto winder.

1980 Nikon F3 replaces F2, with auto exposure, liquid crystal display exposure readout, interchangeable finders, screens, auto flash metering from film surface, special flash and 5fps motor accessories.

1981 Nikon FG is based on EM body but has choice of aperture-priority exposure, program exposure or manual control, LED viewfinder and TTL electronic flash metering.

1981 Nikon FM2 is almost identical to FM but with top shutter speed of $1/4000$ s, with flash sync at $1/200$ s, and provides interchangeable focusing screens.

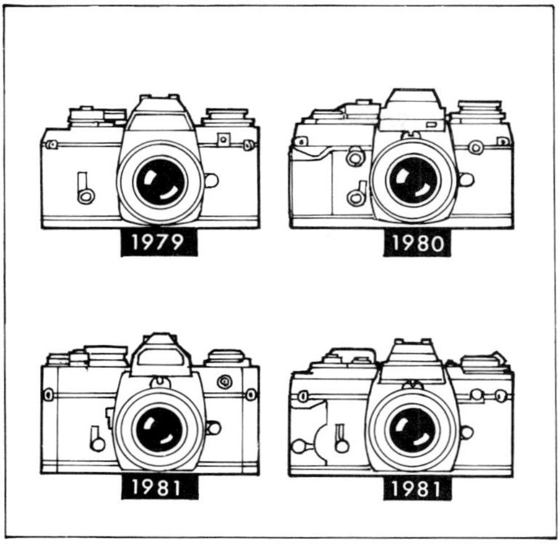

Nikkormats

1965 Nikkormat FT has built-in, averaging meter, manual indexing of lenses, no interchangeable finders or screens.

1965 Nikkormat FS is same as FT but no meter or mirror lockup.

1967 Nikkormat FTN has automatic lens indexing, centre-weighted meter.

1975 Nikkormat FTN modified, detail changes, some had hot shoe.

1975 Nikkormat FT2 has ASA index lock, single PC sync terminal, hot shoe sync, combined split image and microprism screen.

1977 Nikkormat FT3 is similar to FT2 but has automatic aperture indexing.

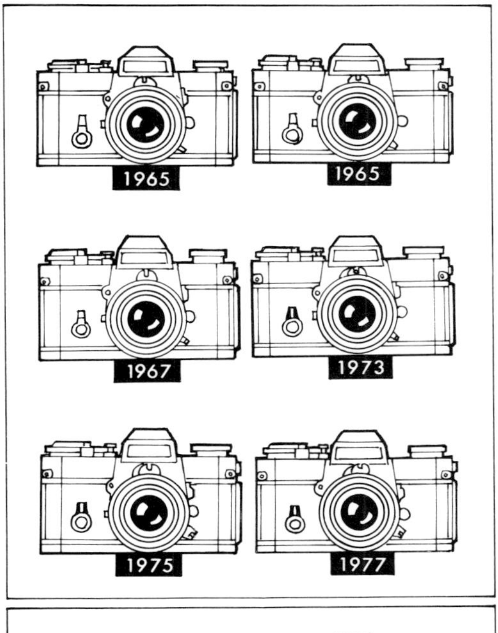

1972 Nikkormat EL has fully automatic exposure available, shutter speeds visible in viewfinder.

1976 Nikkormat ELW is basically same as EL but accepts power winder.

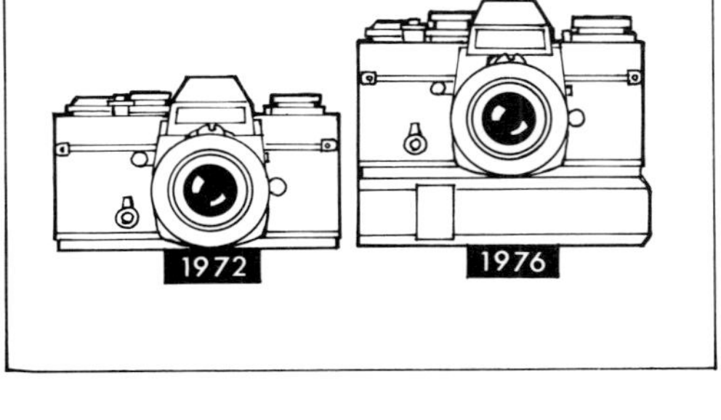

Viewing was through a fixed pentaprism. This Camera Way Book does not describe the operation of Nikkorex cameras. However, much of the information on Nikkormats can be applied to the Nikkorex F.

The Nikkormat (or Nikomat) FT was a redesigned through-the-lens metering replacement for the Nikkorex F. This became the main 'simpler' SLR produced by Nippon Kogaku. The FTn, FT2 and FT3 models differ mainly in their through-the-lens exposure meters and lens-coupling systems. There have been small improvements over the years, such as the addition of an accessory shoe flash contact, ASA setting lock, plastic-tipped wind lever, and an exterior threaded shutter release button to take the standard Nikon collar cable release. The details are described in the section on Nikkormat metering (page 151). For a while, a meterless version, the Nikkormat FS, was available. As well as lacking a meter, this camera differed from the other Nikkormats by the absence of a mirror lock. Apart from these differences, you operate the FS just like the FT, FTn, FT2 and FT3.

The other Nikkormat model is the EL. It has an electronically controlled shutter. This can be coupled to the exposure meter to give fully automatic shutter speed control with any lens. The 1977 improved version is the Nikon EL2.

All Nikkormat cameras as well as the Nikon EL2 have now been discontinued in manufacture (although they are often available in stores with used-camera departments). We will cover the operation of these cameras, as well as all new Nikons as they become available, in the appropriate chapters of this book.

Nikon F2

The Nikon F2 combines the 1972 35 mm camera engineering technology with the basic camera design of its predecessor, the Nikon F. The shutter is a dimpled titanium focal plane type with speeds from 10 seconds to $1/2000$ second plus B and T. Shutter speed selection between $1/80$ and $1/2000$ second is stepless. The built-in self-timer operates between 2 and 10 s. FP and X syncronisation is correctly and automatically adjusted with changes in shutter speeds. M and MF-class bulbs are also usable. The maximum speed for electronic flash is $1/80$ s. The camera had a threaded 3 mm (PC) socket plus a hot shoe contact for cordless flash.

The camera body consists of a die-cast aluminium alloy shell, base-plate mirror box, front cover, top plate, bottom cover and camera back. It takes lenses in the Nikon bayonet. Compared with the F camera, the body has more rounded corners, edges and front escutcheon plate. Wind lever, rewind crank, latching mechanism and shutter release fingerguard have been redesigned. Neck strap eyelets have been moved to improve balance, and have steel inserts to minimise wear. The camera accepts a motor drive unit and 250-exposure magazine without modification. The body is available in satin chrome or black finish.

The body may be fitted with one of a number of viewfinders. As the Nikon F2, the camera has a plain eye-level pentaprism finder in chrome or black. As the Nikon F2 or F2A Photomic, it has an eye-level prism finder with built-in through-the-lens, centre-weighted exposure meter. As the Nikon F2S, F2Sb or F2AS Photomic, the same basic camera comes with more sophisticated through-the-lens metering systems featuring more electronic control and light-emitting diodes (LEDs) for greater accuracy, less chance of shock damage and greater meter-reading visibility in poor light. However, to simplify discussion of the various F2 models, we will simply refer to all F2 cameras, no matter the variations in metering, as the F2 – until we discuss the metering systems themselves. A type-A screen with a matte-fresnel field and central split-image rangefinder is readily interchangeable with screens for special requirements. Speed and aperture indicators are visible in the finder. There is a depth-of-field preview button, an enlarged rapid-return mirror minimising image cut-off even with extreme telephotos, and mirror lock-up control.

The F2 or F2A Photomic finder provides through-the-lens centre-weighted measurement at full aperture or shooting aperture. The meter needle is visible in the finder and on the prism housing. The circuit is powered by two 1.5V silver-oxide batteries located in the camera base plate. There is a battery check button. The meter has a sensitivity range from EV1 to EV17 with a film having an ASA of 100 which is equivalent to a range of *f*/1.4 to *f*/8 at 1⁄2000 s. Films with ASA of 6 to 6400 can be accommodated.

The film-advance lever operates through 120° single or multiple throw. It has a stand-off angle of 20°, and also serves as the meter on/off switch. The removable and hinged camera back has a film box end reminder clip holder. There is a built-in ready light for electronic flash visible in the Photomic finder eyepiece. The take-up spool has six slots for easier loading. The shutter release can be locked.

The camera body is 152.2 × 102 × 65 mm (6 × 4 × 2 9⁄16 in) and weighs 840 g (1.85 lb). Standard lenses are usually chosen from the 50 mm *f*/2, *f*/1.4 or 55 mm *f*/1.2 Nikkor auto lenses. The more recent lenses have multiple layer coating.

Nikon F

The Nikon F, introduced in 1959, has a dimpled titanium focal plane shutter (although a very few early 1959 cameras were made with cloth shutters) with speeds from 1 to 1⁄1000 second plus B and T. The built-in self-timer operates between 3 and 10 seconds. FP and X synchronisation is manually adjustable with a selector. M and MF class bulbs are also usable. Electronic flash can be used at 1⁄60 s or slower. The camera has a 3 mm (PC) socket (threaded on the later models) plus a hot shoe contact for Nikon cordless flash units.

As the Nikon F, the camera has a plain interchangeable eye-level pentaprism finder in chrome or black. 100 per cent of the picture field can be seen. The standard type-A screen with matte-fresnel field and central split-image rangefinder is readily interchangeable. Shutter speed is visible in the finder. There is a depth-of-field preview button and a mirror lock-up control.

The Photomic FTn finder provides through-the-lens centre-weighted measurement at full aperture or shooting aperture; with meter needle visible in finder or on top of the prism housing. The circuit is powered by two 1.3 V mercury batteries within the Photomic finder head. There is a battery check button.

The meter has a sensitivity range from EV2 to EV17 with a film having an ASA of 100, the equivalent of *f*/1.4 at ½ s to *f*/11 at 1/1000 s. Films with an ASA range from 6 to 6400 can be accommodated. Among other features are a 135° single or multi-throw film wind and rapid advance lever with a free throw angle of 15°. (Later models have a plastic-tipped lever.) The removable back allows motor drives and 250-exposure backs to be fitted.

The camera body is 147 × 102 × 67 mm (5 25/32 × 4 1/32 × 2 5/8 in) and weighs 860 g (1.9 lb). It uses the same lenses as the Nikon F2 Photomic previously discussed.

Nikkormat

The 1975 Nikkormat FT2 and 1977 FT3 have a multiple-blade all-metal Copal Square S focal plane shutter with speeds from 1 to 1/1000 s plus B. The built-in self-timer operates at about 8 s. A single screw-threaded 3 mm (PC) flash contact and an accessory shoe contact are used for flash. At speeds of 1/125 s and below they are X-synchronised; at higher speeds they are M-synchronised.

The camera body is made of a die-cast aluminium alloy and finished in chrome plating or black. It has a non-interchangeable eye-level prism finder with built-in, through-the-lens centre-weighted exposure meter. 92 per cent of the picture field can be seen. The standard K screen has a matte-fresnel field and central split-image rangefinder surrounded by a micro-prism collar. The shutter speed and lens aperture are visible in the finder. The exposure meter needle is displayed both in the viewfinder and on the top plate. There is a depth-of-field preview button and a mirror lock-up control. The meter is switched on with the film transport lever; it provides centre-weighted through-the-lens meter measurement at full or shooting aperture.

Shutter speeds are set by a ring round the lens mount, and ASA speeds by an index below the lens. This index is locked unless the catch on the shutter speed setting lever is pulled.

The meter circuit is powered by a 1.5 V silver-oxide cell located in the base plate of the camera. The meter has a sensitivity range from EV3 to EV17 with a film having an ASA of 100, equivalent of *f*/1.4 at ¼ s to *f*/11 at 1/1000 s. Film with an ASA range of 6 to 1600 can be used.

Among the other features are a 135° single throw film and shutter rapid advance lever with a free throw angle of 20° which also serves as the meter switch. There is an independent mirror lock-up control. The back is hinged. The Nikkormat FT2 and FT3 accept most Nikon F and F2 accessories except interchangeable finders, screens, motors and backs. The FT3 differs from the FT2 only in having AI (automatic indexing) of lenses.

The camera body is 148 × 95 × 54 mm ($5^{13}/_{16}$ × $3^{3}/_{4}$ × $2^{1}/_{8}$ in) and weighs 765 g (1.68 lb). This camera closely resembles the FTn it replaced.

The FTn, however, had double 3 mm (PC) flash socket (M or X synchronised), no hot shoe and film-speed setting lock. It was normally supplied with either a split-image rangefinder or a microprism spot in its focusing screen. The meter power is from a 1.3 V mercury cell.

Nikkormat EL, ELW and Nikon EL2

The Nikkormat EL, introduced in 1972, is a fully automatic exposure reflex camera. The shutter is an electronically timed, six-blade, all-metal Copal Square ES electronic focal plane with speeds from 4 to $^{1}/_{1000}$ s. It may be set automatically by the built-in, through-the-lens exposure meter, or set manually (plus B). The Nikon EL2 has an improved metering system and several additional features but is basically the same camera.

The built-in self-timer operates at 10 s. There is a single 3 mm (PC) socket, threaded for a Nikon synchronising cord and a hot accessory shoe contact with built-in safety switch. FP and X synchronisation is available; M and MF class bulbs can also be used.

The camera body is made of a die-cast aluminium alloy and finished in chrome plating or black. It has a non-interchangeable eye-level prism finder showing 92 per cent of the picture field. A screen with matte-fresnel field and central split-image rangefinder surrounded by a microprism grid is fitted as a standard. The shutter speed set is visible in the viewfinder as is a green follow pointer for match needle meter. There is a depth-of-field preview button and a mirror lock-up control.

The meter provides centre-weighted through-the-lens exposure measurement with automatic or manual shutter speed control at full aperture or at shooting aperture. The shutter speed set is displayed in the viewfinder. The circuit is powered by a 6 V silver-oxide or manganese battery located in a compartment within the mirror chamber, below the mirror. The meter has a sensitivity range from EV1 to EV18 with a film having an ASA of 100, equivalent to *f*/1.4 at 1 s to *f*/16 at $^{1}/_{1000}$ s. Films with an ASA range of 25 to 1600 can be accommodated.

Among other features are a plastic-tipped 135° single throw film wind and shutter wind lever with a free throw angle of 30°. The lever also serves as the meter circuit on/off switch. On the ELW or Nikon EL2, which may be fitted with an electric auto-winder, the shutter release button acts as a second switch. The camera back is hinged.

The Nikon F2T of 1979 is identical to the F2 except that titanium metal is used in the pentaprism cover, upper and bottom covers, lens mount area and camera back for maximum professional-use durability. In all aspects it is operated just like the F2.

The Nikon F2H of 1979 has titanium parts similar to the F2T, but is specially designed for high-speed motor drive operation to 10 frames per second with the MD-100 motor. It has a non-interchangeable B screen, interchangeable pentaprism finder but a fixed semi-silvered mirror instead of a rapid return mirror.

Nikon FM, FM2 and FE

The Nikon FM introduced in 1977, FM2 of 1981 and the FE introduced in 1978 share the same body shape. They are smaller and lighter than the older Nikons and Nikkormats. They all have fixed pentaprism viewfinder, and take the new simpler Motor Drive MD-12. The FM and FE use gallium photo diode meters; the FMS, silicon photo diodes.

The FM offers manual exposure with LED read-outs. The shutter speed and lens aperture are seen in the viewfinder. The FM2 has speeds to $1/4000$ s, flash sync at $1/200$ s, and offers interchangeable focusing screens.

The FE uses an auto-exposure system resembling that of the EL2.

Nikon EM

The Nikon EM introduced in 1979 is a much-simplified Nikon camera in a brand new, light, compact body. The auto-exposure system allows the user to set the aperture while the camera's centre-weighted metering system sets the shutter speed (which appears on a scale within the finder). The EM features an audible high and low light warning signal, backlight compensation button (but no manual shutter speed dial), 2 fps motor drive and auto coupled flash with ready signal in the viewfinder. With it, a new series of compact, lightweight, budget-priced Nikon lenses was also introduced.

Nikon FG

In 1981, the Nikon FG appeared, based on the Nikon EM body but offering a choice of aperture-preference exposure (the user sets the aperture, the camera selects the shutter speed), program exposure (in which the camera selects both the aperture and shutter speed) or manual control (the user selects both shutter speed and aperture). Additionally, the FG provides light measurement directly off the film surface during exposure for TTL auto-flash exposure. The viewfinder has a shutter-speed scale with light-emitting diode (LED) readouts.

Nikon F3

The Nikon F3, introduced in 1980, represents a complete departure from the previous F and F2 professional and serious amateur cameras. Instead of a separate metering system built into the interchangeable head, the F3 is provided with a silicon photo diode metering system in which the cell within the mirror chamber 'reads' light reflected to it through the lens (in the case of continuous light measurement) and directly off the film surface itself (for electronic flash). Its shutter speeds are electromagnetically controlled. Besides full auto-exposure capability, the camera can be controlled manually for all speeds between 8 seconds and 1/2000 second. Additionally, the camera has a liquid-crystal display (LCD) viewfinder readout, interchangeable finders and screens plus add-on motor drive with full motorised rewind.

Nikon FM and FM2

The Nikon FM camera is more compact (142 = 60.5 = 89.5 mm or $5^{19}/_{32} \times 2^{3}/_{8} \times 3^{17}/_{32}$ in) than any previous Nikon or Nikkormat SLR. What is equally or more important is its extraordinary lightness (590 g or 20.8 oz). While it works with and readily accepts all Nikkor lenses, the FM features the automatic maximum aperture indexing (AI) and so its exposure system will make readings at full aperture only with the AI lenses having the meter coupling ridge. With all other lenses, metering must be done at shooting aperture, as we'll describe.

The FM shutter is a vertically travelling metal blade focal plane, mechanically operated, having shutter speeds from 1 to 1/1000 s, offering X sync for electronic flash at 1/125 s. It has a fixed prism with non-removable focusing screen similar to that now standard on many other Nikons and Nikkormats – a horizontally split-image rangefinder, microprism collar and full ground-glass focusing screen. Within the finder can be seen a three-light-emitting diode readout metering system, the shutter speed set and also the aperture when an AI lens is fitted. All AI lenses incorporate an ADR (aperture-direct-readout) lens aperture scale.

The FM2 is almost identical to the FM except that its shutter offers a top speed of 1/4000 second, with flash sync at 1/200 s. The 1/4000 s speed provides an ability to stop faster subject action, while the 1/200 s sync speed minimises the danger of secondary ghost images that can be caused by existing light when used in conjunction with electronic flash and relatively slow sync speeds. Additionally, the FM2 provides interchangeable focusing screens. In this chapter, all information applies to both cameras except where I have given specific additional instructions for the FM2.

While the camera has a traditional Nikon centre-weighted metering system, the two cells on either side of the eyepiece reading off the viewing screen are actually gallium photo diodes (GPDs). GPD are superior to CDS cells in the speed of response to quickly-changing light levels and to silicon photo cells in eliminating possible errors caused by infra-red radiation. The FM2 has a similar metering system but uses silicon photo diodes rather than gallium.

The Nikon FM and FM2

The FM and FM2 are small manual exposure Nikon cameras. They couple directly to the Nikon MD-11 or 12 Motor Drive.

1. Neck strap lug
2. Shutter-operation selector
3. Shutter release
4. Shutter speed dial
5. Lens-aperture-display window
6. Meter-coupling lever
7. Meter-coupling release lever (FM only)
8. Lens-mounting index
9. Flash-sync terminal
10. Depth-of-field preview
11. Self-timer
12. Motor-drive shutter coupling
13. Tripod bush
14. Battery cover
15. Motor-drive contacts
16. Mirror
17. Bayonet mount
18. Lens-release button
19. Aperture ring
20. Focus scale
21. Focusing ring
22. Rewind release
23. Motor-drive coupling
24. Memo holder
25. Aperture scale
26. Non-AI meter-coupling prong
27. ADR scale
28. Rewind knob/back release
29. Accessory shoe
30. Shutter-speed dial
31. Shutter-operation selector
32. Frame counter
33. Back-release lock
34. Rewind crank
35. Focal-plane indicator
36. Viewfinder
37. Flash contact
38. Multiple-exposure button (FM only)
39. Film-speed scale
40. Meter-on warning
41. Film transport lever

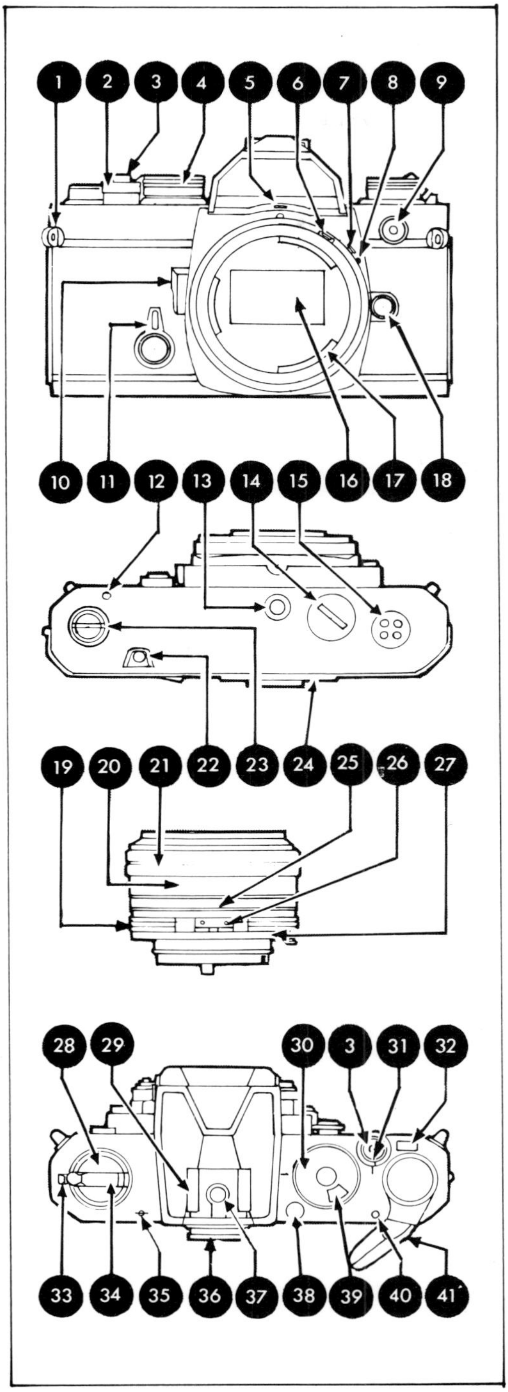

Other major new features include easy provision for making intentional double exposures and direct coupling to an accessory motor fitting snugly under the camera. The motor is capable of speeds up to 3.5 frames per second either continuously or in single exposures.

Power

Before you can operate the camera, two 1.5V silver oxide batteries powering the metering system and diodes in the finder must be installed in the battery clip. The clip is part of the coin-slotted cover of the battery chamber located on the bottom of the camera. Unthread the cover counterclockwise with a coin edge or similar object. Remove battery cover. Place the two cells with their + and − indicators matching those in the battery clip. Replace the cover and fasten it securely by turning it clockwise until it is tight. You can check your batteries easily just by looking through the viewfinder while the camera's film-advance lever is pulled out to the operating position, thus exposing the red dot below it. Look through the finder. One or more diodes should be lighted. If not, the batteries are absent, have been placed in the clip the wrong way round, are exhausted or need cleaning and replacing.

Loading

Now let's load the Nikon FM or FM2. Pull up on the rewind knob while sliding the adjacent safety catch on the rear. The back of the camera will swing open. Insert the film cartridge in the left-hand film chamber with the leader pointing towards the take-up spool, across the focal plane shutter. Push the rewind knob back into the down position and lead the film end directly across the slotted take-up spool. Insert the end in one of the slots but make certain that one or more of the sprocket teeth on the nearby sprocket wheel catch the sprocket holes of the film. Rotate the take-up spool, winding the film end inside out so the film passes under the spool. Advance the film slightly by pushing the film advance lever (if the camera is cocked, of course, you must press the shutter release first) to make sure the film winds on smoothly and the sprockets are still engaging the sprocket holes in the film. Press the camera back closed until you hear it click securely.

Before advancing the film to the first exposure, it is advisable to remove the slack from the film in the cartridge by unfolding the rewind crank and turning it in the direction of the arrow on the rewind knob until you feel a slight resistance. Fold the crank back to its original position. Each time you advance the film, the rewind knob should turn, indicating that film is travelling through your camera properly and that the camera is loaded correctly. (You'd be surprised how many professional photographers ignore this simple precaution and discover only after taking some precious photos that the camera was not loaded properly and the photos were not made.)

FM and FM2 batteries and loading

Unscrew battery cover with a coin to insert 2 to 5 volt silver oxide batteries in the clip following the +, − signs on the clip. Replace battery holder.

To check the batteries on FM, switch on meter by pulling film transport lever out to reveal red dot. On FM2, press shutter release lightly.

Battery power is sufficient if any of the LED exposure indicators light up.

To open the camera, push back the safety lock and pull up the rewind knob.

Put a film cassette in the chamber, push back the rewind knob, and lead film across the shutter. Push the loader into one of the take-up spool stops, and turn the spool to wind a little film on emulsion out. Wind on the film until both perforations engage the sprockets, and close the camera back.

Turn the rewind knob to take up any slack in the film.

Then make three blind exposures, and the camera is ready for the first picture.

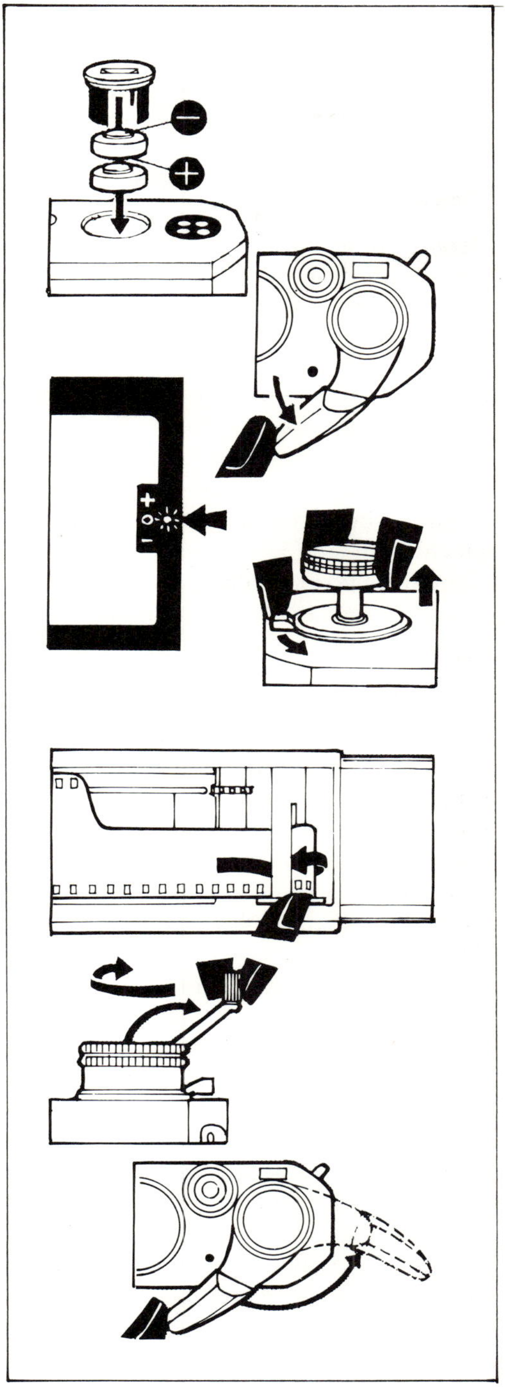

By alternately winding the film and shutter with the film-advance lever (which covers an arc of 135°) and pressing the shutter release, advance the film until number 1 appears in the frame counter located directly in front of the hub of the wind lever. Tear off the end of the film box and insert it in the back memo-holder clip as a reminder of which film you have loaded. Set the ASA film speed of the film you are using (given on the film box or on the film direction sheet) by pulling upwards on the outer knurled collar of the shutter speed dial and turning the collar until the figure appears opposite the red arrow in the inset ASA window within the dial. Then let the collar return to its place. You're now ready to take a picture.

Viewing and focusing

Look through the viewfinder. You will see an extremely bright field of view, slightly less than life size, which is some 93 per cent of the total picture area that will actually be recorded on film. This 7 per cent around the picture circumference is actually a safety factor, since it approximates the amount of picture area generally lost under the cardboard edges of a slide mount or in a glassless negative carrier. The image brightness has been enhanced by a special silver coating of the finder surfaces.

Centrally you will notice a central circle split horizontally. As you point the camera at a subject and focus the lens by twisting the lens focusing ring back and forth, you will see the image in the two halves of the circle move right and left towards or away from each other. When the two parts of the image coincide, you have achieved accurate focus.

Similarly, the outer microprism ring can be used for focusing. When the image is out of focus, the subject covered by the microprism ring seems to shimmer or shatter. When correct focus is achieved, the image snaps into sharpness.

Lastly the entire outer area can be used for focusing. It appears fuzzy when out of focus and is at its sharpest when the image is in accurate focus. All three systems are equally accurate and you have your choice as to which you find preferable with various subjects. However, if you use lenses with maximum apertures smaller than about *f*/5.6, one of the central split-image rangefinder's circles may go black and the microprism collar appear too grainy to focus. At such small apertures you can always focus on the outer ground-glass area.

Besides the focusing screen you will see at the left edge of the picture a black disc section within which is a white numeral indicating the shutter speed you have set. At the top centre, outside the picture area, is a window in which the lens aperture set can be seen (if you have an AI Nikkor with direct aperture readout). With other lenses you will not see the aperture set.

Metering

By pulling the wind lever outwards 30° to the operating position, the metering system is turned on in the FM. For the FM2, press lightly on the shutter release button. The meter will remain on for 30 seconds. You will see one or more red diodes just outside the picture area at the right. There are three LEDs. The centre one is opposite a small circle, the top LED next to a + mark, while the bottom LED is adjacent to a − sign. When you move the aperture ring of the lens and/or the shutter speed dial atop the camera to achieve metered exposure, the centre diode will light up. If your exposure is from ⅕ of an *f*/stop to 1 *f*/stop towards overexposure, the two top diodes will light. If the two bottom diodes light the exposure is under, between ⅕ and a full *f*/stop. If only the top diodes light, the camera is overexposing 1 full *f*/stop or more. The bottom diode alone indicates underexposure by 1 *f*/stop or more. For correct use of the meter the 12 mm circle outlined in the viewfinder indicates the major weighting of the system. This circle should cover that part of the subject on which you wish to make an exposure meter reading. For utmost accuracy the centre diode only should light. However, when shooting fast you can generally rely on getting an acceptable exposure even if two diodes are lighting. (For more explicit information on exposure, see chapter on exposure, page 181.) Note that in dark areas it may be difficult or perhaps even impossible to see the aperture in the finder. If the picture area is dark, the shutter speeds may be hard to see. However, at all times correct exposure can be determined quickly using the quite bright diodes.

The metering range of the cameras is extremely broad with films having ASA speeds from ASA 12 to 300, the range is fully coupled at all apertures and shutter speeds. At ASA 400 the meter can read down to ⅕ at full lens aperture, excellent for low-light photography. Officially the range is EV1 to EV18 at ASA 100.

Shooting

The shutter release on top of the Nikon FM or FM2 has a two-position knurled fingerguard. On Chrome Nikon FM cameras the black line on the fingerguard should be aligned with the black line on top of the camera for camera operation. Black Nikon F camera bodies have white lines instead. When the collar is rotated bringing the red line opposite the black line on the camera body, the shutter release is locked against accidental exposures. (This collar also serves as a switch for the motor release when the motor drive is fitted.) On the FM2, pulling out the film-advance lever to the stand-off position unlocks the shutter release.

Your Nikon lens will show the scene at full aperture, which is the most convenient for viewing and focusing. However, you may wish to see just how much depth of field (zone of sharp focus) you have at any set lens aperture.

The smaller the aperture, the more depth at any given subject distance. While the Nikon lenses do have quite comprehensive depth-of-field scales, you can get quite a good visual approximation of your depth of field by pressing inwards on the depth-of-field button located at the right side of the camera body just to the right of the self-timer lever. The lens will close down to whatever aperture you have set. The view will become darker, since less light is entering the lens, but you will notice that the zone of sharp focus increases, indicating to you the approximate actual sharpness you will achieve if you take the picture at that aperture. You can change the aperture if you want more or less depth of field, but you will then have to change your shutter to achieve proper exposure. Don't take your exposure reading while keeping the depth-of-field lever depressed. Remove your finger from the lever and allow the lens to open fully again first.

When taking a picture, keep the camera as steady as possible, no matter the shutter speed (although the slower the shutter speed selected the more need for steadiness to avoid a blurred picture from camera shake). The camera should be cradled in the palm of your left hand while it is guided and the shutter released with your right. Both of your elbows should be pulled into your body closely to provide support. Finger pressure on the shutter release should be smooth and steady. (The shutter and mirror mechanisms make use of an air-damping system to minimise vibration during exposure.)

Self-timer

Besides the regular shutter release (which is threaded on top to accept a cable release), there is another way to release the camera – using the self-timer lever on the right side of the body. Press the lever downwards fully. When you now release the shutter, the rapid return mirror will fly upwards immediately and the mechanical timer will delay the shutter action for some 10 seconds. This gives you sufficient time to get into the picture yourself. It can also provide a jar-free release for the camera – very useful for long exposures when a cable release and tripod are not available. Put the camera on a firm foundation, set the self-timer and allow the timer to set off the shutter.

The FM and FM2 do not have a lock-up mirror, a feature on virtually every Nikon and Nikkormat SLR made previously. However, the mirror does fly upwards some 10 seconds before the shutter release when the self-timer is operated. This procedure can be used when you require the most jar-free release.

After setting the self-timer, if you decide not to use it, you can cancel it by pushing the lever directly upwards to the original position. You will hear the mechanical escapement mechanism operating, but it will not set off the shutter.

Nikon FM and FM2 operation

Viewfinder layout

1. Aperture direct readout
2. Ground glass/fresnel screen
3. Plain ground glass
4. Shutter speed readout
5. Microprism collar
6. Exposure indication
7. Correct exposure LED
8. Split-image rangefinder

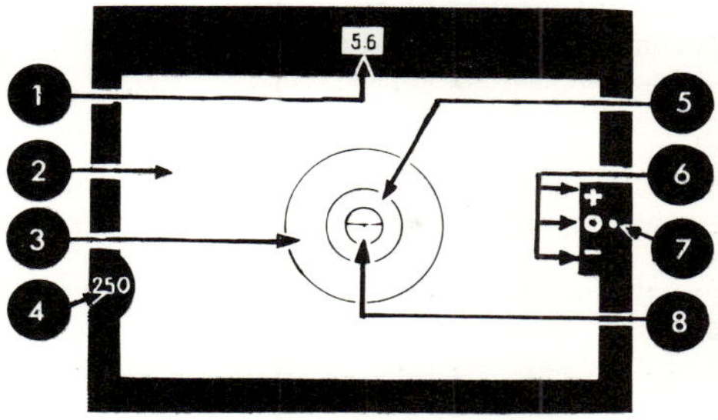

Exposure control

The LEDs light up singly or in combination to display exposure information.

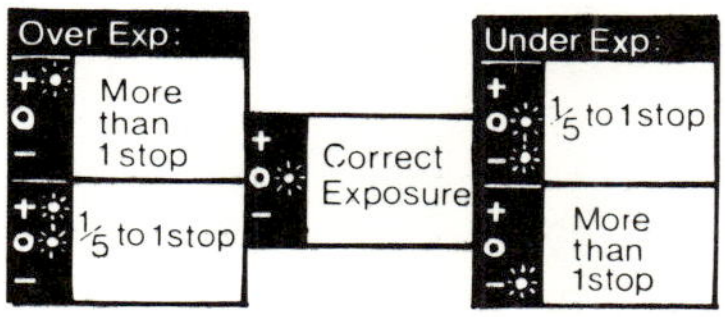

Set the shutter speed by turning the dial to the appropriate figure.

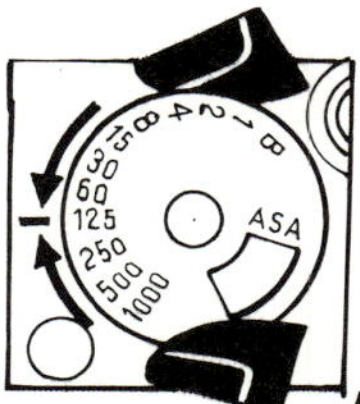

Set the aperture by turning the lens aperture ring.

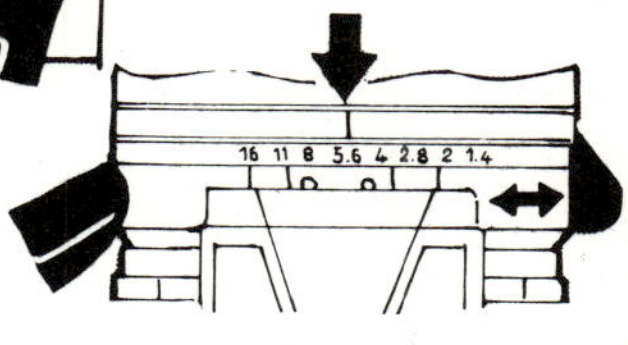

Set the shutter operation mode selector black index to the mark for manual operation. The red mark is for use with the MD-11 or -12 motor drive.

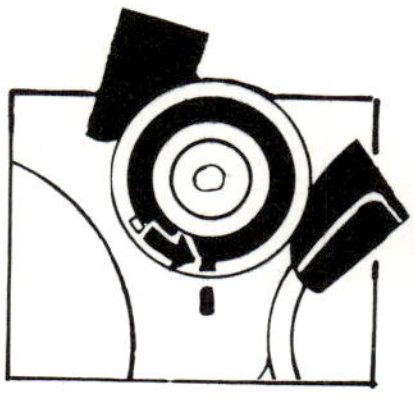

The self-timer is released with the normal shutter release. You can cancel the action by pushing the lever back.

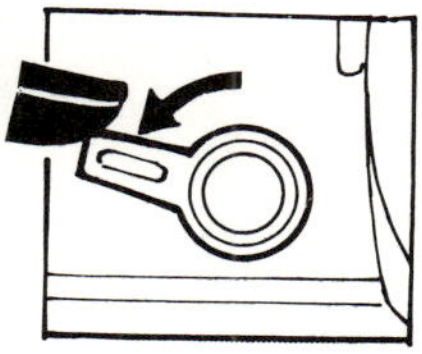

Push the preview lever inward to stop the lens down and display the depth of field.

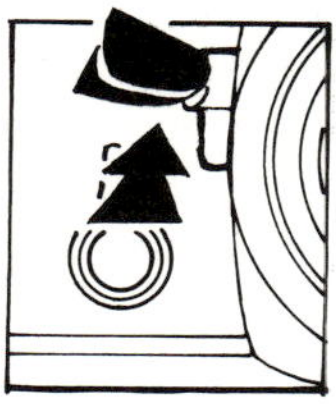

Nikon FM and FM2 operation

The FM focusing screen has a split-image in the centre, surrounded by a microprism collar. Focusing the lens combines the split parts of the image, and removes the shimmer from the microprism area. The whole fine matte screen can be used for focusing, and is particularly useful with very long telephoto lenses, and for ultra close-up work.

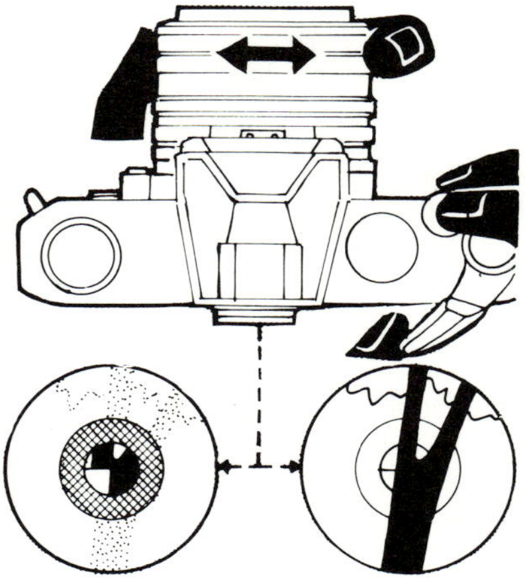

You can release the shutter by squeezing gently on the release, or through a conventional cable release, screwed into the shutter release button.

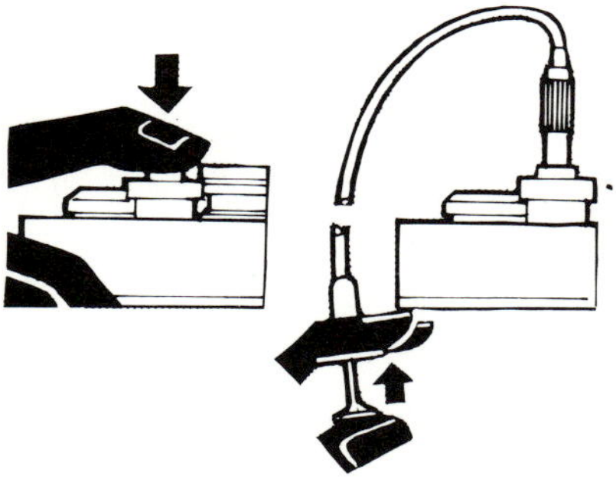

Changing FM2 focusing screens

After removing lens, use tweezer tip (furnished) with accessory focusing screens to slip under release latch at top front of mirror box. Pull outward to open focusing screen holder.

Grasp tab on screen with tweezers and remove. With tweezers, position new screen flat side down, with tab up, in place. Push front edge of holder upwards with tweezers until click is heard. Do not use fingers to handle screens. Accessory screens available are: all-matte or with horizontal and vertical lines for composing.

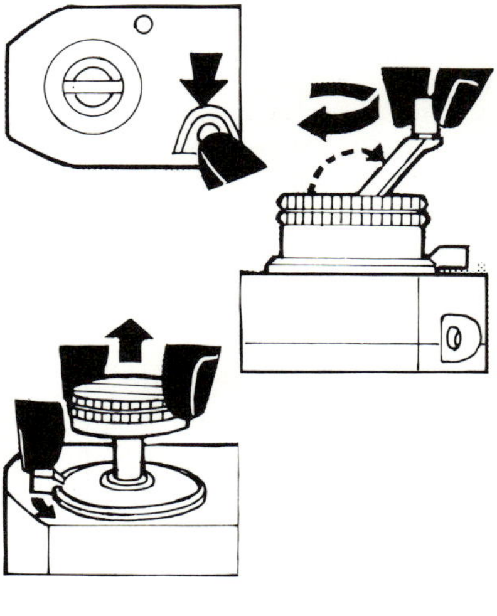

Multiple exposures

The multiple-exposure button allows you to repeat as many pictures as you like on one frame of the film.

1. Taking the first picture.
2. Push the multi-exposure button across and hold it.
3. Operate the film transport lever to reset the shutter.

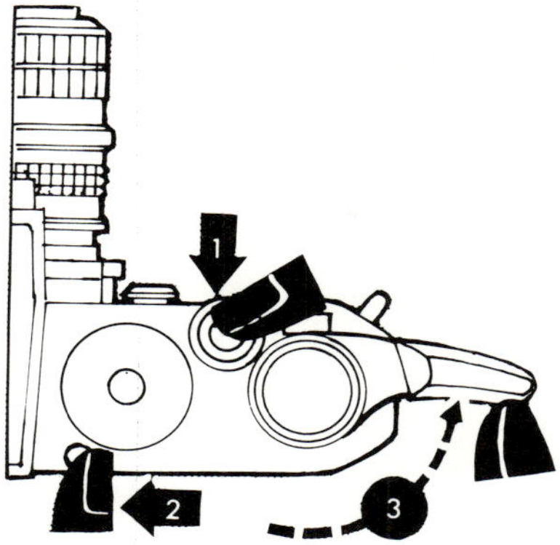

Lens mounting

On the FM only, the lens coupling lever must be pushed up for non-AI lenses. Release it by pressing the small button by the lens mounting index before mounting an AI lens (which has a meter coupling ridge).

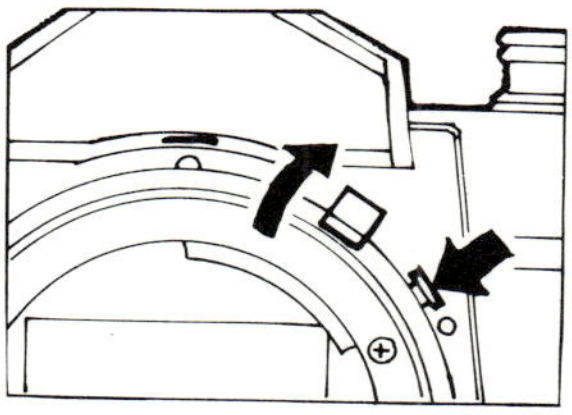

To mount a lens, align the meter coupling prong (or the focus/aperture index if you have removed the prong) with the lens mounting index. Push the lens home and turn it counter-clockwise.

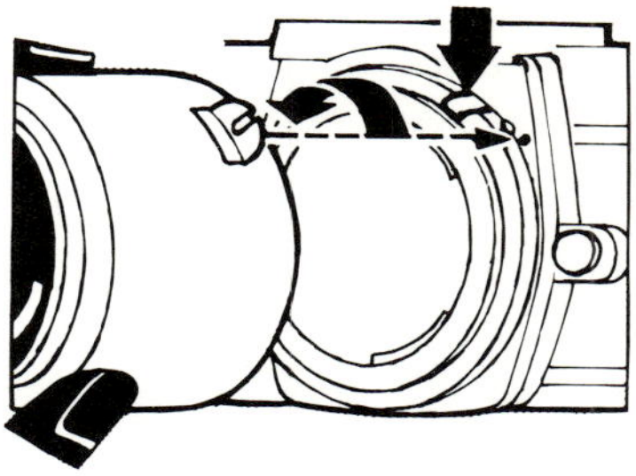

To remove a lens, press the release button, turn the lens clockwise and lift out.

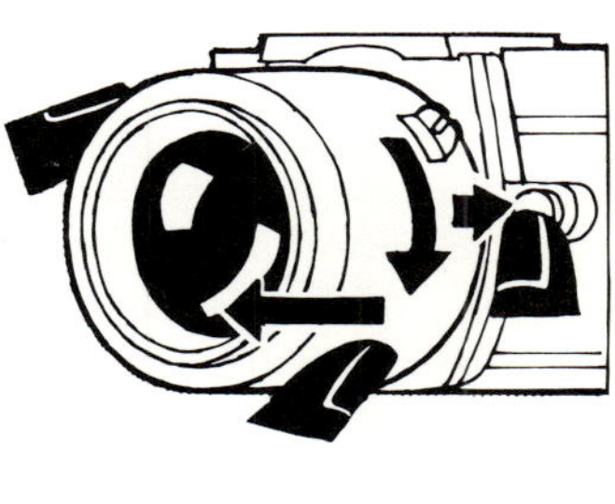

Double exposures

You can make intentional double exposures with the FM and FM2 quite easily. With the FM, following your first exposure, push the small button on the top right-hand side of the camera to the left while rewinding the shutter with the wind lever. The shutter will wind, but the film and the film counter remain stationary. You can now take a second exposure. Repeat for as many images as you wish on the single frame. On the FM2, following the first exposure, pull the multiple-exposure lever, concentric with the wind-lever hub, in a clockwise direction and rewind the shutter. Repeat for each additional exposure. Remember that exposure is cumulative. You will overexpose the picture unless you halve exposures for ordinary subject material when shooting two photos, use a third of the proper exposure when shooting three photos, etc. Of course, if you are multiply-exposing a subject in front of a black backdrop and the subject is not overlapping, you can make each exposure at the full exposure setting without over exposure.

Flash synchronisation

The hot sync accessory shoe atop the Nikon FM and FM2 will accept most footed electronic flash units. Most such allow cordless synchronisation directly through the terminal in the shoe. When the shoe is empty the sync circuit is off. There's a tiny switch built under the right rail which automatically turns on the shoe sync when an accessory is slid into place. The most suitable electronic FM flash shutter speed is 1/125 s, marked in red on the shutter speed dial; use the ×200 setting on the FM2. You can also use any slower speed. You can use flashbulbs if you wish at speeds from 1 s (or B) to 1/30 s. For off-camera flash you will find a push-on and threaded single sync terminal on the left front of the cameras to which you can attach the 3 mm (PC) cord from your flash unit.

On the FM2 only, the Nikon SB-E or SB-10 Speedlight, when directly mounted in the camera's hot shoe, activates the camera's LED ready light inside the viewfinder when the flash is fully recycled and ready to fire. If you have selected an improper flash sync shutter speed, the ready light will blink in warning.

Lens mount

To change lenses on the Nikon FM or FM2, press in the chrome-edged black lens release button on the left front side of the camera. Grasp the knurled chrome ring of the lens and twist the lens clockwise towards the release button. The lens will release from the camera body.

To remount a lens, position it so the black centre line on the len's chrome ring is directly opposite the mounting index dot on the camera. Press the lens firmly into the camera body and twist the chrome ring counterclockwise until you hear a click indicating that the lens has locked in place.

With older Nikkor lenses not having the AI coupling ridge at the back, a slightly different procedure must be followed for the FM camera only in mounting the lens. Push inwards on the small button near the mounting lever on the front of the camera's lens mount ring. At the same time flip the lever upwards. Now mount your lens. The lens will couple to the automatic diaphragm mechanism of the camera and operate perfectly, but you will have to press in the depth-of-field lever while making making an exposure meter reading. This same procedure should be used when bellows units, extension tubes or preset lenses are fitted to the Nikon FM. The FM and FM2 only index lenses automatically if the back ridge of the lens contacts and moves the meter coupling lever.

After using non-AI lenses on the FM, remember to flip the meter coupling lever back down to operating position again.

Unloading

Following your last exposure (usually 12, 20, 24 or 36, depending on the film length you've bought), the end of the film will be indicated by your inability to wind the film and shutter further. Do not try to force an additional shot or you may rip the film end from the cartridge. Press in the rewind button on the bottom of the camera. Using the unfolded rewind crank, wind the film back into the cartridge. You will hear a distinct click as the film leader leaves the take-up spool and is wound completely into the original cartridge. You can then open the camera (as you did originally for loading) and remove the film. Always load and remove film out of bright or direct sunlight to avoid possible fogging through the cartridge lip.

Motor drive for FM, FM2 or FE

Probably the most important accessory for the Nikon FM, FM2 and FE is the MD-12 Motor Drive Unit. It fits directly under the Nikon camera body, secured by a stud threaded into the camera's tripod socket. The MD-12 provides up to 3.5 frames per second either continuously or as single shots. The FM, FM2 and FE body requires no modifications to accept the motor, nor do any special covers on the motor or camera have to be removed.

The MD-12 Motor Drive Unit is powered by 8 AA-type 1.5 V penlight-size batteries which can power the motor for more than 100 rolls of 36-exposure film. To insert the batteries, unthread the battery cover on the left end of the motor, using the edge of a coin or similar object. The entire battery chamber can then be slid from the motor. The sides of the chamber indicate the proper + and − orientation for the batteries. After loading, replace the battery chamber and fasten to the motor by turning the slotted cover clockwise with the edge of a coin.

The camera and motor fasten together very easily. Protruding from the edges of the motor are two drive wheels, one on each side. Bring motor and camera body together so that the mounting screw can enter the tripod socket. Then secure together by turning the two mounting screw drive wheels in a counterclockwise direction – to the right if you look at the camera from the back.

Camera and motor must fasten together securely with no play or looseness. When the motor is in use, the red line on the shutter release guard collar must be opposite the black (or white) line on the camera body. At the rear of the motor there's an on/off switch. Turning it to the 'on' position activates the metering system of the camera without pulling the wind lever away from the body (if the lever is in the out position, the motor will not operate). Remember to shut the motor off to conserve meter battery strength whenever you are not actually taking pictures.

The vertical motor control handle has a two-position S/C mode selector and a chrome S/C locking button. While pressing the chrome locking button down with one finger, move the S/C mode selector to S for single shooting, or to C if you wish the motor to run continuously when you press the release.

With the rear switch in the 'on' position, you're ready to fire the camera by the motor. In the C position, pressure on the motor's shutter release button will release the shutter. Removing finger pressure allows the motor to wind to the next exposure. In the C position, pressure on the release button will fire and wind the camera continuously.

With each firing and winding, a red diode at the back of the motor will light, indicating that the motor is operating properly. The motor will fire at 3.5 frames per second continuously at 1/125 s or faster shutter speeds. At slower speeds the motor automatically adjusts the framing rate to the shutter speed you have selected.

If you wish, you can fire the camera and advance film manually even when the motor is attached. Twist the shutter release collar and line up the black (or white) line on the collar with the black (or white) line on the camera top plate. Operate the camera using the camera's own wind lever and shutter release.

After the last exposure, film can be rewound without removing the motor from the camera. Push upwards on the black ribbed bar with the 'R' at the back of the motor. You can then rewind film with the camera's rewind crank.

When attaching the MD-12, the shutter release pin on the motor, located next to the camera body motor coupling, must be in the retracted position. Occasionally it may be protruding. If you attempt to fasten the motor to the camera with the pin out, the motor will not work. In such a case remove the motor (if already attached), switch on the motor and bring the four copper-coloured motor connecting pins into contact with the chrome bottom plate of the FM or FE. This will activate the motor briefly, allowing the

Motor drive MD-12

The motor drive MD-12 fits directly below the Nikon FM, FM2 or FE and provides continuous (C) or single frame (S) shooting.

To use the MD-12, the camera winding lever must be pushed fully in, and the shutter release collar turned so that the red line is against its index. An earlier motor drive, the MD-11, operates in the same manner but does not have the electronic meter battery power conservation circuit.

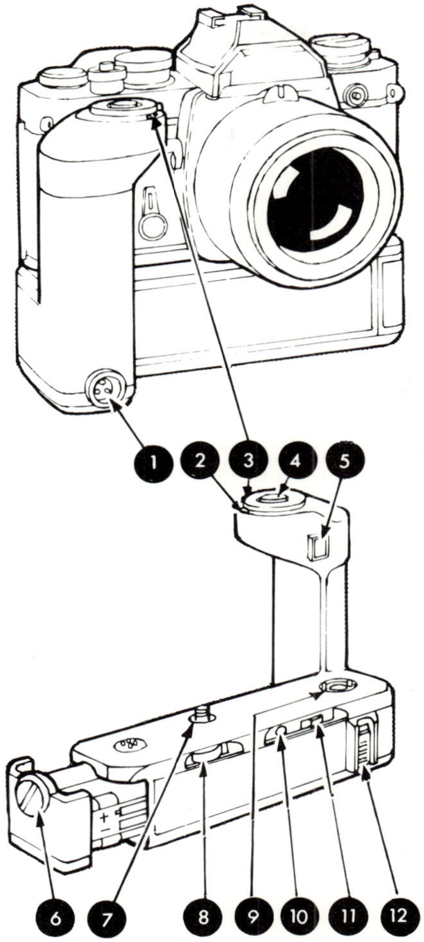

1. Remote control socket
2. S/C control release
3. S/C index
4. Shutter release
5. Protection pad
6. Battery chamber screw
7. Mounting screw
8. Mounting wheel
9. Camera drive
10. Operating light
11. On/Off switch
12. Rewind release slide

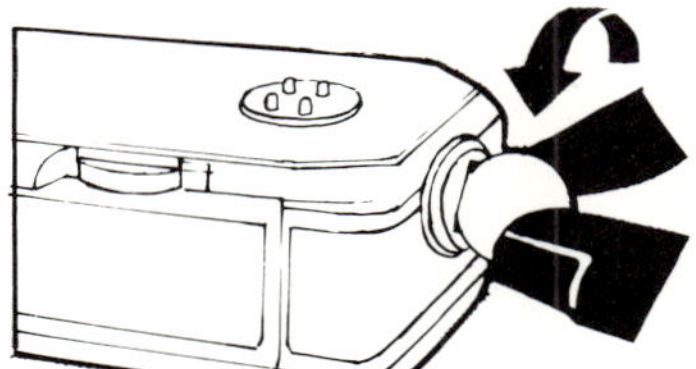

To load or unload the 8 pen cells (size AA), unscrew the magazine with a suitable coin.

shutter release to retract. Then switch off the motor and attach it to the camera as usual.

Besides operating the camera from the motor's shutter release, you can fire the motorised Nikon FM or FE by remote control. Connect the proper cord to the MD-12's front terminal at the base of the hand grip. Then connect the cord to such Nikon accessories as the MT-1 Intervalometer, MW-1 Radio Remote Control and ML Modulite Control described elsewhere in this book.

The MD-12 motor supersedes an earlier MD-11 motor. The MD-11 operates in a like manner to the MD-12 except that it lacks a camera meter battery power conservation circuit.

Data Back MF-12

The Data Back MF-12, which fits the FE, FM and FM2 Nikons, replaces the changeable backs of these cameras, allowing you to imprint either the day, month and year, or day, hour and minute in the lower right-hand corner of all pictures during exposure. The data to be imprinted is shown through the Data Back on a 6-digit, 7-element liquid crystal display (LCD) which also serves as a digital clock. The unit is powered by two 1.5 V silver batteries (or three AA cells via an adaptor). Settings are made with three push buttons: adjust, select and change. A power cable connects the proper sync contact on the camera with the MF-12 back. An LED near the finder eyepiece lights momentarily when data is imprinted, but continues to light if it was not imprinted. Should you wish to power the data back with longer-life, more economical AAA batteries instead of the regular two silver-oxide batteries, there is a Battery Holder DB-3 which provides this alternative using two AAA cells.

Nikon FE

The Nikon FE, introduced in 1978, represents a logical evolution from the Nikon FM (see page 16). It is a fully automatic exposure camera with electronically controlled shutter built into the same basic body shell as the Nikon FM. The exposure system is very much like that in the Nikon EL2 (page 152). As with the EL2, you set the aperture and the metering system sets the shutter speed. The Nikon FE accepts the Nikon DM-11 or DM-12 Motor Drive in common with the FM camera. With AI lenses, the aperture set is visible within the finder, there is a simplified multiple-exposure lever and LED battery check, viewing screens are interchangeable and the camera accepts a new fully coupled electronic flash unit, the Nikon SB-10, which automatically adjusts the shutter speed of the camera to the 1/90 flash speed when it is mounted on the hot shoe. Additionally, a flash ready light can be seen in the viewfinder.

Batteries

Both the Nikon FE's electronically controlled shutter and through-lens meter are powered by two 1.5 V silver oxide batteries located in a battery clip in the bottom of the FE camera body. To fit the batteries, unscrew the cover counterclockwise with the edge of a small coin or similar object until the cover and clip can be withdrawn. Place the batteries in the clip one above the other with their + and − signs matching those indicated on the clip. Replace the clip and cover. Secure both by tightening the cover clockwise in the camera with the coin edge. Check the batteries by pushing down the power check lever on the back of the camera. If the batteries are all right and have been loaded correctly, the central hub of the lever glows red. If the lamp does not light, the batteries are exhausted (a fresh set should last about a year in use) or they have been inserted incorrectly.

Film loading and unloading

The Nikon FE is loaded and unloaded just as is the Nikon FM (see pages 18 and 27).

For proper exposures, there are three main settings that must be made on the Nikon FE: the film speed, the aperture and the shutter speed. The first two you must do yourself. The third will be done by the auto-exposure system of the camera. To set the film speed, depress the film speed dial lock, and turn the ASA film speed dial until the red index mark lines up with the ASA value of the film. The white lines between the marked numerals on the dials indicate in-between settings. After the dial is set, release the lock and make sure the dial is still as set. Since it is quite easy to forget just which film you have loaded – particularly if you put the camera away for a while – do tear off the end of the film box and slip it into the memo holder at the back of the camera.

Viewing and focusing

Hold the camera to your eye and look out through the viewfinder (with the lens cap removed of course). You will see a bright focusing screen with a central circle, split horizontally. Outside of this circle is a thin microprism collar. Surrounding this is a large 12 mm diameter scribed circle which indicates the primary sensitive area of your exposure meter. Aim your camera at a subject, such as the edge of a door, from 1 m (3 ft) to about 5 m (15 ft) away which has pronounced vertical lines. When the camera is not focused properly the image as seen in the two central semi-circles appears to be split and displaced left and right. As you turn the focusing ring in one direction, the image appears to separate further. It grows closer together when you turn the focusing ring in the opposite direction. When you have aligned both halves of the subject precisely, the camera is in focus.

Sometimes you will not have such a pronounced vertical line on which to focus. Then use the microprism collar. When an image is out of focus, the microprism collar will appear to shatter the image into unsharpness. When the image is properly focused the image will snap into clarity.

The outer picture area right to the focusing screen corners can also be used for focusing. Turn the focusing ring until the image on which you wish to focus appears at its sharpest.

The exposure meter

At the left side of the finder, just outside the picture area, you can see a vertical shutter speed scale and two pointers – a black needle and a broad green transparent pointer. These indicate the shutter speed that the camera will set automatically and manually. To turn on the metering system, pull the wind lever out about 30° from its rest position, thus uncovering a red dot beneath the lever. As you aim at your subject and turn the aperture-setting ring of your lens, you will see the black needle travel up and down the shutter speed scale. At the top of the focusing screen is a small window in which you

The Nikon FE

The Nikon FE is an auto-exposure camera, which couples to the Nikon MD-11 or 12 motor drive.

1. Multi-exposure lever
2. Film transport lever
3. Meter-on warning
4. Auto-exposure lock
5. Film plane indicator
6. Viewfinder eyepiece
7. Accessory shoe with flash contacts
8. Film speed dial lock
9. Film speed scale
10. Rewind crank
11. Frame counter
12. Shutter release button
13. ADR scale
14. Aperture scale
15. Coupler for non-AI cameras
16. Focus ring
17. Focus scale
18. Depth-of-field scale
19. Meter coupling ridge
20. Neck strap lug
21. Stop down (preview) lever
22. Shutter dial
23. Lens aperture read-out window
24. Meter coupling lever
25. Flash sync terminal
26. Lens mounting index
27. Self-timer exposure hold lever
28. Viewing mirror
29. Focusing screen release
30. Lens release button
31. Motor-drive coupling
32. Motor-drive shutter coupling
33. Rewind release button
34. Tripod bush
35. Battery compartment
36. Motor-drive connections
37. Film-type reminder holder

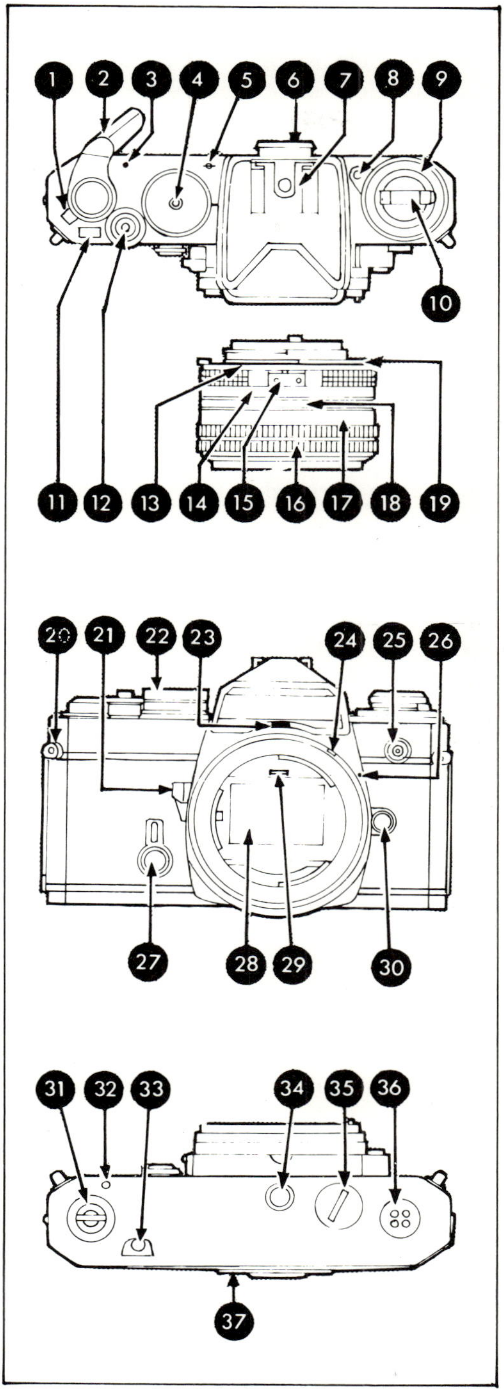

can see the aperture you are setting. For any aperture you set, the metering system will choose the corresponding shutter speed and indicate in with the black needle. For most accurate exposure, place your subject within the 12 mm circle. (If this cannot be done because of compositional requirements, there are some alternatives which we will discuss later.)

The shutter speed scale has black numerals from ½ to 1/1000 s. Speeds below 1/30 s should be avoided unless the camera is being used on a tripod or similar firm support. Fast shutter speeds generally ensure sharper pictures in terms of absence of subject and camera movements. As speed increases, you need a larger and larger lens aperture; meaning that you have less and less sharpness in depth, or depth of field. You must make your own compromise by choosing the most expeditious shutter speed–aperture combination for your particular subject (see chapter on exposure and depth of field, for more information).

There will be specific subjects or lighting situations (also explained in the exposure chapter) when you will wish to alter your auto exposure slightly. If you want to take a close-up reading of your subject for greater accuracy, you can approach the subject, aim your camera, press the self-timer lever *towards* the lens mount and maintain pressure. This is the exposure memory which locks the exposure reading and maintains it until you release the lever or take your picture. Take your close-up reading, move back to camera position and then release the shutter. The camera will provide an automatic exposure as if you were still at the close distance to your subject. The meter needle within the finder, however, will continue to fluctuate with changes in lighting even though the actual meter setting itself is locked.

If you wish to make a series of automatic exposures with a similar exposure adjustment for each photograph – say, increase your exposure between ¼ to 2 full *f*/stops – or decrease it, you can do this by adjusting the auto exposure compensation dial around the rewind knob, opposite the ASA scale. To set the compensation, pull upwards on the auto exposure compensation dial outer ring. Turn it until the red ring dot is opposite the compensation you want. Then let the ring fall into place. The camera's auto exposure system will now provide the additional or subtracted exposure increment dialled. Remember, however, to return the dial to 0 when you are finished or you will most likely under- or overexpose subsequent pictures. The shutter speed pointer in the finder indicates the altered exposure set, but there is no mark in the finder to show that auto compensation is being used.

Manually set shutter speeds

For manual shutter speeds, push in the central hub of the shutter speed dial and turn to whatever shutter speed you wish. In the viewfinder the green transparent pointer descends from its top A ('automatic') position to indicate the shutter speed you have chosen. Meanwhile the black pointer continues to

Getting ready

The FE is powered by two 1.5V silver oxide cells. They go in the holder, with the positive (+) side towards the camera.

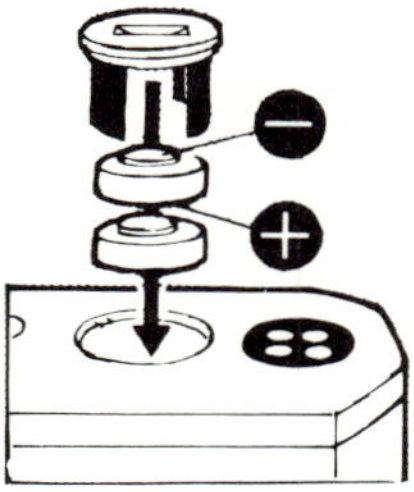

To check the batteries, push down on the check lever. If the indicator lights, the batteries are in good condition.

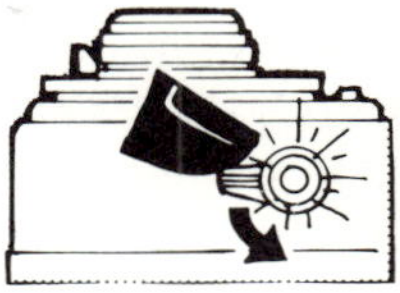

To open the camera back, push the safety lock backwards, and pull up the film rewind knob as far as possible.

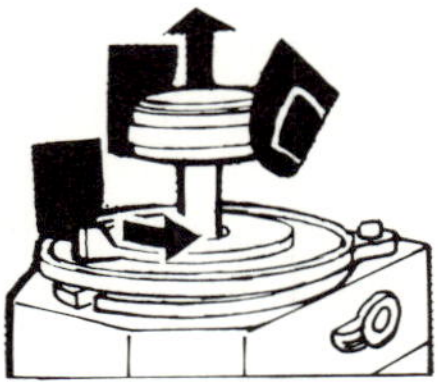

Put the film cassette in the camera and push back the rewind knob. Pull the film leader across the shutter, and push the end into a slot in the take-up spool. Turn the spool by hand to wind the film underneath (emulsion outward). Wind on until both sets of sprockets engage in the film perforation. then close the camera back.

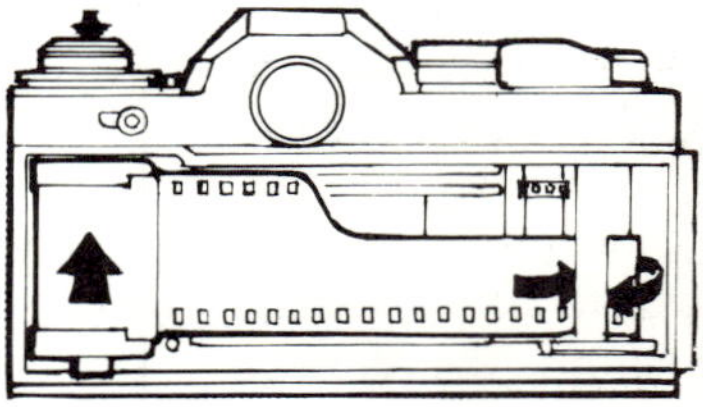

Take up any slack by turning the film rewind lever.

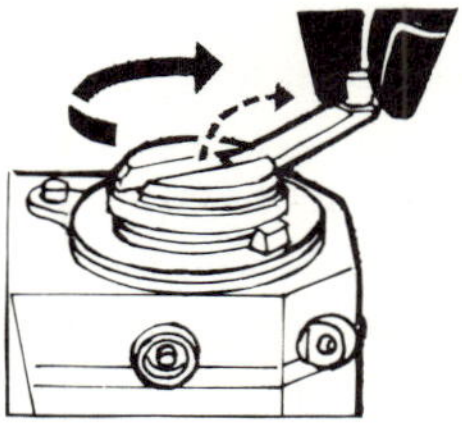

Operate the film transport lever three times. The counter now indicates that the camera is ready for the first exposure.

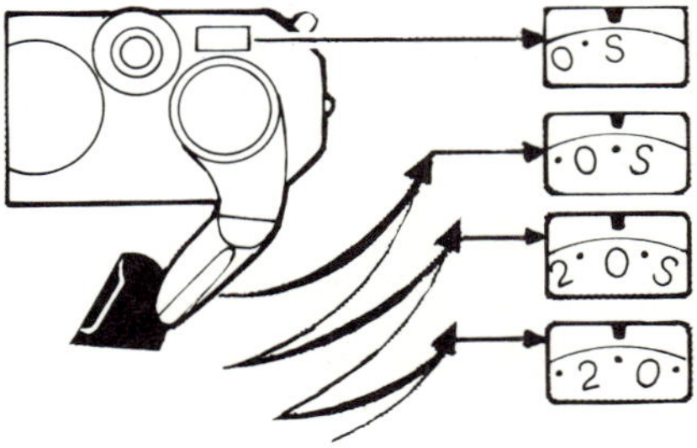

indicate the meter's suggested shutter speed for whatever aperture you have set. You can thus follow the camera's advice by matching the green and black pointers or choose a speed higher or lower than the black pointer indicates. At all times the green and black pointers show you how far away from the suggested exposure your manual exposure will be.

At the bottom of the shutter speed scale are M and B settings. When you turn the shutter speed dial to B for bulb exposures (in which the shutter will remain open as long as the release is pressed and closed when you relinquish pressure), the green transparent pointer moves to the B setting in the finder. The green pointer indicates M setting when the shutter speed dial is at the M90 speed; which is available even when the camera batteries have failed, and is correct for electronic flash.

The FE can be operated with flashbulbs at speeds up to 1/30 s or for electronic flash at speeds to 1/125 s. The hot shoe atop the camera not only has special connections to accommodate a fully coupled Nikon electronic flash unit (which we will discuss) but can be used with any electronic flash unit having flash sync built into its foot. For flash units using a PC cord, there is a threaded PC connection on the front left side of the camera.

Other controls

The self-timer (which is combined with the memory hold lock already described) can be used to release the shutter after an 8 to 14 second delay. This affords the photographer enough time to get in front of the camera and take his own picture. The self-timer can also be used instead of a cable release to release the camera shutter gently. After setting all camera controls and advancing the film fully, push downwards on the self-timer, away from the lens. When the shutter release is pressed, the lens diaphragm will immediately close down to the preset aperture and the rapid return mirror will lock upwards for the length of the delay; thus locking in the auto exposure at the moment the release is pressed. Thus if you shield the viewfinder eyepiece from extraneous light while pressing the release, you can then leave the finder unattended, being assured that no extraneous light will have any effect on the finder or exposure until the shutter is released.

Should you wish to cancel the self-timer after setting it, you can do it by pushing the self-timer lever upwards again and then towards the lens mount. The clockwork will be heard to release, but the shutter mechanism will not operate.

Multiple exposures can be made easily with the FE. After taking your first exposure, push the multiple exposure lever adjacent to the hub of the wind lever backwards while operating the wind lever. The shutter will be rewound, but neither film nor frame counter will move. When making multiple exposures, remember to cut your individual exposures to prevent overexposure on the single frame. For instance, if you intend to make two

Operating the FE

To focus, turn the lens focus ring until the viewfinder image is sharp.

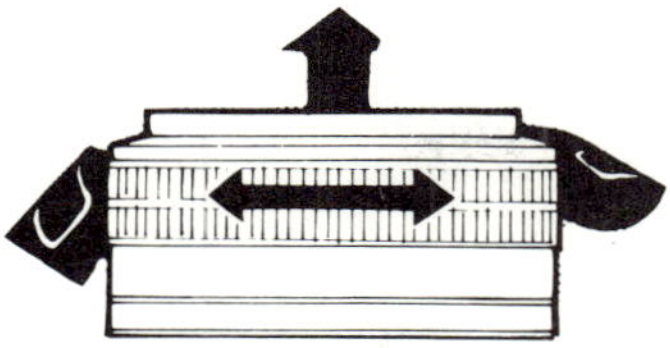

The microprism collar and the split-image area are of considerable help in most situations.

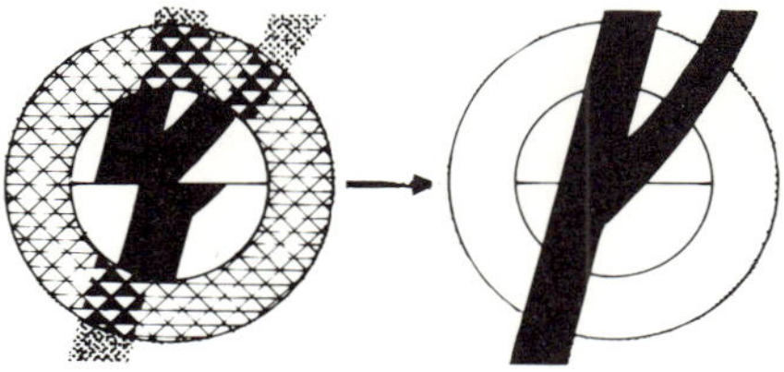

If you want to hold an automatic exposure, press the self-timer lever toward the lens mount.

To preview the depth of field, or meter with a non-AI coupled lens, you can press the stop-down button.

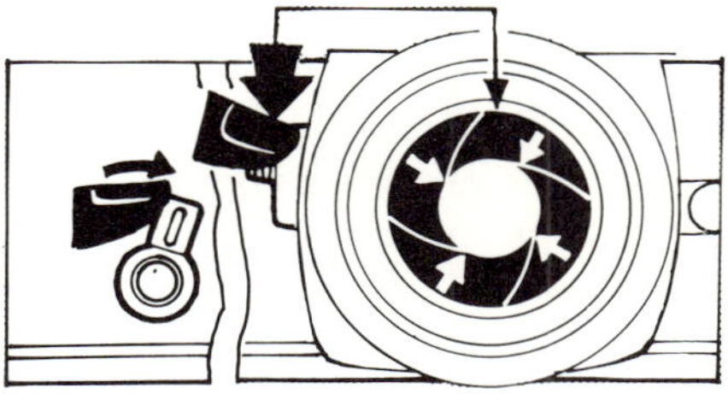

To take your pictures, depress the shutter release gently.

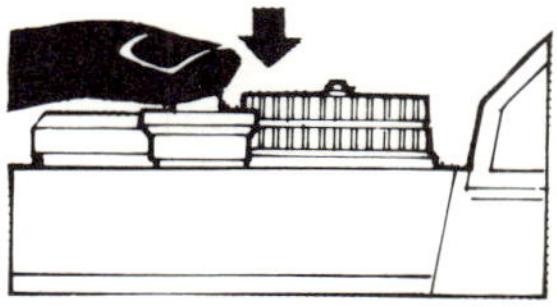

When you have finished a cassette of film, depress the rewind release button, and rewind the film.

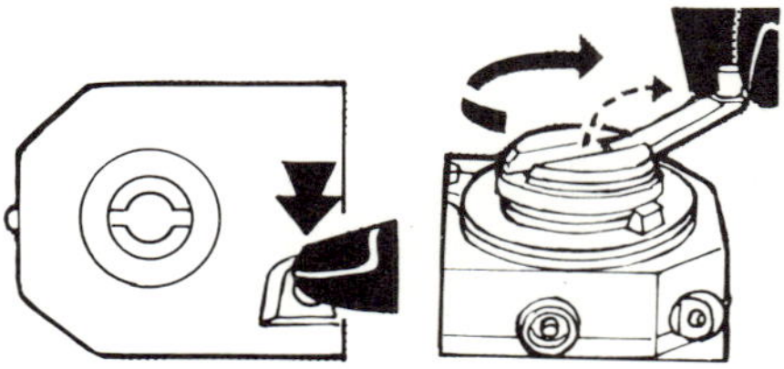

Pull up the rewind crank to open the camera back and remove the cassette.

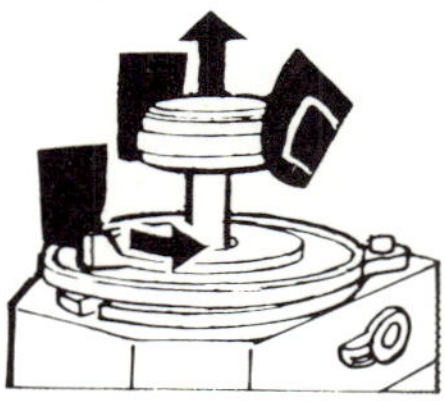

pictures on the frame, each exposure should be half the normal exposure. If you make three exposures on a single frame, each should be ⅓ normal exposure. However, if you are photographing against a black background and your subjects are not overlapping each other, you can give each shot full exposure.

As with all Nikons and Nikkormats, most normal viewing and focusing is done at full lens aperture to provide the brightest image and crispest focusing. However, this view at full lens aperture does not indicate to you just how much sharpness you will actually preserve in front of or behind your focused-upon subject at actual shooting aperture – your depth of field (see chapter on exposure and depth of field). To view your approximate depth, press in on the Nikon FE's depth-of-field preview lever with your lens aperture set to some opening other than maximum. Through the viewfinder, you will see a gradual darkening of the picture image and an increase in sharpness in front of and behind the main subject, indicating the approximate gain in depth of field you will experience when the photograph is actually made. We stress 'approximate', since for a more precise indication of just how far depth extends before and behind the subject you should refer to the lens's depth-of-field scale (see chapter on exposure and depth of field), or consult the depth-of-field tables which came with your lens.

Lens coupling

The Nikon FE takes Nikon AI lenses, which mount directly in the usual way (see page 208). With older automatic diaphragm. Nikkor lenses not having the AI coupling ridge on back and thus not providing full aperture metering, mount as follows. Push inwards on the small button near the mounting lever on the front of the camera lens mount ring. Flip the lever upwards. Now mount the lens. The lens will couple to the automatic diaphragm mechanism of the camera perfectly, but you will have to press in the depth-of-field preview lever while making an exposure meter reading or during auto exposure. This same procedure should be used when automatic extension tubes are mounted to the Nikon FE.

When using non-automatic extension tubes or bellows units where the lens's automatic diaphragm mechanism is not coupled to the camera, the lens must be closed down to the shooting aperture manually. You need not press the depth-of-field preview lever when making an exposure reading or shooting the picture.

With lenses or optical systems having only a single aperture – mirror lenses, microscopes and telescopes – make your meter readings and exposures at the single opening. (However, for all of these operations remember the lens coupling lever must be in the flipped up position.)

If you wish, you can also use your AI lens for stop-down aperture meter readings and exposure. Simply flip up the coupling lever, as already

Viewing and exposure

The viewfinder contains exposure and focusing information.

1. Automatic exposure indicator
2. Shutter speed, auto exposure pointer
3. Shutter speed scale
4. Meter needle
5. Lens aperture readout
6. Main metering area
7. Microprism grid
8. Split-image rangefinder
9. Underexposure area

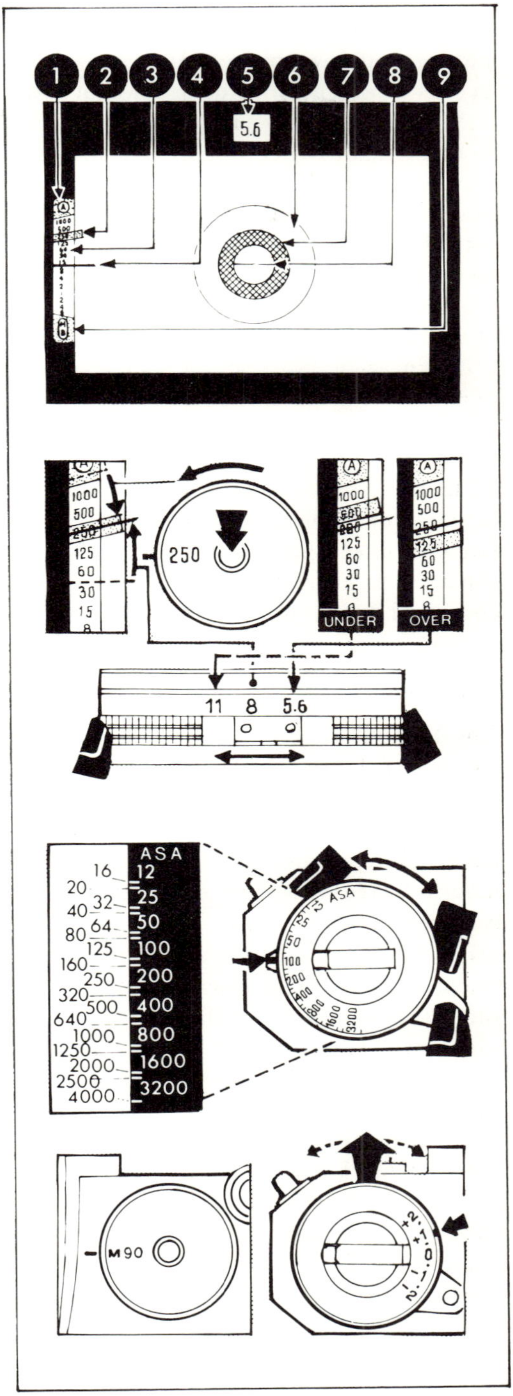

With the shutter dial on 'AUTOMATIC' the camera sets the shutter speed indicated by the meter needle. To set the shutter speed manually, depress the centre button on the shutter dial, and turn it to the desired speed. The green pointer then indicates that speed in the viewfinder; altering the lens aperture changes the meter needle position.

The meter only indicates (or sets) the correct exposure if it is set to the correct film speed. To change the film speed setting, depress the lock button, and rotate the dial until the correct ASA speed (number or intermediate mark) lines with the index.

The camera has a battery-less speed of 1/90 second. It is convenient to set this speed for flash pictures, but you can use any setting up to 1/125.

In unusual conditions, you can adjust the automatic exposure by up to two stops either way. To change the setting, lift the film speed ring, and turn it one way or the other. Return it to 'O' for normal pictures.

described, and proceed as if the lens were a non-AI lens. But do not try making stop-down meter readings or auto exposures with AI lenses while the lever is in the downwards position or improper exposure will result.

At stop-down aperture, the Nikon FE can be operated in the auto exposure mode or manually. For auto exposure, simply set the shutter speed dial to 'auto' and the camera will provide the proper exposure. On manual, use the shutter speeds to match up the green transparent pointer in the viewfinder with the black meter indicating pointer, if you wish to follow the camera's metering suggestions, or you can set whatever shutter speed you wish.

Make sure when remounting your AI lens to the FE, following stop-down operation, that you flip the lens mounting lever back downwards.

Focusing screens

The Nikon FE focusing screens can be readily interchanged by the user. While the standard screen supplied with the camera (type K – with its three methods of focusing: split-image rangefinder, microprism collar and full focusing outer areas) is probably the most suitable for general photographic applications, there are some special picture-taking situations which may best be served by a specialised screen. Additionally, some users prefer other screens.

To change screens, just remove the lens from the camera. At the top front of the camera body lens mount interior there is a small horizontal latch. Press upwards on the latch and the focusing screen frame holder drops down, giving you access to the screen itself. Each accessory screen is provided with a small pair of tweezers for exchanging screens. Do not touch them with your fingers. If you do, you may dirty the screens' optical surfaces. To insert a new screen, place it carefully in the frame holder, flat side upward and tab out to the right side. Press the front edge of the holder upwards into position until it locks securely.

Besides the K screen, two others are available. First, there's a type B which has a plain fine focusing area in place of the split-image rangefinder and the microprism collar. Type B is particularly useful when using wide-angle, tele and small aperture lenses as well as in close-up work where one or the other semi-circles of the split-image rangefinder might darken. The fine-focusing area is contained in the 12 mm circle which approximates the centreweighting of the metering system.

The Type E screen is exactly the same as the B but in addition has a superimposed etched grid. This can be used as a help in architectural photography to align buildings (or in copying where you wish to line up texts or pictures). It is excellent for use with the Nikkor perspective control lenses since the grid pattern offers precise information for non-parallel line correction. The Type E is also used by some photographers as a compositional aid.

The focusing screen interchange allows the user access to the interior of his

Focusing screens

You can exchange the focusing screens on the Nikon FE. To release the screen frame, push up on the small catch the screen and frame then drop down. Take out the screen with the tweezers supplied with alternative screens. Do not touch the surface with your fingers.

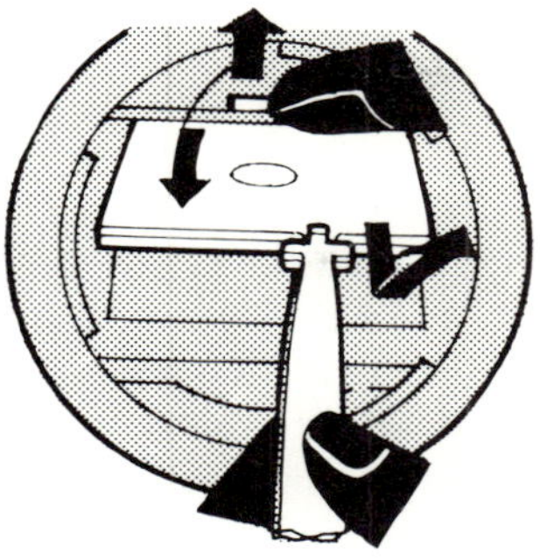

Three screens are available. Type K, as normally fitted with split-image and microprism areas; type B, a matte screen with a 12 mm diameter fine ground spot, and the similar type E, which also has horizontal and vertical lines so that you can align buildings and other man-made articles accurately.

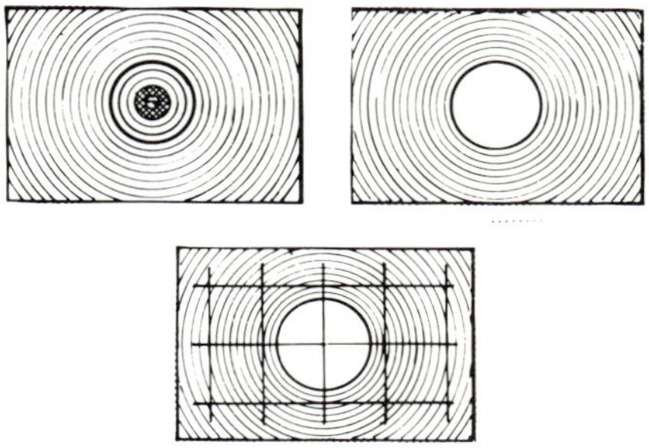

Lens mounting

To mount the lens, align the aperture/focus index with the camera lens mounting index; push in the lens; and turn it counterclockwise until it locks.

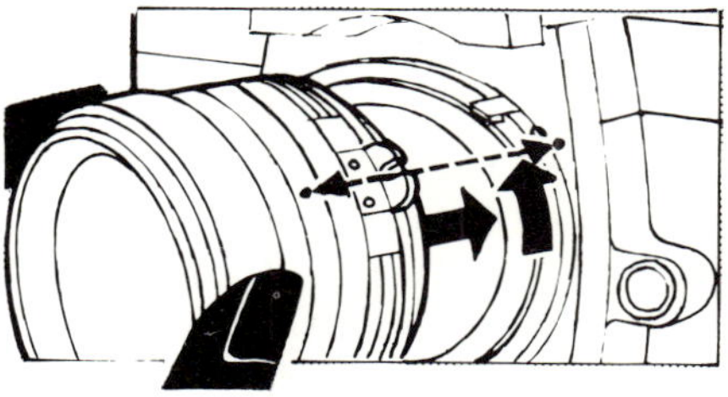

To remove a lens, depress the release button, and turn the lens clockwise until you can lift it out.

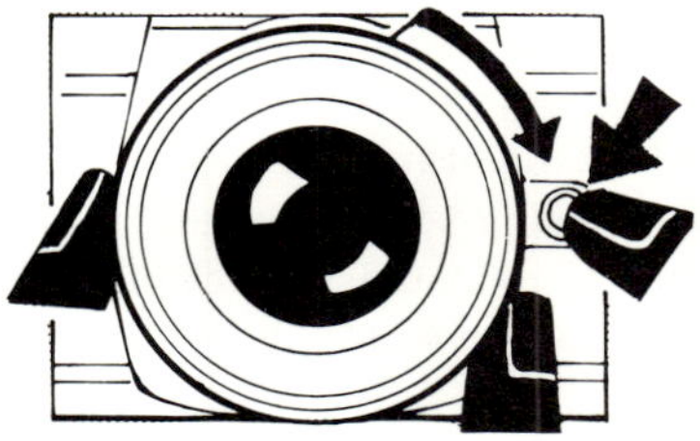

viewing system so he can remove any stray pieces of dust or dirt which may be lodged there. Remove with a clean, fine-quality paint brush or brush with air blower.

Flash

While the Nikon FE can be used with any electronic flash unit, the special one designed just for the FE, the Nikon Speedlight SB-10, is certainly the most convenient. It is a fully automatic electronic flash with a front mounted silicon cell that reads the amount of flash falling on the subject during the exposure and adjusts the duration of the light during the exposure. The SB-10 also has a power-saving circuit. Should the flash be fired at a closer range than its maximum, the extra energy saved by shooting closer is stored in the flash unit for use the next time. In this way the flash unit can provide far more flashes per charge or set of batteries than a non-energy-saving unit.

The SB-10 provides coverage of 56° horizontal and 40° vertical which is sufficient to cover the angle of a 35mm lens. (An accessory panel provides 28mm coverage but a loss in overall brightness.) Its foot slides into the hot coupling shoe atop the camera. Using four penlight-size manganese alkaline cells, the unit will deliver upwards of 160 shots. When the SB-10 is completely recycled, the ready-light in the top of the FE's viewfinder will glow red, indicating the flash is fully charged for the next picture. The flash unit also has its own ready-light. The recycling time is around 8 seconds.

Load the SB-10 with four AA cells by pressing inwards on the two battery compartment latches and pulling the battery compartment from the unit. Insert the batteries as indicated on the compartment interior. Replace the compartment. Slide the SB-10 into the FE's hot shoe as far as it will go and then tighten the foot and shoe together by rotating the foot-locking ring clockwise.

Set the ASA index of your film at the bottom window of the large calculator dial on top of the flash unit by turning the outer ribbed collar. The two coloured markings, red and blue, at the top of the dial indicate the two possible aperture settings of the lens during auto exposure. With ASA 100 film, these are *f*/4 and *f*/8. These two markings also provide the auto exposure distance range. Read the footage scale opposite them. At ASA 100, *f*/4 is opposite the 6m (20ft) marking, indicating that the auto exposure range will be to 6m (20ft). At *f*/8, the range is to 3m (10ft). Both of these ranges extend from the closest marked distance on the calculator scale, 0.6m (2ft). Distance ranges and aperture choices change, of course, with various speed films. The higher the film speed the greater the distance ranges possible. For the most depth of field, you will probably wish to use the short distance range. For greatest coverage, the larger aperture setting will be needed.

For automatic use, set your camera's aperture ring to the aperture indicated on the SB-10. Press in the shooting mode selector switch on the

Flash with the FE

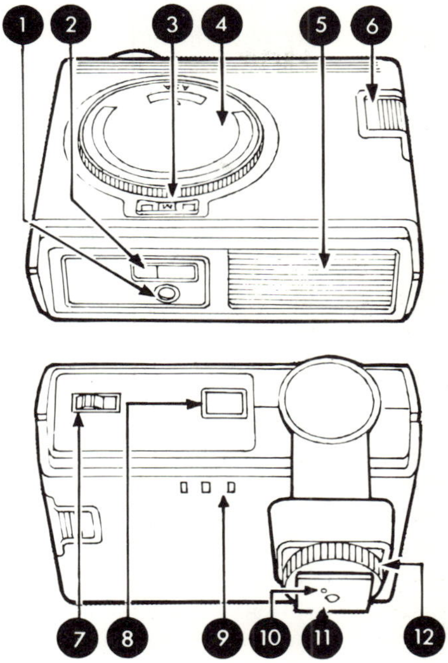

The Nikon Speedlight SB-10 is specially designed to work with the Nikon FE, as it contacts with the camera's built-in ready-light.

1. Light sensor
2. Shooting mode selector
3. Shooting mode indicator
4. Exposure calculator/auto exposure aperture indicator
5. Flash tube
6. Battery compartment
7. Main switch
8. Ready-light/open flash
9. Sync lead socket
10. Ready-light contact
11. Mounting foot
12. Locking screw

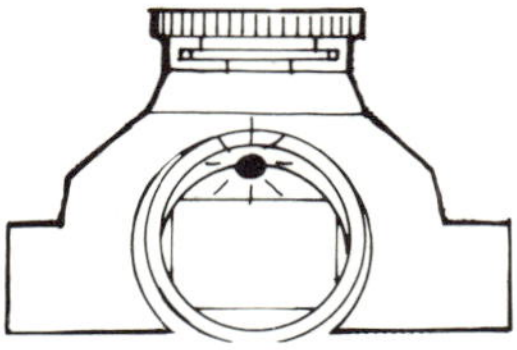

The Speedlight illuminates a second 'ready' light in the FE viewfinder.

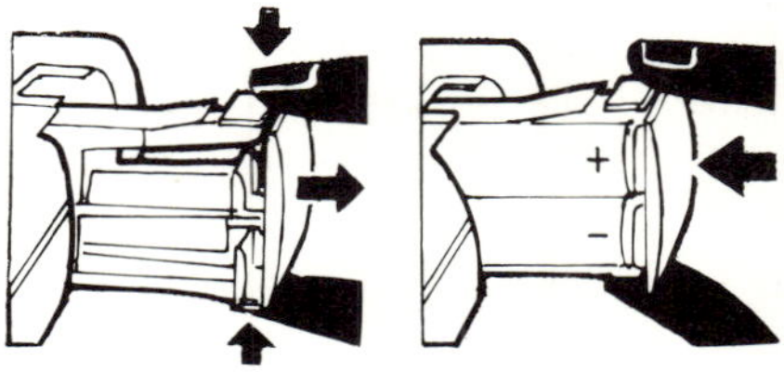

To remove the battery holder, press the two sides, and pull it out. Load it with 4 pen .cells, oriented correctly, and push it back in.

The Nikon FE has X-synchronisation. It can be used with electronic units at all speeds (including M90) up to 1/125 second. It can be used with bulb flash at all speeds up to 1/30 second.

		Shutter Speeds															
		1000	500	250	125	60	30	15	8	4	2	1	2	4	8	M90	B
Electronic																	
Bulb	FP	Cannot be used															
	M																
	MF																

front of the SB-10 and slide the switch to move the pointer in the small window just above the calculator dial to red or blue. Your shutter speed dial should be set to the 'auto' position. Turn on the SB-10 using the off-on switch at the back of the flash unit. Within 8 seconds the ready-light on the flash unit and that inside the viewfinder will begin to glow. Although the black viewfinder pointer will continue to indicate various shutter speeds, the camera's electronic circuitry sets the shutter at 1/90 s, the proper flash speed. If your subject is fairly centrally located (so the front silicon cell can get a reading of it during the flash) you will achieve proper exposure within the focusing range indicated on the calculator dial.

The SB-10 can also be used on manual shutter speed for existing light flash fill-in or to employ the even faster 1/125 s sync speed available which reduces the possibility of ghost images caused by existing light. Move the shooting mode selector switch to the central position. The indicator above the calculator dial moves to 'M'. However, should you inadvertently select a speed too fast for proper electronic flash synchronisation (1/125 s or faster) the warning recycling signal light within the viewfinder will begin to blink. When any flash other than the SB-10 or a similar specially designed unit is fitted to the Nikon FE the shutter speed will not be set automatically. You must therefore manually shift the shutter speed dial to 1/90 or 1/125 s. The 1/90 s and B speed settings are non-electronic and will operate even if there are no batteries in the camera – quite useful for emergencies if your batteries do go dead.

Motor drive

The Nikon MD-12 or earlier MD-11 Motor Drive, which can provide 3.5 frames per second continuous sequence photography or single frame shooting with automatic shutter and film winding, is exactly the same as that already fully described in the Nikon FM and FM2 chapter. All instructions for its use are precisely the same except that the FE does not have a two-position locking collar around the camera body shutter release. To operate the MD-11 or 12 with the FE, please refer to the FM and FM2 chapter.

Nikon EM

The Nikon EM is the smallest, lightest and easiest-to-operate camera Nippon Kogaku has ever produced.

Batteries

Before you can use your EM, you must insert the batteries. Using the edge of a coin or similar object, turn the slotted battery chamber cover on the bottom of the camera in a counterclockwise direction until the entire battery clip connected to the cover can be removed. Insert two fresh 1.5 V silver oxide batteries in the clip, one atop the other, with the + marks on the batteries facing upwards, away from the cover. Reinsert the slip and cover. Push the blue battery check button near the hub of the rapid wind lever. The adjacent light-emitting diode should glow red if the batteries are all right.

You can operate the camera in an emergency without the batteries. Simply set the shutter operation mode selector switch next to the shutter wind hub to M90 to give you a 1/90 s mechanical shutter speed. You can then select the proper aperture for this speed using the printed directions which usually accompany the film (or use a separate meter if one is available).

Loading

To open the camera back for loading, pull up on the rewind knob. The camera back swings open. Insert a 35 mm film cartridge into the empty left-hand chamber and draw the film leader into one of the slots of the take-up spool. Each slot has a small tooth which should engage a sprocket hole of the film. Using the rapid wind lever and pressing the shutter release when necessary, advance the film until the full width of the film covers the top and bottom teeth of the sprocket wheel. The teeth should engage the sprocket holes of the film, both top and bottom.

Close the camera and push the rewind knob downwards. Unfold the rewind lever and turn it in the direction of the arrow on the rewind knob until you feel the tension of the tightened film.

Whenever you begin to wind film to the first exposure, watch the *rewind* knob closely. It should turn, frame by frame, indicating that the film has been loaded properly and is advancing through the camera.

Film speed

Each type of film has a certain sensitivity, usually indicated as its ASA speed (see the chapter on films) printed on the film box or in the instructions accompanying the film. To set the speed, lift up on the outer rim of the dial and turn the rim until the white dot is opposite the correct ASA number. You will see that the scale does not have all the possible numbers. For instance, you may have film with speeds of ASA 64, 80, 125, 160 and the like. However, you will find small dots between the printed numerals. The ASA 64 is one dot higher than the 50 numeral; the ASA 80, two dots. ASA 125 is one dot above the 100 numeral, while 160 is two dots above the 100. After setting the speed, let the rim drop in place.

As a reminder as to which film you have loaded and how many exposures it contains, tear off the cardboard end of the film box and insert it in the memo holder on the back of the camera. Some ends are rather large and you may have to trim them with scissors. Don't forget to remove and replace the box end when you change film types.

Preparing to start

Check your shutter operation mode selector. The white setting dot should be opposite the green 'auto' position. Use the shutter release button alternately with the film and shutter winding lever to advance film from the 'S' marking in the frame counter window to the numeral 1. This usually takes three strokes and releases of the shutter. You can advance film with the wind lever either in one full stroke or a series of strokes.

Normally the metering circuit of the camera turns on with slight pressure on the shutter release. However, you cannot turn on the metering until you reach frame 1. This feature prevents the camera from possibly selecting very long exposures while you are attempting to wind to the first frame.

Automatic exposure control

After you have reached frame 1, you can press the shutter button and watch the speed-indicating needle in the viewfinder drop from the top red area to a position on the shutter speed scale. As you change the aperture of your lens, you will note that the position of the meter needle changes, indicating the shutter speed which will be set by the metering circuit to provide the proper exposure.

The Nikon EM

The Nikon EM is a simple-to-use automatic exposure Nikon camera.
Here are its main features:

1. Frame counter
2. Shutter-release button
3. Film transport lever
4. Film plane indicator
5. Viewfinder eyepiece
6. Flash contacts
7. Accessory shoe
8. Film rewind/back release knob
9. Film-speed scale
10. Shutter mode selector
11. Battery check button
12. Lens aperture ring
13. Battery check LED
14. Focus scale
15. Depth-of-field scale
16. Focus ring
17. ADR scale
18. Self-timer
19. Motor-drive coupling
20. Rewind-release button
21. Nikon AI bayonet lens mount
22. Tripod bush
23. Lens mounting index
24. Battery compartment
25. Lens-release button
26. Exposure-compensating button
27. Motor-drive contacts

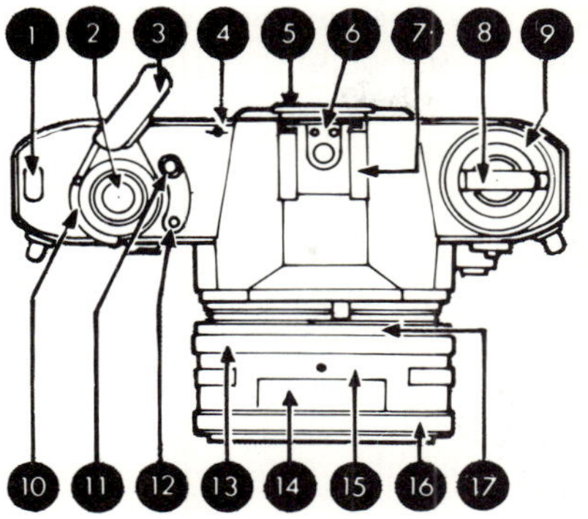

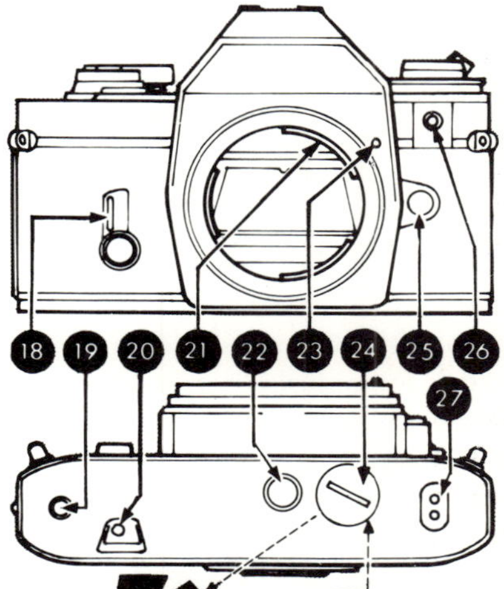

To power the EM, put 2 1.5V silver oxide batteries in the holder, with the plus (+) side facing up.

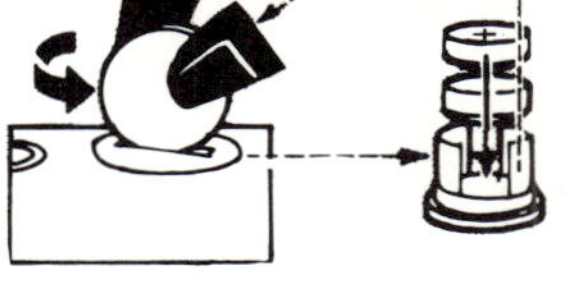

To check battery power, press the button. If the LED lights, all is well.

If you have no battery power, set the shutter to M90 (1/90 second) and choose a suitable lens aperture.

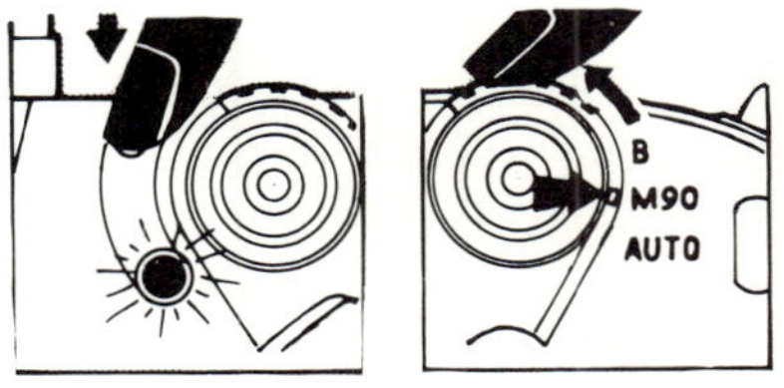

If your exposure meter needle stays within the top red sector when you select a lens opening, you will have an overexposed picture. If the needle remains in the bottom red sector, your picture will be underexposed. In either event, change your lens aperture or light level so that the needle swings over one of the numeral shutter speeds from 1 to 1/1000 s. The shutter speeds below 1/60 s are marked in red to advise you to put the camera on some firm support (such as a tripod) for steady exposures. At speeds below 1/30 s, or if overexposure will occur because of the camera setting, you will hear an audible electronic beep warning signal from your camera when you press the shutter button to turn on the meter.

There will be times when you will not wish the camera to make a continuous audible signal – as when taking pictures in the theatre or when making candids. You can stop the continuous beeping by taking your finger off the shutter release. The metering system will remain on for 20 seconds without any audible signal. You can then set the exposure you wish in silence and take the picture without a beep by pressing instantly down on the shutter release. If you press down too slowly, however, the camera will beep again.

The Nikon EM's auto exposure system will provide you with excellently exposed photographs most of the time with no need to override the setting or try to operate the camera manually. The meter is centreweighted with about 60 per cent of its sensitivity concentrated within the 12 mm circle you see in the viewfinder. Place your main subject (if there is one) within the circle and you will achieve proper exposure. However, when there is a great deal of backlight behind your subject (such as bright windowlight or sunlight), it can create an underexposed picture. To avoid this, press in the blue exposure compensation button at the front of the camera just below the rewind knob. Hold it in while taking the picture. It lowers the shutter speed by two full settings. For instance, if the original shutter speed was 1/125 s, pressing the button would lower it to 1/30 s. The shutter speed needle will drop accordingly in the viewfinder.

Exposure compensation

There are times when you do not want the metered exposure (see chapter on exposure and depth of field). The Nikon EM has no manual shutter speeds except 1/90 s bulb, but you can still vary your exposures to achieve the same results. You do this by readjusting your ASA film speed index scale. Changing the ASA dial setting to a higher index provides less than normal exposure. Setting a lower index increases the exposure. If you wish to decrease your exposure by one *f*/stop, double your ASA index. If you were using an ASA 100 film, you would set ASA 200 instead. If you wish the equivalent of 1/3 *f*/stop less exposure, you would multiply the ASA by 1 1/3. This would be 125. To increase exposure by 1/3 *f*/stop, divide the ASA index by 1 1/3; to increase by one stop, divide by two; to increase by two stops, divide by four, and so on.

Loading the EM

Like all other Nikons, the EM uses normal perforated 35 mm film in cassettes (type 135). (Note: Nikon FG loads in the same manner.)

1. Pull up the knob to open the back
2. Put in the cassette
3. Engage the film in the take-up spool and wind on until sprockets engage top and bottom

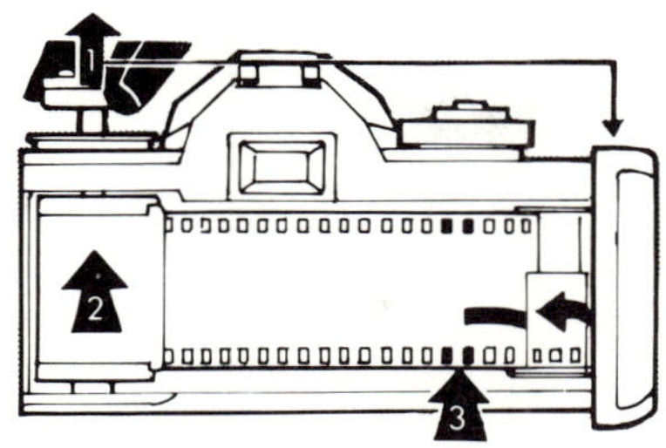

After closing the back take up any slack in the cassette. Then set the camera for the correct film speed (ASA).

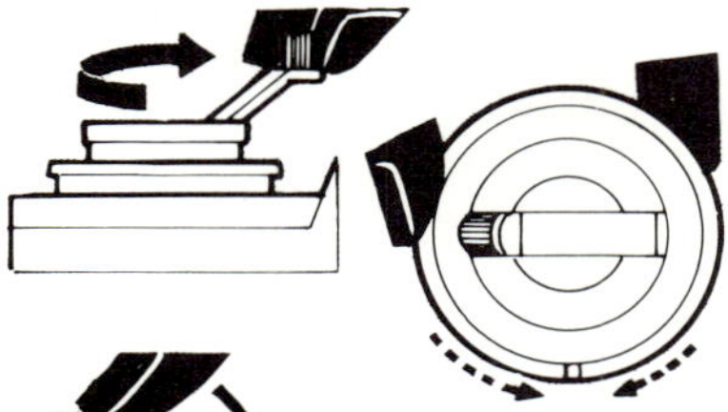

Select automatic shutter operation.

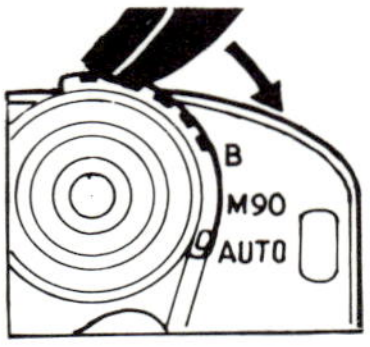

Wind on and release shutter until the frame counter reads 'I'.

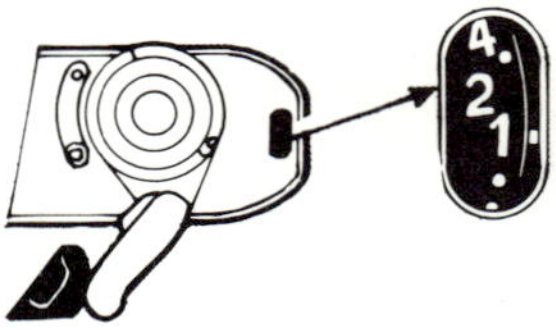

Unloading

At the end of the film, you rewind it into its cassette before removing it for processing.

Press the rewind button to disconnect the film transport mechanism. Then turn the rewind crank until you feel the beginning of the film pull clear of the take-up spool with a click.

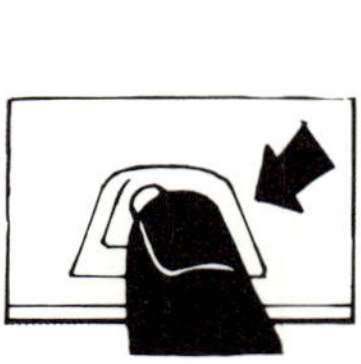

Lift the rewind knob to open the back and remove the cassette.

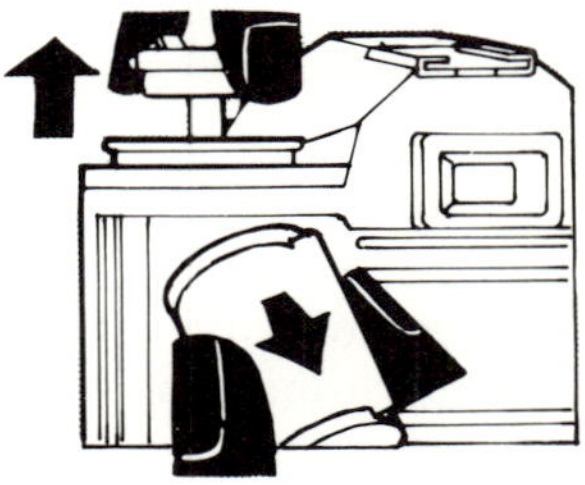

Remote release and self-timer

Whenever you are using a slow shutter speed below 1/30 s and have mounted your camera on a tripod or placed it on a steady support, your finger pressure may jar the camera, causing a blurred picture. To overcome this danger, use a cable release. The shutter release button is internally threaded to accept such a release.

The self-timer, located on the right front of the camera as you hold it, serves two purposes. It delays the exposure so you can get into the picture yourself, and also provides an alternative method of preventing camera movement when you want to make long exposures. To use the self-timer, push the lever down, away from the lens as far as it will go. When you depress the shutter release, the timer will begin its 10 second countdown, releasing the shutter automatically at the end. This gives you enough time to leave the camera and get into the picture. Warning: since your eye will not be at the eyepiece of the camera when you are using either the cable release or the self-timer, there is some danger that bright extraneous light behind the camera may enter the eyepiece and produce an inflated exposure reading, thus causing underexposure of your picture. To avoid this, always cover the eyepiece when taking such a picture, either with your hand, if you are using a cable release, or with a piece of black tape when using the self-timer.

If you decide that you don't want to use the self-timer after having already set it, you can cancel its action by pushing the lever upwards all the way. Remember that the self-timer will only work when film and shutter are wound.

Multiple exposures

You can make double or multiple images with a little dexterity. Take your first picture. Now take all the slack out of the film by tensioning it with the rewind lever (as you did when loading). Hold the rewind knob so it won't turn, and press in the rewind button on the bottom of the camera. At the same time, reset the shutter with the wind lever. The film will not move and you can take another picture on the same film. Repeat as often as you wish (depending on the number of images you want to place on the single film). The frame counter will continue to advance, so remember to subtract the total number of additional exposures from its total.

Long exposures

The longest automatic exposure possible with the Nikon EM is 1 second at the maximum aperture of the lens. However, you will find subjects which require longer exposures: night scenes, fireworks, lightning, for instances. For exposures longer than 1 second, turn the shutter mode selector switch to the B position, attach a cable release to the camera and place it on a tripod or similar steady support. To begin your exposure, press the plunger of the release. Keep it pressed for as long as the exposure is required. Release it to end the exposure.

Taking pictures

What shutter speed and aperture is best for each type of picture-taking situation? Please read the chapter on exposure and depth of field.

Shutter speed and aperture are two important picture-taking controls; your third control is focus. You have three focusing aids within the viewfinder. The central circle on the viewfinder screen is bisected horizontally and is known as a split-image rangefinder. When the image is not properly focused, the top and bottom halves of the prism of the rangefinder image will not line up. By turning the lens focusing ring, you can line up the two halves, thus bringing the image into sharp focus.

Directly surrounding the split-image rangefinder is a microprism collar. The image is focused properly when it appears crystal sharp in this area. When the image is out of focus, it seems fuzzy and shattered. The outer finder area can also be used for focusing. When the image is out of focus, it will appear blurred. When sharp focus is achieved, the subject will become clear and crisp in this outer area. You can use all or any of these focusing aids. Sometimes your subject will govern which to choose. For instance, a flagpole or building edge is easily focused with the central rangefinder. However, a shaggy dog or wheat field is far more easily focused by the microprism or outer focusing area.

There is a fourth way to focus the camera. In candid situations where you won't wish to hold the camera to your eye until you're ready to make the picture (or when shooting flash in pitch darkness where you can't see through the finder at all), you can estimate the camera-to-subject distance and set this footage directly on the focusing scale of your lens.

Should you have difficulty in viewing and focusing your EM because of eyesight problems, see your photo dealer and try one of the eyepiece correction lenses available for the Nikon EM. The camera uses regular Nikon eyepiece correction lenses, but the camera must first be fitted with an eyepiece correction adapter. When in place, you cannot open the camera back. Just slide the adapter upwards slightly and the back can then be easily opened. Do not let it fall again before you close the back.

While you are actually focusing on one specific plane in your picture, sharpness actually falls off gradually in front of and behind your main subject. The further away the subject, and the smaller the aperture, the more slowly sharpness decreases. The amount of depth in which sharpness is considered acceptable is known as depth of field. Your EM lens always shows full aperture and thus minimum depth of field (since the camera has no depth-of-field preview button). However, your lens does have colour-coded depth-of-field indicators on its barrel, adjacent to the focusing scale. You can use these to judge your depth of field or you can consult the depth-of-field tables which come with your lens. Full instructions on controlling depth of field are given in the chapter on exposure and depth of field.

Unloading

After the last exposure you make (usually 12, 20, 24 or 36 frames, depending on the number of exposures provided by the film you have purchased), the film must be rewound into its original cartridge before it can be removed and replaced. Do not accidentally open the camera before rewinding or you will fog a large number of the pictures you have taken.

To rewind film press in the rewind button on the bottom of the camera, unfold the rewind crank and turn it in the direction of the arrow atop the rewind knob. You will be able to detect when all film is rewound, as you will hear a pronounced click of the film leader entering the cartridge and notice a considerable loss of tension as you turn the rewind crank. Now you can open the camera back and reload with fresh film.

Lenses

The Nikon EM is usually fitted with the special compact and light E series Nikon lenses designed for this camera. (Note they are *not* marked Nikkors, but *Nikons*.) A full listing of all Nikon E lenses is provided in the chapter on lenses. The EM can also accept regular Nikkor AI (auto indexing) or AI modified lenses as well. It is not recommended that non-AI Nikon mount lenses be fitted as they can damage the EM auto indexing lever. The EM lenses can be attached to any Nikon or Nikkormat, past or present. On older non-AI camera bodies, exposures must be made by stopping the lens down to shooting aperture since the E series does not have the full aperture meter coupling prong necessary to activate the meter systems on these older cameras. However, the E series can be fully used on all Nikon or Nikkormat cameras having AI, beginning with the Nikkormat FT3 and Nikon EL2.

To attach a lens to the Nikon EM, match the white dot lens mount index at the centre of the lens's depth-of-field scale to the white dot on the front of the camera lens mount. Insert the lens and twist it counterclockwise until it clicks into place. To remove a lens, press the lens release button on the camera and turn the lens clockwise until it becomes loose from the camera.

While we have stated that the Nikon EM does not have an official provision for previewing depth of field, I use an unofficial way of releasing the lens and turning it so that I can preview the depth of field. Here's how you do it. Press the lens release button. Turn the lens clockwise only until the right-hand orange depth-of-field scale line is directly below the 'k' on the

Features of the Nikon EM

To mount a lens, line up the centre index with the camera's index, seat the lens and turn it counterclockwise until it clicks. To remove, depress the release, turn the lens clockwise and lift it out.

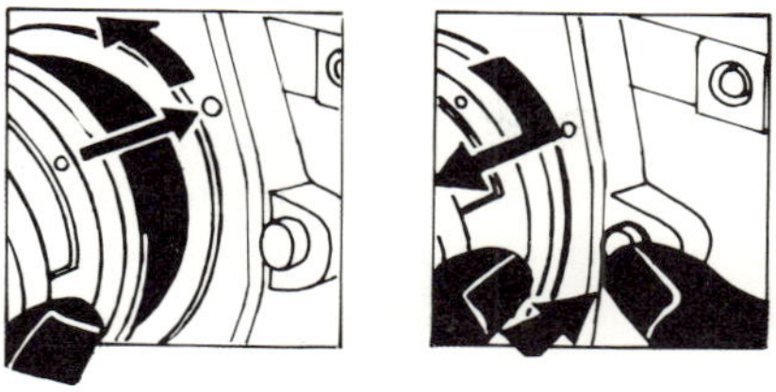

The viewfinder screen shows you the information you need.

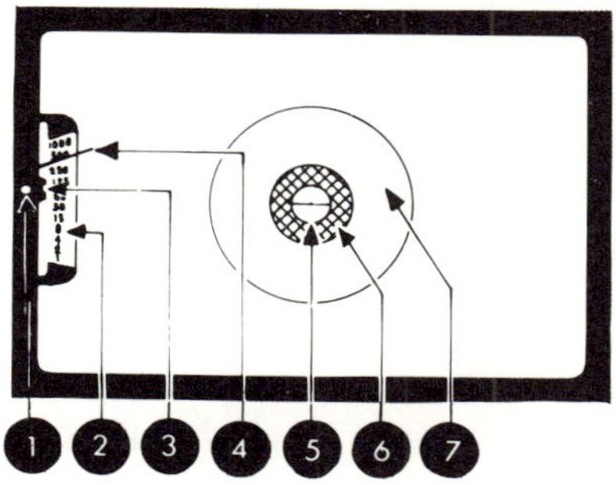

1. Flash ready-light
2. Shutter-speed scale
3. Flash-sync speed bracket
4. Shutter-speed needle
5. Split-image focusing aid
6. Microprism focusing aid
7. Fine matte field, main metering area

To compensate for backlit subjects, depress the compensation button. This gives about 2 stops extra exposure. When the shutter speed is too slow for hand-held shots, or would need to be shorter than 1/1000 s, the camera emits a high-pitched sound to warn you to adjust the lens aperture.

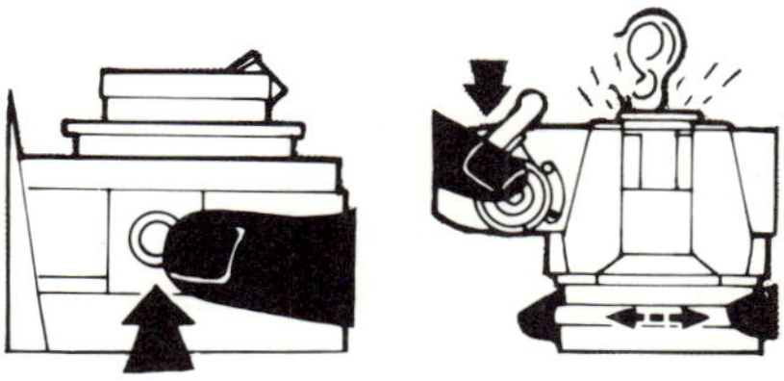

To use the self-timer, pull the lever down to the side. Then operate the shutter release button. Remember to obscure the viewfinder eyepiece to be sure to correct exposure.

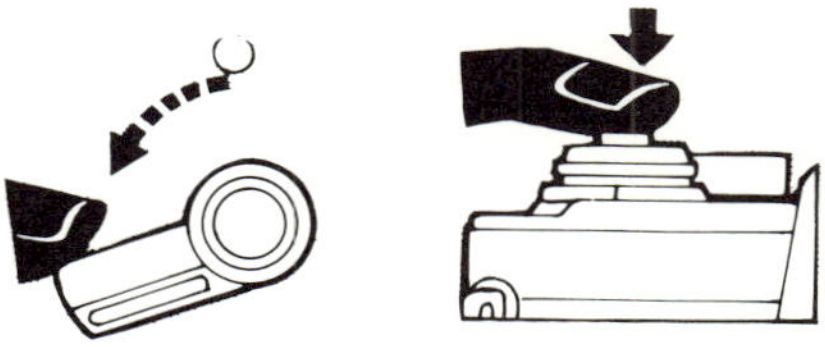

You can operate the winding lever with a single stroke, or with two or more short strokes.

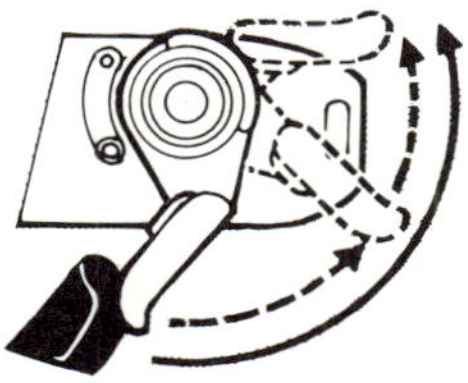

Nikon nameplate. You will find that the lens is still quite secure on the camera. Now if you set any aperture, the lens will actually close down to that opening. You can therefore set the aperture you intend to use. Look through the viewfinder and you will see the approximate depth of field just as well as if you had a depth-of-field preview lever. Afterwards, make sure you twist the lens counterclockwise as far as it will go to lock it again.

Be very careful in selecting any lens accessories such as bellows units, extension tubes, microscope and telescope adapters, manual, preset or single aperture lenses which do not specifically have AI mounts. They can damage your Nikon EM auto indexing lever. When in doubt, consult a reliable photo dealer.

Flash with the SB-E unit

While the Nikon EM can be fitted with a vast variety of electronic flash units, the Nikon Speedlight SB-E specifically designed for it provides the photographer with many conveniences he wouldn't enjoy with other flash units. The SB-E automatically sets the EM's shutter speed to the proper sync speed, warns you when your aperture is out of flash range and shows a red LED in the viewfinder when the flash has completely recycled. It covers the angle of a 35 mm or longer focal length lens.

The SB-E is powered by four AAA alkaline cells. Before loading the batteries, make sure the power switch is off. Then slide open the knurled battery compartment cover and insert the batteries, following the + and − markings within the chamber. Close the lid. Slide the flash unit into the accessory hot shoe of the EM as far as it will go. Set the EM's mode selector switch to 'auto'. Slide the camera selector/power switch on the back of the SB-E to the 'EM' setting. Check the table at the back of the flash unit and note the suggested aperture ranges for your film speed. If your particular film's ASA isn't listed, you will find a line just above the lower ASA index which will correspond to it. Starting from the top of the table, the lines represent ASA 40, 64, 80, 125 and 160. At the largest aperture suggested, your auto flash distance is 0.6 to 6 m (2 to 20 ft). The middle aperture will give you 0.6 to 4 m (2 to 13 ft), while the smallest aperture provides 0.6 to 3 m (2 to 10 ft). The lines representing higher ASA speeds than those on the table provide ⅓ *f*/stop additional range. For instance, if you were using an ASA 160 film speed, you would note that *f*/5.6 is the smallest advised lens opening for ASA 100. The first line greater is ASA 125, providing ⅓ *f*/stop more exposure. The next line is 160, allowing ⅔ *f*/stop more exposure. For ASA 160, then, you could use any aperture from *f*/2.8 + ⅔ *f*/stop to *f*/5.6 + ⅔ *f*/stop. However, you needn't worry if you find this confusing since the diode in the finder will blink to warn you if you have chosen a wrong aperture.

Look through the viewfinder. As soon as the SB-E has reached full power, the red diode will light. So will the diode on the back of the SB-E. If the viewfinder diode starts blinking, you have not set the right aperture. Select

Nikon Speedlight SB-E

The Speedlight SB-E especially designed to go with with Nikon EM. It gives you fully automatic flash operation. All you need do is select one of the lens apertures marked on the table on the back. The SB-E sets the EM shutter to $1/90$ when the shutter switch is on AUTO.

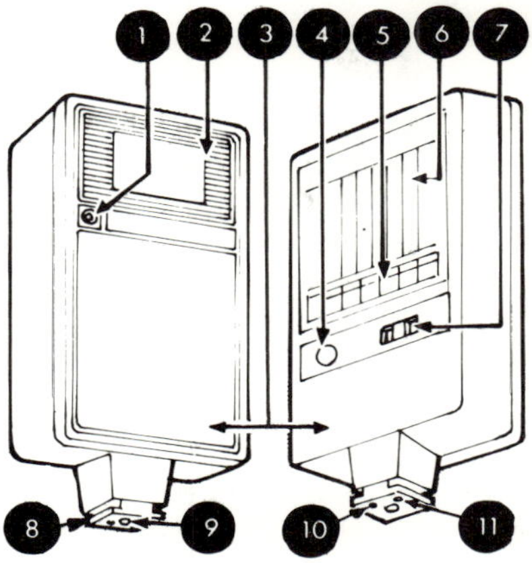

1. Light sensor
2. Flash tube
3. Battery compartment
4. Ready-light
5. Aperture-setting scale (FE/FM)
6. Aperture-setting scale EM
7. Camera type/off switch
8. Mounting foot
9. Sync contact
10. Ready-light contact
11. EM electrical contact

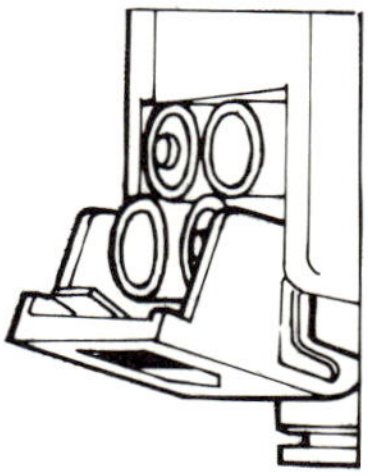

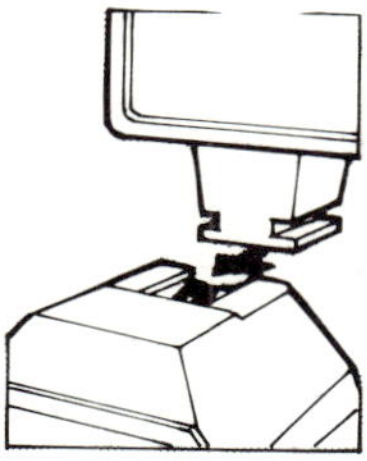

To load the SB-E with four AAA type batteries, press in and down on the compartment lid. Follow the +/− marks in the flash.

The flash is synchronised through the contact on any hot shoe Nikon. To select the aperture to suit your film, refer to the table on the back. On the EM, with Nikon AI mount lenses (not converted lenses or independent lenses), use the top table, and set the flash switch to EM. Then you have a choice of aperture.

On other cameras, or on the EM with a converted Nikkor lens, choose the aperture indicated at the bottom; and set the flash switch to FE/FM. The EM has a ready-light beside the flash sync bracket in the viewfinder. It glows steadily when the flash is ready to fire. If it blinks, you have chosen an aperture outside the correct aperture range.

	ASA \ F	2	2.8	4	5.6	8	11
EM	25	o	o				
	=						
	50	o	o	o			
	=						
	100		o	o	o		
	=						
	200			o	o	o	
	=						
	400				o	o	o

AUTO-FLASH RANGE 0.6-3m(2-10ft)

FE FM						
	ASA	25	50	100	200	400
	F	2.8	4	5.6	8	11

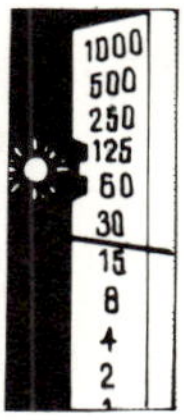

another that will cause the diode to remain on without blinking. You are now ready to take a flash picture. (Note: the LED will blink only with AI or E series lenses. It will not activate by AI modified lenses, or lenses in Nikon AI mount by other makers. For such lenses, you must switch the SB-E to the FE-FM setting on the back of the unit. Look up the correct single aperture on the bottom table at the back of the flash. You will have but a single flash range from 0.6 to 3 m (2 to 10 ft).

After you have made the picture, the diodes will light again when the flash unit has recycled to full power. Since it is an energy saving unit, it will recycle swiftly at short distances and larger apertures, providing more flashes than at small apertures and longer distances. You should be able to get more than 80 flashes per set of batteries. When recycling takes 30 seconds or more, it's time to replace the batteries.

For maximum depth of field, try to select the smallest aperture possible. For greatest number of flashes, use the largest aperture.

The SB-E can also be used on the Nikon FE, FM and other cameras. Set the operating switch to the FE-FM position. On the FE and FM2, the SB-E will cause the finder diode to light when fully recycled but will not give warning when the flash is out of aperture range. However, the diode will blink if the shutter speed is outside the proper electronic flash shutter speed range. Also, only one aperture can used with the camera. The table on the back of the SB-E provides you with this aperture. The range is 0.6 to 3 m (2 to 10 ft). The SB-E does not have any manual operation but always delivers auto exposure. After using the flash, remember to push the switch back to the central 'off' position.

Motor drive

The MD-E Motor Drive is powered by six AAA cells and fits directly beneath the Nikon EM or the FG. It will advance film either as single shots or continuously in bursts at speeds up to 2 frames per second. The vertical post extending upwards from the motor serves as a handgrip.

To load the batteries, squeeze the battery chamber knurled lid opening buttons and pull the lid down. Insert alkaline batteries into the chamber as indicated by the battery diagram within the chamber. Refasten the battery chamber lid.

To attach the motor, make certain the operating switch on the left end is in the 'off' position. Align the motor and bottom of the Nikon EM. Use the motor attachment screw to thread the motor onto the camera via the tripod socket. The motor and camera must be firmly attached. Slide the motor power switch on. Press the EM's shutter release. For single shots, press and then remove finger pressure immediately. This film will automatically be advanced to the next frame and the shutter will be wound, ready for the next picture. If you wish to take sequence pictures, keep your finger on the release.

Nikon Motor Drive MD-E

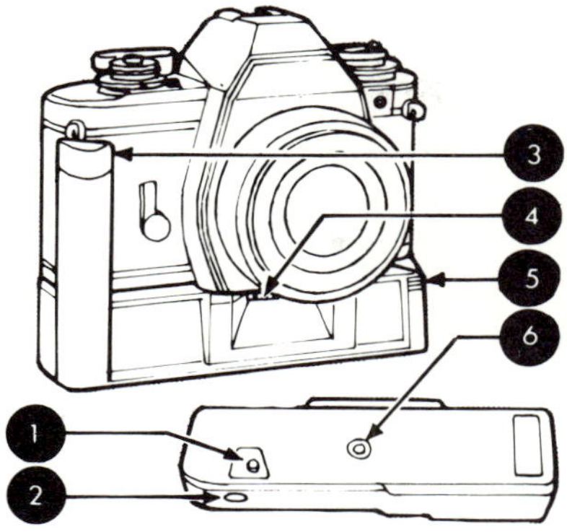

The MD-E provides a convenient power winding facility for your Nikon EM.

1. Rewind-release button
2. Pilot lamp
3. Grip
4. Mounting thumb wheel
5. Battery compartment release
6. Tripod bush

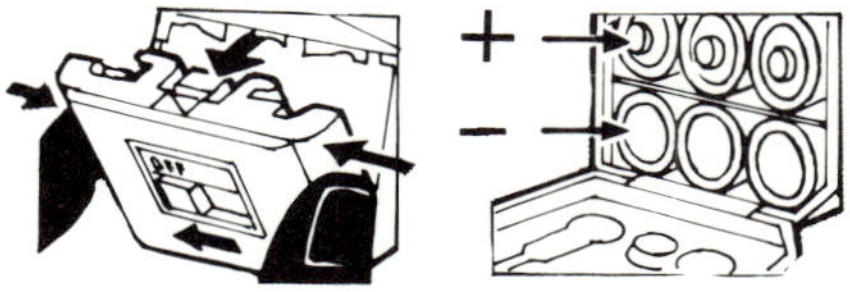

To load batteries, slide the switch to off, and squeeze the release buttons to open the cover. Put in six size AAA manganese alkaline cells – follow the +/– orientation marked inside and shut the cover. To mount the camera, line up the contacts, stand it on the MD-E, and tighten the attachment screw.

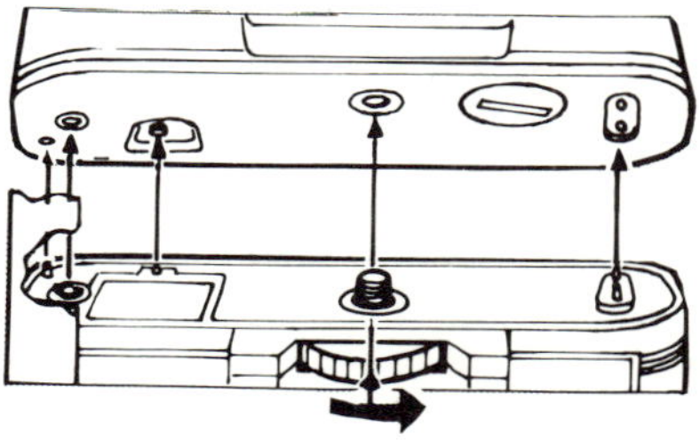

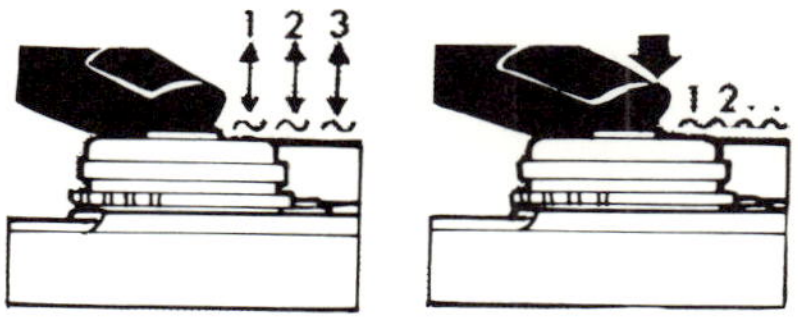

To take single shots, turn on the power, and press and release the shutter button. If you hold the button down, the camera fires continuously at about 2 frames a second.

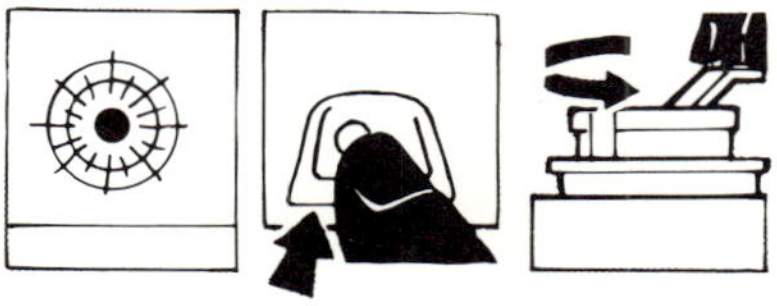

When you have used up your film, the red light stays on. Turn off the power, press the rewind-release button on the MD-E, and you can rewind the film.

The EM will continue to advance film and make the exposures as long as you maintain finger or cable release pressure. The faster your shutter speed, the more swiftly you can take sequence pictures. The LED at the back of the motor will light up during the motorised film advance.

After the last exposure on the roll, the LED on the motor back will remain lit. Turn off the motor, press in the rewind button on the bottom of the motor (you needn't remove the motor to rewind or change film). Rewind the film and replace it with fresh film. The motor will drive about 50 rolls of 36-exposures through the camera on a fresh set of batteries. However, if you are operating in cold weather, a lower number of rolls will be realised.

If you wish, you can wind the camera manually with the motor attached. Simply leave the motor switch in the 'off' position and wind the film by hand using the rapid wind lever.

Nikon FG

The Nikon FG, introduced in 1981, represents Nippon Kogaku's successful attempt to provide a highly versatile, sophisticated camera of remarkably small size and moderate price. To accomplish this, Nikon engineers based the design on the basic camera body of the Nikon EM. However, unlike the EM which provides aperture-preference auto exposure only, the FG incorporates some of the advanced features which amateurs and professionals most want. These include not only aperture-preference automation but program auto exposure (in which the camera's metering system selects both shutter speed and aperture), manual control with a full set of quartz-timed electronic speeds which can be set in conjunction with the camera's metering system, a light-emitting diode (LED) viewfinder information system plus the advantages of through-the-lens electronic flash metering. While incorporating all these conveniences, the camera retains basic shooting signals so that a tyro can still operate the camera with no difficulty. The camera body measures 136 mm long × 87.5 mm high × 54 mm deep (5⁵⁄₁₆ × 3⁷⁄₁₆ × 2⅛ in), weighs 490 g (17.3 oz) and accepts all AI-indexing lenses. Earlier Nikkors which have not been modified to AI or lenses of other makes also unmodified should not be fitted. If they are, they can damage the camera. (Check chapter on lenses if you have any doubt about AI and non-AI lenses.)

Inserting batteries, attaching the lens and loading the camera with film are done as shown in the Nikon EM chapter's drawings. However, for simplicity we will describe them here. Unthread the battery compartment lid at the bottom of the camera by turning the lid counterclockwise with the edge of a coin. Remove the lid and insert two 1.5V alkaline manganese, 1.55 silver oxide or a single 3-volt lithium battery into the lid's battery clip with the + signs up, away from the lid. The batteries must be clean of all moisture or grease. Replace lid and clip in the camera and tighten. Batteries should last up to a year depending on camera use. It's always advisable to keep spares in your gadget bag. You can check the battery strength or correct loading by pressing the shutter release slightly after the batteries are inserted. One or more LEDs in the finder should light.

To mount a lens, line up the distance-scale index dot or line with the mounting index dot on the face of the camera, insert the lens and twist counterclockwise until it clicks into place. The aperture index dot or line should now be directly on top. To remove a lens, press the lens release button and twist the lens clockwise until it can be withdrawn from the camera.

Loading

To load the film, open the camera back by pulling upwards on the rewind knob. The back will swing outwards. Place the film cartridge in the empty left-hand chamber with the film leader pointing to the right, across the film plane. Press the rewind knob down (it may be necessary to rotate it slightly to do so). Pull the film leader end across the film plane and insert the end into any one of the take-up spool slits. Turn the take-up spool's knurled edge inwards slightly with your finger so that the film sprocket holes engage the teeth of the sprocket wheel. Advance the film by alternately pressing the shutter release and winding with the advance lever until the full width of the film covers the sprocket wheels and both sets of sprocket holes are engaged, top and bottom. Close the camera and turn the rewind knob in the direction of the arrow, using the unfolded crank until tension is felt. If you have loaded film correctly, the rewind knob will rotate each time you wind film to the next exposure.

Continue alternately pressing the shutter release and winding film until the no. 1 appears in the frame counter at the far right top end of the camera. Tear off the film box end and insert it into the memo holder at the camera back. Check the film directions for the ASA film speed. Set this number on the ASA speed scale concentric with the rewind knob by pulling upwards on the outer ring, turning the ring until the ring dot is opposite the proper numeral, and then let the ring drop into place.

Exposure

For beginners and all photographers who wish to make setting exposures on the FG as easy as possible, the programme mode of auto exposure is probably the most convenient to use. To prepare the camera for this, rotate the shutter-speed dial until the 'P' is opposite the indicator marking. (If the camera is set to 'A', it will be necessary to press the A/P setting lock release next to the dial before turning it.) Turn the lens aperture ring to its smallest setting (usually *f*/22). Turn on the camera-shake audible warning signal by pushing the signal lever forward, uncovering the small engraved audio indicator. Raise the camera to your eye with your left thumb and forefinger, grasping the camera lens from beneath (for focusing). Your right hand should hold the right side of the camera body with your second finger resting on the shutter release. Press the release gently. This will turn on the single

Nikon FG features

1. Frame counter
2. Shutter-speed/mode selector
3. Film-advance lever
4. Audio warning lever
5. Viewfinder eyepiece
6. Accessory shoe
7. Exposure-compensation dial lock
8. ASA film-speed dial
9. Folded rewind crank and knob
10. A/P-setting lock button
11. Hot shoe sync contact
12. Exposure-meter coupling prong
13. Aperture scale
14. Meter-coupling lever
15. Exposure-compensation dial index
16. Exposure-compensation dial
17. Neckstrap eyelet
18. Lens focusing ring
19. Distance scale
20. Aperture/distance-scale index
21. Lens-mounting index
22. Exposure-compensation button
23. Hand-grip mounting screw
24. Hand grip
25. Self-timer lever
26. Lens-mount bayonet
27. Rapid-return mirror
28. Lens release button
29. Motor-drive positioning hole
30. Motor-drive coupling
31. Film rewind button
32. Film-box end memo holder
33. Tripod socket
34. Battery-chamber lid
35. Motor-drive electrical contacts

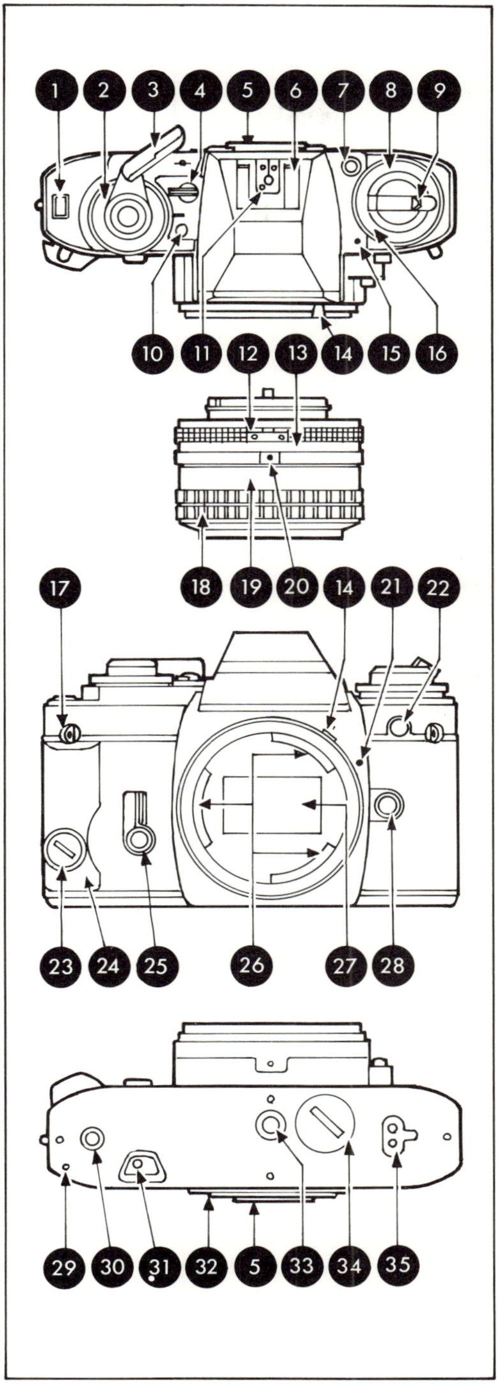

silicon-diode cell metering circuit which provides the traditional Nikon centre-weighted metering pattern in which the light on the focusing screen itself is measured. At the right side of the finder is a vertical shutter-speed scale with a red LED opposite each numeral. Black numerals run upwards from 1/60 second to 1/1000 second. Red numerals (indicating the danger of camera shake if you attempt to use them without a tripod or other suitable support) run downwards from 1/30 to 1 second. The LEDs remain lighted for about 16 second. If they go out before you have taken your picture, just press the shutter release again. Wherever you point the camera, the metering system will set both the shutter speed and aperture for you, choosing a combination of lens opening and speed to provide the best possible exposure and subject control under prevailing lighting conditions. The shutter speed chosen is indicated on the shutter-speed scale. The aperture is not shown, but if you wish to know it, you can check the programme-exposure chart on page 67 where all aperture and speed combinations are given.

If the picture illumination falls beneath the level which provides an adequate speed for a sharp image, 1/30 second, you can see this on the scale, and the audible signal will beep a warning. If light falls even further to the point where an auto exposure isn't possible, a red LED at the bottom of the shutter-speed scale will blink a warning. If you should see two red arrows, top and bottom in the finder, blinking alternately, this means the aperture ring is not set to an aperture of *f*/11 or smaller; in which case, reset the aperture as already described.

Under nearly all adequate lighting conditions, you need not worry about exposure when in the P mode. You will be warned as already described. If, however, the highly unlikely situation should arise where there is too much light to make a proper exposure, the top red arrow will blink in warning and the audible signal will beep. (If it is important to operate your camera as quietly as possible, you can turn off the audible beep signal; but normally it is best to have it operating as often as possible.)

For FG owners who prefer their auto exposure with a bit more personal control, there is aperture-preferred automation in which you can select whatever aperture you wish and the camera metering system will set the appropriate shutter speed. You can choose an aperture that will give you precisely the amount of depth of field you wish or, by watching the shutter-speed scale as you change aperture, select an appropriate speed to stop the type of action you are photographing. (This is explained fully in the chapter on exposure and depth of field.)

To set the FG for aperture-preferred auto exposure, turn the shutter-speed dial to the 'A' setting, again pressing the lock release button if necessary. Now you can select whatever aperture you wish, and the camera selects the shutter speed and indicates it in the viewfinder. The audible-beep and warning-arrow signals operate in the same manner in 'A' setting as in 'P', except that there is no need of a warning for not using the small apertures as

How to set the FG for program auto exposure

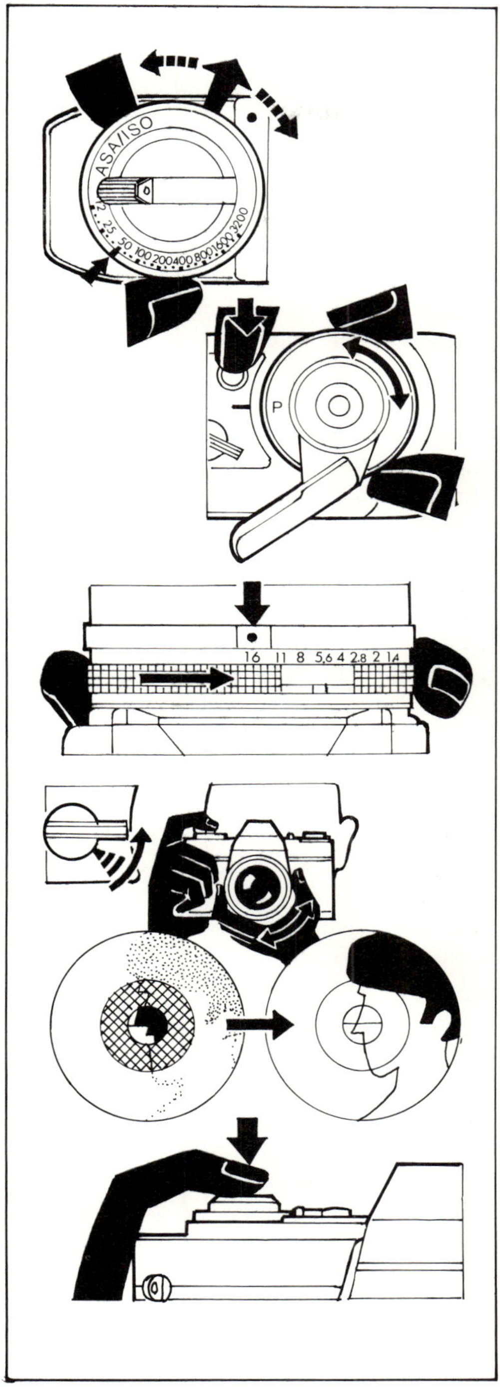

To set the film-speed index, lift up to the ASA/ISO film-speed dial rim and rotate it in either direction until the film-speed index is oppo- site the film speed you are using. Let the rim fall back in place.

While keeping the A/P setting lock button depressed, rotate the shutter-speed/mode selector until the P is opposite the index. Remove your finger from the lock button.

Set the aperture ring at the smal- lest lens opening, usually *f*/16 or *f*/22.

If you wish the audible warning signal to tell you when exposure is below handholding speeds or beyond exposure capabilities, push lever forward uncovering the audio-warning mark.

Hold camera and focus as shown. If image is out of focus (not lined up in the central rangefinder, shimmering in the microprism collar and fuzzy outside), turn focusing ring until image comes together in centre, sharpens in both microprism and outer area.

Press shutter release slightly. If you don't hear audio-warning sig- nal, continue pressing to take the picture.

you are setting the aperture yourself. While shooting, particularly with fast film such as ASA 400, the shutter-speed scale may light an LED and then, as light falls further, change immediately to an underexposure warning arrow. This is an indication that the exposure is probably outside the meter-coupling ability of the camera. For instance, the lowest possible exposure at full aperture with ASA 400 film is ¼ second. Should ½ or 1 second be needed, the camera cannot set it. Check the meter-coupling chart in the 'Facts and figures' section at the back of this book to see what the limits are for each film speed and lens used.

The third method of setting the camera is for full manual operation where you choose and select both aperture and shutter speed. Happily, the FG's metering system will continue to indicate the proper metered exposure so you can compare your settings with what the camera advises. For manual operation, turn the shutter-speed dial to the actual shutter speed you wish, then select and set the aperture on the lens aperture ring. When you press the shutter release lightly, an LED glows opposite the shutter speed you have selected. However, another LED blinks at the speed that the camera's metering system has determined is correct. If you wish to follow the camera's recommendation, just turn the aperture ring until the blinking LED matches the steady one and only the steady LED remains lit.

One of the most useful techniques needing manual control is exposure bracketing. Here you usually take at least three or more exposures at the proper setting, as well as slightly faster and slower. When you have the film developed, you can select the best negative or transparency from the bracketed group. With the FG, you can make your first exposure by matching the blinking and steady LEDs. Then make a second with the blinking LED one reading above the steady LED, and a third with one LED below the steady LED. You now have three exposures taken at correct exposure, 2× and ½×. Many professional photographers who always prefer to set their own exposure controls often use the FG in manual at all times. It is often called match-diode manual control. Although the under- and overexposure warning arrows light when needed, the audible signal does not sound in manual control.

Exposure compensation

There are two more methods of altering exposure. The first is auto-exposure compensation. On the opposite side of the ASA dial concentric with the rewind knob is a scale marked from 0 upwards to 2 on one side and from 0 to −2 on the other. In normal shooting the dial should be at 0. However, for special lighting situations where you may wish to underexpose or overexpose a series of pictures deliberately, these markings are quite useful. For instance, in shooting distant scenics, it is often advisable to reduce exposure by one *f*/stop. You could do this by setting the auto-exposure compensation scale to −1. If you were shooting a series of pictures involving a subject heavily

Nikon FG features and controls

The finder contains the following viewing, exposure and focusing information:

1. Main metering area
2. Split-image rangefinder
3. Microprism collar
4. Fine-focusing area
5. Electronic flash ready/insufficient-light warning signal
6. Shutter-speed/exposure-control scale
7. Under/overexposure warning arrows
8. LED indicator lamps

For aperture-priority auto exposure, press A/P setting lock button and turn dial until the A letter clicks into place opposite the index.

For manual exposure control, press button and turn dial until shutter speed you want is opposite index.

Whether using camera in auto-exposure, aperture-priority or manual mode, select and set your aperture by turning the aperture-setting ring until required opening is opposite index marking.

In manual exposure control, lighted LED 1A represents speed you have selected while blinking LED 2A is speed selected by FG metering system.

For aperture-priority or programme auto exposure, LED will light opposite shutter speed selected 3A and set by FG metering system.

To set auto-exposure compensation dial, press lock button and turn dial until setting required is opposite indicator dot. +2 for white backgrounds, +1 white backgrounds occupying half of picture, −1 spotlit subject occupying half of picture with black background, − black background.

Pressing auto-exposure compensation button at A or P setting automatically lowers shutter-speed equivalent of two *f*/stops.

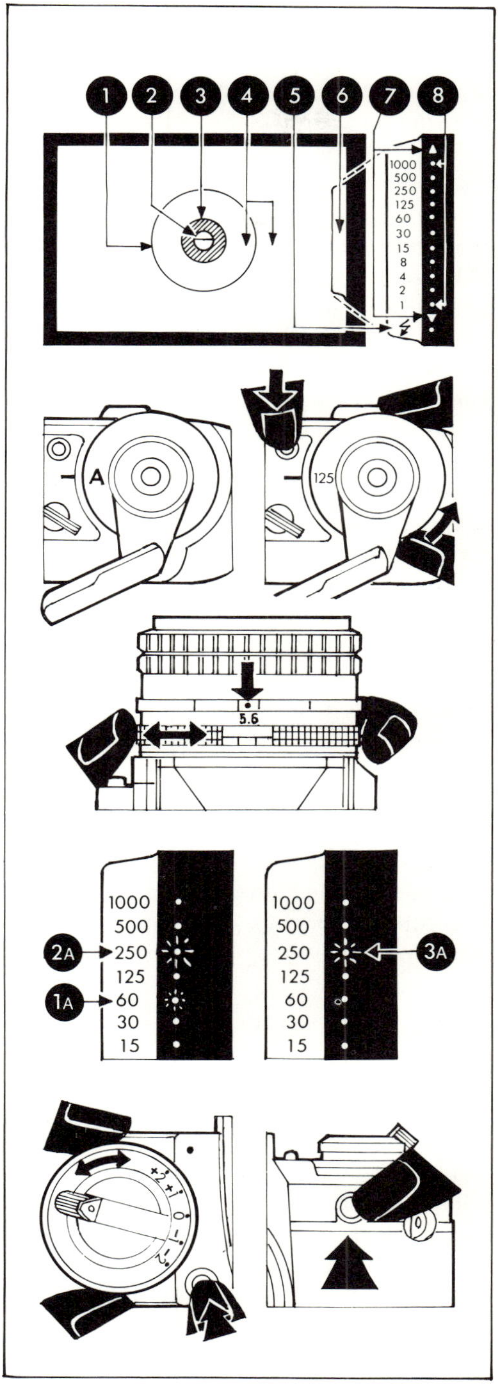

backlit, but wished to retain detail in the main subject, you might wish to increase exposure by 1 or even more stops. You would then set the dial to +1 or more. Other auto-exposure compensation setting needs are shown in the drawing on page 65.

To set the auto-exposure compensation dial, press the adjacent dial lock and rotate the entire dial to the required setting. Since there is no indication in the viewfinder that the auto-exposure compensation has been set, you must remember to return the dial to the neutral zero setting after use.

In some instances you will wish to provide additional exposure compensation for a single picture or two – or perhaps require additional pictures in a hurry to solve a quickly-occurring problem. By pressing the exposure-compensation button on the front of the camera directly below the rewind knob, you can immediately get a full two *f*/stops of additional exposure when you're at either the P or A settings. On P, the exposure is shifted 2 EV lower on the programme scale. On A, the shutter speed is slowed by two settings. For instance, if your speed is to be 1/500 second, pressing the button and keeping it depressed during the exposure causes the speed to shift to 1/125 second. The shutter-speed scale within the viewfinder shows the new speed.

The button is particularly useful for backlit scenes in which you wish to retain detail in your main subject, in brilliant snow or beach scenes.

Besides finger pressure on the shutter release button, there are two additional ways of making the exposure. A standard tapered and threaded cable release can be inserted into the centre of the shutter release button. Pressure on the release's plunger will activate the shutter with less chance of camera movement. This is the preferred release method when you have the camera on a tripod or similar steady support and intend to make an exposure longer than 1/30 second.

When the exposure you require is beyond the 1 second longest auto speed possible, set the shutter speed on B, press the cable release plunger for the requisite number of seconds needed and release the plunger at the end of the timed period.

Self-timer

The FG may also be set off by the self-timer, either to allow you to get into the picture yourself or to provide a vibration-free exposure when a cable release isn't available.

The self-timer on the front of the camera can be set either after exposure or following film and shutter wind. The lever must be turned completely down counterclockwise as far as it will go. When you press the shutter release (with the film and shutter wound), the rapid-return mirror will automatically rise and stay upwards for the duration of the self-timed period. This provides exceptional vibration-free operation since it eliminates any camera movement that could possibly be caused by the rising of the mirror just prior to

More Nikon FG controls

To activate self-timer, turn fully counterclockwise. Press shutter release to start 10 second exposure delay.

To remove hand grip for attachment of motor, insert coin edge into slotted screwhead and turn counterclockwise.

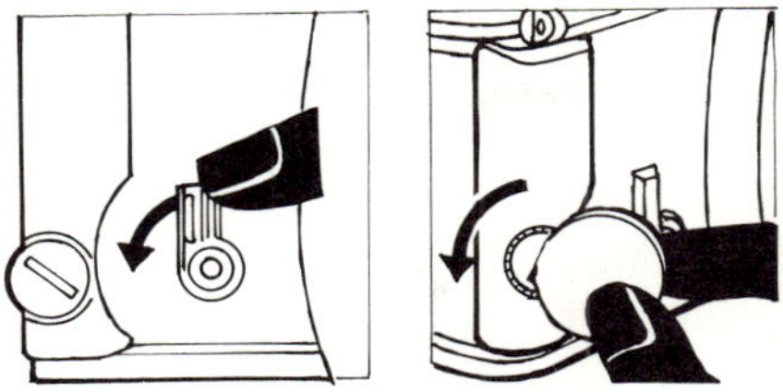

To remind you which film is loaded into camera, tear off film container end and insert in back memo holder.

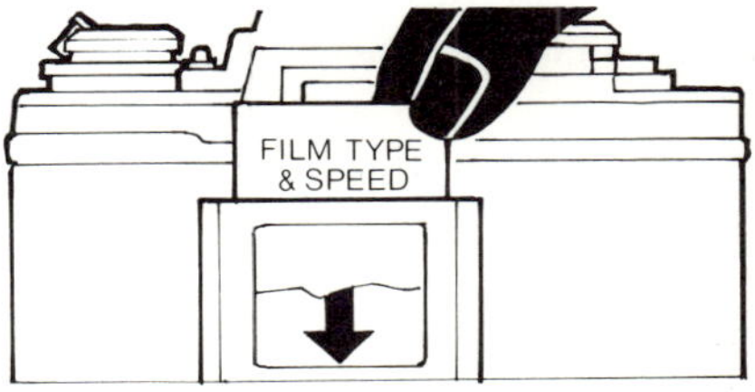

Solid line in graph shows shutter and aperture couplings when camera is used in P setting. With lenses slower than *f*/1.4, exposure couplings begin on that aperture line at left until they join solid graph line. (Example shows *f*/4 aperture lens.) However, following lenses will cause slower shutter speeds: early *f*/1.2s, 50–300 mm *f*/4.5, AI converted 85 mm *f*/1.8, 105 mm *f*/4 Micro, 85–250 *f*/4.

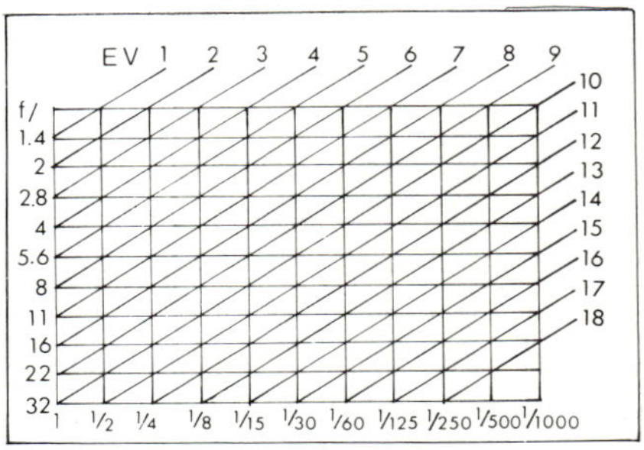

Exposure capability of FG meter becomes limited in shutter-speed reading and setting with films having ASA indexes over 100. Find ASA index group of your film at right, read usable EV range centre and shutter-speed range at left by following appropriate diagonal graph lines.

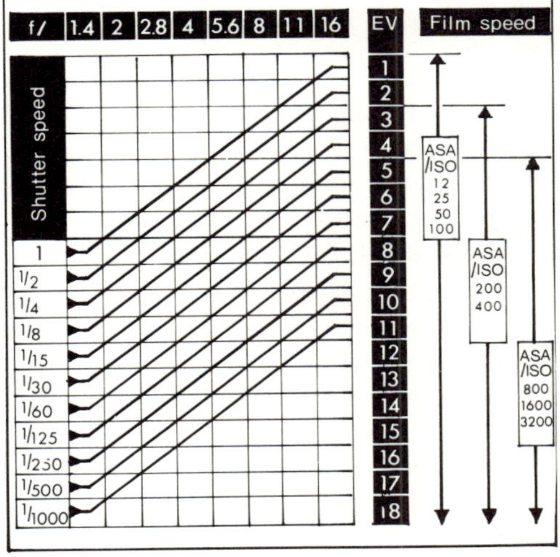

exposure. This is an important advantage when doing scientific work such as photomicrography or astrophotography, or even when using extremely long telephoto lenses or doing close-up work.

The self-timer provides a 10-second interval between the moment the shutter release is pressed and the actual exposure of the film. Once set it cannot be overriden but must be used.

Following the last exposure on the roll (usually 12, 20, 24 or 36 – check your film directions!), the film must be rewound into the original cartridge before it can be removed. Some camera owners attempt to make one or more additional exposures on each film, but do not try if you can detect any pressure on the wind lever. Quite often this last 'stolen' frame won't come out in any event, due to its closeness to the film end.

To rewind film, press inwards on the film rewind button at the bottom of the FG while turning the unfolded rewind-lever crank in the direction of the arrow. Once rewinding begins you need not keep your finger on the button. While some camera owners like to rewind only until the film releases from the take-up spool, thereby leaving the film leader sticking outside, I prefer to rewind the film leader into the cartridge completely so there is no danger that the film can be mistaken for an unexposed roll. In opening the camera to remove film and reload, make certain the film and camera back are protected from direct sunlight to prevent accidental fogging of the film through the cartidge's felt light-trap lip.

There are two features not found on the FG which are usually a part of other Nikon cameras. There is no depth-of-field preview control. To determine what will and will not be in focus at any aperture, check the depth-of-field scales on your lens. The chapter on exposure and depth of field explains the use of these scales.

Flash

The FG has electronic-flash synchronisation exclusively through the accessory shoe and has no PC terminal for off-the-camera flash or flash units not having an accessory foot with sync contact. If such a flash units are to be used, a PC adapter foot which fits the accessory shoe can be found at, or ordered by, your camera store. However, this is not made by Nikon.

Flash with the FG, however, is extremely comprehensive and provides far greater control, convenience and flexibility than do most cameras – including many Nikons. While the camera can accept any shoe-mounted flash with a sync connection in the foot, it offers the most control when used with flash units made specifically for it, principally the Nikon Speedlight SB-15. The SB-15 provides automatic flash control by adjusting its flash output according to the illumination reflected from the subject itself reaching the film during the actual exposure. A silicon cell at the bottom of the camera's mirror chamber points backwards. It measures the amount of illumination

SB-15 speedlight for Nikon FG

While the Nikon SB-15 is specially designed to provide off-the-film flash auto exposure with the Nikon FG, it can be used on other Nikons with hot sync contacts in their accessory shoes.

1. Light sensor (for non-TTL operation)
2. Tilting flashtube unit
3. A2 aperture band indicator (blue)
4. Mode setting knob.
5. A1 aperture band indicator (red)
6. Exposure calculator dial
7. ASA film-speed setting ring
8. Wide-angle lens flash adapter SW-6
9. Battery chamber
10. A1/A2 aperture-selection switch
11. Shooting-mode selector
12. On/off switch
13. Ready-light/open-flash button
14. Sync/multiple-flash terminal
15. Mounting foot
16. Ready-light contact
17. Knurled locking nut
18. Colour-coded auto-shooting range indicators
19. Distance scale
20. MD (motor drive) index
21. Normal lens angle setting index
22. Battery holder
23. Flashtube unit lock
24. Monitor contact
25. TTL flash auto-stop signal contact
26. Flash contact
27. Wide-angle lens setting index
28. Auto sync *f*/stop scale
29. ASA film-speed index
30. ASA film-speed scale

For through-the-lens auto-flash exposure control with Nikon FG, move selector switch 1A to far right TTL setting. Turn on flash by sliding switch 2A to right. Ready light 3A on flash unit and in finder will glow when flash is ready to fire; will blink after exposure if flash illumination was insufficient.

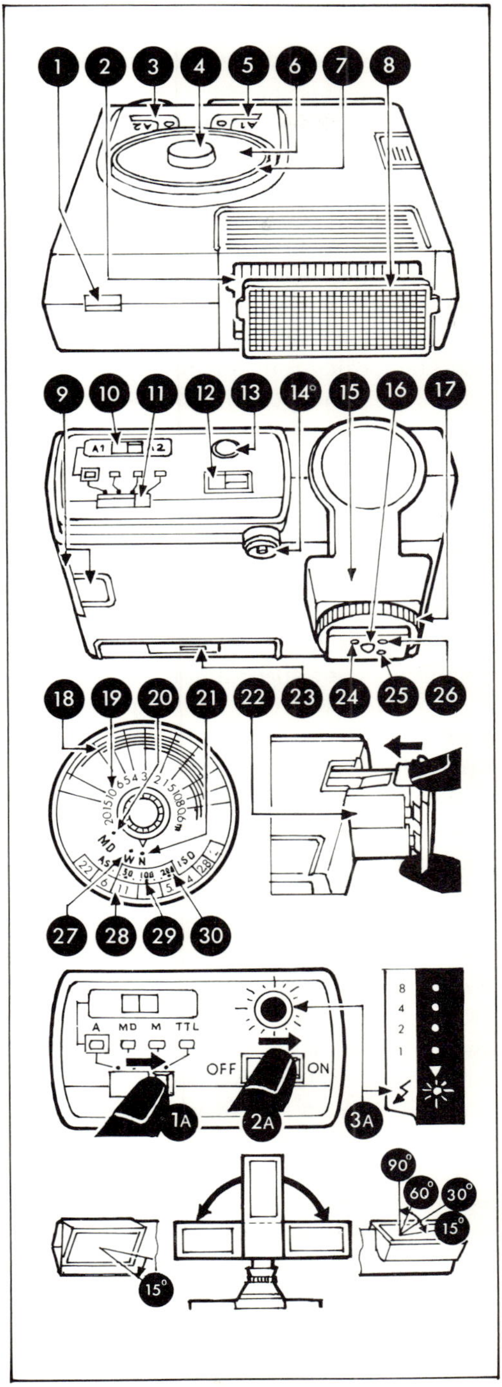

when the film is fully exposed at the actual shooting aperture. It cuts off flash exposure when it detects that the proper amount of illumination has been reached. In this manner correct autoflash exposure is assured within the limits of the flash unit specifications, no matter what lens or what lens accessory is placed on the camera.

Before use, four AA cells must be inserted in the battery-holder located on the left side of the flash unit. Press the knurled battery-holder release locks, top and bottom. The battery-holder will pop out. Insert the batteries, preferably alkaline energisers, in the holder according to the holder diagram, and reinsert the holder into the SB-15. Attach the flash to the FG by sliding the mounting foot forward from the rear of the accessory shoe as far as it will go. The locking nut, directly above the foot, must be rotated counterclockwise first or the foot will not slide in properly. Following insertion, turn the nut clockwise as far as it will go to lock the flash unit to the camera properly.

For use, the flash head should be in the horizontal position so the front nameplate is readable left to right. Set the mode selector switch on the top calculator dial to 'N' (for normal operation). (If you are using a 28 mm wide-angle lens, set it to 'W'.) Turn the exposure-calculator dial, using the central knob, until the N (or W if you are using it) is opposite the ASA speed of the film you have loaded. (This must be between ASA and 400.) Set the shutter-speed dial to either P or A. The flash unit will set the shutter speed to the proper sync speed automatically.

You can now decide what lens aperture you wish to use. On the top of the dial are colour-coded circular lines, each indicating the distance range of an aperature. Depending on the maximum subject distance at which you are shooting, choose one of the apertures. For instance if you have ASA 100 film and want to shoot subjects at distances up to 6 m (20 ft), you can see from the dial that you can use *f*/2, *f*/4, or *f*/2.8. The greatest distance is represented by *f*/2, but the orange *f*/4 line provides a range between 1 and 6.2 m (3 and 20 ft) and offers the greatest depth of field. So it would usually be your logical choice. Set your lens's aperture to the opening you select (in this case *f*/4). Switch the SB-15's mode selector at the left side of the unit's back to the TTL (through-the-lens) position. Turn on the flash unit by sliding the on/off switch to the 'on' position. The small green light beneath the TTL indication will glow, indicating that you are ready for TTL flash. However, before using the unit, you must wait until it is fully charged by the batteries, which is indicated by the red ready light above the on/off glowing. Simultaneously the red LED opposite the lightning mark at the bottom of the viewfinder's shutter-speed scale will glow. This finder light will tell you when the unit has recharged after each shot, so you needn't take the camera away from your eye to examine the ready light at the back of the flash unit itself.

After focusing, press the shutter release. If the ready light within the finder does not blink immediately following the exposure, you have made a picture with the correct exposure. If it does blink, this is an indication that exposure was insufficient. Retake the picture again using a larger lens aperture or move closer to the subject. After your last flash exposure, remember to turn off the flash unit. Do so also between shots in order to conserve battery life if you don't intend to take another picture within a minute or so.

The maximum number of flashes per set of batteries at longest auto distance is about 160 with recycling at 8 seconds. However, because of the SB-15's energy-saving circuitry, the number of flashes will increase markedly and the recycling time shorten, the closer the subject is to the camera, the faster the ASA of the film and the larger the lens aperture you use. Batteries should be replaced when recycling at maximum distance reaches 30 seconds or longer.

When using the SB-15 with its wide-angle adapter (which snaps in front of the flashtube), your maximum flash distance ranges will not be as long as in normal operation.

Besides direct flash, your SB-15 also furnishes proper exposure for bounce flash (see chapter on lighting for an explanation of this useful type of flash). To tilt the flashtube upwards for ceiling bounce, slide the lock directly beneath the tube to the right and at the same time move the flashtube to any desired angled position from 0° to 90°. If you are taking a vertical picture, bring the entire flash unit to the vertical position first and then tilt the flashtube sideways.

A few warnings concerning bounce flash. You can no longer rely on the calculator dial to show the maximum distance possible with each aperture since the flash illumination must now travel to the bounce surface and then be reflected downwards to the subject, a considerably greater distance. Also a certain amount of illumination will be lost at the reflecting surface. The amount depends on the surface's reflectivity. The further away the reflecting surface, the more light you will lose. As a starting point, in a normal room with average-height ceilings, try using an aperture at least two *f*/stops greater than the direct-distance scale calls for. Make an exposure and check the flash confirmation signal in the finder. If it does not light, you are all right. If it does, open your lens aperture further.

The tilting flashtube can be used advantageously for shooting close-ups by tilting it downwards instead of upward. Rotate the SB-15, when attached to the camera, 180° from its standard horizontal position so it is upside down. The flashtube can now be pointed downwards at near subjects as required.

When shooting colour film you will face another bounce-flash problem. The colour of the reflecting surface will affect the colouration of your picture unless the surface is a flat white. For instance, a light-blue ceiling will turn your picture a light blue. A yellowish surface will give your photographs a cast of that colour.

When using TTL flash you may wish to give your subject slightly less or more exposure than normal. This can be done easily with the auto-exposure compensation dial as already explained.

The SB-15 has three other means of providing flash exposures: regular automatic flash, manual flash and motor drive flash (the latter is useful if you want to make sequence pictures with a motor drive attached to the camera). Let's take up automatic flash first.

Instead of TTL flash operation, you may wish to operate with the unit's own front-mounted auto sensor. Set the mode selector switch to A instead of TTL. Use either the A1 or A2 switch setting above the mode selector. The A1 offers a smaller shooting aperture than A2. With the unit turned on, the A1 or A2 indicators below the calculator dial will light opposite the required aperture. You must set the lens to whichever aperture has the lighted LED. The circular lines atop the scale will show you the distance ranges for those apertures.

Regular automatic flash does have one distinct advantage: you can check the exposure prior to taking the actual picture. After waiting for the ready light to go on, aim your camera at the subject while looking through the viewfinder. Press the ready light, which is also the open flash button. The unit will flash. If there is enough light, the confirmation flash signal in the finder will not light. If the light does blink after the flash, use the larger aperture A2, switch to TTL and a larger aperture or try manual flash. When using 'A' automatic flash, remember that it is not as precise and accurate as TTL flash, particularly with wide-angle and tele lenses; and it won't give you correct exposure if you are using various lens accessories such as filters, extension tubes or bellows.

You may wish to ignore auto flash entirely and set your camera manually for maximum distance range. To do this, focus on your subject and read off the distance from the lens's focusing ring. Find that distance on the top of the caclulator dial and set your lens's aperture ring to the aperture which appears directly above the distance on the calculator dial.

To shoot sequence pictures with your camera and SB-15 in which very fast recycling or recharging of the unit between shots is needed, turn both the shooting mode selector and mode setting knob to MD. At this setting, you'll be able to shoot up to four flash shots in a row as fast as 3.5 frames per second (top speed of the accessory MD-14 Nikon Motor Drive). The exposure, however, must be calculated and used manually. The amount of illumination is considerably less for the SB-15 at the MD setting than in normal operation. Use the calculator to find your proper aperture at any shooting distance. For instance, with ASA 100 film and the subject 1.3 m (4 ft) from the camera, the proper aperture would be *f*/5.6. For MD operation, we suggest loading with high-speed film to maximise your possible shooting-distance ability.

The SB-15 can be used off-camera, or a second flash unit can be connected to it in sync for multiple flash operation with the aid of a connecting cord threaded to the terminal at the bottom of the flash head. For off-camera use, screw one end of the accessory SC11, 10 or 15 sync cords into the terminal

Motor drive with the Nikon FG

The MD-14 Motor Drive provides speeds up to 3.2 fps for the FG (and EM too). However, Motor Drive MD-E (see Nikon EM chapter) will also operate on FG at speeds of 2 fps.

1. Battery-chamber locking screw
2. Battery-chamber with battery clip
3. Electrical contacts
4. Attachment wheel
5. Mounting screw
6. Camera-positioning pin
7. Anatomical grip
8. Rewind-button pin
9. Motor drive coupling
10. LED indicator
11. Power switch/high-low fps selector
12. Rewind slide

Unscrew battery-chamber locking screw as indicated. Remove clip from chamber. Load with eight AA cells following + and − indication on clip.

Before mounting motor drive, Nikon FG handgrip must be removed. Use coin edge to unthread slot-headed screw.

Line up motor and camera bottom electrical contacts, mounting screw and socket, motor couplings, camera-positioning pin and motor hole. Thread together using wheel turned in direction of arrow.

Select either L (for 2 fps) or H (for 3.2 fps) firing rates and move selector from 'off' to desired position.

Holding camera as shown, take picture. When film ends, LED lights. Turn off motor immediately. Push up rewind slide and rewind manually using unfolded rewind crank atop Nikon FG rewind knob.

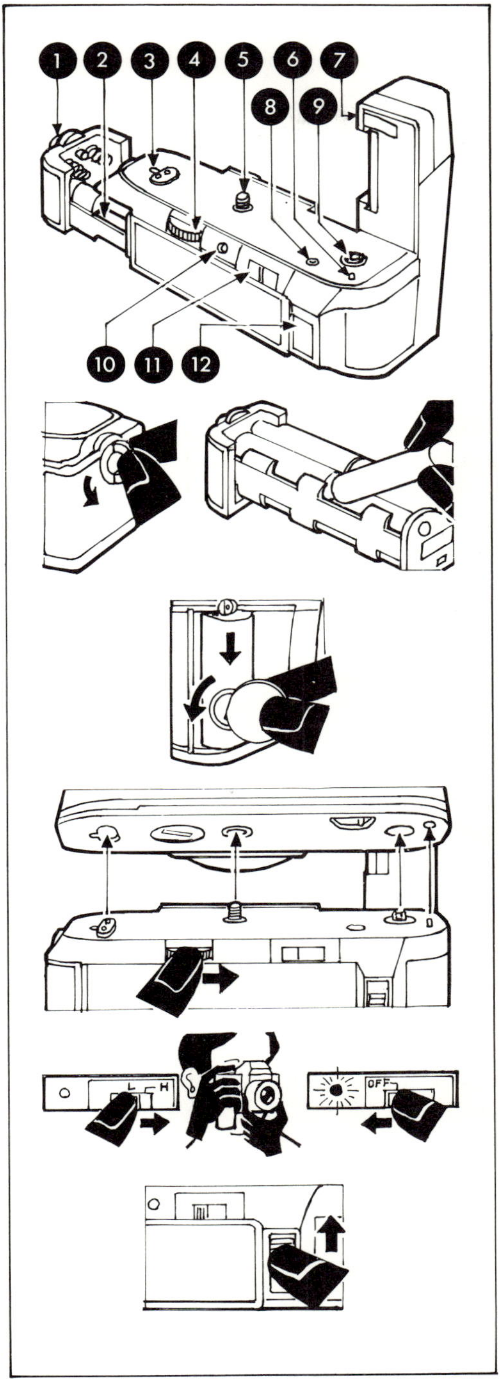

and the other end into the camera's flash terminal. However, in off-camera flash the camera's ready light signal will not operate in the finder, nor will the finder confirmation light be usable. Additionally you must set the camera shutter-speed dial manually to the M90 or 125 sync speeds.

For multiple flash units in which other Nikon units will be attached to the SB-15, see your Nikon dealer to obtain the proper connecting cord.

Motor drive

Two different motor drives are available for the Nikon FG camera. The MD-E 2 fps motor drive, already described and explained in the Nikon EM chapter, can be attached and operated on the FG in exactly the same manner as on the EM. Additionally, with the FG, Nikon made available the more powerful MD-14 3.2 fps maximum-speed motor drive which fits both cameras.

Before use, unthread the motor's battery-chamber locking cover. Lift the outside ring and unscrew it. Remove the battery clip and place eight AA penlight cells in the clip as per the directions on the clip. Alkaline manganese batteries provide sufficient power for approximately 50 rolls of 36 exposures. Replace the clip in the chamber. Remove the FG's handgrip by unthreading the grip-fastening screw counterclockwise using the edge of a coin. Check to make certain the on/off switch at the back of the MD-14 is off and the camera film-advance lever is in the cocked position. Place the FG camera body atop the motor so the camera tripod socket and the motor's mounting screw can be threaded together. The camera's positioning pin should line up with the corresponding hole of the motor drive. Fasten the motor and camera firmly together by turning the attachment wheel clockwise.

Load the camera with film in the normal manner as though the motor drive was not attached. Make the required blank exposures to bring the frame 1 numeral into the proper place on the frame counter.

Position the firing rate selector at the back of the motor to either (L)2 or (H)3.5 fps. This also turns on the motor. You can now use the camera motorised by pressing the shutter release. For single shots, set the L position and remove your finger from the camera shutter release as soon as the exposure is made. For continuous operation, keep the shutter release depressed. Top 2 or 3.2 fps speeds can only be achieved at camera shutter speeds of 1/125 second or greater.

At roll end, the motor automatically ceases to operate but the red LED indicator at the back of the motor lights continuously. At this point, turn the motor off. Push the motor rewind slide upwards and rewind the film manually using the unfolded rewind crank. If you have difficulty pushing the slide upwards, remove the motor from the camera and use the camera's own rewind button.

Nikon F3

Approximately 20 years after the introduction of the Nikon F and 10 years after the Nikon F2, Nippon Kogaku announced the successor, the Nikon F3. Like the F and F2, the F3 was designed and engineered for the professional and serious amateur photographer seeking the most rugged, reliable and yet most flexible and convenient 35 mm SLR possible. The concept of the F3 differs radically from that of the F and F2. Rather than being a mechanically controlled modular add-on camera in which the metering system was actually an attachment to the basic camera body, the electronically controlled F3 has an internal metering system of very advanced design. The metering system provides aperture-preferred automatic exposure (you set the aperture and the camera sets the shutter speed), but still allows full manual speeds from 8 s to 1/2000 s with continuous metering capability. The speeds are displayed within the viewfinder on a liquid crystal (LCD) panel. The panel with the aperture readout can be illuminated from within the camera when the exernal light is insufficient to read the numerals normally. Perhaps more exciting, however, is the availability of automatic flash exposure via a meter readout of the film's surface during the actual flash exposure itself. The new F3 weighs but 960 g (34 oz) with a 50 mm *f*/1.4 Nikkor lens and is 148.5 mm long, 96.5 mm high and 9.3 mm deep (5⅞ × 3 13/16 × 3⅝ in), far smaller than the Nikon F2 it replaces and only a shade larger than the Nikon FE but 4 oz heavier. The F3 has its own motor-drive system and related accessories, a special dedicated flash, an F3 interchangeable finder system and an improved interchangeable finder screen. The camera retains the traditional Nikon lens mount and accepts all AI (auto indexing) or AI-modified lenses for full aperture auto-exposure metering, and all non-AI and manual lenses for auto exposure at shooting aperture.

The metering system and electronically controlled titanium foil focal plane shutter are powered by two 1.5 V silver oxide batteries located in a chamber on the bottom of the camera. Using the edge of a coin or similar object, unthread the silver-coloured battery chamber lid by turning it counterclockwise until the lid with its attached battery clip can be removed. Insert the two batteries with their + signs up, away from the lid. Make certain you keep your fingers off the broad battery surfaces since finger grease can impair the electrical contact. Reinsert the clip and lid into the battery chamber and refasten clockwise with the same coin edge until the lid is adequately tight. Do not use undue force.

To check battery power, move the power switch on the top of the camera at the front of the shutter release collar to the right, uncovering a red dot. Press gently on the shutter release sufficiently to turn on the metering system, but not enough to trip the shutter. The meter remains on for approximately 16 seconds after which it will automatically turn off to conserve battery power. (The F3 has only about a fifth the battery drain in operation that is experienced with many cameras using light-emitting diode digital readouts.) Look through the viewfinder at the rectangle above the picture area and to the left of the central aperture readout window. You should see a shutter speed displayed on the LCD panel. If you do, the battery is operating properly. If nothing appears, either there are no batteries in the battery chamber, their electrical contact is poor, they have been placed in the clip improperly, or they are dead. If there is no LCD reading, reopen the battery chamber and investigate the power failure cause.

To mount the lens on the camera, match up the focusing index mark of the lens with the white dot on the camera body lens mount. Insert the lens into the camera body and, holding the mounting ring, twist it counterclockwise until the lens clicks into place. To remove a lens, push in the lens-release button and twist the lens clockwise.

To open the camera back for loading, push the camera-back lock lever on the rewind knob collar to the right, and at the same time lift the film rewind knob. The back will swing open. (This dual-locking system is designed to prevent accidental opening of the camera back while it is loaded with film.)

To load film, place the 35 mm film cartridge in the left-hand chamber, with the film leader across the camera's film plane, pointing towards the right. Push the rewind knob down (you may have to turn the knob slightly to allow its keying mechanism to mesh with that of the film cartridge). Pull the film leader across the film plane and insert it into one of the take-up spool slots, making certain that a tooth of the take-up spool slit engages a sprocket hole of the film leader. Wind the film using the rapid wind lever and shutter release until the film is engaged on the take-up spool properly and part of the leader has been wound inside out on the take-up spool. (While winding and releasing during loading and also while winding to the first frame after you shut the camera, the electronically controlled shutter will provide a 1/80 s exposure when the shutter speed dial is set to 'A' for automatic. This prevents the shutter remaining open during film wind, causing improper loading, film fogging and excess battery drain.)

After you have closed the camera back, unfold the rewind crank and turn it in the direction of the arrow until it stops. This removes any slack from the film in the film cartridge and allows the rewind knob to turn each time the film is advanced, providing a check on proper loading. If the film rewind

The Nikon F3

1. Film frame counter
2. Shutter release
3. Film advance lever
4. Shutter speed dial
5. Viewfinder eyepiece
6. Viewfinder releases
7. Eyepiece shutter lever
8. Exposure compensation locking button
9. Back release catch
10. Multiple exposure lever
11. Power on/off switch
12. Self-timer lever
13. Viewfinder illuminator button
14. Accessory shoe
15. Hot-shoe contacts
16. Film rewind crank
17. Aperture readout scale
18. Meter coupling shoe
19. Focusing ring
20. Aperture/focus index
21. Focusing scale
22. Aperture ring
23. Meter coupling flange
24. Carrying strap lug
25. Depth-of-field preview button
26. Mirror lock-up lever
27. Speed dial lock button
28. Aperture readout window
29. Viewfinder illuminator
30. Flash sync contacts
31. Film rewind knob
32. Film speed dial
33. Self-timer LED
34. Exposure memory lock
35. Lock button
36. Bayonet mount flange
37. Reflex mirror
38. Meter coupling lever
39. Meter coupling release button
40. Lens release button
41. Lens mounting index
42. Motor-drive locating hole
43. Interlock release button
44. Motor-drive coupling
45. Tripod bush
46. Battery chamber cover
47. Motor-drive electrical contacts
48. Electrical contacts cover-plate

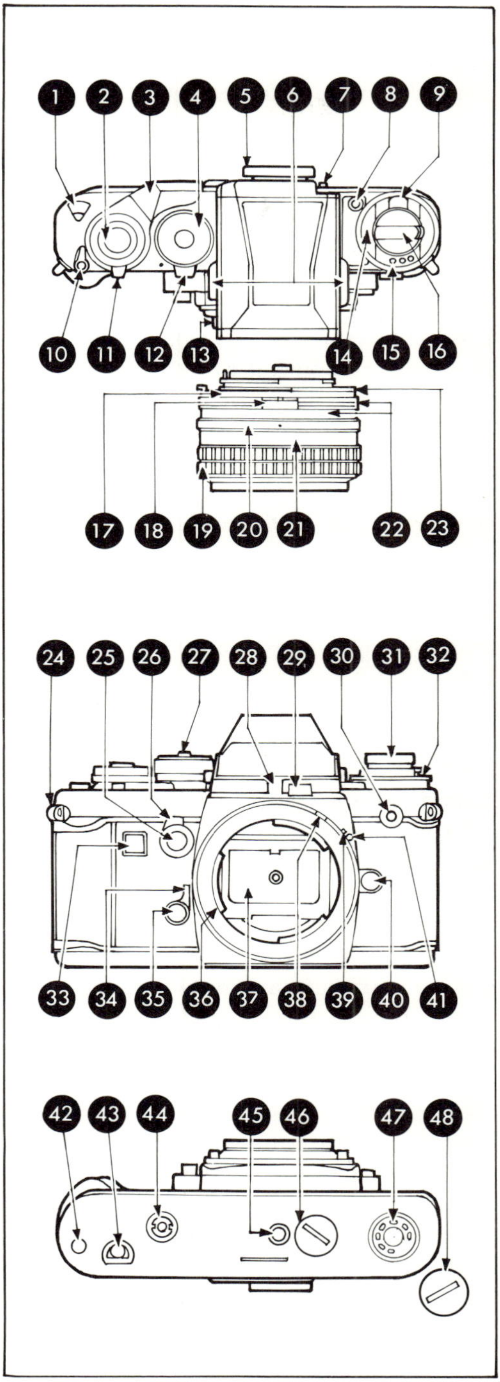

knob does not turn when you advance the film with the rapid wind lever, there is either no film in the camera or the film leader has not been caught properly on the take-up spool.

Using the rapid wind lever and shutter release button, advance the film until frame 1 shows in the frame counter window.

Before taking pictures, you must set the ASA index film speed ring rim around the rewind knob and turn it in either direction until the white dot matches the ASA film speed you intend to use. Let the rim drop back into place. Check the shutter speed dial. It should be set to the 'A' for automatic setting if you intend to use the automatic exposure provision of the camera. If the dial is set to 'X', you will have to press the central hub lock release of the dial before turning it to 'A'. For any other manual shutter speed you can simply rotate the dial until you reach 'A'. When the dial clicks into the 'A' position, it will lock in place and cannot be changed unless you push the central hub button. This safety device prevents an accidental shift off 'A'.

Viewing and focusing

You will find a very complete description of how best to hold your camera and how to carry it in the chapter 'Practical camera operations'. Make certain before proceeding further that you can hold the camera both horizontally and vertically while operating the controls. To focus the camera, turn the rubberised focusing ring of the lens using your thumb and first or second finger (whichever is most convenient) of your left hand. If your camera is equipped with the standard K focusing screen, you will see a small circle bisected horizontally in the centre of the viewfinder. This circle is the split-image rangefinder. Place the horizontal split over your main subject and turn the focusing ring until the top half and bottom half of the subject are aligned within the circle. If the subject has no lines which are easy to focus on even if you turn the camera vertically, use the outer microprism collar and focus until the image snaps into sharp crispness. When shooting with lenses having maximum apertures smaller than *f*/5.6, the split-image rangefinder and/or microprism collar become too dark to use conveniently. In this case, use the outer fine-focusing screen and bring the image into sharpness there.

Within the viewfinder, the F3 provides exposure information besides the focusing aids. If you have an ADR (aperture direct readout) Nikon mount lens, the aperture you set will appear in the top centre window just above the finder screen. To the left is the LCD panel which indicates approximately the shutter speed selected by the camera's built-in metering system. The metering circuit uses a single silicon cell mounted at the bottom of the rapid-return mirror chamber. This cell angles backwards, towards the filmplane. When photographing with continuous light illumination, be it daylight or tungsten, light from the lens is transmitted to the rapid-return mirror. In the centre of the mirror is a darkish rectangle which in reality is an

Preparing the F3

Insert the batteries into their holder and screw this into the base of the camera. If the LCD lights when the shutter release is slightly pressed, the batteries have been inserted correctly and have sufficient power.

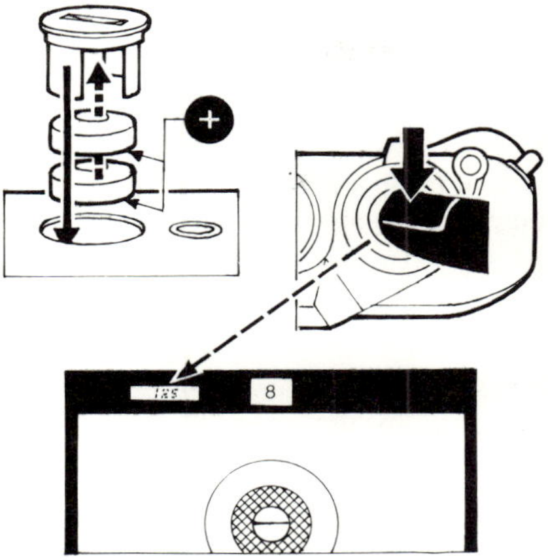

Open the camera by pushing the small catch sideways and pulling up the rewind knob. The back will spring open.

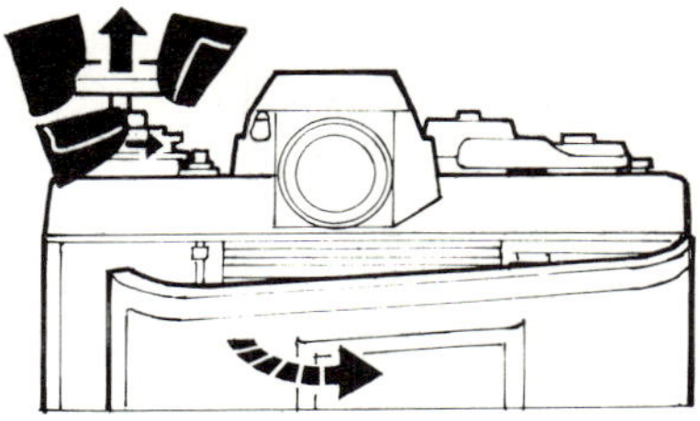

Pull up the rewind knob, insert the film and engage its tongue in the take-up spool, to wind emulsion side out.

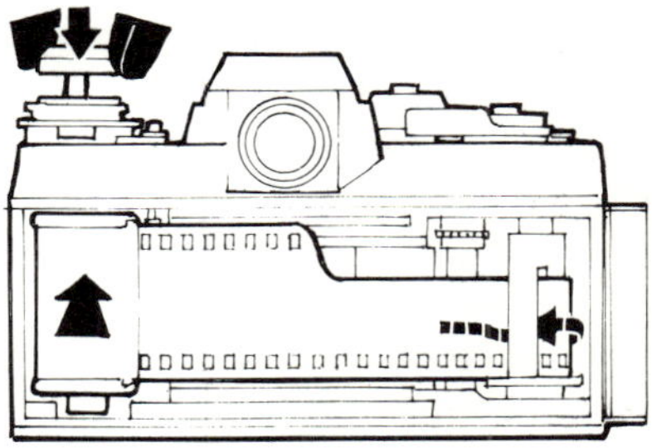

Take up the slack film in the cassette by turning the rewind crank in the direction of the arrow. Advance the film winding lever until No. 1 shows.

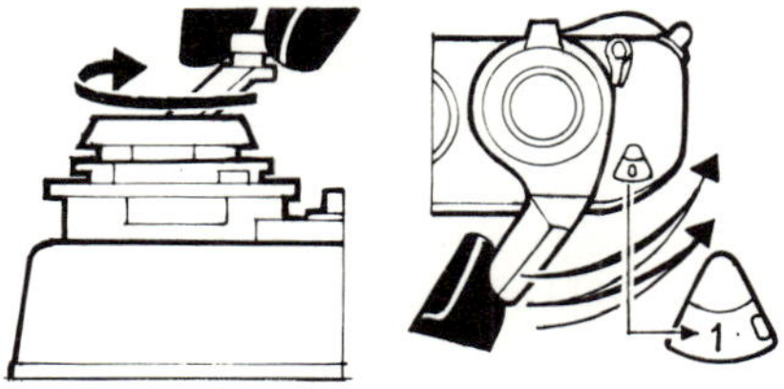

area with some 50 000 clear oval areas. These allow 8 per cent of the light from the lens to be retransmitted to a hinged secondary mirror at the rear of the rapid return mirror. This three-piece mirror concentrates the light and reflects it to the silicon cell. The metering pattern is heavily centre-weighted. It has been traditional in Nikons to have some 60 per cent meter sensitivity weighted within the outer scribed circle in the viewfinder, with 40 per cent in the remaining area. Responding to the requests of professionals for even greater centre-weighting, the Nikon F3 has 80 per cent of the meter weighting contained within the circular area. This increased centre-weighting further minimises the possibility of illumination outside your main picture interest, producing an inflated exposure reading and possibly causing underexposure of your main subject. Later, we'll see how you can also use this to advantage even if your subject is not located centrally in the viewfinder area.

Looking around your viewfinder, note that you can easily see the entire picture frame area plus the shutter speed and aperture readouts even if your are wearing glasses. This is due to the .8× magnification of the Nikon F3 finder which allows greater eye relief (distance from the eyepiece) while still providing full area viewing.

Exposure control

When the shutter release is pressed slightly, turning on the metering system for its 16 seconds, the shutter speeds selected by the metering system will be seen on the LCD panel. As the light level changes and/or you shift the camera from one subject to another, the exposure will shift to the proper one for your subject. In order to prevent confusion, the LCD shutter speeds change only at half-second intervals. They also only show full marked speeds, the same ones as on the shutter speed dial. However, in reality, the auto-exposure system provides almost instantaneous shifting of actual shutter speeds to the exact speed required. In other words, even if your LCD shows 1/250 s and takes half a second to do it, the actual speed set almost immediately may be 1/233 s. The automatic speeds set are continuously variable between 8 s and 1/2000 s. The LCD readout simply indicates the nearest marked setting and is sufficient to give you a close indication of the real speed which will be used. The display panel shows fractional speeds as direct numerals, e.g. 1/250 s is shown as 250. For speeds of 1 to 8 s the numeral appears followed by a short dash, e.g. 4– indicates 4 seconds, *not* 1/4 s.

If the light is too bright for the aperture set and the speed needed is beyond 1/2000 s, a '2000+' will appear meaning you should use a smaller lens aperture or a slower film. At the opposite end of the shutter speeds, an '8–' will appear if the necessary speed at the aperture set would be longer than 8 s. Although the F3 can sometimes provide speeds slightly longer than 8 s, it is advisable to heed the warning and use a larger lens aperture or increase the

Metering

The mirror reflects the image for viewing and transmits the central portion to a secondary mirror, which reflects it to the meter cell.

The 'holes' in the mirror through which light is bled for the meter cell.

During flash exposures with the Speedlight, the meter cell 'reads' light reflected from the surface of the film.

The alternative finder heads and twenty focusing screens for the Nikon F3.

To change the finder head, push back the clips and lift out the head. To change screens, tilt the rear edge with a fingernail or something similar and lift out.

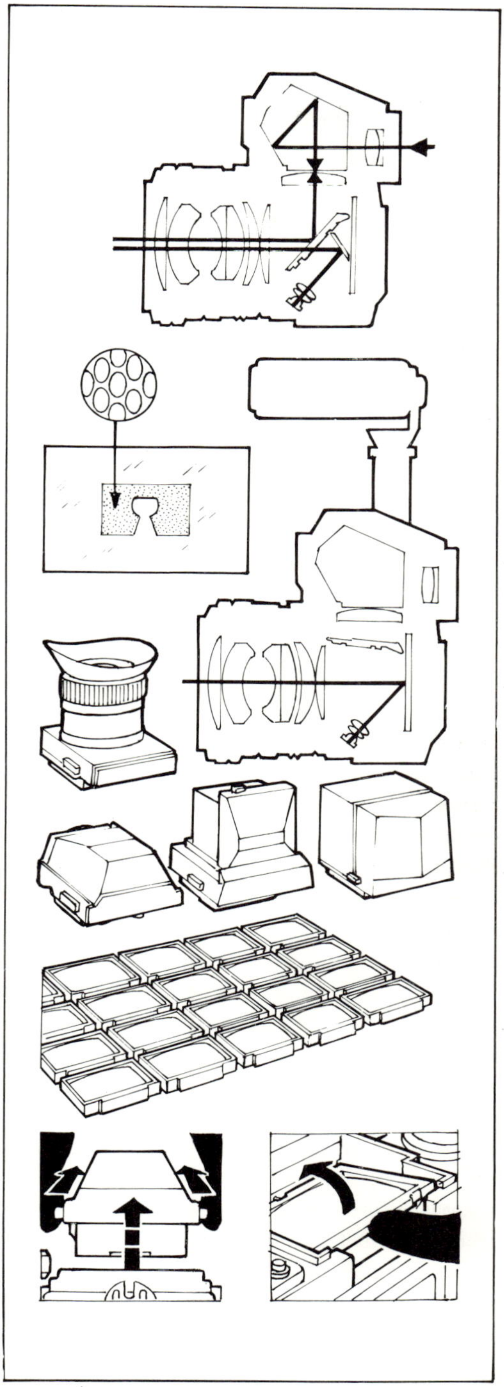

illumination to shorten the exposure to 8s or less. If you do not, the shutter may open for the exposure and not close at all. If this does happen at any time (and it often does inadvertently if you press the shutter release when you have the cap over the lens), turn the shutter-speed dial to any of the manual shutter speeds and the shutter will close. Remember to set it back to 'A' again afterwards.

While the centre-weighted metering system will handle most subjects which are either centrally located or of overall even illumination levels, there are many instances where you must take steps to ensure correct exposure. Perhaps your subject is not in the centre of the picture and the surrounding area is far brighter than the subject. In such circumstances you should use the exposure memory lock button located in the front of the camera below the chrome depth-of-field preview plunger. Pressing the memory lock button will hold the exposure reading until you either take the picture or release the button. You can point your camera directly at your subject or even up close to it, make an exposure reading, press the memory-hold button and, while still holding the button, recompose your picture as you wish and then release the shutter. Your original meter reading will remain. The shutter speed shown on the LCD will not change while the memory lock button is depressed. This is a particularly useful technique when shooting heavily backlit subjects.

Another exposure alternative is the exposure compensation dial to the right of the rewind knob. It is calibrated in ⅓ *f*/stops from 0 to +2. While pressing the dial release button just to the rear of the scale you can turn the outer knurled rim of the rewind knob collar. Match the while index dot to whatever auto-exposure compensation you wish. For instance, if you are shooting distant scenics or aerial photos you might wish to cut the exposure by a full *f*/stop, i.e. set the auto exposure compensation dial to −1. While the auto compensation dial is set to −1, the camera's auto-exposure system operates with half the normal shutter speed, thus giving you a continuous *f*/stop cut in exposure. When doing opaque or slide copying, you may need to give an additional 1⅓ stop exposure for letters or figures on a light background or reduce exposure by ⅔ stop if the background is dark. Use the auto exposure compensation dial when you must make a number of photos in a row which require the same exposure compensation.

Additional information on handling exposure problems of this nature is given in the chapter 'Exposure and depth of field'.

There is yet another alternative exposure system: the use of manual speeds. Press the hub of the shutter-speed dial and rotate the dial to whatever manual shutter speed you wish. Now, instead of a continuously variable shutter speed, you have precise quartz time marked shutter speeds. Whenever you use manual shutter speeds, a lower case 'm' appears in front of the shutter speed in the LCD panel. If the speed you select is lower than that which the metering system would choose, a '−' appears above the m. If the

Viewing and exposure

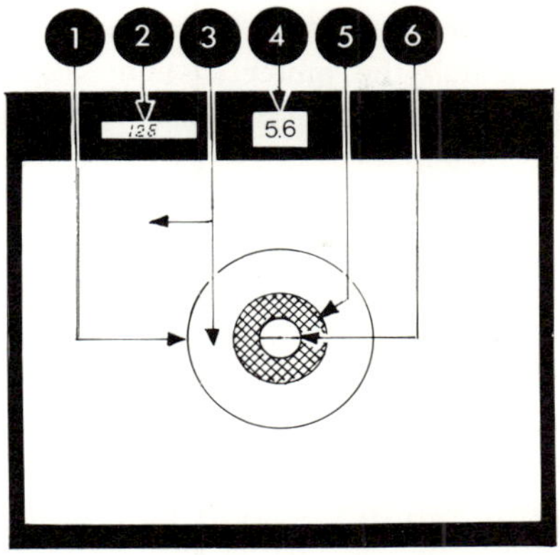

1. 12 mm diameter reference circle
2. LCD exposure readout
3. Fine matt/fresnel outer field
4. Aperture readout
5. Microprism collar
6. Split-image rangefinder

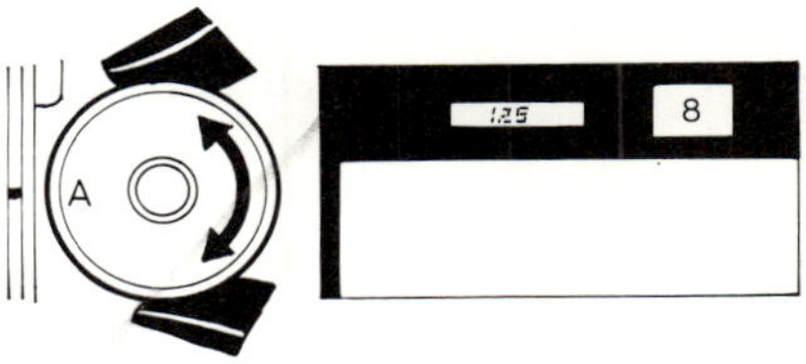

Viewfinder display when the camera is set to automatic exposure control.

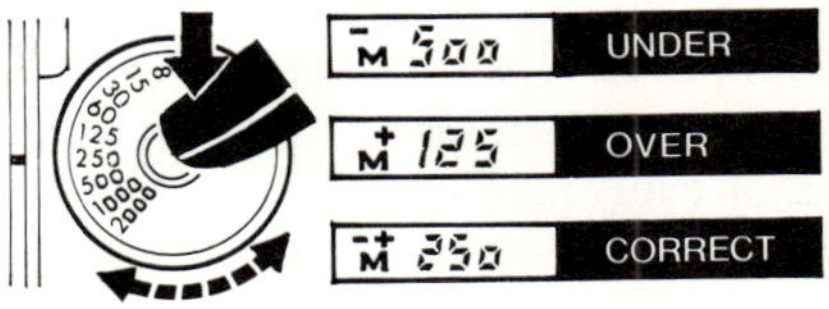

Viewfinder display on manual.

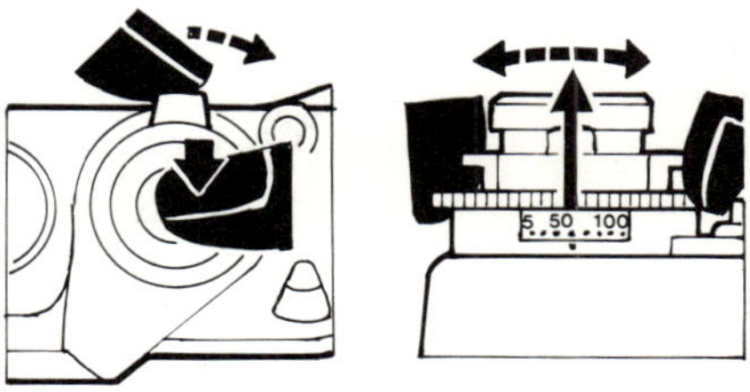

Left: Move power switch to on. Light pressure on shutter release switches on meter.
Right: Lift and twist to set film speed.

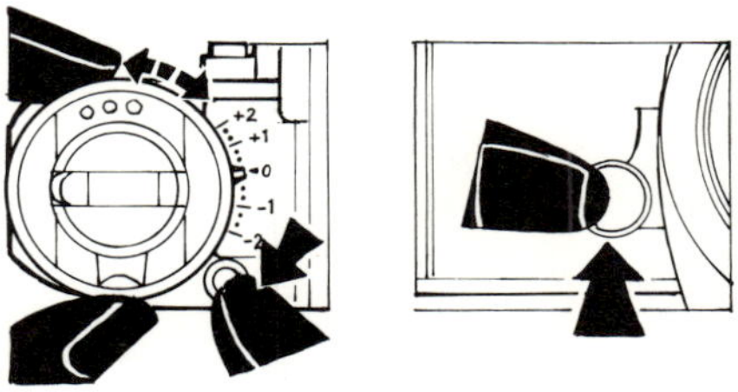

Left: Depress button and rotate collar to set exposure compensation dial.
Right: Depress to lock exposure setting.

speed is faster than the metering system would select a '+' appears above the m. When both a + and − appear above the m, you have matched the shutter speed which the meter system would select. Besides providing you with complete control, the manual system is ideal for photographers who wish to bracket their exposures by approximately one *f*/stop faster or slower. Bracketing provides the photographer with 'insurance' against a poor exposure and gives him a choice of three or more shots exposed with slight differences. To bracket, shoot one shot with both the + and − in view; then shoot one each by turning the aperture ring right and left just enough to make the + and − appear separately. After using the manual speeds of the auto exposure compensation dial, remember to return the shutter dial to A for auto exposure and the auto compensation dial to zero. While the LCD will always warn you with the m that you are on manual control, there is no finder warning when the auto exposure compensation dial is in use, so be careful to watch its setting carefully.

Nikon has officially listed auto exposure limits depending on the ASA film speed set. At maximum aperture, the slowest shutter speed claimed usable for 25 ASA film is 4 s; for 50 or 64 ASA film, 2 s; for 80 or 100 ASA, 1 s; for 160 or 200 ASA, ½ s; for 400 ASA, ¼ s; and for 1600 ASA, 1/15 s. However, as in other electronically controlled auto exposure Nikon cameras, I have found these official limitations to be very conservative and have no compunction in shooting down to 8 s with 400 ASA film. However, before you do so, check your own camera without film in a simulated low-light condition, using the ASA of your own film.

Following the last exposure on your film, be it 20, 24 or 36, the film must be rewound into the original film cartridge before removal from the camera. (While the F3's frame counter does count as high as 40 frames for those intent on squeezing the last few additional pictures on the roll, I don't recommend this. The photos made after the last official frame can often be ruined in processing if they are colour, or you may tear the film from the cartridge spool while trying to get that last frame on the roll.)

To rewind, press in the rewind button on the bottom of the camera. With the unfolded rewind crank, rewind the film back into the original cartridge by turning the crank in the direction of the arrow. When film is completely rewound, you will feel the tension on the crank lessen and can often hear the click of the film leader end as it enters the cartridge lip. Open the camera and remove the film in subdued light.

Additional features

While the foregoing instructions should suffice for much of your picture taking, there are many additional features of the Nikon F3 that you will wish to use from time to time.

If your batteries within the camera are not operable, you can still shoot pictures with the F3 by using the back-up mechanical release lever concentric with the exposure memory lock button. Move the lever outward from the camera body to its 45° rest position. By pressing it further down, the shutter can be released at 1/60 s, regardless of the setting on the shutter speed dial. You can also use this speed for electronic flash photography. Additionally, you can set the shutter speed dial to 'T' for long time exposures, and release the shutter with the mechanical release lever.

Directly above the mechanical release lever is the chrome depth-of-field preview lever. If your lens is set to any aperture but maximum, pressure on the plunger will close the lens down to the selected aperture, so that you can see the depth of field. This plunger must be used when shooting with auto diaphragm lenses, but with non-AI lenses push the plunger and hold it while adjusting your shutter speed. Make the exposure when the necessary shutter speed appears in the viewfinder.

Directly above the depth-of-field preview plunger is the mirror lock-up lever. To lock up the mirror, press and hold in the depth-of-field preview plunger and move the mirror lock-up lever 90° counterclockwise. With the mirror in the up position do not attempt to operate the camera in the auto exposure mode. Use manual shutter speeds even though the LCD and ADR windows in the finder will show numerals. These should not be followed.

The mirror should be locked out of the way to ensure the least possible camera vibration when making extreme close-ups, photomicrographs or astrophotography through high-powered telescopes. Two Nikkor lenses, the 6 mm *f*/5.6 Fisheye and 10 mm *f*/5.6 OP Fisheye fit deep into the camera body and also require the mirror to be locked up. Each lens is equipped with its own direct viewfinder which fastens to the accessory shoe.

Multiple exposures can be made with the F3. Take the first photo and push the multiple exposure lever forward at the top right of the camera. Wind the shutter again with the rapid wind lever. The film will not move and frame counter will remain stationary. Then take the next exposure. Be sure to adjust your exposure if the multiple images are to overlap; for two images, each exposure should be half the normal; for three, 1/3 of normal exposures; for four, 1/4 normal exposure, and so on. After each exposure the multiple exposure lever will automatically return to the off position, so you must push it forward for each additional multiple exposure.

When existing light is too low for you to read the aperture and shutter speeds properly in the viewfinder, you can illuminate both by pressing in the red viewfinder illuminator button on the right side of the prism. This will cause a small grain of wheat bulb to light up both the lens aperture scale and the LCD panel.

At the rear of the camera is a memo holder which allows you to insert the film box end as a reminder of just what film is loaded within. Don't forget to change the box end when you change film.

The Nikon F3 self-timer is fully electronic. To activate it, push the self-timer lever, which is in front of the shutter speed dial, to the left, towards the prism housing uncovering a red dot. When the shutter release button is pressed, the 10 second delay self-timer action will begin. For the first 8 s a red LED at the front of the camera will blink slowly. This blink rate will increase during the last 2 s as a warning to your subject that the shutter is about to be released. The self-timer action will continue for each exposure until the self-timer lever is again returned to the forward position covering the red dot. The self-timer can be used for gentle release of the camera when a cable release is not available.

The electromagnetic shutter release button of the F3 is threaded for a standard tapered cable release, an accessory which should be used whenever the gentlest possible shutter release is needed, especially when the camera is operated on a tripod at slow shutter speeds.

If you make self-timed exposures with the self-timer, or photograph with the camera mounted on a tripod and do not have your eye at the viewfinder eyepiece during the exposure, there is some danger that extraneous light from behind the camera may enter the eyepiece and inflate the exposure. This will cause underexposure in the auto exposure mode. To avoid such exposure inflation, the eyepiece can be covered by pressing the eyepiece blind lever to the left at the back of the prism. Remember to return the lever to its upright position after use.

To remove the pentaprism viewfinder, to clean the viewing system or to change it for another finder or focusing screen, slide the two finder release levers backward on either side of the prism and lift the finder out. The standard DE-2 Eye-Level Finder can be replaced with four other finders. The High-Eyepoint Viewfinder DE-3 resembles the DE-2, but provides 25 mm viewing distance from the eyepiece for spectacle wearers or action photographers so that they too can see the entire finder area and controls. The DW-3 Waist-Level Finder is excellent for low level horizontal picture taking or for shooting over the heads of crowds with the camera held upside down. The DA-2 Action Finder allows you to view and focus at eye level while seeing the entire picture area with your eye some distance from the finder eyepiece. It is fine for photographers wearing helmets, goggles or if the camera is to be used in an underwater housing. The DW-4 6× Magnification Finder provides critical high magnification in the waist-level position for close-ups or photomicrography. No matter what finder, the F3 provides full use of its metering systems.

The prism must be removed before you can change viewing screens. After removal, insert your fingernail (or similar shaped instrument) under the rear edge of the focusing screen and lift out the screen. The fingernail lift lip can be used as a handle if you do not want to hold the screen by its frame edge. To replace a screen, slip the front edge (with the slot in the middle) under the pin and push the rear edge of the screen downwards.

Operating the F3

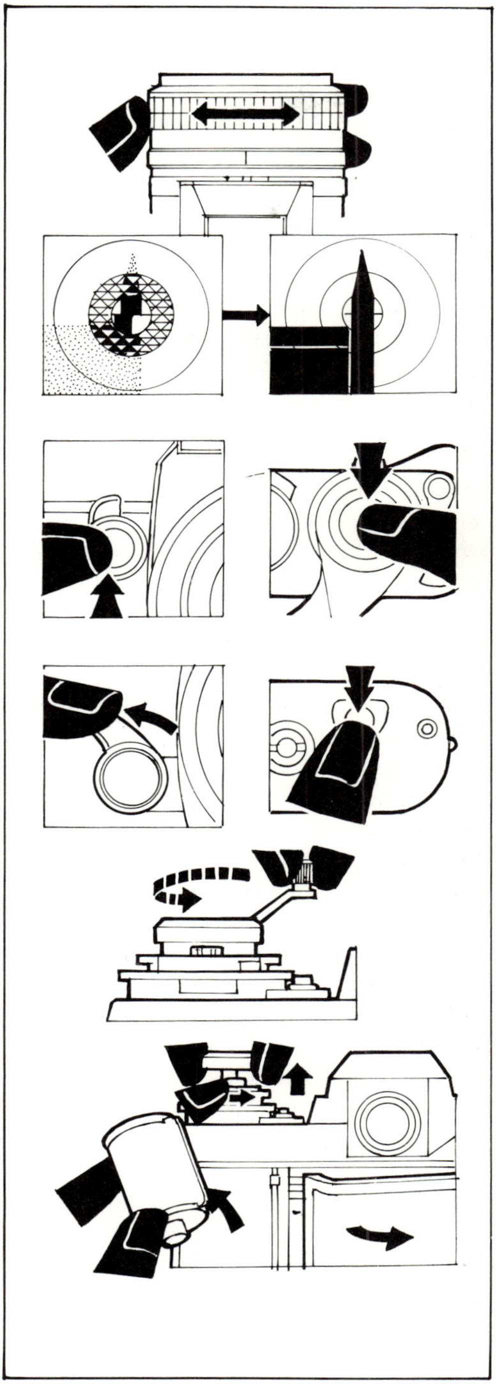

Rotate the focus ring until the microprisms cease to shimmer and the subject is continuous in the rangefinder circle in the viewfinder.

Left: Preview depth of field by pressing the stop-down button, used also for meter readings with non-AI lenses.
Right: Slight pressure on the shutter release switches on the viewfinder display for 16 s. Further pressure fires the shutter.

Left: Should the batteries fail, use the mechanical release to fire the shutter at 1/80 s regardless of the setting on the speed dial.
Right: To rewind the film, first press in the interlock release button in the base of the camera.

Rewind film in the direction of the arrow.

Push the catch sideways, lift the rewind knob and remove the exposed film.

There are 20 different screens available, similar in type to those provided for the Nikon F2. However, the screens from the F and F2 cameras are not interchangeable with those from the F3. The choice of screen depends greatly upon the lens. For a table of suggested screens see pp. 427–428.

To mount a non-AI lens on the F3, push the meter coupling lever release button on the camera lens mount and lock the meter coupling lever in the up position. We have already explained how to make an auto exposure using a non-AI lens with an automatic diaphragm. To use such a lens manually, select your shutter speed and set it on the shutter speed dial. Then, while holding in the depth-of-field preview plunger, turn the aperture ring until both the + and − signs appear above on the LCD panel.

If you are using a non-AI lens or accessory with no auto diaphragm, proceed as you did with a non-AI auto diaphragm lens but close down the lens manually to the aperture needed, instead of pressing the depth-of-field preview plunger.

When attaching the body to a fixed aperture optic such as a mirror lens, a microscope or telescope, no special procedure is needed when shooting on automatic. The LCD panel will show you the shutter speed that the camera meter will set, and with manual shutter speeds you can get proper exposure by adjusting the shutter speed dial until both the + and − appear on the LCD panel.

When and if you do lock the meter coupling lever in the up position, do not forget to push it downwards again before remounting the AI Nikkor lens.

Before passing on to flash and the motor drive, there are a few additional helpful hints about camera operation. In normal use, the manufacturer claims that fresh 1.5 V batteries will last about a year. However, I always carry a spare set for safety, since batteries can grow weak before that period, particularly since you have no control over how long they may have been on a dealer's shelf before you got them.

The batteries will work down to about 0 °C or 32 °F, but battery efficiency deteriorates at low temperature. Use fresh batteries under such conditions for maximum capability. In very cold weather, it is recommended that the F3 be used with the MD-4 motor drive whose greater battery capacity will then power the camera. It will then operate down to −20 °C (−4 °F) if the NiCad battery pack is used.

At temperatures of −10 °C (14 °F), or below, the LCD panel may show a slight delay in providing the shutter speed information. It will in no way harm the LCD which will return to normal operating speed when the temperature rises. At temperatures of 60 °C (140 °F) the surface of the LCD may turn black and be illegible. The LCD will return to normal as the temperature drops. However, prolonged exposure to such temperatures may damage the LCD permanently.

The LCD panel has a life expectancy of about 6 or 7 years after which it will lose contrast and become difficult to read. Your local Nikon service centre can replace the LCD element at a small charge.

Operating the F3

For multiple exposures, make the first exposure (1) and then push the multiple exposure lever forwards (2). Recock the shutter with the film advance lever (3) and then take the next exposure (4). Repeat as many times as required.

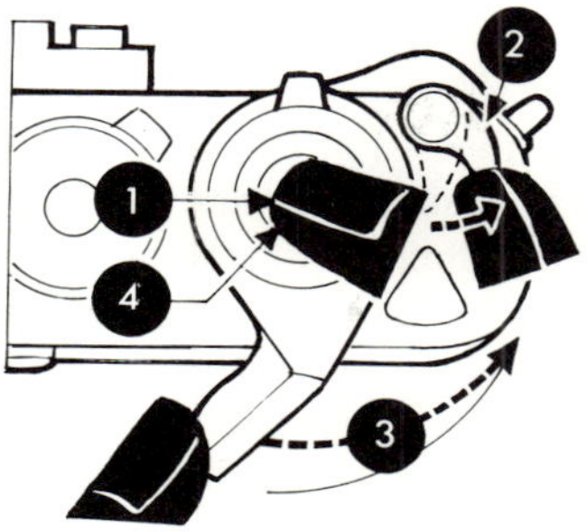

To lever up the mirror, for example when using fisheye lenses, press and hold down the stop-down preview button and pull down its surrounding lever.

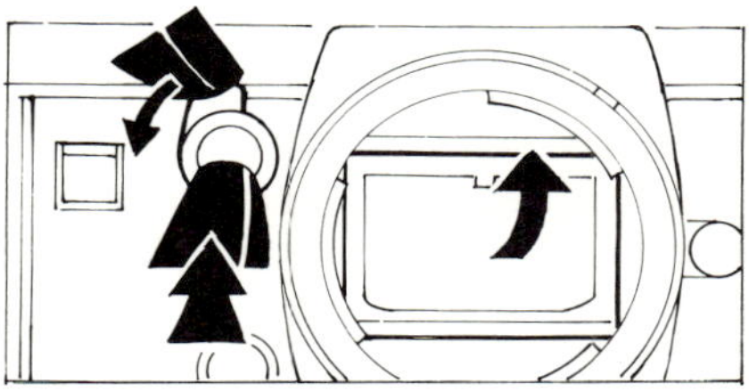

Left: When the ambient light is too dim to read the figures on the LCD, press the red button beneath the viewfinder to switch on a small light next to the display.
Right: Close the viewfinder blind when the shutter is set to Auto and the camera used away from the eye.

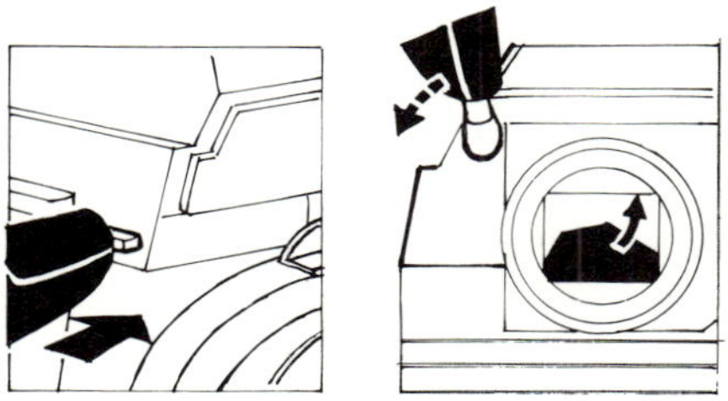

To set the self-timer, move its lever to reveal the indicator spot (1). The timer starts when the release is pressed and an LED on the front panel blinks (2) at half-second intervals for 8 seconds and then more rapidly for a further 2 seconds.

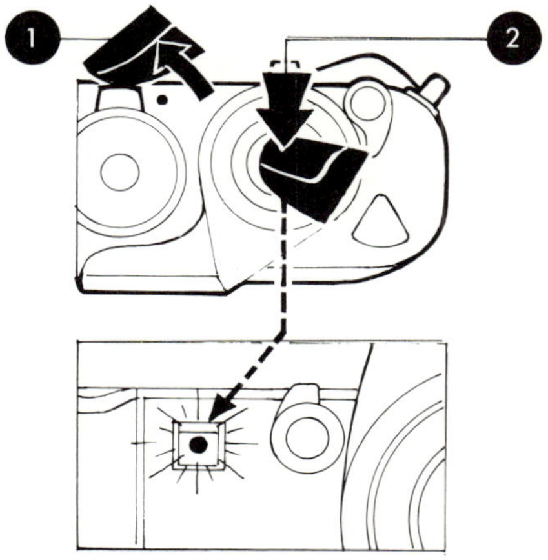

Flash

While the Nikon F3 can be fitted with any standard electronic flash unit, it does have its own advanced auto exposure flash system in which the proper amount of flash illumination is metered from the film surface and is set by a circuit operating during the actual exposure itself. The same silicon cell used for continuous light measurement also provides measurement for this flash system. When you press the shutter release, the rapid-return mirror rises with the hinged secondary reflecting mirror folded against it. The shutter curtain opens at X sync (1/80 s) or slower. At this instant, the electronic flash is activated. The silicon cells reads the flash reflected from the film surface itself and regulates its duration based on the needed exposure. Thus, accurate automatic flash exposures can be made through any lens, bellows unit, lens accessory or microscope. Using the proper flash unit, the light can be removed from the camera and placed anywhere with the guarantee of correct exposure. Even slide duplication can be undertaken with auto exposure by pointing the flash at the translucent panel of the flash duplicator.

Besides flexibility of placement and the advantages of measuring the light directly through any lens, the system has another decided advantage. Unlike almost all other autoflash units in which specific lens apertures must be used, the Nikon system allows you to set whatever aperture you wish. Light will be measured at actual shooting aperture and the proper exposure determined and set accordingly. The danger of possible underexposure has been obviated by having a LED warning indicator in the finder to the right of the aperture window. Before exposure, the appearance of the red LED indicates that the unit has charged fully for proper exposure and is ready to make a picture. After exposure, if the red LED blinks immediately, it is a signal that there was insufficient light to make a picture, the problem generally is too small an aperture for the distance. In such a case, you would select a larger aperture or decrease the flash-to-subject distance until you could make pictures without causing the LED to blink.

Two Nikon flash units have been designed specifically for through-the-lens autoflash coupling. The SB-12 is a rectangular box-shaped flash unit 40 × 105 × 84 mm (1 5/8 × 3 5/16 × 4 in) powered by four AA cells. Its foot slips over the flash accessory shoe around the rewind knob. It has energy-saving thyristorised circuitry so that all the flash energy not used in each exposure is automatically recycled in the unit. Therefore, the larger the lens aperture, the faster the film and the closer the subject, the greater the number of pictures that can be taken on one set of batteries and the faster the flash unit will recharge or recycle and be ready for the next picture. Depending on aperture and shooting range, you will be able to achieve upwards of 160 shots per set of alkaline batteries at an initial maximum recycling time of 8 seconds. Usually you will far exceed this number of flashes and at much

Flash

Slide the SB-12 on to the accessory shoe surrounding the rewind knob and turn its locking collar to secure it in place.

The F3's accessory shoe has synchro contacts for the SB-11 and SB-12 Speedlights and an auto film speed programme.

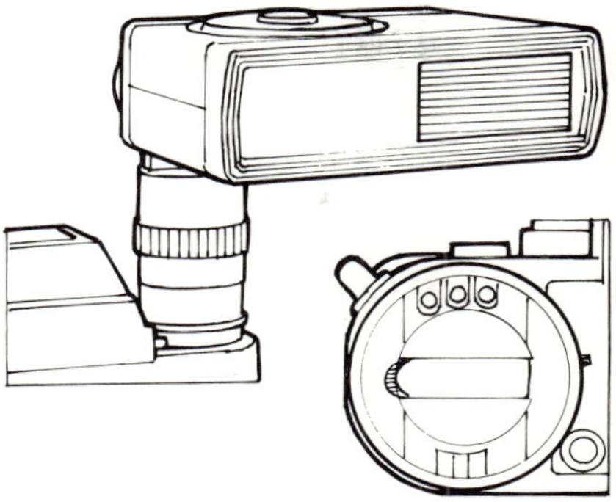

All of the SB-12 controls are neatly grouped and clearly labelled.

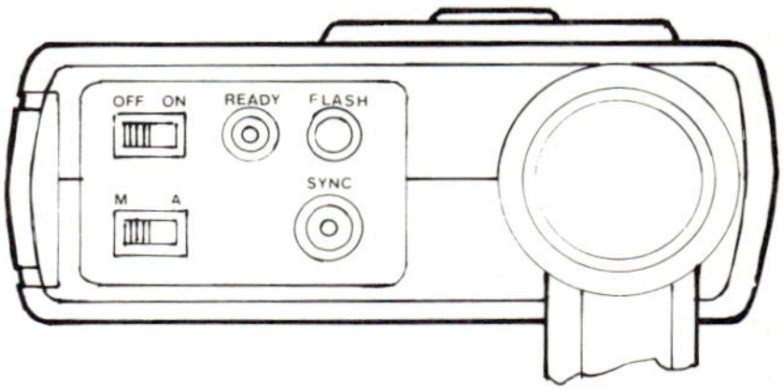

To change the batteries, slide the cover, remove the old batteries and replace all of them with fresh ones. Make sure that the new ones are inserted the right way round.

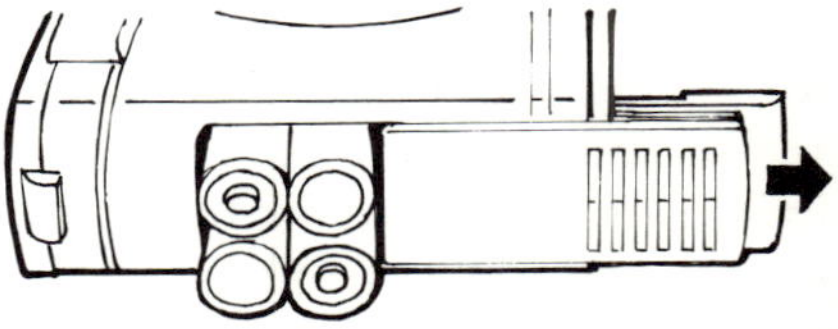

When the SB-12 is used off the camera or with models other than the F3 calculate the correct lens aperture for the film speed and flash–subject distance. The viewfinder LED glows when the flash is fully charged and ready to fire.

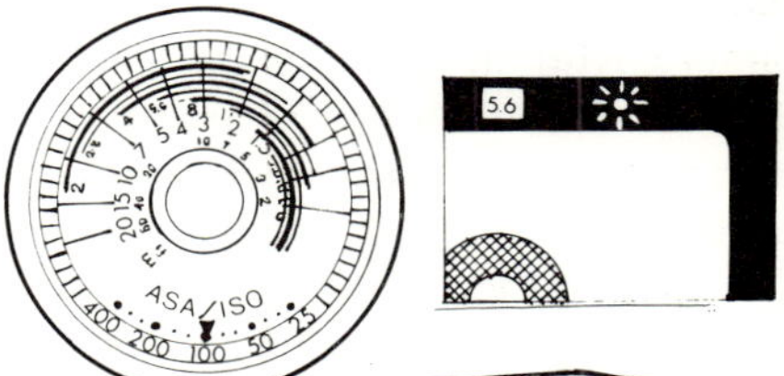

The pro-type SB-11 Speedlight can be fitted with a TTL sensor cable SC-12 which allows through-the-lens flash metering for auto flash. The cable attaches to the F3 over the rewind knob.

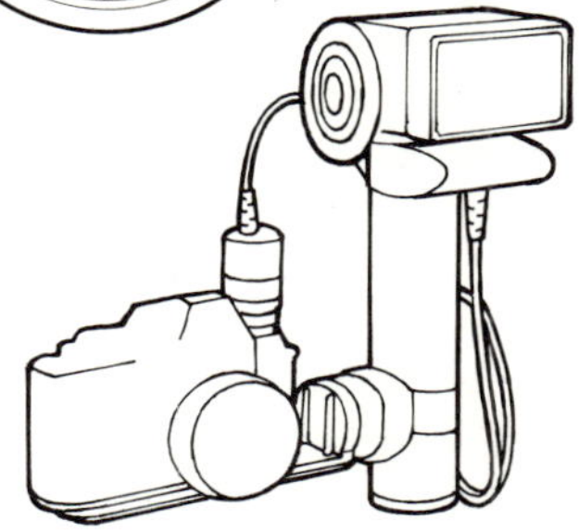

shorter recycling times. The angle of flash coverage is sufficient for a 35 mm lens but an additional wide-angle panel is furnished which fits over the flash tube lens and extends the coverage sufficiently for 28 mm lens.

The control panel at the rear of the SB-12 has an on/off switch, a flash-ready signal, open flash button, manual and automatic switch and a PC sync terminal for manual off-camera use. On top of the flash unit is an indicating dial. After setting it to the ASA film speed, coloured lines representing apertures from *f*/2 to *f*/22 indicate the possible distance ranges available to help you select the proper lens aperture for your needs.

Before using the SB-12, load with four AA cells; alkaline cells give the maximum number of flashes but NiCad cells can be used although they give fewer flashes before they need recharging. Slide open the battery chamber cover on the left end of the unit, as indicated on the cover. Insert the four batteries following the battery placement diagrams inside the battery chamber.

Slide the SB-12 foot backwards from the front of the camera onto the accessory shoe around the rewind knob. Rotate the locking collar at the base of the flash unit foot to the left, locking the flash unit in place. (This also automatically keys the flash unit to the film's ASA speed as set on the camera.) Turn on the flash unit. Set the M/A switch to A for automatic. If the red LED at the back of the unit and in the viewfinder flashes, the flash unit has been mounted improperly or the ASA set is outside the range of the unit (the SB-12 can handle films from ASA 25 to 400). Normally, the LEDs on the flash unit and in the finder should light within 8 seconds. After referring to the dial on top of the flash unit, set the required lens aperture for your needs and distance. When the flash unit cycles fully and is ready, it will automatically set the camera to the flash sync of $\frac{1}{80}$ s whether the camera is set to A operation or any manual speed faster than $\frac{1}{30}$ s. At slower manual speeds which you may use when combining flash and natural light, the slower speed will be set by the camera and so shown on the panel. Autoflash exposure, of course, operates only when the camera is set to the A position.

After exposure, watch for the blinking LED which would indicate insufficient light. If the LED simply lights continuously, your exposure was sufficient and you can proceed to the next shot. The SB-12 has a manual 100 ASA guide number of 25 m (82 ft) and 18 m (60 ft) when used with the wide-angle panel. With 100 ASA film the auto exposure range, depending on the aperture selected, is 1.9 ft to 39 ft. With faster films, the maximum range is correspondingly greater; with slower films, the maximum distance is abbreviated. When flash recycling exceeds 30 seconds, the batteries should be replaced or NiCads recharged.

The SB-12 can be used horizontally directly over the camera or swung outwards, which also avoids red-eye (p. 321). Accessories to allow the SB-12 to be used off camera, for bounce, close-up and slide duplicating work are to be made available.

The SB-11 flash unit powered by 8 AA cells is a more powerful head-and-handle flash unit designed to provide bounce flash and off-camera flexibility while retaining the autoflash capabilities of the SB-12. It fits the F3 with an under-camera bracket and connects to the camera via a flashcord. It has its own autoflash sensor so it can be used for autoflash operation on other cameras not having the F3's built-in flash sensor. It is 50 per cent more powerful than the SB-12.

However, the SB-11's primary advantage with the Nikon F3 camera is its ability to operate fully automatically while measuring flash directly through the shooting aperture of the lens of other optical equipment at the moment of exposure – as does the smaller SB-12 Speedlight already described.

To load the SB-11 with batteries, unscrew the handle base cap, remove the battery clip, insert AA-type cells (preferably manganese alkaline types) into the clip as per the symbols on the battery clip and reinsert it into the battery chamber. Replace the cap.

You can attach the bracket-mounting adapter to the Speedlight handle by first loosening the two bracket-mounting adapter screws using the screw-driver provided with the flash. Slide the adapter about 1 in over the end of the Speedlight's handle and turn it so its flat side is on the same plane as the calculator dial. The locking wheel should face towards the back of the flash. Tighten the screws.

Attach the bracket to the camera by threading the bracket-attaching screw into the camera tripod socket. Insert the Speedlight's bracket-mounting pin into the bracket-mounting adapter hole with the two dots aligned. Rotate the camera forward and tighten the locking wheel.

Rotate the SC-12 TTL sensor cable's locking ring counterclockwise so that the mounting foot is fully open. Slip the mounting foot onto the camera accessory shoe and then tighten by rotating the locking ring counterclockwise fully.

With the TTL cable sensor plug's Nikon nameplate upwards, push the plug into the sensor socket of the SB-11 flash unit until it clicks into place. (To remove if following use, press the sensor release catches and pull out the plug.) Set the sensor plug A-M switch to 'A' for automatic operation. If you wish to use the flash unit manually, set the switch to 'M'. Turn on the SB-11 flash unit using the on-off switch located within the back calculator dial. The ready-light at the rear of the unit and within the viewfinder will glow when the unit's capacitor has been charged fully and is ready to fire. You need not worry about the shutter speed setting. At any speed, whether on automatic or on manual between $\frac{1}{125}$ s and $\frac{1}{2000}$ s, the proper X sync $\frac{1}{80}$ s shutter speed will be set automatically. At speeds below $\frac{1}{125}$ s, the actual speed will be set so the unit can be used for auto exposure fill-in flash at slow shutter speeds if desired.

For any aperture set on the lens, the SB-11 will provide the proper amount of illumination if the light is sufficient for the flash-to-subject distance. If it is incorrect, the ready-light at the back of the flash or in the viewfinder will blink. The SW-3 wide angle adapter which clips to the front of the SB-11 flash head and increases the covering angle from that of a 35 mm focal length lens maximum to 28 mm, but it does shorten the distance range.

Besides being used on-camera for straight flash, the flash head of the SB-12 can be tilted upwards at 30° click-stop intervals for bounced flash, while the entire head and handle can be removed from the bracket and camera for off-camera flash, whether direct or bounced. (See the chapter on flash for a description of such uses.) In all instances, the absence of a blinking red light on the flash or within the finder following exposure indicates an adequate amount of light reached the subject.

With the SB-11's off-camera flash ability, the unit can also be employed as the lighting for photomicrography or slide duplication. In both cases proper exposure will be provided automatically at any lens aperture set or, in the case of optics with no aperture settings (such as with mirror telephoto lenses or microscopes), correct exposure will be achieved at the single given aperture of the optical instrument. In all cases, absence afterwards of a blinking warning light indicates there was enough illumination to make the picture.

There are but two other warnings to keep in mind. If the ready-light blinks before taking the picture, it indicates that the flash unit hasn't been mounted on the camera or the cable with its contacts. Another possible cause is that the ASA index has been set above ASA 400, indices with which the flash unit will not couple.

Secondly, although the flash ready-light blinking following exposure is an indication of insufficient light, there is no indication of too much light which would cause overexposure. If there is a danger of overexposure, then by all means use a smaller lens aperture or drape a clean white handkerchief over the flash head.

Motor drive

The ultracompact and light MD-4 motor for the Nikon F3 is a triumph of microelectronics and brilliant engineering. It adds but 60 mm (7⁷⁄₁₆ in) to the total height of the F3 and 709 g (25 oz) with NiCad battery pack making it just slightly larger and heavier than the far less versatile and slower auto winders on other SLR cameras. It not only offers single-frame film advance, continuous firing to 6 frames per second, but also features motor rewind of the film. It has its own frame counter which can be set to fire any specific number of frames.

To attach the MD-4 to the F3, the camera's power switch should be turned off. With the edge of a coin, unthread the black motor drive coupling cover on the camera bottom by turning the cover counterclockwise. Remove the motor drive battery clip from the MD-4 by pressing the battery clip release

Motor Drive MD-4

1. Rewind slide 2
2. Rewind slide 1 and lock button
3. Frame counter
4. Frame counter setting dial
5. Battery test button
6. Battery test LEDs
7. Auto-rewind stop terminals
8. Battery clip
9. Battery clip release catch
10. Electrical contacts
11. Remote terminal
12. External power terminal
13. Camera attachment screw
14. Motor drive coupling prong
15. External release terminal
16. Shutter release
17. Mode selector dial
18. Film rewind release link
19. Battery clip

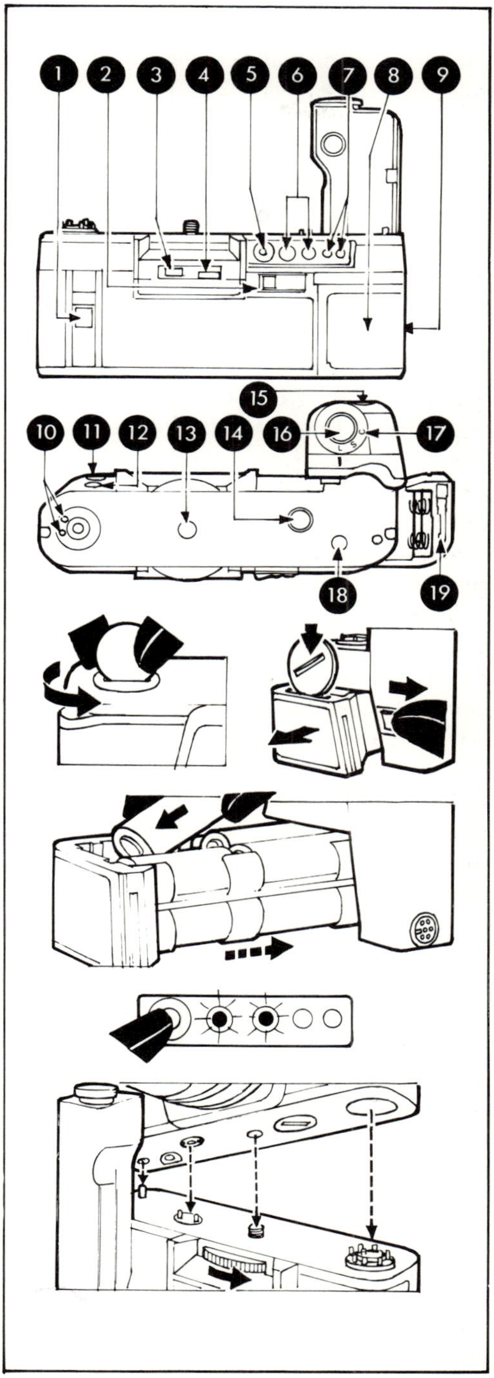

The cap protecting the electrical contacts in the camera base is stored in a slot in the battery clip of the MD-4.

Check the batteries by pressing the test button. Both lights should glow if they have been correctly inserted and have sufficient power.

Carefully line up the various contacts and locating points on the camera and motor before mounting the motor drive.

catch forward in the direction of the arrowhead next to the catch. Remove the clip and for safekeeping, insert the motor drive coupling cover in the small slot at the end of the clip. Insert 8 AA cells into the battery clip following the + and − indicators on the clip. All batteries will provide sufficient power for 60 36-exposure rolls of film at maximum firing speed. Alkaline energisers allow 80 more rolls to be fired at reduced speed before exhaustion. Zinc carbon cells provide 20 more rolls while the special NiCad pack allows 10 more.

Push the battery clip back into the motor. It will click into place. To check battery power, press the battery check button at the back of the motor. If two LEDs light, the batteries have been loaded properly and more than 50 per cent of the battery power is still available. When power falls below 50 per cent only one LED will light.

To attach the motor drive to the camera, make certain that the S-C mode selector on top of the motor handle is at the 'L' (lock) position. Bring motor and camera bottom together so that the mounting screw of the motor can be inserted into the tripod socket of the camera. The camera positioning pin must also align with the motor drive coupling hole. Fasten camera and motor securely together by turning the attachment wheel counterclockwise.

Load film into the camera as already described and close the camera back. Take up the film slack with the rewind crank. From this point on until the film is removed from the camera you should not separate the motor from the camera, or you may fog part of the film roll when light enters the motor drive coupling shaft.

Set the MD-4 frame counter to the orange dot by turning the adjacent knurled wheel. Set the S-C mode selector to the 'S' (single frame) operating position. Press the button on top of the MD-4 handle slightly and check whether the LCD panel is providing a shutter speed reading. (As previously explained, the batteries in the motor power the camera itself when the MD-4 is attached.) Press the release button fully. The motor will fire the shutter and advance the film one frame. Continue pressing until the first frame is reached.

While using the MD-4, you can either continue to shoot single frames or shift to multiple shots by turning the S-C mode selector to the C setting. The speed of operation depends on the shutter speed and the power source. Highest motor speed can only be reached at shutter speeds of 1/125 s or over. With through-the-lens viewing, zinc carbon or alkaline batteries provide speeds of 3.8 frames per second. The MN-2 NiCad battery pack raises the speed to 5.5 fps while the MA-4 AC/DC converter can allow speeds of 5 fps. By locking the rapid-return mirror in the up position, speeds of 4, 5, 6 and 5.5 fps respectively can be achieved.

If you wish to shoot only a specific number of frames, set the frame counter to that number. The counter will count down to zero as you operate the camera and will stop operation after the last frame.

Operating the MD-4 motor

For continuous shooting turn the wheel until the orange dot shows.

Preset the counter with the number of pictures required for a particular sequence and the motor will automatically stop when the subtractive counter reaches zero.

A red LED flashes after each exposure.

The counter can be set for single picture shooting (S) or continuous sequences (C).

To rewind the film, depress the lock button on the rewind slide and push the slide left. Hold the slide there while pushing rewind slide up. The film will then rewind.

The MF-6 camera back prevents the film tongue from being rewound into cassette.

The charger and NiCad battery pack.

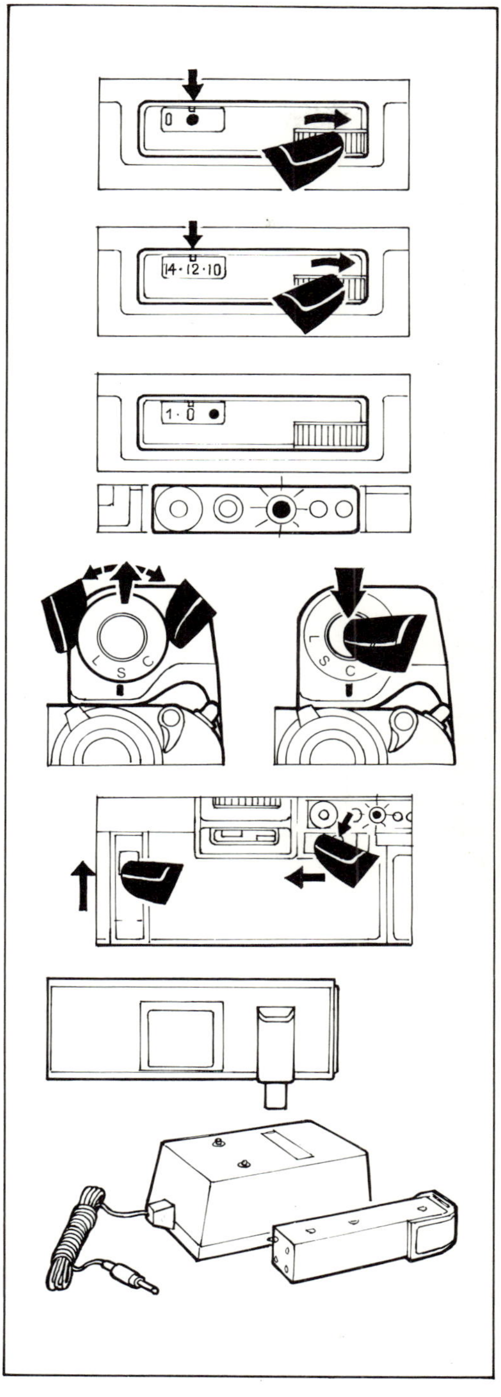

For F3 owners who use their MD-4 motor a great deal, and/or will be working in low ambient temperatures, the NiCad Battery Unit MN-2 and MH-2 Quick Charger are strongly recommended. They allow the motor to operate at temperatures down to −20°C (−4°F) along with the camera's metering system exposure control and electromagnetic shutter release. The NiCad battery provides the fastest firing rate, up to 5.5 fps (6 fps with the camera mirror locked up). One charge of the battery permits 60 rolls of 36 exposures to be shot before recharging. The battery is capable of being recharged more than 100 times, providing constant motor users with considerable savings in replaceable battery expense. The battery, known as the MN-2, replaces the standard MD-4 motor drive battery clip. The MN-2 should be recharged when it is new, when it has not operated for a month, or when it has been exhausted or partially exhausted in use.

Turn the Quick Charger on its back and plug in the female end of the appropriate main cord into the three-pin connector. Plug the charger into a wall receptacle. Insert the charging plug attached to the charger into the female receptacle of the MN-2 battery. Immediately, a green lamp will light on the charger. When charging is complete, a red light will light, indicating that charging is complete. You should charge batteries only at temperatures between 5° and 40°C (41° and 104°F). If you charge at other temperature ranges, you will not receive a full charge. The best range is 15° to 30°C (59° to 86°F).

While moderate overcharging will not harm the battery, the unit should be disconnected as quickly as possible after the red light shows. Under no circumstances should the battery and charger remain connected and plugged in to power for more than four hours following the red light.

If the red light fails to come on after five hours of charging, the line voltage is insufficient or there is some defect in the charging unit and/or battery. In the latter case they should be returned to a Nikon dealer for inspection and, if necessary, service.

When not being used, NiCad batteries gradually lose their power even though they may still light up the red, fully charged, lamp. It's wise to give the battery an hour or so charge each month if it has not been used. Additionally, if the battery isn't used nearly to exhaustion occasionally, it will lose its power to hold a maximum charge. To avoid this, fully discharge and charge your battery three or four times at least once every six months. (Discharge by dry-running the motor without film. While this is somewhat time-consuming, it will prolong the life and ability of your battery.)

The MD-4 can be connected up to a number of different power sources and remote-control alternatives. These are the MA-4 AC/DC Converter and MC-11 External Power Cord which allows the motor to be driven by mains current. In the remote-control area there are the 3 m long MC-10 Remote Cord with Button Release; the MW-1 Radio Control Set and MC-5 Connecting Cord, providing wireless radio control in three separate channels for three cameras at distances up to 0.7 km (2300 ft); the ML-1 Modulite Remote Control Set with two channels which can release the camera by a wireless double pulse electronic flash signal; the Pistol Grip Model 2 with MC-3 Connecting Cord; the MC-4 Remote Cord with plus and minus banana plugs to be used to fire three motor-driven F3s simultaneously; and the MT-1 Intervalometer and MC-5 Connecting Cord, which provides time-lapse exposure ability for the F3 and MD-4 motor.

The remote releases attach to the Remote Terminal at the front of the MD-4 motor, while the power sources can be connected to the front External Power Terminal. Those items requiring additional explanation are more fully described in the later chapter on motor drive and bulk film backs.

For MD-4 users who do not wish the MD-4 rewind to return the film leader completely back into the film cartridge, a MF-6 Camera Back is available which replaces the Nikon F3 standard back and provides automatic film rewinding which stops with the leader still outside of the cartridge.

To remove the standard F3 back, either for replacement with the MF-6, the F3 Databack or the 250-exposure bulk film back, first open the F3 back as if to load film. Press downwards on the small chrome button located on the back at the hinge of camera and back. The top of the back can now be swung outwards away from the camera and the back removed. The back can be replaced by first inserting the lower hinge-pin of the back into the camera body lower back-pin receptacle. While holding the chrome button downwards, swing the top of the back into position until the top pin and top receptacle meet. Then release the chrome button so that the upper pin will enter the receptacle. The back is now reattached.

For those who require continuous shooting for more than the standard 36 exposures – as for industrial, scientific or other technical work – Nikon makes the 250-Exposure Magazine Back MF-4 to be used with the F3 in conjunction with the Motor Drive MD-4. The bulk film loader for the Nikon F2's 250 Exposure Back and the film cassettes (see the chapter on motor drives and bulk film backs) can be used with the MF-4.

MF-4 bulk film back

While the MF-4 bulk film back for the Nikon F3 is similar in construction and operation to the MF-1 for the Nikon F2 camera, there are sufficient differences to make a single set of instructions for both impossible. Thus we'll cover the MF-4 here and deal with the earlier bulk film back in the chapter on motor drives and bulk film backs.

Before attaching the MF-4, connect the MD-4 Motor Drive to the F3 camera body and remove the camera back. Turn the open/close supply-side knob on the MF-4 until it clicks in the open position and 'OPEN' aligns with the orange square index. Apply pressure to the camera-clamp lock-release button and turn the camera-clamp lever clockwise to release the clamp.

MF-4 250 Magazine

Here are important features for the Nikon F3's magazine back:

1. Open/close knob index
2. Open/close knob (for take-up)
3. Frame coutner reset ring
4. Frame counters
5. Camera holder
6. Camera clamp
7. Camera clamp lever
8. Open/close knob (for supply)
9. Open/close knob index
10. Shutter release button lock ring
11. Shutter release button
12. Neckstrap eyelet
13. Tripod socket
14. Film pressure plate
15. External connecting cord
16. Camera clamp lock release button
17. Tripod socket
18. Power cord
19. Supply cassette spindle knob
20. Supply cassette ejector lever
21. Take-up cassette ejector lever
22. Take-up spindle knob
23. Rear cover hinge
24. Supply cassette compartment

25 & 28. Cassette spindle

26. Frame counter signal terminal
27. Film sprocket
29. Take-up cassette compartment
30. Latches
31. Rear cover latch
32. Rear cover support pin knob
33. Battery check button
34. Battery check indicator

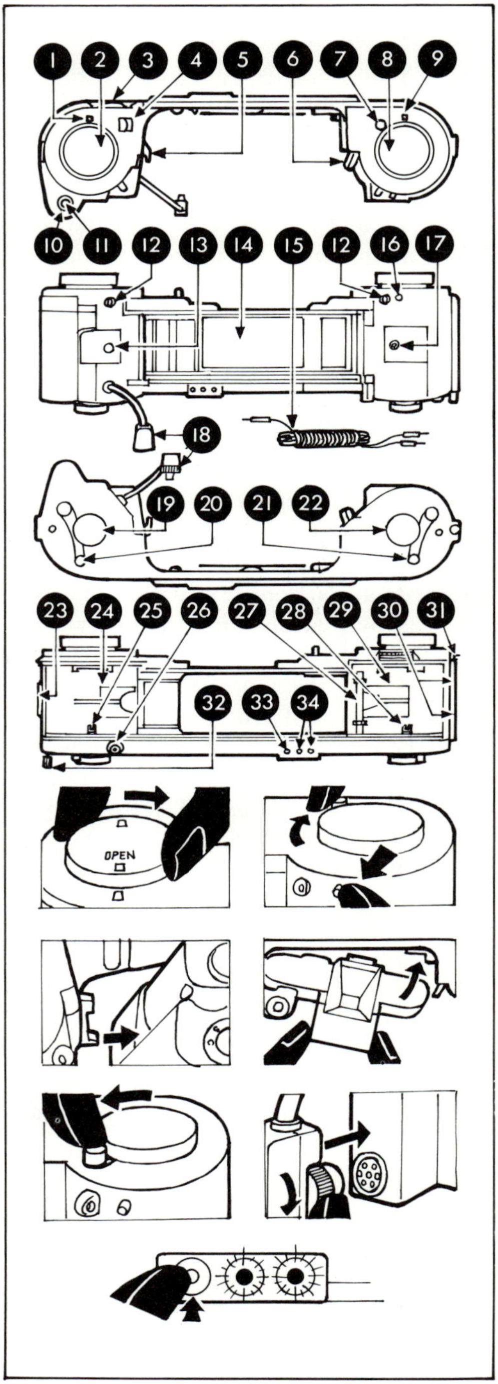

Set supply-side magazine knob to 'OPEN' position.

Press camera-clamp lock-release button, turn clamp lever clockwise to release clamp.

Attach magazine to the camera body by lining up claw A with space B.

Fit magazine back carefully into place.

Lock magazine back by turning camera-clamp lever counterclockwise while pushing magazine back and camera body end together.

Connect magazine cord to motor drive magazine back terminal.

Check battery by pushing check button. Both LEDs should light.

Connecting the Nikon F3 to the MF-4 250 Magazine

After locking shutter release buttons, turn knobs to 'OPEN' position and pull up cover latch to open back.

Unscrew rear-cover support pin until it stops. Remove the rear cover.

Pull out cassette spindles at bottom of both chambers.

Load cassettes in both chambers. Line up top pins with chamber cutouts.

Remove slack from film by rotating spindle knobs. Replace the rear cover.

Turn rear-cover pin knob clockwise until it stops.

Close the rear cover forcefully until it clicks.

Set both open/close knobs to 'CLOSE'.

After 5 blank exposures (see text), set subtractive counter (left side in frame counter) while holding knob under reset ring.

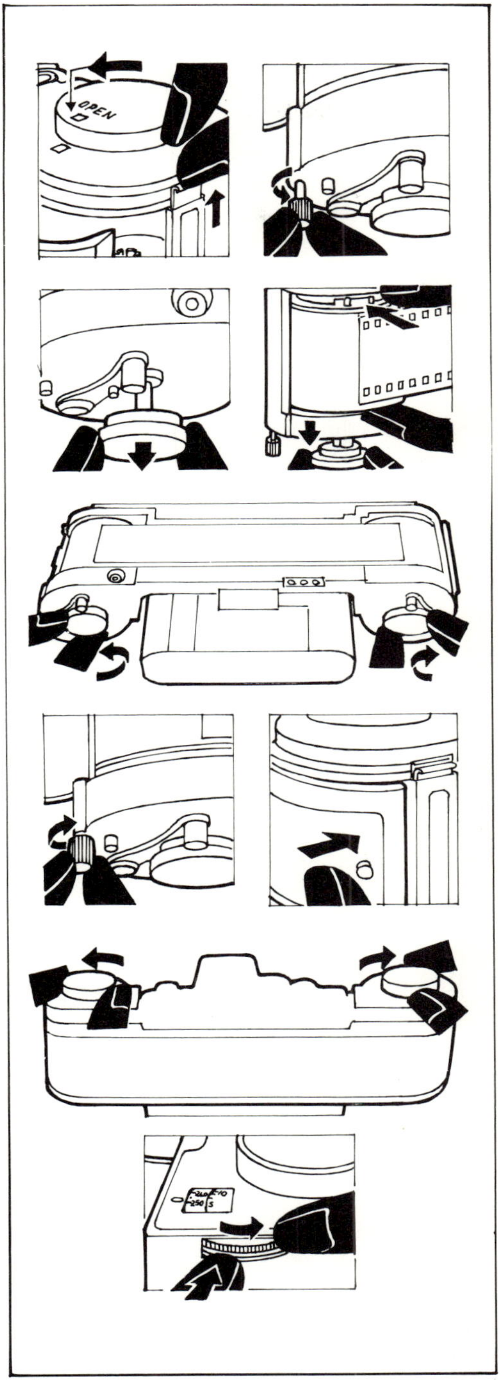

Attach the magazine to the camera body, lining up the claw at the bottom of the camera holder with the space between the grip of the motor drive and the camera body. Using the claw as a guide, fit the magazine back into place. Lock the magazine back by pushing the magazine's supply side and the camera body end together. Turning the camera-clamp lever counterclockwise until it stops and the camera-clamp lock-release button clicks.

Connect the magazine back to the motor drive by plugging the cord into the magazine back terminal at the motor drive grip base. Check battery power by pressing the back battery-check button. Both LEDs should glow. If none or only one glows, replace the Motor Drive batteries since the bulk film back with its own micromotor and added film weight pull will consume power faster than when an ordinary film cassette is used.

The MF-4 accepts the same type of reloadable 250-exposure MZ-1 Nikon cassettes as does the MF-1 for the Nikon F2. The supply cassette is loaded in precisely the same manner for either camera and can be seen easily in the illustrations on page 293. The film end should protrude from the first cassette loaded and the second take-up cassette should be opened, the film end fastened to the spool and the cassette closed in the same manner as the first. You will now have two cassettes oriented left and right with film connecting them.

To load the film cassettes into the bulk film back, ascertain that the shutter-release lock ring of the back is in the L position and that the motor's S-C selector is also at L. Open the rear cover of the magazine back by setting the take-up and supply knobs to the 'OPEN' position. The back will pop open when you pull up on the rear-cover latch. Unscrew the rear-cover support pin counterclockwise until it stops, and remove the rear cover. Pull out the film-supply side and take-up side cassette spindle knobs at the cassette chamber bottoms. Load the supply cassette and take-up cassette into the cassette chambers. The pins atop each cassette must slide into the cassette chamber cutouts fully. Keep pulling down on the spring-loaded spindle knobs until the cassettes are properly seated.

Rotate the supply-side cassette-spindle knob counterclockwise and the take-up knob clockwise to remove slack from the film. The sprocket wheel teeth must engage the film perforations. Replace the rear cover and turn the rear cover support pin knob clockwise until it stops. Close the cover.

Set the open/close knobs to the 'CLOSE' position. Rotate the spindle knobs again to remove any film slack. Unlock the shutter release button on the bulk back and motor drive. Set the motor drive's mode selector to S or C depending on whether you want to make single exposures or continuous burst. Set the motor-drive frame counter to the orange dot.

Make five blank exposures using the bulk film back shutter release button. The white dots on the cassette spindle knobs should rotate indicating that film is being transported properly. Use a fairly high manual shutter speed to make the blank exposures. Do not attempt to use the camera's own rapid-wind lever when you have the bulk film back attached to the camera.

After making the five blank exposures, set the MF-4's subtractive frame counter. It is on the left in the frame counter's window. (The additive counter on the right in the window automatically begins at S when the bulk film back is open, and will count frames in succession after the 5 blanks are fired.) To set the subtractive counter which shows the number of frames left to shoot, turn the counter-reset ring in the direction of the white arrow until it indicates the entire roll of 250 exposures or just that number you wish to shoot in sequence at one time. In either case, when the subtractive counter reaches zero, the motor drive automatically stops. While setting the subtractive counter, press in and hold the knob under the reset ring to prevent it rotating and thus changing the additive counter number.

You can operate the camera with bulk film back using the camera shutter release, the motor release or the film back release, whichever is the most convenient. When using the bulk film back or motor drive release, set the S-C mode selector on the motor drive to the setting you wish. The exposure meter on the F3 will be activated by pressing any of the release buttons halfway.

After a roll of film has been fully exposed and the subtractive frame counter reads 0, reset the frame counter to read 5 frames or more and make 5 blank exposures to wind on the film still in the centre of the bulk film back. The supply-cassette spindle knob will cease turning when the cassette runs out of film. Set the open/close knobs on both sides to the 'OPEN' position and open the rear cover. While pulling out the cassette spindles of both chambers, press the cassette-ejector levers and lift out the cassettes.

To detach the magazine from the camera, remove the connecting plug from the motor drive and set the open/close knob on the supply cassette side to 'OPEN'. Turn the camera-clamp lever clockwise while pressing the camera-clamp lock-release button.

With the Motor Drive's batteries, about 20 250-exposure cassettes can be driven on one set of alkaline-manganese batteries and 12 with regular carbon cells. The MN-2 NiCad battery unit will handle about 10 rolls before recharge. With carbon or alkaline-manganese batteries, additional rolls can be fired if slightly slower firing rates are acceptable. The camera with motor and bulk film back can also be powered by the AC/DC Converter MA-4. All methods of releasing the F3 via remote control are equally applicable when the bulk film back is attached.

Camera controls

F and F2

Since the Nikon F and F2 are similar, let's examine them together. (The Nikon F2T and F2H have controls similar to the F2.)

At first glance of the untrained eye, the two cameras may indeed look virtually identical. A more careful scrutiny reveals the more rounded edges and corners of the F2, the slightly lower and slimmer Photomic prism housing (if fitted), and the fact that the controls are not placed in precisely the same position. The first controls that your right hand reaches usually are the rapid wind lever and shutter release. Both cameras allow the wind lever to be pulled away slightly to a stand-off position – that of the F2 slightly more. You expect to let your first finger fall onto the shutter release button, so you'll note that the button of the F2 is placed considerably further forward than that on the F. When winding film and shutter and then releasing the shutter, the forward position on the F2 allows you to keep your first finger on the release or very near it at all times. The position of the F requires you to remove your finger for winding on.

With either F or F2, you can operate the rapid wind lever in one full stroke or a series of small strokes. In either case, it's important to advance the lever firmly until it can move no further. If you fail to do this, the film and shutter won't be wound properly and you can't take a picture; rather embarrassing if you're about to take an important subject that won't wait. Many photographers continue to press forward on the rapid wind lever throughout exposure. It's not advisable to do this. On the F, such pressure prevents the locking mechanism from releasing after exposure, and so you have to remove pressure before you can wind. On the F2, the locking mechanism will release properly, pressure or not, but I have found that occasionally the shutter will accidentally release while winding if pressure is constantly applied forward. Therefore, after winding film, by all means keep your finger on the wind lever ready to advance directly after exposure, but don't press forward until after exposure.

Nikon F2 and F2A Photomic features

1. Frame counter
2. T-L fingerguard
3. Film advance lever
4. ASA film speed dial
5. Film speed index ring
6. Viewfinder eyepiece
7. Flash ready-light contact
8. Finder release button
9. Flash contact
10. Shutter release button
11. Finder release lever
12. Meter window.
13. Accessory shoe
14. Rewind knob
15. Rewind crank
16. Aperture ring with aperture scale
17. Depth-of-field scale
18. Focusing ring with distance scale
19. Meter coupling prong
20. Neckstrap eyelet lug
21. Mirror lock lever
22. Shutter speed scale
23. Shutter speed selector
24. Battery checker
25. Photomic finder
26. Maximum aperture indicator (F2 only)
27. Sync terminal
28. Depth-of-field preview button
29. Self-timer
30. Meter coupling lever (F2A only)
31. Coupling lever release (F2A only)
32. Lens release button
33. Motor drive coupling
34. Motor shutter release coupling
35. Rewind button
36. Camera back
37. Tripod socket
38. Battery chamber
39. Memo holder
40. Open-close key

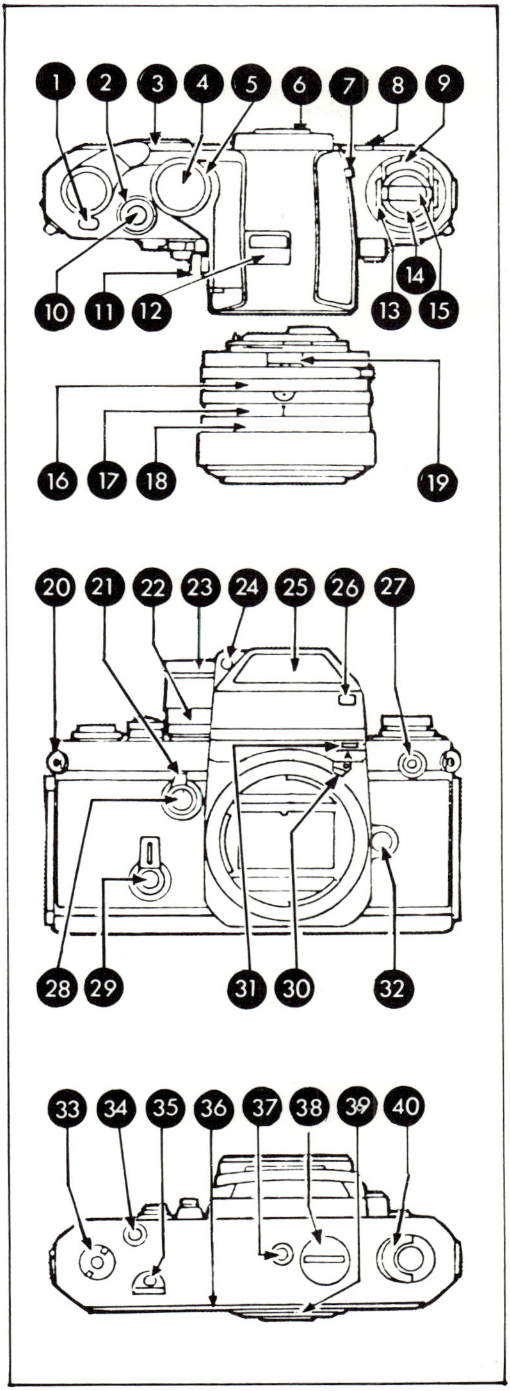

Both shutter release buttons are threaded for the special Nikon threaded cable release collar. While in the past a few photographers have expressed annoyance at this special cable release socket, it's an improvement over the standard tapered screw-tipped release found on the majority of other cameras. It offers a more secure fixing, and obviates the possibility that over-enthusiastic use can damage the shutter release mechanism.

The rotating collars around the shutter release buttons on the Nikon F and F2 appear similar, but have somewhat different functions. On the F2, the collar has three positions. At the far left, marked T, it sets the camera for time exposures and allows the front self-timer to act as the slow-speed mechanism (to give you speeds from 2 to 10 seconds). For regular speed operation (1 to 1/2000 s) the collar should be set with its indicator dot pointing forward, click-positioned in an unmarked setting equally distant between the T and the right L setting. L indicates a lock position, to prevent accidental exposure.

The collar on the F has two positions. On the left is the A or advance position for normal operation. On the right is R for 'rewinding'.

The shutter speed dials on the Nikon F and F2 housings look very much alike, except that the F2 has a top speed of 1/2000 s (instead of 1/1000 s on the F) and a red line marking its top electronic flash shutter speed of 1/80 s (instead of a red 1/60 s mark indicating the top speed of the F). Shutter speeds from 1 to 1/60 s on the F2 and to 1/30 s on the F are engraved in white. The F has both B and T on the dial while the F2 has only B. When the Photomic metering heads are attached to the cameras, the same speed scales are visible on the vertical rim of the connecting rings.

Speeds on the F must be set precisely in the click positions. If you try to set speed midway, you will get the speed closest to the click position. On the F2, at 1/80 s or shorter you can set your speed half-way between marked speeds and get an in-between speed.

The F2 has an additional range of slow speeds, from 2 to 10 seconds, making use of the self-timer mechanism. Set the top shutter speed dial to B, turn the collar around the shutter release button to T. Now push downwards on the front-mounted self-timer lever until the black dot on the side of the lever hub is opposite the number of seconds of exposure you want. A press on the shutter release or cable release gives you the exposure (with no need to maintain pressure throughout). If you press the self-timer release button in the front of the camera (underneath the self-timer), the self-timer just delays the exposure in the usual way.

The B for 'Bulb' and T for 'Time' settings have always confused photographers. Basically, on B, the shutter opens you press the release, and closes again when you take your finger off the button. On T, the shutter opens when you press the button, and remains open whether or not you remove your finger from the release. It closes only when you press the release a second time. This is the accepted function, but on the Nikons the T setting

Nikkormat FT2, FT3 features

Note: Nikkormat FTN and earlier Nikkormats quite similar except as noted.

Shutter-release button
2. Frame counter
3. Film advance lever
4. Film plane indicator
5. Finder eyepiece
6. Hot shoe sync contact (FT2, some FTN only)
7. Accessory shoe (FT2, some FTN only)
8. Meter window
9. Rewind crank
10. Depth-of-field preview button
11. Shutter speed scale
12. Aperture indicator dot
13. Depth-of-field scale
14. Focusing ring
15. Distance scale
16. Meter coupling (not on FS)
17. Aperture scale
18. Maximum aperture scale
19. Neck strap eyelet lug
20. Shutter speed index dot
21. Self-timer
22. Lens release button
23. Shutter speed selector lever
24. ASA lock (FT2 and FT3 only)
25. Meter coupling pin (not on FS)
26. Mirror lock (not on FS)
27. Rewind button
28. Camera back
29. ASA film speed scale (not on FS, FT)
30. ASA film speed indicator (not on FS, FT)
31. Tripod socket
32. Battery chamber (not on FS)
33. Meter coupling lever (FT3 only)
34. Coupling lever release (FT3 only)
35. Lens mounting index (FT3 only)

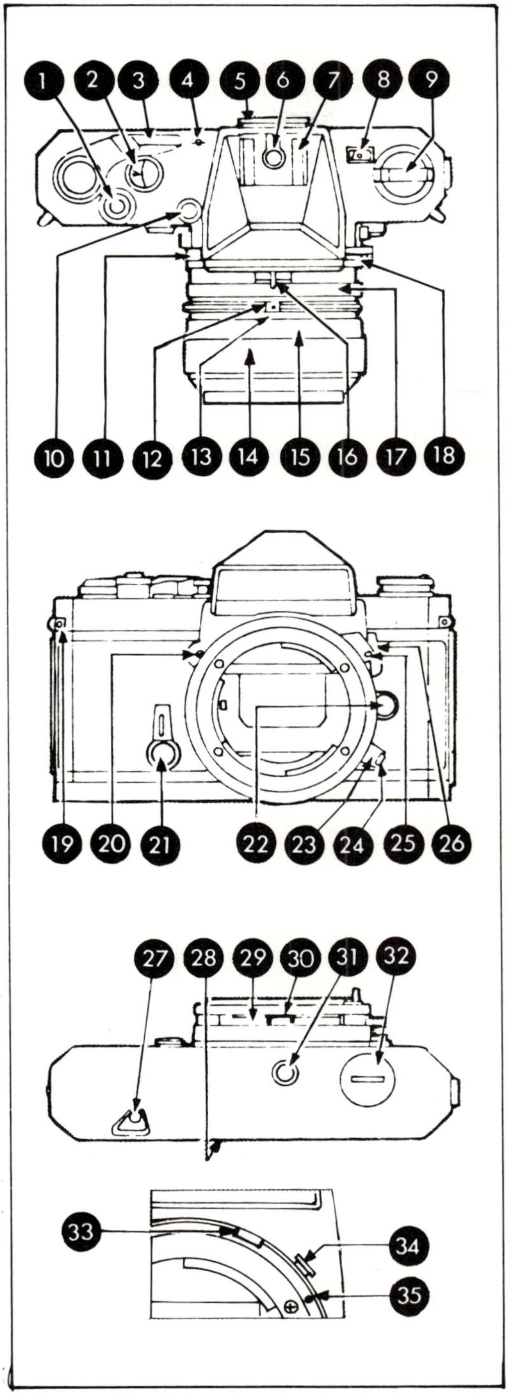

works in a slightly different way. The shutter remains open after the first press on the release, but no amount of further pressure closes it. On the F (where you set T by turning the shutter speed dial to the appropriate place) you close the shutter by turning the dial to any other speed setting. On the F2 there is no T on the speed dial. Set the speed dial to B. Turn the collar around the shutter release to T. After exposure, apply slight pressure to the film wind lever to close the shutter.

Nikkormat operation

Nikkormats (except the Nikkormat EL and ELW; see page 152) have the same basic features aside from the metering systems. The rapid wind lever is non-ratcheted. In other words, unlike the Nikon cameras, you just make one complete throw of the lever to wind shutter and film. If you stop half-way through, you will have to continue from the same position onwards to wind the camera.

The shutter release is located forward, somewhat as it is on the Nikon F2, and it is possible for you to keep your first finger on the shutter release while winding between shots. However, you must remove all pressure from the release after exposure or the winding mechanism doesn't unlock. Early Nikkormats had only the central tapered thread for a standard cable release. Later cameras have, in addition, the Nikon external threaded release for the special Nikon collar adapter or release. This is preferable because it gives a more positive fixing than the standard tapered release which pulls away from the camera easily.

Shutter speeds are set on a click-stopped ring round the lens mount. Use the small lug below the lens release button to turn the speed ring around the mount until the desired speed is opposite the black or white indicating button on the opposite side. Speeds are in white up to the top 1/125 s electronic flash speed and thence red to 1/1000 s. There is no T setting on the Nikkormats. This type of shutter speed control is fitted because it simplifies connection to the Copal Square shutter, which has its control levers on the front.

Loading

On the Nikon F, twist the release key on the camera bottom from CLOSE to OPEN and slip off the camera back. On the F2, twist the key and the camera back automatically swings open on its hinges. The Nikkormats (except EL and ELW) have an opening latch at the left bottom of the cameras. Pull this down to let the back swing open. If you've nowhere to put the separate back of your Nikon F, turn it so the back faces you with the bottom plate to your left. Slip the curved left end of the back between the first and middle fingers on your right hand and let it hang from there while you go about the business of loading the camera.

Nikon F and Photomic FTN

Finder features

1. Film load reminder
2. Film advance lever
3. Shutter release button
4. Advance-rewind ring
5. Shutter speed dial
6. Pentaprism viewfinder
7. Accessory shoe
8. Finder release button
9. Flash sync contact
10. Frame counter
11. Sync type selector window
12. Depth-of-field preview button
13. Lens aperture ring
14. Lens release button
15. Film rewind crank
16. Film speed reminder dial
17. Meter coupling prong
18. Self-timer
19. Mirror lockup knob
20. Tripod socket
21. Folding open-shut back key
22. Focusing ring with distance scale
23. Distance indicator with depth-of-field scale
24. Aperture indicator dot
25. Viewfinder eyepiece

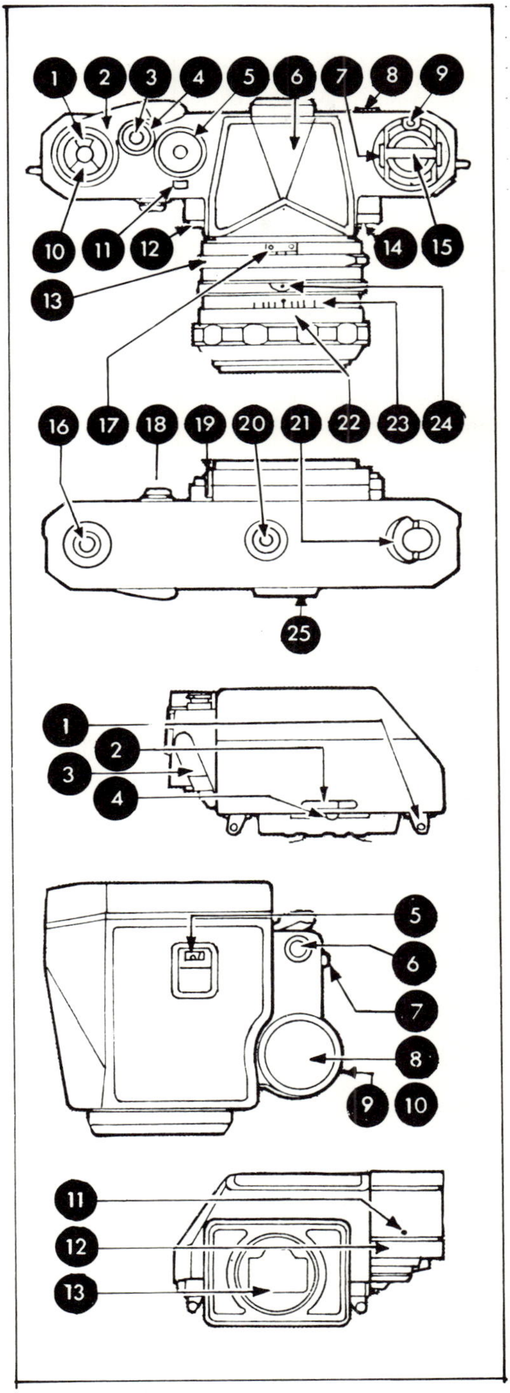

1. Prism clamp
2. Maximum aperture scale
3. Finder lock lever
4. Meter coupling pin
5. Meter window
6. Meter switch-off button
7. Meter switch-on button
8. ASA film speed dial
9. ASA scale index ring
10. Shutter speed selector ring
11. Shutter speed index dot
12. Shutter speed scale
13. Viewfinder eyepiece

Loading Nikon cameras

Note: Except for the method of opening and closing the camera back, loading a Nikon F is much like a Nikon F2 or F2A described here. You'll find more information on the Nikon F at the bottom of this page.

Fold out O/C key on camera bottom, turn counterclockwise until arrow points to O. Pull up rewind knob as far as it will go.

Drop film cartridge into chamber with film leader to right and push down rewind knob. Thread leader across film plane, insert end in take-up spool slot so slot tooth catches film perforation. Turn spool edge as indicated winding film inside out. Make certain film sprocket wheel teeth are securely caught on film sprocket holes.

Close camera back. Take slack out of film by winding film tight using rewind crank.

Advance film using lever and shutter release button until indicator for frame 1 appears in frame counter window. Rewind knob will turn while advancing if film has been loaded properly. Immediately set ASA index for your film if camera has meter prism.

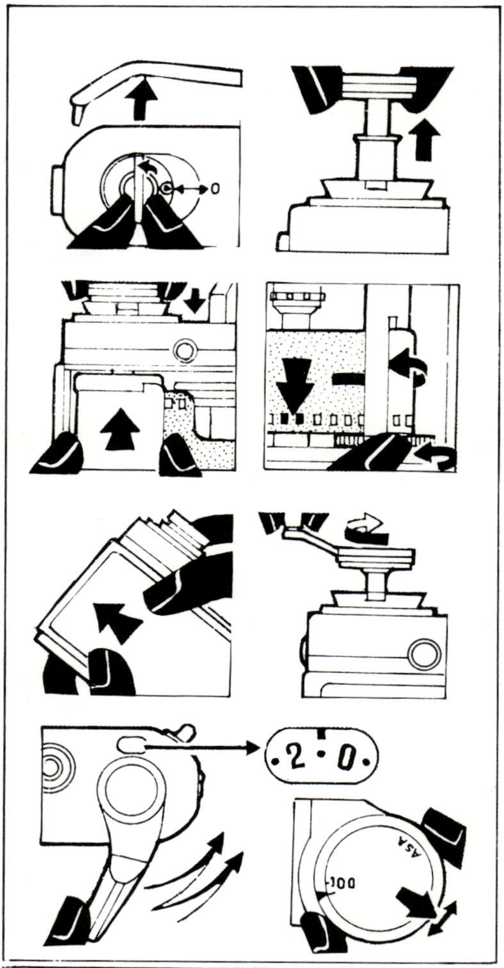

Separate Nikon F camera back

Entire Nikon F back slides off when bottom key is turned. For convenience hold back between fingers as indicated when loading film.

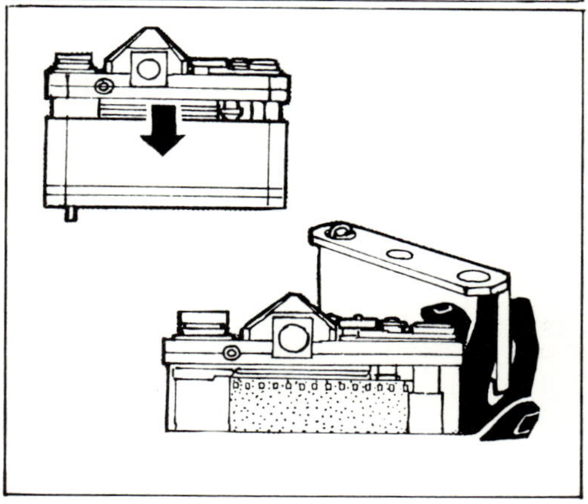

Loading Nikkormats (except EL, ELW)

Pull downwards on side catch. Back will swing open. Pull up on rewind knob and drop film into chamber with film leader to right. Push down knob.

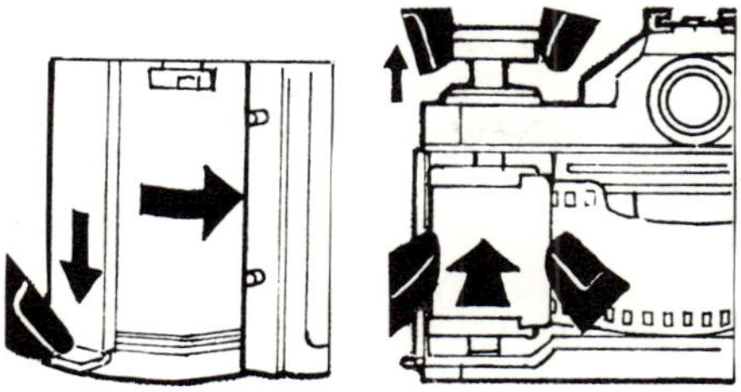

Pull film leader end across film plane and insert end only into slot of take-up spool. Make certain that tooth in slot catches leader perforation. Turn take-up spool rim, winding film emulsion out at least two full turns. Make sure sprocket teeth on sprocket wheel engage film sprockets securely.

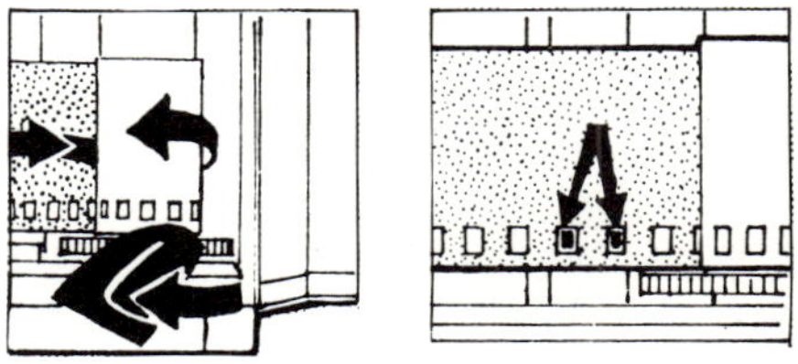

Close back of camera. Take slack out of film by winding with rewind crank.

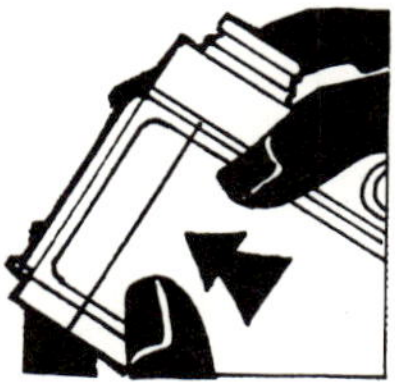

Using rapid wind lever and shutter release, wind film until indicator frame 1 appears in counter window.

With Nikkormat FTN, just set ASA index by pushing index prong on lens mount bottom to proper setting. With FT2 and FT3 release lock on shutter speed setting lever before pushing prong. With Nikkormat FT, ASA index is on side of lens mount. Maximum lens aperture must be set next to proper ASA.

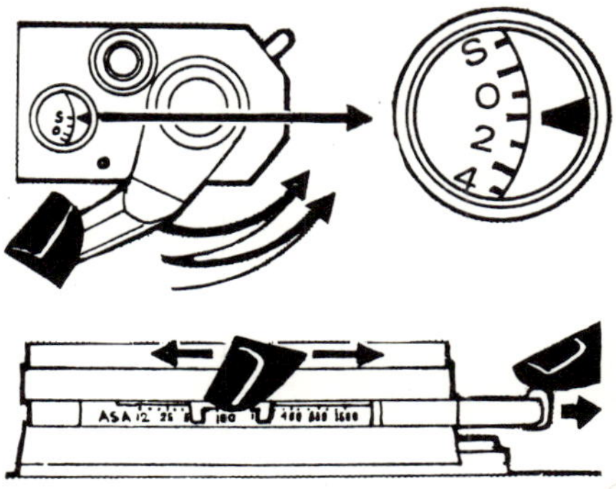

Unloading Nikkormats

Press in rewind button, turn rewind crank clockwise until you hear film end leave take-up spool.

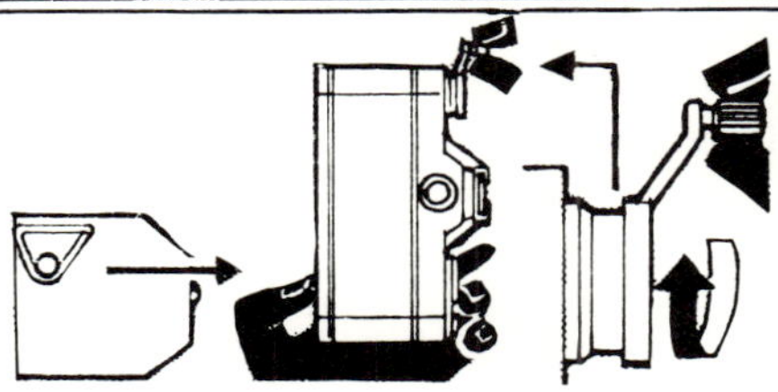

Loading the Nikons or Nikkormats is much the same. The film cassette slips straight into the left-hand film chamber of the Nikon F with its cutaway bottom chamber. On other Nikons and Nikkormats you must move the rewind spindle up out of the way. You can do this by pulling up on the rewind knob, but it is more convenient to push upwards on the spindle from inside. With the cassette in the chamber, push down on the rewind knob. You may have to turn the knob slightly to engage the spool.

I find that holding the camera vertically with the supply chamber at bottom and take-up spindle at top is the easiest position to load it. Ascertain that the film cassette core is engaged by the take-up spindle lugs. Pull the film leader straight across the film guide rails and fasten the end of the leader to the take-up spool. The leader engages directly into one of the take-up spool slots; make certain that one of its sprocket holes is caught by the tooth in the slot. With your right thumb, wind downwards on the milled right end of the take-up spool (the bottom end with the camera in upright position). By winding downwards you will be winding as the camera winds, with the film *emulsion side out.* Wind in a small length of leader.

The film should now be held securely. It should pass evenly from take-up spool across the film channel over the sprocket wheel which should also engage a sprocket hole. If it has missed the sprocket wheel, move the film over it so it does catch. Release the take-up spool and make sure the sprocket remains engaged.

Close the camera and lock it. On the Nikon F, have the release collar set to A for advance. Turning the rewind knob in the direction of the arrow, remove all slack from the film. Advance film to the first exposure with the transport lever (releasing the shutter each stroke) until the number 1 appears in the frame counter. The counter is near the wind lever of the Nikon F2 and Nikkormats, and in the wind lever hub of the Nikon F. *Important!* If you have loaded your film correctly (and have taken the slack out of the film), the rewind knob of your camera revolves each time you advance film. This is your assurance that film is advancing through your camera. Improper loading and failure to check the movement of the rewind knob during winding is a major cause of photographic disasters even among professional photographers.

Double exposures

Although I have never wished to make double exposures on a single frame myself, many owners like to try this procedure. The Nikon F2, F, and the Nikkormats can produce double exposures with varying degrees of ease.

You can produce accurate double exposures with the Nikon F2. After you have taken the first scene, push in the rewind button on the bottom of the camera and hold it in while winding the shutter using the film transport lever. This resets the shutter mechanism without advancing the film. It also stops the frame counter from going on to the next exposure number.

Making double exposures

It's possible to expose as often as you want on one frame for special effects with Nikons and Nikkormats. Here's how to do it.

With all Nikon F2 models, take your first exposure. Then, while pressing in the rewind button on the bottom of your camera, wind the shutter for the second exposure. The film remains in place.

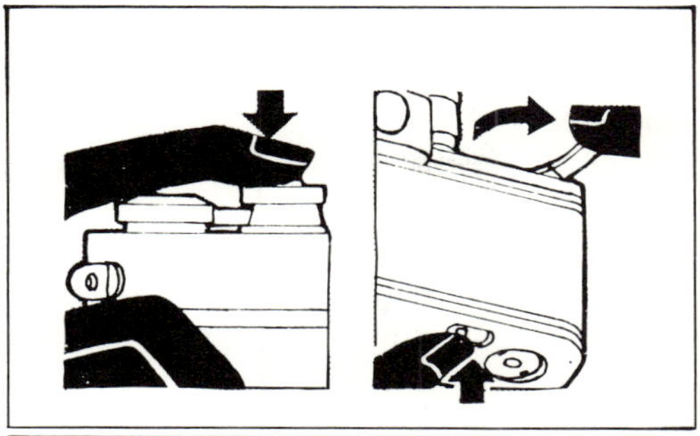

With the Nikon F, make your first exposure, then turn the A-R collar around the shutter release button to the R position. Very carefully rewind your film while watching the dot on the shutter release button. Rewind until the dot has made one complete circle and has come back to the exact same spot. Lastly, return the A-R collar to the A position and wind shutter and film in the normal way. This method does provides double exposures, but is not sufficiently accurate for precise superimpositions.

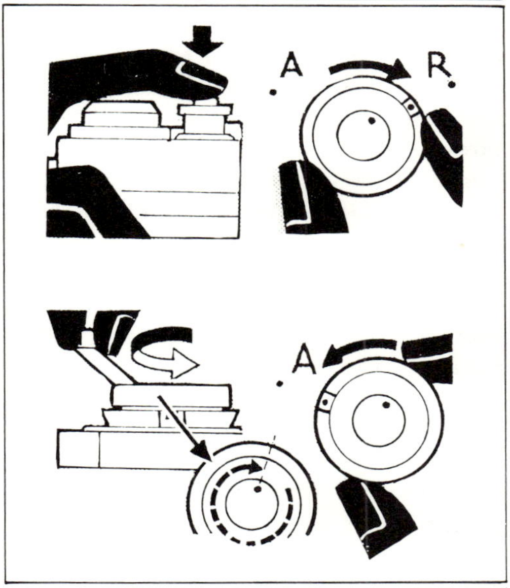

With Nikkormat cameras, take your first exposure. Then take all slack from film by tightening with rewind crank. While holding rewind knob securely with one finger, press in rewind button and recock shutter with film advance lever for second exposure.

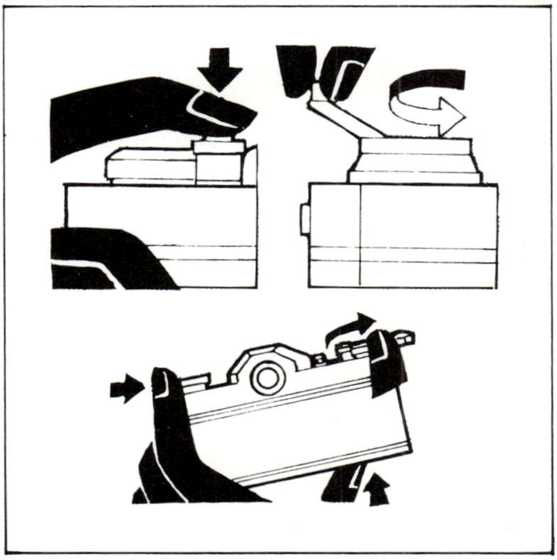

With the Nikon F, after you have taken the first exposure, turn the shutter release collar to R for rewind. Notice the small dot on the shutter release button edge. It revolves one complete turn every time film is advanced one full frame. With the rewind crank, carefully wind back one complete frame by allowing the dot to revolve exactly one complete turn. Then turn the release collar back to 'A' for advance and wind both film and shutter back to the same exposure. The frame counter itself will advance by one, but you will be able to superimpose a second exposure on the same original frame (although not with the exact same precision of the Nikon F2).

Making a double exposure with the Nikkormats takes somewhat more digital dexterity. After the first exposure, turn the rewind crank to take out all slack from the film. Hold the rewind crank tight. Push in and hold the rewind button on the bottom of the camera, and rewind the shutter mechanism with the film advance lever. The film remains in about the same place, the frame counter advances one number.

One short warning about superimposed double exposures. Exposure is cumulative. If images overlap you will have to use something like half normal exposure with each shot, or the resulting double exposure is apt to be overexposed.

To become really adept at loading, practise it in the dark or while not looking at your camera. You may be surprised how often you will be called to load your camera under just such circumstances.

Rewinding

On to the rewinding. Let's assume you have now shot the last picture on the roll. When you detect the slightest amount of hesitation during winding, stop. Do not try to squeeze one extra picture onto the film. It's not worth it.

To rewind, you turn the rewind collar (around the shutter release) on the Nikon F or press in the rewind button (on the bottom) of the Nikon F2 or Nikkormat. Then rewind the film with the rewind crank. The crank of the F2 can be extended upward to make it easier to hold. Although some experts in the past have warned that too rapid rewinding can set up static electricity on the film, causing lightning-like streaks, properly manufactured film and camera interiors of the right materials virtually eliminate such possibilities.

You may prefer to wind the entire film leader back into the cassette. Alternatively, you may feel that film so wound may cause light leakage through the empty felt cassette lip. I prefer to wind film right into the cassette so that I can distinguish exposed cassettes from yet-to-be-shot films. As long as I avoid brilliant light falling on it, I have never experienced light leaking through the felt tip.

One additional winding matter. You may quite often find that you want to remove a film from a camera when it is halfway shot and replace it with another; then shoot the rest of the original film at some later time. Perhaps

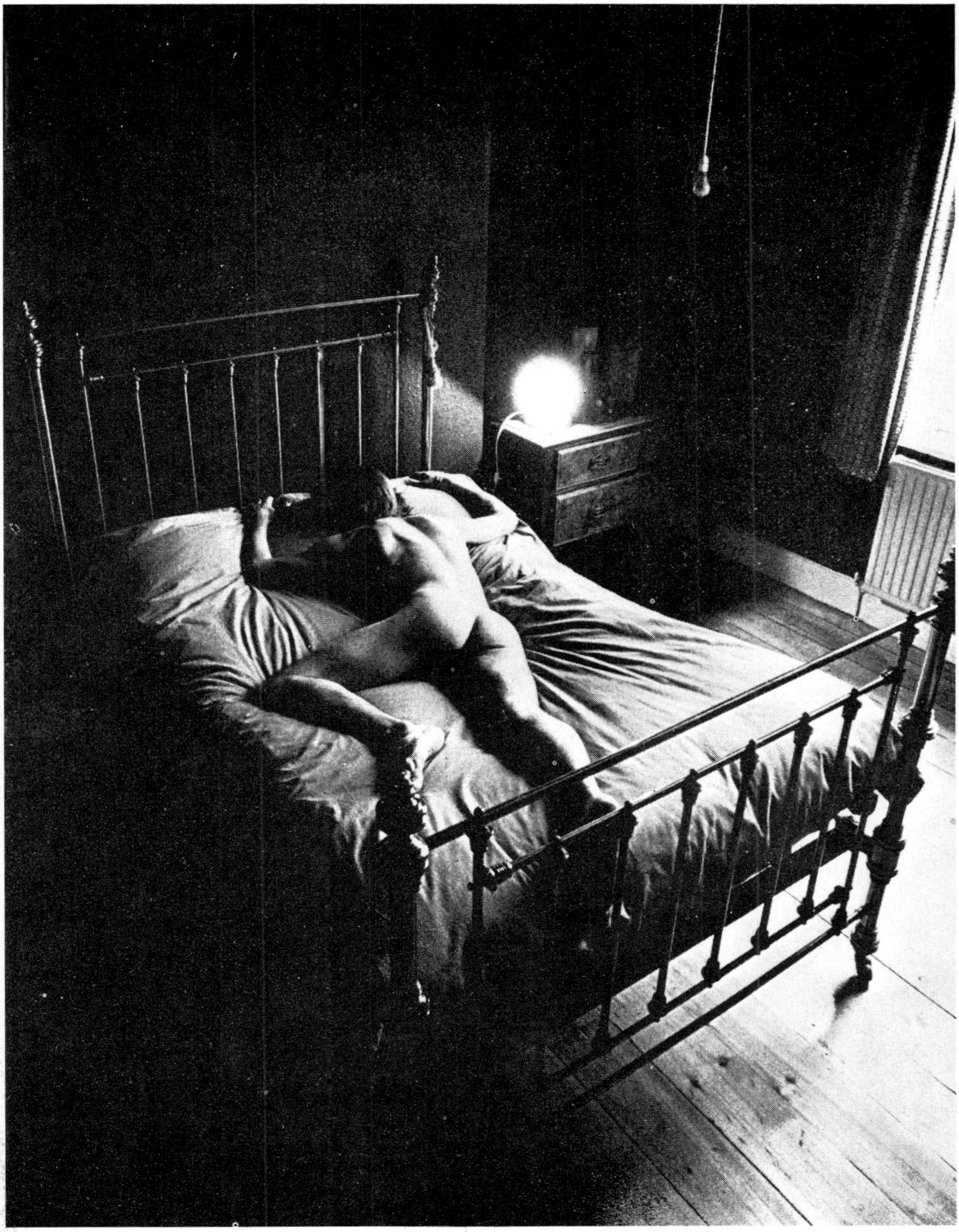

Self-portrait

Camera set on a tripod, the photographer trips the self-timer and takes up his pose. 20 mm *f*/4 Nikkor takes in the scene as well. *Ed Buziak.*

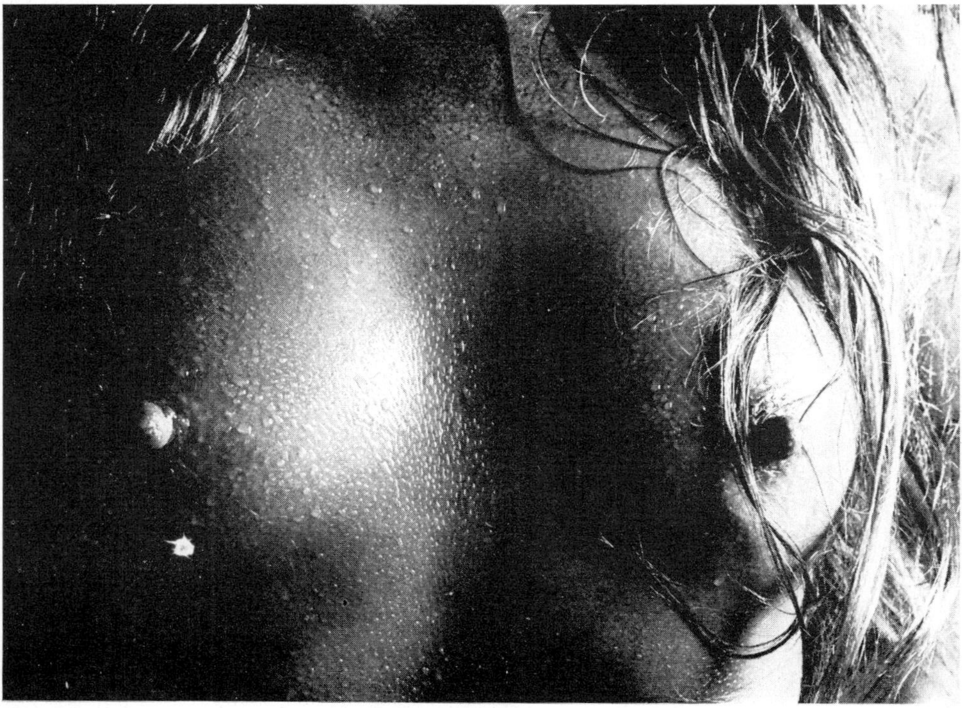

Close-up

Careful control of the lighting and judicious use of water turns a woman's body into a more-or-less abstract pattern. *Colin Ramsey*.

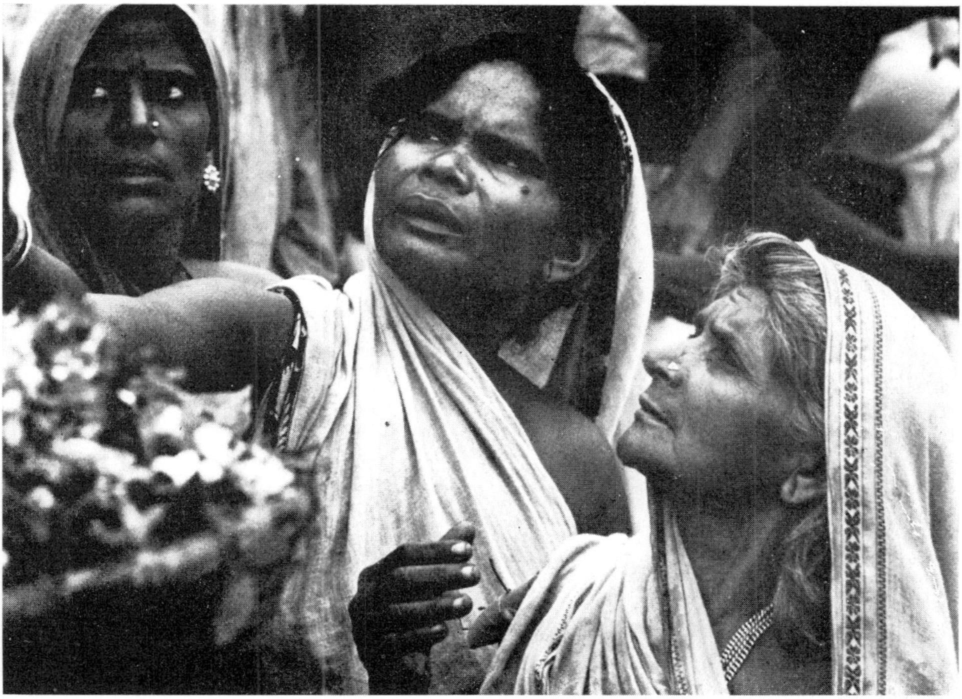

The candid approach

Three Hindu pilgrims in Benares, India stop to buy garlands of flowers, completely oblivious of my Nikon F with 105 mm *f*/2.5 Nikkor. Exposure on medium-speed black-and-white was about 1/125 second at *f*/5.6. This is only two-thirds of actual negative. A 135 mm lens would have been better in this circumstance.

Out of chaos, order

Overleaf, left. The jumble of sampans filled with Hong Kong Chinese awaiting the dragon boat races was fascinating. Biggest jam was in foreground. I chose the 105 mm *f*/2.5 Nikkor lens to narrow view and foreshorten distances making sampans appear more jammed than they were. Nikon F, medium-speed colour film, 1/125 second at *f*/11.

Solitude

Overleaf, right. The lone fisherman set against a wintry background. A normal lens would have reproduced the distant hills hardly bigger than him. Here the photographer used a 500 mm Reflex Nikkor to dramatise the isolation. *Ed Buziak.*

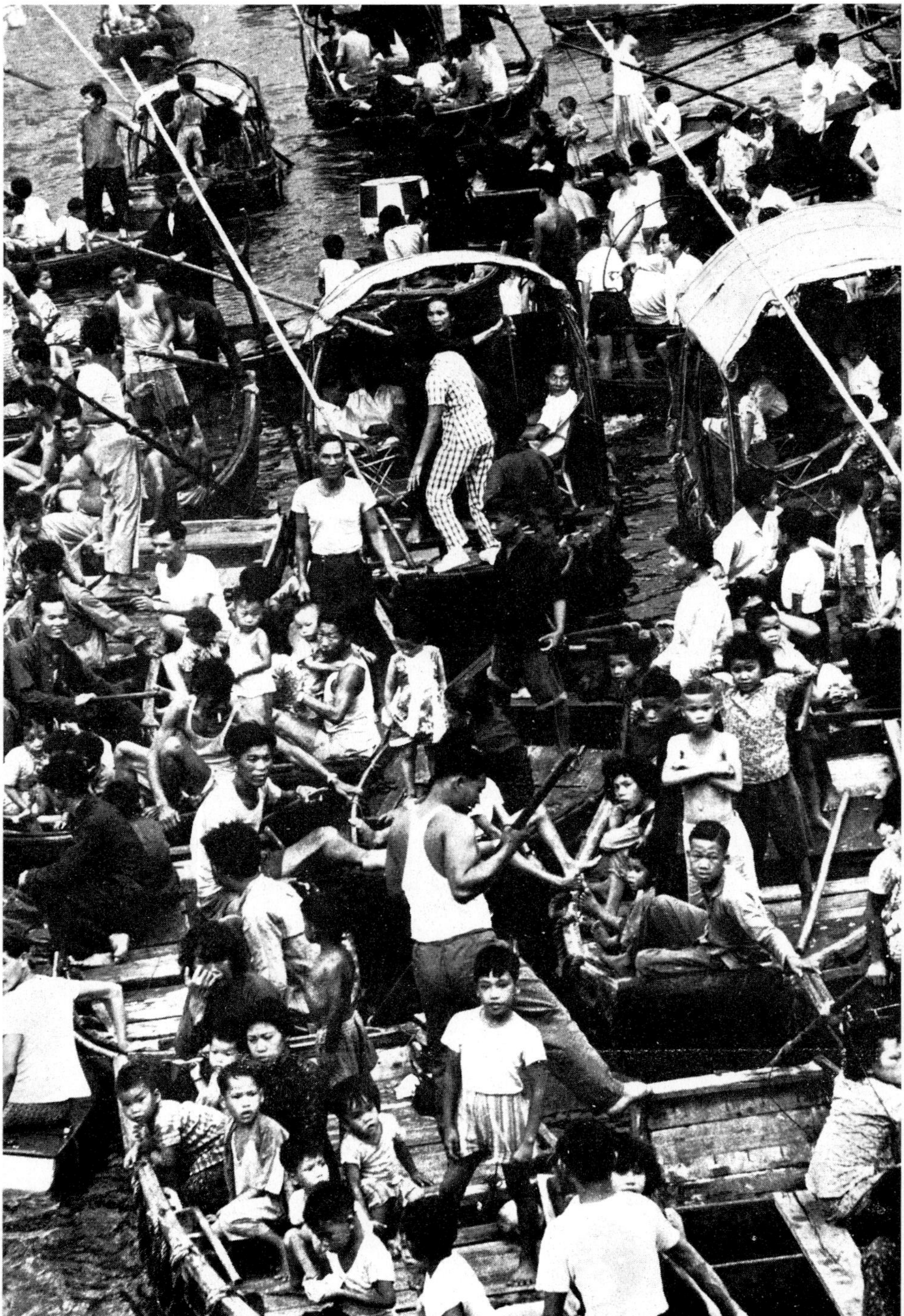

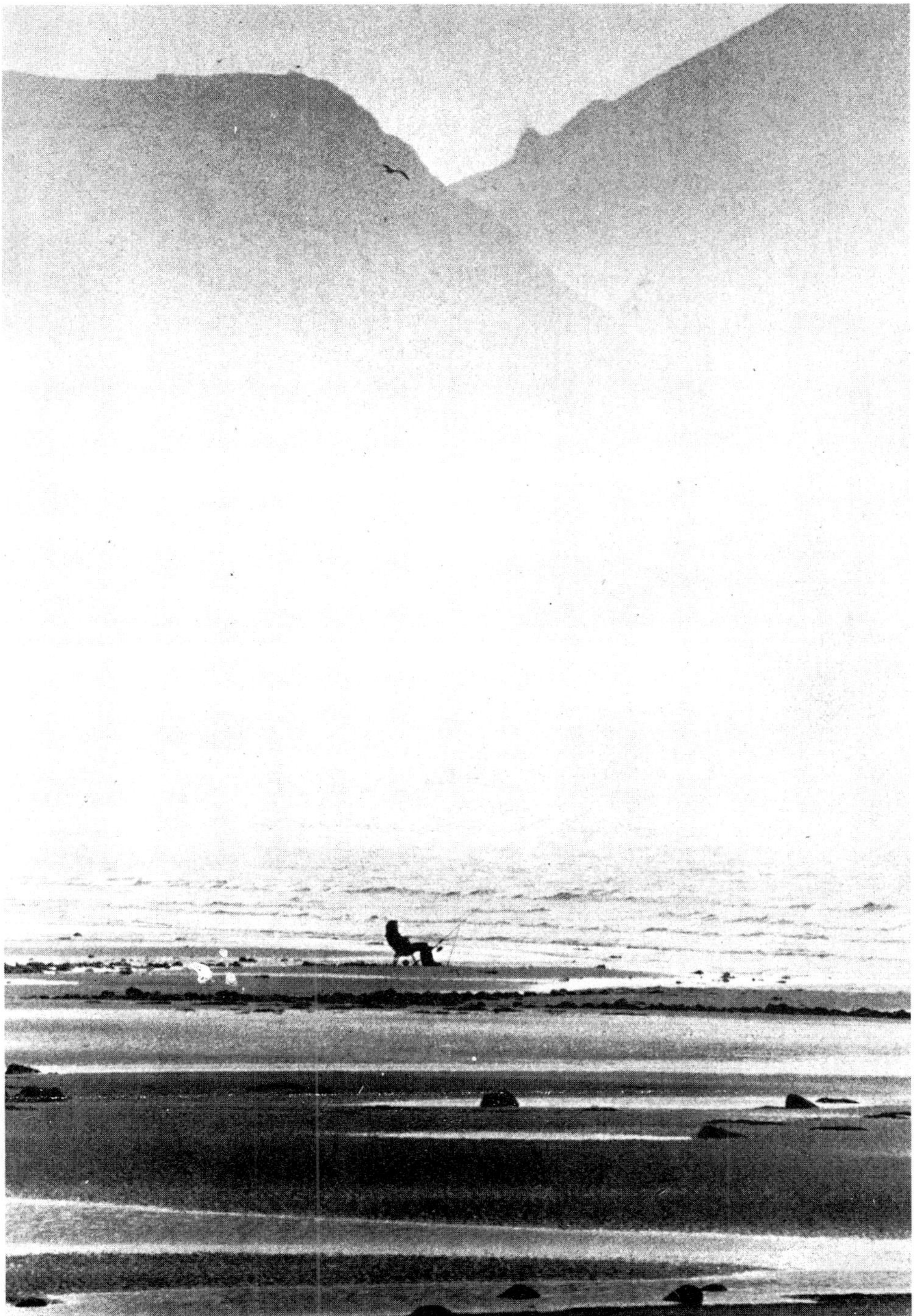

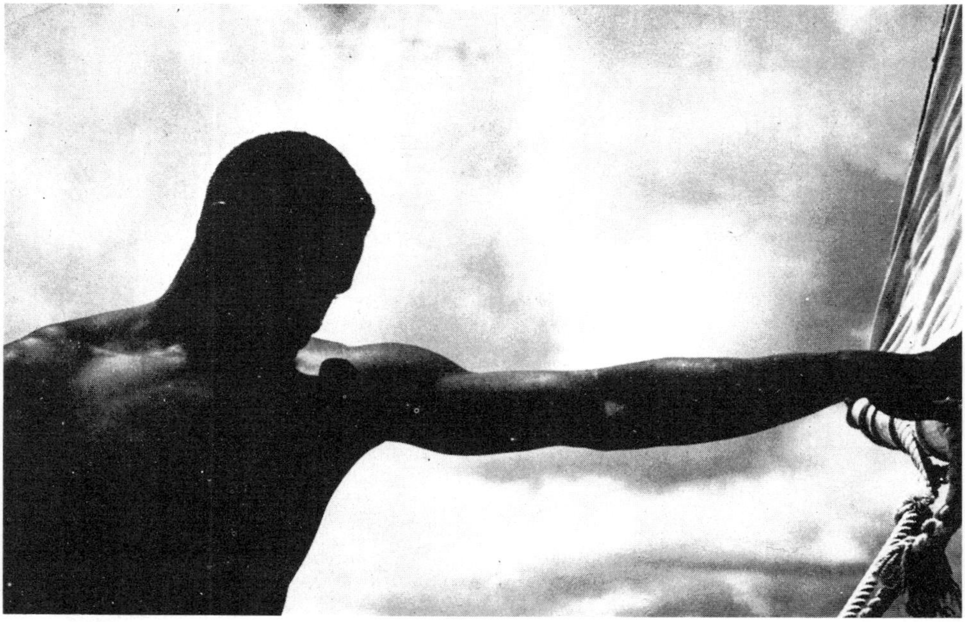

Printer's choice

Above. While an averaging meter reading produced an exposure of about 1/125 second at *f*/8 on medium film, there was ample detail in the negative to print it as a silhouette or as a detailed photo of the man pushing the sail outwards to catch the wind. However, as I saw it on that bright day, the sky was proper and the man a dramatic almost detail-less foreground statue and so it was printed. Nikkormat FT, 50 mm *f*/1.4 Nikkor.

Another silhouette

Opposite. Here the photographer took the shot as a silhouette, exposing for the background. Low shooting position produced statuesque quality.

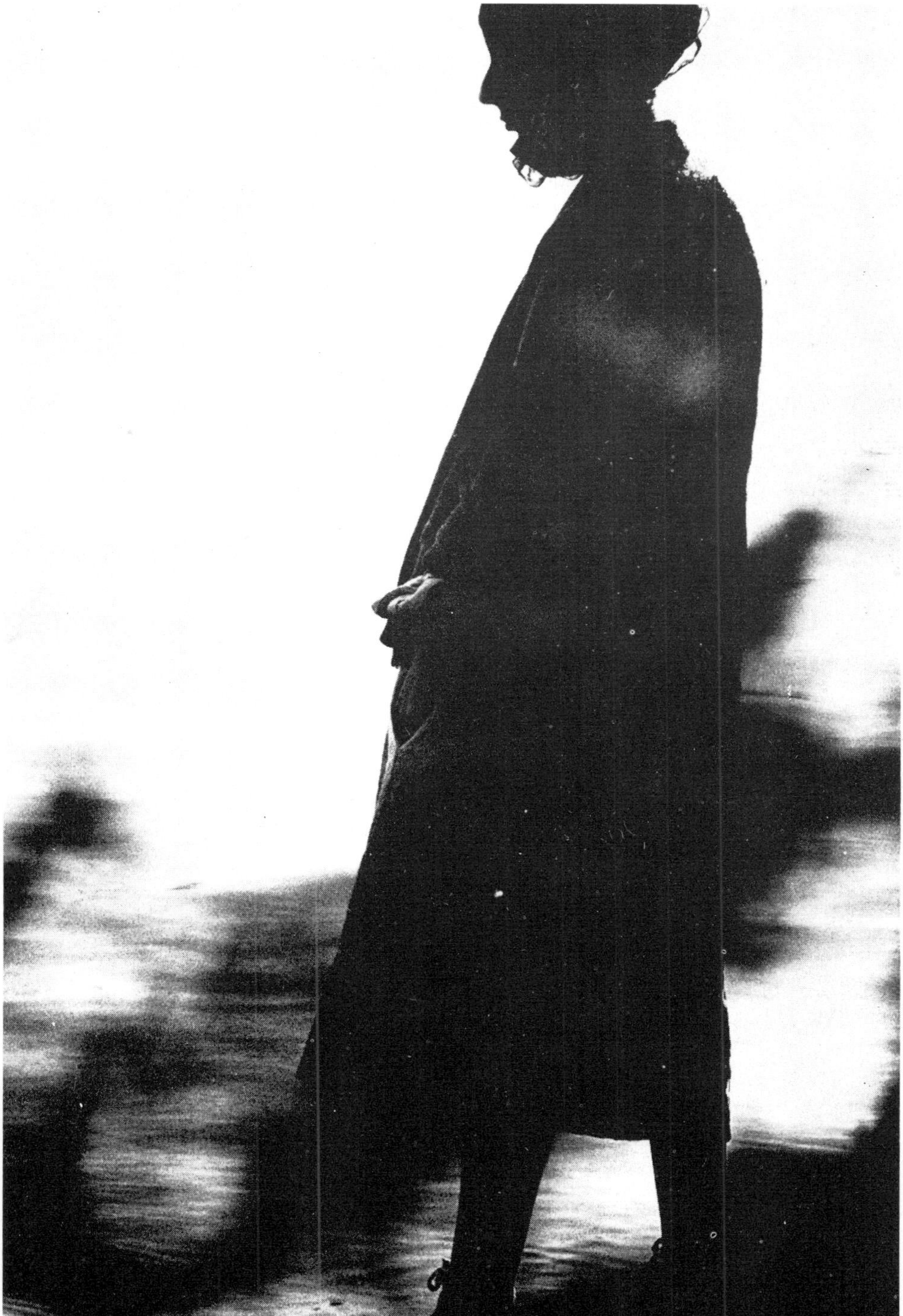

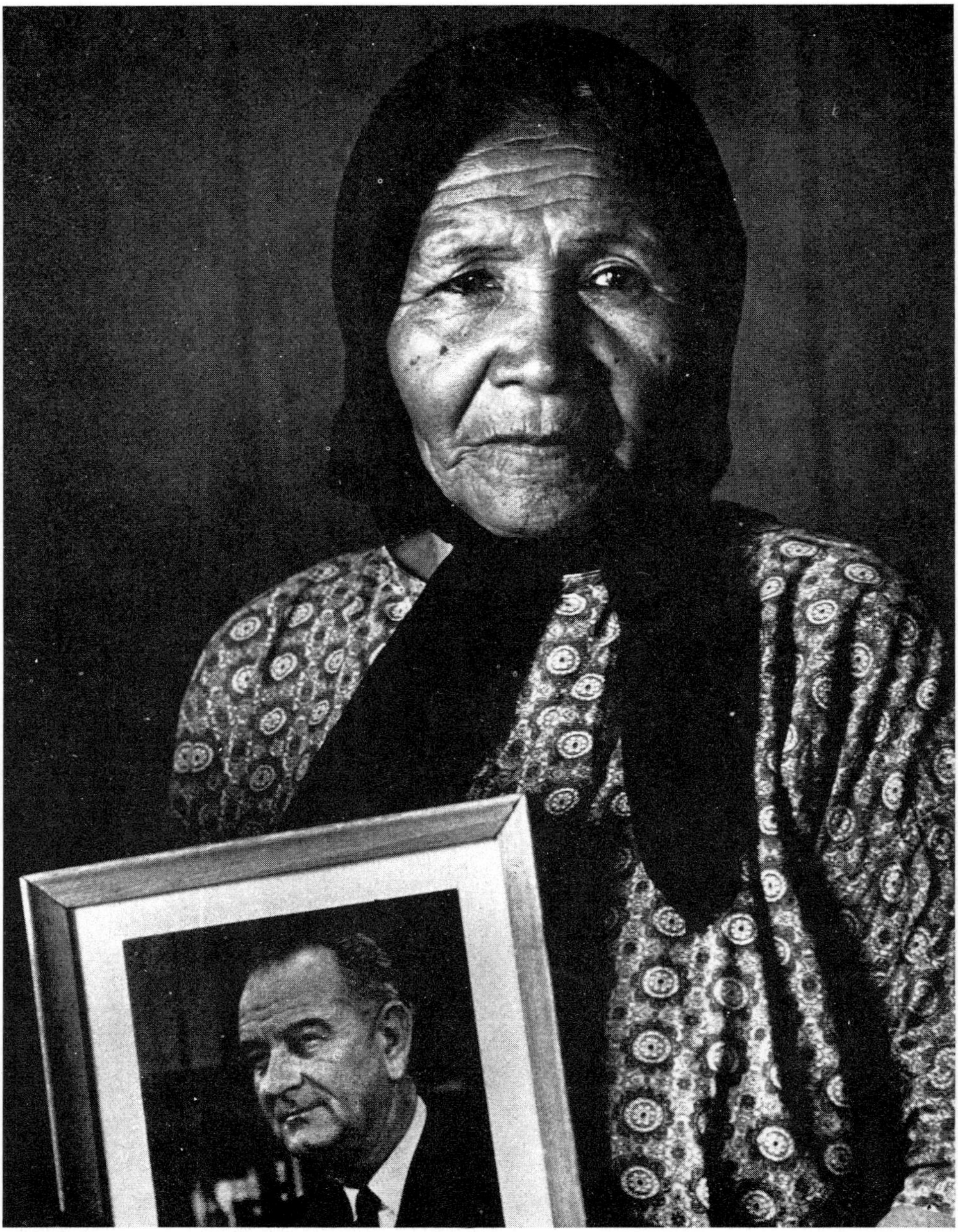

Windowlight indoors

Daylight filtering through a small window in a dilapidated frame house on a Cheyenne Indian reservation, Ashland, Montana delineated the face of an Indian squaw holding her prize possession – an autographed framed portrait of a former president of the United States. I found a fast film and windowlight provided facial lines and tones no artificial light could have accomplished. 105 mm *f*/2.5 Nikkor Nikkormat FT, *f*/4, 1/30 second.

Film load reminders

On all Nikon F2 models, slip torn-off film box end into holder on back of camera. With Nikon F, push control lug in hub of wind lever so either 20 exposure or 36 appears in window. On camera bottom, turn ASA film speed reminder dial so proper film appears opposite black arrow for black and white film or red arrow for colour film.

Nikkormats have no film reminders but you can slip torn-off film box end between camera back and carrying case.

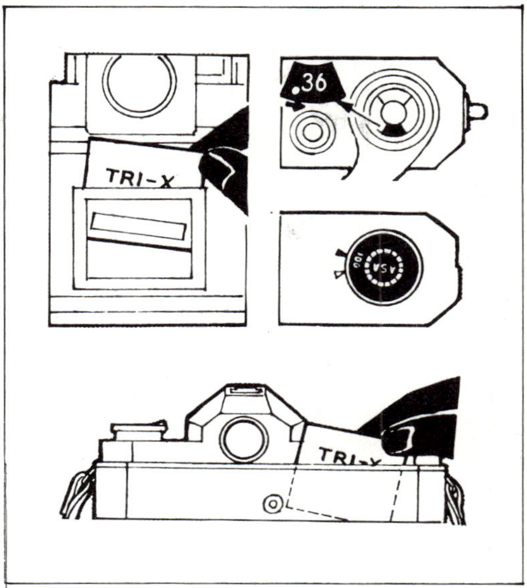

Locking-up mirror

All Nikon F2 models: Press downwards on lock-up lever.

Nikon F: Turn mirror lock knob up so black and red dots align. Wind and release shutter.

Nikkormats: Push downwards on mirror lock-up lever. (Nikon 8 and Nikkormat EL models have flip-up lever in same position but push upwards on it.)

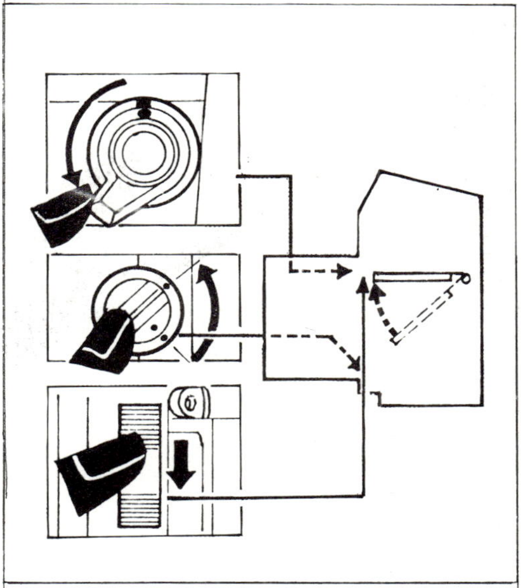

Avoid these dangers

Make certain tripod screw thread is not too long for tripod socket or screw may penetrate and damage camera. Some large tripod heads may be so large they interfere with lens focusing rings or controls on some Nikkormats.

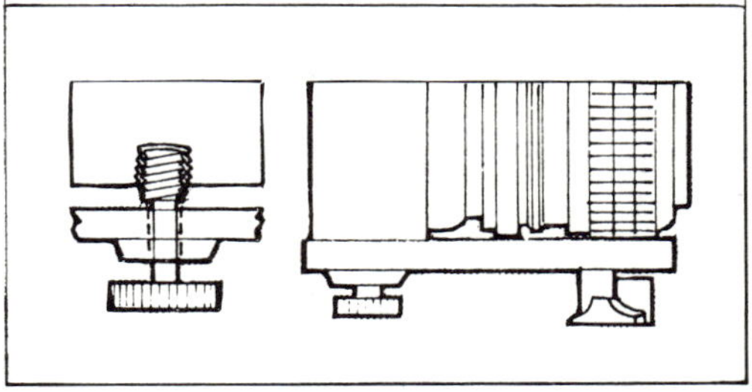

you have one sort of colour film in the camera and need to shoot another, or want to switch to black-and-white or vice versa. Unless you are almost to the very last frame of the first film, you won't want to waste the unshot frames.

Note the number appearing in the frame counter and whether at this point your camera is wound or unwound. In the normal way, rewind the film into the take-up spool; but be careful to stop when you feel the fall-off in tension as the leader comes loose from the take-up spool. When you take the film out of the camera, write the number of frames used on a piece of paper or on the film leader; note whether the camera was cocked or not. Wrap the note around the cassette with a rubber band. When re-using this film, load it quite normally, place the cap on the lens, select a fast shutter speed, small lens aperture and dark area to prevent any film fogging. Then wind on the film again, releasing the shutter each frame until you have reached the frame number you noted before.

For good measure, I then advance the film one more full frame even though I am perhaps losing a frame in doing it. This is my insurance against a partial overlapping double exposure. I can't over-emphasise the importance of marking the film removed from the camera. On more than one occasion I have forgotten to do so and have replaced a film in my camera with an already partially used film in the mistaken idea that it was brand new. Result: film wasted and two sets of pictures lost.

Self-timers

All Nikon and Nikkormats have self-timers, but they operate in different ways.

On the Nikon F2 you push downwards on the self-timer lever past the spot where the marked red dot on the timer lever hub indicates the slow speed 2. On the Nikon F you push the self-timer index mark past the second white dot on the camera facing. The further you push either lever beyond this point, the longer the self-timing interval.

To release the self-timer after you've cocked the shutter, push in on the small button above the self-timer on the front of the camera itself. If you set the self-timer and then decide you don't want to use it, simply ignore the setting and shoot as you normally would using the shutter release.

On the Nikkormat cameras, there is no minimum point for the self-timer to be set. After winding the film, press the self-timer down for as great an interval as you wish. Once the self-timer is set, you cannot release it. You must press the ordinary shutter release button and your exposure is delayed by whatever interval you have set with your self-timer. Incidentally, as we'll see, the self-timer has more important functions that simply allowing the photographer to get into the picture – although I admit that's just how I get my whole family into our annual photographic Christmas card!

Mirror lock

Older Nikons and Nikkormats have provision for swinging the mirror manually upwards out of the light path. Originally this feature was primarily used to allow deep wide-angle lenses to be inserted. With modern inverted telephoto lens designs we can get equally wide lenses which do not require the mirror to be moved. However, there is a second reason why you might wish to swing the mirror upwards. Both the Nikon and Nikkormat cameras have special damping devices to minimise any camera vibration caused by the mirror action during exposure. These are more than sufficient to give you crisp pictures in almost all photographic circumstances. However, when the Nikon or Nikkormat is mounted on a microscope or a telescope, or is used with extremely long lenses, the tiny amount of residual vibration can be magnified immensely. To eliminate this possibility, you can focus and view, then swing the mirror out of the light path before the exposure. It is easiest done on the Nikon F2 by just pushing outwards and downwards on the black lever surrounding the depth-of-field preview button on the right side of the camera. The mirror can be moved either up or down whenever you please.

On the Nikon F, the mirror control is a small inset disc on the right side of the camera body lens mount. To flip the mirror up, turn this counter-clockwise until the black dot on the disc matches a red dot on the disc rim. Now press the shutter release and the mirror will remain in the up position after exposure. To bring the mirror back down again, you turn the disc in the opposite or clockwise direction until the black dot matches a black dot in the disc rim. The mirror will then immediately return to the down position. The advantage of the F2 over the F in this matter is obvious, of course. With the F you cannot immediately swing the mirror out of the way, but must release the shutter with the mirror down first.

With the Nikkormat cameras, pushing the sliding lever mirror control downwards on the left side of the lens mount immediately raises the mirror. Pushing the lever back upwards returns the mirror to the down position. It's important to remember that the action of the lever is exactly opposite to what the lever does. There is another very convenient way to flip the mirror upwards before exposure. Use the self-timer. When you push the self-timer down and press the shutter release, the mirror immediately swings upwards some 8 seconds or so before exposure, coming down again immediately after exposure. Any possible vibration set up during downward mirror travel after the shutter has closed has no bearing on the exposure itself. The simplicity of this Nikkormat function made it my favourite camera body for still-subject telephotography.

Film reminders

Unless you load film into one camera only, and use it immediately, you may forget what sort of film you've loaded and how long it is. If you use two camera bodies with different films, you can easily get mixed up as to what film each contains. The film reminder systems are designed to obviate these problems. The easiest one to use is on the Nikon F2. On the back of the camera is a metal frame into which you can slide the end of the film box. On the Nikon F, there is an ASA speed reminder dial on the bottom of the camera plus a 20- or 36-exposure window in the hub of the wind lever operated with a moving lug. The Nikkormats have no reminder at all. The F2 reminder system is excellent. That on the F is so hidden most people either forget to set it or to reset it.

If you have difficulty remembering which film you're using with the F or Nikkormat, try tearing off the end of the film box and keeping it with your camera inside the ever-ready case (if you use one). If you plan on using two cameras, you might buy one black and one chrome. I keep black-and-white film in a black body and colour in a chrome one. If you have two similar camera bodies, you can code them with masking tape. If you use more than two types of film, you can then note the film loaded by writing on the tape. I am embarrassed to tell you how often I have mixed up films in cameras and thus have exposed them improperly, or used colour when I wanted black and white or vice versa.

Tripod bush

On the bottom of your camera is an essential fitting – the tripod socket. Never buy a tripod or other tripod-socket fastening device without carefully fitting it to the camera before purchase. First, note that on each camera, Nikon or Nikkormat, the thread is of a very definite depth. Many camera owners have punctured the bottom of their cameras by fastening them to tripod devices whose screws were longer than the thread; and thus damaged the camera internally. Many good tripods have threads of variable length. Whether variable or fixed, the thread must always be shorter than the depth of the tripod socket before you try to fix the camera.

When buying a tripod for the Nikkormat, select the tripod head with care. If it is too large it may extend so far forward as to prevent easy setting of the ASA index on the bottom of the lens mount, or could interfere with the shutter speed setting lug.

Practical camera operation

Inevitably, if you have acquired a new Nikon or Nikkormat you'll want to make a few practice dry runs before committing film to the camera. So you should become thoroughly familiar with camera handling.

Safety

Every year thousands of Nikons and Nikkormats are dropped on to hard floors where they are severely damaged. Make sure yours isn't one of them; never handle it unless the neckstrap is around your neck (or twisted around your wrist).

When you fit it, adjust the strap so that the camera rests at about chest level. The shorter the strap, the less danger of banging the camera into a wall or door as you turn around. Use the Nikon or Nikkormat strap fitted directly into 'O' rings through the neckstrap eyelets. Avoid those accessory straps with swivel locks that can rub against the camera finish and ruin it. The swivel locks are also prone to open when you least expect them, allowing the camera to fall. Remember, the faster a strap can be removed from a camera, the more likelihood there is that it can happen when you don't want it.

There has been much controversy about whether a camera should be kept in an ever-ready case. These cases, consisting of a camera body holder and a swivelling and snap-off front, are undeniably bulky. Many camera owners lose good pictures because they take too long to open the camera case. However, those who carry cameras naked with no case do have the most scratches, dents and damaged finish. A good compromise is to use the ever-ready case camera body holder but leave off the front, except when you are transporting the camera and there is no chance that you might take a picture. Always remember that a camera has never taken a picture inside a case. (An additional disadvantage of a full ever-ready case: it makes lens interchangeability difficult, since tele and wide-angle lenses often won't fit inside the front snap-off lens cover.)

An alternative to the ever-ready case, if you do have accessory lenses, is one of the many Nikon compartment cases. In these the camera is properly cradled and protected without a regular carrying case, and the case has compartments just the right size for the particular lenses. There are cases designed for just a few accessories and others for very comprehensive camera outfits including bulk film backs and motor drives.

Whether it's naked or in an ever-ready case, avoid carrying your camera over your shoulder. It is too exposed, easy for someone to pull it off your shoulder; and, perhaps more important, in a very awkward position if you want to shoot a picture quickly. The best place to carry a camera, the safest and most convenient, is around your neck, hanging on your chest. A few professional photographers who do not wish to have subjects noticing the camera so prominently displayed do remove the camera from their necks, and then wrap the strap securely around their wrists and carry the camera in their hands.

Holding

Virtually all modern 35 mm camera are designed with the major controls for the right hand and with the eye-level finder placed best for right-eyed use. However, whether you are right- or left-eyed, or right- or left-handed, the best way of holding the camera is basically the same. Functions must be divided between both hands to even out the support, aim and operation of controls as much as possible.

Place the camera on the palm of your left hand so that the lens rests naturally between your left thumb and first finger. Your palm becomes the camera's main support. Use your thumb and first or middle finger (whichever you find most comfortable) to grasp the knurled focusing ring of the lens mount. With your left hand alone, you should be able to raise the camera to your eye and operate the focusing control ring. If you can, you have the camera positioned properly in your left hand.

The right hand is your aiming, firing and film-advance hand. But you also steady the camera with it. With the camera held in your left hand as we've suggested, grasp the right side of the camera with your right hand so that your right thumb comes to rest naturally on the tip of the film transport lever when it's pulled out to the offset position. Your right first finger should rest on the shutter release button, and your right index finger falls over the depth-of-field preview button.

Which eye?

Now bring the camera to eye level. Keep your elbows well into your body and your arms close in for maximum support of the camera. Note what eye you use for viewing. If you have naturally brought the camera up to your

Carrying your camera

Carry your camera at the ready around your neck at chest level (not at waist where it may bounce). Leave front case part open or remove completely.

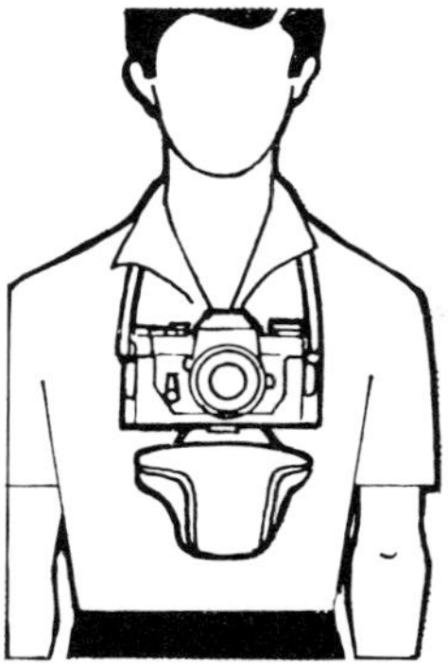

When travelling, you can carry camera without front of case, over your shoulder. Keep strap short and your arm and shoulder will protect camera.

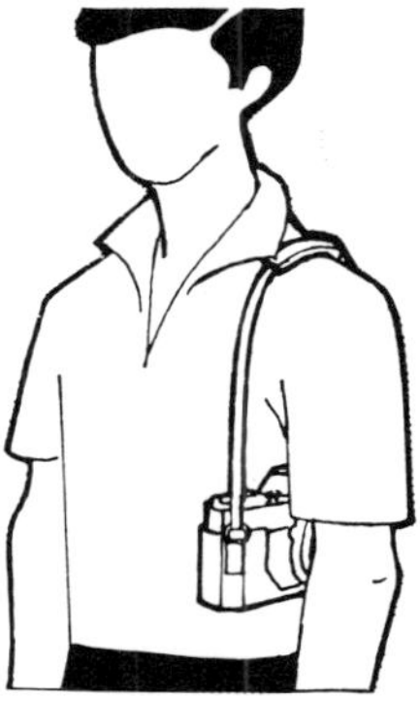

For candid shots, remove case completely, wrap neckstrap securely around wrist, pre-set controls, keep finger on shutter release. You can move camera quickly to eye level for fast shooting.

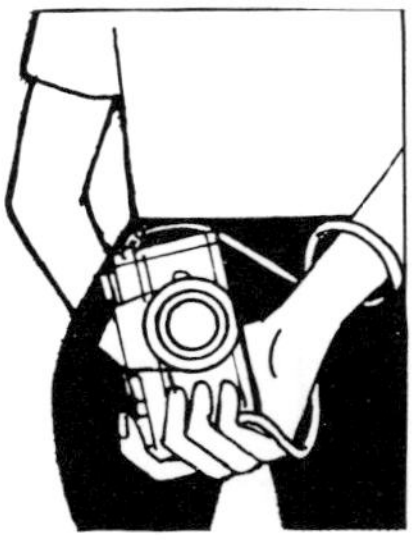

One of the most secure strap fasteners is a strong split-O ring which can be threaded into neckstrap eyelet of camera. More recent Nikon and Nikkormat cameras come already furnished with a triangular split ring which is even more secure than, and superior to, the split-O ring.

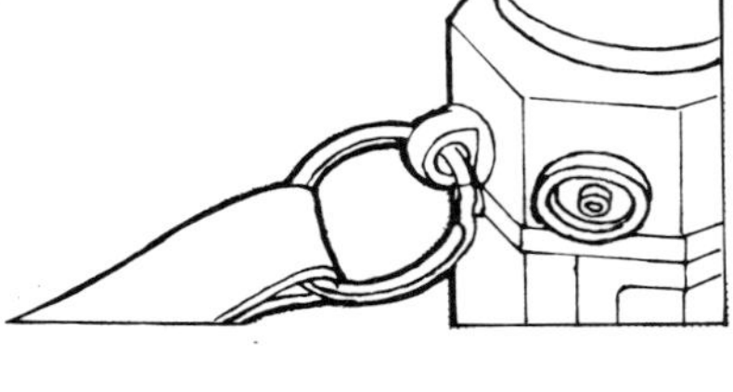

right eye, fine. If you have brought it to your left, try using your right. It may well be that you use your left through force of habit and could train yourself to use your right just as well, and this can be easier. However, if you know you are left-eyed, or you do find that switching is somewhat uncomfortable, difficult to focus with or inconvenient, you'd better continue left-eyed.

If you're a right-eyed photographer, holding the camera as we've suggested, you should be able to view and focus, push the shutter release and advance film with no need to remove the camera from your eye. You can look through the finder the whole time, making it an extension of your eye, and eventually almost forget the camera as more and more you operate it virtually subconsciously.

Left-eyed photographers may find that they need to remove the camera slightly from their faces to wind film. Otherwise, noses or eyes may get in the way of the wind lever. However, you may be able to squeak by without removing the camera too far between shots.

Taking vertical pictures is another matter. Most photographers find it convenient to continue to control the camera with their right hand. Swivel it so that the left side of the camera rests in your left palm. Grasp the focusing ring with the same fingers, and operate the camera as before. Depending on how your head is shaped, you may have to tilt the camera away slightly to wind film.

Left-eyed photographers generally find turning the camera in the opposite direction, with the right side of the palm of their left hand, more convenient.

Stand with your feet sufficiently parted to give yourself a firm balance. Breathe naturally. Stop breathing just for the moment you shoot the picture. (Many successful professional photographers tell me that they don't even do that and still get sharp pictures.)

Setting the controls

With the Nikon F2, F2S Photomic or F3 (in which shutter speeds and apertures are visible in the finder), you can set both controls without removing the camera from eye level. With the Photomic FTn Nikons or Nikkormats (in which shutter speeds are visible in the finder) you should be able to change speeds naturally at eye level. You can set the apertures, too, by counting the clicks from full aperture. For instance, with the 50 mm *f*/2 Auto-Nikkor, the end of the aperture scale is *f*/2, then there are clicks at each whole *f*/stop smaller. So, just open up the lens, and count off the clicks until you reach the stop you want. I don't advise starting from the smallest aperture reading, since it's far easier to remember the maximum aperture of a lens than the minimum.

Operating the shutter speed control, aperture ring, wind lever and shutter release will come easily; but do spend time focusing. This is often most

Film wind and cable release

The Nikon F2 wind lever can be pulled 20° away from the camera body for more convenient operation. This also serves to turn on the metering circuit. Actual film and shutter wind can be made one or a series of lever strokes totally 120°.

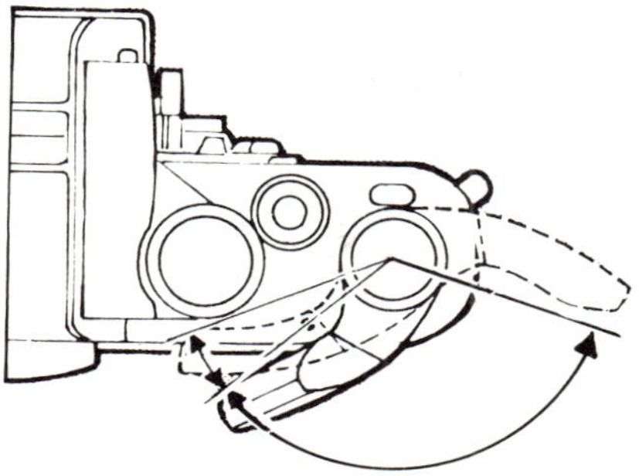

The Nikkormat wind lever also pulls away 20° from the camera body for more convenient operation. This also serves to turn on the metering circuit. However, the actual film and shutter wind must be made in a single 135° lever stroke.

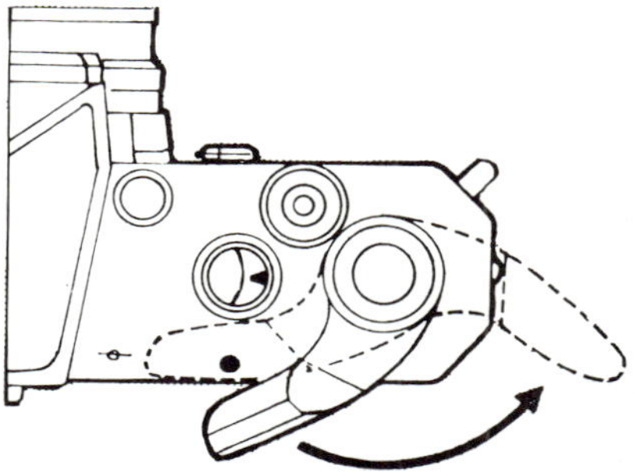

The Nikon F wind lever can be pulled away from the camera body 15° for convenient operation, but does not control any metering systems as in the cameras above. Actual film and shutter wind can be made in one or a series of lever strokes totalling 136°.

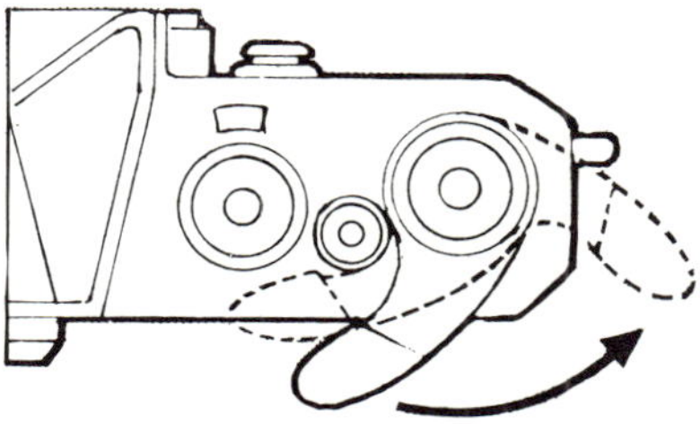

Nikon F, F2 camera shutter release buttons take a special cable release collar which threads over shutter button, left. All Nikkormats accept standard tapered cable release tip, right, but newer Nikkormats also accept collar as an alternative fastening method.

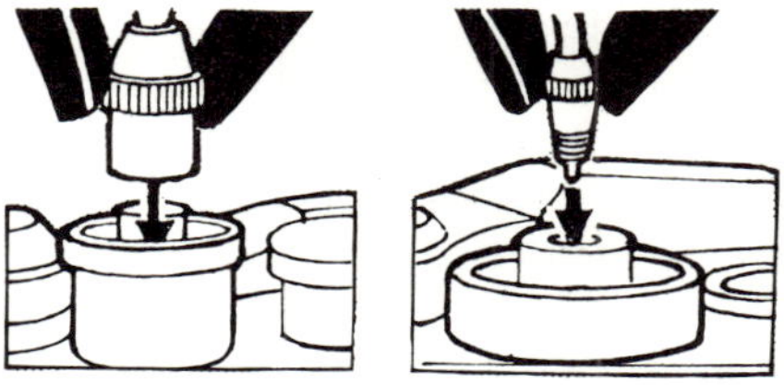

difficult to master. With the camera resting in your left palm, the fingers of your left hand should be able to turn the focusing ring of a normal 50 or 55 mm lens from infinity to about 2 m (7 ft). At that point, let go of the ring, bring your fingers back to normal position and give the ring a second twist. This will probably bring you to about 1 m (3½ ft). The total focusing span may take you four such twists. However, you are not likely to want to whip suddenly from end to the other. Most subjects stay at round about the same distance away.

Practise focusing on everything in sight. You'll soon find that some objects with pronounced contours are easily brought into sharp focus while others, like people's faces, are not. Focus again and again on the same spots, and check the focusing ring to see whether you are finding the exact same point of sharpest focus each time. There is no short cut to good focusing. Just practice.

Releasing the shutter

Squeezing off an exposure takes some practice. The greatest cause of unsharp pictures is camera shake. The pressure on the shutter release should be smooth and even, as you might squeeze the trigger of a gun. Ask a friend to watch you. If you're releasing the shutter properly he shouldn't be able to detect at what instant the shutter will be released. While he's watching, ask him to check also that you don't sway about.

Unobtrusive photography

Carrying a camera around your neck is a giveaway that you are taking pictures. Some people get embarrassed when they see you are going to take their picture. Others freeze or try to pose, ruining a good shot. To avoid this, keep the camera out of sight. Take it from your neck and wrap the strap around your right wrist a number of times. Hold the camera with your thumb on the wind lever and your first finger on the shutter release. Keep the camera down at your side or behind your back and whip it up to eye level just before you shoot. As you bring it up, move your left hand up to the focus ring. Raising the camera and firing smoothly takes practice, but it is, I find, a most effective method of carrying a camera, particularly when touring.

I am not suggesting that this quick-firing method should be a way of taking pictures of places where you are not supposed to take pictures, or of capturing people who do not want their pictures taken. You should at all times observe the local laws and the sensibilities of possible subjects: as you might wish them to observe yours.

Setting shutter speed controls

All Nikon F2 models have fingerguard rings around release button (left) and have three positions: T for shutter speeds 2 to 10 s or 'time', straight ahead for all other speeds, L to lock button against accidental exposure. Nikon F fingerguard (right) has two positions: A when advancing film normally and R when rewinding.

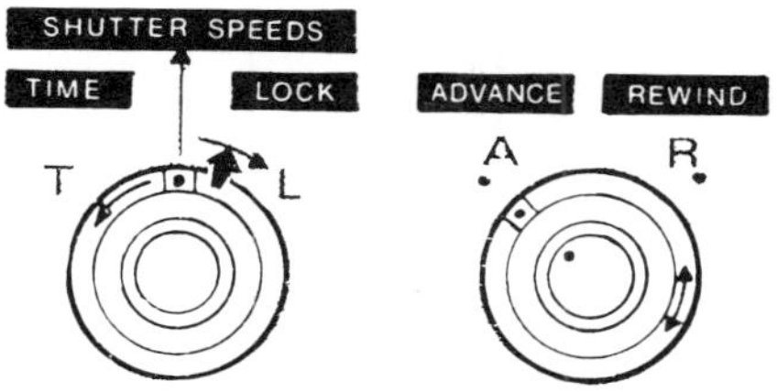

All Photomic heads of Nikons have shutter speed scales set by turning top knob as indicated.

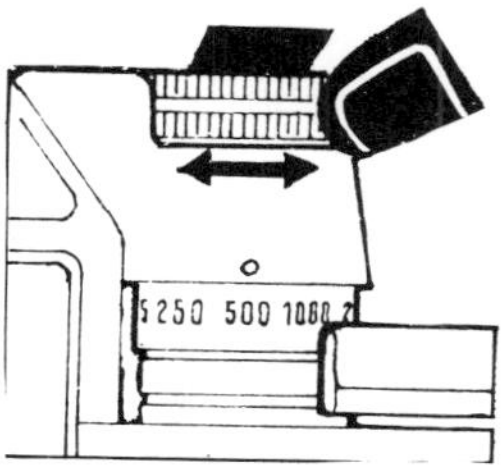

For exposures between 2 and 10 s with Nikon F2 models, set shutter speed scale to B, fingerguard to T and move self-timer lever until indicator matches speed desired.

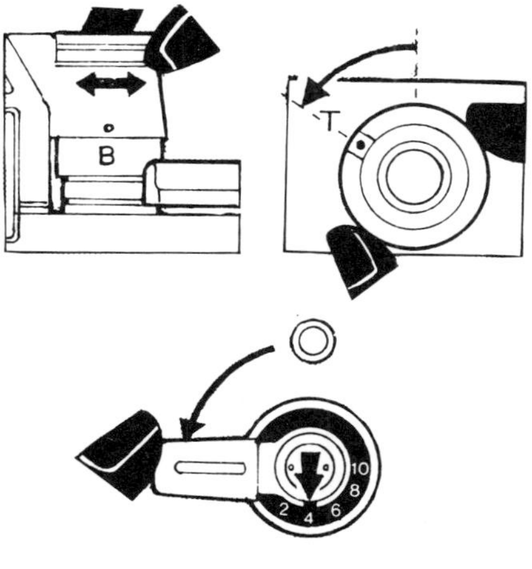

Setting Nikkormat shutter speeds

Grasp lever around lens mount as indicated, left, and move until desired shutter speed is opposite dot indicator on opposite side of lens mount, right.

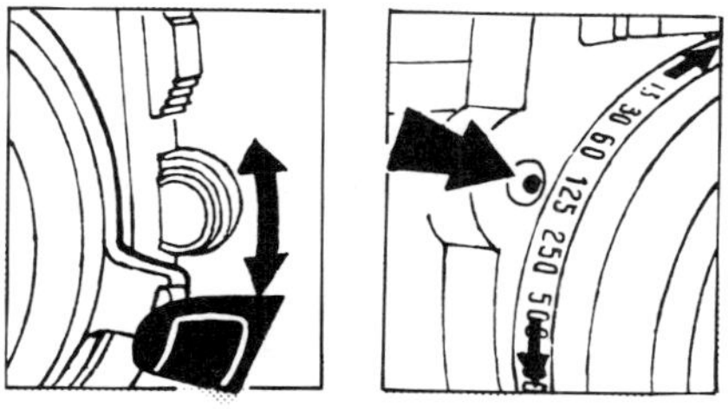

Try out your camera

Before you use a new camera for really important pictures, take a trial roll. Use colour transparency film, because it shows up exposure errors easily. Try a variety of conditions, but take at least some on a bright hazy day. This'll show you the sparkling results you can expect. With fast shutter speeds and wide apertures (at least *f*/2.8) you'll be able to see how well you're focusing. Have the films processed by a good-quality processor. (If you wish to experiment with lower-priced processing, do it at some other time.) When you get the slides back, if you don't have a projector hold them over a clean white surface that's well illuminated and examine them with a 10× or better magnifier. Colours should be rich and focus should be exactly in the right spot.

Using the viewfinders

The viewfinder shows you what the lens sees; lets you adjust focus and composition, observe perspective, make your judgement on camera angle, subject placement, lighting lenses – and even exposure if your camera has a prism housing with metering system. Learning to use this to view and focus the image properly is the key to successful picture taking.

With a 50 mm lens on your camera, probably at first you will think that the image you see through the viewfinder is the same size as the image you see directly. In fact, it isn't: on all Nikon and Nikkormat cameras, the image with a 50 mm lens is about four-fifths life size. Many experts have suggested in the past that photographers should keep both eyes open when viewing and focusing. This is fine for horizontal pictures if you put your left eye to the eyepiece. In other situations I would not recommend it. The disparity between the image sizes can cause eyestrain, and I have found attempting to keep both eyes open during exposure very much a handicap for accurate focus. Some people have difficulties in keeping one eye shut. If you are one of them, practise, or use your left eye. The lack of strain can be well worth it.

Screen focusing

An SLR viewfinder does not actually let you see through the camera lens. Your eye focuses on a screen, where the viewing images are focused by the lens. The Nikon and Nikkormat eyepieces form a virtual image of a subject in focus at a distance of about 1 metre (40 in) from the observer. Different makes of camera form their images at different distances. Nippon Kogaku engineers feel that their distance is suitable for most people. If normally you don't need glasses to see perfectly at this distance you will not need glasses to see the Nikon or Nikkormat screen. However, if you do need correction eyeglasses at that one-metre distance, you should use one of their nine eyepiece correction lenses: −2, −3, −4, −5, 0, +0.5, +1, +2, or +3 if you don't want to wear your own glasses. Even if you have been getting away without glasses for many years you may find that a slight diopter correction will sharpen up your focusing ability. Special corrections can be ground for you by an optician for insertion in the eyepiece. Photographers who claim they can't focus a reflex accurately suddenly find the problems clears up completely with the proper eyepiece correction. It should be noted that the corrective eyepieces for the Nikon and Nikkormat are not marked with the correction for the eyepiece alone but for the total corection of the camera finder system with corrective eyepiece attached. In other words, for instance the 0 eyepiece is not a piece of plain glass but actually a +1 by itself which, when combined with the Nikon-Nikkormat's −1, creates a total viewing system of 0.

As you get older, your eyes tend to lose their ability to accommodate. This leads to the need for 'reading glasses' (or bifocals). As the Nikon and Nikkormat viewing systems form comparatively close-up images, the lack of accommodation may be a problem. If this is your difficulty, try fitting a 0 or +0.5 eyepiece corrector. You will then be able to focus without reading glasses.

Focusing aids

For many years the standard focusing screen on the Nikon cameras was the A screen which has a split-image rangefinder spot in a 12mm diameter reference circle. Recent Nikons and Nikkormats have K-type screens which consist of central split-image rangefinders and microprism collars, plus full focusing areas to the picture edges.

Earlier Nikkormats offered the (factory-fitted) choice of microprism or split-image rangefinders. Further, you can fit Nikon F and F2 cameras with different microprisms for different lenses, or any one of a dozen other screens for special uses.

Which screen is best? There is no empirical answer. Optically, the split-image rangefinder or microprism can both operate successfully on all Nikon lenses with apertures greater (larger) than *f*/5.6, although with specific lenses you may wish to refer to the outer fine-focusing collar as a check. With a suitable subject, the split-image finder is the most positive. When the image is not in focus, the top and bottom of the image bisected by the split in the prism appear to be misaligned. When the image is in focus, they line up exactly. This is simple when you have a flagpole or a corner of a building to focus on. If you've just got horizontal lines, you can turn the camera vertical. However, if there is no straight-line object, you may find it difficult to focus. For such subjects, like shaggy dogs, or cornfields, a microprism helps. A microprism area shimmers when the subject is out of focus. The shimmer disappears when the subject is focused. It works on field of grain and shaggy dogs; but some people still can't find the exact point of sharpest focus. If possible, try both types of focusing on a number of different subjects so you are satisfied you have selected the best choice for your own

Previewing depth of field

With automatic diaphragm lenses on your Nikon or Nikkormat, you view your subject at full lens aperture no matter where the diaphragm ring is set. Press the depth-of-field preview button (on the front of your Nikon or Nikkormat EL – on the top of the other Nikkormats) to stop the lens down to the preset aperture so you can see an approximation of what will and what will not be sharp. At full aperture your depth will always be very shallow before and behind the subject you focus on (middle subject at right). Stopping down increases the focal depth (so you get all the subject sharp). Note: The Nikon EM and FG do not have a depth-of-field preview provision.

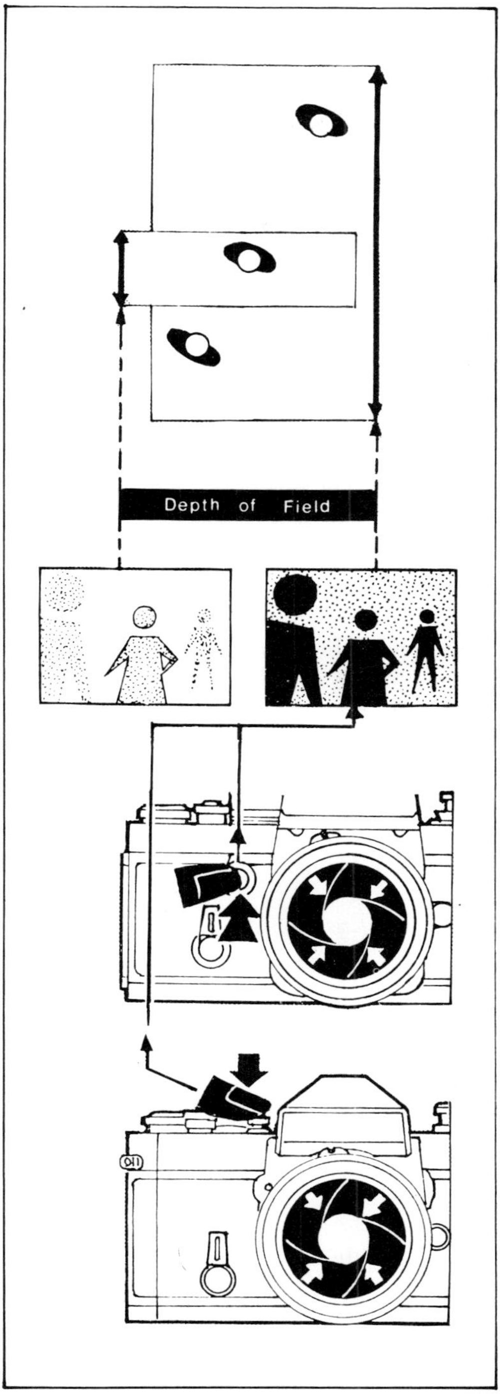

eyes. Even so, you may find a number of circumstances when you will wish to focus on the outer fine focusing collar rather than use the central rangefinder or microprism collar.

Neither split-prisms nor microprisms work well at lens apertures smaller than about *f*/5.6. At small apertures, either the top or bottom of a split-image centre darkens. You may be able to get both halves to appear clear by shifting your eye slightly from side to side. Similarly, at small apertures, a microprism becomes rather grainy and doesn't shimmer when out of focus. The more modern Nikons and Nikkormats have a combination to suit most users. If you own a Nikon F, F2 or F3 and find neither aid to your liking, you might prefer a plain central focusing spot of the B screen; especially if you are used to the plain ground-glass screen of view or press cameras. If not, it does take practice. It requires a very subjective ability to distinguish minute differences between in- and out-of-focus images.

Lenses with automatic diaphragm mechanisms (that is, all the normal lenses except those at the extremes of the focal length range) allow you to view and focus at full aperture. Turning the aperture ring makes no visible difference on the viewing screen. What you see on the finder screen represents the image at the full aperture of the lens. You can get a good approximation of the sharpness at other apertures by pressing the depth-of-field preview button. This closes the lens diaphragm to the set aperture. The image darkens and the depth of sharpness on the finder screen increases. But don't use this as a precise measurement, since the magnification through your finder eyepiece cannot give you the exact amount of sharpness you might require in a big enlargement or projection of a transparency. Instead, use the depth-of-field preview button as a general guide and refer to the depth-of-field scale on your lens. For even more precise control, consult a set of depth-of-field tables designed for your purpose.

Alternative finder systems

The most popular finders on the Nikon F and F2 are the Photomic heads. However, don't overlook alternative viewing and focusing accessories.

Eye-level finder

Simply labelled the eye-level finder for the Nikon F, the F2 version has a DE-1 designation. These are just like the Photomic finders, but with no metering. Consequently they are much smaller. The DE-1 has a ready-light for use with Nikon electronic flash units.

Waist-level finder

Called the Waist Level Finder II for the Nikon F, the DW-1 for the F2 and the DW-3 for the F3, this finder has a folding hood and sides with a fold-away 5× magnifier to critical focusing. It's especially suitable for use on

Finders and attachments

Eye-level finder for F, F2: No built-in meter, but has built-in ready-light for Nikon and similar flash units.

Waist-level finder for F, F2, F3: Shows right side up but reversed image. Has built-in hinged mangnifier for critical focus. For low angle or copy stand pictures.

Action finder for F, F2, F3: No built-in meter but special optical design of prism provides entire picture area to be seen 20mm distant from finder. For eyeglass, goggle or mask wearers, underwater camera housings, sports photography.

Focusing finder: Provides 6× magnification of entire finder screen, variable eyepiece diopter correction from −5 to +3. For technical applications close-ups, macro photography.

Right-angle viewing attachment: Threads into back of Nikon, Nikkormat prisms, permits waist level or other angle viewing. Turns 360°. Has diopter correction −5 to +3.

Eyepiece magnifier: Threads to back of Nikon or Nikkormat prism, provides 2× magnification of image centre for critical focusing. Swings away when not in use. Has diopter correction −5 to +1.

Rubber eyecup: Attaches to Nikon or Nikkormat eyepiece to shield eyepiece from extraneous light when viewing.

Photomic illuminator: Attaches to back of Nikon F2 Photomic head, provides illumination for meter needle within F2 prism meter head.

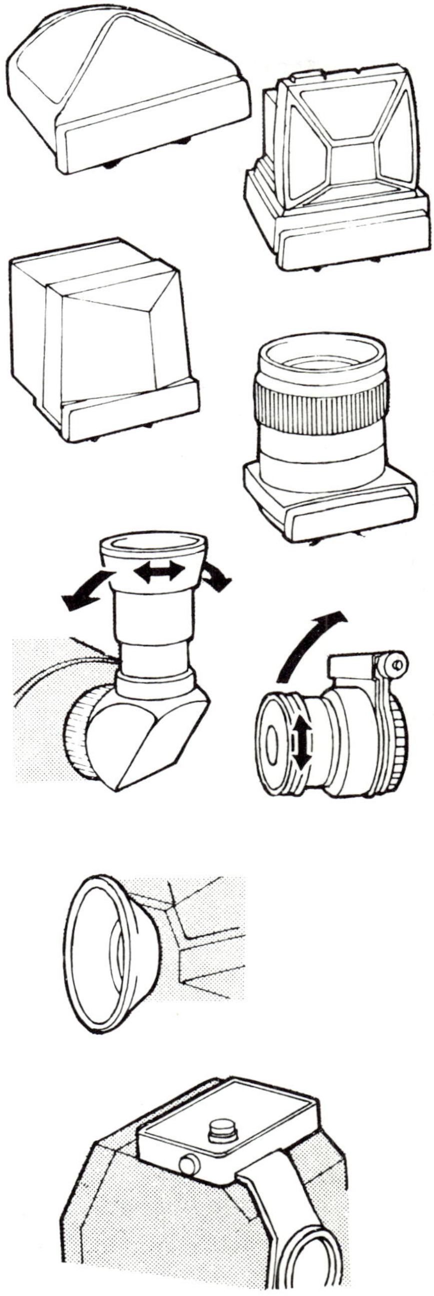

a vertical copying stand or for work at a low level where it is impossible to get your eye behind the eyepiece of an eye-level finder. It can also be used for holding the camera overhead or upside down, or to get photographs over the heads of crowds. It has no metering capability and, of course, the image is reversed left to right. It is particularly irritating if you want to take vertical-format pictures. You must look sideways into the viewfinder, and the image is upside down.

6× focusing finder DW-2, DW-4

This critical magnifier, which can be fitted to either the F or F2, or the DW-4 for the F3, features a helicoil thread 6× focusing finder providing adjustment from −5 to +3 diopters. The finder magnifies the entire focusing screen and is particularly suitable for parallax focusing with cross-hair screens as well as most precise work with any of the other Nikon screens. Although well suited to special applications such as astrophotography and macrophotography, it is also excellent for any work where the regular waist-level finder may be used. Its only disadvantage compared with the waist-level finder is that the 6× Focusing Finder is not collapsible and is therefore rather bulky and will not fit into any of the Nikon standard ever-ready camera cases. Note: The DW-2 is adapted for the F cameras by removing two small screws underneath the finder. They hold on the nameplate, which also must be removed.

Action finder

The DA-2 Action Finder for the Nikon F3 (identified as the DA-1 in the F2 version) provides an extremely large full-frame viewing and focusing image as far away from its eyepiece as 2½ in or 60 mm. While it was originally created for the use of astronauts wearing space helmets, it is splendid for following sports or other action, for use when the photographer must wear protective goggles or a helmet, or for underwater photography where the camera must be encased and the swimmer must wear a diving mask. It has no metering system.

High-Eyepoint Viewfinder DE-3

Just slightly larger than the standard DE-2 finder for the Nikon F-3, the High-Eyepoint finder allows eyeglass-wearers and photographers of action who cannot put their eyes close to the finder, access to the entire viewfinder screen even if their eye is as much as 25 mm from the eyepiece. Finder magnification is 0.7×, just slightly less than the DE-2. An eyepiece shutter is built in.

Photomic illuminator DL-1

Fitting both the Nikon F and F2, this small battery-powered illuminator mounts on top of the Photomic T, Tn, FTn, or DP-1 finders. The attaching bracket ring threads into the Photomic eyepiece. The illuminator contains a small lamp powered by a 1.3V mercury battery similar to that used in Photomic finders (but not in the F2S). The lamp lights up the meter needle window on top of the Photomic finder so that the metering needle is readily visible even when the camera is used where no existing light can strike the camera top. The illuminator, which has an 'on' button at the side and an 'off' button on top, will operate for about 10 hours on one battery. (The F3 has a built-in illuminator.)

Viewfinder accessories

You can't change the viewfinder on a Nikkormat, but you can fit accessories to aid viewing and focusing. You can fit the same accessories to your Nikon viewfinder if you want. Often they're more convenient and portable than unchangeable finders.

Right-angle viewing attachment

This single accessory unit, equally usable on all eye-level Nikon and Nikkormat finders, threads into the rear eyepiece of Nikon finders or replaces the removable eyepiece protection lens of Nikkormats. It provides right-angle viewing so that the camera can be used either at waist-level or on a vertical copying stand. Of course, there is no loss of metering as there is when the waist-level or focusing finders are used. The eyepiece is focusable from −5 to +3 diopters and shows a reduced-size full focusing screen image area or 0.6× with a 50mm lens. The view shows a reversed right to left image for both horizontal and vertical picture taking. The meter needles, shutter speed and aperture indications within the finder area are visible, although they too are reversed right to left. Although numerals are rather small for easy reading through the right-angle finder, metering is quite convenient.

Eyepiece magnifier

This is a common accessory which threads directly into the eyepiece of all Nikon eye-level finders or in place of plain optical glass cover of Nikkormats. It provides 2× magnification of the central image only and has a focusing eyepiece variable from −5 to +3 diopters. The metering system cannot be seen through the magnifier, but the magnifier can be swung out of the way quickly on its hinge and the regular finder eyepiece employed. The magnifier is especially useful for all applications where extremely critical focusing is needed.

Rubber eyecup

This is designed for all Nikon and Nikkormat eye-level finders. It minimises stray light and prevents it from entering the finder eyepiece, which could cause erroneous meter readings and loss of finder brightness.

Older exposure metering systems

In pre-F3 Nikon and Nikkormat camera series, the model designations indicate differences only in the metering system. The basic camera body design on these cameras, Nikon F, F2 and Nikkormat, has actually changed only in minor detail. With metering systems installed, names such as Nikon Photomic FTn, Nikon F2 Photomic, F2S Photomic and Nikkormat FTn or FT2 define the models. The word 'Photomic' indicates an interchangeable prism with built-in metering system. Since the Nikkormat has a non-interchangeable prism and the meter is permanently mounted, the word Photomic has never appeared with this camera. A Nikkormat FS had no meter.

The meters in the later pre-F3 models have basically the same operational features. Two metering cells, one on each side of the viewfinder eyepiece, 'read' the light from the finder screen. Aspheric lenses and special diaphragm plates in front of the cells give a centre-weighted reading of the picture area. Approximately 60 per cent of the total sensitivity of the metering system is concentrated within a central circular area of about 12 mm diameter (the fine-focusing collar surrounding the rangefinder spot). This constitutes but 13 per cent of the viewing field. The remainder of the sensitivity recedes gradually towards the edges and corners of the finder area. The cells of the Photomic finders are set vertically and their view is redirected horizontally by wedge prisms. The cells of the Nikkormats are set horizontally.

Three different types of metering cells have been used in Nikon and Nikkormat cameras. For your specific type of camera model, check for details throughout this book.

CdS 'cells' were used in the first through-the-lens metering models. They are not actually cells, but light-dependent resistors. However, as even engineers commonly call them cells, so shall we. The CdS resistor cell does not generate electrical current when light falls on it. Instead, light hitting the resistor cells allows current to pass through the circuit. The more light, the more the current flows.

The silicon cell meter circuit behaves in a somewhat different manner. Silicon cells actually generate electricity when light strikes them. The more light, the more electricity. The amount of current, however, is exceedingly small, so it is amplified by the battery circuit to a more usable level. Silicon cells react more swiftly to light changes than do CdS cells and they recover almost instantly from excessive exposure to bright light, an important factor when making readings in low light after shooting in higher light levels.

The gallium photo diode (GPD), behaves like and has the advantages of the silicon cell but needs no filtration to correct it for infra-red light rays.

Current from all metering circuits is displayed in the viewfinder by a moving meter needle or LEDs (light-emitting diodes). All Nikon F and F2 cameras and all Nikkormats (save for the EL and ELW) show needles or diodes on top of the Photomic prisms or top plates. By centering the meter needles, causing both red diode arrows to light (on the F2S Photomic) or lighting just the centre diode, you can achieve proper exposure.

First you must set the speed of the film you intend to use. On Photomic finders, lift upwards on the outer film speed setting ring and align the red ring marker with the correct numeral. On the Nikkormats, set the pointer on the underside of the lens mount to the correct setting. On the FT2 and FT3, you must pull out the ASA locking latch on the shutter speed setting lever before you can move the pointer.

The number you set is the ASA meter setting. To begin with, use the number suggested by the film manufacturers on the film box or on the instruction sheet. As you get to know your equipment, film and exposure techniques, you may wish to devise your own optimum settings for particular materials.

There isn't room on the film speed scales for every single film index you might wish to set. In-between markings are represented by dots. A guide to in-between settings is to be found on page 139.

On either side of the F and F2 red film speed index indicating triangle, you'll notice dots and numerals. These are special focusing screen compensation markings. The metering system of the Nikon Photomic finders gives accurate readings with standard focusing screens and most normal, tele and wide-angle lenses. For these, simply set the ASA index opposite the red triangle. Some of the special screens do not transmit to the metering cells the same percentage of illumination, so the metering system must be compensated when such screens are used. The numerals on either side of the red triangle indicate increments of exposure in *f*/stops. The 1 above the triangle indicates a full stop less exposure; the 2, two full stops less; while the dots between indicate half stops of exposure compensation, and the single dot below the red triangle indicates a half stop less exposure. See page 428 for a chart showing how to set the ASA index ring for special screens and special lenses. We'll also be discussing them when we take up the use of these lenses themselves.

Inside Nikon F2 Photomic

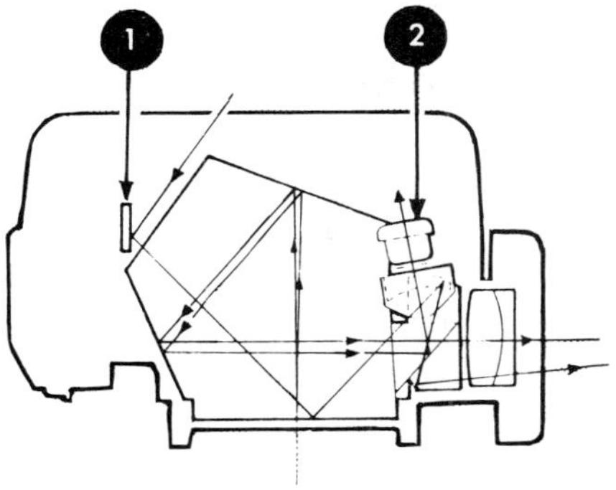

Nikon F2 Photomic prism: Light from above prism enters translucent opal diffuser, is reflected forward to mirror (1) that deflects light to various prism surfaces until it illuminates meter needle at bottom of eyepiece. Light coming from lens enters prism from below, is reflected by various prism surfaces until it enters split prism at right just before eyepiece. Split prism deflects portion of light to meter cells (2) through condensing lens while remainder travels through split prism and viewfinder eyepiece.

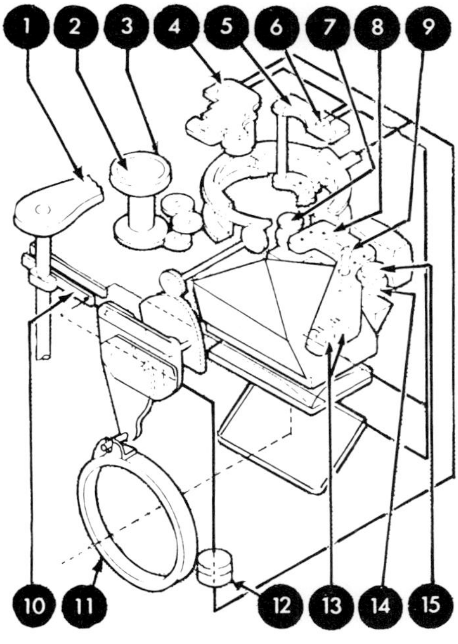

Here are some of the major internal electronic and mechanical parts of the Nikon F2 metering circuit.

1. Film wind lever
2. ASA setting dial
3. Shutter speed dial
4. Ammeter
5. Printed circuit
6. Resistor
7. Right side CdS cell
8. Printed circuit
9. Resistor
10. On/off switch
11. Aperture control ring
12. Silver oxide batteries
13. Resistors
14. Condenser lens
15. Left side CdS cell

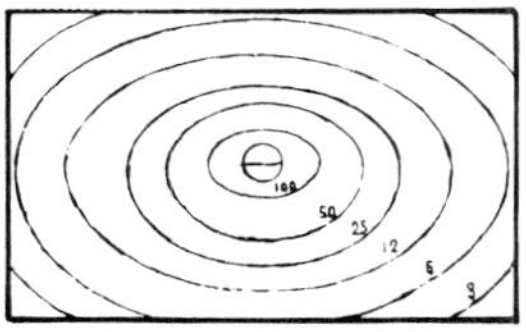

Centre-weighted metering. All modern Nikons and Nikkormats have metering systems which stress the centre of the finder area. Here is a finder screen showing the actual sensitivity from the centre outwards in percentages.

Once the film speed has been set, turn on the metering system. This is done by pulling the wind lever away from the camera body of all Nikon and Nikkormat cameras, except the Nikon F Photomic on which you push in the meter button on the side. When the metering systems are on, red dots appear on the camera body housings near the shutter wind lever, except a red band can be seen around the pop-up battery check button on the Nikon FTn Photomic prism.

Look through the viewfinder; as you change shutter speeds and apertures the needle moves. Centre it in its cut-out and you have the camera set to the meter exposure. This is fine for most average subjects. There's more detail on modifying the exposure to suit special situations in the chapter on exposure. If you can't centre the meter needle with the shutter speed and aperture controls, there is too much or too little light for the film you are using, or the exposure is outside the capabilities of the metering system.

You'll find meter coupling limit ranges for most Nikon and Nikkormat cameras at the back of this book. The range limits are usually reached when attempting to set exposures with fast film (such as ASA 400) while using large apertures and speeds below ¼ second.

If your camera is a later model, it will be equipped with automatic maximum aperture indexing (AI) as shown on page 207. If so, you can only make exposure readings at full aperture if you use properly coupled AI lenses, as explained on pages 206 and 207. If you use older Nikkor lenses without the coupling ridge, you can make exposure meter readings at actual shooting aperture while pressing the depth-of-field preview button on some Nikon and Nikkormat cameras. On newer Nikon cameras on which the meter coupling lever cannot be lifted for such use, non-AI lenses should not be fitted as they may damage the camera. With manual lenses having no automatic diaphragm connections at all, close down the diaphragm manually while making your meter reading.

DP-2, 3 and DP-12 finders

The DP-2 Photomic finder mounted on the Nikon F2 makes it into the F2S. Instead of a meter needle, red light-emitting diodes display the read-out. They are situated bottom right of the viewfinder frame. Both glow to indicate correct exposure. If the one at left glows alone, it shows that you'll get overexposure; the right alone, underexposure. The signal lights are arrow shaped and indicate the direction you need to turn the diaphragm ring for correct exposure. The display is repeated with circular lights on the top of the prism so that you can see it without looking through the finder.

As well as being visible even in the darkest of places, and illuminating the shutter speed and aperture numerals, the F2S finder has two advantages. First it allows you to read illumination at a much lower level than you can with any other Nikon through-the-lens metering system. You can also read

Metering systems

To set ASA index on Nikon with any Photomic head, pull upwards on outer ring of setting dial and turn it. On older Nikon FS without lens indexing, set ASA to lens max aperture.

On Nikkormats (except EL and ELW) slide ASA index prong to set speed in cut out. With FT2 and FT3, pull lock (on shutter speed setting lever) to release prong. On FT, set ASA index to lens maximum aperture on side of lens mount.

Intermediate values.

On all Nikon F2s and Nikkormats except EL and ELW, pull wind lever away from body to turn on meter. On Nikon FTn Photomic, press switch at side of prism, off-switch pops upwards.

Nikon F2: Shutter speed and aperture controls centre needle in viewfinder or on prism.

Nikon F2S and F2A: Both red arrows in viewfinder or red dots on finder light up at metered exposure.

Nikon F2Sb and F2AS: Central red diode lights alone in viewfinder or on finder.

Nikkormats: Centre meter needle within viewfinder or on prism for measured exposure.

Nikon FT or FTn Photomic: Centre needle within viewfinder or on prism.

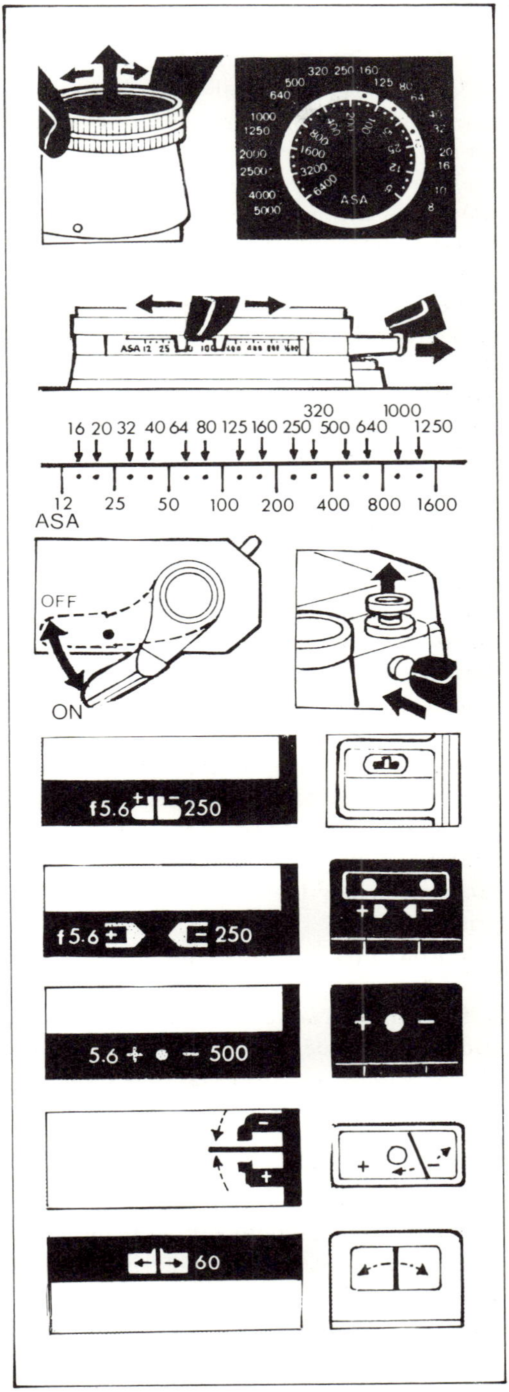

right down to 8s at full aperture. For readings below the normal range, set the shutter speed dial to B. Depress its locking button and turn the shutter speed selector until both signal lights glow. Read off the number on the extra-long shutter speed scale which appears opposite the white dot. You can set this shutter speed using the self-timer, as explained on page 125. Note that the shutter speed read-out (in the viewfinder) remains indicating B. One word of warning. When using such long speeds it may take the metering system 2 or 3 minutes to reach a steady reading.

A refinement of the F2S finder is the F2Sb Nikon Photomic. The finder alone is called the DP-3. Instead of a CdS cell circuit, the F2Sb employs a silicon-cell circuit which reacts more swiftly to light changes and is less liable to be affected by sudden major shifts in picture-taking light levels. The similar DP-12 couples to the AI lenses on F2A and F2AS cameras. When fitted to an F2 camera body, the camera designation is Nikon F2AS. The following metering instructions apply to both.

In the viewfinder you'll see a central diode light, a plus (+) sign to the left of it and a minus (−) sign to the right. At the left is a window for aperture numbers, and at the right one for shutter speeds. When exposure is correct, only the central red diode will light. It has a tolerance of ±⅕ *f*/stop. If the exposure setting is towards the overexposure side by ⅕ to 1 stop, both the centre diode and the + indicator will light. If the overexposure is greater than that, only the + will light. The operation is similar on the minus side: underexposure by ⅕ to 1 stop will cause both the − and central dot to light up, while greater underexposure will cause only the − to light.

With such a system, not only pinpoint exposure accuracy can be maintained, but you can tell when you are over- or underexposing up to 1 *f*/stop for special lighting situations.

You can illuminate the shutter speed setting within the F2AS finder when shooting in low light by pushing the illuminator switch forward atop the prism.

On the top of the prism finder you will see a single diode which will light when exposure is correct.

The other advantage of the DP-2, DP-3 and DP-12 finders over the DP-1 and DP-11 finders is that they couple with special EE aperture control attachments. This gives you fully automatic exposure.

Lens coupling

Newer cameras (Nikon F2A, F2AS, FM, EL2 and Nikkormat FT3) have automatic aperture indexing systems which immediately couple AI lenses to the metering systems. With older cameras, the meter coupling prong of each lens directly behind the *f*/5.6 aperture numeral must attach to the meter coupling pin beneath the front of the Photomic housing (Nikons) or the pin on the camera lens mount (Nikkormats).

Long exposures with all Nikon F2 models

Preset aperture by turning the aperture ring of the lens.

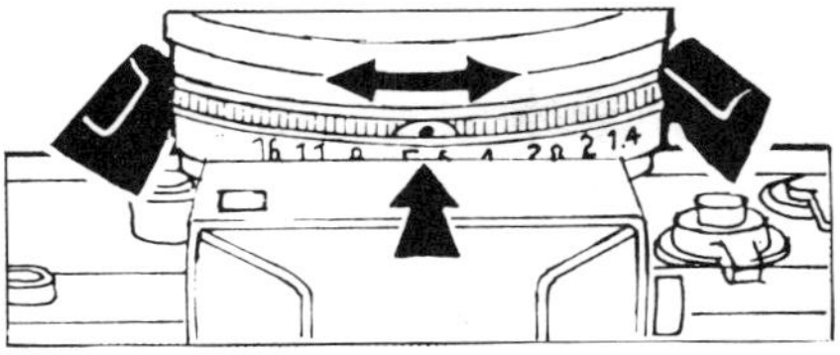

With shutter speed set to B, depress lock button in centre of ASA film speed dial and turn shutter speed selector until both arrows in finder or red dots light on prism. With F2Sb, red central dot only with light. Read off exposure in seconds opposite the white dot on the long shutter speed scale (here it is 4 s). Note that dot to left of 8 second mark represents 10 seconds.

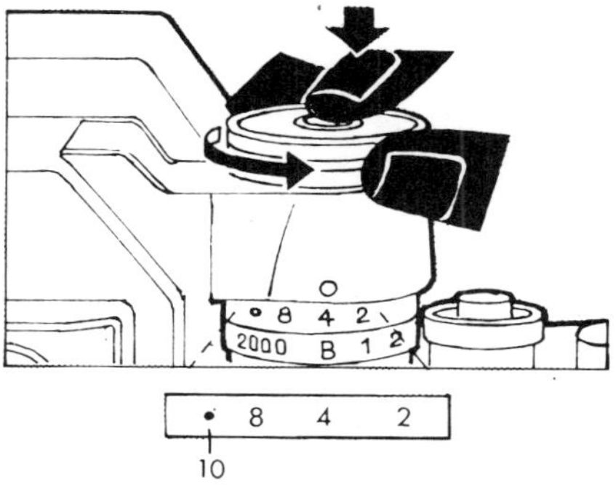

To make long exposure make certain shutter speed scale is on B. Turn shutter release button guard to T. Push down self-timer lever until indicator points to shutter speed desired.

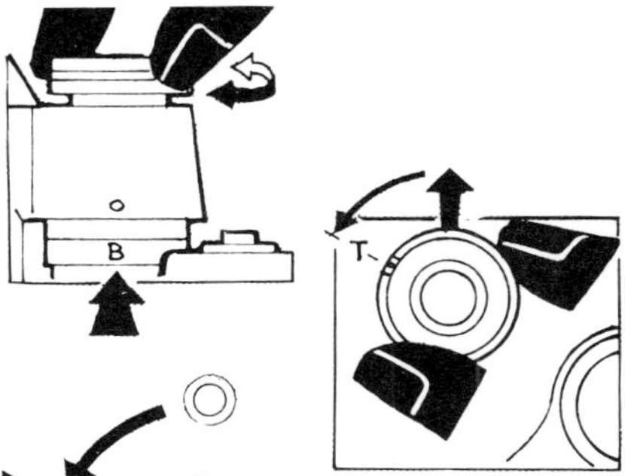

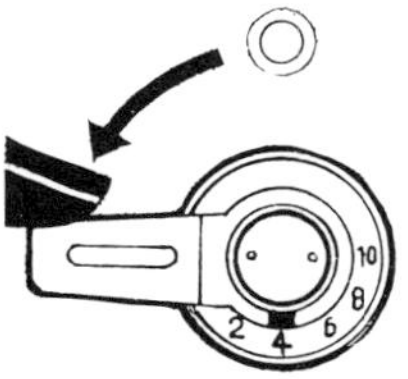

Focusing screens

Special focusing screens require alterations to your ASA exposure index setting on all Nikon F and F2 camera models. The numbers on the outside ring correspond to such corrections which are indicated in the exposure screen table at the back of this book. For normal screens always set ASA index opposite arrow.

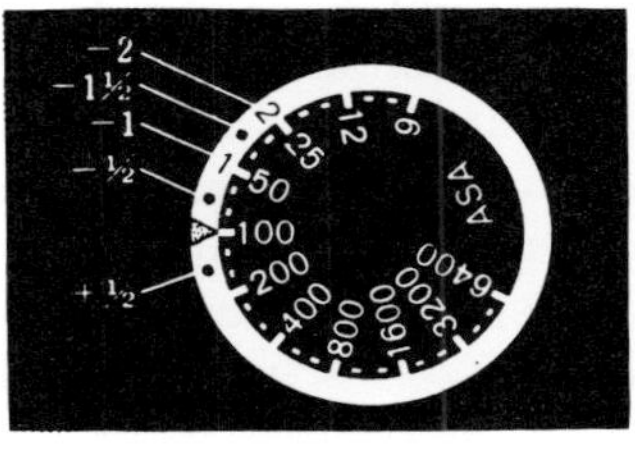

Not only must the coupling pin fit into the prong, but the maximum aperture of the lens must be indexed properly, each time the lens is mounted on the camera. The maximum aperture set appears in a small window on the front of the Nikon F2, F2S and F2Sb Photomic finders; on a scale of the front plate of the Nikon Photomic FTn; or on the side of the lens mount of the Mikkormat FT2 and FTn. On the Nikon Photomic finders the aperture scale reads 1.2, 1.4, 2, 2.8, 4 and 5.6 with in-between dots indicating *f*/2.5 and *f*/3.5. The scale on the Nikon Photomic FTn, Nikkormat FTn and FT2 cover the same range, but are marked only at 1.2, 2.8 and 5.6. On a Nikon F2 Photomic, an *f*/3.5 lens, for instance, should have a window showing the dot between the 2.8 and 4 markings. On the Nikon Photomic FTn and Nikkormats, the red dot on the scale should rest between 2.8 and 5.6, but closer to 2.8.

If the index does not match the maximum aperture of the lens, it is best to remove the lens completely and remount it. Push in the lens mount release button on the left side of the camera and turn the lens clockwise with its chromed ring until it is released from the body. Be careful when removing the lens to uncouple the maximum aperture pin and prong without damage. This is simplified if you set the lens aperture to *f*/16 on the Nikons and *f*/5.6 on the Nikkormats.

Lens mounting

To remount the lens on a Nikon, match the aperture index mark to the dot on the left front of the camera lens mount and twist the lens counterclockwise until it clicks into position. With all the Nikkormats, except the FT3, set the lens to *f*/5.6; then the procedure is much the same, except that you must first push the coupling pin on the camera body clockwise as far as it can go. Otherwise it will not couple to the prong on the lens. (With the lens set to *f*/5.6, the meter-coupling prong lines up with the dot.)

With all Nikons and Nikkormats prior to the F2A, F2AS, EL2, FE, FM and FT3 you must set the meter to maximum aperture. After the lens clicks into position, turn the aperture ring to set the smallest aperture, and then the largest. Check your maximum aperture scale: it should now indicate the proper maximum lens aperture. If it doesn't, try unfastening and fastening the lens again. Once you become accustomed to it, you will recognise the ratchet noise from the camera when it is indexing. If you do not hear this, the meter is not being set properly.

After changing lenses with these older, non-auto indexing cameras, always check the maximum aperture index scale. Even when you haven't changed lenses, it's wise to read the scale periodically to make sure it is correct.

Older Nikon Photomic finders or Nikkormats cannot be adapted to automatic maximum aperture indexing; but you can fit any Nikon F2 body with a DP-11 or DP-12 finder. Additionally many older Nikkor lenses can be converted to AI by Nikon at a modest cost, making them suitable for all Nikons and Nikkormats.

Non-AI Nikkors with prongs allow full aperture metering on older cameras; the new AI lenses allow it on both old and new Nikons and Nikkormats. The Nikon E series lenses have no coupling prong and cannot be used for full aperture metering. There are also many special-purpose lenses having neither prongs nor auto indexing. Some have manual diaphragms. With these, exposure readings are made at shooting apertures. With the new AI cameras, push the meter coupling lever below the Photomic housing faceplate to the right (F2A and F2AS), or depress the meter coupling lever button on the lens mount and push up the coupling lever (EL2, FE, FM, FT3) prior to mounting the lens. With older Photomic finders, push upwards on the coupling pin (on the finder itself) until the maximum aperture indexing scale slides to *f*/5.6. With older Nikkormats (FT2, EL and FTn) facing you, push the aperture coupling pin clockwise to the right as far as it will go. Now fasten the lens to the camera.

With all Nikons and Nikkormats, old or new, make your exposure readings while pressing in or on the depth-of-field preview button or lever. With manual or preset lenses (having no automatic diaphragm coupling) the lens' own diaphragm control ring stops the lens down directly. Of course, you can set the aperture first and then, still keeping the lens closed down, turn the shutter speed dial until the correct exposure is indicated.

With auto indexing Nikons F2A and F2AS, release the coupling lever before fitting AI lenses by sliding the coupling lever release (on the front of the Photomic housing) to the right. With the FE, FM, EL2 and Nikkormat FT3, push this lever down to its original horizontal position.

You must take stop-down meter readings when using non-coupled lenses or accessories such as extension bellows or tubes. This metering method is also used when the camera is attached to an optical system without a diaphragm control such as a mirror lens, microscope or telescope. In these cases you just centre the needle in the finder, or zero your reading using the LED lights (in cameras with them), by altering the shutter speed.

Battery check

The Nikon F2 Photomic and Nikon Photomic FTn have battery check buttons. So you can test whether the meter system batteries are operating. There are no battery checks on the Nikkormats.

On the F2 Photomic, turn on the metering system by pulling the wind lever away from the camera body to expose the red dot. Push in the battery check button at the top right front on the finder. With a good battery the needle swings to the centre position in the viewfinder or within the meter window on the finder. You can also check the battery on the F2S Photomic. If the signal light in the viewfinder or on top of the finder glows brightly when the wind lever is pulled away from he camera, the batteries are OK.

On the Nikon Photomic FTn, push down the tiny battery check button on the top right of the finder and the meter needle should centre in the viewfinder or top window.

The battery checkers on the Photomic finders are worry-prevention devices, but the batteries on both Nikon and Nikkormats should just 'drop dead' suddenly, not grow progressively weaker and weaker. However, this does not always happen. The simplest solution is to replace your Nikkormat battery every year or so. In any event, you should carry a spare new battery. If you suspect your old one, change it for the new. If you get the same readings, you can put the old one back again. If the meter needle in the Nikkormat (or a Photomic finder for that matter) doesn't respond to light and movement of the controls, no current is flowing through the metering circuit. This may mean the battery is dead. Quite often, however, the problem isn't the battery but some corrosion of the battery contacts, causing an oxidation film to form between the battery and the interior contacts of the camera. In a hot, moist atmosphere, the battery can exude corrosive materials, turning battery terminals green. To remove light oxidation, one of the major battery manufacturers I consulted recommends rubbing the battery and terminals gently with a pencil eraser.

For heavier corrosion, it may be necessary to scrape the contacts with a small flat blade. After cleaning, hold the camera with the battery compartment opening downward and brush out the corrosive scrapings before inserting the battery. If after cleaning the battery and contacts, the meter system still does not work, you probably do need another, fresh battery. Don't substitute batteries of other designation for those recommended. They may fit and perhaps work, but can give erroneous readings, and may even damage the electrical circuitry in the meter.

In general use, your batteries should last at least one year, but many owners find that they get two or even more years. To reduce corrosion problems, if you do not use your camera for more than a week, it is best to remove the battery and store it in a cool place – in the refrigerator (sealed in a moisture-proof plastic bag) is ideal.

Other problems

The battery is not the only source of meter failure. If the meter cell is suddenly brilliantly illuminated, the metal needle may swing violently upwards. There is a danger of the needle sticking there. You can usually bring it down, however, with a gentle tap on the meter housing. CdS cells used in most older SLR meters have what is called a memory. They remember bright light for some time afterwards and give inflated readings in lower light. It's difficult to determine just how long you should wait before attempting a low light reading after a bright one. Much depends on the relative brightness levels of the two scenes and the length of time that the

Checking and installing batteries

Nikon F2 and F2A. Pull wind lever away from camera body to uncover dot.

Push battery check button on right front of prism. If needle swings to right edge of notch or further left, batteries are alright.

To install batteries: remove bottom battery cover with edge of coin or similar object. Place two fresh 1.5V silver batteries in chamber with negative side facing camera. Refit cover. Check the battery again.

Nikon F2S and F2Sb: pull wind lever away from body as with F2. If one or more of the red diodes on the prism light, batteries are OK. If not, replace them.

Nikon FTn Photomic: push down battery check button on top of prism. If needle swings to centre or beyond, batteries are OK.

To install new 1.3V mercury batteries in Nikon FTn Photomic finder, remove finder, turn upside down, unthread battery cover, replace batteries with positive side towards cover. F2AS finder has a LED check light on top. If it lights, batteries are OK.

Nikkormats have no battery check. If the needle moves, the battery is OK. Unthread bottom battery cover with coin edge and replace with 1.5V silver battery (1.3V mercury on all Nikkormats before FT2). Replace cover.

Batteries may appear to be dead and still be OK. Wipe oxidation from batteries using rubber eraser end of a pencil. Scrape corrosion from battery chamber contact very gently with blade edge of fine knife.

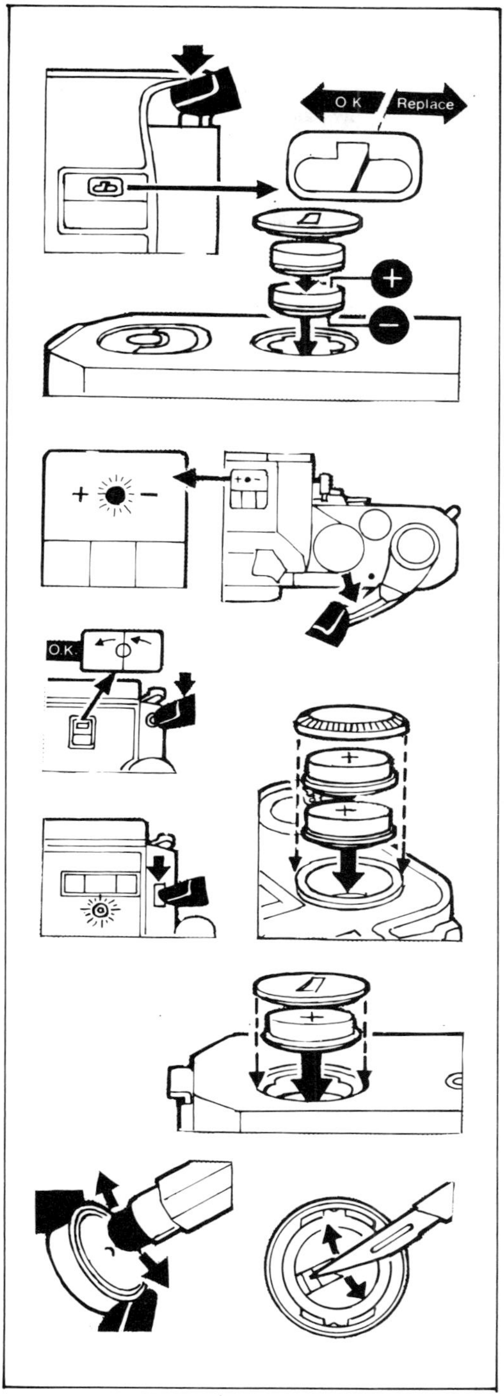

cells were exposed to the bright one. Never deliberately point the meter at any subject that you would have difficulty seeing because of its intense brightness. After shooting a bright scene, allow the meter time to recover its sensitivity before trying to take a reading in subdued light.

When carrying the camera, always keep the lens cap on if you are not actually taking picures. Your meter cells, even when they are not turned on, are still sensitive to light. A vast amount of illumination may inadvertently be let through to the cell when the camera is accidentally pointed at the sun or other bright object. This can cause the meter to give inflated readings for some hours afterwards.

Temperature

The batteries should be protected from below-freezing temperatures. If you must shoot in very cold weather, keep the naked camera with neckstrap inside your own clothing, next to your chest, where your body warmth will protect it. Expose it to outside temperatures as little as possible. I have used Photomic finders as well as a Nikkormat outdoors in below-freezing weather. The metering systems have worked well; but the warning against freezing temperatures by the manufacturer is a good one. Don't automatically expect the meter to work under such circumstances.

Eyepiece light

One last word about through-the-lens metering systems. While illumination can enter (and is supposed to enter) the camera through the lens, some illumination also enters through the viewfinder eyepiece. In situations where you might be photographing a fairly dark subject with brilliant light behind you, there is a possibility that some light may enter the eyepiece and give you an inflated meter reading. If you don't wear glasses, the chance of this is fairly small provided you keep your eye close to the eyepiece while taking a reading. Of course, eyeglass wearers will have a more difficult time of it since light can enter the finder from the sides. To minimise this, Nikon provides an accessory rubberised finder eyecup. This also reduces the chances of scratching your glasses on the metal eyepiece surround. Even many who don't wear glasses find this an excellent aid and use it continuously.

When reading from the meter needle windows on the Photomic finders, Nikkormat FT2, 3 or FTn cover the eyepiece with a piece of tape if it is liable to be exposed to bright light.

Low light levels

The meters of the Nikons and Nikkormats are sensitive to slight changes in subject illumination levels. Make sure needles are centred properly or LED

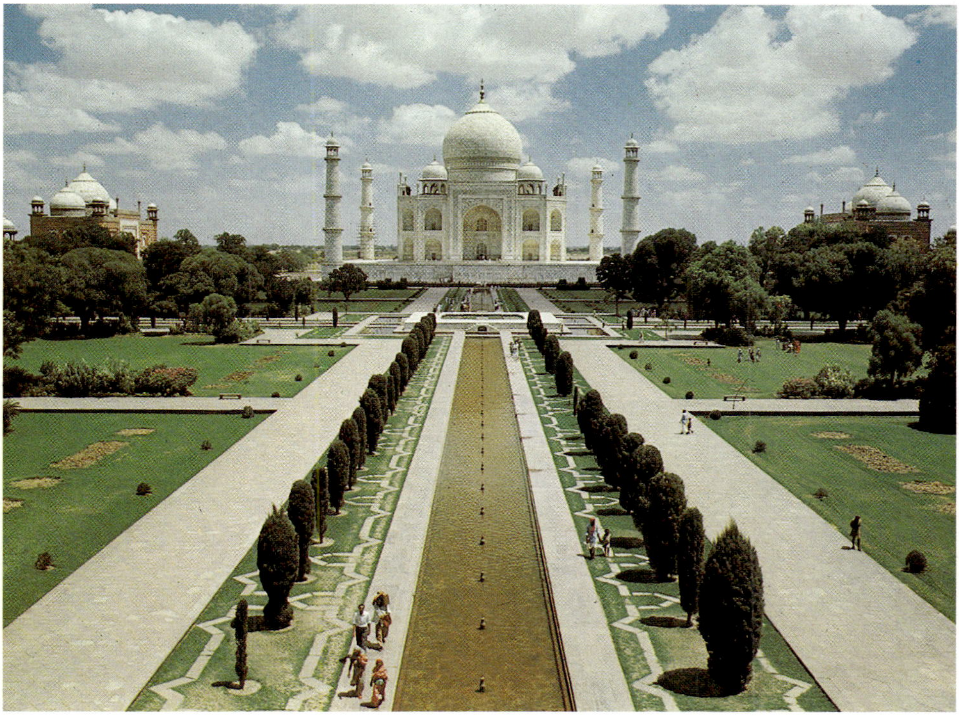

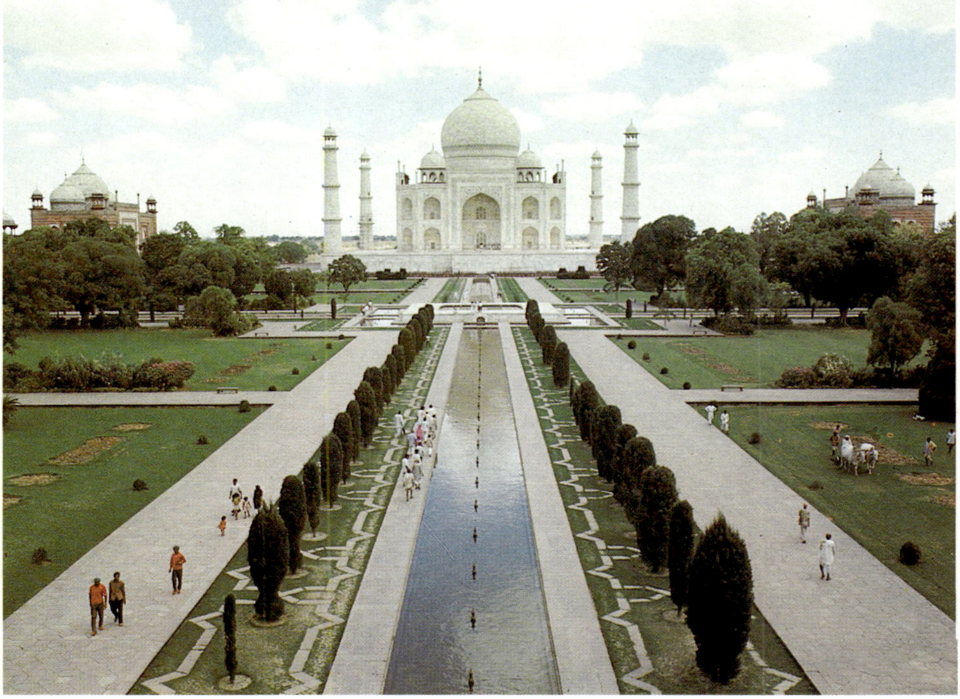

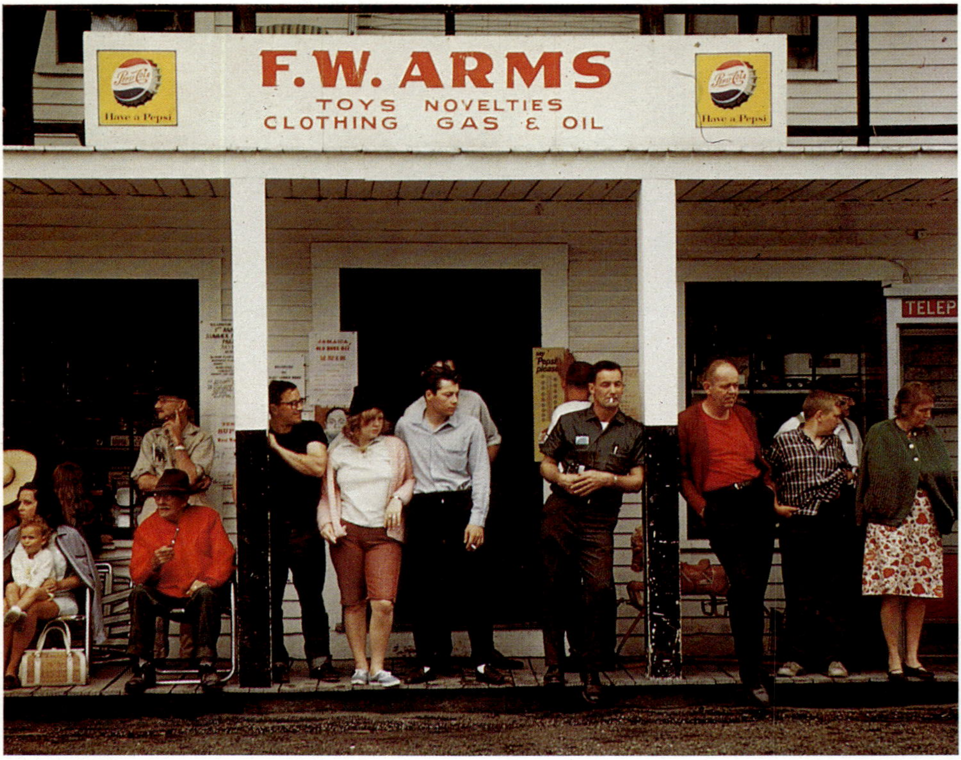

Zoom for quick composition

Above. Residents of small New England U.S.A. village await arrival of July 4 independence day parade. With 43-86 mm *f*/3.5 Nikkor zoom, I was able to crop picture in Nikkormat FT finder instantly to include figures I wished before anyone had chance to move.

Use of polarising filter

Previous page. Polarising filter near noon, top photo, shows maximum effect with sunlight, darkening sky in band around horizon, eliminating sky reflection from pool in foreground top photo of Taj Mahal, Agra, India. When the sun went behind a cloud, I removed polariser, bottom photo. Sky lost rich saturation but pool reflection returned.

Fixed focal length for studies

Opposite. My daughter sat in an old rocking chair on the porch in late afternoon. Best angle to depict her face and doll's equally was from just below her eye level. Fine-grained slow colour slide film, and my favourite portrait lens, the aperture at 1/30 second with Nikkormat FT, 105 mm *f*/2.5 Nikkor.

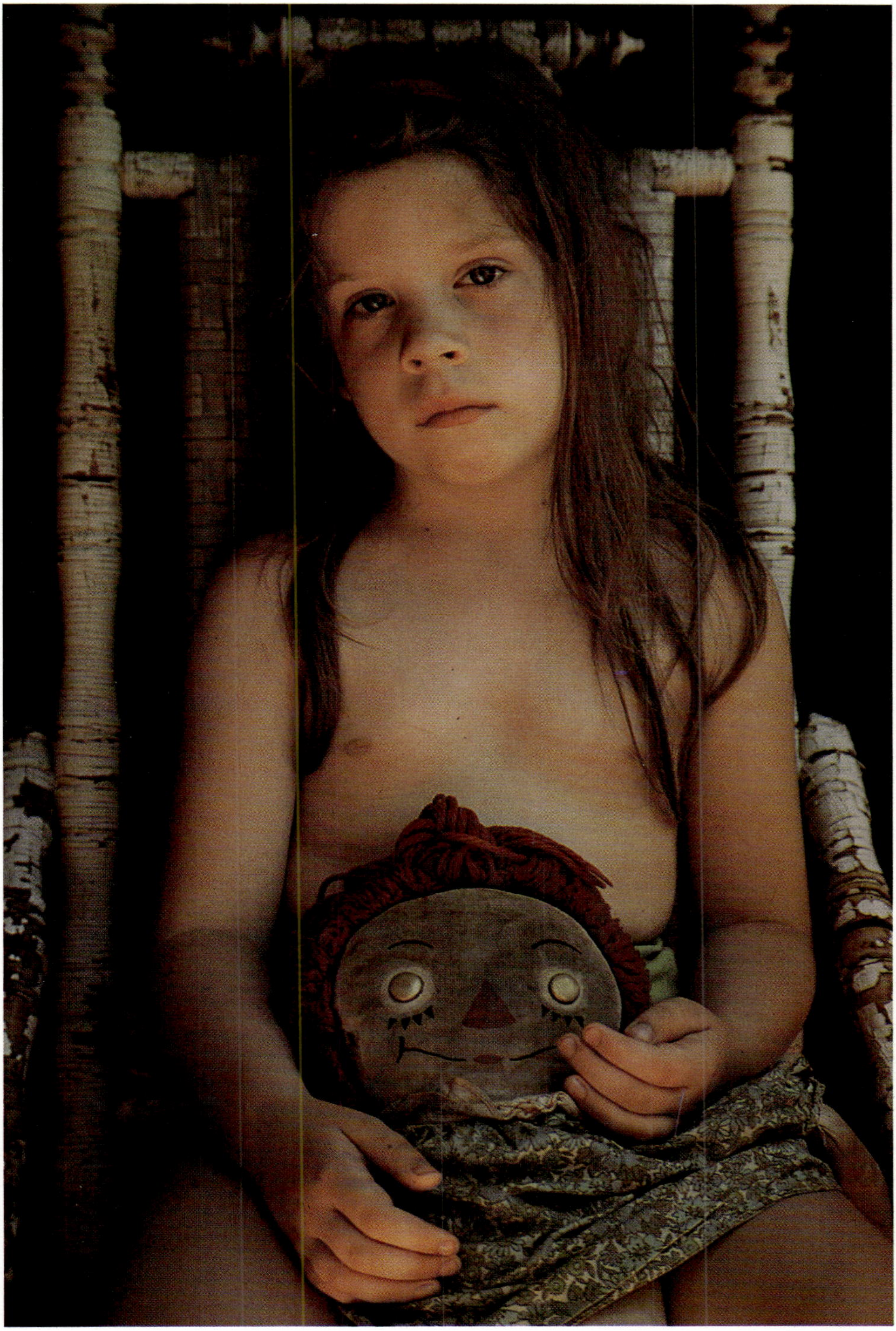

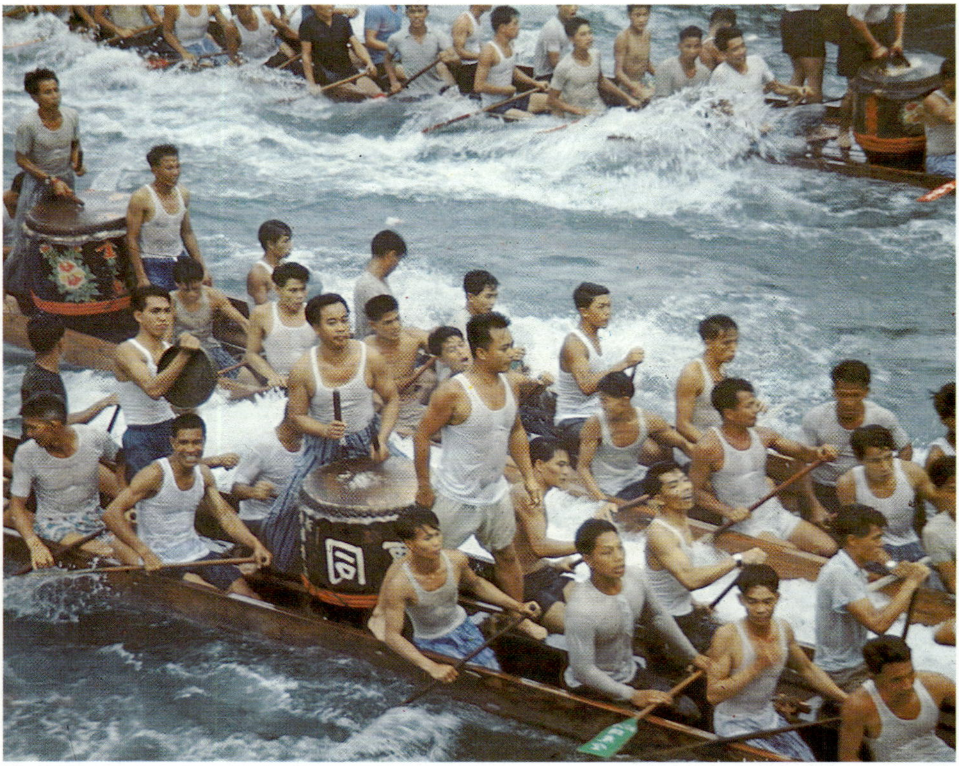

Choosing the right film

Dragon boat races in Hong Kong occur but once a year. In the rain I chose a medium-speed film with strong colour saturation and good contrast even in the rain.

Doorways

Opposite. An open doorway makes a fine dark background. Of course you must expose to suit conditions outside. *Colin Ramsay.*

Always carry a pocket flash

Overleaf, left. I came across this striking statuette of Kali adorned with garlands in a dark temple. Nikon F, 105 mm *f*/2.5 Nikkor at *f*/8 medium-speed colour film, direct on-camera flash.

Crop portraits tightly

Overleaf, right. For this portrait of a holy man in Benares, India, I used 43-86 mm *f*/3.5 zoom at *f*/8 on my Nikon F for best cropping.

Choose lenses for dramatic effects

Final page. When faced with overphotographed monuments, such as the 16th century Tsar cannon in Moscow's Kremlin, try an unusual angle or different focal length lens. 18 mm lens, 1/30 second at *f*/8, on medium-speed colour film.

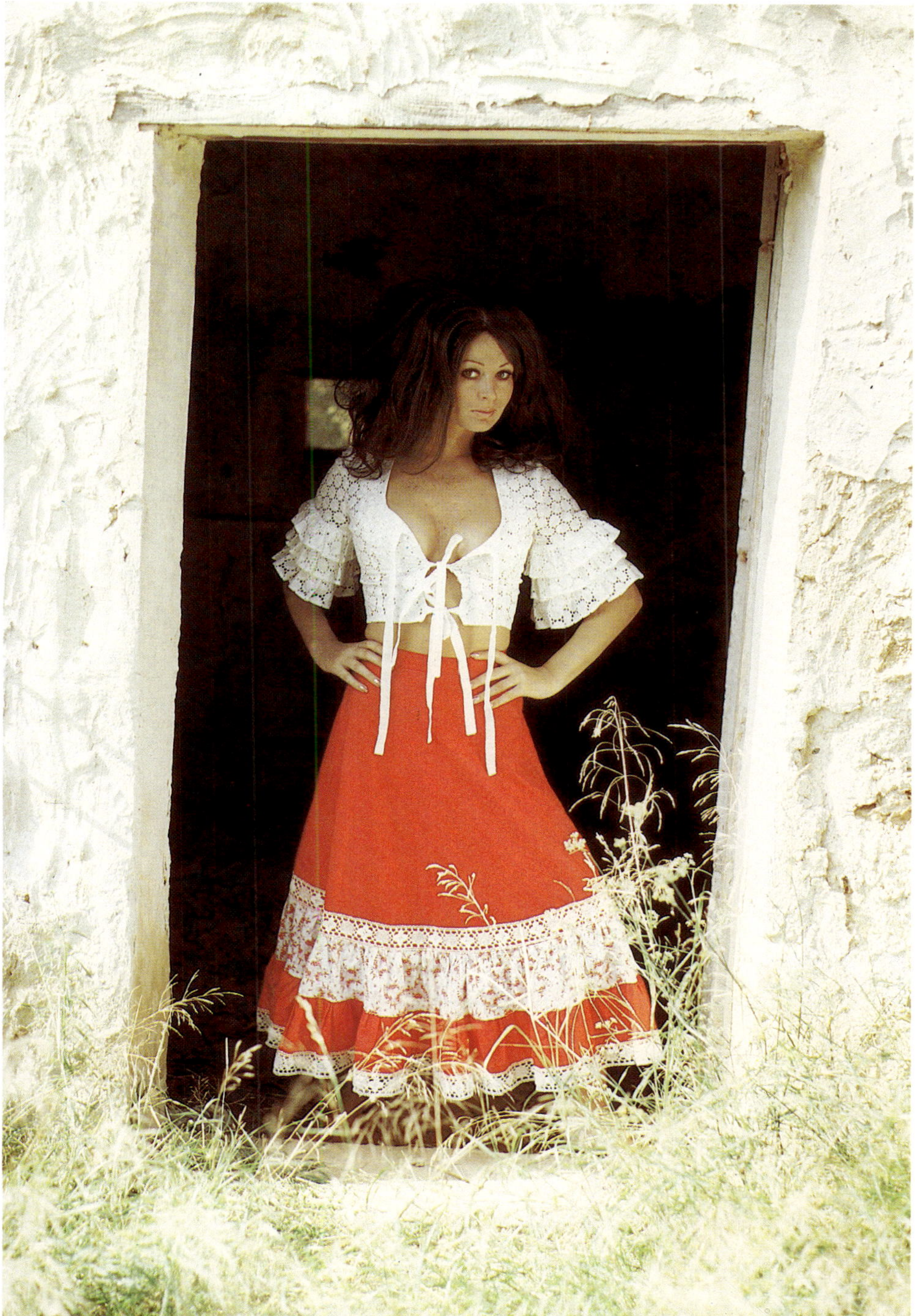

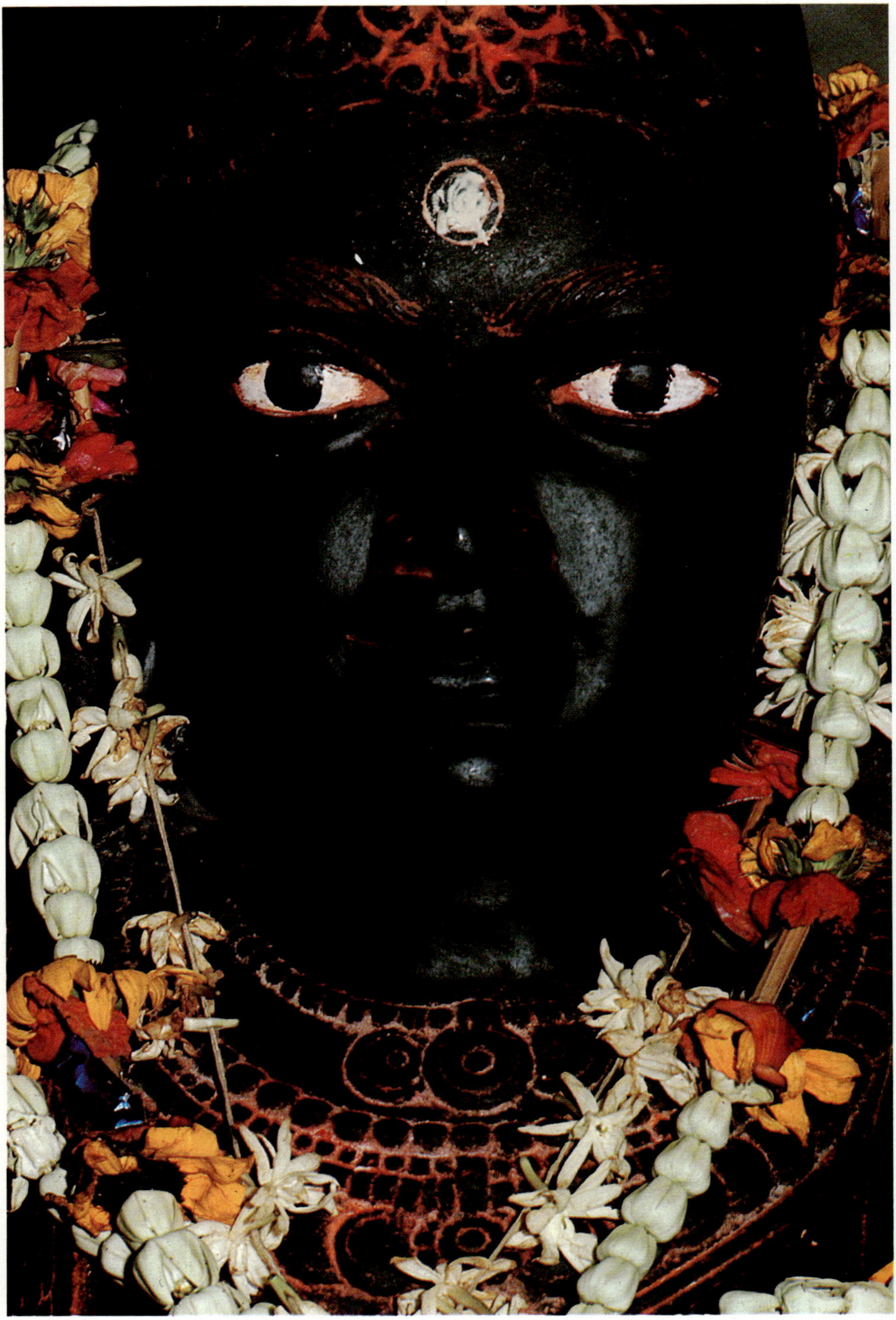

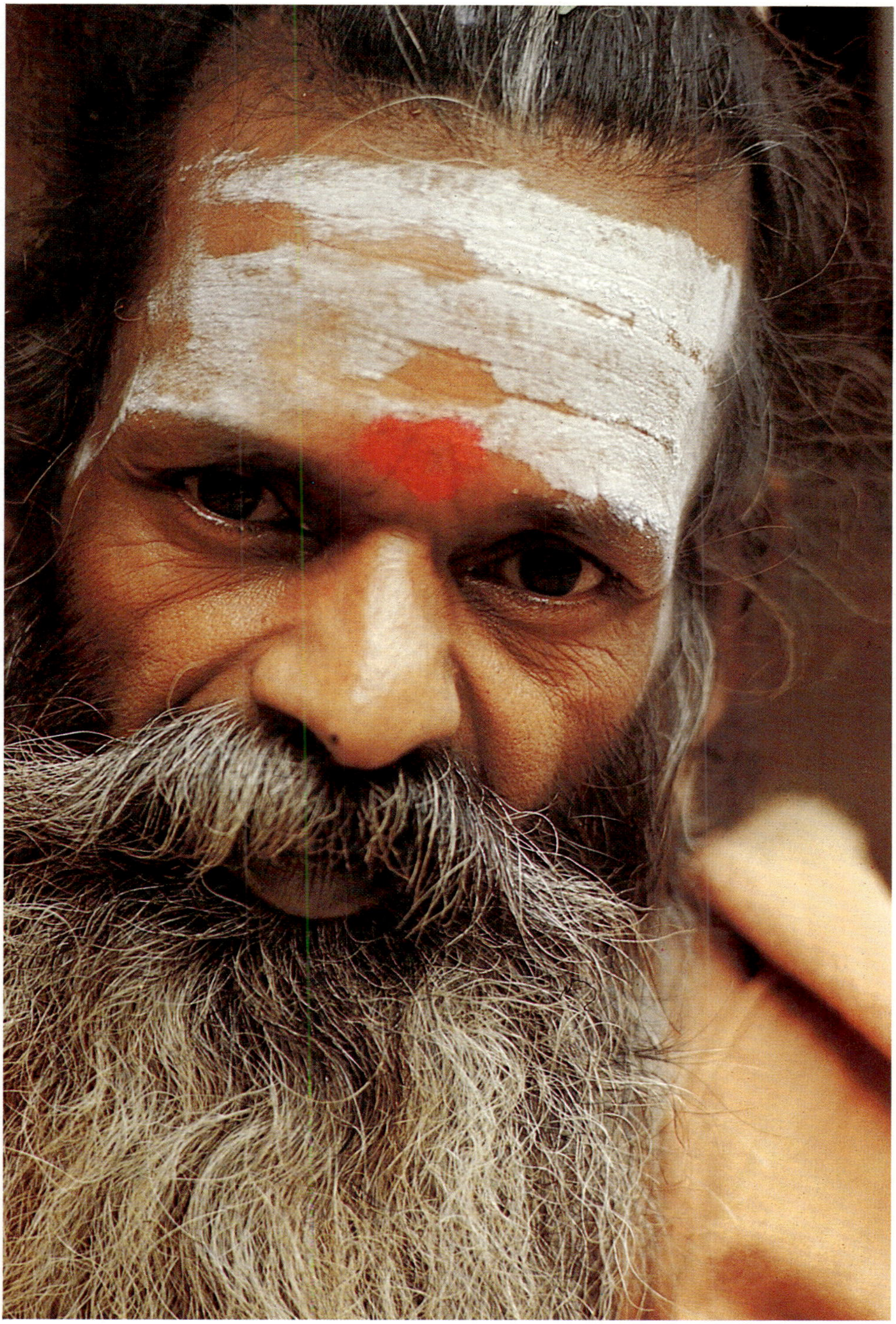

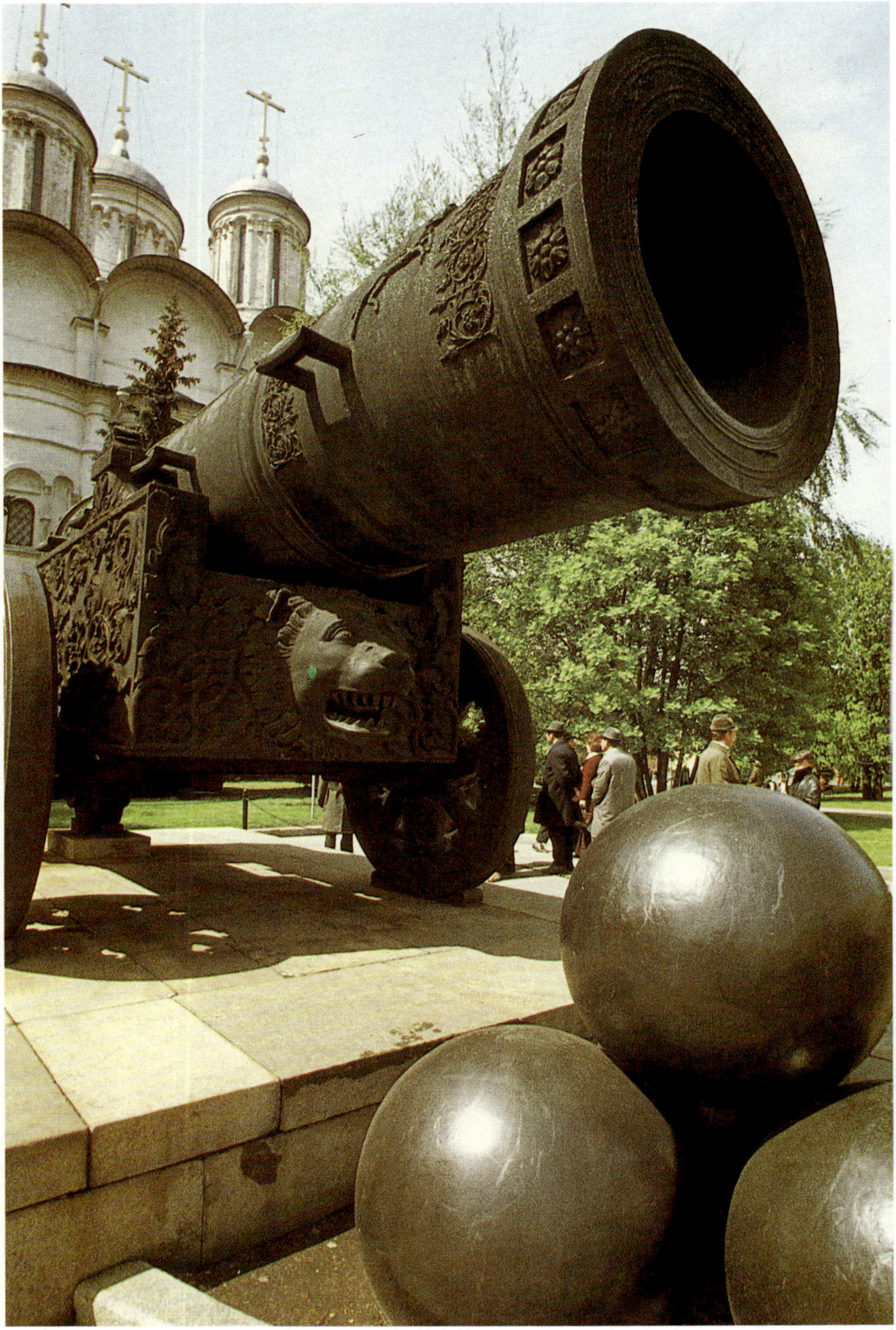

Removing Nikon F, F2 and F2S finders and screens

Pushing in finder release button on back of prism and release lever on right side of prism, remove prism from camera.

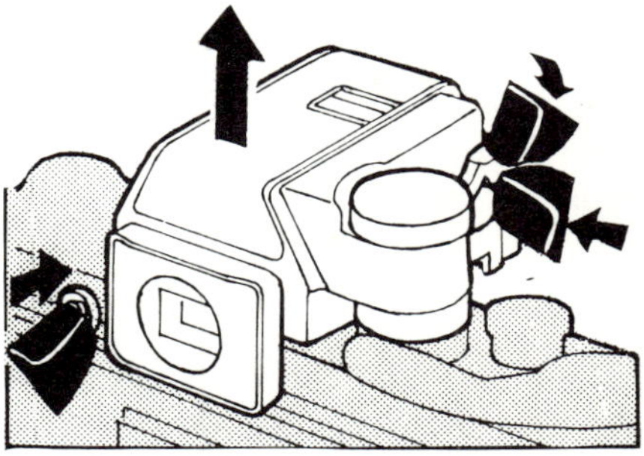

To remove finder screen, turn camera without prism upside down, spread clean lintless cloth, push finder release button further with end of ballpen or similar blunt pointed instrument. Screen will fall out.

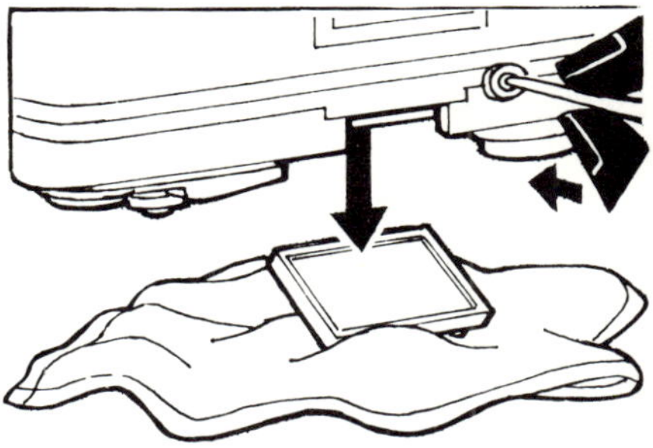

To insert screen, drop as flat as possible ('Nikon' forward) into screen chamber. Push in finder release button with finger or pointed instrument. Finder screen should seat itself.

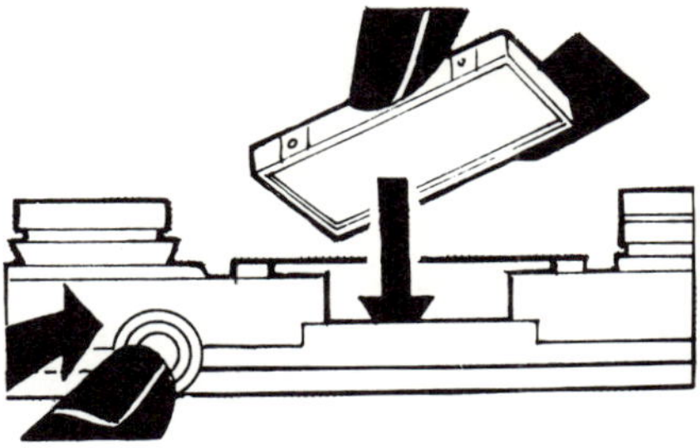

To attach Photomic F2A or F2AS finder, with lens in place, set lens to maximum aperture. Place finder over focusing screen chamber. Press finder down until it clicks and two clamps lock over pins on camera body. Attaching an older F2, F2S or F2Sb Photomic finder is done in the same way but the meter coupling pin must be centred and the aperture winder must read *f*/5.6 as shown at right. Twist shutter speed selector knob right and left until it engages shutter speed dial and both rotate together. Rotate lens to index maximum aperture.

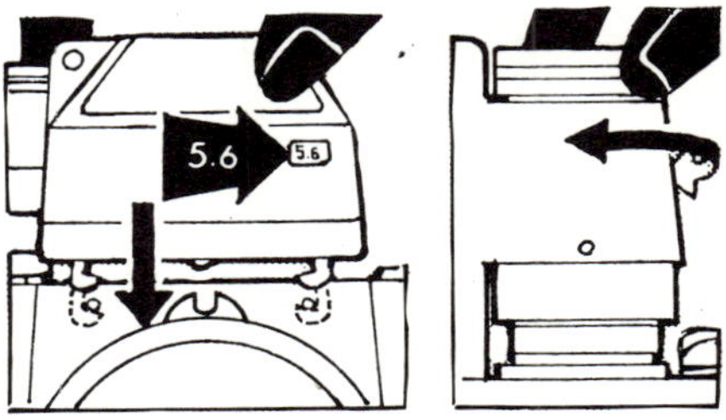

lights are correct when you are making a reading. Note that sometimes you obtain a meter reading with the shutter speed set on bulb. If the meter does read properly and the needle is centred with the shutter set to 'B', you have the lens set to an aperture suitable for a two-second exposure to give a correctly exposed picture. Of course, a tripod should be used for very slow speeds.

After exposure, turn your metering system off. Nikons and Nikkormats with meter needles in their exposure systems have a battery life of up to a year, even if you leave the meter on. The newer meter circuits using light-emitting diodes, though, will drain a battery in a matter of a few hours to a day or so. Always carry replacement meter batteries with you. They are small and take up little room.

Changing the Nikon viewfinders

All Nikon F and F2 prism heads are removable. You can fit various accessory finders in their place. The removable prism also provides focusing-screen interchangeability and means for you to clean any possible dust or dirt from the finder or screen area.

To remove any F2 Photomic head, press in and depress the lever on the top right of the finder and push in the finder release button on the back left side of the camera. (This button is most easily pressed with a small blunt pointed instrument.) The finder can then be lifted away from the body. To remove the focusing screen, turn the camera body upside down over a soft, clean, lintless cloth area (or someone's outstretched palm in an emergency) and push again on the finder release button. The screen drops out. Keep your fingers well away from the finder and screen surfaces. Finger marks are hard to remove.

To insert a screen, drop it carefully into the screen chamber opening as horizontally as possible. The flat side of the screen goes downwards and the word 'Nikon' faces the front of the camera. Press in on the finder release button and screen should slip into place. In a very few instances, the screen may not drop properly in place. If it doesn't, remove it and start again.

To attach the finder, set the lens (if it is attached) to its maximum aperture, centre the meter coupling pin (on older Photomic heads without AI); locate the prism base over the rectangular focusing screen chamber and press the finder gently into place. Correctly seated, it is secure and can't be moved. (When being secured it generally makes a clunking sound.) If you have just fitted a Photomic finder, check the shutter speed dial. There is a small keying slot on the underside of the Photomic speed dial which must connect to a lug on the shutter speed dial of the camera body. Turn the Photomic speed dial in first one direction and then the other until it clicks into place and the two dials move together. Before it is connected, the upper dial just rotates by itself.

Lastly, on Nikons without AI, check the meter coupling pin and prong on the lens to make sure they, too, are mating. If not, follow the directions already given for properly indexing the lens for maximum aperture setting (see page 142).

Viewfinder information

With F2, F2S, F2Sb, F2A and F2AS finders, at the right bottom of the picture area you can read the aperture set at the left and the shutter speed at the right. Either apertures and shutter speeds can be used on the click positions. Apertures and shutter speeds faster than 1/80 can be used in between to provide accurate exposure. Light for the shutter scale comes through a translucent panel atop the Photomic finder, directly below the secondary meter window. This also allows you to see the F2 or F2A finder needle quite clearly, even if the subject is darkly lit, as long as you have a fair amount of light overhead. If there is insufficient light overhead to illuminate the window, you can use a small flashlight, or the Nikon window illuminator. In the F2S finder, the figures are sufficiently illuminated by the light-emitting diodes, so need no further illumination.

The Nikon Photomic FTn finder provides a meter needle window directly above and outside the picture area. Shutter speeds only are visible directly to the right of the window. Aperture can be set between click stops, but for correct exposure all shutter speeds *must* be set on marked values. Like the F2 Photomic finder, illumination for the needle window and shutter speed scale comes from the top of the finder. Like the F2 Photomic, the window can be illuminated overhead when working under extremely low light conditions.

Nikkormat viewfinders on FT, FTn, FT2 and FT3 models

Older Nikkormats have a meter needle moving between under and overexposure control (marked '+' for overexposure and '−' for under) at the right of the picture area. The shutter speed set appears outside the picture area at the bottom of the finder. The next faster and next slower speed also appear, in yellow on adjacent sides of the speed set. Apertures can be set between click positions, but shutter speeds slower than 1/250 s must be on the exact markings. All the illumination for the meter needle and the shutter speed scale is obtained directly through the lens of the camera. Needle brightness depends on the brightness of the subject itself. There is no way to boost it when shooting in low light.

Old Nikon meters

As well as the latest systems, there are thousands of older, now discontinued Nikon metering attachments and systems still in daily use throughout the world. Here's how to distinguish and use some of them.

Nikon reflex exposure meter, model III

One of the first meters available for the Nikon F, a selenium cell meter introduced in 1960, fastened to the Nikon F nameplate for pincer fingers. A slide pin underneath the cell fitted the Nikkor lens coupling prong and the meter's own shutter speed dial fitted and locked on the Nikon F shutter speed dial. After setting the proper ASA film index on the large dial on top of the meter (ASA 6 to 4000), you moved the shutter speed dial or aperture ring to centre the meter needle within the forked pointer in a window. In low light, the meter automatically shifted to its low light scale. Its range was 1/1000 s to 2 s and from *f*/1.4 to *f*/22. A selenium cell amplifier grid attachment was available to increase low light sensitivity four times. The camera meter had to be held at waist or chest level to read from this meter. It was very compact and could be switched from one camera to another in seconds. It operated like any separate selenium-celled meter. Its angle of view was fixed.

Photomic finder

The first built-in Nikon F finder was the Photomic, introduced in 1962. Like later metering systems, it was built into a prism housing and its shutter speed dial fitted over the camera body shutter speed dial; an aperture pin underneath the front plate fitted the Nikkor lens prongs.

Unlike the present metering systems, the single CdS cell did not read through the lens. The cell port was located on the front of the housing where it made a direct 75° reading of the scene. Correct exposure was obtained as in present finders, by centering the meter needle within the finder or on the meter housing.

The meter was supplied with a small tube. This threaded into the front of the cell window and narrowed the view to 15° for central area or tele readings. Since the meter did not read through the lens, there was no need for full aperture indexing. Instead, you just set the ASA index (10 to 1600) of the film on the meter's shutter speed dial, centred the needle and shot.

Photomic T finder

The Nikon F Photomic T, introduced in 1965, was Nikon's first through-the-lens meter. In operation it was much like the later Nikon Photomic FTn or Nikon F2 Photomic systems, but had a full area averaging meter system instead of a centre-weighted one. No apertures or shutter speeds were visible in the finder and it was necessary to set the maximum aperture of each lens in use opposite the ASA index on the shutter speed dial each time the lenses were changed.

Photomic Tn finder

The Nikon F Photomic Tn, introduced in 1967, was similar to the Photomic T, but the metering system was now centre-weighted instead of averaging. It was still necessary to set the maximum lens opening opposite the ASA index, and no shutter speeds or apertures were visible in the finder.

Meter switches and batteries

On the Photomic finder, the metering system is turned on by pulling up a small red inset flag located directly behind the cell. Lowering the flag turns off the meter. The Photomic T and Tn meters are turned on by pressing a small side button which causes a top button to pop up. To turn them off you simply depress the top button. The Photomic finder uses a single 1.3 V No. 625 battery, while the Photomic T and Tn employ two such batteries. All will last about a year in service.

Nikkormat FS and FT

In 1965 the Nikkormat FS and FT were introduced. The FS was meterless. The FT employed two horizontally set CdS cells which made an averaging reading of the finder screen. Shutter speeds were not visible in the finder and you had to set the maximum aperture of the lens in use opposite the ASA index of the film on the camera lens mount ring. Pulling the rapid wind lever away from the camera body to expose the red dot turned on the meter. Returning it to body position turned the meter off, as on later Nikkormats. A single No. 625 1.3 V battery furnished the meter power.

Upgrading your camera

All Nikon F cameras having plain prisms or the older metering systems can be fitted with the latest Photomic FTn finder systems. However, some of the older models need a slight modification of the prism chamber. This was once done in some countries by a Nikon dealer for a modest fee.

Nikkormat cameras cannot be upgraded.

Operating the Nikon EL2, Nikkormat EL and ELW

The Nikkormat EL (or Nikomat EL) is a fixed-pentaprism SLR with an automatically controlled, electronically timed shutter. A second version, the ELW, allows you to fit on an accessory auto-winder which advances the film electrically. The third version is called the Nikon EL2. Control operation on all three are similar except where noted in this chapter.

Exposure meter

The exposure meter on the EL cameras is used in two distinct ways:

1. On automatic exposure with the shutter speed dial set at 'A' you adjust the aperture and a black needle in the finder shows you the shutter speed that *will* be set. You can alter your shutter speed by turning your aperture ring until the black needle indicates the shutter speed you want. You can hold any reading by pressing the self-timer lever inward (towards the lens mount). All speeds on automatic are stepless.
2. On manual exposure with the shutter speed dial set at any marked speed but 'A', the green translucent pointer indicates the shutter speed set. No in-between marked speeds are possible. The black needle shows metered shutter speed. The meter acts independently in this mode, and does not influence the aperture or shutter speed actually set. If you match the black and green pointers you will be following the suggested meter reading. However, you can adjust the camera for more or less exposure by using a higher or lower aperture than the matched needle position.

Automatic exposure

The EL cameras provide what is called an aperture-preferred control system. You set the lens aperture and the camera electronically adjusts the shutter speed according to the meter reading. The all-metal Copal Square SE shutter is set to any speed from 1/1000 to 4 second (8 s on the EL2) without regard to

Nikon EL2, Nikkormat EL, ELW

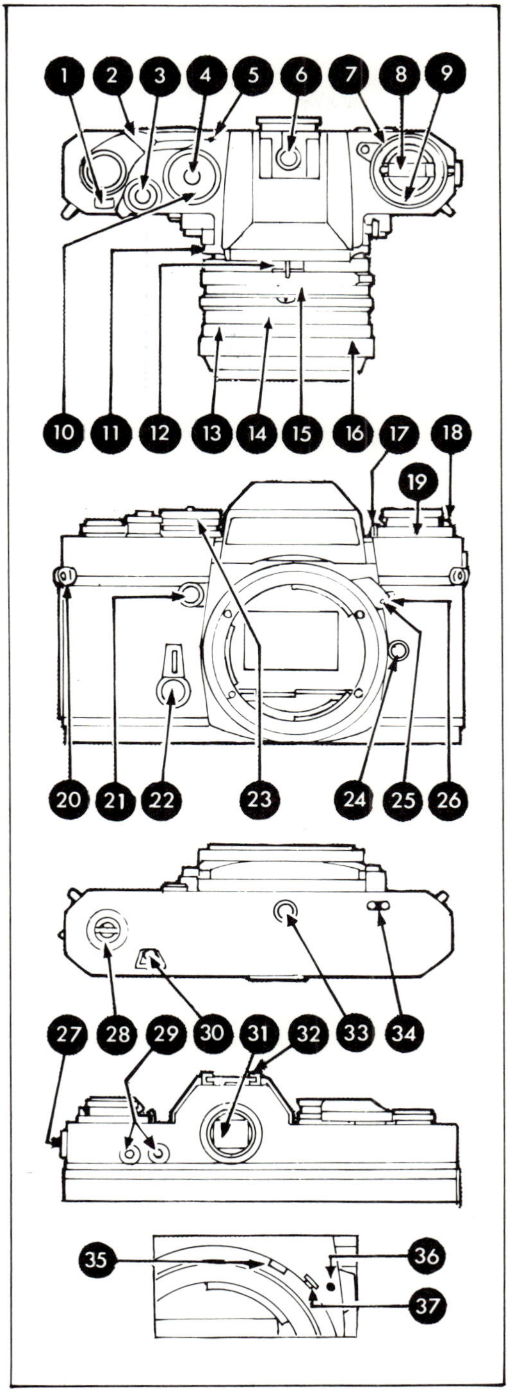

Here are the controls:

1. Frame counter
2. Film advance lever
3. Shutter release button (with lock on ELW and EL2)
4. Shutter speed dial lock
5. Film plane indicator
6. Hot shoe contact
7. ASA film speed dial
8. Folded rewind crank
9. ASA setting ring
10. Shutter speed dial with sync type window
11. Maximum aperture scale
12. Meter coupling prong
13. Distance scale
14. Depth-of-field scale
15. Aperture scale
16. Focusing ring
17. Film speed dial lock
18. Camera back safety lock
19. Exposure compensation ring (EL2 only)
20. Neckstrap eyelet lug
21. Depth-of-field preview button
22. Self-timer/memory lock
23. Sync selector ring
24. Lens release button
25. Meter coupling pin
26. Mirror lock-up lever
27. Sync terminal
28. Auto winder film advance coupling (ELW and EL2)
29. Battery check button and battery check light
30. Rewind button
31. Finder eyepiece
32. Accessory shoe
33. Tripod socket
34. Auto winder electrical contacts (ELW and EL2 only)
35. Meter coupling lever (EL2)
36. Lens mounting index (EL2)
37. Coupling release lever (EL2)

the usual steps. So, if the metering system demands neither 1/60 s nor 1/30 s, but, say 1/43 s, that is just the speed the shutter gives. The speed is indicated by a needle moving on a scale located on the left-hand side of the viewfinder. You can control your speeds, if you wish, by turning the aperture ring until a suitable speed is set.

The metering system 'chooses' the shutter speed necessary for the light coming in through the lens. Naturally, it takes account of the film speed you set, the maximum aperture and the chosen aperture on automatic lenses. It can, equally well, measure through non-coupled optical systems at the picture-taking aperture. So, you can get automatic exposure on a microscope, telescope, mirror lens, lens on bellows, plain extension tubes, through manual or preset lenses.

Lens mounting

The Nikon EL2 features automatic maximum aperture indexing (AI) with all auto indexing Nikon lenses so all you need do is mount a lens to the camera to have the camera meter set properly. The Nikkormats EL and ELW have a somewhat less convenient method of lens mounting, similar to that on the Nikkormat FT2 and 3 except that the maximum aperture scale is on the right side of the lens mount instead of the left. The meter systems of the EL and ELW provide proper automatic exposure only if the lenses are properly indexed when mounted.

For full details on how to use AI and non-AI lenses, and for directions for using the EL and ELW, see pages 142 and 143.

Model differences

While all three camera models have the same body casting and many of the same features, there are specific differences between them which should be understood. The Nikkormat EL was the original camera. The Nikkormat ELW was almost identical except that it accepted a 2 frames per second motor drive accessory coupled to the camera bottom, had an additional improved meter turn-on switch with which you need only press the shutter release to switch on the circuit, and had a shutter release locking collar.

The Nikon EL2, as already mentioned, has automatic maximum aperture indexing. Additionally it incorporates a silicon-cell metering system rather than CdS for faster readings, also eliminating the danger of inflated readings caused by the meter being exposed to very bright light prior to low light operation. The EL2 automatically sets shutter speeds down to 8 rather than 4 seconds. Flash synchronisation need no longer be set for bulbs or flash, but instead automatically switches over as manual shutter speeds are set; an additional exposure compensation dial is fitted opposite the ASA index dial to allow automatic exposures up to 2 *f*/stops under or over exposure. Like the

Nikon EL2, Nikkormat ELW auto winder features

While the Nikon EL2 and Nikkormat ELW resemble a standard Nikkormat EL, there are specific features of the former which are different. Here they are:

1. Camera motor coupling slot
2. Camera rewind button
3. Tripod socket
4. Electric contacts to motor
5. Battery chamber cover
6. AW-1 winder connecting spindle
7. AW-1 rewind connecting rod
8. Pilot lamp
9. Camera attaching screw
10. Power switch
11. Camera connecting terminals

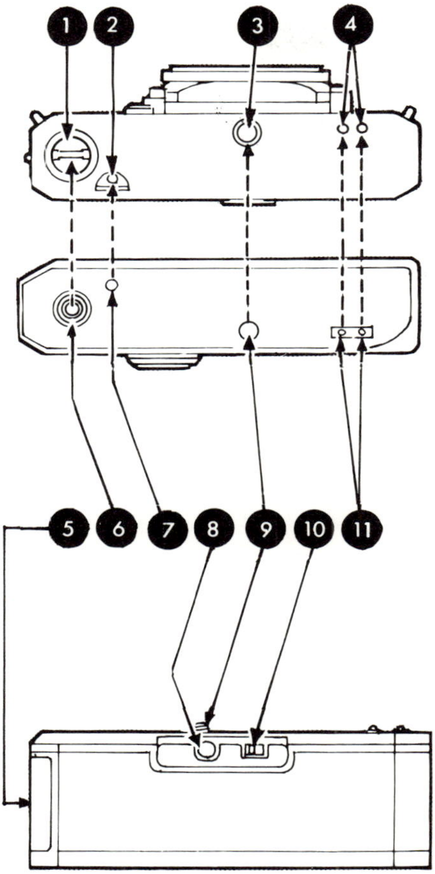

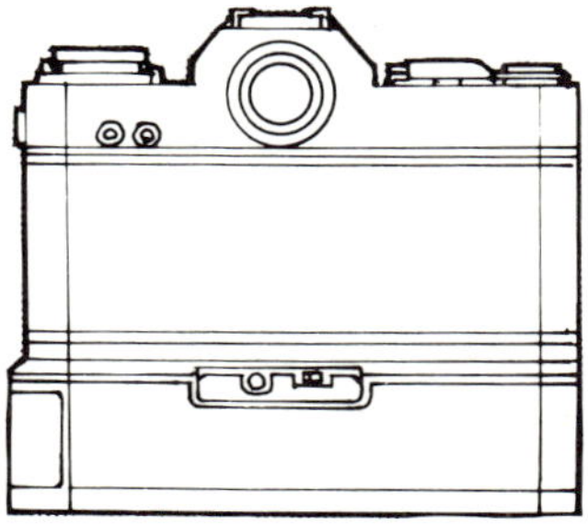

AW-1 Auto Winder when connected to the Nikon EL2 or Nikkormat ELW becomes a single interconnected entity.

Nikkormat ELW, it accepts the Nikon AW-1 auto winder which we shall discuss.

While the cameras are obviously quite alike in basic features and operation, it is not possible to have a Nikkormat EL upgraded to an ELW or an EL or ELW upgraded to a Nikon EL2. None of these cameras offer interchangeable prism finders or viewing screens.

Making double exposures

Camera owners often wish to make double exposures on the same film frame. Using such a technique, you can make trick photos showing the same images twice or more in the same photo. Superimpositions of two complete scenes can be made directly in camera. A sun or moon can be added to a landscape by first photographing the landscape and then adding the celestial body during the second exposure. (Remember, however, that obtaining double or triple or more images on a single frame requires a plain dark background while superimposed images require halving, reducing by two thirds or quartering each exposure, depending on how many photos you wish on a single frame.)

With the Nikkormat EL, you can make double exposures, but it is more difficult than with the ELW or Nikon EL2. As with other Nikkormats, to reset the shutter you must hold the EL rewind lever taut, push in the rewind button and wind the shutter, all at the same time. On the ELW and EL2, you can rewind the shutter for the second exposure simply by pushing in on the rewind button and operating the film advance lever. The frame counter advances one additional frame, but the film remains stationary, and you now ready to make a second exposure on the same frame of the film.

Auto winder

The Auto Winder AW-1 fits the Nikkormat ELW and Nikon EL2 (the EL cannot be adapted). It is powered by six AA-sized cells which are loaded into the Auto Winder as indicated on the winder itself. Alkaline cells last for approximately 150 rolls of 36-exposure film; standard carbon zinc batteries last for only about 40 rolls, but operate more efficiently in low temperatures than alkaline batteries.

To attach the Auto Winder, you thread it to the bottom of the camera baseplate using a coin edge in the slotted screw head on the Auto Winder base. At the back of the winder is an on/off switch and red pilot lamp, which lights each time the winder is activated. With the Auto Winder switched off, you can advance film and wind the shutter manually, using the camera's own rapid wind lever. When batteries are exhausted the winder slows and it is best at that time to replace the cells. Under no circumstances should you attempt to wind film with the lever when the Auto Winder is turned on.

The winder has a slip clutch which lets the motor go on turning, but not pull the film end from the cassette. Even so, don't leave the motor running when you come to the end of a roll. Although the Auto Winder doesn't provide motor rewind, there is a rewind button on the bottom so it need not be detached for film rewinding.

Firing as fast as you can, the Auto Winder lets you expose up to 2 frames per second at fast shutter speeds. In addition, left-eye users are able to operate the camera at eye level with no need to remove the camera to rewind the film. The Auto Winder provides great convenience in obviating the need for winding film. It also provides the motive power for operation at a remote distance with a long cable release.

Meter battery

In the EL, EL2 and ELW, the meter battery powers both the exposure meter and the electronic shutter timing mechanism; thus the silver-oxide battery is considerably larger than those used in non-electronically controlled shutter cameras. The battery fits in a compartment in the bottom of the mirror box. The battery operates in temperatures from 55°C (113°F) down to −15°C (5°F). Battery life is about one year.

To insert the battery, lock up the mirror. At the base of the mirror chamber you will find a small lug. Push it to the left to open the battery compartment. Insert battery firmly with the (+) terminal to the right and snap the top shut. Return mirror to down position.

To check the battery, press the battery check button. (You may need a small blunt instrument for this.) If the meter lens lights up, your battery is OK. Without a good battery in place, the camera gives 1/90 s regardless of similar speed setting. You can tell this is happening if the battery fails during shooting because the exposure meter needle drops to 1/15 s on the viewfinder scale, and stays there. It pays to check your battery every time you load a film and whenever you haven't used it for more than a few days. There is a chance that a failing battery may give you erroneous readings or automatic exposure.

If you want to remove the battery, press it against the right spring terminal and pull the left end out with a fingernail. If it doesn't come out easily, turn the camera upside down so that the battery drops into your hands.

Operation

To turn on the metering system, pull the film transport lever out to its stand-off position (revealing a red dot); or just depress the ELW or EL2 shutter release a little. For correct exposure, you must set the speed of your film on the meter. To unlock the ASA scale around the rewind knob, push in on the film speed dial lock to the right of the knob. Turn the milled outer

Installing Nikon EL2, Nikkormat EL, ELW battery

Remove lens and lock mirror up. Press battery chamber cover to left.

Push cover upwards. After removing old battery, replace with new 6 V battery, positive terminal facing right. Close lid, return mirror downwards, replace lens. Push battery check button at back of camera. Adjacent light should go on.

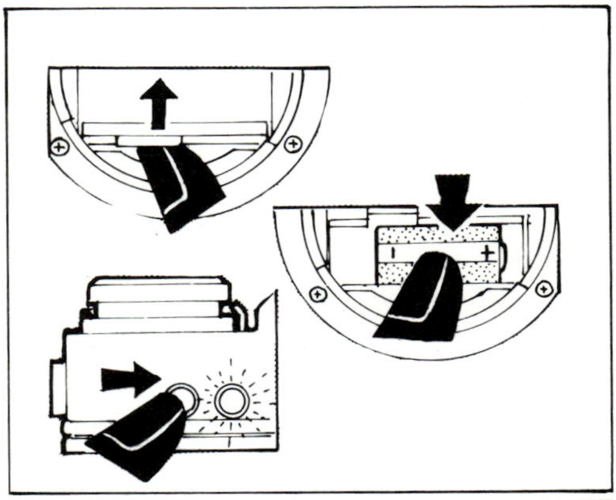

Loading EL, EL2, ELW

Push camera back lock backwards, freeing rewind knob so it can be pulled upwards fully. Back will swing open. Insert film cartridge in chamber with film leader pointing to right.

Pull film leader across focal plane and insert end into slot of take-up spool making sure slot tooth catches leader perforation. Turn spool to left using knurled end. Make certain sprocket teeth engage sprocket holes of film. Advance film using shutter release button and film advance lever until full width of film covers sprocket drive. Close back.

Remove film slack with rewind crank until resistance is felt. Advance film to frame 1. Rewind knob will turn if film is loaded properly.

Set proper ASA index of your film by pushing in ASA ring lock and turning outer ASA setting ring.

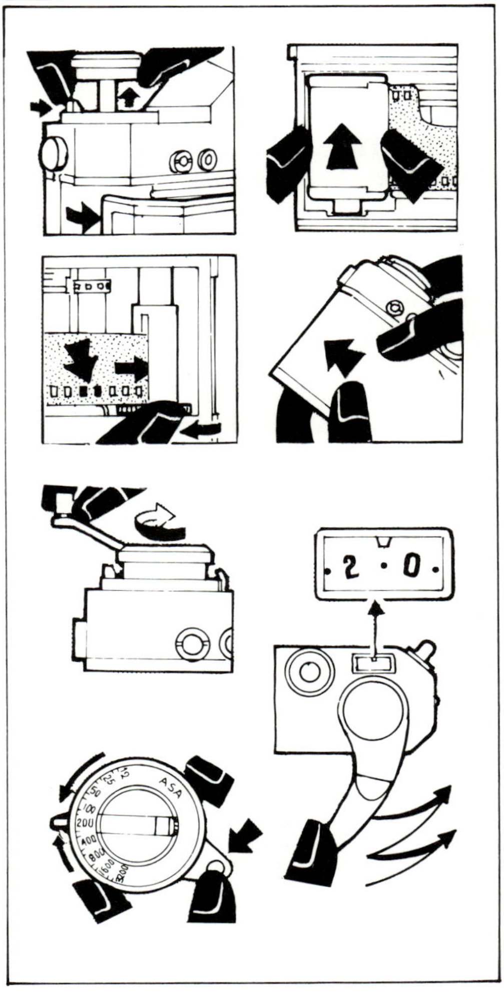

Using Nikon EL2, Nikkormat EL, ELW meter

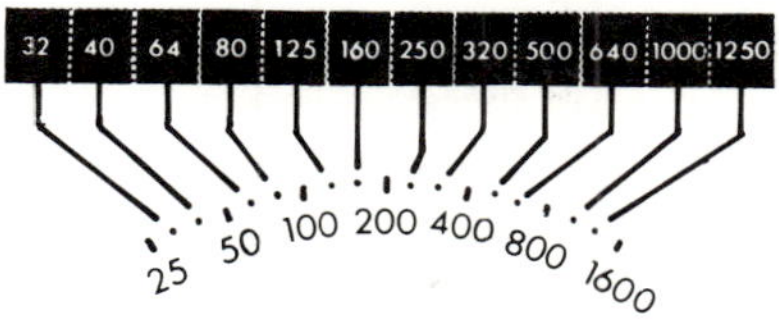

To set film speed (ASA), push in lock and turn outer ring (round rewind knob) until mark on ring is opposite appropriate ASA index. Dots are for intermediate speeds.

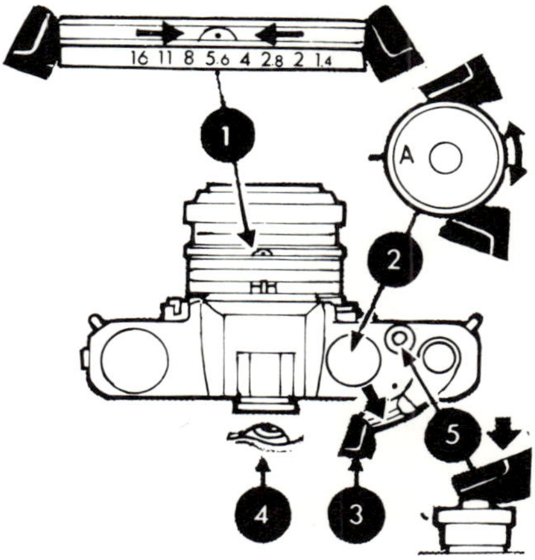

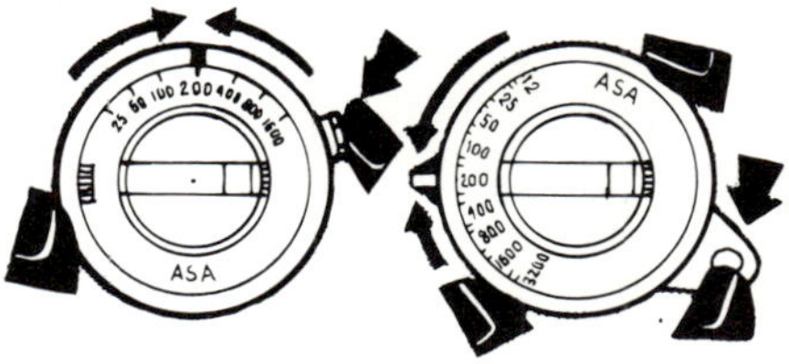

To make a picture using automatic exposure control, set aperture desired (1), set the shutter speed dial to A (2), swing film advance lever outwards (3), thus turning on meter circuit. Look through viewfinder (4) to determine that shutter speed needle is within scale limits. Press shutter release button (5) to take picture.

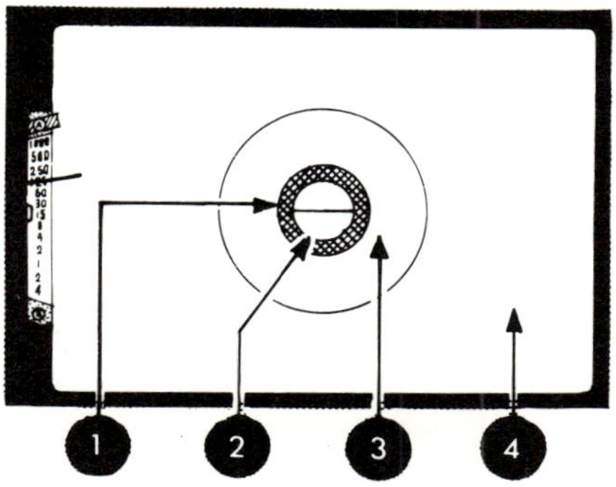

Here is view through EL, ELW, EL2 finder with camera set for automatic exposure. Transparent green needle at top of shutter speed dial covers A for automatic. Long black meter needle indicates shutter speed for exposure will be about 1/125 s. 1. Microprism. 2. Split-image rangefinder. 3.Main ground collar. 4. Fresnel condenser.

collar until the red mark indicates the ASA setting. The scale runs from 12 to 3200 ASA on the EL2 and 25 to 1600 ASA on the EL and ELW, but there isn't sufficient room to engrave every numeral. If you have trouble interpolating the ASA speeds between numerals, look at the scales on page 139.

For automatic exposure, set the shutter dial to 'A'. It locks here, and you must press the central shutter dial lock to shift it again. Look through your finder at a fairly bright subject, with the meter circuit on. To the left of the focusing screen you'll see a needle which moves against the shutter speed. For any aperture you set, the needle indicates the metered shutter speed. When you press the shutter release, the electronically controlled shutter opens for precisely the time indicated by the meter.

Long exposures

Watch your shutter speeds carefully. If you are hand-holding your camera, you will want to keep your shutter speeds at 1/30 s or faster. Slower speeds may cause blurring of the picture; and the camera can set speeds as long as 4 seconds. It can be rather difficult to watch the shutter speed scale before each picture, but you should be able to note if it goes below the small central black tab at the 1/15 s mark. This tab indicates the position of the meter needle when the metering circuit is turned off, but it's also a useful minimum speed mark when you are using the standard lens. If speeds drop below, you'll have to use a larger aperture, or support the camera. At the opposite end of the scale, you mustn't let the meter needle rise beyond the 1/1000 s marking, or you will get overexposure. If the needle rises too high, you need a smaller lens aperture.

When familiarising yourself, practise making readings of various objects indoors and out until you are completely at home with shifting aperture to gain the shutter speed you want.

Metering exposures

There are two ways you can think about setting your camera. You can either set your aperture and let the camera select the correspondingly correct shutter speed; or you can turn the aperture ring until the meter needle indicates the shutter speed you want. You can then maintain this speed by altering aperture whenever necessary to keep the meter needle at the proper speed setting.

Remember when using the meter that it is centre-weighted – that is, it is most sensitive in the 12 mm diameter outer circle within the viewfinder – so you should keep your principal subject within this area.

Using the Nikon EL2, Nikkormat EL, ELW memory lock

In special lighting situations such as a heavily backlit subject you may not want to let the camera exposure to work automatically without help. Here bright background would cause camera to set $1/250$ s, thus underexposing girl in foreground.

With camera close to subject push self-timer/memory lock lever in, towards lens mount, and hold there.

Return to original camera position and take picture while holding memory lock lever in place. Although shutter speed scale will show $1/250$ s, actual speed will be $1/60$ s.

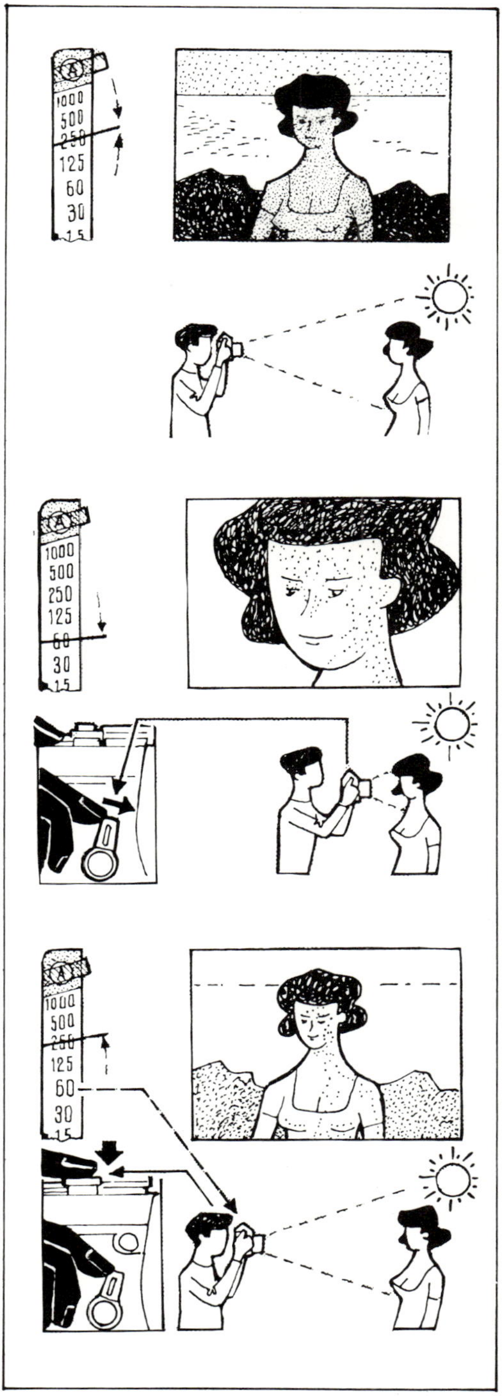

Automatic exposure override and compensation

Most photographers achieve consistently better and more even exposures when they use an intelligently designed, fully automatic exposure camera. However, there are some instances when you may want to override the automation. There are two methods on the Nikon EL2 and one on the Nikkormat EL and ELW.

The quickest and easiest with all three cameras is to use the memory lock switch. Leave the shutter set to 'automatic'. Push the dual-purpose self-timer lever towards the camera. The shutter holds the speed set by the meter just as the switch was pressed. This is quite useful if you wish to make a close-up reading of a specific part of the subject or your hand. You can take your reading, push the lever towards the lens mount and hold the exposure until you press the shutter release.

One word of warning, however. The meter needle is not affected by the memory lock switch and continues to show variations of shutter speeds even though you actually are holding the reading with the switch.

With the Nikon EL2 you have an additional means to compensate for the automatic exposure. Simply lift up and turn the outer exposure compensation ring around the rewind knob and set it to any additional exposure up to 2 *f*/stops, or less exposure up to 2 *f*/stops. (See the chapter on 'Exposure and depth of field' as to when such compensation might be necessary.) Remember to return the ring to 0 when there is no longer need for compensation.

Auto exposure compensation, EL and ELW

While the EL and ELW do not have an exposure compensation dial, here is how I used the ASA index dial with an EL to accomplish the same thing.

I took some pictures of guests seated around a large dining table with a white cloth. I had a wide-angle lens on the Nikkormat EL. Obviously, the white tablecloth would inflate my exposure reading, and cause me to underexpose the guests. Because the lighting varied, and I was working in a hurry, I wanted to shoot on automatic.

In this situation, you can alter the range of shutter speeds set automatically by altering the film speed (ASA index). Each doubling of the ASA speed set halves the exposure time the meter will calculate, and each halving doubles it. You can determine what film speed to set by taking a suitable selective reading, or just by applying your experience to the problem.

For my dinner party, I took an exposure reading from the guests themselves, noted the shutter speed, and moved back to my general picture-taking position. I then turned the ASA film speed scale until I got the same shutter speed reading as the guests' faces gave. Instead of 400 which I normally set for the film I was using, I had turned to a speed of 200 and used that for all shots in which the tablecloth was predominant. This gave me

Nikon EL2, Nikkormat EL, ELW manual control

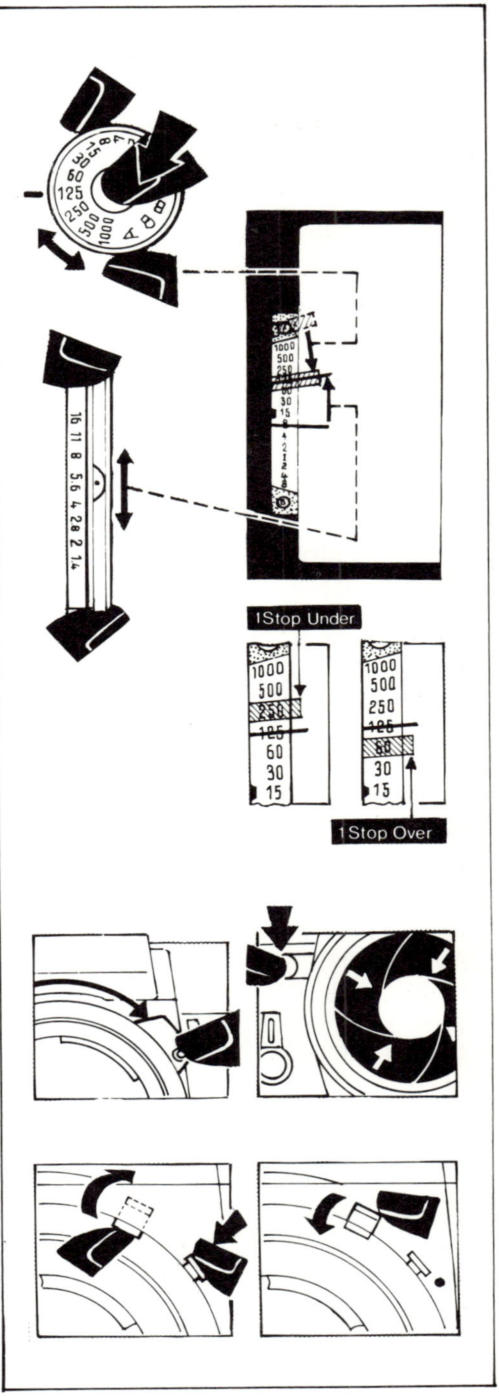

To set camera for manual control, push in shutter speed dial lock and turn dial to whatever shutter speed you wish. Green transparent pointer then shows the speed you set on shutter speed scale. Black meter needle continues to point to measured shutter speed. Align green and black needles for recommended exposure.

For special effects you may wish to give less or more exposure than the camera meter suggests. To underexpose, use a faster shutter speed causing the green needle to rise above the black. To overexpose, use a slower shutter speed so green needle drops below the black needle.

If you are using lenses which have no coupling prong to attach to the EL or ELW camera meter coupling pin, you can't make exposure measurements at full aperture. Instead push meter coupling pin clockwise as far as it will go. If the lens has an automatic diaphragm, push in depth-of-field preview button to close lens down to the aperture you select. Make reading and exposure while holding in button. With Nikon EL2, only AI lenses with back coupling ridge can make exposure readings at full aperture. For all others, push in coupling lever release button, flip up coupling lever, make reading and exposure as with EL and ELW.

precisely double the normal meter exposure. I then shot all the pictures on automatic exposure, knowing that I had compensated for the unusual lighting.

If you need to compensate like that, do it; but don't forget to reset it properly when you go back to taking standard pictures!

Manual exposure

The camera can also be used with manual, fixed shutter speeds and apertures. You can determine the exposure in any way you like, but it is usually most convenient to use the built-in meter. Looking through the viewfinder with the shutter speed dial on 'A', you can see a green translucent pointer over the 'A' marking at the top of the viewfinder shutter speed scale. This signifies that the camera is set to automatic operation. Push in the central shutter speed dial button and turn the dial to one of the marked speeds. The translucent pointer travels down to the viewfinder scale to indicate the shutter speed. The meter needle still moves just as it does in the automatic mode. It indicates the shutter speed measured to suit the lighting, lens aperture and film speed setting; but now the shutter just gives you whatever speed you've set. If this is what the needle indicates, you've got the camera set for the recommended exposure. This is immediately obvious; because when the meter recommends the speed you've set, the needle lies over the green pointer.

The basic advantage of this method of operation is that you can set a specific shutter speed and adjust exposure using the diaphragm only. It also lets you make exposure alterations easily. You can just open or close the aperture exactly as you want. By seeing how far above or below the green pointer the black needle is positioned you can set any specific amount of exposure adjustment. For instance: set the shutter speed dial to 1/125 s and the green pointer inside the finder lines up at 125. If you adjust your aperture so the needle matches the translucent green pointer, you will get exactly the exposure the meter suggests. Set the black needle to the 1/60 s marking and you double the exposure, giving one stop more exposure than the meter reading suggests. Set 1/30 s for two stops more and so on. Correspondingly, set the black needle to rest at 1/250 s, one mark above the 1/125 s, and you halve the exposure, giving one stop less; and so on.

Non-coupled lenses

As we've indicated before, the EL camera's automatic exposure system works with any lens or optical system. With non-coupled optics, lock the meter coupling lever on the Nikon EL2 in the up position by pushing in the coupling lever release button located on the right side of the camera lens mount, as the camera faces you, and lift the lever up and out of the way of operation. (Make sure to return this lever downwards when you wish to remount a regular automatic indexing lens.) With Nikkormat EL or ELW cameras, push the meter coupling pin to the far right as the camera faces you, so that the pin is by the mirror lock-up lever. The meter now reads at picture-taking aperture, and displays its calculated shutter speed on the viewfinder scale. With the EL2, EL or ELW set to 'A', you get the same fully-automatic shutter speed selection, and the same option to hold any shutter speed reading you wish. Alternatively, you can operate the camera in match needle non-automatic mode by turning the shutter dial off 'A'.

Manual exposure compensation

Suppose you have the EL, EL2 or ELW on a microscope in which there is a small central subject surrounded by a huge dark field. Exposure based on the whole area, even with the centre-weighted system, may cause overexposure of the tiny subject. To cut down exposure, you can switch to manual speeds and use one, two or three shutter speeds faster than the black pointer indicates. There are instances in special lighting situations, such as copying or shooting distant scenics through mirror lenses, where you might not wish to take full advantage of automatic exposure. These are covered in detail in the chapters on 'Exposure and depth of field' and 'Close-ups and copying'. However, in most instances when using non-coupled optical systems, you will be safe to use full automation.

Loading

Loading the EL, EL2 or ELW is exactly like loading other Nikons and Nikkormats (see page 108) except that these three have a different back opening mechanism: you pull up the rewind knob. But first, the lock beside the rewind knob must be pushed backwards to release the knob. In winding film, it's best to set the shutter dial to a fairly fast manual exposure speed. On automatic, with the lens cap on, the shutter may remain open after you press the release during loading.

Flash synchronisation

You can fit a flash-gun to the hot shoe, or connect it to the single 3 mm (PC) contact on the camera. Either way you get the same synchronisation. With the Nikon EL2, synchronisation automatically switches as you change shutter speeds. With the Nikkormats EL and ELW you choose it by raising the ring round the shutter dial and turning it one way or the other, to reveal a symbol in the cut-out (between 'A' and 'B'). For electronic flash you need X-sync, which is denoted by a lightning symbol (⚡): for any kind of bulb you need M-sync, denoted by a bulb symbol (💡).

You can't use automatic exposure with flash on the EL, EL2 or ELW. For electronic flash, 1/125 s manual speed is best but you can use slower speeds. Check the synchronisation charts in 'Facts and figures' at the back of this book to see what shutter speeds should be used with which flashbulbs. If you exceed the maximum speed allowed for flash, part of your picture will be darkened if not totally blank.

Handling

Shutter wind, release and rewind is very similar to that on the Nikon FM and FM2 (page 18) or Nikkormats (page 12). There are two important operating procedures on the EL models which must be kept in mind when operating automatically.

First, when the speed calculated by the meter is longer than 4 seconds (8 seconds on the EL2), the maximum which the camera can handle, the mirror may remain up and the shutter open. If this does happen, you must get the shutter closed as swiftly as possible. If it remains open, the film gets continuously exposed and, perhaps more important, your camera battery drains. The simplest way to close the shutter is to turn the shutter speed dial to any single set speed. Of course, you must press the release catch in the centre of the shutter dial to let you turn it from 'automatic'.

Second, extraneous light can enter the eyepiece of most SLR cameras from the rear and cause an inflated exposure meter reading. This is generally avoided by keeping your eye close to the finder. If you wear glasses and find you can't get your eye sufficiently close, a rubber eyecup helps. Do be careful, though, when shooting with a bright light from directly over your shoulder. If you are in any doubt, shade the gap behind your glasses with one hand, and make sure this doesn't alter the exposure reading. If there is a change, you'll have to shoot on manual until you get into different conditions. There are occasions when you may want to shoot without your eye to the finder. For example, you may want to use the self-timer or put your camera on a microscope stand. It is essential that whenever you take a picture with your eye not at the eyepiece, you shade the eyepiece from external light. Black tape does nicely.

How the EL, EL2 and ELW work

For those of you who would like a closer look at the electronics of these cameras, let's discuss the major features briefly. Basically the electronic mechanism works like a miniature computer. The 'input' is the ASA speed index, the aperture set and the light level. The 'output' is the suitable shutter speed. This can be fed directly to the timing mechanism of the focal plane shutter blades. Even when you select shutter speeds manually, the blinds are controlled electronically. You are merely substituting fixed values for the meter's ever-changing timing information.

However, apart from exposure timing, the camera retains the normal mechanical features: winding film, rewinding, the automatic aperture diaphragm mechanisms, the rapid return mirror, and the spring drive of the Copal Square SE shutter. Perhaps a more accurate description of the camera would be an electronically controlled (or timed) mechanically operating camera.

The heart of the electronic timing circuitry is a single highly complicated 2 mm square IC (integrated circuit). As all the electronic functions are confined to one small area, this reduces the mat of wiring, and minimises the effects of temperature change. The single IC can be pulled out and replaced with considerable ease by a qualified repairman. (Warning! If anything does indeed go wrong with your camera in or out of warranty, make sure you take it to an authorised repair agency. The electronic circuitry must be repaired and adjusted by experts in electronics, and very few independent servicemen are prepared or equipped for such services – even if they do fine work on most mechanical components.)

Besides the IC, another essential element in the EL2, EL and ELW's electronics is the Functional Resistance Element (called the FRE for short). This is a metallic thin-film resistor prepared on a hard glass baseplate located underneath the rewind knob. It integrates the ASA film speed and aperture set to provide continuously variable shutter speeds on the 'A' or automatic setting. To avoid wear on this critical resistor, it has been designed so that the tracing brush making electrical contact with it does not contact the resistor section directly. Instead, the brush only touches precious metal taps connected to the resistor. The resistor is protected by a silicone dioxide coating; the tracing brush is made of gold alloy.

The Nikon EE aperture control attachments

The Nikon F2 can be turned into a fully automatic exposure camera when it is fitted with the Photomic F2S, F2Sb or F2AS Photomic heads. For such automation, the F2S or F2Sb must be fitted with the EE Aperture Control Attachment DS-1, while the F2AS accepts a new version only, the DS-12.

Unlike the electronically controlled automatic exposure system used in the Nikkormat EL and Nikon EL2, the DS-1 or DS-12 provides shutter speed priority. You set the shutter speed, and a miniature servo motor drives the aperture setting ring to the correct *f*/stop for that shutter speed. If there is any movement in front of the camera, or the slightest change in light level, you will hear the slight whir of the motor constantly adjusting the lens opening for the precisely correct exposure.

Within the finder, you can check the shutter speed and aperture set. The DS-1 will work with all automatic diaphragm Nikon mount lenses with meter-connecting prongs. The DS-12 works only with the new auto indexing (AI) Nikkor lenses. Both units operate at all shutter speeds on the F2 shutter speed dial, can be manually overriden whenever desired and operate from a rechargeable DN-1 NiCad battery, C-cells or an AC power source. The DS-1 and DS-12 provide accurate automatic exposure even when used in conjunction with continuous-burst motor-driven shooting.

Fitting the EE attachment

To attach the DS-1 or DS-12 to your camera, first remove the lens from the camera body and pull up on the rewind knob. With its A-M switch lever set at the M position, slide the DS-1 into place. (To put the lever into the M position if it's on A, just push in on the central lever button and the lever will spring into M.) The top back fork of the unit should slide into the accessory shoe, while the lens mount ring should settle around the camera body lens mount.

EE aperture control attachments

Here are the parts:

1. Loop arm
2. Lens mounting index
3. Battery checklight
4. Lock knob
5. Battery housing
6. Drive gear (DS-12 only)
7. Lens release button
8. Auto-Manual switch
9. Sync terminal
10. Run, battery check switch
11. Control switch

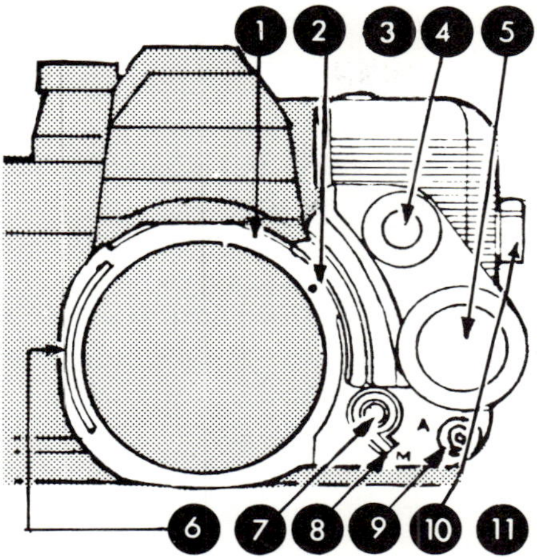

To attach to camera, remove lens from camera, push lens release button on attachments so A-M switch points to M. Pull up rewind knob of camera and slide attachment fork onto accessory show. Fasten attachment by turning lock knob clockwise until attachment is tight.

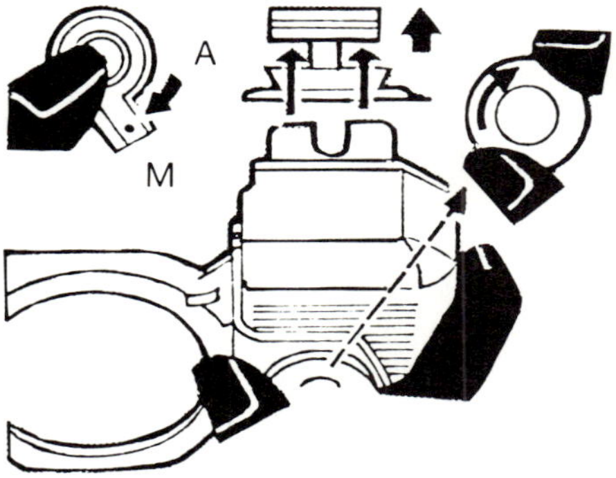

DS-1: With meter coupling pin of prism centred so *f*/5.6 appears in window, push recessed catch on tooth gear drive as far right as it will go. Set lens aperture to *f*/5.6. Insert lens and fasten it. Twist to minimum and maximum aperture as you would without FE attachment.

DS-12: Push loop drive arm.

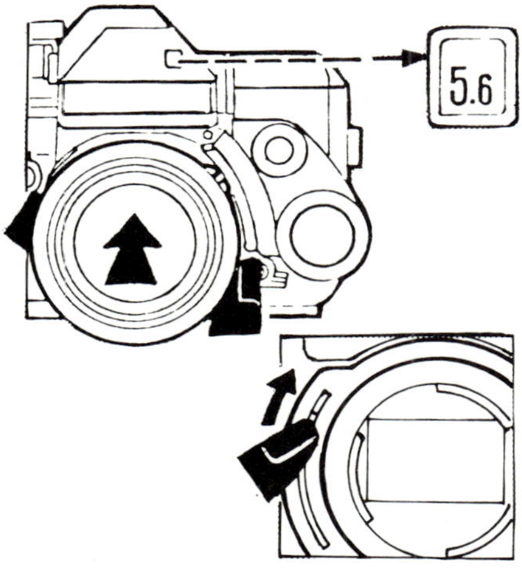

Once you have the fork in the shoe and the lens mount ring is flush with the lens mount, secure the EE attachment to the camera body. To do this, press the EE unit close to the camera body and turn the milled lock knob on the attachment. The milled lock knob threads a continuously turning screw into the 3 mm (PC) flash contact on the camera. The knob does not stop turning when the thread is all the way home, but it does get slightly harder to turn. It is made this way to prevent overtightening and possible damage to the flash terminal thread. When the EE attachment is locked securely there is no play between it and the camera body. It's important to make certain of this complete lock-up when you fit it, and to check it when the EE attachment is in use. The slightest slackness can produce poor electrical contact between the EE attachment on the meter prism. This causes malfunction of the EE attachment. Now attach the Photomic finder to the camera body. This connects the circuitry of the DS-1 or DS-12 to the finder via the electrical contacts in both units.

With the DS-12, push the ring's drive gear up as far as it will go. Set your lens to its smallest aperture. This correctly aligns your AI len's EE Servo Coupling Post for proper gear-drive engagement. Align the indices of the lens and mount, inset lens and twist counterclockwise until it clicks into place.

With the DS-1, push the recessed coupling arms on the unit's lens mount ring as far to the right as you can. Set the aperture ring of the lens you intend to mount to *f*/5.6 and mount the lens as you normally would. Be certain that the lens's coupling prong fits in between the recessed coupling arms of the DS-1's lens mount ring. Once the lens settles into the mount, twist it in to the left, counterclockwise, until it locks in place with a click. Turn the lens aperture ring all the way to the minimum aperture setting and then all the way to the maximum aperture. The prisms's coupling pin should now be secured properly in the lens's prong; the prong should nestle between the arms of the lens mount ring. The maximum aperture indicator of the finder should show the proper maximum aperture of the lens.

One point to bear in mind: if you intend to use a neckstrap with either EE attachment in place, make sure that the triangular split ring to which the Nikon neckstrap fastens is in the up position. Once the EE unit is in place it cannot be moved up and down. Only the Nikon triangular split rings can be used, since the usual commercially available round rings that most professional photographers have on their straps are too large or too thick to allow the EE attachment to be fastened properly to the camera. Only a suitably thin strap can be attached to the Nikon rings.

Power sources

There are three different power sources for the DS-1 and DS-12: the single DN-1 NiCad battery, which fits directly into the battery well at the front of the EE attachment; a voltage-stabilised battery pack holding four 1.5 V cells; and the MA-4 power pack which powers the motor drive unit.

The most convenient power source is the NiCad battery. To fit this, unthread the large milled cap on the front of the EE unit. Put the battery into the battery compartment, making certain that the plus (+) side faces outwards. You can't replace the cap if the battery is the wrong way round.

When supplied new, the battery for the DS-1 or DS-12 is charged. However, the battery will drain, even when not in use, so it is advisable to recharge it to full capacity even before you use it for the first time.

You check the battery by pushing the lever on the run control (on the left side of the unit) down until the black dot on the chrome button matches the CH lettering. The lamp on the top of the EE attachment lights brightly if the battery is satisfactory.

Automatic operation

To set the EE for automatic control, push the A-M switch lever (at the bottom front of the unit) until the white dot matches the A marking. Switch on the metering system by pulling the wind lever away from the camera body, exposing the red dot beneath. Unlike normal operation, the red diodes won't light immediately. To start the unit, you press in on the chrome run control knob button its side. Then the viewfinder diodes light, and you hear the servo-motor start to drive the lens aperture ring. Keep the chrome button depressed until the motor ceases and both lights glow in the finder, indicating that proper exposure has been set. Keep the button depressed, and changing the shutter speed or the light level causes one of the lamps to go out, and the servo-motor to go back into action to reset the lens aperture.

Operating range

The range of possible shutter speeds settings on automatic exposure stretches from 1 s to 1/2000 s; and the range of aperatures possible to set stretches from maximum opening with any lens to *f*/16. Nothing is outside of the full shutter speed and aperture range, no matter the ASA rating of the film in use.

Of course, it is possible to set a shutter speed either too fast or too slow, so that the servo-motor drives the aperture ring to its largest or smallest setting which is still insufficient for that shutter speed. In such a case the aperture ring halts at the limit, but the servo-motor goes on whirring, and only one of the two exposure read-out lights glows. In such a case you must reset the shutter to a suitable speed, and then the servo-motor will move the aperture ring to the correct lens opening.

Continuous control

Once the motor stops moving, you can take your picture while still depressing the run button. You can alternatively release the button. This turns off the meter circuit so that the unit maintains the last exposure set. This can be a convenient way of working, and does save your battery. However, the unit is probably more useful in allowing continuous automatic exposure monitoring and control.

To switch on the unit for continuous operation, push in the run-control button and at the same time turn the ring surrounding it by pushing back on the lever at the top. The lever should click into position and stay there. The word 'ON' is now set against the black dot. Switch the unit off by turning the meter ring back round the run-control button, so that the protrusion returns to the top neutral position. Do this whenever you're not actually shooting. To conserve battery power, switch off when you're not actually shooting.

Manual override

If you wish to override the automatic exposure control of the EE, push in the A-M switch lever's central button on the front of the unit and the lever will spring back to the manual (M) position. With the EE unit in place, the run control still switches on the light-emitting diodes in the pentaprism. So for manual measure, you must either press in on the run control knob button and hold it during the setting, or lock it to continuous operation. As with automatic operation, switch off to prevent battery drain when you're not metering.

Lens changing

The centre of the A-M switch lever button also serves as the lens mount release lock button when pressed inwards to interchange lenses. Lenses can only be changed with the A-M switch in the M position, since it is only in the M position that the control arms moving the aperture-setting prong are free to turn, allowing the lens to be removed. Lenses can be removed from the DS-1 unit in the same manner as lenses in the regular F2S Photomic.

Removing the DS-1 or DS-12

To remove the unit from the camera, first remove the lens. Then loosen the milled lock knob on the attachment and pull the DS-1 or DS-12 away from the camera body.

Battery charging

How long will the NiCad battery last before recharging? In my tests I found it would give 48 minutes of continuous aperture changing before becoming exhausted. In practical use, you certainly wouldn't have it operating constantly under such conditions. However, it would be advisable to carry around a spare fully-charged DN-1 battery at all times.

The DN-1 NiCad battery for either EE attachment is recharged with the Nikon Quick Charger DH-1. First, before plugging in the charger, make certain that the slotted voltage selector on the back is set for the proper voltage: 100, 117, 200 or 220 volts. The selector can be set easily by using the edge of a coin or similar object.

Unscrew the milled screw cap on the front panel of the charger and insert the battery with the plus (+) side facing out. The unit will not operate if the battery is reversed. Screw the cap back on to switch on the charger. The top neon lamp at the front of the charger glows green. Also, the red lamp below glows during the charging period. When the battery has reached 80 per cent of capacity (in about thre hours of charging from near exhaustion) the red lamp goes out. The battery may be removed for use, but you can leave it in the charger longer to top it up fully.

Since the EE unit's battery cover is of the same size and thread as the DN-1 battery charger's cover, it is fairly easy to mix them up. If you do, you won't charge the battery. However, you can easily keep them sorted out by remembering that the cover with the chrome trim is for the charger while the all-black trim cover matches the all-black finish of the EE attachment.

Alternative power sources

To operate the EE attachment constantly, you need an alternate power source to the compact DN-1 NiCad battery.

A battery pack holding four 1.5V with built-in voltage stabiliser is available. The pack, housed in a leatherette container, has a removable, over-the-shoulder carrying strap. To connect the pack to the EE unit, remove the NiCad battery from the unit and connect the pack to the EE battery compartment with its connecting cord. Check to make certain the pack is operational after connecting by depressing the run-control button on the EE. Note if the battery checker on the battery pack lights. Keep the battery pack switched off when not in use.

The DS-1 or DS-12 can also be run off house current, using the AC/DC Converter MA-4 (which is described in the chapter on the MD motor drive). To connect the DS-1 or DS-12 with the converter, remove the NiCad battery from the EE unit, push in the cord supplied to the battery well, and to the 3.6V output jack of the converter. Plug the converter to any proper power source. As with the battery pack, check for proper operation before use. Press the run-control button, and the indicator should light.

Problems in handling

The EE unit, although bulky-looking, is quite convenient for standard camera hand-holding operation, with or without the motor drives. It gives accurate and fast response to changing conditions.

It is, however, most important that the directions for connecting the DS-1 or DS-12, as given, be carried out scrupulously or the attachment will fail to operate. Generally, failure of more than one diode to light with the DS-1 and the motor continuing to whir indicates that a faster or slower shutter speed must be chosen, or the unit is not secure to the camera. If no lights operate, the NiCad battery of the unit is exhausted, not in place, or the alternative power supply not connected. In such a case the diodes will not light even if the F2S's own batteries are all right. As soon as the EE unit is attached to the camera's internal batteries, they are switched out of circuit.

Likewise if the two MS76 batteries in the camera bottom are exhausted or inoperative, the diodes will work while the DS-1 or DS-12 is attached, but will cease to work when the unit is removed. However, once the basic interconnections and operating controls of the DS-1 or DS-12 are learned, using it will become quite simple and enjoyable.

Nikon data back

The ability to imprint useful information directly on the picture at the moment of exposure has become more and more popular. Nikon data backs, which replace regular camera backs, provide this ability. With one, a Nikon owner can immediately identify the negative, print or slide by date, time and, in some instances, by consecutive number. This information appears in the lower right-hand corner of the picture where it is least likely to interfere with picture content. The imprintings can be used or not used as desired. The data back does not interfere with normal camera operation. However, imprinting can be difficult to read in the picture if there is a white, bright or fine background, such as grass or against a red colouration.

Attaching the data back

To prepare a Nikon camera for a data back, open the camera back, locate the locking catch on the interior of the back's hinge and push it downwards. This allows the top of the back to be swung outward. You can then remove the back completely.

With the MF-12 Nikon Data Back for the FE, FM and FM2 cameras, load the batteries by sliding the battery chamber cover open with your finger or the tip of a ballpoint pen. Insert two 1.55 volt SR-44-type silver-oxide batteries in the chamber with the + signs facing up. Close the chamber. Attach the back to camera, starting with the bottom hinge pin. Then depress the top pin by pushing the data back's locking catch downwards. Swing the back into place and release the catch so the top pin can enter the top hole of the hinge. Attach the connecting cord's plug into the data back's socket with the plug's projection fitting the groove inside the socket. Fasten the other end of the cord to the camera body sync terminal.

Setting the data

To set the date of the LCD display panel, make certain that the panel shows the year/month/day display and not the time display. If the display shows a colon (:), it is in the time display and must be changed by pressing the 'CHANGE' button.

Push the 'SELECT' button. This allows you to adjust the year. Set the year by pressing the 'ADJUST/R' button until the proper year appears on the LCD panel. To set the month, push the 'SELECT' button again. The centre number indication for the month will now appear. Again push the 'ADJUST/R' button until the correct numeral for the month appears.

To set the day, push 'SELECT'. Then push 'ADJUST/R' until the proper day appears at the right of the panel.

To set the time, push the 'CHANGE' button so the display switches to show day/hour/minute. Press the 'SELECT' button. You'll see that the day already set automatically reappears correctly. Push the 'SELECT' button again. The first push allowed you to activate the 'ADJUST' button for the day (which you need not do, since it has been done previously). The second push will provide you with the mode for the hour. Push the 'ADJUST/R' button until the proper hour appears. The hours operate on 24-hour time so PM times begin at 12, 1 PM is 13, 2 PM is 14 and so on. After you have set the hour, push the 'SELECT' button again for the minute. During the minute setting the clock actually stops. This is indicated by the absence of the blinking diamond at the far right of the display (which continues blinking when all other modes are being set). The clock stops so you can activate the minute at an exact time signal.

To set the clock precisely, first advance it one minute beyond the actual time using the 'ADJUST/R' button. At the precise time signal, push the 'SELECT' button one more time and the entire day and time will appear with the clock running from the signal. You can now switch back and forth between date and time display by pressing the 'CHANGE' button.

The data back can also imprint a one or two digit number-only if you wish. For example, you might wish to record pictures in a numbered sequence. The easiest way to do this is in the year/month/day mode. In setting the data back, simply use the year numeral to set the numbers from 00 to 99, bearing in mind that you will have to change numerals after each picture for an advancing set of numerals.

Before using the data back, you must input the ASA film speed. After loading film, turn the film-speed selector until the indexing dot clicks at the proper ASA/ISO speed of the film being used. Use only film with speeds indicated by the scale. For instance, with black-and-white film you cannot use films other than in the ASA 100–400 range.

To imprint data on the film during exposure, press the 'CHANGE' button to display the appropriate data on the LCD display. When you want to

Nikon Data Backs MF-12, 14 and 15

Here are the major features of the MF-12 for Nikon FE, FM and FM2 cameras:

1. Socket
2. Data imprint ON/OFF switch
3. Battery chamber
4. LED indicator
5. Display panel
6. Connecting cord
7. Locking catch
8. CHANGE button
9. SELECT button
10. ADJUST/R button
11. ASA/ISO film-speed scale
12. Film-speed selector

LCD panel can either show and imprint the year/month/day or day/hour/minute on the film.

Here are the major features of the MF-14 for the Nikon F3 and the MF-15 for the Nikon FG:

1. ASA/ISO film-speed table
2. Display panel
3. Locking catch
4. Control panel cover
5. Battery chamber
6. Alarm set indicator
7. Time indicator colon
8. LCD imprinting data
9. Picture counting indicator
10. L/M/H film-speed indicator
11. Data imprint indicator
12. Alarm mode indicator

Control panel buttons are clearly marked.

LCD panels offer full informational data.

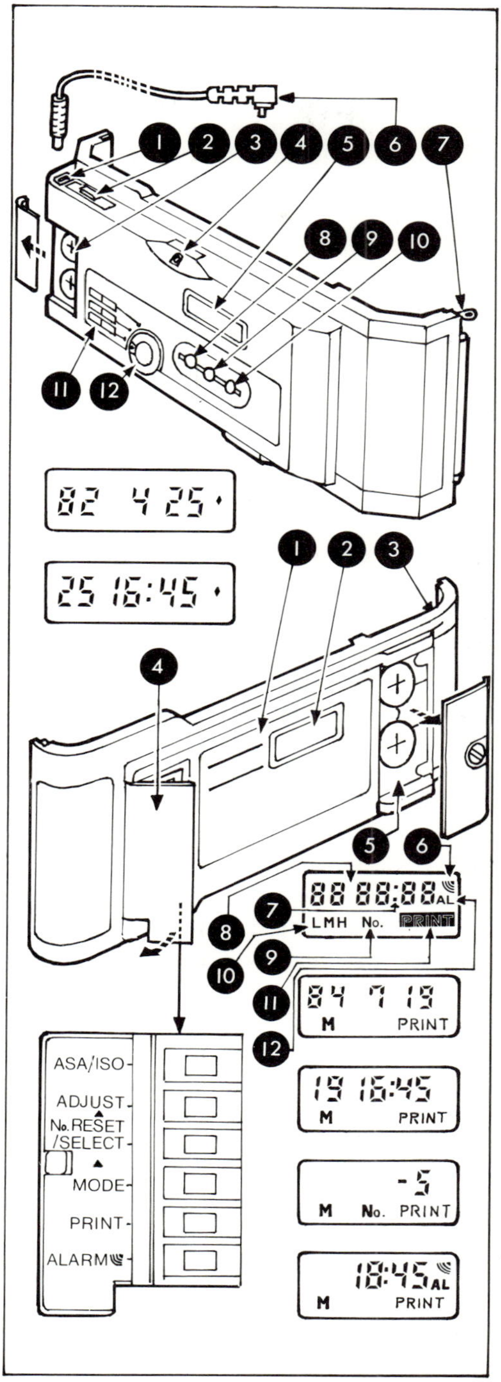

imprint, turn the 'ON/OFF' switch to 'ON'. The back's LED indicator will light at the time of exposure to indicate that data is being imprinted.

If the LED indicator remains continuously lit, change both batteries (unless the back is being used in temperatures below −10°C (14°F), in which case you should turn off the LED by pushing the 'ADJUST/R' button). Before discarding the batteries, however, try them again in normal temperature. The may be perfectly all right for use under such conditions.

The MF-14 for the Nikon F3, or MF-15 for the FG, are quite similar to each other but are a bit different to the MF-12. They provide all the information available on the MF-12 but additionally have automatic consecutive numbering and a built-in audible alarm system which you can use as a regular alarm clock. The operating batteries are located under a battery-chamber lid which can be removed by unscrewing the locking screw with a coin edge. Insert two 1.55 volt alkaline-energiser cells with both + signs upwards and replace the battery cover. Replace the regular camera back with the data back, as already described with the MF-12 back and the F3.

To set data, open the cover of the control panel. The buttons therein allow all settings needed. Check the panel display before setting. If the batteries are fresh and inserted properly, the panel should show 82 1 1 with an M underneath the 82 and the word 'PRINT' blinking beneath the right-hand 1. (Note: the MF-14's clock starts working at 0:00 on January 1, 1982, hence the 82 1 1 starting date.) Before setting, the display should show this indication. If it doesn't but shows any setting with a blinking colon (:) or with a 'NO' lettering at the bottom of the display, change the display by pushing the button marked 'MODE' until the proper year/month/day display appears. Push the 'RESET/SELECT' button to activate the 'ADJUST' mode for the year. Set the proper year by pushing the 'ADJUST' button. Warning: all numerals set by the 'ADJUST' button will advance by 1 numeral unless the button is held down for more than 2 seconds. If this occurs, the numerals advance first to the nearest denominator of 5 and then advance by 5. This is an aid in reaching the right minute or numbered picture frames quickly, but is certainly not needed in getting to the proper date. So push the button singly in setting the year. Push the 'RESET/SELECT' button again and you can set the month with the 'ADJUST' button. Another push of the 'RESET/SELECT' button allows you to set the day with the 'ADJUST' button. Following the date setting, push the 'RESET/SELECT' button to cancel the setting mode. The display will now read the date completely.

Push the 'MODE' button to switch the display to day/hour/minute setting. The day, already set, will appear. Push the 'RESET/SELECT' button twice. Now you can set the hour by pushing the 'ADJUST' button. Remember that the clock is of the 24-hour type so PM numerals should be set higher than 12 (for instance, 6:45 PM is 18:45). Press the 'RESET/

SELECT' button. Push the 'ADJUST' button to 1 minute beyond the actual time. When you hear an actual hourly time on the radio or TV or similar source, or wish to start the time, push the 'RESET/SELECT' button and the clock, previously stopped, will begin running.

To view the data back picture counter, press the mode selector until the 'NO' indication appears in the bottom of the display panel. Whenever the data back is opened for film loading, the counter is automatically set to −2, thus reaching 0 at frame 1. When the shutter release is pressed for frame 1, the picture counter will also automatically read 1. It can count from 1 to 2000, provided the back isn't opened. It also can be reset to whatever numeral you wish, whether the back is opened or not, by first pressing the 'RESET/SELECT' button and then the 'ADJUST' button until you reach the numeral desired. When 2000 is reached, the counter stops. It will not automatically begin over again unless it is reset or the back is opened.

Adjusting film speed

Before imprinting you must adjust the film speed according to the film you have loaded in the camera. Each time you press the ASA/ISO button, a M, H or L appears at the bottom of the display. At the left of the LCD display on the back of the data back you will see a chart indicating what ASA/ISO speeds are covered by these three settings. Then simply set the M, H or L accordingly. Do not use films whose ASA indexes are beyond the ranges shown on the chart.

Imprinting data

To imprint data, select the data you wish to print by pressing the 'MODE' selector. Then push the 'PRINT' button until the word PRINT blinks on the LCD display. The data will now be imprinted when the picture is made. Push the button again when you don't want data imprinted.

The data back alarm operates very much like the alarm on a regular LCD watch and has no printing function. To set the alarm timer, push the 'ALARM' button and keep it held down during the entire setting procedure. The alarm mode will immediately appear with the radiating wave alarm mode indicator. To set the hour for the alarm, press the 'RESET/SELECT' button and set the alarm hour with the 'ADJUST' button (keep that alarm button depressed during this entire time). Also remember that the time is on a 24-hour system, so, for example, 4 PM would require that 16 be set. Push the 'RESET/SELECT' button again to set the minute and then set the alarm minute using the 'ADJUST' button. Push the 'RESET/SELECT' button one more time to cancel the adjust mode. The display should now read the alarm time you require. When you remove your finger, the alarm time will be set but the display will return to one of the other modes. To activate the alarm so it will sound, the small radiating alarm wave signal must appear in the upper right-hand corner of any mode. If it does not, press the 'ALARM' button again and it will. The alarm will ring at the time you have set for 20 second or until you press the alarm button to cancel it. If you keep the alarm on, it will ring each day at the same time.

If the MF-14 LCD display begins to blink, it's a sign that the batteries are nearly exhausted and should be replaced. The display must then be reset again. The display may also blink in very cold weather. Push the print button to stop the blinking. Batteries should last approximately 1 year under normal use.

No matter which LCD data back you are using, the data display may go black if temperatures go over 60°C (140°F), but will still print properly. The display will return to normal when temperatures lower. Below freezing, display changes may be sluggish. After six or seven years of normal use, the display numerals may become difficult to see or may lose contrast. If so, contact your Nikon dealer about a complete panel replacement.

Exposure and depth of field

To a large number of photographers, exposure is nothing more than setting the ASA index for the film, then centering the meter needle or letting the camera determine the exposure automatically. For them, camera manufacturers have done everything possible to assure the highest percentage of correctly exposed, acceptable results in both colour and black and white. The centre-weighted metering system employed in all currently manufactured Nikon and Nikkormat cameras was created with just users in mind. In emergency circumstances, as when shooting fast-breaking news or quickly-changing action, even the professional may have no time to set exposure to his liking and so just centres the needle and shoots.

However, there are any instances where blindly following the needle will not give you the best results or the picture you really want. Sometimes, even a compromise exposure (which is what following the needle always is) may yield a compromise which gives you nothing of what you sought. The purpose of this chapter is to give you a practical working knowledge of exposure with both black-and-white and colour materials.

Colour or black and white

Proper exposure should not really be divided between handling colour and black and white. Rather it is divided between films which yield negatives for printing and reversal films which produce positive transparencies directly. The reasons for this are twofold. First, because there is no intermediate (printing) stage, your reversal film exposure determines exactly the density of your final print. Secondly, because they must reproduce the scene directly, the contrast of transparency materials is considerably higher than that of negative materials. It is an important differentiation since exposure of colour negative films have far more in common with that of black-and-white negatives than they do with colour slide films. In like manner, if you do ever intend to shoot black-and-white reversal slide film directly, you had best follow our suggestion in shooting colour slides.

Exposure aims

First, what type of quality should you seek in a negative or slide?

1. Every part of the negative or slide that you wish sharp should be sharp.
2. The overall density should be such that long printing times with negative materials are not necessary, and slides produce brilliant images on the screen with your projector.
3. The contrast or density range of any black-and-white negative should allow printing on a so-called normal grade of paper (2 or 3) so that adequate detail is visible in both shadows and highlight areas if both are desired. The contrast of the print or projected slide should provide as close a representation of the scene as possible.
4. The image should be no more grainy than can be expected from the material used.
5. The negative or slide should be free from dust, dirt, pinhole scratches, static marks or faults caused by improper processing.

Our aim should be to fulfil as many of these criteria as possible.

It is generally accepted that the best-quality negative or slide is one when the film is given the least exposure necessary to record the shadow detail. To allow some latitude, it is normal to aim to give slightly more exposure than that. The exposure latitude of a film is the amount that you can vary from the ideal exposure and still get a satisfactory negative or slide. Of course, if you are near the minimum exposure, there will be little latitude on the underexposure side. You can expose negative materials at several times the minimum exposure and still get printable negatives, despite their density and need for longer printing times. They will probably also need a lower-contrast paper grade and, perhaps most important, show increased graininess.

Slide material is somewhat different, particularly colour. Overexposure causes irretrievable loss of colour, resulting in a washed-out slide. To avoid this, many photographers prefer slight underexposure. This gives darker and more saturated colour with no real loss of shadow detail.

With today's powerful slide projectors, such slides can offer richer, more satisfying projected images. To aid them, Nikon and Nikkormat exposure systems are deliberately calibrated to give about ½ *f*/stop less exposure than that theoretically demanded by the film speed. This still provides sufficient exposure for good negatives.

Metering

An exposure meter, whether in your hand or built into the camera, does not have a mind of its own. It is designed to indicate the correct exposure when pointed at an average subject, which reflects about 18 per cent of the light striking it. You can substitute a neutral grey test card for your average

Using your behind-lens meter

Simply pointing your camera at the subject from camera position may not always yield you best possible exposures.

For average scenes, a direct reading is often adequate. With older models, having averaging rather than centre-weighted meters, point the camera down slightly to exclude excessively bright sky.

If part of the subject is in bright light and part in shadow but you wish detail in both, make reading of both areas from close to and then average them.

Take a close-up reading of your subject when possible, particularly when photographing people. When the main subject is not in the same general lighting as the rest of the area, such as in backlit situations, you can't use the overall readings. However, if you want a silhouette, ignore reading from darkened subject and expose for bright background only.

Can't get close enough to take a reading from your subject? Try taking a meter reading from your hand held in the same lighting. Better still, make a reading from a neutral grey card available from most photo dealers.

Beware of arches or other foreground framing devices which can give you erroneous readings of scene outside. If possible move forward to make a reading.

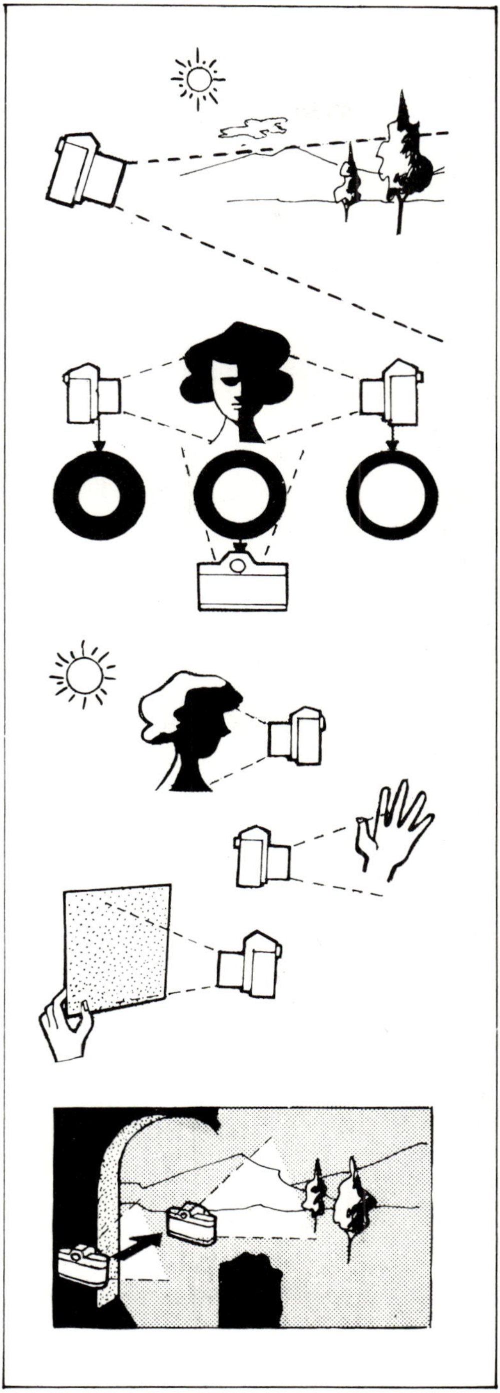

subject, and get just the same reading. Whatever you aim your meter at, following its reading will produce pictures which average out to a neutral grey. In other words, if you follow a reading from a dark-skinned person, his skin will come out lighter, and that's not what you want. To preserve the tones of your subject, you should read from a suitably neutral-toned object. The most convenient is the palm of your hand. (If you wish to work even more precisely, you can buy a neutral grey card from your photo dealer. You can then hold the card in the same light as the subject and make a reading.) However, be warned that having the tones in the correct relation may not be all you're trying to get in the picture. If you want detail in your highlight and shadow areas and they don't fall within your film's acceptance range, you have to modify the lighting, with extra lights, reflectors or fill-in flash, to reduce the brightness range.

Subject contrast

One of the major exposure problems is that the brightness range of many subjects, from deepest shadow to brightest highlights, often exceeds the film's ability to record it. The film's brightness range is related to its exposure latitude. Most negative materials have a greater exposure latitude than most slide films. If the subject range between the brightest and dullest parts of the subject exceeds the ability of the film, either the highlights or the shadows (or both) will be recorded without details.

If you think that you may have this problem, you must determine your exposure with care. First, you must decide whether it is the shadows or the highlights that contain the detail you want. Then bias your exposure towards that.

Suppose you are to picture a girl in a white wedding dress. If her face is in shadow but the dress is sunlit, you don't want to sacrifice the face for detail in the dress, so you ignore the dress. Take a meter reading from the face, and use that. The dress will be overexposed in a colour slide and appear white but without detail.

Selective metering

The best way to make selective exposure determination is to approach the subject as closely as possible and read those areas that are important. Then determine if an average is within the range of your films. If not, decide which area (or areas) must be sacrificed to get the more important one. I have seen too many scenes in contrasty bright sun in which a photographer attempted a compromise right down the middle, causing underexposure of the shadow areas in which he wished detail, and overexposure of the highlights. In effect, he got nothing at all of what he wanted.

Making close-up readings isn't always possible (although if you have time and a long-focus lens, you can meter from a distance through the lens). When time is short and you can't approach the subject, try making substitute readings from similarly lit close-by objects of similar brightness as your subject. For instance, the palm of your hand makes a good substitute for facial tones.

Bracketing

The next best thing, if you have enough time, is to bracket exposure. Take one shot at the meter's suggested exposure, one at one *f*/stop less exposure and a third one at one *f*/stop more than the meter indicates. With automatic cameras, you need manual control to achieve this bracketing.

Bracketing, of course, is time- and film-consuming. What if you have time and film only for one shot under a different circumstance? Now you have to make a quick decision. Either go with the reading that the meter indicates or adjust it depending on the subject matter. But how?

When people are in the picture, I have found (in almost every case) you get the most suitable exposure by measuring from a pale skin area. Faces are fine for subjects with light skin. But reading from a dark-skinned person, the meter suggests that you use a larger aperture or slower speed than you need.

Bright sun

Bright sun is the most difficult type of lighting to handle. This is true not only of exposure, but in composition and handling the subject as well, you get trouble with shadow areas and the sun that always getting into people's eyes. In every way, it is easier when there are overcast skies or the sun is behind a cloud. Immediately, contrast is cut, the deep shadows disappear and a general average reading with a centred meter needle will give you a good, acceptable result. If you are out on a day with no clouds but can take your subject in bright shade, such as under a tree, do so. Exposure will be easier and better. But you may need a filter if your colour slides are not to come out too blue (see page 197). I would rather photograph under any other lighting condition than bright sunlight.

Special cases

There are a few specific subjects which require specific handling.

Distant scenes or aerial pictures are often better with one *f*/stop less than the meter recommends. You get a deeper, richer, more detailed picture. This is important because skylight tends to inflate exposure readings.

To produce silhouettes, your subject must be lit considerably less than the background. Take your reading from the background only. Use this single reading for your picture-taking. On the other hand, when you wish to retain in a backlit subject, go as close as possible to exclude the backlight for your reading. If you can't approach the subject, take a reading from the palm of your hand held in the same light.

Sunsets do not lend themselves to any definite rule. I have photographed the same sunset at many different settings and got very acceptable results in all pictures even though they varied from a high-key, sun-filled picture (made by taking a reading of the foliage) to a rich, deep, dark sun (made by reading the sun itself and cutting the exposure further by half an *f*/stop). Never point your camera at the sun until it is well down toward the horizon where you can easily get a meter reading right from it. Extreme brightness can cause your metering system temporarily to read erroneously and refuse to give readings at lower light levels for up to an hour. It can even damage the cells permenantly.

Exposure controls

You control exposure with two variables, aperture and shutter speed. Many different combinations of these give you any particular exposure. The problem is to choose the right combination for the picture you want. This is probably well-known ground for most readers of this book, but for those less familiar with photographic practice we should first look at the basics of shutter speeds and apertures.

Lens apertures

The apertures of your (or any) camera are marked in *f*/stops from maximum *f*/1.2, *f*/2, *f*/3.5, or whatever, to *f*/16 or more. These mysterious numbers are really nothing more than the ratio of the focal length of the lens divided by the diameter of the aperture. In other words, a 50 mm lens with a measured 12.5 mm aperture would be marked *f*/4. Except for maximum apertures, all Nikkor and Nikon lenses are marked in full *f*/stops – *f*/1.4, 2, 2.8, 4, 5.6, 8, 11, 16 and sometimes beyond to 22, 32 and 45. Each successive number transmits half the amount of light as did the number before it. In other words, *f*/2 lets in just half as much light as an *f*/1.4 lens.

Large aperture means a large opening, not a large number. Small aperture means a small opening. Large maximum apertures are often said to be 'fast', and those with small ones are 'slow'.

All Nikkor and Nikon lenses are click-stopped at full apertures. A few have click detents at half stops as well. For purposes of exact exposure setting, the lens diaphragm rings can be set in-between full *f*/stop markings when needed. The variation of the light transmission is accomplished by a multi-bladed iris within the lens element.

The only exceptions to full *f*/stops marked settings are the maximum apertures of some lenses.

Shutter speeds

The shutter speeds of the Nikon or Nikkormat are also arithmetical. Each successive one allows either twice as much light to enter, or half as much. Thus 1/60 s allows half as much light as 1/30 s. Shutter speeds are produced by the focal plane shutter's curtains or blades. One curtain or set of blades opens, allowing light to strike the film. The delay before the second set of blades or curtains follows (closing the film from light) determines the shutter speed.

Combinations

Since both shutter speed and apertures arithmetically double with each adjacent setting, the series of settings to give one exposure is simple to determine. For instance, if you need an exposure of 1/60 s at *f*/4 there are a whole range of equivalent settings. You can shift your shutter speed or aperture any set number of markings providing you shift the other control the same number of markings to compensate. If you halve the light coming through your lens by closing down your aperture from *f*/4 to *f*/5.6, you can restore the correct exposure by using a shutter speed which allows the film to be exposed twice as long – 1/30 s. In like manner, 1/500 at *f*/4, 1/250 at *f*/2, 1/125 at *f*/2.8, 1/60 at *f*/4, 1/30 at *f*/5.6, 1/15 at *f*/8, 1/8 at *f*/11, and 1/4 at *f*/16 all allow the same amount of light to strike the film and thus give equal exposures. You needn't keep these equivalent in your head. If you centre the meter needle or check the combination set by an automatic camera, you can then shift the aperture or shutter speed setting. As you recentre the needle, using the other control, you still set the same exposure. With an automatic camera, when you change the manually-set control, the other automatically shifts itself to provide proper exposure. Therefore, even with an automatic camera, you the photographer must decide what the proper aperture and shutter speed combination should be.

While all the various combinations of shutter speeds and apertures give you the metered exposure, each combination gives you a different picture – in some cases, radically different.

Movement

The faster the shutter speed you choose, the less chance there is your main subject coming out blurred because it moved. In other words, if you could use 1/1000 or 1/2000 s you would be best assured that all action of the subjects would be frozen as far as possible. Also, most pictures are taken with a hand-held camera. Even the most practised professional photographer is nowhere near as steady as a tripod. So at slower shutter speeds you may blur the picture by moving the camera. Although subject choice and the photographer's ability to hold steady vary considerably, I have found as a general rule that for subjects in motion, speeds of 1/125 s and higher are needed. Speeds below are best reserved for stationary subjects and photographers who have good ability to hold very steady. You need a great deal of practice to be sure of taking sharp pictures at 1/30 s. There are some professional photographers who claim that they can hand-hold speeds of 1/15 s or even 1/8 s; but they can never by absolutely sure of being able to do so every time. Note that the speeds we talk of are when you've got the standard lens fitted. With longer focus lenses, any shake or subject movement is magnified, so you need higher speeds still to be sure of sharp pictures.

Of course, when we say 'stop action', this is a relative term. No ordinary camera can 'stop' a bullet in mid-air. If the action is continuing in a direction so you can follow it, holding the subject fairly steady against a moving background, you may be able to produce an adequately sharp subject against a blurred background. This technique is called panning.

Action going across your view at right angles to the camera needs a higher shutter speed than action coming towards or going away from the camera. Action at a distance does not require as fast a speed as close-up action as long as it remains in the distance in your picture. But if you enlarge the distant image, the action is every bit as blurred as if it had originally occurred close to the camera.

In many books there are tables purporting to give you specific suggestions as to what shutter speeds are needed to halt various types of action. I have found them to be misleading. If, for instance, the shutter speed is sufficient to stop the forward movement of a runner, it may not be enough to halt his arms or legs, which are moving faster and in somewhat different directions.

Apertures

I have stressed shutter speed first in the setting of shutter speed and aperture because I feel that it is the prime consideration for most picture taking. However, it is by no means the only one. Aperture affects sharpness, too. It has no relationship to the movement of the subject or the photographer. It affects the depth of sharpness.

Whenever a lens is focused, only one plane is actually in true focus (through an ideal lens). In real lenses this two-dimensional plane may be slightly curved; but for purposes of discussing aperture, consider it as an absolutely flat plane. Sharpness falls off progressively in front of and behind the plane of focus. At a large aperture and close to the camera, sharpness falls off swiftly. At a small aperture and further away from the camera, sharpness falls off more slowly. If you have a photograph with an important subject near the camera but you wish to register the background (perhaps a beautiful cloud or mountain) also sharply, you may have to use a very small lens aperture to do so. As we've seen, the smaller the lens aperture, the slower the shutter speed you need for correct exposure. So it may be possible to provide a sharp subject and background, but the necessary shutter speed may be too slow, so that any movement comes out a blur. You may have to sacrifice either the sharpness of a moving subject or the sharpness of the picture in depth (or both) to get a correct exposure on film. (As we've seen in the chapter on choosing films, you may be able to help by selecting a film having a faster ASA speed, too.) However, even if nothing is moving in the scene, you need a steady tripod if you are to avoid camera shake with slow shutter speeds.

While your ability to stop action with an adequate shutter speed is not possible to guarantee, achieving sharpness in depth with any lens at any distance and at any aperture can be calculated and controlled.

Depth of field

A theoretically perfect sharp image on film is composed of pinpoints of light. As sharpness falls off before and behind the plane of focus, each pinpoint blurs and becomes a circle. The further away from the plane of sharpness you go, the bigger becomes the circle. The larger the lens aperture, the faster the circle grows away from the plane of sharpness.

Our eyes cannot distinguish between a pinpoint of light and a tiny disc. At normal viewing distances we cannot distinguish a pinpoint from a small disc in a picture, so everything that is made up of these small discs and smaller is indistinguishable from an absolutely sharp image. The sharpest-focused part of the subject looks just like subject-matter before or behind, which is not really as sharp. Of course, sooner or later, as objects get less and less sharp away from the plane of focus, we eventually reach a distance before and behind the point of focus where we realise that the picture is no longer sharp. We can measure the distance either side of the focus plane at which the image becomes noticeably unsharp. The total distance from the closest sufficiently sharp subject to the furthest sufficiently sharp subject is called the depth of field. By actually measuring on film the diameters of the circles of light at these two extremes, we can determine just what the maximum circle diameter of a pinpoint of light can be before we find it no longer sharp. This is called the circle of confusion. Nikon choose a figure of 1/30 mm for all Nikkor lenses, and Nikkor tables and scale are computed using this figure. This works well for normal-sized enlargements from more or less the full negative area, or for looking at transparencies at a comfortable distance from the screen. If, however, you make enlargements from small parts of the negative, you may find you need to use stricter limits.

Depth-of-field scale

Let's first look at the most close-at-hand and usable depth-of-field indicator to see how depth of field and circle of confusion relate to practical picture taking. Note that apertures from *f*/4 to *f*/16 have a different engraved colour. These colours match the colours of the depth-of-field scale lines on the chrome ring just behind the distance scale ring. On the chrome ring the heavy black central line represents the focusing and distance and the full aperture of the lens. The closest lines on either side are engraved in green and indicate the depth-of-field markings for *f*/4 aperture (which is also in green). In like manner, the next lines are red for *f*/8. The *f*/11 lines are in yellow to match the yellow *f*/11 on the aperture ring, while *f*/16 lines are in blue to mark the *f*/16 on the ring. Nikkor and Nikon lenses all follow this colour coding as closely as practicable. However, always look at the aperture scale on the lens you are using, to see which colours correspond to which apertures.

If you set your focusing scale to 3 metres (10ft), what will be the focus at *f*/11? Check the distance scale numerals opposite the yellow lines which are the depth-of-field limits on either side of exact focus and full aperture. At the left side, the yellow line seem opposite 4.6 metres (15ft). On the right side, the yellow line is slightly beyond 2.1m (7ft). So at *f*/11 when the lens is set to 3m (10ft), the depth of field extends approximately from a little over 2.1m (7ft) to about 4.6m (15ft). If you were to use *f*/16 instead of *f*/11 (blue depth-of-field lines), your depth would extend from a little less than 2.1m (7ft) to nearly 9m (30ft).

This is a practical help in the field, but not exact. It is, however, far more exact than trying to determine depth of field by pushing the depth-of-field preview button and observing what is or is not sharp on the focusing screen. The focusing screen is too small and the image magnification too low for you to translate accurately what you see.

Depth-of-field tables

If you need something more exact than the scales, you can refer to the depth-of-field tables which Nikon supplies with every lens. Coming back to the same *f*/11 setting at 3m (10ft), the table will show you that the exact depth of field is 2.2m (7ft 1¼in) to 5.2m (17ft 1in). If you had followed your depth-of-field scale, you wouldn't have been very far off. However, in many instances neither depth-of-field line will be near a distance marking. Now you must interpolate, but beware: half-way-between distance settings do not indicate half-way between the distances. In other words, the mid-way point between the 1.5m and 2.1m (5ft and 7ft) markings on the focusing ring is not 1.8m (6ft). As the scale goes from closest focusing to furthest, note that the distances bunch up. The scale distance between 3m and 4.5m (10 and

15 ft), for instance, is much less than between 1.5 and 2.1. This means in terms of determining depth of field that the 1.8 m setting is closer to the marked 2.1 m engraved figure than to the 1.5. Technically, to find a correct depth of field you would have to go to the depth-of-field tables and interpolate there.

While you can achieve a fairly accurate determination of depth of field that way, you can calculate an even more accurate one if we give you the formulae for determining depth of field near depth:

$$\text{near depth} = \frac{D}{1 + Dcf/F^2}$$

and far depth:

$$\text{far depth} = \frac{D}{1 - Dcf/F^2}$$

where D = focused distance, c = circle of confusion, f = *f*/number of lens, F = focal length of lens. Remember, however, to keep all numbers either English or metric. If you are working in feet, convert your distances to inches and take 0.085 in instead of 1/30 mm for the circle of confusion and use the focal length of the lens in inches as well. Of course, for precise use of the table, the actual distance from the film plane to subject must be measured accurately by tape measure.

Practical depth of field

In practical picture-taking terms, unless you are doing architectural photography or studio work where you can take the time for precise depth-of-field determination, calculations or even reference to depth-of-field tables is seldom possible. The depth-of-field scales of the camera must be relied upon. I have been able to do this very successfully and also have managed to guarantee even better depth-of-field standards for my pictures. I call the system the safe-side depth-of-field system. At the left, the 4.6 m (15 ft) setting falls opposite the yellow line, so that I would use as my criterion. On the right, although the yellow line is just to the left of the 2.1 m (7 ft) marking and should thus give depth from just a little over 2.1 m onwards, I would take no chances and establish 2.4 m as my closest distance, thus giving me some room for error. In other words, at the left side of the depth of field use the closer footage than you would normally decide, and at the right side use a further distance.

Circle of confusion

While the depth-of-field formula appears very impressive and appears to give you an exact method of determining what is sharp and what isn't sharp in a picture, there is one very subjective number built into the formula – the circle of confusion. We have said that with Nikkon lenses it is 1⁄30 mm in diameter. The question is: who sets this criterion and what makes any of us feel that it is correct? If we set a smaller circle, while the depth wouldn't be as great at any setting, wouldn't we be able to enlarge our pictures further or look at them more closely with less chance of being dissatisfied with sharpness at the depth-of-field limits? Yes, but perhaps we're being too hard on ourselves. Perhaps the circle should be larger, meaning the depth would be greater. Would people really be able to notice the difference?

The 1⁄30 mm maximum blur circle limit isn't arbitrary; it is considered the limit of sharpness viewable if a normal-sized picture is seen at a normal viewing distance. Some manufacturers use formulae related to the focal length of the lens. These, however, assume that you're going to look at wide-angle lens pictures close to, and long-focus lens pictures from far away. In truth, you generally view all photographs at the same distances regardless of the lens with which they were taken. And the distance is, more often than not, closer than the focal-length-related formula calls for (except with wide-angle lenses).

The 1⁄30 mm formula assumes a normal enlargement and viewing distance, but we often blow up part of the negative, or look at the prints close up. The same can hold true in viewing slides at home, where we often sit our audience fairly close to the screen to impress them with the size, colour and sharpness of our projected transparencies.

Consequently, the 1⁄30 mm depth-of-field circle has come under criticism as being too generous for today's audiences. I would therefore again recommend that critical Nikon owners might well use the depth-of-field scale line or numerals for the next largest lens aperture to make certain of picture sharpness. However, if you stick to 8 × 10 prints or smaller and have a fairly small projection screen, you'll be happy with the regular depth-of-field tables and apertures.

Focus distance

If you want maximum sharpness, you must focus exactly on the right point. If not, you 'waste' some of your depth of field. Here's how. Let's say you are photographing a man standing some 5 m (16 ft) from your camera. Looking at the depth-of-field scale on your 50 mm Nikkor and Nikon lens, you see that at *f*/11 your depth of field extends from about 3 m to 9 m (10 ft to 30 ft) if you focus on the subject itself. Suppose there is no important subject matter in front of the main subject but there are some lovely mountains behind. If you maintain focus directly on your subject you are wasting the depth of field in front. You can shift the whole zone of sharp focus backward and get the mountains sufficiently sharp without any appreciable loss of sharpness of your main subject. Bring the infinity marking of your focusing mount to the

Proper use of depth of field

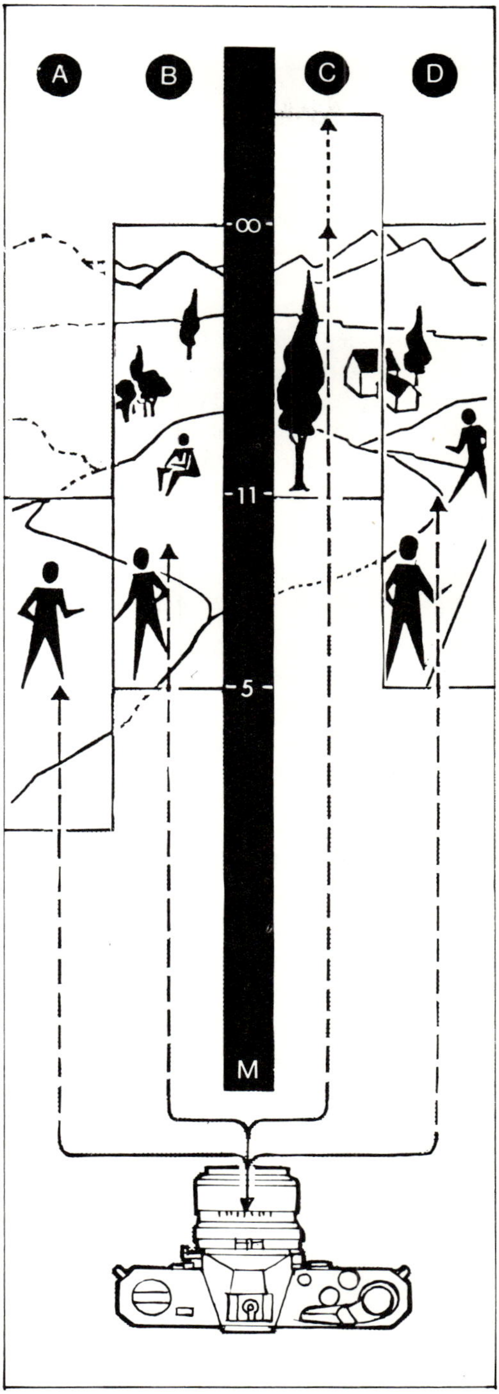

Here are two examples illustrating how you can shift your depth of field so it does more work for you.

A. Here you have focused upon a main subject at 5m (15ft). The depth of field in front of subject is wasted because there is no useful subject material. However, the landscape behind is out of focus, outside the depth of field.

B. By changing your focus setting so that the 5m (15ft) distance is at the near depth-of-field mark instead of at centre point, you have now shifted your depth of field so that it extends from your main subject backwards to infinity, thus producing an adequately sharp background.

C. Here's another case of misused depth of field. You have focused your camera at infinity for a landscape. But much of your depth of field is lost beyond the infinity point.

D. By shifting the infinity setting on the focusing mount until it coincides with the near depth-of-field mark on your lens aperture scale, you have also shifted your depth of field into a more useful position. Depth now extended from 5m (15ft) to infinity.

left-hand yellow line of *f*/11. You're set to get the mountain sharp. Now the right yellow line is still to the right of the 5 m marking, so the man is also in focus.

In other words, to make maximum use of your depth of field, place your nearest important subject not at the exact point of sharpness but at the edge of the depth of field for the aperture you are using. You then gain the additional depth behind the subject for a sharper background.

The same technique can be used in reverse to gain additional foreground sharpness. If you just set your lens to infinity, you're wasting the depth of field beyond infinity where it can never do any good at all. To achieve more foreground depth, never keep infinity marking at midpoint on the focusing scale. Always bring it left to the marked aperture line indicating the lens opening you are using. The amount of depth you gain will be appreciable.

You'll find this a bit of a problem at first, because with the lens full open, none of your subject looks sharp. After a while, though, you can begin to ignore the unsharp viewfinder when you know all the subject will be sharp on the film.

Focal length and depth of field

Regarding depth of field, there are a few myths which must be laid to rest. Many photographers believe that wide-angle lenses inherently have more depth than normal or tele lenses. This is true in some ways and untrue in others. Short-focus lenses are good for close-ups because you don't need so much extension to focus them. However, if you frame the subject in the same manner and produce the same image size on the negative as you would with a long lens, you gain no depth of field at all. Depth of field is not a function of the focal length of the lens, but of distance and aperture alone. You can only gain depth by shooting with your wider lens at the same distance as the original picture with the longer lens. Now if you enlarge the central portion of the wide-angle picture to the same image size as the picture with the longer lens, you will indeed achieve more depth. Of course, the danger is that you will lose sharpness of the picture and because you enlarge the unsharpness present in any image, possibly to a noticeable level. However, in moderate use, such as shooting with a 35 mm lens instead of a 50 mm and using very fine-grain film, you will be able to get more usable depth with the wide-angle lens at the same *f*/number when you enlarge the wide-angle picture. From any given distance, then, a long-focus lens indeed allows you less depth that a wider-angle lens – as a glance at your depth-of-field scale readily shows.

Hyperfocal distance

Before leaving depth of field, we should cover one additional important term, hyperfocal distance. When your lens is set at infinity, the hyperfocal distance is the distance between your camera and the closest acceptable point of sharpness for the aperture set. This is more useful than it sounds at first. Let's say you are using a *f*/16 with your 50 mm lens. The right-hand blue *f*/16 depth-of-field marker is just about opposite the 5 m (16 ft) numeral on the distance scale. The hyperfocal depth, then, is 5 m (16 ft). What good is that?

If you set the lens's distance scale directly to the hyperfocal distance, everything will be in focus from half the hyperfocal distance to infinity – that is from 2.3 m (7½ ft) onwards at *f*/16. Basically it is another tool to make sure that you are actually getting maximum depth-of-field sharpness in your picture with whatever aperture you are using.

The hyperfocal distance is a function purely of your effective lens aperture. (In general terms, this is the product of focal length and *f*/number.) In fact, depth-of-field tables are calculated from theoretical hyperfocal distances for each lens.

Filters

Filters tend to be divided into two categories – those for use with black and white, and those to aid colour photography. A few filters are intended for both types of films. In black-and-white photography, filters are generally employed to emphasise certain colours, by making them darker shades of grey or to de-emphasise colours by lightening them. Perhaps the most common use in black-and-white photography is to bring out clouds.

Filters for black and white

In black-and-white photography, the film renders different colours in terms of grey shades. Today's panchromatic films do a remarkable job, but two problems occur. No matter how able the film is, certain colours don't come out quite right. Secondly, in rendering colours in shades of grey, important differentiations are sometimes lost. For instance, brilliant red and bright blue, easily discernible by eye or on colour film, may turn out identical shades of grey, and be indistinguishable from one another. With various coloured filters you can change the grey shade of one colour or another to produce a needed difference.

The colour of the filter determines just what colours pass through to the film and which ones won't. Filters transmit strongly their own colour: red filters transmits red; green, green; yellow, yellow; and so on. While transmitting its own colour, the filter holds back (or absorbs) other colours. A red filter holds back blue and green, a green filters holds back red and blue, a yellow filter holds back blue, and so on. The deeper the colour of the filter, the more strongly it acts. Colour filters darken the tone in a black-and-white print of colours they hold back or absorb. Because they hold back some of the light, you have to give more exposure than you would without the filter. This lightens the tone of the colour the filter transmits.

Nikon filters

While there are many excellent filters on the market, the Nikon filters have been specially manufactured for the Nikon lenses' optical qualities and are

Filters for B & W

Here is the complete spectrum of colours as seen by your eye, by panchromatic film and various filters plus film. Yellow filter darkens blue and violet. Light green makes foliage lighter but makes red appear almost black. Orange filter lightens yellow, orange, red slightly, makes green slightly darker, darkens blue and ultra-violet considerably. Strong red filter makes red and orange nearly white, has nearly same effect on yellow. Blue is very dark, green almost black. Strong green filter makes red appear black, darkens orange, violet and blue, lightens greens and yellows.

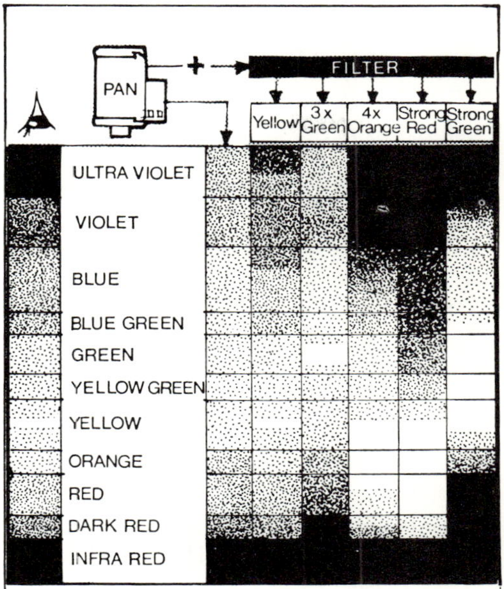

Polarising filters behave in a unique manner to dark blue skies, minimise reflections and penetrate haze. Sky is darkened only if sun is shining at 90° from sun. At noon, band of sky around horizon will be darkened. When sun drops towards sunset, note how band rises into sky keeping same 90° to sun.

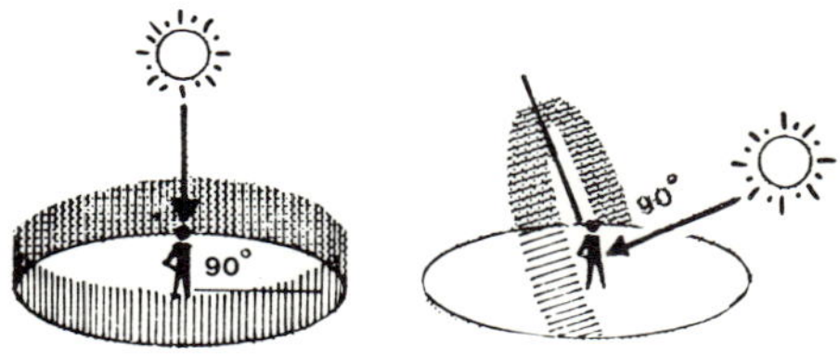

Unpolarised light striking shiny non-metallic surface at about 35° becomes polarised and can be blocked out completely with polariser at 90° from light wave.

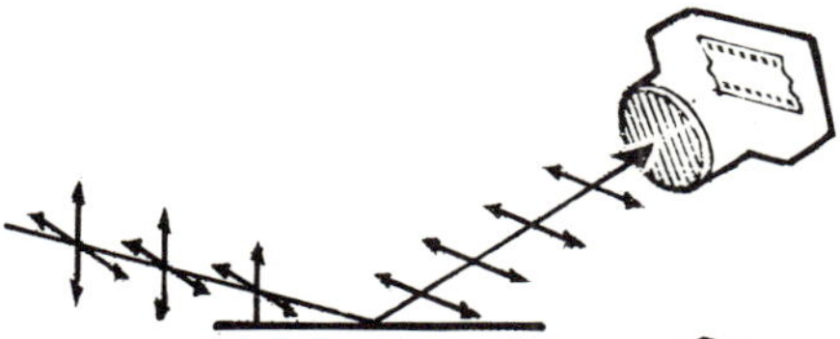

Diffused reflecting surfaces. Polarising filter has no effect on reflecting surface.

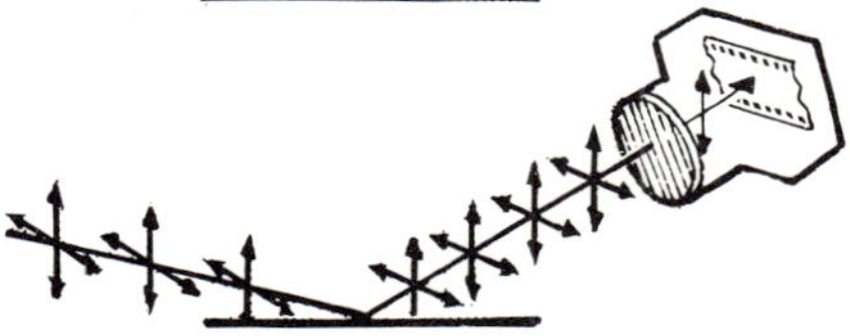

By placing polarising filter over light source, light striking glossy metal surface remains polarised, can be controlled by polariser over camera lens.

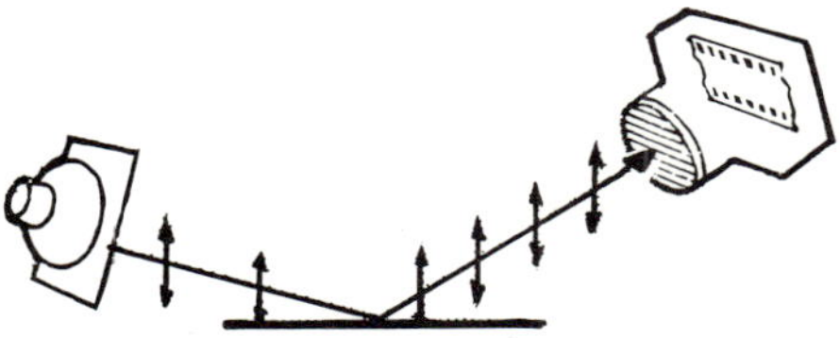

recommended. They are made of dyed-in-the-mass optical glass with both sides ground and polished, optically flat and parallel. The glass is spring-mounted in the frame to prevent strain, a fine point not always attended to by other filter makers. By far the greatest variety of filters is available for the standard 52 mm screw-in lens mount size, but a selection of filters in other screw-in or series mounts are also available. There is a complete listing at the back of this book.

All screw-in filters have a female thread at the front to accept additional lens accessories or a lens hood. Series filters are attached with a filter retaining ring and lens hood which is supplied with the lens. The filters available for lightening or darkening colours for black-and-white photography are:

Light Yellow (Y44): This filter absorbs ultra-violet radiation, violet and blue light moderately, darkening skies and thus making clouds stand out. Skin tones are rendered more natural in outdoor portraiture.

Medium Yellow (Y48): Performance is similar to light yellow, but more pronounced. This is best general yellow filter for most purposes, rendering most natural blue sky and cloud differentiation.

Deep Yellow (Y52): Performance similar to medium yellow, but effects even more pronounced, providing dramatic skies beyond the natural look.

Orange (O56): Has a wider absorption range than the yellow filters, resulting in more effect. It accentuates any subject in which yellow, orange or red predominates. It is good for aiding detail in textures of trees and sculpture.

Red (R60): Creates very striking contrasts, rendering skies almost black against black clouds, good for distant scenics, useful in infra-red photography, can provide simulation of night time if you underexpose the picture.

Light Green (X0): Absorbs ultra-violet, blue and red, darkens sky, lightens foliage, produces good skin tone, but can cause problems since it tends to cut out both blue and red simultaneously, producing both colours with about the same tone.

Deep Green (X1): Performance similar to light green, but more pronounced. Also good for cutting over-emphasis on red tones under tungsten light.

Filters for colour

So much for the black-and-white only filters. Now let's see what the problems are with colour films and why filters are needed.

Today's colour films render subjects with amazing fidelity. However, as we've seen, the colour slide or print can vary in overall rendition if the colour temperature of the lighting does not match the colour balance of the film. Colour compensation filters provide colour alterations to balance the film to the lighting, while colour-correction filters allow films of a particular balance to be used under lighting conditions for which they were not originally designed.

Colour correction

Let's look at th colour-correction filters first:

Deep Amber (A12): To be used with tungsten-balanced films when shooting outdoors in fair weather.

Medium Blue (B8): To be used with daylight film when exposed by clear flashbulbs. Filter eliminates red-yellow cast.

Deep Blue (B12): To be used with daylight films exposed with photoflood lamps indoors to avoid a strong red-yellow cast.

Colour compensation

There are two Nikon colour-compensating filters:

Light Amber (A2): To be used with daylight film when pictures are taken in the shade, in cloudy weather or indoors by north light from a window in fair weather. The filter reduces the blue tinge.

Light Blue (B2): To be used with daylight film when pictures are made three hours before sunset or after sunrise. It prevents a red-yellow cast.

Ultra-violet absorbing filters

There are three filters which can be used with both colour or black and white to reduce ultra-violet, thereby cutting haze and reducing the blue in shadow areas. These are:

Skylight (L1A): Probably the most used filter for colour film. It helps cut haze in both colour and black and white, but its principal use is to reduce the bluish cast often resulting in colour shots made in shade or in bad weather. Many photographers simply leave this filter on the lens at all times, since it can never harm the colours and may help. It protects the lens surface and require no additional exposure. There is, however, one disadvantage to this practice. The filter is a flat piece of glass right at the front of the lens. If oblique light strikes the surface, especially if it is in the slightest soiled, the filter can introduce flare. To minimise the possibility, always keep your filter spotlessly clean (and unscratched) and fit a suitable lens hood (shade).

Ultra-violet (L37): Greater haze correction than Skylight, with greater reduction of blue in shadows, produces more prominent effect in black and white than skylight. It virtually eliminates ultra-violet radiation shorter than 370 millimicrons. It's best thought of as a stronger Skylight filter.

Ultra-violet (L39): Still stronger effects than the L37 and is perhaps preferable to use with black-and-white for more pronounced differences. It should not be left on the lens at all times, as it tends to introduce a pale yellow cast to colour transparencies.

Neutral density filters

A neutral density filter cuts down the amount of transmitted light uniformly, without changing its colour. Many of the filters sold as *neutral* density are not truly so. I have examined and used many that coloured transparencies – usually a bit yellowish. The best, however, including Nikon's own filters, are genuinely neutral in tone.

Neutral density filters allow you to use a longer shutter speed, wider aperture, or both. Sometimes the light may be so bright that you need high shutter speeds and a small opening for outdoor pictures even with quite slow films. Perhaps you want to use selective focus and render the foreground or background unsharp. To allow you to open up your lens to a suitable aperture, fit a neutral density filter.

Mirror lenses, such as the Reflex-Nikkors, cannot be fitted with a conventional diaphragm, so they operate always at full aperture. Such lenses are supplied with neutral density filters (normally to fit the camera mount end) to give you alternative light transmissions.

In one other case, such a filter is essential. If you have been employing special high-speed film for indoor photography, and decide to take pictures outdoors while the film is still in your camera, the lighting may be so bright that without a filter you need higher speeds and smaller lens openings that you can set to get the right exposure.

The difference between one neutral density filter and another is the amount of illumination that they transmit. Nikon supply four strengths, ND4×, ND8×, ND10× and ND400× which transmit $\frac{1}{4}$, $\frac{1}{8}$, $\frac{1}{10}$ and $\frac{1}{400}$th of the light striking their surfaces. In normal photography, you're likely to need only 4× and 8× filters, to make 2 or 3 stop changes. However, you may find the 400× filter useful for special effects, such as using full aperture on a bright sunny day or giving several seconds' exposure to blur movement out of extant.

Polarising filters

We have deliberately left the polarising filter to last. While it is a useful filter, it is also the most difficult to comprehend. With other filters, the effect is always predictable. With polarising filters, it isn't.

Most light travels in waves, up and down, from side to side, and every way around its axis. Some light, however, is *polarised*; that is, most of it is vibrating in one plane – vertical, horizontal or somewhere in between. A polarising filter absorbs light vibrating in all planes but one. So it lets through polarised light only if the filter is aligned to pass light polarised just in that plane. To provide the photographic effects (such as reducing or eliminating reflections or darkening skies), the polarising filter absorbs or transmits light that is *already* polarised. By rotating the polarising filter you can vary the amount of polarised light transmitted from almost all to virtually none.

Luckily, many of the surfaces from which you want to eliminate reflections polarise light. For instance, light reflected from water, glass or a similar shiny surface at a suitable angle is polarised. By rotating a polarising filter over the lens you can absorb the polarised reflection from the surface and sometimes virtually eliminate it. However, reflections from the surfaces of metals are not polarised, so a polarising filter normally has no effect. Indoors, you can control metallic reflections by placing a sheet of polarising material over the light source.

A diffused surface such as a sandy beach or matt paper depolarises light. Therefore, even if polarised light strikes it, you cannot eliminate glare or reflection with a polarising filter.

Light is polarised by a shiny *non-metallic* surface if it is reflected at a suitable angle. The angle varies slightly from surface to surface, but is usually between 30° and 40°. Point the camera from the optimum angle and you can eliminate most of the reflections. At any other angle, your ability to eliminate reflections is less. For instance, if you wish to photograph through a store window which is being hit by a street light reflection, you cannot eliminate it by standing directly in front and using a polarising filter. Instead, you should move off to the side and point the camera at a 33° angle to the window.

When you use a polarising filter outdoors, the picture is again somewhat different. The sky-light 90° from the sun position is polarised in a broad band. For example, with the sun directly overhead, light from the entire horizon is polarised. When the sun goes down, the band tilts, so that at sunset (or sunrise) it forms an arch with its apex directly above you. By turning your polarising filter to a suitable angle you can darken the sky of this band, producing some very high-contrast, dramatic results. This is just as effective with colour film as with black and white. With your Nikon and Nikkormat cameras you can readily see the results through the finder as you turn the polarising filter. Be warned, however, that we are speaking of a sunlit day. No sun means no polarised light and, therefore, no effect.

Nikon makes polarising filters in 52 mm and 72 mm screw-in diameters. Polarising filters are thicker than regular filters, so you must take care fitting them to wide-angle lenses; or using additional accessories in front, such as lens-shades, since these can cause vignetting. The 72 mm polariser is especially recommended for photographers wishing to use polarising filters with moderate wide-angle lenses.

Exposure

All filters (except water-clear ultra-violet filters) absorb or fail to transmit part of the illumination. This means you must make some adjustment to get the proper exposure. Accordingly, filters are given filter factors which indicate directly the amount of additional exposure needed. If a filter has a factor of 2× it simply indicates that twice as much exposure must be given for it as without it. You could therefore either halve the shutter speed or use the next largest lens opening. You may want to employ a combination of both when employing filters with large exposure factors (such as the red, which has a factor of 6×). Trying to determine the precise factor for a polarising filter, however, is difficult, since the effect is variable with the degree of polarisation of the light. Usually the factor is between 2 and 4×.

Fortunately, few Nikon or Nikkormat owners have to compensate for filter factors. If you are using a behind-the-lens meter for your readings, the meter reads through the filter over the lens and automatically gives you more or less the correct exposure. Readings can even be made through the polarising filter with good accuracy, although these filters will not read accuately with some other SLR cameras. In a few other SLR cameras, the light path to the meter cell includes a semi-reflecting mirror or surface. These partially polarise the light and can produce an incorrect meter reading if a polarising filter is used. The Nikons and Nikkormats read from their focusing screens, and thus don't introduce this problem.

With strong-coloured filters, however, there can be some difficulty. The meter cells do not measure all colours equally well. They are calibrated to measure daylight. If you measure through a strong-coloured filter, you may not get exactly the effect the filter manufacturer expected. So, with strong colours, it is better to take a separate reading first, and alter it by the manufacturer's factor. If this gives you the same result as a reading through the filter, then you can read through it from then on.

Nikkor and Nikon lenses

Nippon Kogaku manufacture a vast range of lenses for Nikon and Nikkormat cameras. They range from a 6 mm fisheye covering an angle of 220° – literally seeing behind itself – to a 2000 mm reflex lens covering 1° 10′. Nippon Kogaku design and supervise the manufacture of every part of their lenses, including more than 200 different types of glass.

Most Nikon-made lenses are designated as Nikkors. With these lenses, the owner receives optimum optical performance, the latest advances in glass manufacturing and coating techniques, mounted in barrels, which while as compact and light as possible provide no compromises. Nippon Kogaku has also a second series of lenses called the Nikon E series which, while usually of equal optical performance, are of simpler design, mounted in compact, ultra-light barrels using plastics in non-critical areas. These lenses bear the name Nikon rather than Nikkor and are not equipped with meter-coupling prongs to operate with the older Nikon and Nikkormat cameras.

Modern developments

Many modern lenses are given multiple-layer anti-reflection coatings. Very thin layers of different chemical coatings are deposited one after another, singly or in combinations. This can reduce flare, increase light transmission, minimise ghost images and improve the colour performance of some lenses. The improvements, however, over a single-layer coating are not great except for lenses with a vast number of elements or wide aperture. Nippon Kogaku's version of multiple coating is called Nikon Integrated Coating (NIC). It is used whenever the manufacturers feel it is needed. Lenses for small format cameras are normally designed to work well at medium and long distances, so they do not produce the same image quality when focused at close objects. This is specially so with large-aperture wide-angle optics. Specially computed lenses are made, but many photographers do not wish to forsake their standard lenses for specialised optics when shooting at close distances. The problem has been overcome with designs that incorporate 'floating' rear elements. These elements are shifted precisely to compensate for close focus distances. Nikon call their system 'automatic image-quality correction'. Introduced in 1967, this system allows wide-angle lenses such as the 24 mm *f*/2.8, 28 mm *f*/2 and 35 mm *f*/1.4 Auto Nikkor lenses to maintain image quality at close focusing distances.

Three other innovations bear discussion. First, a Nikon exclusive: the use of extra-low dispersion glass in lenses, particularly telephotos (identifiable by the letters ED on their identification rings). While optical engineers have concentrated principally in correcting chromatic aberrations in camera lenses to bring the red and blue wavelengths of light to a common focus, they have usually left a certain amount of secondary colour aberration. This causes some undesirable residual light dispersion which may produce slight loss of contrast and sharpness, particularly at large apertures. The longer a lens is in focal length, the more it can be so affected.

To minimise this secondary colour aberration, many lens manufacturers have made use of calcium fluorite crystal optical elements, but Nippon Kogaku's unique development of the ED glass provides even more advantages. It maintains a constant refractive index over a wider temperature range and is therefore less liable to focus shift. It is harder and more scratch-resistant than calcium fluorite and can therefore be used as front or rear elements for optimum correction over the complete wavelength range. The Nikkor ED lenses are so fully corrected that sharpness extends even into the infra-red and therefore no infra-red focus correction is needed. ED has also made it possible to produce some lenses which are far more compact for their focal length than was previously thought possible. Producing such lenses is more costly than the regular lenses, so these remain available.

Traditionally, long tele lenses have been focused by moving a group of elements or the entire lens forward in a large cumbersome helical focusing mount. Nippon Kogaku optical engineers have overcome this problem by adopting another method of focusing: moving the lens elements internally. The helical, weight and bulk have been eliminated, convenience of focusing improved and extra correction added, particularly in image fall-off at close focusing distances. Tele lenses with internal focusing are marked with the letters IF.

Lastly, Nikon is now employing some aspherical surfaces in their high-speed lenses such as the 58 mm *f*/1.2 Noct-Nikkor whose first surface is aspheric. In most optics the curve of each element remains at constant radius over its surface. In an aspheric lens element, the curvature varies, allowing the edge light rays to come to focus at the same point as the central ones. As a result, such lenses with aspheric surfaces, particularly high-speed lenses, have far less flare and much better sharpness at large apertures.

Nikkor lenses

1. Aperture ring
2. Depth-of-field scale: Lines colour-coded to match aperture scale
3. Distance scale: Usually feet and metres
4. Screw-in thread: For accessories
5. Focus distance index
6. Focusing ring
7. Meter coupling prong: Connects aperture control ring to meter coupling pin on older cameras
8. Lens retaining ring: With detail information
9. Iris diaphragm: Controls picture-taking aperture
10. Meter coupling ridge
11. Aperture direct read-out scale
12. Locking detent: Couples with spring pin on camera
13. Auto diaphragm lever
14. Lens mount bayonet flange

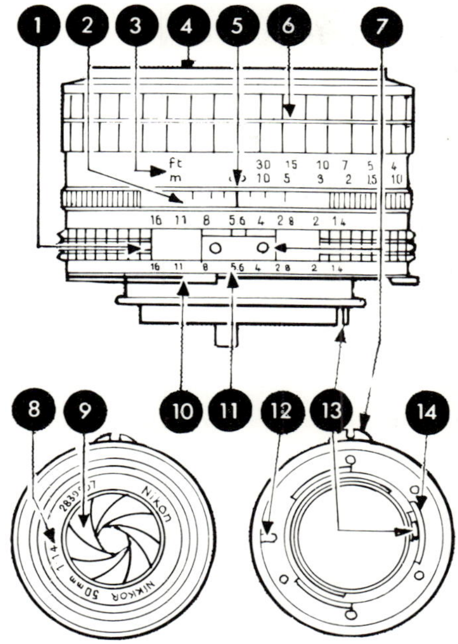

Focal length (*f*) determines image size, measured from principal points H,H′ to focal plane. Back focus (Bf) from rear of last lens element. Total length (L) has no direct effect on image. Effective lens diameter (D) is used with focal length to determine *f*/number.

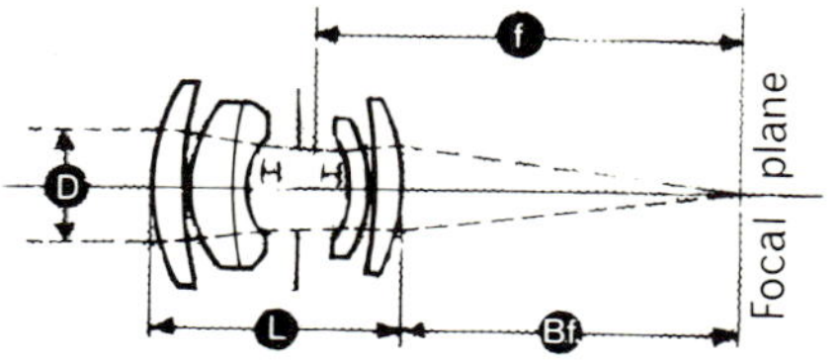

Picture angle (1) is image angle subtended by picture frame diagonal (2) at film plane. When close-focusing, picture angle decreases.

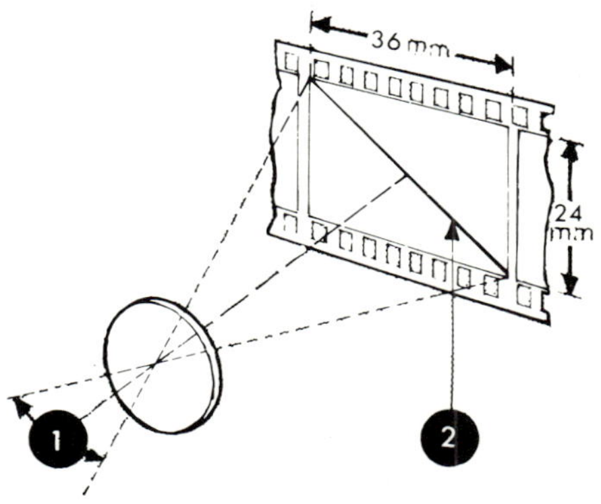

Auto indexing lenses

In 1977, Nikon introduced a new automatic maximum aperture indexing (AI) system on all their new cameras. This makes lens-to-exposure-meter coupling more convenient. Instead of the prong and pin arrangement, the new cameras have a spring-loaded lever on the front of the lens mount or below the Photomic head faceplate which automatically makes contact with a ridge on the back of the lenses. Most Nikkor lenses with prongs are now available in a revised mount with the necessary back ridge for automatic indexing. These new lenses, although called AI (for auto indexing), are not so marked. You must examine the lenses themselves to check whether they do have auto indexing.

AI lenses have three points of identification differentiating them from non-AI lenses. Most quickly seen are the two large holes on the meter coupling prong (which has been retained for full coupling on older cameras). These holes are designed to allow light from in front of the camera to reach the secondary aperture scale behind the regular aperture scale. This secondary scale, another AI identification point, is reflected by means of an optical system into the viewfinder of many new Nikon cameras and Photomic heads so the aperture can be read in the viewfinder. This is called aperture direct readout (ADR). The last method of identification is the coupling ridge, already mentioned.

Non-AI lenses can fit many of the new cameras only if these older lenses are modified to the new AI specifications through a Nikon dealer (at a moderate cost). Not all older Nikon can be so adapted. (See the 'Facts and figures' section at the back of this book for details.) Older lenses without coupling prongs cannot be modified but may be used on the new cameras exactly as they were on the old – making readings at shooting aperture.

When a non-AI lens is used on the newer auto-indexing cameras which allow it, the camera body must be set for stop down metering. With Nikons having Photomic finders, push the meter coupling lever beneath the Photomic finder's Nikon name-plate to the far right, as you look at the camera front. Afterwards, when mounting an AI lens, remember to release the lever by sliding the lever release (located just above the lever) to the right.

As a simple rule, do not expect to fit non-AI Auto Nikkor lenses to any Nikon camera lacking a depth-of-field preview control.

On all other Nikons and Nikkormats with auto indexing, prepare the camera for stop-down metering by pushing in the coupling lever release button (right front of lens mount) and lifting the adjacent coupling lever up and out of operation. Remember to flip the lever down again when refitting an AI lens. If the camera's coupling lever cannot be lifted, non-AI lenses should not be used.

To make stop-down meter readings, press and hold in the depth-of-field preview button or lever, thus closing the lens down to take the meter reading.

Lens changing and meter coupling

To remove a Nikon or Nikkormat lens, depress the release button, turn the lens clockwise and lift it out.

To replace a lens, line the focus/aperture index with the camera's lens mounting index, push in the lens and turn it counterclockwise until it locks.

To use a non-AI lens with AI camera body (or Photomic head) the coupling lever must be pushed out of the way. On the F2A and F2AS heads, push the lever up before mounting the lens. To release the coupler for fitting an AI lens, push the switch above the 'A' or 'AS' designation.

On the FE, FM, EL2 or FT3, press the release button and push in the coupler before mounting a non-AI lens. Push the coupler back towards the lens mount to return to AI coupling.

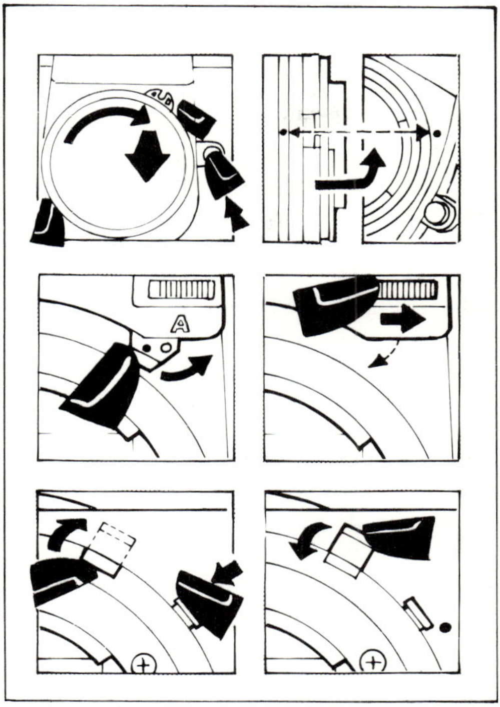

On older (non-AI) cameras, the exposure meter must be coupled to the lens' prong. Mount the lens so that its prong couples with the pin on the camera. With the Nikkormats, set the lens to *f*/5.6. The meter must then be set for the full lens aperture. Turn the diaphragm ring to the smallest aperture and then to the largest.

The maximum lens aperture should then show on the scale beside the lens mount of the FT2 or FTn, or on the Photomic finder.

On the original Nikkormat FT, match the lens' maximum aperture to the speed of the film you are using.

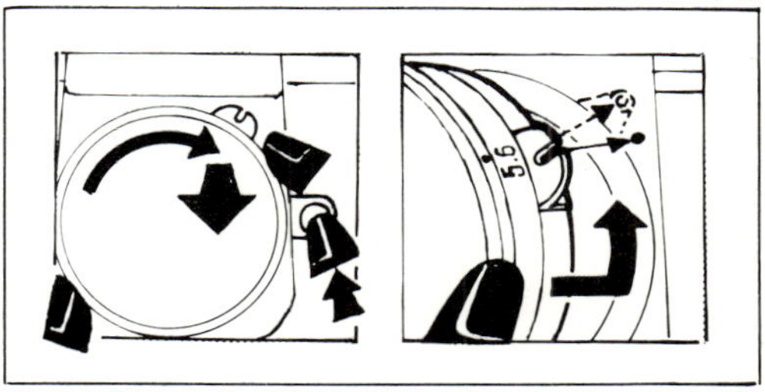

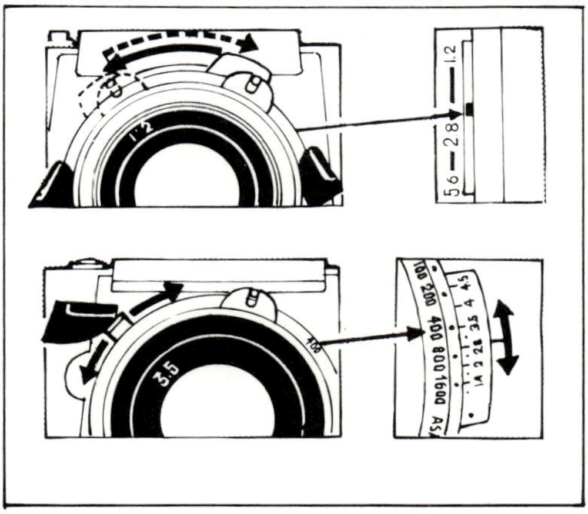

Names preceding the work 'Nikkor' on a lens indicate optics made for special purposes. Fisheye-Nikkor lenses show an extreme wide angle with distorted circular image. The PC Nikkors feature perspective control. A Zoom Nikkor can be used over a range of focal lengths. A Reflex Nikkor contains both mirror and lens components. An EL-Nikkor is for enlarging. As we'll see later, however, many special-purpose Nikkors have excellent uses outside their primary design fields.

Aperture markings on Nikon and Nikkor lenses can be confusing to the tyro. They are generally written with a 1 followed by a colon (:) followed by another number. This is because the aperture of each lens is actually a ratio – e.g. 1:1.2 for an *f*/1.2 lens. This can be confusing at first glance: the figures 1:4 do not mean an *f*/1.4 lens, but rather an *f*/4.

The focal length of each lens may be indicated with an equal sign. For example, a 50 mm lens is labelled f = 50 mm. Lastly, each lens has its own serial number (as does the camera body). You should always keep a list of all your serial numbers for insurance purposes or to aid in case the camera is lost or misplaced.

Aperture and focus settings are engraved on the appropriate control rings. They both align with the same central dot.

Lens mounting

To grip for lens changing, wide-angle and normal focal length lenses have knurled matt-chrome rings just forward of the aperture control ring. The lens mount itself uses a three-tab bayonet requiring a ⅙ counterclockwise revolution of the lens to seat and lock in on the camera body. To fit a lens, you match up the meter coupling prong (at *f*/5.6) or *f*/number index dot on the lens barrel with the index mark on the front plate of the Nikon, or dot on the Nikkormat. When the *f*/number index on the lens is at top centre position mounted on the camera body, a slot on the rear of the lens locks in place over the camera body's spring-loaded locating pin. When removing a lens with a corresponding ⅙ clockwise revolution, this locating pin must first be retracted by pushing on the lens release button on the camera body. When mounted properly the Nikkor lenses fit snugly, with no play.

Stop-down metering lenses

There are a few Auto-Nikkors which do not have a meter coupling pin or auto indexing. Meter readings with them must be made by closing down the diaphragm to shooting aperture. These are the older models of the 55 mm *f*/3.5 Micro-Nikkor when used for 1:1 magnification with the M2 extension ring, 200 to 600 mm Zoom, the 400 mm *f*/4.5, 600 mm *f*/5.6, and 800 mm *f*/8 Nikkors.

Accessories

Nippon Kogaku have tried to standardise, as far as possible, on the front accessory threads of their lenses. Most accept 52 mm threaded accessories such as filters, lens caps and close-up lenses. Care must be taken, however, in selecting the proper lens hoods (shades) for each lens. The mere fact that the hood is of the proper attaching diameter does not mean it has the correct angle. The angle of acceptance of the hood must match the angle of acceptance of the lens. If it is too wide, it will not be efficient; if too narrow, it will cause darkening of the picture corners, the edges, or both. Nikon hoods are generally marked with indications as to which lenses they should be used with.

Focal length

The focal length of a lens determines the size of the image that will be reproduced on the film. From any given camera-to-subject distance, short-focal-length lenses produce smaller images on the film than do longer ones.

Just what is focal length and how is it determined? Light rays from infinity pass through a lens parallel along the optical axis, and converge at a point called the focal point. Focal length is the distance from the optical centre of a lens (or its rear nodal point) to the focal point where the image is formed. Usually the rear nodal point is within the lens, but seldom coincides with the physical centre of the lens. The distance from the back of a lens to the film plane is known as the back focal distance, and from that mechanical mounting point the flange focal distance. This is a most important linear measurement because it determines whether a lens focuses properly when fitted on the camera body. The flange distance in the Nikon-Nikkormat system is 46.5 mm.

Angle of view

In discussing different focal-length lenses, we often differentiate between them by the angle of view which they deliver. Long-focal-length lenses, or 'teles', see a very narrow angle of view, while wide-angle lenses see just that – a wide angle of view. This angle is actually the picture angle at the image side principal point subtended by the diagonal of the picture frame – 43.2 mm in a 24 × 36 mm frame (which is considered the standard for a 35 mm camera such as the Nikon or Nikkormat). Sometimes angles are given for the vertical or horizontal measurement of the picture area; but always the diagonal unless otherwise specified. In this book all angles given are measured at the picture diagonal with the lens set at its infinity focus. This must be specified since the angle of view does decrease somewhat as you focus closer. Incidentally, for maximum optical performance, Nikkor and Nikon lenses are designed to give a full definition in a circle just more than 43.2mm diameter and are not designed to cover any much larger picture format.

Aperture

Lens aperture, *f*/number and speed of lenses all mean the same thing in practice. The aperture is the hole through which light passes. It is formed by the diaphragm leaves and altered by moving the aperture ring. The larger the aperture, the more light can pass through the lens. The effective aperture can be thought of as the diameter of the 'bundle' of light rays that pass through the front element of the lens, *and* through the aperture in the diaphragm. This rather complicated definition is needed because the aperture is effectively enlarged or reduced by the elements in front of it.

For practical measurement we use *f*/numbers. The *f*/number is simply the diameter of the effective aperture divided into the focal length of the lens. It may be written in a number of ways – e.g. *f*/, f/8 or 1:8. Apertures are usually calibrated on a scale of *f*/numbers running 1, 1.4, 2, 2.8, 4, 5.6, 8, 11, 16, 22, 32 and 64. Each step indicates a transmission of either twice as much light or half as much light as the adjacent number. Most lenses start and finish their aperture range within this scale. The maximum aperture of a lens is often loosely called its speed. The large the aperture (lower *f*/number), the more light can pass, and the faster the lens is said to be. For instance, *f*/2.8 lets in twice as much light as *f*/4 and four times as much light as *f*/5.6 but only half as much light as *f*/2. The *f*/stop markings on the Nikkor aperture rings are equi-distantly spaced and click-positioned at these marked apertures. However, you can set lens opening mid-way between any markings. The maximum aperture is marked on each Nikkor lens as 1:8 or 1:1.4, etc. A number of Nikkor lenses, such as the 55mm *f*/1.2 or 105mm *f*/2.5, have maximum apertures which do not fall precisely on these numbers. The rest of their apertures, however, do fall on the scale; including unmarked click positions on the aperture scale indicating the *f*/1.4 and *f*/2.8 apertures on the two lenses above.

Lenses are produced with intermediate maximum apertures because the apertures is limited by the lens design. When the design constrains the maximum aperture to somewhere between stops, it would be wasteful to restrict its use to the next smaller aperture.

The *f*/stop is a physical indication of the lens's ability to transmit light. However, this is a theoretical figure, not an actual measurement of the light transmitted. While for all practical picture-taking purposes we do rely on the *f*/stop for making our exposures, true light transmission as measured at the film plane is generally given in 'T' (transmission) stops. The T-stop of a lens is always smaller than the *f*/stop. The difference is negligible in practical picture-taking, but inevitably the term T-stop will come up, so it's worthwhile knowing what it is.

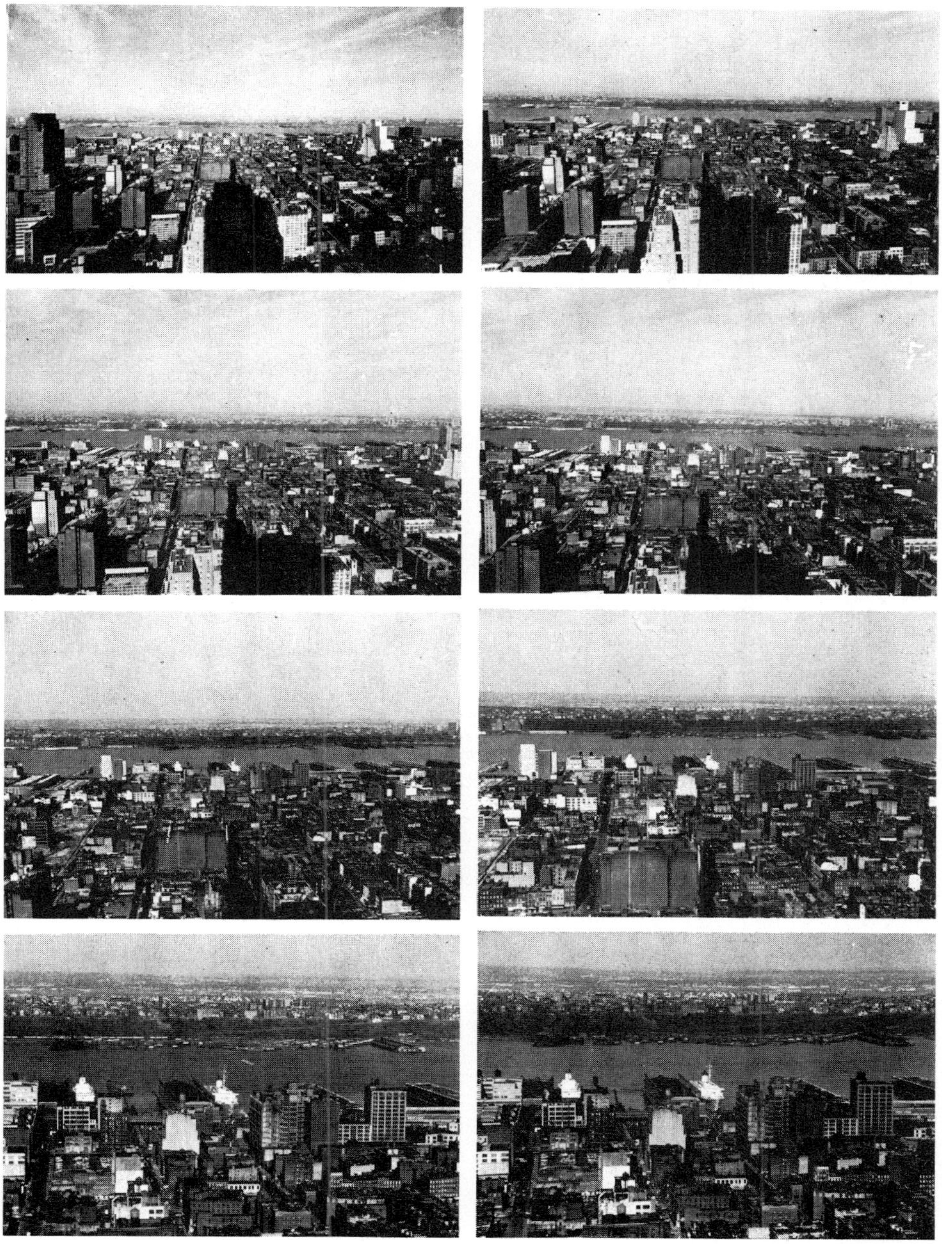

Left to right, top to bottom. 15, 20, 24, 28, 35, 50, 85, and 105 mm lens.

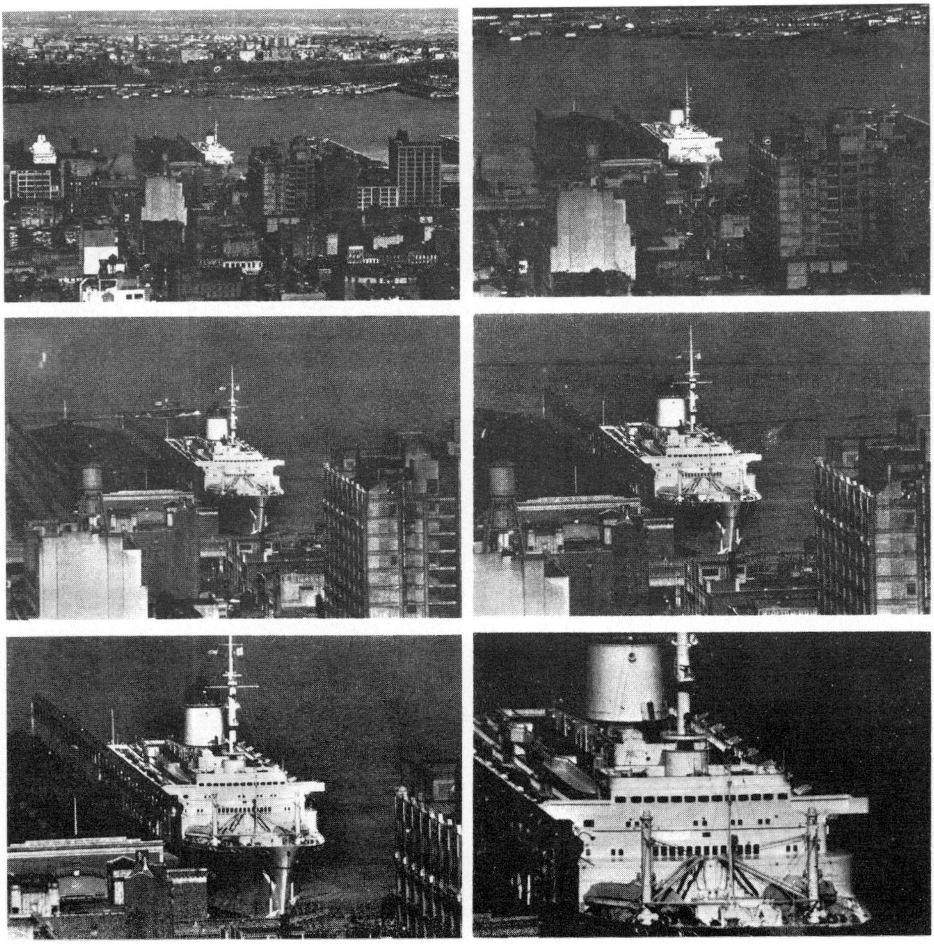

Focal lengths change distance

A New York harbour scene photographed with lenses from an ultrawide 15 mm covering 110° to a 1000 mm on this and the last page limited to a narrow 230′. To use this series of photos properly, locate the normal 50 mm scene and note how much change various focal lengths make.
Left to right, top to bottom, 135, 200, 300, 400, 500 and 1000 mm lenses. Choose your additional lenses accordingly.

While the foregoing series of photographs, all taken from the same viewpoint and distance from the subject illustrate the angles of coverage, the series of photographs on the next two pages by Mitchell Funk indicate the change in apparent perspective with different focal lengths.

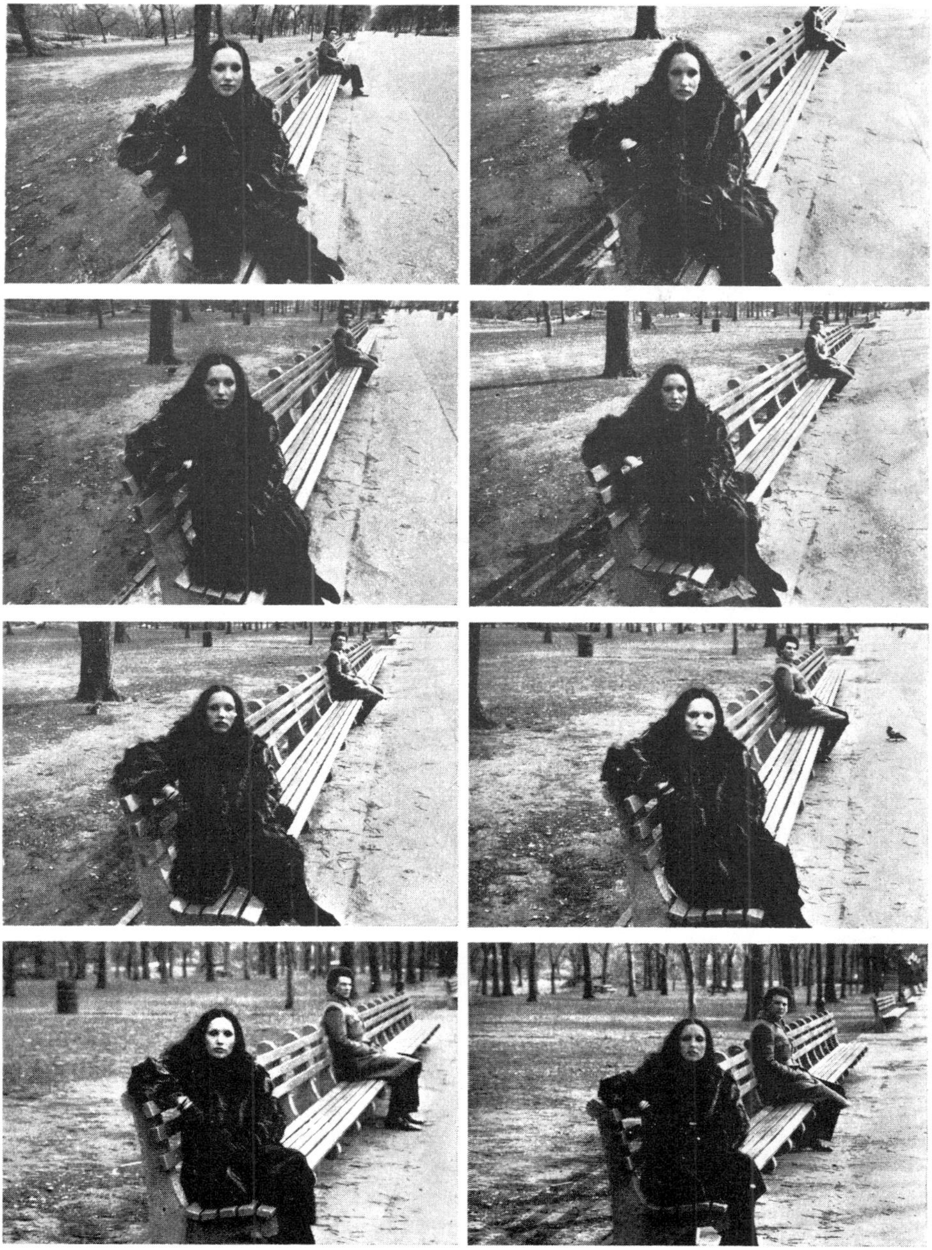

Left to right, top to bottom. 15, 20, 24, 28, 35, 50, 85, and 105 mm lens.

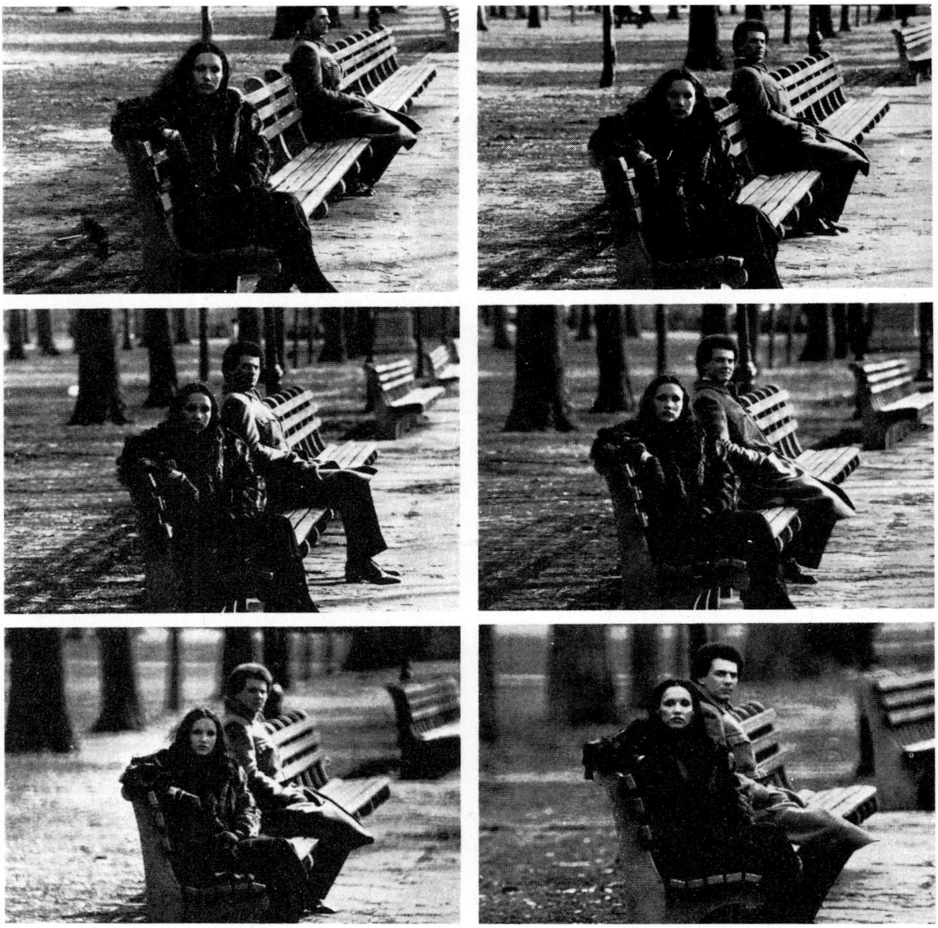

By varying the distance from the camera to principal subject – the girl in the foreground – so that she remains the same image size in each picture with each lens, the amount of apparent elongation between her and the young man sitting behind her on the same bench can be varied immensely. This series of photographs illustrates the apparent distorted elongation of distances possible with wide-angle lenses and the apparent perspective for shortening with telephoto lenses. However, even with the vast apparent disparities in distance between the two figures in these photos, all would look precisely alike if viewed at the right distance from this page. The viewing distance should be the focal length of the lens times the magnification of the print. Here the prints are 2×. Try it and see!
Left to right, top to bottom. 135, 200, 300, 400, 500 and 1000 mm lenses.

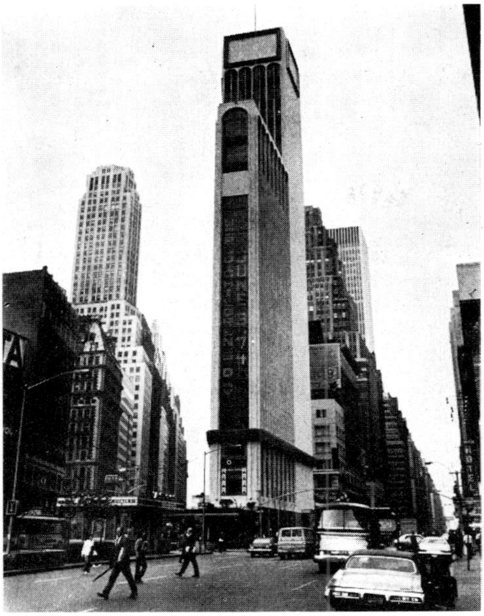

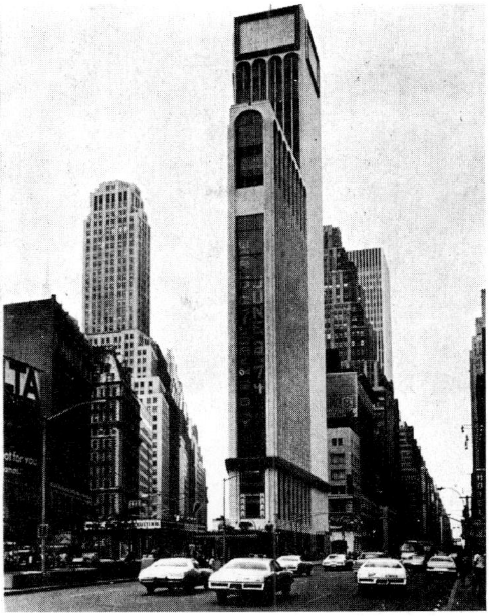

Verticals

When a camera is pointed upwards to include an entire building or to centre it in the picture (left), vertical parallel lines, at the edge, appear to converge toward the picture top, thus making the building appear to fall over backwards. To prevent this phenomenon, the camera back must be kept plane parallel to the buildings and the lens itself shifted upwards towards the buildings. Using a 35 mm *f*/2.8 PC Nikkor, the author corrected the view at right.

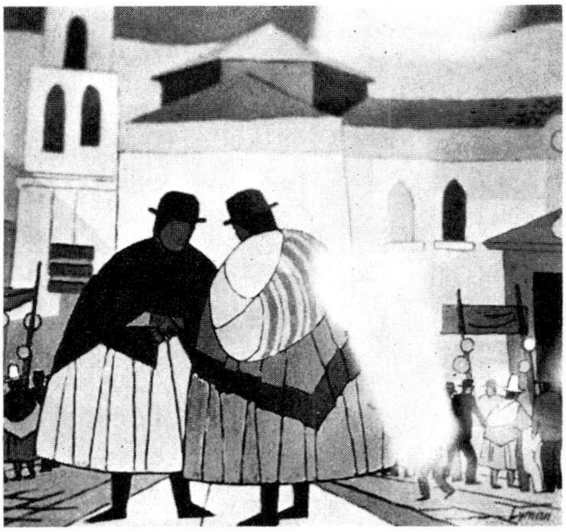

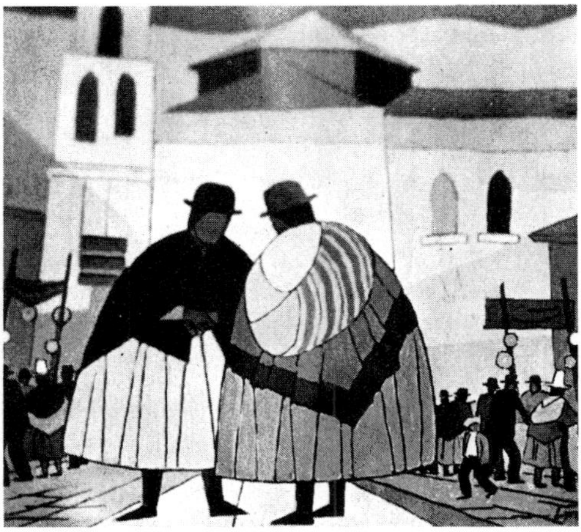

Reflections

When standing directly in front of glass-covered artwork front illumination can cause a bad reflection (left). Sometimes the photographer himself may be mirrored in the glass. To minimise this reflection or prevent the photographer's image from appearing, move to the side of the artwork, keeping the film plane parallel. Then shift the PC Nikkor lens towards the artowrk until it is centred properly (right).

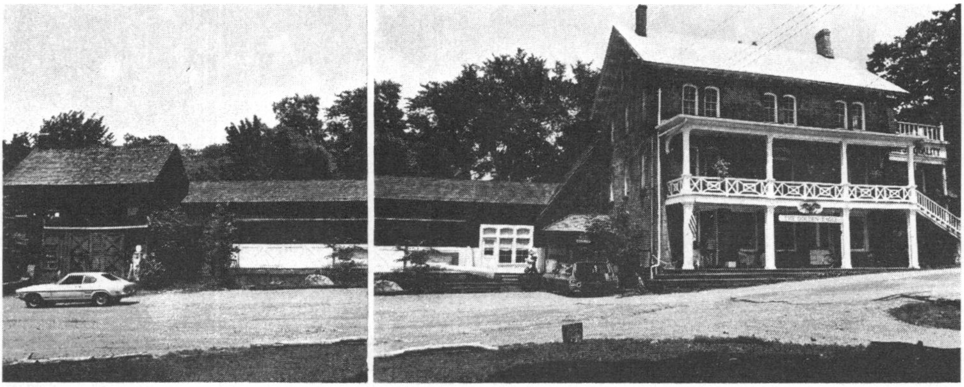

Panoramic view by swinging camera

If you take one picture, then swing the camera to make a matching one, you'll find the two photos will not line up in the centre, as above.

Panoramic view using PC Nikkor

Take first picture with PC lens shifted far right. Then take second with shift far left. Join them. They will match exactly.

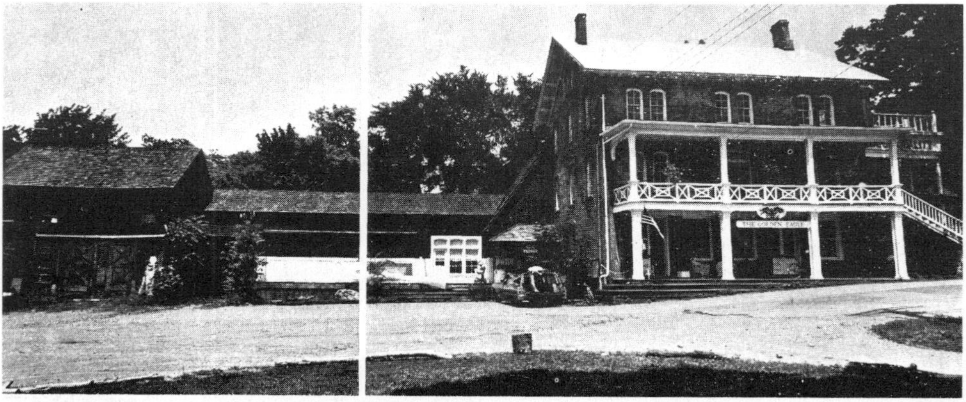

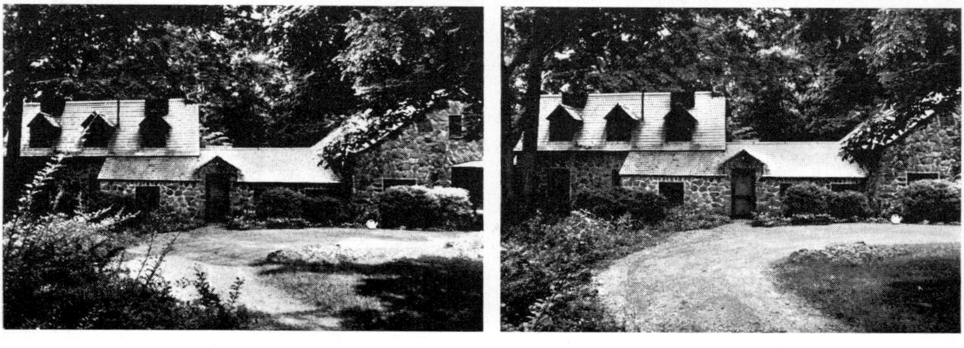

Eliminating unwanted foregrounds

Scruffy foreground bushes in lower left-hand corner of picture (left) were eliminated by shifting PC Nikkor lens and moving to the right (right).

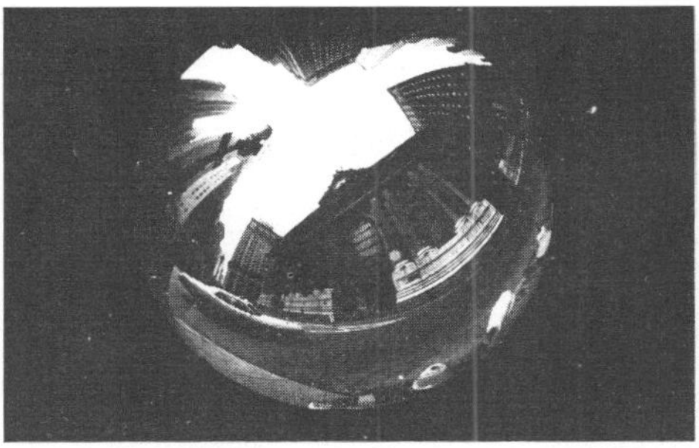

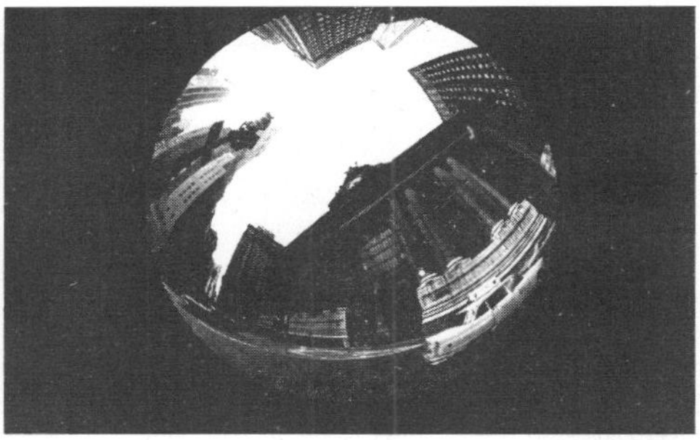

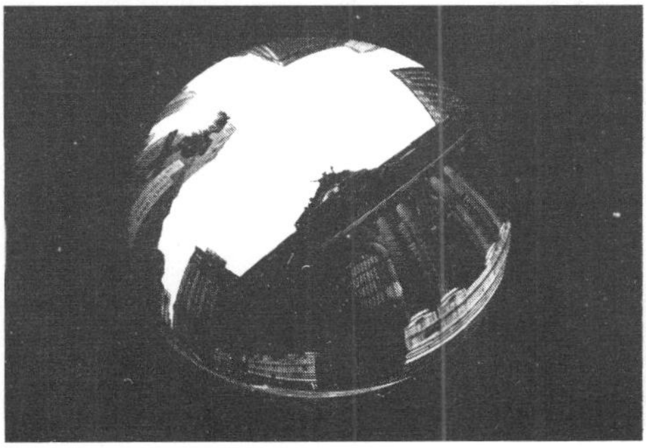

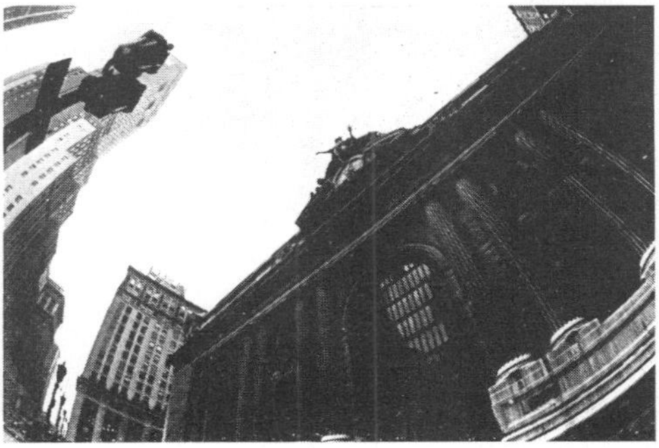

Using the fisheyes

What coverage differences are there between the four different Nikkor fisheye lenses? Joe Marvullo managed to round up all four lengths. Top left is 6 mm fisheye view of famous New York City landmark, Grand Central Station; top right, same view with 8 mm fisheye. The 10 mm *f*/5.6 OP fisheye, above left, records an orthographic projection of the image in which the amount of subject curvature is continuous as opposed to the varying curvature of other fisheyes. The 16 mm view, above right, fills the entire picture frame. Below, a well known auto front becomes a caricature through the author's 8 mm fisheye. Camera to subject distance was inches from the radiator.

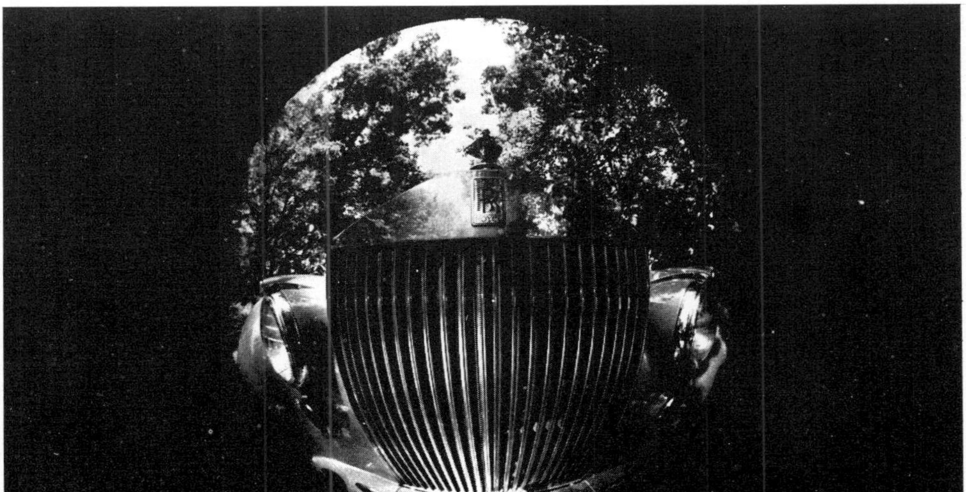

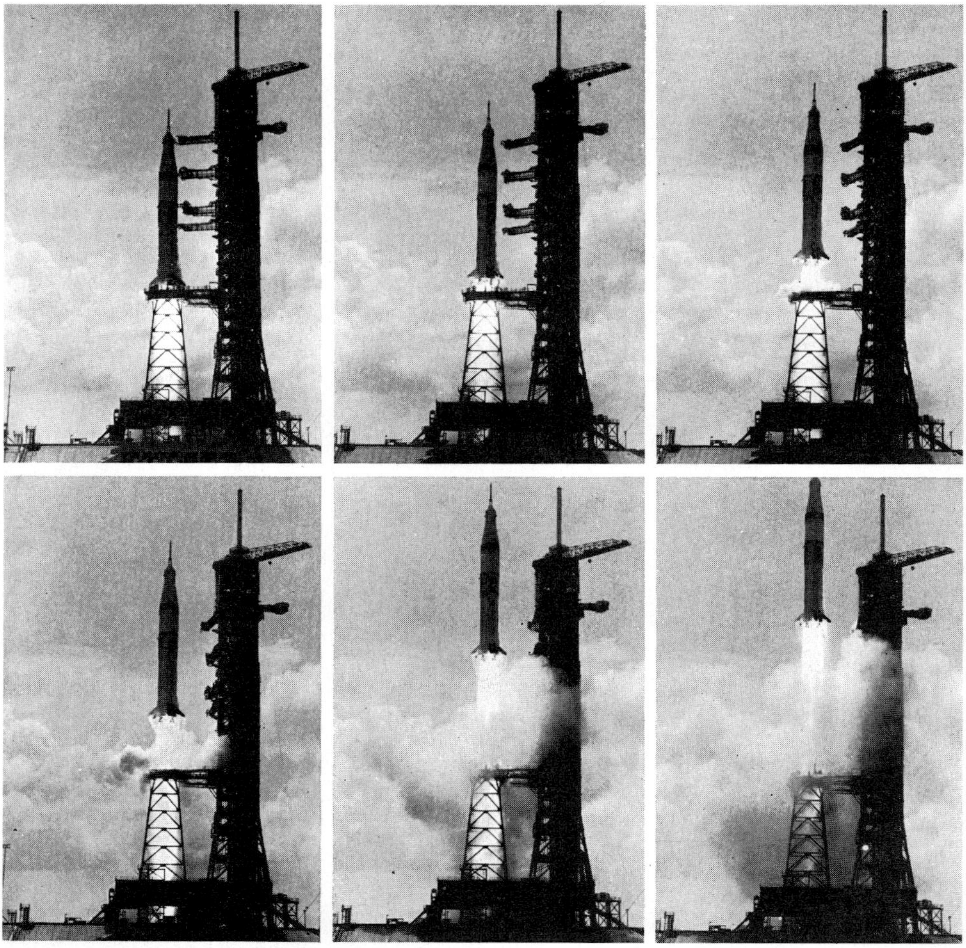

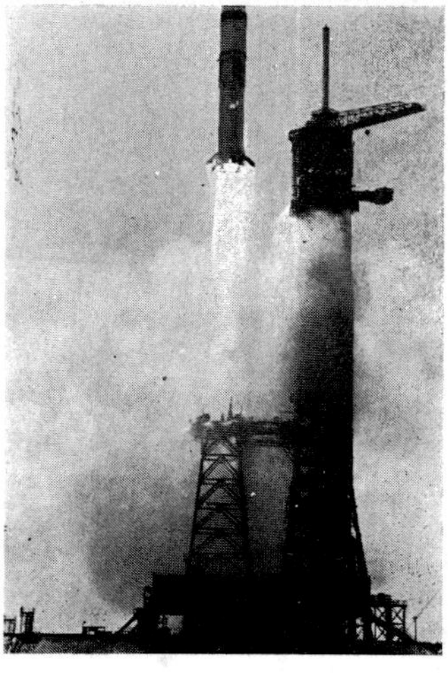

Motor drive sequence

While there are many uses for the Nikon motor drives, especially sports, it is particularly useful to record once-only events at high speed from which selected frames can be chosen later. Joe Dimaggio, JoAnne Kalish and Ron Thompson collaborated on this Nikon F2 sequence of an Apollo rocket launching using a 55 mm *f*/3.5 Micro Nikkor and a MD-2 motor drive at 3 frames per second.

Focusing

Set at its focal length from the film plane, a lens focuses subjects at infinity. To focus nearer subjects, it must be moved further away. Nikkor and Nikon lenses are almost all built in helical focusing mounts. As you turn the focus ring, you move the lens further from (or closer to) the film plane. Normally you can see the focus through the viewfinder, but Nikkor and Nikon lenses have a focus scale as well. The figures line up against the central index to show the distance on which the lens is focused. Most distance markings are given in both feet and metres. However, lenses for specific markets may be marked only in one or the other. Directly adjacent to the scale index on each lens are colour-coded depth-of-field scale lines which match in colour the aperture markings on the aperture rings. This colour coding provides a swift method of determining depth of field at any aperture and distance.

The focusing distance scale on each lens represents the distance from the object right to the film plane (not to the front of the lens). For purposes of measurement, you'll find a small circle with white horizontal line engraved on the top plate of each Nikon or Nikkormat camera except the Nikon F2. The line represents the placement of the film within the camera and can be used for accurately measuring object distances. On the F2, the top edge of the serial number digits represent the film plane.

Nikkor and Nikon lenses (except the ED and reflex Nikkors) have red dot or line infra-red scale markings to the left of the standard central focus indicator. You'll have to look closely, since these dots or lines are very small.

You need these marks for infra-red work, because infra-red rays focus at a point further from the film than light. As a result, you should use the red dot or line in place of the central focusing index when shooting with infra-red film. In other words, footages should be set manually, not by regular focusing. However, if you are using apertures of *f*/8 or smaller on standard or wide-angle lenses, the depth of field will cover the discrepancy between the infra-red focus and visual focus.

Choice of focal length

The focal length you need depends on the work you are doing. Some 'experts' say that 35 mm is best for everyday use, others argue in favour of 85–90 mm. The compromise that SLR manufacturers have accepted is to call lenses in the 45–55 mm range 'standard'. These focal lengths produce pictures which, when viewed normally, give an impression of perspective, closely matching the apparent view of the human eye. Nikon's three principal general all-purpose lenses in this category are the 50 mm *f*/1.4 and *f*/1.8 Auto-Nikkors, the 55 mm *f*/1.2 Auto-Nikkor and the 50 mm *f*/1.8 Nikon Series E. Also often used as a general-purpose lens is the 55 mm *f*/2.8 Micro-Nikkor.

We'll cover this in the 'special-purpose' category, and herewith discuss the principal all-purpose lenses which are differentiated mainly by their maximum apertures.

Optical performance

Ideally, every lens should be able to gather the light rays at the subject and form an exactly accurate image in the proper shape and colour on the film plane – centrally and right to the corners of the picture area. However, it isn't optically possible to reach this ideal. Light rays do not always go precisely where the designers might wish. The slight unwanted deviation of the rays is generally referred to as the aberrations of the lens. For the purpose of simplification, we'll divide aberrations into six types: chromatic aberrations, spherical aberrations, astigmatism, curvature of image field, and distortion. No lens is completely free from all of these aberrations, but lenses are judged on just how well they are corrected for these aberrations.

We don't want to get too involved in aberrations, but it's useful to know more or less what their effects can be. Chromatic aberrations cause colour-fringing around images. Spherical aberrations produce flare of bright objects and possible shift of focus at various apertures, and may spread light pinpoints or circles to become streaks (particularly at picture edges). Astigmatism turns images, particularly in the picture corner, to blurry streaks. Curvature of field causes the plane of sharp focus to become a curve rather than a flat plane, so making overall sharpness centre and edge difficult to achieve. Distortion results in straight lines curving inwards or bowing outwards. Note: parallel lines, as in a building, seeming to run together, is not distortion but apparent perspective distortion. This is not a lens fault but a picture-taking effect, as we'll see later on.

Resolution

How are we to classify the quality and ability of a lens? The most commonly known method is in terms of the lens's resolution – its ability to photograph separate lines of different thickness and adjoining white areas clearly. Usually a series of vertical and horizontal line patterns is photographed in groups. The patterns begin with large thick lines and gradually diminish to small thin pairs of lines. The smallest pair of lines disposed both horizontally and vertically which can be distinguished on film is known as the lens's maximum resolution. It is generally expressed in the number of lines that can be resolved (seen clearly under a microscope) per millimetre.

While this might at first seem a very logical objective method of demanding a lens's resolution, there are many variables such as the size of the charts, the distances at which they are photographed, the contrast of brightness between the lines and background, the illumination, the film used,

Lens faults and testing

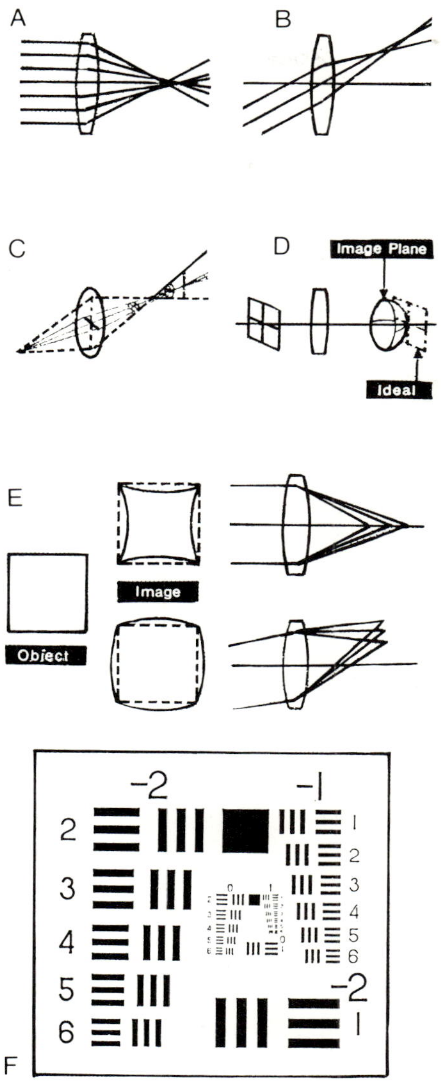

A. Spherical aberration: Light rays through lens edge and centre may not focus on single plane. Can be corrected somewhat by closing down lens.

B. Coma: Off centre light rays focus at different points causing unsymmetrical light blurs often resembling teardrops instead of circles. Can be minimised by using smaller lens opening.

C. Astigmatism: Horizontal and vertical lines focus at different points. At smaller apertures, increased depth of field masks problem.

D. Curvature of field: Sharpest image not on flat plane so it is not possible to obtain sharp image of entire subject. Closing down lens extends depth of field masking this problem.

E. Distortion: If image magnification increases outwardly through lens, a square object is rendered in shape of pincushion. If magnification decreases outward, lines of square bulge outward causing 'barrel distortion'. Closing down lens does not improve distortion.

F. Traditional lens test: Maximum number of lines that a lens can resolve (horizontally and vertically) is determined by photographing resolution chart such as this one.

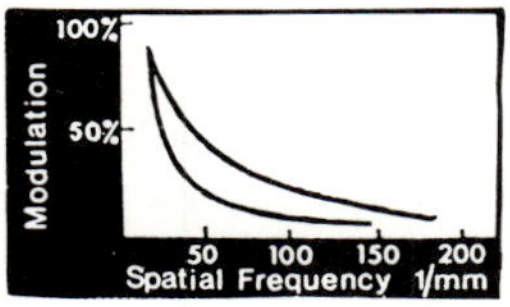

Modern lens testing: Using electronic means, the lines per millimeter resolution can further be expressed in terms of its modulation transfer response function or, simply put, contrast.

the method of focusing, the processing of the film, and the magnification of the examined image. If you add to these variables the eyesight and judgement of the person reading the test patterns, you have some indication of the problems involved in coming up with any sort of objective information. In addition, the resolution is different at centre, edges and in the picture corners; and varies with every aperture selected. Moreover, recent optical studies indicate that resolution is but one aspect of measuring a lens's quality. Optical engineers now lean more heavily on measuring resolution electronically in terms of a lens's contrast.

As you can readily see, unless tests are carried out with rigid standards for every lens tested, no valid comparisons can be made between lenses. Indeed, wide-angle lenses cannot be directly compared with teles or normal lenses, mirror lenses with all-glass lenses, or large-aperture lenses with moderate-aperture lenses. More-or-less maximum optical ability is required from each lens, depending on its use. For instance, it is important for an *f*/1.2 normal lens to yield acceptable results at full aperture. To do this it may sacrifice some degree of resolution, contrast and freedom from aberrations in order to allow pictures to be taken under very poor light. Better correction and higher resolution may be expected from a 55 mm *f*/2.8 micro-focusing lens in return for a sacrifice of speed.

The standards by which lenses are tested by their own manufacturers is seldom released, since each make has his own methods of determining these and would rather not have his results compared with another manufacturer's lenses and results achieved in a different manner.

While to a great extent the reputation of the manufacturer must be relied upon for the quality of the lenses produced, there are two optimum optical points on which all lens makers do agree. Large-aperture lenses are more difficult to compute and make than smaller-aperture lenses, so smaller-aperture lenses from the same maker usually give slightly better performance. Secondly, general-purpose lenses for 35 mm photography do not give their very best performance at maximum aperture, because of residual aberrations present. The optimum aperture for a lens, for best possible quality, is usually two or three *f*/stops smaller than its maximum aperture. All Nikkor and Nikon lenses are designed to give professional-quality results at full aperture or wide open, but, even so, do better at smaller apertures. Usually, there are two or three *f*/stops that give more-or-less equal optimum resolution. After this, closing down further, quality begins to drop off slowly – although again, not enough to discourage you from using the smaller apertures.

Lenses also behave best at specific focusing distances. Lenses for 35 mm cameras are usually corrected for an infinity distance, which provides highest optical ability from infinity to about 26 times the focal length of the lens. Most such lenses are not really suitable for close-up work, although they can be used for it. To accommodate photographers who wish to have the best possible results in close work, Nippon Kogaku has provided a variety of lenses such as the 55 mm *f*/2.8 or *f*/3.5 Micro-Nikkor, 120 mm *f*/4 IF or 200 mm *f*/5.6 Medical Nikkor, 105 mm *f*/4 Micro-Nikkor and 200 mm *f*/4 IF Micro-Nikkor. These lenses not only produce excellent close-up definition, but are remarkably free from linear distortion. Except the Medical Nikkor, they can be used for distant subjects with no loss of image quality. Of the more general all-round lenses also quite capable of good close-up performance, you can choose between the 50 mm Nikon and Nikkor *f*/1.8 lenses. However, if you intend to concentrate on close-up work, you'll probably want one of the former lenses.

So these are basically the optical problems of lenses; but how do they affect you? You will almost certainly find that any Nikon or Nikkor lens produces superb image quality, even under the most adverse conditions. In fact, most photographers are perfectly happy with the results from lenses which are considerably inferior in measured performance. If, however, you are proposing to use your equipment at the limits of its performance, you undoubtedly need the best optical quality you can get. Another point is that lower-cost lenses (of the same nominal specification) are liable to vary more between one example and another than the Nikkor and Nikon optics. You should bear in mind these considerations (and the mechanical constraints we mentioned earlier) when choosing your lenses.

Flare

Flare around a subject can be caused by aberrations. Overall flare in part or all of the picture can also be caused by light reflected from the camera body, the lens elements, or the inside of the lens barrel. This light may be part of the subject, or it may come from just outside the subject area. The larger the aperture and the more lens elements, the greater the possibility. Of course, such flare does depend on the brightness of the extraneous light involved. The effect is to reduce contrast, sometimes even to the extent of fogging the film. While deliberate use of flare can produce some interesting high-key results, most flare is unwanted, undesirable and detrimental to picture quality. In particular, light reflected back through the diaphragm of the camera and thence back again to the film can cause bright spots, which are images of the diaphragm aperture.

Flare can be eliminated by preventing the extraneous light from entering the lens, using a lens hood (shade). However, this cannot affect flare from light sources within the subject area. Modern lens coating techniques have helped immeasurably, reducing reflections from lens element surfaces to less than 1 per cent.

Normal lenses

50 mm f/1.4 Nikkor 7 elements in 5 groups, 46° picture angle, graduated in both metres and feet to 0.45 m and 1.5 ft (older models to 0.6 m and 2 ft), *f*/16 minimum aperture, fully automatic diaphragm, meter coupling prong for non-auto indexing cameras, 52 mm accessory size, dimensions 64 mm diameter × 49 mm length (2½ in × 1¹⁵⁄₁₆ in), weight 255 g (9 oz).

This is probably the most famous of all Nikkor lenses, if not the most famous SLR lens of all time. The first *f*/1.4 Nikkor for the Nikon F had a slightly different formula, yielding a 58 mm focal length. The current design yields 50 mm length. The *f*/1.4 aperture provides a bright, easy-to-focus image in the viewfinder. The displacement of focus resulting from stopping the lens down to a small aperture is virtually absent. At maximum aperture, there is a small amount of flare which disappears at *f*/2.8 or smaller openings.

50 mm f/1.8 Nikkor 6 elements in 5 groups, 46° picture angle, graduated in metres and feet to 0.45 m and 1.5 ft, *f*/16 minimum aperture, fully automatic diaphragm, meter coupling prong for non-auto indexing cameras, 52 mm accessory size, dimensions 63.5 mm diameter × 48 mm length (2½ in × 1⅞ in), weight 220 g (7.8 oz).

50 mm f/1.8 Nikon Series E 6 elements in 5 groups, 46° picture angle, graduated in both metres and feet to 0.6 m and 2.25 ft, *f*/22 minimum aperture, fully automatic diaphragm, 52 mm accessory size, dimensions 62.5 mm diameter × 33 mm length (2½ in × 1⁵⁄₁₆ in), weight 135 g (4.8 oz).

50 mm f/2 Nikkor (discontinued) 6 elements in 4 groups, 46° picture angle, graduated in metres and feet to 0.45 m and 1.5 ft, *f*/16 minimum aperture, fully automatic diaphragm, meter coupling prong for non-auto indexing cameras, 52 mm accessory size, dimensions 63.5 mm diameter × 50.5 mm length (2½ in × 2 in), weight 220 g (7.8 oz).

Perhaps the most versatile of the normal lenses, although slower than the *f*/1.4, aberrations are corrected to a greater degree. Even at full aperture, flare is virtually eliminated. The lenses are noted for high resolution, outstanding colour rendering and good results with minimum distortion in close-up work using bellows or tubes. The newer *f*/1.8 lenses have higher contrast and more even illumination.

50 mm f/1.2 Nikkor 7 elements in 6 groups, 46° picture angle, graduated in both metres and feet to 0.5 m and 1.7 ft, *f*/16 minimum aperture, fully automatic diaphragm, meter coupling prong for non-auto indexing cameras, 52 mm accessory size, dimensions 70.5 mm diameter × 59 mm length (2¾ in × 2⁵⁄₁₆ in), weight 390 g (13.8 oz).

This lens has the widest aperture, brightest viewing and focusing image of any Nikkor lens. Because of its very shallow full-opening depth of field, focusing is very easy. Besides general photography, this is the most useful lens for photography under adverse lighting conditions.

Lens types

Normal lens: 50 mm *f*/1.4 Nikkor uses 7 glass elements in 5 groups. 55 mm *f*/1.2 has almost identical construction. 50 mm *f*/1.8 is similar but has last 2 elements combined.

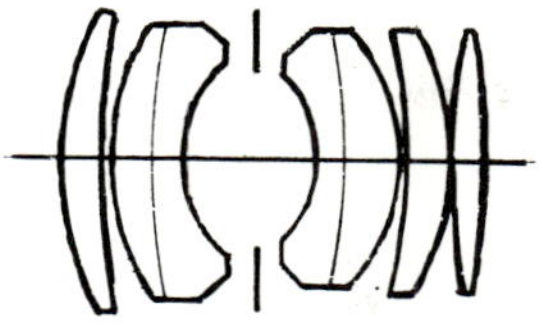

Telephoto lens: To minimise physical length of long focus lenses designers make the distance from front lens element to focal plane (D) much shorter than true lens focal length (L).

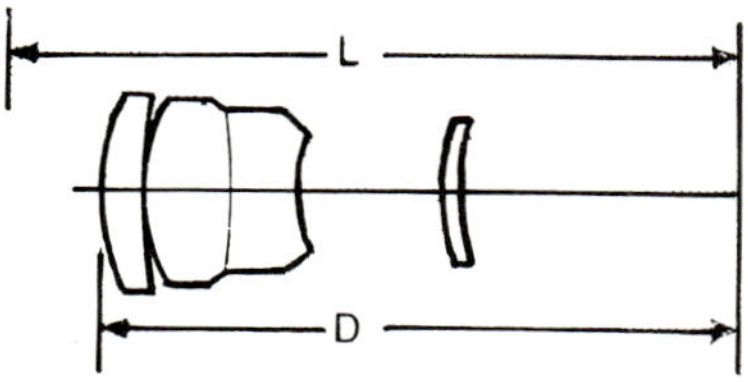

Wide angle lens: Because of the SLR mirror, wide angle lenses must be designed so last element surface will clear mirror edge. Hence back focal distance (Bf) is made greater than focal length (L). Such lenses are called inverted telephotos.

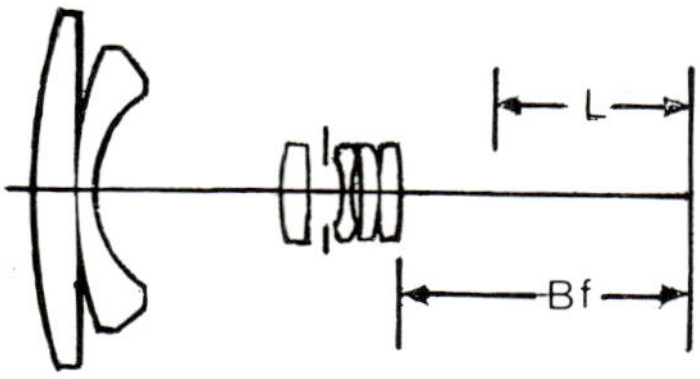

Catadioptric lens: To shorten lenses further, a combination of mirrors and glass optics is used in Reflex Nikkors to 'fold up' light path. Light from subject at left enters front glass corrector plate, is reflected from mirror surface, right, to smaller secondary mirror at left, and is then redirected through optical clear hole with glass correcting lenses to film plane at far right.

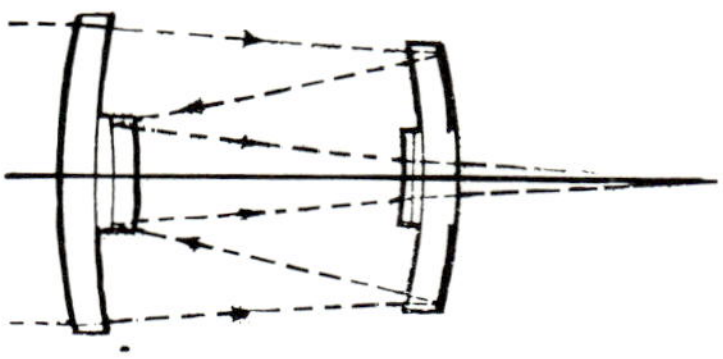

Floating element lens: for best quality images when close focusing high speed wide angle lenses, rear element group (2) shifts depending on focus. Normal focusing (1) also takes place.

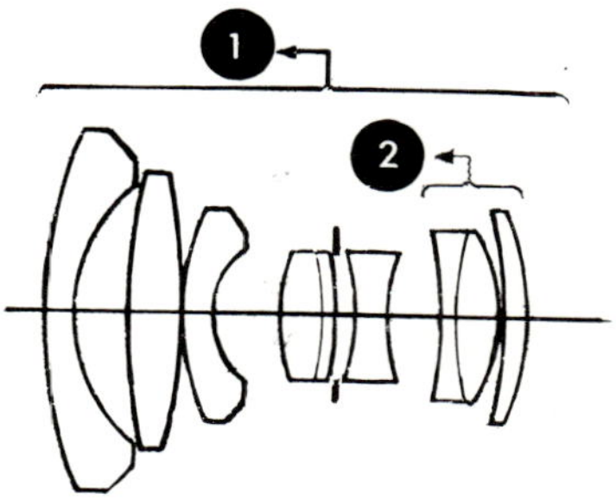

The choice between the four 50 mm lenses: *f*/1.4, *f*/1.8, *f*/2, or *f*/1.2 is determined by the use to which it will be put. Unless you work in low light, the *f*/1.8 or *f*/2 aperture lens is certainly your best optic (and least expensive, too). If you expect to shoot under poor conditions, the *f*/1.4 is the right choice. To squeeze the very last bit of detail and shutter speed under 'impossible' lighting conditions, the *f*/1.2 improves over this by about ⅓ *f*/stop. There is one other lens you might consider for 'standard' use: the 55 mm *f*/3.5 Micro-Nikkor, if you are interested in close-up photography and don't need a wide aperture. This lens is described later in this chapter.

While the foregoing 50 mm *f*/1.2 Nikkor represents the choice in high-speed lenses in general use, there is another specialised optic of superior quality but far more costly.

The 58 mm f/1.2 Noct-Nikkor has a first surface aspherical curve (as already discussed) which provides less flare and sharper images at maximum apertures. It has 7 elements in 6 groups, 40° 50′ picture angle, graduated in both metres and feet to 0.5 m and 1.7 ft, *f*/16 minimum aperture, fully automatic diaphragm, meter coupling prong for open aperture metering, 52 mm lens accessory size, dimensions 74 mm diameter × 63 mm length (2⅞ in × 2½ in), weight 485 g (17 oz).

Wide-angle lenses

Lenses with shorter than normal focal length give you a wider angle of view. In rangefinder or view cameras, normally-constructed wide-angle lenses are mounted fairly close to the film plane. In an orthodox SLR this is impossible if you are to have through-the-lens viewing and focusing. For this there must be room behind the lens for the mirror to rise out of the way. So optical manufacturers resort to the inverted tele-photo design for SLR wide-angle lenses. This design gives a back focal length distance much greater than the focal length, so you get a wide-angle lens with the space behind it to allow the mirror to swing up and down without hindrance. At one time such lenses were not optically equal to the regular wide-angle lenses. However, now you can have superb optical quality in just as short a focus lens with just as wide an aperture as a non-retro-focus lens design.

How wide an angle should the lens cover? Wide-angle lenses are generally sought after because they allow the user to get subject matter into the picture that he cannot with a normal lens. You want to photograph the whole building but cannot back up sufficiently far to get it all in; you wish to get an interior picture but your normal lens doesn't show enough of the room. Obviously a lens with a greater angle of view is essential for such photography. It might at first seem most sensible to get the widest-angle lens possible to achieve the broadest coverage and thus get the most in your picture.

The danger of settling for the widest lens you can get is clear. The wider the angle and greater the coverage, *and* consequently the smaller the individual subjects in your picture. Mountains which appeared so dramatic and imposing to your eye suddenly seem small and far away. That tremendous stormy sea stretching from horizon to horizon comes out as a thin strip. So you need to be wary in choosing too broad a view.

Wide-angle lenses have other apparent peculiarities. As angle gets wider, distance from foreground to background seems to grow. Suppose you picture a man standing a few feet in front of a tree. With your standard lens, the tree comes out quite large. With a wide angle, keep the man the same size (by going closer) and the tree comes out much smaller. (The opposite happens with a long focus lens.) Many buyers of wide-angle lenses use this phenomenon deliberately to make photographs showing very exaggerated apparent perspective with extreme wide-angle lenses – a hand close to the camera looking gigantic compared with the face or body further away, and so on.

Because the size of their effective aperture is smaller at any given *f*/number, wide-angle lenses have greater depth of field than do standard or long focus lenses at the same setting. This adds to the possibilities of picturing grossly distorted subjects.

The inherently great depth of field is also most handy when photographing action where it's impossible for you to follow and constantly focus directly on the subject. The moderately wide-angle lenses are generally those which should figure as your first choice; we'll start with them and work ourselves into the wider angles as we go along. We'll start with the 35 mm lenses. These have a 62° angle of view, and some photographers prefer them to the 45–55 mm lenses for general use.

35 mm f/2.8 Nikkor 6 elements in 6 groups, 62° picture angle, graduated in both metres and feet to 0.3 m and 1 ft, *f*/22 minimum aperture, fully automatic diaphragm, meter coupling prong for non-auto indexing cameras. 52 mm accessory size, dimensions 63.5 mm diameter × 54 mm length (2½ in × 2⅛ in), weight 240 g (8.5 oz).

35 mm f/2.5 Nikon Series E 5 elements in 5 groups, 62° picture angle, graduated in both metres and feet to 0.3 m and 1 ft, *f*/22 minimum aperture, fully automatic diaphragm, 52 mm accessory size, dimensions 62.5 mm diameter × 44 mm length (2⁷⁄₁₆ in × 1¾ in), weight 150 g (5.3 oz).

These are compact and light wide-angle lenses, and perhaps are the most useful and versatile 35 mm. Definition even at full aperture is outstanding with minimal spherical aberration and curvature of field. They are fine for landscapes, architecture, candids, groups, interiors, and good for flash photography, too, since their angle of coverage is inside the angle produced by most flash units.

35mm f/2 Nikkor 8 elements in 6 groups, 62° picture angle, graduated in both metres and feet to 0.3m and 1ft, *f*/16 minimum aperture, fully automatic diaphragm, meter coupling prong for non-auto indexing cameras, 52m accessory size, dimensions 63.5mm diameter × 61mm length (2½ in × 2 13/32 in), weight 285g (10.1oz).

Although this lens is a full *f*/stop greater than the *f*/2.8 35mm lens, it has gained little in size and weight. Its optical design virtually eliminates coma and other aberrations to produce a sharp image of high contrast with maximum corner brightness fall-off even at full aperture. While its maximum opening allows the lens to be used for low-level existing light photography and candids, perhaps just as important is the very shallow depth of field produced at full aperture, providing excellent, crisp focusing ability, a most desirable but seldom achieved feature in a wide-angle lens.

35mm f/1.4 Nikkor 9 elements in 7 groups, 62° picture angle, graduated in both metres and feet to 0.3m and 1ft, *f*/16 minimum aperture, fully automatic diaphragm, meter coupling prong for non-auto indexing cameras, 52mm lens accessory size, dimension 66.5mm diameter × 74.5mm length (2⅝in × 2 15/16 in), weight 415g (14.6oz).

Another *f*/stop faster, this remarkable lens is ideal for shooting under the poorest indoor or outdoor light. The large aperture makes focusing even easier, and is a boon for low-light viewing. The rear group of lens elements are floating to compensate for close focusing. The *f*/22 minimum aperture provides enormous maximum depth of field for unusual picture taking.

While most photographers seem to prefer a 35mm focal length as a general all-round wide-angle, I feel that the function is best performed by the shorter 28mm length. This is confirmed by many experienced photographers. Note, in particular, that the difference between a 50mm lens and a 35mm may well not be great enough to justify owning (or carrying) both. A 28mm is a much better companion to the 50mm. It is particularly useful for architectural and interior photography, where you often need a greater angle of view than the 35mm lens can accomplish. The 28mm takes in more of the scene, and with its greater depth of field is useful for quick 'grabbed' shots. It also allows you take a closer view than the 35mm lenses, to get even greater 'wide-angle' distortion.

28mm f/3.5 Nikkor 6 elements in 6 groups, 74° picture angle, graduated in both metres and feet to 0.3m and 1ft, *f*/22 minimum aperture, fully automatic diaphragm, meter coupling prong for non-auto indexing cameras, 52mm accessory size, dimension 62.5mm diameter × 54mm length (2 7/16 in × 2⅛in), weight 240g 8.5oz).

Although this was one of the first accessory lenses introduced for the Nikon F in its updated form, it remains an outstanding performer with good contrast and brilliance even at full lens opening. Coma and distortion are well corrected, as are spherical aberrations, providing constant focus even as the lens is closed down to minimum aperture. Because of its low weight, the lens is a favourite of photographers who like to travel as lightly as possible.

28mm f/2.8 Nikkor 8 elements in 8 groups, 74° picture angle, graduated in both metres and feet to 0.2m and 0.7ft, *f*/22 minimum aperture, fully automatic diaphragm, meter coupling prong for non-auto indexing cameras, 52mm accessory size, dimensions 63mm diameter × 53mm length (2½ in × 2⅛in), weight 250g (8.75oz).

28mm f/2.8 Nikon Series E 5 elements in 5 groups, 74° picture angle, graduated in both metres and feet to 0.3m and 1ft, *f*/22 minimum aperture, fully automatic diaphragm, 52mm accessory size, dimensions 62.5mm diameter × 44mm length (2 7/16in × 1¾in), weight 150g (5.3oz).

Some of the newer lens designs, these optics have exceptionally well-corrected spherical and coma aberrations over the entire picture area even at full aperture. They are remarkably light and compact for their speed.

28mm f/2 Nikkor 9 elements in 8 groups, 74° picture angle, graduated in both metres and feet to 0.3m and 1ft, *f*/22 minimum aperture, fully automatic diaphragm, meter coupling prong for non-auto indexing cameras, 52mm accessory size, dimensions 64.5mm diameter × 70mm length (2 17/32in × 2¾in), weight 345g (12.2oz).

Faster than any other Nikkor lens with this angle of view, the 28mm *f*/2 provides high resolution and contrast even at full aperture. Using a rear floating group of elements, the lens is able to maintain optimum image quality as the lens is focused to its minimum distance. The *f*/2 lens provides a wide aperture for natural-light photography under adverse conditions, making it an excellent photojournalist's or newspaper photographer's tool. The aperture also makes viewing and focusing very much easier than it normally is with 28mm lenses.

If you already have a 35mm lens, and want something wider, a 28mm may seem too close to the 35mm, and a 20 or 21mm lens too 'way out' for you. The solution is provided by a 24mm lens. Still acceptable for normal views, this focal length has great possibilities for taking strikingly unusual pictures.

24mm f/2.8 Nikkor 9 elements in 9 groups, 84° picture angle, graduated in both metres and feet to 0.3m and 1ft, *f*/22 minimum aperture, fully automatic diaphragm, meter coupling prong for non-auto indexing cameras, 52mm accessory size, dimension 63.5mm diameter × 56.0mm length (2½in × 2 3/16in), weight 270g (9.5oz).

This optic is relatively compact for its very short focal length. It provides uniform brightness to the picture corner even at full aperture, excellent definition even at close focusing and has more and more become one of the most used wide-angle lenses among working photographers. It's a fine performer for travel, landscapes, architectural work and candid picture taking.

24mm f/2 Nikkor 11 elements in 10 groups, 84° picture angle, graduated in both metres and feet to 0.3 m and 1 ft, *f*/22 minimum aperture, fully automatic diaphragm, meter coupling prong for non-auto indexing cameras, 52 mm accessory size, dimension 63 mm diameter × 61 mm length (2½ in × 2⅜ in), weight 300 g (10.6 oz).

A surprisingly compact and light alternative to the *f*/2.8 provides one full *f*/stop additional illumination for brighter viewing and better focusing as well as the ability to take picture under poorer lighting conditions.

Now we're ready to drop down to some extraordinary lenses for photographers needing the greatest angle of coverage with linear perspective (you can, of course, achieve even wider angle with the deliberately distorting fisheye lenses, as we'll see).

20mm f/3.5 Nikkor 11 elements in 8 groups, 94° picture angle, graduated in both metres and feet to 0.3 m and 1 ft, *f*/22 minimum aperture, fully automatic diaphragm, meter coupling prong for non-auto indexing cameras, 52 mm accessory size, dimensions 63.5 mm diameter × 50.5 mm length (2 15/16 in × 2 in), weight 235 g (8.3 oz).

This remarkable extreme-wide-angle lens has minimal coma aberrations, high contrast even at full aperture, and brightness to the corners for picture taking and viewing. With its immense depth of field even at *f*/3.5 there is hardly any need to focus for subjects at most distances. With careful use, keeping the subject parallel to the film plane and keeping important subjects away from the picture edges, apparent picture distortion can be eliminated for remarkably accurate coverage of interiors and architectural work. However, if you want it, the apparent perspective distortion possible when the lens is used at close distances provides a fine opportunity for creative exaggerated effects. Since the lens can be used for full open aperture viewing and focusing, all results can be instantly observed, corrected or changed.

18mm f/3.5 Nikkor 11 elements in 10 groups, 100° picture angle, graduated in both metres and feet to 0.25 m and 10 in, *f*/22 minimum aperture, fully automatic diaphragm, meter coupling prong for non-auto indexing cameras, 72 mm acessory size, dimensions 75 mm diameter × 72.5 mm length (3 in × 2 9/10 in), weight 370 g (13 oz).

The spread between Nikon's 20 mm and the very wide and costly 15 mm *f*/5.6 lens was a wide open one. To span the gap, Nikon introduced this optic which has an exceptionally flat field, commendable edge-to-edge illumination for bright and sharp images over the entire field even at maximum aperture. By exaggerating the apparent perspective, striking dramatic effects are possible. It is also excellent for general indoor photography and architectural work where extremely wide angles must be covered from a limited subject distance.

15mm f/3.5 Nikkor 14 elements in 11 groups, 110° picture angle, graduated in both metres and feet to 0.3m and 1ft, *f*/22 minimum aperture, fully automatic diaphragm, meter coupling prong for non-auto indexing cameras, rear bayonet type filters, dimensions 87.5mm diameter × 94mm length (3½in × 3¾in), weight 630g (22.2oz).

This, next to widest of all the straight-line Nikkors, features superb linear correction, extremely even illumination right to the corner of the picture even at full aperture. It is an essential tool for the serious photographer, amateur or professional, who must squeeze every bit of subject material out of a very confined space. This is a fine lens for architectural photographers, for shooting interiors and creating very unusual effects with exaggerated 'perspective' distortion.

13mm f/5.6 Nikkor 16 elements in 12 groups, 118° picture angle, graduated in both metres and feet to 0.3m and 1ft, *f*/22 minimum aperture, fully automatic diaphragm, meter coupling prong for non-auto indexing cameras, rear mounting bayonet filters, dimensions 115mm diameter × 102mm length (4½in × 4in), weight 1.2kg (2.71lb).

An incredibly wide wide-angle lens with true linear perspective – not a fisheye – with excellent all-round correction for best definition and minimisation of aberrations. To provide sharpest possible focusing ability even at close distances, the rear lens elements are 'floating' – that is moving separately in respect to the regular focusing movement. The 13mm *f*/5.6 Nikkor opens up a new world of possibilities to the creative photographer.

Long focus lenses

In many ways the wide-angle lenses are the most useful of interchangeable optics, since they allow you to include subject material in your picture you could not without them. But the long focal length or 'tele' lenses are the glamour stars (although zooms are giving it a run for it these days). Like telescopes, lenses of longer than normal focal length narrow your angle of view, thus apparently bringing distant objects closer. Really long 'supertelephotos' summon far-away subjects to what seems like arm's length.

In years past the telephoto or long focal length lens had one simple duty, to provide an enlarged image of a distant subject when it was impossible for the photographer to approach closer. However, serious photographers now employ the longer lenses also to present the subject the size they want. Because they can enlarge a portion of a distant scene, long lenses appear to compress the distance between subjects. Different parts of the scene seem pressed together with little distance separating them. The longer the focal length lens, the greater this apparent effect. This ability aids moderately long and normal lenses which seem to operate in the opposite manner. With normal focal length lenses, and even more so with wide angles, we have noted the apparent perspective distortion of hands or facial features: those close to the camera appearing overly large. This, of course, is actually a function of the short camera-to-subject distance needed to fill the frame with normal and wide-angle lenses; and has nothing more than that to do with the focal length of the lenses. To prove this, close one eye, have a friend hold his hand out towards you inches from your eye and note how very large the hand appears in relation to his head behind his hand.

To avoid such distortion, you must shoot at a greater distance from the subject. You can enlarge the subject either by magnifying the image through printing, or by using a longer lens on the camera. The somewhat elongated nose, lengthened face, and too small ears characteristic of a very close portrait are thus avoided. Most professionals use an 85 mm, 105 mm or in some instances even a 135 mm focal length to allow themselves to stand well back.

Remember, your camera-to-subject distance is the sole governing factor. The focal length makes no difference. Try it for yourself. Take two pictures of the same subject from exactly the same spot. Use a wide-angle lens for one and a long focus optic for the other. Enlarge the right part of the wide-angle shot so that it matches the picture area of the long focus shot. You will find that the perspective is exactly the same in the two pictures.

The apparent compression of distances coupled with the inherent lack of depth of field makes long lenses snap in and out of focus more crisply than shorter lenses at the same *f*/number. This also means you must take additional care when focusing! With very long lenses, focusing is difficult on normal screens; this can be solved by changing focusing screens (on Nikons).

One last important point to cover before we look at the Nikon and Nikkor long lenses is the difference between telephoto and long focal length lenses. In today's general parlance, little effort is made to distinguish between them. A long focal length lens of normal construction has its optical centre at about its focal length from the film. In other words, the middle of the elements of a 300 mm lens is 300 mm from the film. Such an optical construction can provide excellent results, but makes for rather long and unwieldy lenses. To shorten them, telephoto construction is used for most long focus lenses. The front lens elements converge the light rays strongly and a negative group towards the rear diverges them again somewhat. This makes it possible to shorten the back focus distance considerably. In telephoto lenses the back focus may be only ½ or ⅓ as great as in a long focal length lens. Telephoto lenses are more difficult to make and more expensive, but they are obviously much handier and more compact. In discussing the various long focal length lenses we won't pay too much attention to their optical construction, since in practical terms few photographers ever do. They are all long lenses and all tend to be referred to as telephotos (or teles).

We'll start by examining the moderately long lenses of the 85 mm, 100 mm, 105 mm and 135 mm focal length. It's in this group that you will probably make your first choice of a longer than normal focal length lens. In terms of traditional popularity, the 135 mm leads the 105, 100 and 85 mm. It has always been the prime, easy-to-hold long lens for bringing distant objects closer. For the traveller and holiday-maker or candid photographer it can indeed be the best choice. Another old favourite focal length is the 85 mm. This gives a nice-sized image for portraits, and manufacturers have concentrated on producing wide aperture 85 mm lenses. It is popular with stage photographers since it provides a large image than the standard lens and also has great speed for low-light photography. The 105 or 100 mm focal length have gained popularity in more recent times as a compromise, retaining some of the speed of the 85 mm but giving a longer 'reach' nearer the 135 mm. Many Nikon owners prefer this for portraiture. Of the four lengths, I feel the 105 or 100 mm are the most useful, all-round moderate-long lens – unless you have specialised interests which really call for the others.

All three focal lengths are available in a number of lenses whose principal difference is in maximum aperture. The larger the aperture, the greater the focusing and viewing brightness, the better for low-light level photography. However, as apertures get larger, so do size and weight (as you can see in our descriptions), and price.

85 mm f/2 Nikkor 5 elements in 5 groups, 28° 30′ picture angle, graduated in both metres and feet to 0.85 m and 2.5 ft, *f*/22 minimum aperture, fully automatic diaphragm, meter coupling prong for non-auto indexing cameras, 52 mm accessory size, dimensions 63.5 mm diameter × 61 mm length (2½ in × 2⅜ in), weight 310 g (10.9 oz).

85 mm f/1.4 Nikkor 7 elements in 5 groups, 28° 30′ picture angle, graduated in both metres and feet to 0.85 m and 3 ft, *f*/16 minimum aperture, fully automatic diaphragm, meter coupling prong for non-auto indexing cameras, 72 mm accessory size, dimensions 80.5 mm diameter × 72.5 mm length (3⅛ in × 2⅞ in), weight 605 g (21.4 oz).

105 mm f/2.5 Nikkor 5 elements in 4 groups, 23° 20′ picture angle, graduated in both metres and feet to 1 m and 3.5 ft, *f*/22 minimum aperture, fully automatic diaphragm, meter coupling prong for non-auto indexing cameras, 52 mm accessory size, built-in telescopic-type lens hood, dimensions 64 mm 173 mm diameter × 445 mm length (613/16 in × 17½ in), weight 6.2 kg (13.7 lb).

105 mm f/1.8 Nikkor 5 elements in 5 groups, 23° 20′ picture angle, graduated in both metres and feet to 1 m and 3.5 ft, *f*/22 minimum aperture, fully automatic diaphragm, meter coupling prong for non-auto indexing cameras, 62 mm accessory size, dimensions 78.5 mm diameter × 88.5 mm length ($3\frac{1}{8}$in × $3\frac{7}{16}$in), weight 580g (20.5 oz).

100mm f/2.8 Nikon Series E 4 elements in 4 groups, 24° 20′ picture angle, graduated in both metres and feet to 1 m and 3.5 ft, *f*/22 minimum aperture, fully automatic diaphragm, 52 mm accessory size, dimensions 62.5 mm diameter × 57.5 mm length ($2\frac{1}{2}$in × $2\frac{1}{4}$in), weight 225 g (8 oz).

135mm f/2 Nikkor 6 elements in 4 groups, 18° picture angle, graduated in both metres and feet to 1.3 m and 4.5 ft, *f*/22 minimum aperture, fully automatic diaphragm, meter coupling prong for non-auto indexing cameras, 72 mm accessory size, built-in telescopic-type lens hood, dimensions 81 mm diameter × 103 mm length ($3\frac{3}{16}$in × $4\frac{1}{16}$in), weight 860 g (30 oz).

Very effective flare and ghost control – highly important with such a wide maximum aperture – are special features of this optical design which makes maximum use of Nikon's Integrated Coating (NIC) also for maximum contrast and optimum colour rendition. The lens is especially suitable for action photography under poor lighting conditions although it is equally capable of use as a standard 135 mm all-round objective.

135mm f/2.8 Nikkor 5 elements in 4 groups, 18° picture angle, graduated in both metres and feet to 1.3 m and 4.5 ft, *f*/22 minimum aperture, fully automatic diaphragm, meter coupling prong for non-auto indexing cameras, 52 mm accessory size, built-in telescopic-type lens hood, dimensions 64.5 mm diameter × 91.5 mm length ($2\frac{9}{16}$in × $3\frac{5}{8}$in), weight 430 g (15 oz).

A modern, more compact, far lighter in weight lens with close focusing, this optic was designed to replace the famous older 135 mm /2.8 Nikkor. Optical corrections and definition have been improved with the newer version.

135mm f/3.5 Nikkor 4 elements in 4 groups, 18° picture angle, graduated in both metres and feet to 1.5 m and 5 ft, *f*/32 minimum aperture, fully automatic diaphragm, meter coupling prong for non-auto indexing cameras, 52 mm accessory size, dimensions 66 mm diameter × 93.5 mm length ($2\frac{19}{32}$ in × $3\frac{11}{16}$in), weight 400 g (14.1 oz).

Remodelled in 1969 and again in 1975, the new lens has improved chromatic aberration correction at maximum aperture for best resolution. It is furnished with a separate snap-on lens hood. This lens is less expensive than the *f*/2.8 version. It appeals especially to those who carry their equipment around.

The next group of longer lenses (from 180 mm to 400 mm) should be considered specialised lenses for specific purposes. In years gone by, any lens longer than 150 mm (on 35 mm cameras) needed a tripod for every shot.

Today, many professionals rely on hand-holding even quite long lenses for maximum picture-taking flexibility. However, even so, you will undeniably get sharper results consistently with a good tripod. The 180 and 200 mm lenses are not provided with their own tripod mounts and the camera's own tripod mount should be used with these lenses. The longer 300 and 400 mm focal lengths do have their own tripod sockets. The lens barrels are longer and a lens fastened to the tripod instead of a camera body gives superior balance and stability on the tripod. However, since the camera body is unsupported there is added danger from camera body vibration. Therefore an even sturdier tripod than usual is recommended.

Lenses in this group are ideal for isolating individual subject matter from its surroundings. Photography of sports, action, animals and birds, children at play, and candid pictures at distances spring immediately to mind. Which lens you choose depends on your needs. While each is a longer focal length and provides you with a larger image, each also has a smaller maximum aperture and is harder to hold steady.

180 mm f/2.8 Nikkor 5 elements in 4 groups, 13° 40′ picture angle, graduated in both metres and feet to 1.8 m and 6 ft, *f*/32 minimum aperture, fully automatic diaphragm, meter coupling prong for non-auto indexing cameras, 72 mm accessory size, built-in telescopic-type lens hood, dimensions 81 mm diameter × 141 mm length (3³⁄₁₆ in × 5⁹⁄₁₆ in), weight 880 g (31.6 oz).

180 mm f/2.8 ED Nikkor 5 elements in 5 groups, 13° 40′ picture angle, graduated in both metres and feet from 1.8 m and 6 ft, *f*/32 minimum aperture, fully automatic diaphragm, meter coupling prong for non-auto indexing cameras, 72 mm accessory size, built-in telescopic-type lenshood, dimensions 78.5 mm diameter × 138 mm length (3⅛ in × 5⁷⁄₁₆ in), weight 830 g (29.3 oz).

Newsmen and photo-journalists have found these the ideal quick-acting sports lenses, capable outdoors, but also equally usable indoors. They are suitable not only for sports, but also for stage action, candids and close portraits of important news figures that photographers cannot approach closely. Even at full aperture, resolution and contrast are high.

200 mm f/4 Nikkor 5 elements in 5 groups, 12° 20′ picture angle, graduated in both metres and feet to 2 m and 7 ft, *f*/32 minimum aperture, fully automatic diaphragm, meter coupling prong for non-auto indexing cameras, 52 mm accessory size, built-in telescopic-type lens hood, dimensions 68 mm diameter × 126 mm length (2¹¹⁄₁₆ in × 4¹⁵⁄₁₆), weight 530 g (18.7 oz).

This lens can be considered an outdoors alternative to the 180 mm lens, being considerably smaller and lighter. Note that unlike the 180, the 200 can use the standard 52 mm lens accessories.

200mm f/2 Nikkor ED 10 elements in 8 groups, 12° 20′ picture angle, graduated in both metres and feet to 2.5 m and 9 ft, *f*/22 minimum aperture, fully automatic diaphragm, meter coupling prong for non-auto indexing cameras, 122 mm accessory size, dimensions 128 mm diameter × 214 mm length (5 1/16 in × 8 7/16 in), weight 2.3 kg (5 lb).

An unbelievably high speed lens of this focal length has been made possible thanks to Nikon's extra dispersion (ED) glass and the use of IF (internal focusing) plus Nikon Integrated Coating (NIC). Because of its vast light gathering, it offers superb focusing and viewing brightness. The lens can be used hand-held.

300mm f/4.5 Nikkor 6 elements in 5 groups, 8° 10′ picture angle, graduated in both metres and feet to 4 m and 13 ft, *f*/22 minimum aperture, fully automatic diaphragm, meter coupling prong for non-auto indexing cameras, 72 mm accessory size, built-in telescopic-type lens hood, tripod socket, dimensions 80 mm diameter × 203 mm length (3 5/32 in × 8 in), weight 1.1 kg (2.3 lb).

Remodelled in 1969, the new optic replaces the Nikkor-P. The new lens has improved colour balance. It's a full 50 per cent longer in focal length than the 200 mm lens and is ideal for spectators sports photography where the user cannot leave his seat. It is also most useful in bird photography.

With the use of low dispersion (ED) glass and internal focusing (IF), Nikon is able to offer a smaller, lighter and close focusing alternative to the regular 300 mm *f*/4.5 Nikkor just described.

300mm f/4.5 IF-ED Nikkor 7 elements in 6 groups, 8° 10′ picture angle, graduated in both metres and feet to 2.5 m and 10 ft, *f*/22 minimum aperture, fully automatic diaphragm, meter coupling prong for non-auto indexing cameras, 72 mm accessory size, built-in telescopic-type lens hood, tripod socket, dimension 80 mm diameter × 200 mm length (3 5/32 in × 7 7/8 in), weight 990 g (35 oz).

This lens is particularly useful for close nature photography, and is extremely hand-holdable due to its light weight.

There are additional ED telephoto lenses in this series of one-piece lenses (as well as ED lens heads in the super-telephoto series we'll be discussing a bit later).

300mm f/2.8 Nikkor IF-ED 8 elements in 6 groups, 8° 10′ picture angle, *f*/22 minimum aperture, fully automatic diaphragm, meter coupling prong for non-auto indexing cameras, 122 mm accessory size, built-in telescopic-type lens hood, dimensions 138 mm diameter × 249 mm length (5 7/16 in × 9 3/4 in), weight 2500 g (5 lb 8 oz).

Nikon Internal Focusing (IF) provides this lens with convenient hand-holding balance. The focusing ring has a special click-stopped preset ring to aid rapid refocusing to any specific needed distance. Extra low dispersion glass (ED) allows this lens the crispness and colour correction one would expect only in a much shorter focal length optic. Correction is so good on this and other ED lenses that it is not necessary to provide a separate infra-red focusing index mark. Sharp focus can be achieved even in the infra-red wavelength.

400mm f/3.5 Nikkor IF-ED 8 elements in 6 groups, 6° 10′ picture angle, graduated in both metres and feet to 4.5 m and 14 ft, *f*/22 minimum aperture, fully automatic diaphragm, meter coupling prong for non-auto indexing cameras, 122 mm accessory size, built-in tripod socket, dimensions 134 mm diameter × 304 mm length (5¼ in × 11 13/16 in), weight 2.58 kg (5.7 lb).

Another famous ED lens from Nikon offering shorter total focal length and closer focusing than is generally available in such a length lens, thanks to its internal focusing (IF) system, it incorporates all the advantages of ED glass already described, and is especially suitable for distant shots, action and sports photography where highest posible detail and colour correction are needed under a variety of temperature conditions. The lens has a gelatin filter holder which is reached by sliding the filter lock button towards the camera body and pulling the filter out. Keep the filter holder alone, or one of the 41 mm gelatin filters in place, at all times to prevent stray light entering the filter holder slot.

400mm f/5.6 ED-Nikkor 7 elements in 6 groups, 6° 10′ picture angle, graduated in both metres and feet to 4.6 m and 15 ft, *f*/32 minimum aperture, fully automatic diaphragm, meter coupling prong for non-auto indexing cameras, 72 mm accessory size, built-in tripod socket, dimension 83 mm diameter × 254 mm length (3⅓ in × 10 in), weight 1.18 kg (2.6 lb).

This is an ideal combination of lightness, compactness and superb optical quality due to the ED glass used in its construction. Although meant for tripod operation, careful photographers will find it an easy matter to make hand-held exposures at 1/125 second or faster. It's a good choice for sports or nature photography where the lens must be carried by the photographer in the field.

600mm f/5.6 IF-ED-Nikkor 7 elements in 6 groups, 4° 10′ picture angle, graduated in both metres and feet to 5.5 m and 18 ft, *f*/22 minimum aperture, fully automatic diaphragm, meter coupling prong for non-auto indexing cameras, behind-lens filters, built-in tripod socket, dimensions 125 mm diameter × 382 mm length (4⅞ in × 15 1/16 in), weight 2.5 kg (5 lb 8 oz).

600mm f/4 IF-ED-Nikkor 8 elements in 6 groups, 4° 10′ picture angle, graduated in both metres and feet to 6.5 m and 21 ft, *f*/22 minimum aperture, fully automatic diaphragm, meter coupling prong for non-auto indexing cameras, behind-lens filters, built-in telescopic-type lens hood, dimensions 173 mm diameter × 445 mm length (6 13/16 in × 17½ in), weight 6.2 kg (13.7 lb).

800 mm f/8 IF-ED-Nikkor 9 elements in 7 groups, 3° picture angle, distance scale graduated in metres and feet to 10.7 m and 35 ft, *f*/32 minimum aperture, fully automatic diaphragm, stop-down metering system, behind-lens filters, built-in telescopic-type lens hood, dimensions 134.6 mm diameter × 459.7 mm length (5.3 in × 18.1 in), weight 3.8 kg (8.4 lb).

1200 mm f/11 IF-ED-Nikkor 9 elements in 8 groups, 2° picture angle, distance scale graduated in metres and feet to 13.7 m and 45 ft, *f*/22 minimum aperture, fully automatic diaphragm, stop-down metering system, behind-lens filters, built-in telescopic-type lens hood, dimensions 134.6 mm diameter × 576 mm length (5.3 in × 22.7 in), weight 3.8 kg (8.4 lb).

Super telephotos

At this stage of long-lens growth Nikon provides us with two alternative lines of optics – all-glass lenses and mirror-lens (catadioptric) types. We'll stay with the all-glass lenses for the moment, but give the assets and limitations of the catadioptrics vs all-glass when we discuss the latter type.

The series of Nikkor lenses which Nikon considers super telephotos consists of an integrated group of four focal length heads which are used individually with either of two common focusing units. (Note: some of these heads are in short supply and may be discontinued.) The older focusing unit is a 1.4 kg (3 lb), 312.5 mm (12 5/16 in) long intermediate tube which fits the Nikon or Nikkormat camera body on one end and accepts any one of the 400, 600, 800 or 1200 mm lens heads at the other. It has a large scalloped focusing ring and an automatic diaphragm with click stops for *f*/4.5, 5.6, 8, 11, 16 and 22. A more modern focusing unit is the AU-1. It has a removable metal lever for fast and convenient focusing, and provision to accept standard 52 mm Nikkor filters. The maximum aperture possible with either focusing unit depends on the lens head. The 1200 mm lens head does not operate with the automatic diaphragm and none of the lenses couples to the camera's full aperture metering system. So readings are made by the stop-down method. A shoulder strap is provided with the focusing unit, and an accessory cradle for a firmer support is available. The lenses and focusing unit must used on a tripod. A tripod socket is built into the focusing unit on a revolving collar so the entire unit, lens head and camera body can be rotated for either horizontal or vertical shots. Each lens comes with its own removable distance scale, which attaches to the focusing unit with screws.

The advantage of the common focusing unit plus four separate lens heads is obvious. Cost is kept down for those needing more than one focal length,

Super telephotos and focusing units

Here are the controls of the AU-1 Focusing Unit:

1. Focusing handle
2. Holder release button
3. Infra-red indexes and distance scale index
4. Distance scale and changeover knob
5. Focusing ring
6. Tripod mounting collar
7. Collar locking screw
8. Aperture ring and scale
9. Alternative focusing handle mounting thread
10. Mounting index
11. Carrying strap eyelet
12. Filter holder

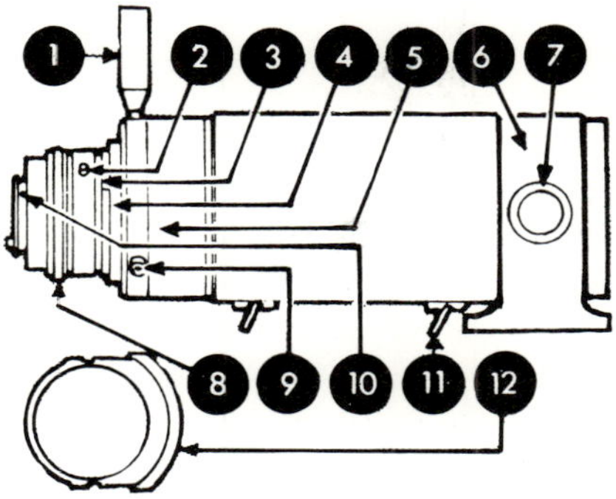

Here are the controls of the standard Focusing Unit:

1. Mounting index dot
2. Aperture ring
3. Carrying strap
4. Focusing ring
5. Locking screw
6. Mount thread
7. Tripod socket

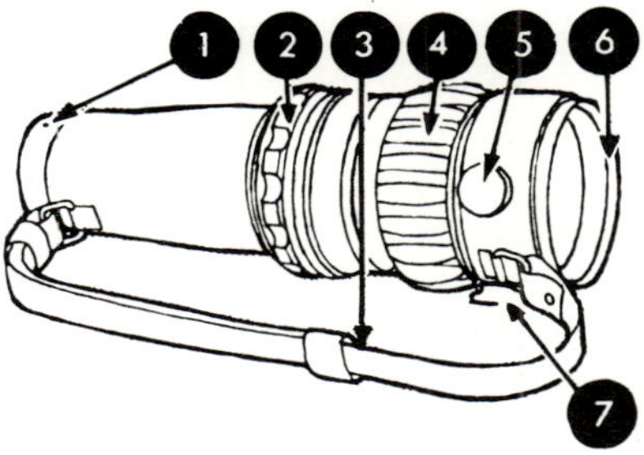

Here are the lens heads which thread into either the standard Focusing Unit or the Focusing Unit AU-1 for use.

These heads are available in normal or ED glass.

1. Mounting screw thread
2. Lens hood
3. Separate aperture scale and aperture ring

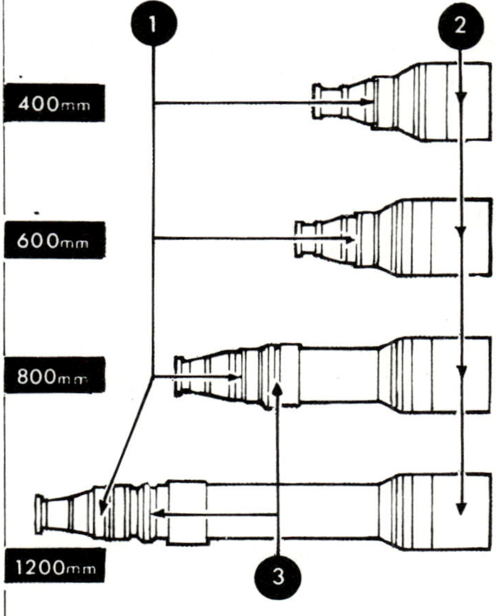

and lenses break down into two parts for ease of carrying. The advantage in portability is enhanced if you carry more than one lens head with your focusing unit. These lenses are designed for extreme sports photography or nature picture work from a great distance.

The separate lens head simply screw into the focusing unit which then attaches to the camera body as a standard lens. The focusing unit measures 102 mm diameter × 312.5 m length (4 1/32 × 12 5/16 in) and weights 1.4 kg (3 lb). To attach the distance scale plate supplied with each lens to the focusing unit, first mount the lens and focusing unit on a tripod and focus on infinity by aiming at and bringing into focus a very distant subject. Turn the focusing collar until the subject attains its maximum sharpness. Place the distance-scale plate around the focusing unit so that the infinity mark is opposite the white line on the focusing unit. The focusing unit has six tapped holes to accept the scales in the proper position. There are rectangular slots at both plate ends to allow thermal expansion compensation movements. Screw the plate into place using the two screws supplied.

The Nikon Focusing Unit AU-1 measures 101 mm diameter × 313 mm length (4 in × 12 5/16 in), weight 2.4 kg (5.3 lb). It is a more modern and convenient control and coupling device to use than the standard focusing unit. Besides the provision for accepting standard 52 mm Nikon filters in an internal filter holder, the AU-1 has a removable focusing lever fixed to the standard rubberised focusing ring. Lens heads are mounted to the AU-1 and the AU-1 mounted to the cameras in the same manner as to the standard focusing unit. However, the AU-1 has its own changeable focusing scales so that owners of the lenses need not attach the accessory distance scales for each lens in use to the focusing unit. Photographers having more than one lens head can quickly change heads with no mismatch of distance scales. These distance scales, in metres and feet, are colour-coded, matching the colours of the various focal lengths marked on the AU-1 itself. The scales can be set as follows: for the 600 or 1200 mm lenses, turn the distance scale clockwise, using the changeover knob. Blue graduations for the 1200 mm focal length and yellow for 600 mm will appear. By turning the scale counterclockwise, green (800 mm) and pink (400 mm) graduations appear.

Once you have the right distance scale in place, you must calibrate it. Find an infinity subject (preferably at least 1/4 mile distant) and focus the lens on it. Align the distance scale infinity mark (∞) with the white distance-scale index line. Your distance scale is now properly set. Note, however, that the various lens heads can be focused closer than their marked close-focusing distances. The 400 mm can reach 3.8 m or 12.5 ft; the 600 mm, 8 m or 26.4 ft; the 800 mm, 14 m or 46.2 ft, and the 1200 mm, 31 m or 102 ft. These distances are considerably shorter than those possible with the standard focusing unit; however, they do vary slightly with temperature effects on the standard glass lens heads. This is minimised, if not eliminated completely, with the new Nikkor ED series of lens heads.

Installing and removing filters is a simple matter. To remove the holder, push the release button, grasp the holder at the milled-end surfaces and pull the holder vertically out of the AU-1 focusing unit. Filters can be removed and replaced by threading them directly into the filter holder. Be certain, however, to thread the filter into the recessed side of the holder. Replace the holder and it locks automatically into the AU-1.

A few hints on using the AU-1 and the lens heads. Although the AU-1 has apertures to *f*/4.5, remember that you are limited to the maximum aperture of your lens. Only the 400 mm lens has an *f*/4.5 aperture; the others are smaller. The 800 mm *f*/8 has an additional manual aperture range to *f*/64 for maximum depth of field when possible, but it is more convenient to use the AU-1 automatic diaphragm between *f*/8 and *f*/22. The 1200 mm lens has a manual preset diaphragm only. When using a manual diaphragm, you must open the auto diaphragm aperture scale of the AU-1 to *f*/4.5. When using infra-red film with the regular lens heads, focus the image through the finder. Then turn the focusing ring counterclockwise until the point focused aligns with the proper coloured-coded infra-red index for the head you're using. Colours are the same as the distance scales. With the ED series lens heads, you need not reset focus when shooting infra-red.

400 mm f/4.5 Nikkor Auto 4 elements in 4 groups, 6° 10′ picture angle, distance scale graduated in metres and feet to 5 m or 16 ft (to 5.5 m or 18 ft with the AU-1), *f*/22 minimum aperture, fully automatic diaphragm, stop-down metering system, built-in lens hood, 122 mm accessory size, dimensions with focusing unit 135 mm diameter × 275 mm length (5$\frac{5}{16}$ in × 10$\frac{9}{16}$ in), weight with focusing unit 1.9 kg (4.2 lb).

Ideal for sports and action photography from a tripod, this lens provides almost one additional *f*/stop of light transmittance over the 400 mm *f*/5.6.

600 mm f/5.6 Nikkor Auto 5 elements in 4 groups, 4° 10′ picture angle, distance scale graduated in metres and feet to 11 m or 35 ft, *f*/22 minimum aperture, fully automatic diaphragm, stop-down metering system, built-in telescopic lens hood, 122 mm accessory size, dimensions with focusing unit 135 mm diameter × 297 mm length (5$\frac{5}{16}$ in × 11$\frac{3}{16}$ in), weight 2.4 kg (5.3 lb).

This lens provides a good intermediate super-telephoto. It extends the range of the sports or wildlife photographer without being too difficult to handle.

800 mm f/8 Nikkor Auto 5 elements in 5 groups, 3° picture angle, distance scale graduated in metres and feet to 19 m and 61 ft, *f*/22 automatic diaphragm minimum aperture and *f*/64 manual aperture setting, fully automatic diaphragm, step-down metering system, built-in telescopic lens hood, 122 mm lens accessory size, dimensions 135 mm diameter × 510 mm length (5$\frac{5}{16}$ × 20 in), weight 2.3 kg (5.1 lb).

Unlike the shorter focal lengths of this lens group, the 800 mm has a separate manual diaphragm which can be set from *f*/8 to *f*/64 to provide greater depth of field than is possible with the *f*/22 minimum available with the automatic diaphragm. Whichever diaphragm you use, the other must be at full aperture. Because of the relatively small maximum aperture, Focusing Screens Type G4 or H4 are recommended for best viewing and focusing.

1200 mm f/11 Nikkor 5 elements in 5 groups, 2° picture angle, distance scale graduated in metres and feet to 43 m and 139 ft, *f*/64 minimum aperture, manual diaphragm, stop-down metering, built-in telescopic lens hood, 122 mm accessory size, dimensions with focusing unit 135 mm diameter × 731 mm length (5⅚ in × 35 in), weight 3.1 kg (6.9 lb).

Designed as an apochromat, virtually eliminating chromatic aberration for best image quality, this longest of the Nikon super telephoto lenses is useful for sports, photo-journalism or wildlife photography. The mannual diaphragm of the focusing unit tends to produce vignetting, so it must therefore be left at *f*/4.5. Because of the small maximum aperture, Focusing Screen Types G4 or H4 are suggested for best viewing and focusing.

Following the introduction of the four super-telephoto lens heads and common focusing units, Nikon announced three additional heads in the same 600, 800 and 1200 mm focal lengths and apertures, known as the Nikkor ED series. These three heads incorporate extra low dispersion (ED) optical glass, developed by Nikon, which is particularly effective in minimising secondary colour aberration.

Although this glass has optical characteristics similar to those of calcium fluorite crystal, ED has a more constant refractive index over a wider range of temperatures, and therefore lenses made of this glass experience less shift of focus during temperature variations. ED glass is also much harder and more resistant to scratching, and can thus be used for both first and last elements to obtain best possible correction of chromatic aberration over the widest possible wavelength range. These lenses have exceptional sharpness and full contrast extending even to the infra-red region, and use separate infra-red focus index. They have the same uses of the first group of four, but perform to a higher level for the most critical user.

600 mm f/5.6 ED-Nikkor 5 elements in 4 groups, 4° 10′ picture angle, distance scale graduated in metres and feet to 11 m or 35 ft with focusing unit; to 40 ft with Focusing Unit AU-1, *f*/22 minimum aperture, fully automatic diaphragm, stop-down metering system, built-in telescopic hood, 122 mm accessory size, dimensions with focusing unit 133 mm diameter × 515 mm length (5¼ in × 20 9/32 in), weight with focusing unit 3.5 kg (7.7 lb); with Focusing Unit AU-1 4.7 kg (10.4 lb).

800 mm f/8 ED-Nikkor 5 elements in 4 groups, 3° picture angle, distance scale graduated in metres and feet to 19 m and 61 ft with Focusing Unit; to 20 m

Attaching and operating focusing unit lenses

To attach any of the front lens group to the Au-1 Focusing Unit, simply screw lens into focusing unit end.

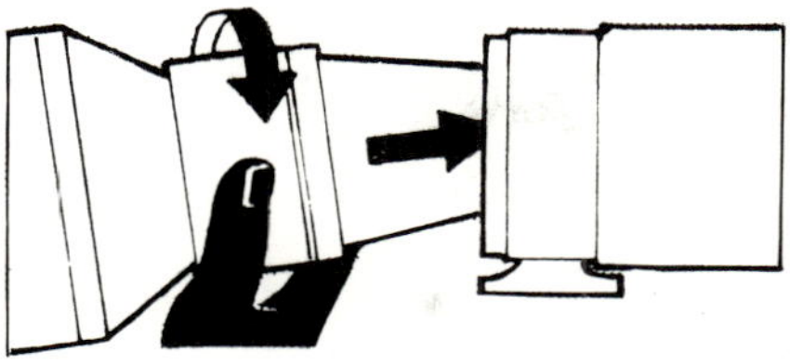

Position unit so its mounting index dot is aligned with that on camera. Bring camera and unit together, twist camera body clockwise until click is heard.

To remove filter holder, push holder release button, grasp holder's milled end and pull out. Holder accepts threaded 52 mm filters in recessed side.

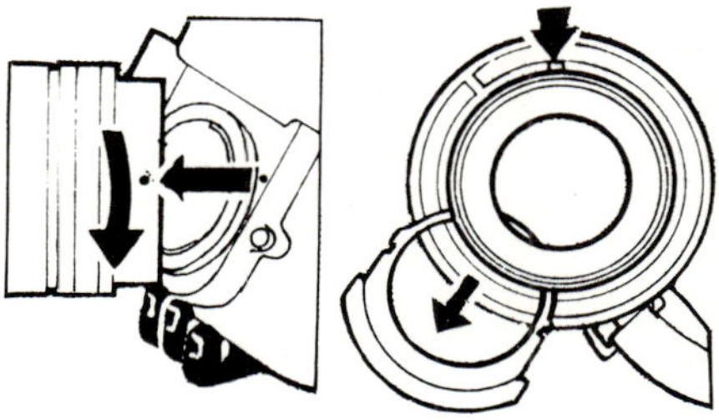

Focusing handle attaches in either of two mounting positions. Use it or the focusing ring.

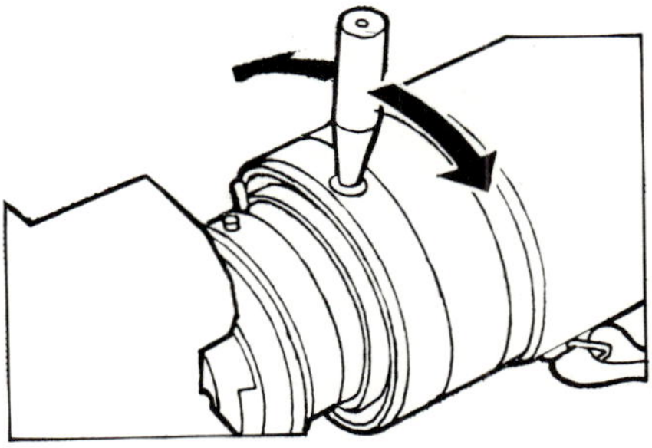

Adjustable focusing scale must be matched to focal length lens in use. Using scale changeover knob, set distance scale to blue scale for 1200 mm, yellow for 600 mm, green for 800 mm and pink for 400 mm.

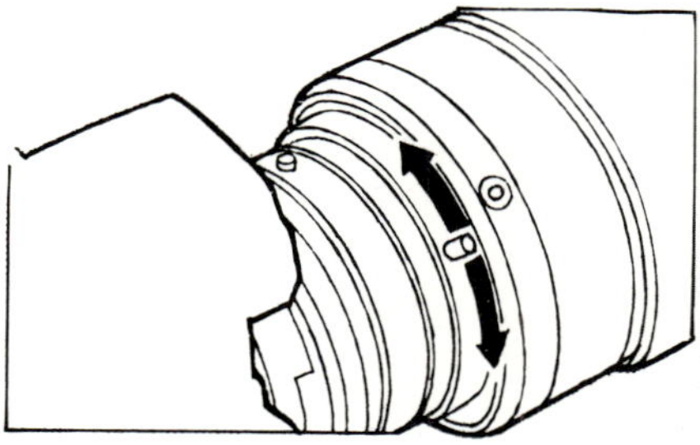

After setting proper distance scale, calibrate by focusing lens carefully on infinity subjects. Using changeover knob, align infinity mark on scale with broad white distance scale index line.

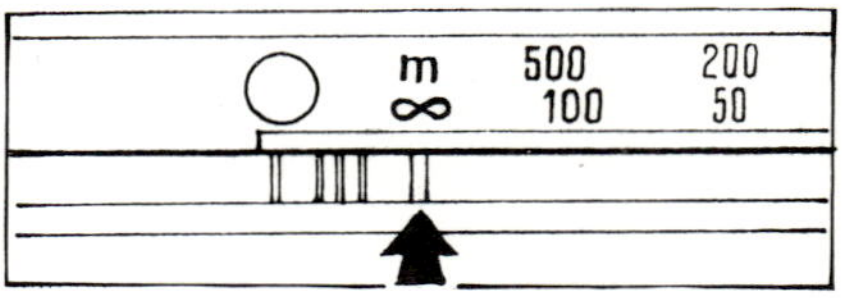

and 70 ft with Focusing Unit AU-1, *f*/22 minimum aperture, fully automatic diaphragm, stop-down metering system, built-in telescopic hood, 122 mm accessory size, dimensions with focusing unit 133 mm diameter × 693 mm length (5¼ in × 27 9/32 in), weight with focusing unit 4.1 kg (9 lb); with Focusing Unit AU-1 5.3 kg (11.7 lb).

1200 mm f/11 ED-Nikkor 5 elements in 4 groups, 2° picture angle, distance scale graduated in metres and feet to 43 m and 139 ft; to 50 m and 150 ft with Focusing Unit AU-1, *f*/64 minimum aperture, manual diaphragm, stop-down metering system, built-in telescopic lens hood, 122 mm accessory size, dimensions with focusing unit 133 mm diameter × 898 mm length (5¼ in × 35 11/32 in), weight with focusing unit 4.9 kg (10.8 lb); with Focusing Unit AU-1 6 kg (13.5 lb).

Reflex Nikkor lenses

Since World War II, photographers have been given a very useful alternative to all refracting lenses: the catadioptric lens. Although sometimes called a mirror lens, the catadioptric lens actually consists of a combination of reflecting and refracting elements. The basic principle is quite simple. Instead of the light entering a refracting lens and travelling directly through a tube with glass transmitting elements, the light path is 'folded' by optical mirrors. It enters through the front glass corrector plate of the catadioptric to the main mirror at the rear of the lens. There it is reflected forward and concentrated to a second mirror attached to the back of the corrector plate. This redirects the light back out through a central hole in the mirror to the film plane. Corrective lens elements may be mounted in this hole.

Because the light path is folded, the lens fits into a tube less than half the length of a regular lens of the same focal length. Many such lenses, including Nikkors, can be focused by changing the distance slightly between the front corrector plate and the main mirror. Since the light path has been folded between them, any movement between plate and main mirror has the effect of changing focus to about three times as much as the same movement could in an all-refracting lens. As a result, these catadioptric lenses can be made to focus from infinity down to extreme close distances. So mirror lenses are generally far shorter, lighter and focus closer than comparative refracting lenses. Catadioptric lenses have a further advantage. Mirrors produce virtually no chromatic aberrations, thus fewer lens elements are needed to yield good-quality images with these lenses.

As in almost all things, with such great assets come distinct limitations. Catadioptric lenses have only a single operable aperture and cannot be used at smaller ones since a standard diaphragm cannot be fitted to them. Therefore an *f*/8 or *f*/11 lens must always be used at *f*/8 and *f*/11. The adjustment of exposure can only be done with a change in shutter speed or through the use of various filters, including neutral density filters which cut the light down but do not actually change the aperture of the depth of field. However, the relatively modest apertures do provide a workable depth of field, either for distant subjects or in closer individual subjects such as birds where the photographer wishes to single out the subject.

Glass mirror lenses have another characteristic which some photographers find useful and others find objectionable. Out-of-focus highlights, instead of appearing as just discs of bright light, become rings with black centres produced by the secondary mirror of the catadioptric lens. While such out-of-focus images may disturb some photographers (since they do not exist in nature), others find them intriguing and have deliberately used catadioptric lenses to produce just such rings for creative purposes. In addition, when out-of-focus lines such as twigs and branches are photographed with catadioptric lenses, they tend to appear as double lines. However, these are seldom noticed unless actually pointed out to a viewer.

In terms of optical quality, catadioptric lenses yield pictures of approximately equal contrast and definition to those taken at the same aperture through equivalent refracting lenses. But most mirror lenses do tend to show some illumination fall-off at the corners. In addition, the true total light transmission of mirror-glass lenses is generally about half an *f*/stop less than the marked *f*/stop.

Problems in using catadioptric lenses often stem from their light weight, which makes them easier to shake. In particular, shutter vibration may cause more deterioration of the image than it would with the same camera attached to a heavier lens. For sharpest possible results, support the mirror lens with a solid tripod. If you can, steady the camera body as well, locking up the mirror if possible.

The dilemma in choosing between an all-refracting lens and a catadioptric can be understood quickly when you realise that the 500 mm *f*/8 Reflex-Nikkor is just about half the length of the 400 mm *f*/5.6 Nikkor, weighs nearly half a pound less and focuses 0.6 m (2 ft) closer – which can be crucial if you are a nature photographer. Now let's look at the three Reflex-Nikkor catadioptric lenses Nikon offers.

500 mm f/8 Reflex-Nikkor 5 elements in 3 groups, 5° picture angle, distance scale graduated in metres and feet to 4 m and 13 ft, provision for rear screw-in 39 mm filters, front screw-in 88 mm lens hood, tripod platform with vertical and horizontal spring-catch positions, dimension 93 mm diameter × 142 mm length (3 21/32 in × 5 19/32 in), weight 1 kg (2.2 lb).

Easily portable for sports or wildlife photography, it is possible to hand-hold this lens at reasonable speeds (over 1/125 s). It has become one of the most important lenses for newsmen and photo-journalists.

1000 mm f/11 Reflex-Nikkor 5 elements in 5 groups, 2° 30′ picture angle, distance scale graduated in metres and feet to 8 m and 25 ft, built-in rotating filter wheel with L39, Y48, O56 and R60 filters, 108 mm accessory size, tripod platform with horizontal and vertical positions, dimensions 117 mm diameter × 238 mm length (4 19/32 in × 9 1/3 in), weight 1.9 kg (4.2 lb).

An excellent nature study, sports and journalists' lens, the 1000 mm *f*/11 Reflex-Nikkor is well corrected for all aberrations, particularly chromatic, and has remarkably good contrast. The filters, a UV, medium yellow, orange and red, can be interchanged for light yellow, deep yellow, deep green or four grades of neutral density by removing the outside metal cover with its four screws and the crescent-shaped cover with its three screws. The revolving turret filter has threaded mounts allowing easy filter interchange. Since the filters are part of the optical system, there must always be a filter in position. For standard picture taking, set the filter turret to the L39 (UV) filter. When used on a Nikon camera, a Type B or E screen is recommended for easiest focusing.

2000 mm f/11 Reflex-Nikkor 5 elements in 5 groups, 1° 10′ picture angle, distance scale graduated in metres and feet to 20 m and 60 ft, built-in rotating filter wheel with L39, Y48, O56 and R60 filters, 254 mm accessory size, built-in rubber-ringed lens hood, accessory forked pedestal mount allows tilting and turning. Lens mount provides full 360° camera adjustment, dual-sized tripod sockets, dimensions 563 mm high × 320 mm wide (22 9/16 in × 13 in), weight 17.5 kg (38.6 lb).

This, the longest focal length lens in the Nikon arsenal, is 40× the length of a normal lens. Three rotations of the rear focusing knob changes focus from infinity to closest distance. Distances can be read in a glass-covered window above the knob. The four filters, UV, yellow, orange and red, are controlled by a knob on the left side of the rear of the lens. A locking knob on the rear of the lens allows the camera body to be rotated to any position in 360°. Because of the difficulties in sighting a lens with such a narrow angle of view, a direct peepsight is built into the handle on top of the lens barrel for initial aiming. Area seen through the sight is approximately three times that of the lens proper. Besides a normal 1/4-inch tripod socket thread, the lens has a heavy-duty 3/8-inch thread as well. It can be mounted on a yoke to provide horizontal and vertical movement.

To attach the lens to the accessory yoke, first position the mount so that the Nikon trademark faces away from the camera. Loosen the wingscrews on the mounting sockets and swing back the covers. Remove the rubber caps from the lens mounting bushes and set the lens on the mount. Then close the covers and retighten the wingscrews. The camera can now be rotated horizontally through 360° downward. The wingscrews and knurled knob on the side of the mount clamp the lens in the angle wished. There are three 10 mm tapped holes at the bottom of the mount to attach it to a support.

For easiest focusing and viewing, you should use Type B, D or E screens in Nikon cameras.

Zoom lens coverage

Zoom lenses can be divided roungly into four categories: wide angle, wide to moderate tele, tele and super tele zooms. An example of each is shown at right coupled to the maximum and minimum picture area coverage of each. Arrows above some lens elements indicates direction of travel for these elements when lens is zoomed. Note: While the 43–86 mm and 28–45 mm lenses have now been replaced in the line with 35–70 mm and 25–50 mm optics, the comparisons shown are still relatively valid.

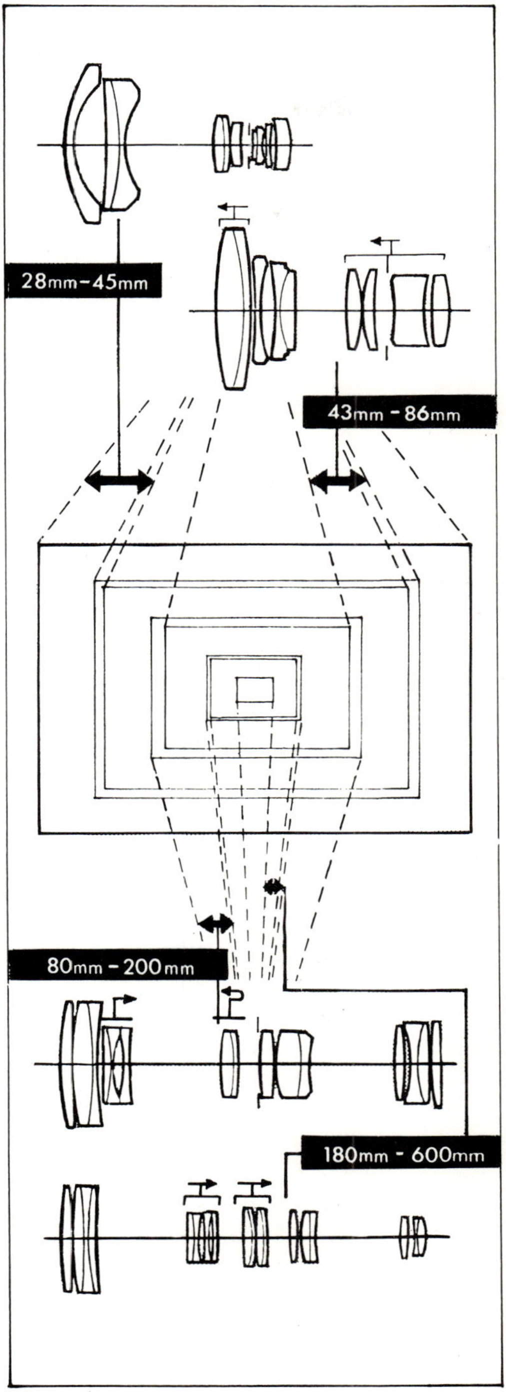

Zoom lenses

Zoom lenses were originally designed before World War II for motion picture camera work. Later they were adapted to television photography, and since then have been developed to give good enough images to be used for still cameras. Basically, a zoom lens allows you to change the focal length ot the lens over a given range while the focus and relative aperture remains constant. They differ from varifocal lenses in that these require you to refocus whenever their focal length is changed.

The basic zoom lens design generally requires a moving set of lenses which shifts the focal length. Most designs employ a compensator group of elements that move to maintain the focus during the zoom. The complexity of such designs – which today provide optical performance approaching that of single focal length optics – is immense. The 50 to 300 mm *f*/4.5 Zoom Nikkor (zoom ratio 6:1), for instance, has 15 lens elements.

In practical use, zooms are generally divided into so-called 'one touch' and 'two touch' systems. A one touch means that the zoom and focusing controls have been combined into a single control ring which allows you to zoom by pushing it forward or back while focusing by twisting it. This is very convenient, since it allows the practised photographer to change focal length and adjust focus simultaneously, even on a subject moving away or towards the camera.

The two-touch lenses have separate zoom and focusing rings. This sytem is most often used today on the lenses with the greatest zoom ranges, in which it is optically difficult (or well nigh impossible) to construct a single-touch system.

Zoom lenses allow you to select at will the exact cropping needed without altering your camera position or changing lenses. Each one replaces two or more prime lenses. Many a picture has been lost while a photographer fumbles for the right focal length lens. It cannot happen if you have a suitable range zoom lens fitted.

Why, then, should anyone use single focal lengths? Apart from the fact that many of them still can't approach the best single lenses, there are three basic reasons:

1. Size and weight: Because of the complex designs, zoom lenses are almost always longer and heavier than lenses they can replace. For instance, the 50 mm to 300 mm *f*/4.5 Zoom-Nikkor Auto weighs 4.9 lb and is 9.7 in long, while the 300 mm *f*/4.5 Nikkor single focal length lens is about half as heavy and is nearly 3 inches shorter. At shorter focal lengths the comparison becomes even more disparate. For instance, a 135 mm *f*/3.5 Nikkor lens weighs only one-fifth as much as the 50–300 mm zoom and is about one-third as long.
2. Zoom lenses generally have smaller maximum apertures. Again looking at a lens such as the 50 to 300 mm zoom, its maximum aperture is *f*/4.5

throughout its range. This is fine at 300 mm, but somewhat restricted at shorter focal lengths. If you need a large aperture for indoor work, few zooms can provide them.

3. Zoom lenses have focusing ranges restricted by their maximum focal length. Again let's take the 50 to 300 mm *f*/4.5 Zoom-Nikkor. While its closest focusing at 300 mm setting is a useful 8.5 feet, this remains the same throughout the zoom. In other words, even at the 50 mm setting, where a normal 50 mm Nikkor would focus to less than 2 feet, the zoom still only focuses to 8.5 feet minimum.

The same considerations apply to other zooms. So, all in all, zoom lenses are fine provided the maximum aperture, minimum focusing distance, size and weight are sufficient and convenient for the photographic work you intend to do with the lens. If not, you needn't discard the zoom completely. Often professionals may use a zoom plus one or more single focal lengths even within the zoom range to cover particular requirements the zoom will not meet.

Zooms do provide one additional useful feature. You can create interesting effects by zooming the lens over a long exposure, or by varying the subject size for multiple exposures on the same frame.

25–50 mm f/4 Zoom-Nikkor 11 elements in 10 groups, 80° 40′ (at 25 mm) to 47° 50′ (at 50 mm) picture angles, graduated in both metres and feet to 0.6 m and 2 ft, *f*/22 minimum aperture, fully automatic diaphragm, meter coupling prong for non-auto indexing cameras, 72 mm lens accessory size, separate zoom and focusing controls, dimensions 75 mm diameter × 112 mm length (2 15/16 in × 4 7/16 in), weight 600 g (21 oz).

This wide-angle to normal focal length lens offers a choice between a zoom covering a full 2:1 range from a remarkably wide 25 mm to a normal 50 mm. Despite the complex optical construction of this lens, it provides all-over brightness, good contrast and definition comparable to that which would be expected from single focal length lenses. It is excellent for interior, scenics and photographing groups.

43–86 mm f/3.5 Zoom-Nikkor 11 elements in 8 groups, 53° (at 43 mm) to 28° (at 86 mm) picture angles, graduated in both metres and feet to 1.2 m and 4 ft, 1 in, *f*/22 minimum aperture, fully automatic diaphragm, meter coupling prong for non-auto indexing cameras, 52 mm accessory size, single-touch control, dimension 65.5 mm diameter × 81.5 mm length (2 9/16 in × 3 1/4 in), weight 450 g (15.7 oz).

One of the handiest zooms for everyday use because of its moderate size, weight and single control, it is suitable for all general photography such as portraiture, landscapes, sports, journalism or candids. Although this lens has been discontinued, I still list it because of its popularity.

35–70mm f/3.5 Zoom-Nikkor 10 elements in 9 groups, 62° (at 35mm focal length) to 34° 20′ (at 70mm) picture angles, graduated for regular zoom mode in both metres and feet to 0.7m and 27.6in; to 0.35m and 13.7in for macro modes, *f*/22 minimum aperture, fully automatic diaphragm, meter coupling prong for non-auto indexing cameras, 62mm accessory size, separate focusing and zoom controls, dimensions 66.5mm diameter × 101mm length (2.6in × 4.1in), weight 510g (18.3oz).

A very compact wide-angle to moderate tele general-purpose lens with almost no distortion, this lens can substitute for a wide-angle or normal lens whenever extremely large apertures are not required. It provides continuous zooming at the same focus, making it ideal for precise composition of 35mm slides. The lens's ability to focus to a magnification of 1:4 in the macro mode at 70mm makes it an excellent choice for ultra-close-ups.

36–72mm f/3.5 Nikon Series E Zoom 8 elements in 8 groups, 62° (at 36mm) to 33.5° (at 72mm) picture angles, graduated in both metres and feet to 1.2m and 4ft, *f*/22 minimum aperture, fully automatic diaphragm, 52mm accessory size, combined zooming and focusing controls, dimensions 67mm diameter × 71.5mm length (2.7in × 2.9in), weight 380g (14oz).

50–300mm f/4.5 Zoom-Nikkor ED 15 elements in 11 groups, 46° (at 50mm) to 8° 10′ (at 300mm) picture angles, graduated in both metres and feet to 1m and 3.5 *f*/22 minimum aperture, fully automatic diaphragm, meter coupling prong for non-auto indexing cameras, 95mm accessory size, two-touch control, separate focusing and zooming controls, rotatable tripod socket platform, dimensions 98mm diameter × 247mm length (3⅞in × 9¾in), weight 2.2kg (4lb 13oz).

70–210mm f/4 Nikon Series E Zoom 13 elements in 9 groups, 34° 20′ (at 70mm) to 11° 50′ (at 210mm) picture angles, graduated in both metres and feet for regular zoom to 1.5mm and 5ft, for macro mode to 0.56m and 1.8ft, *f*/32 minimum aperture, fully automatic diaphragm, 62mm accessory size, combined zooming and focusing controls, dimensions 72.5mm diameter × 156mm length (2.9in × 6.2in), weight 760g (26.6oz).

A remarkably light, compact and inexpensive lens with excellent optical ability and capable of 1:5 magnification in macro mode for ultra-close-ups.

75–150mm f/3.5 Nikon Zoom Series E 12 elements in 9 groups, 31° 40′ (at 75mm) to 17° (at 150mm) picture angles, graduated in both metres and feet to 1m and 3.5ft, *f*/32 minimum aperture, fully automatic diaphragm, 52mm accessory size, single focusing and zooming control, dimensions 65mm diameter × 125mm length (2 9/16in × 4 15/16in), weight 520g (18.4oz).

Nikon owners desiring a very light, compact convenient and very close-focusing zoom at the expense of maximum focal length (when compared with the 80 to 200mm zooms which follow) should be pleased with this optic.

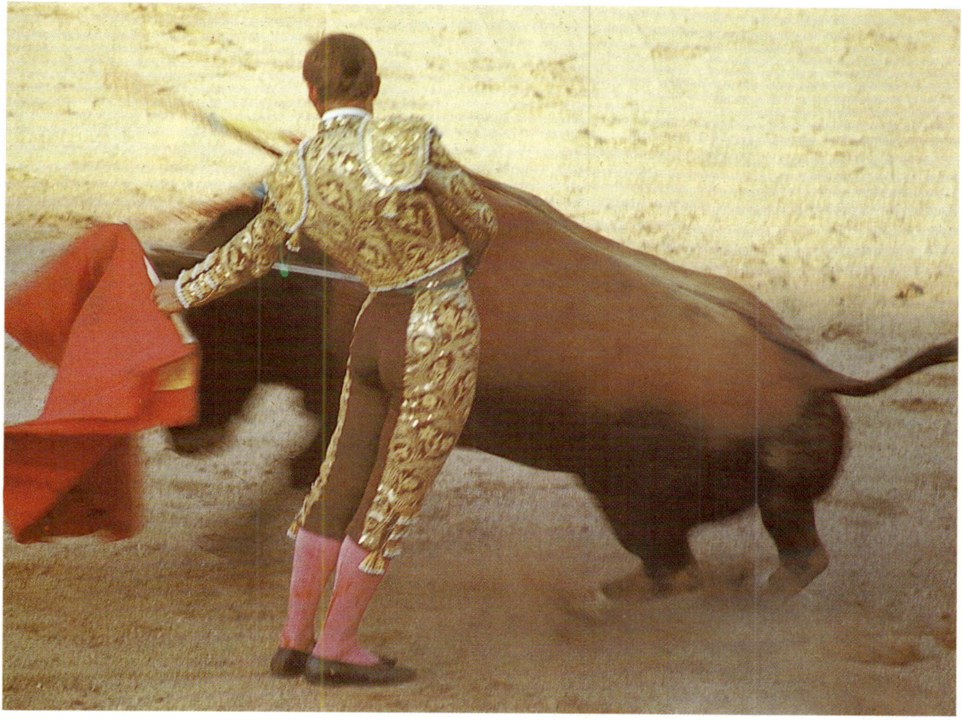

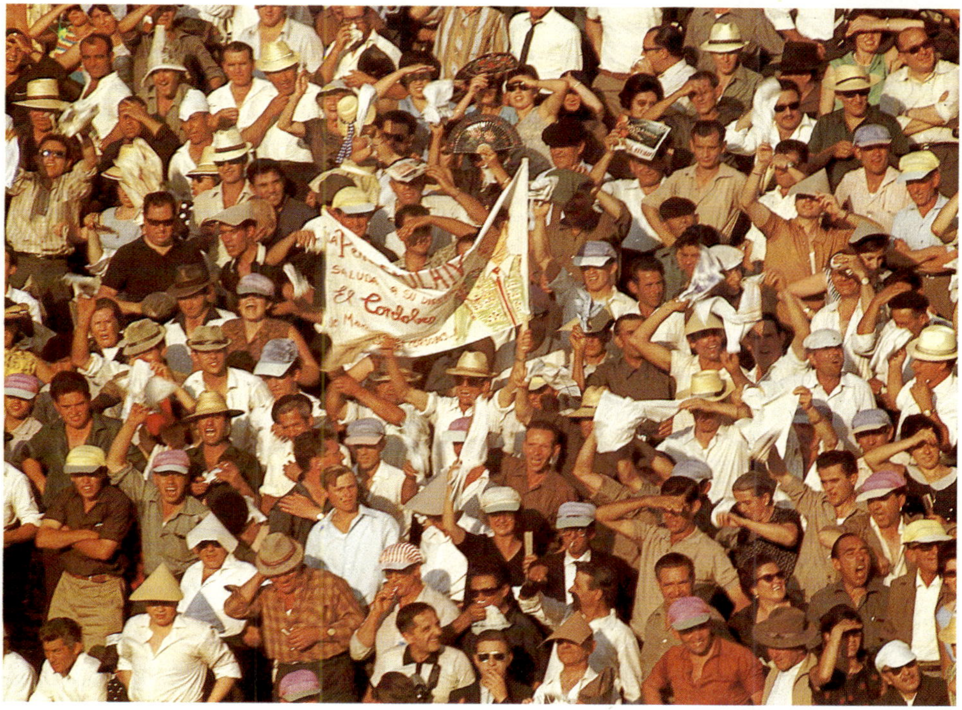

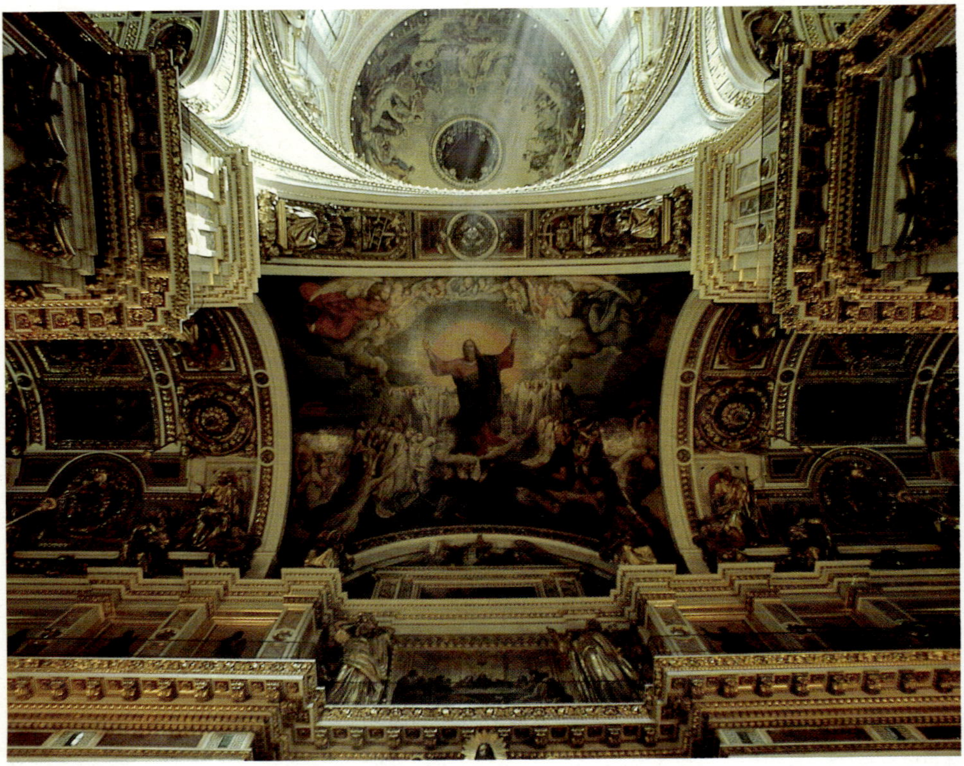

Auto exposure for church interior

Above. How to photograph the incredible ceiling of St Isaacs in Leningrad? Put a Nikkormat EL on the floor, facing upwards, with an 18 mm lens. Make an automatic exposure at about 2 seconds, at *f*/3.5 on fine-grained but slow colour film.

500 mm mirror lens for sport

Previous page. While I do not approve of bull-fights, they are undeniably colourful Spanish spectacles, visually very exciting. For such spectator sports a 500 mm *f*/8 mirror lens in a Nikkormat FT with high-speed colour film was ideal for photographing both El Cordobes, the matador, top, and his cheering fans, bottom. Don't attempt to halt all action with a fast shutter speed. Some blur is essential for the illusion of fast motion.

Soft-focus still life

Right. Dreamy effect of vase and flowers was achieved at outdoor buffet picnic lunch table using plain glass filter sprayed with semi-clear plastic over 50 mm *f*/2 Nikkor on Nikkormat EL at *f*/4, 1/125 second with slow colour film.

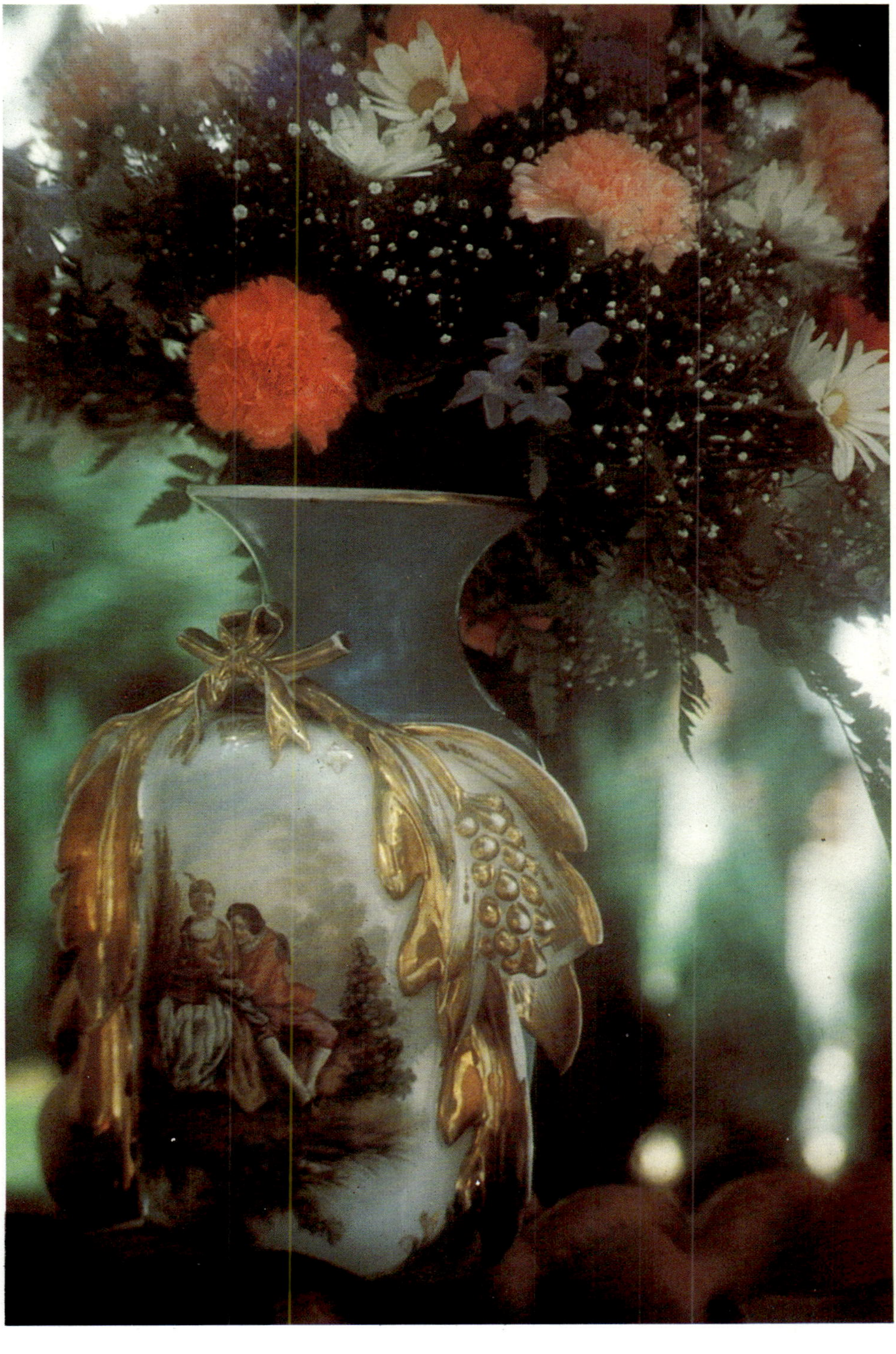

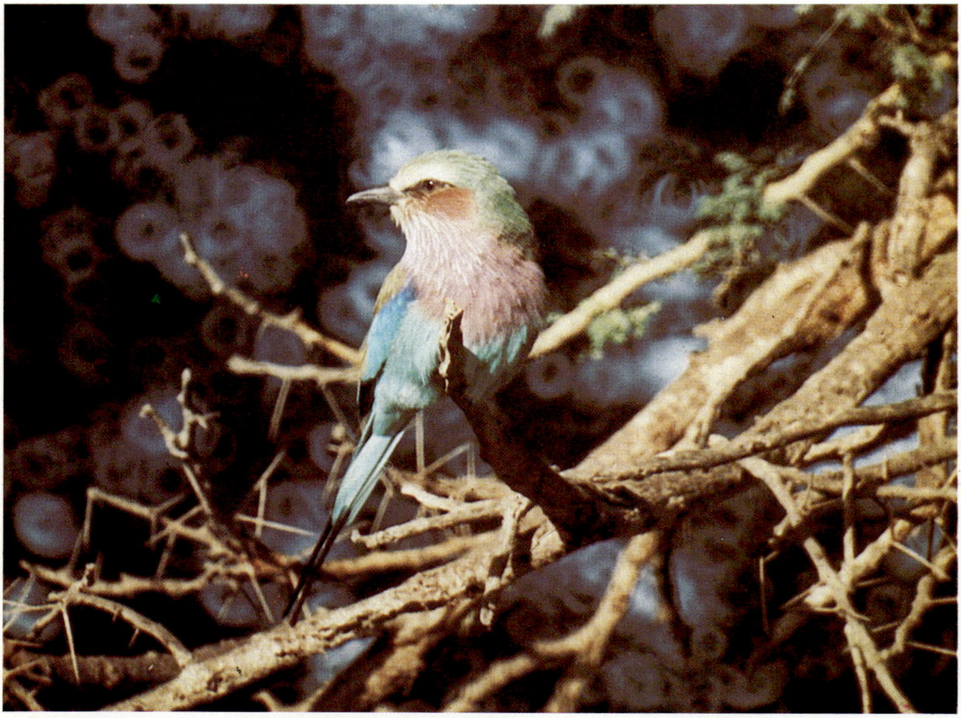

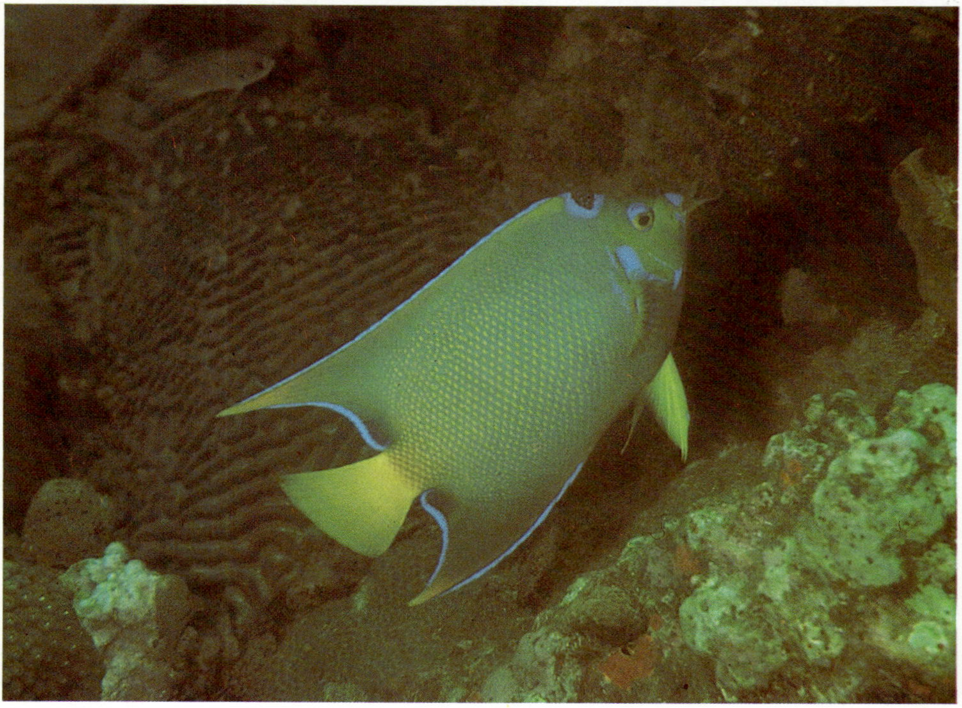

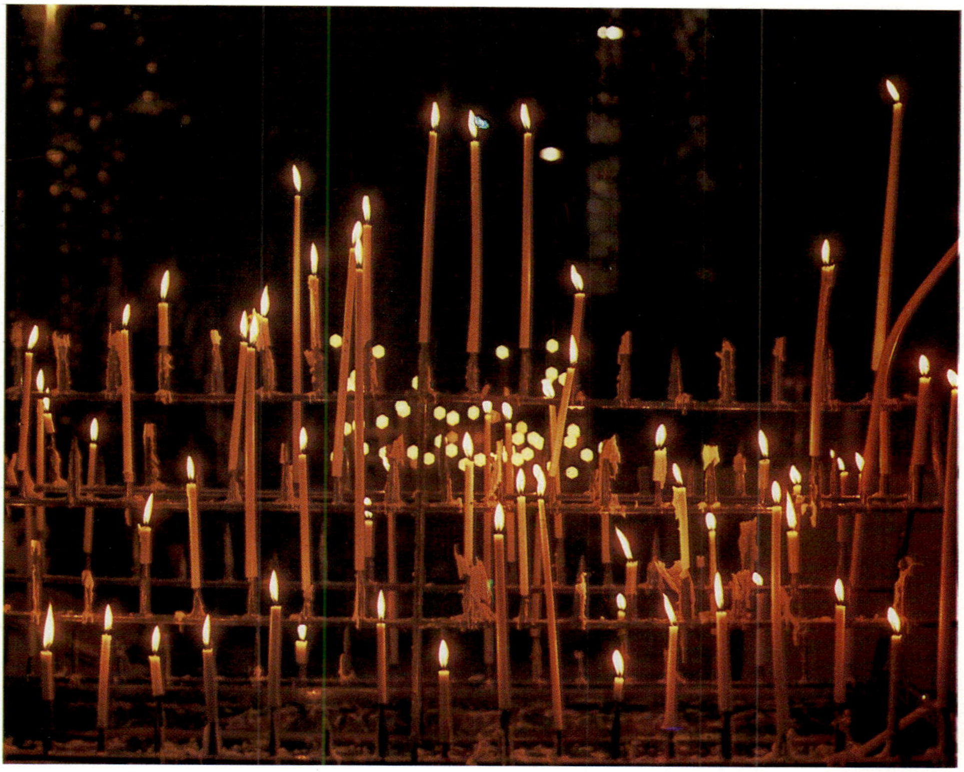

Colour in low light

Above. Votive candles. Chartres Cathedral, France, captured on high-speed colour film, tungsten type, using 50 mm *f*/1.4 Nikkor at full aperture. Shutter speed: about 1/15 second.

Bird photography

Opposite, above. Remarkably small and convenient 500 mm mirror lens at its closest 4 m focusing captures lilac breasted roller during late afternoon. Nikkormat FT 1/60 second. Note the circular out-of-focus light points typical of mirror lenses.

Underwater

Opposite, below. Queen angel fish at depth of 10 m off St Vincent in the Caribbean is captured by electronic flash with Nikkormat FTN and 50 mm *f*/3.5 Micro-Nikkor Ikelite underwater housing on medium-speed colour film.

Wild animals

Overleaf, left. Did I poke my camera right into the nose of the King of the Beasts? No. Leaning out of a car I shot from 4 m with a 500 mm *f*/8 lens, 1/30 second on medium-speed colour film.

Domesticated animals

Overleaf, right. English afternoon sunlight proved ideal soft illumination for this Golden Labrador using 43-86 mm *f*/3.5 Nikkor Zoom at maximum focal length, *f*/5.6, 1/60 second medium-speed colour film.

Filters for sunsets

Final page. Fascinating Caribbean sunset off St Vincent was helped along using two filters on 105 mm *f*/2.5 Nikkor – a radial diffraction filter for multi-coloured sunrays and a graduated brown filter.

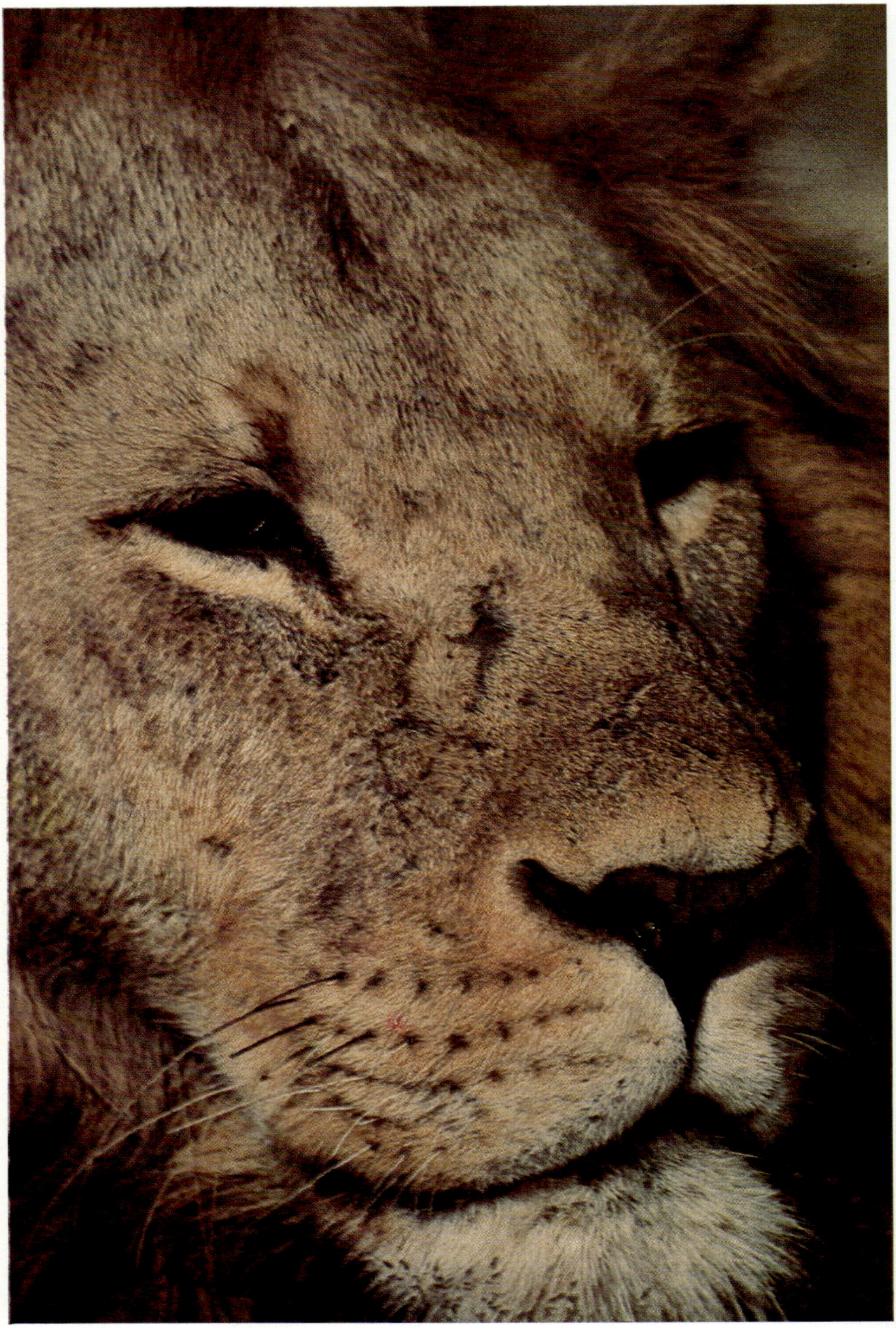

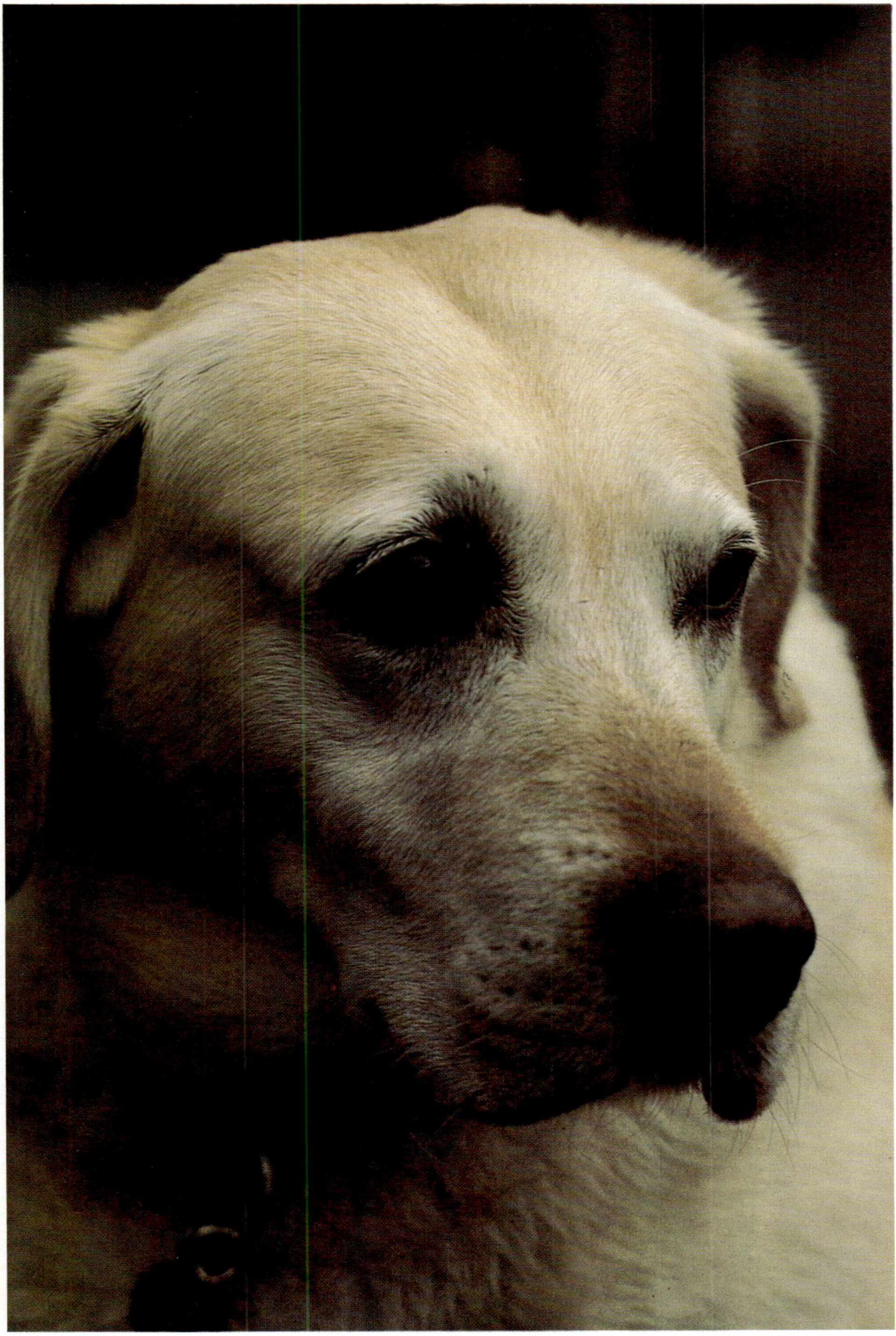

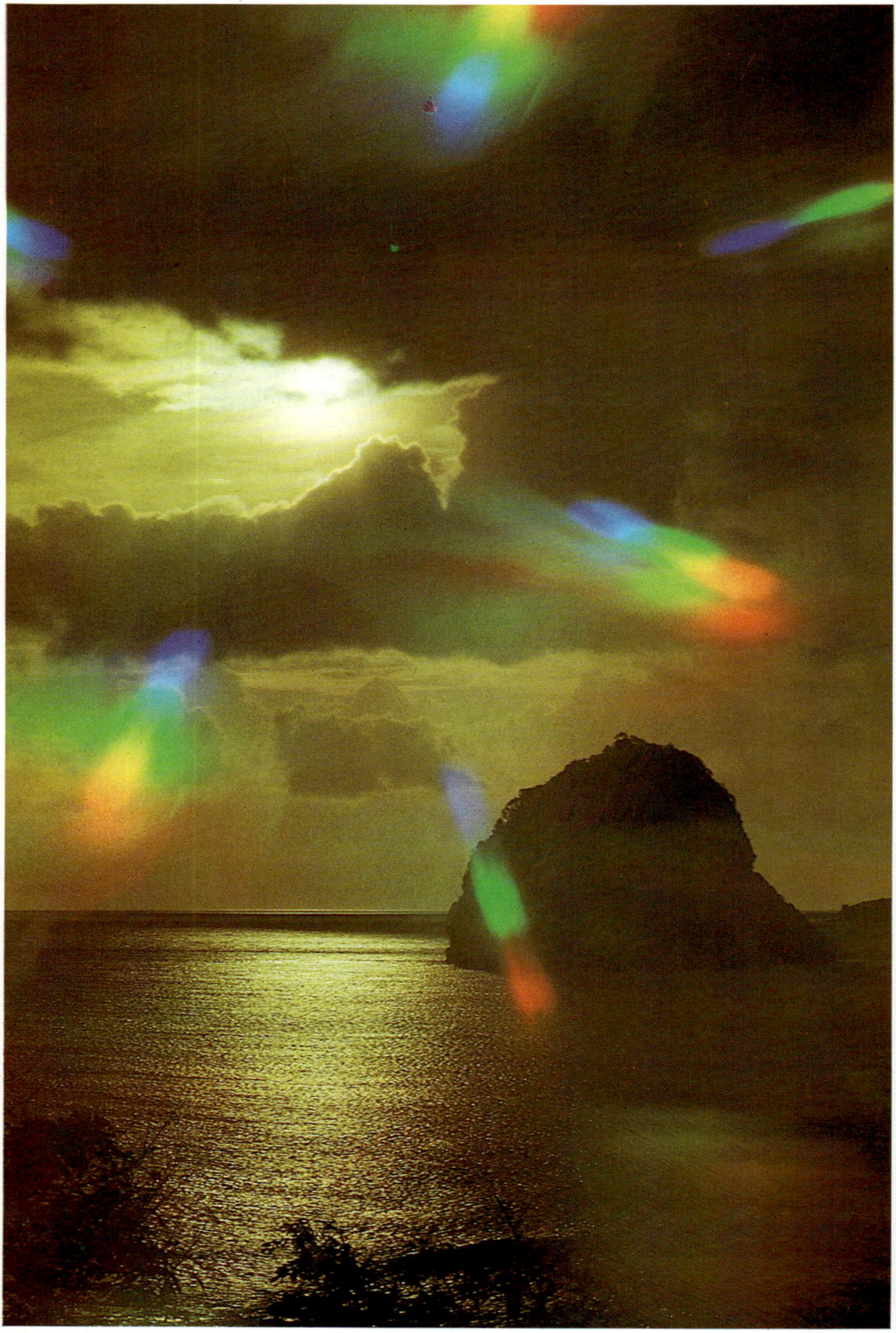

80–200mm f/4 Zoom-Nikkor 13 elements in 9 groups, 30° 10′ (at 80mm) to 12° 30′ (at 200mm) picture angles, graduated in both metres and feet to 1.2m and 4ft, *f*/32 minimum aperture, fully automatic diaphragm, meter coupling prong for non-auto indexing cameras, 62mm accessory size, single-touch control, dimensions 73mm diameter × 162mm length (2.87in × 6.28in), weight 810g (28oz).

This lightweight, compact and convenient zoom is actually only a little heavier and longer than a 200mm focal length Nikkor. The range of focal lengths is very good for sports, news, magazine, industrial and general photography where a moderate long to 200mm tele would be used. Because of its light weight and small size, it can easily be hand-held for picture taking and needs no tripod. The lens has no tripod socket. If a tripod is needed for slow speeds, it should be attached to the tripod socket of the camera itself.

80–200mm f/2.8 ED Zoom-Nikkor 12 elements in 9 groups, 30° 10′ (at 80mm) to 12° 20′ (at 200mm) picture angles, graduated in both metres and feet to 2.5m and 10ft, *f*/32 minimum aperture, fully automatic diaphragm, stop down metering for non-auto indexing cameras, 86mm accessory size, separate zoom and focusing controls, dimensions 91.5mm diameter × 204mm length (3⅝in × 8⅛in), weight 1700g (3lb 12oz).

Although considerably larger and heavier than the better-known 80–200 mm *f*/4 Zoom-Nikkor, this lens provides a full *f*/stop greater maximum aperture speed making it an excellent choice for low existing light photography.

180–600mm f/8 Zoom-Nikkor ED 18 elements in 11 groups, 13° 40′ (at 180mm) to 4° 10′ (at 600mm) picture angles, graduated in both metres and feet to 2.49m and 8ft 2in, *f*/32 minimum aperture, fully automatic diaphragm, stop-down exposure measurement, 95mm lens accessory size, single-touch control, lockable, rotatable (full 360°) tripod mount, dimensions 105mm diameter × 403mm length (4⅛in × 15⅞in), weight 3.4kg (7.6lb).

By using several new glass elements with different dispersion properties, this super tele zoom effectively reduces chromatic aberration usually present in long focal length lenses to a minimum. With the aid of NIC (Nikon Integrated Coating), the lens can produce photographs of excellent sharpness and contrast throughout the zoom range and at all apertures. An important extra feature is the lens's ability to focus close with no need of accessories. This zoom Nikkor is a superb choice for action photography or news work where the photographer is not free to move. Of course, you need to mount it on a steady tripod.

200–600mm f/9.5 Zoom-Nikkor 19 elements in 12 groups, 12° 20′ (at 200mm) to 4° 10′ (at 600mm) picture angles, graduated in both metres and feet to 4m and 13ft with accessory close-up attachment from 4m and 13ft and 2.3m and 7.5 ft, *f*/32 minimum aperture, fully automatic diaphragm, stop-down metering system, Series 9 lens accessory size, single-touch control, rotatable click-stopped (at 90°) tripod socket platform, dimensions 89 mm diameter × 382 mm length (3½ in × 15¹⁄₃₂ in), weight 2.3 kg (5.1 lb).

For the sacrifice of half a stop in speed, and convenience in close focusing, this lens provides a lower-cost lighter-weight alternative to the 180 to 600 mm *f*/8 Nikkor. With good aberration correction over its entire focal length range, this lens is most useful for astronomical, scientific, nature, sports or any action subjects at far distances. The special screw-in close-up lens extends the focusing range considerably. The lens barrel has an orange focusing scale for use when the close-up attachement is in use. The focusing ring has a locking screw to secure the focus and zoom at any settings you want. While the lens is designed primarily for use on a tripod, it can be fitted easily to the Pistol Grip Model 2 through the tripod socket on the lens. It is provided with a shoulder strap for carrying convenience. For easiest focusing with the 180 to 600 mm or 200 to 600 mm zooms, type G4 or H4 focusing screen is recommended for Nikons.

360–1200 mm f/11 Zoom-Nikkor-ED 20 elements in 11 groups, 6° 50′ (at 360 mm) to 2° (at 1200 mm) picture angles, graduated in both metres and feet to 6 m and 20 ft, *f*/32 minimum aperture, fully automatic diaphragm, stop-down metering system, 122 mm lens accessory size, single-touch control, lockable rotatable tripod mount, dimensions 125 m diameter × 704 mm length (5 in × 27¾ in), weight 7.12 kg (15.7 lb).

A most amazing tele-zoom with a similar optical construction to the 180–600 mm zoom Nikkor. The second and third lens groups move to change focal length and maintain the focusing point accurately by a special cam arrangement. Chromatic and other aberrations are well controlled through the use of newly developed glass elements. Nikon Integrated Coating enhances contrast, definition and picture brightness throughout the entire zooming and aperture ranges.

This is probably the ultimate in versatile tele-zoom lenses for sports, action photography and news work. Although covering a vast zooming range with a reasonable maximum aperture, the lens focuses surprisingly close and is relatively compact and light.

Teleconverters

In recent years the lens extender or tele converter has gained much favour as a measure to increase the focal length of the lens in use. This device increases the focal length of the lens in use. To do this, the teleconverter, incorporating usually between four and seven lens elements, acts as a negative lens group and extends the focus point of the converging light rays furthe back. By doing so, of course, some lens illumination is lost. In the case of a converter which

PC-Nikkor features

Here are the features of the PC-Nikkor 35 mm *f*/2.8.

1. Aperture scale
2. Aperture preset ring index dot
3. Stop-down ring
4. Distance scale
5. Infra-red mark
6. Shift-scale index dot
7. Maximum permissible shift index dot
8. Maximum permissible shift scale
9. Aperture preset ring
10. Stop-down ring index
11. Focusing ring
12. Shift knob
13. Depth-of-field scale
14. Shift scale

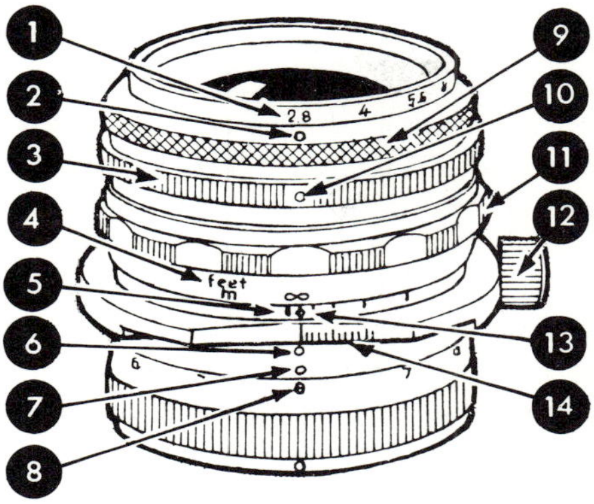

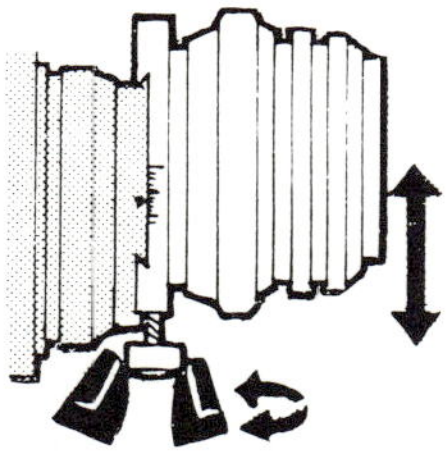

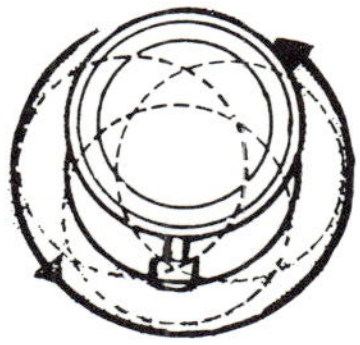

The PC-Nikkor's front part can be shifted up to 11 mm from the centre by turning the knurled shift knob. Each scale marking represents 1 mm of shift. This movement can be combined with a 360° rotation of the lens for a vast variety of lens adjustments. PC-Nikkor 28 mm *f*/4 operates in a similar manner.

Distortion occurs in the picture corners if the lens is shifted too far. Scale shows maximum allowable shift in mm for each direction of lens rotation when shifted in directions indicated on circle below. 1 is maximum shift while 2 represents picture area when there is no shift.

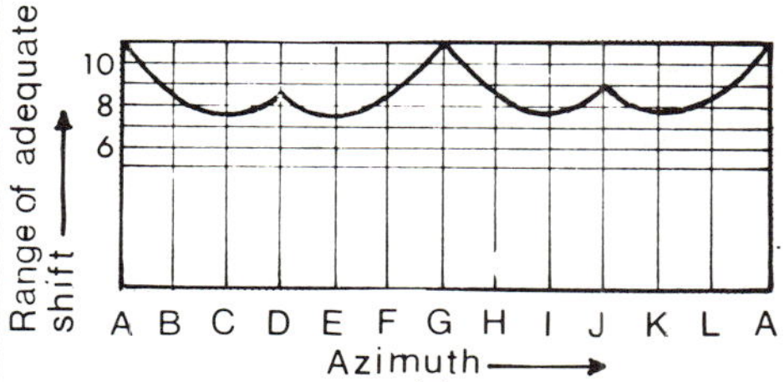

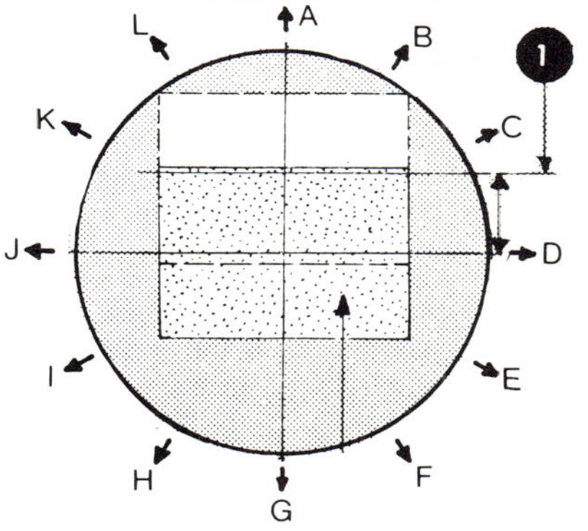

doubles the focal length (usually referred to as a 2× converter), the actual set aperture of the lens is reduced by two full *f*/stops. Thus a converter on a 135mm *f*/2.8 lens would make it into a 270mm *f*/5.6.

There are some other advantages and a number of disadvantages. On the plus side is the maintenance of the same focusing ability as the lens alone. For instance, a 135mm *f*/2.8 lens might focus as close as 1.3m or 4½ft. With a 2× converter, this very close focusing is maintained, making the combination excellent for very close photography. Viewing and focusing take place right through the camera's own system, and many such converters couple fully to both the camera's metering and automatic diaphragm mechanisms, making them very convenient to use. Moreover, a single converter generally fits almost any lens, so it has as many uses as the owner has original lenses.

Nikon first introduced two Teleconverters, the TC-1 and TC-2 with full diaphragm and meter coupling. The AI versions are the TC-200 and TC-300. The optical performance of Nikkors with these matched converters in place, while not equal to that of the original lens, is still amazingly good.

Teleconverter TC-1 (TC-200) 7 elements in 5 groups, doubles focal length, designed for 200mm lenses or below (except fisheye lenses which require mirror lock-up), 50–300mm *f*/4.5 Zoom-Nikkor (with some vignetting) and 500mm *f*/8 Reflex Nikkor. Depth of field: half that of lens in use, aperture coupling range *f*/2 to *f*/32 (effectively *f*/4 to *f*/64), fully automatic diaphragm, meter coupling prong for open-aperture reading, dimensions 65mm diameter × 57.4mm length (2½in × 2¼in), weight 220g (7½oz).

Teleconverter TC-2 (TC-300) 5 elements in 5 groups, doubles focal length, designed for 300mm lenses or more (except 500mm *f*/8 Reflex-Nikkor and 50–300mm *f*/4.5 Nikkor-Zoom) and 105mm *f*/4 Micro-Nikkor. Depth of field: half that of lens in use, aperture coupling range *f*/2.8 to *f*/32 (effectively *f*/5.6 to *f*/64), fully automatic diaphragm, meter coupling prong for open-aperture reading, dimensions 65mm diameter × 115mm length (2½ in × 4⅜in), weight 290g (10oz).

Teleconverter TC-14 5 elements in 5 groups, increases focal length by 1.4×, designed for 180mm *f*/2.8 Nikkor, all 300mm to 1200mm lenses, except Zoom-Nikkors, Reflex-Nikkors. Depth of field: 1/1.4 that of lens in use, decreases marked lens aperture by one *f*/stop, aperture coupling range *f*/2 to *f*/32 (effectively *f*/2.8 to *f*/45), fully automatic diaphragm, can only be used with AI lenses; when used with non-AI camera bodies, exposures must be measured in the stop-down aperture.

Perspective control lenses

Thirty-five-millimetre cameras have long been thought quite unsuitable for architectural photography. This is mainly because they lack the movements available on view cameras. So you have to use extremely wide-angle lenses, or tilt your camera upward to take in a complete building. The ultra-wide angle lenses then show an enormous amount of foreground; or if you tilt the camera, the resulting photograph shows the sides of the building as converging lines. This makes it look as if the building is falling over backwards.

You can cut out excess foreground while printing from a wide-angle negative, but this may need considerable enlargement. A certain amount of distortion can be corrected while making prints by tilting the enlarger easel. However, obtaining overall adequate sharpness with such techniques is difficult. If you can, you may also tilt the negative carrier to shift the plane of sharp focus to match the easel tilt. Of course, neither option is open to the photographer shooting colour transparencies who needs the transparency itself to be correct. While it would be patently untrue to say that the 35mm SLR can approach the versatility of a view camera, the photographer with a 35mm *f*/2.8 or 28mm *f*/3.5 PC-Nikkor does have considerable perspective control. Nikon's original 28mm *f*/4 and 35mm *f*/2.8 lenses have been replaced by the newer optics listed which operate in the same manner but are optically superior and more modern in construction.

35mm f/2.8 PC-Nikkor 7 elements in 7 groups, 62° picture angle, graduated in both metres and feet to 0.3m and 1ft, *f*/32 minimum aperture, preset diaphragm, 360° rotation with click stops at every 30°, 11mm shift (on calibrated scale) in any direction by lead screw, dimensions 62mm diameter × 66mm length (2⁹⁄₁₆in × 2⁹⁄₁₆in), weight 320g (11.3oz).

A conveniently wide-angle for most scenes, with a degree of shift that allows you to 'correct' most converging or diverging parallels.

28mm f/3.5 PC-Nikkor 9 elements in 8 groups, 74° picture angle, graduated in both metres and feet to 0.3m and 1ft, *f*/22 minimum aperture, preset diaphragm, 360° rotation with click stops at every 30°, 11mm shift (on calibrated scale) in any direction by lead screw, dimensions 78mm diameter × 68mm length (3¹⁄₁₆in × 2¹¹⁄₁₆in), weight 380g (13.4oz).

For photographers needing an even broader coverage for controlling perspective, the 28mm *f*/3.5 lens has the same amount of shift available and same type of controls as the 35mm *f*/2.8 lens.

Basically, these are wide-angle lenses with extended film plane covering ability. Their most general use is to prevent buildings from appearing as if they were toppling over backwards. This occurs because the camera normally pictures buildings just as you see them. When you look at a picture, though, your eyes don't compensate for the converging effect produced by looking up at the building. However, by keeping the camera's film plane parallel to the building (instead of tilting the camera) you can picture the verticals parallel. To get the top in, you shift the *lens* upward until the building is completely with your picture frame. Either of the PC lenses can be set to a shift of up to 11 mm. The setting can be duplicated over again by noting the setting on the scale. A Type E focusing screen on a Nikon camera is etched with a horizontal and vertical line. These are ideal guides for aligning linear subjects: you simply operate your lead screw until the converging lines run parallel to those etched on the focusing screen.

Since the picture area is rectangular but the lens provides a circular coverage pattern, the amount of allowed lens shift varies according to the direction of the shift. The maximum allowance in any direction is marked clearly at each clicked position. You can, however, exceed the maximum recommended shifts if you can compose your picture in such a way that an unwanted part of the subject will fall into the danger area.

To photograph a tall building, hold the camera so that the film plane is parallel to the face of the building. Now rotate the lens mount so that the micrometer screw knob is pointing downward. Observe the building through the camera's finder while rotating the knob until all the building is visible and its vertical lines are parallel. Be sure, however, always to check the scale to make sure you haven't shifted further than permissible or, if you have, that you won't be spoiling anything important. Although the shift facility immediately strikes you as useful for taking vertical format pictures of high buildings, don't overlook its use in horizontal views. Even a landscape with just one or two houses can be improved by shifting your lens to make their sides parallel.

The PC Nikkors are not just confined to vertical shifts. If you wish to photograph a building but cannot place yourself directly in front of it, get as close to the centre as you can, and turn the lens so that you can shift it toward the centre of the building. Now, keeping the camera film plane parallel to the building, turn the knob until it appears in the finder as if you are actually standing directly in front. Shifting sideways like this is especially useful if there is an unwanted object such as a tree or flagpole in front of the building.

The shifting ability of the PC Nikkor can also be used for making superior wide panorama pictures. When a normal lens is used to make panorama pictures, one picture is first taken and then the camera is swung slightly to right or left for one (or more) additional photos, which after processing can be joined. If the film plane is not kept parallel for the two pictures, the angles of each picture will appear differently and make perfect joining impossible.

However, you can use the shift of a PC Nikkor to take two pictures without rotating the camera, set up on a tripod with the lens as far to the left or right as possible. Take the first picture, then rotate the lens 180° so that it can be shifted in the opposite direction, for the second exposure. The two photographs will join exactly. The resultant picture with the 35 mm *f*/2.8 PC Nikkor covers a horizontal angle of 78°, about 4° more than a 24 mm lens – and with a much larger image size of course. The 28 mm *f*/3.5 PC Nikkor covers a horizontal angle of 92°, slightly more than you get with an 18 mm

Using the PC-Nikkors

To maintain the sides of buildings parallel, film plane should be parallel to building. With normal lens, photo shows too much foreground, and cuts off building top.

If camera is pointed upwards to encompass entire building, parallel sides of building converge, making building appear as if it were falling over backwards.

By keeping film plane parallel to building and raising PC-Nikkor lens, entire building can often be brought into picture with no converging verticals.

In making panoramic photos by joining two pictures, shift in camera angle produces unjoinable centre in which lines in picture will not match. By keeping camera stationary but shifting PC lens in each direction between photos, perfect matching can be obtained with both photos.

Since panorama made by joining two PC Nikkor photos causes some overlapping, final shot is not equal to 24 × 36 mm frames joined end to end. However here is comparison between PC 35 mm panoramic photo V5, coverage of 24 mm and 35 mm lenses alone on single 24 × 36 mm negative frame.

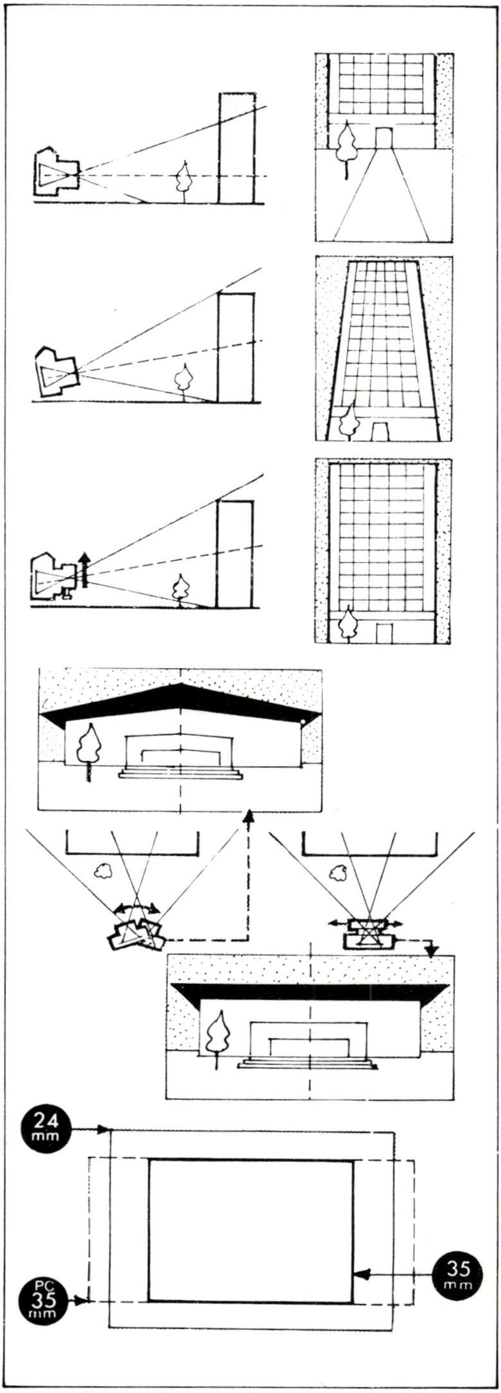

lens. Vertical panorama pictures are also possible (top and bottom of frames matching instead of end to end), but naturally they don't cover so great an area.

For best panorama results, the camera must not budge an iota between the first and second pictures. If it does, they won't line up properly.

A few hints on using your PC Nikkor. It can, of course, be used as a standard wide-angle lens when in its normal non-shifted position. However, when shifted for linear correction or panorama pictures, we'd advise attempting to keep the aperture no wider than *f*/5.6 or *f*/8 for best definition. Remember that you are now shifting the coverage of the lens to its limit where sharpness does slowly diminish. Because you can move them around, the PC Nikkors can't have mechanical connections to the camera. So they have a preset diaphragm instead of an automatic and they do not couple to the camera's full aperture metering system.

The lens diaphragm itself remains open until the stop-down ring is turned (by two knobs on the 28 mm *f*/3.5 lens). This closes down the diaphragm to the preset aperture. Since the lens is rotatable, there are two sets of *f*/numbers engraved on opposite sides of the lens rim, so one scale or another can be read easily regardless of lens position. Meter readings must be made by manually closing the lens down to the shooting aperture you will use. You set the aperture by pressing the aperture preset ring (inwards towards the camera) and turn it until the white dot is opposite the aperture you want. When you release the ring, it springs into a lock position.

Macro lenses

There are five lenses designed specifically for close-up photography use, the 55 mm *f*/2.8 Micro-Nikkor, the 105 mm *f*/4 Micro-Nikkor, the 200 mm *f*/4 Micro-Nikkor IF, the 120 mm *f*/4 IF Medical Nikkor, and the 200 mm *f*/5.6 Medical Nikkor. We'll start with the most popular lens, perhaps the most renowned close-focusing lens for any 35 mm camera in the world. That's the 55 mm *f*/2.8 Micro-Nikkor. (The earlier *f*/3.5 Micro-Nikkor, which did not have the *f*/2.8's superior close-focusing resolution due to its floating design, has been discontinued but operates in a similar way.) Not only can it be used for extreme close-ups, but it is suitable for picture taking at any distance to infinity and can double as a standard lens.

55 mm f/2.8 Micro-Nikkor 6 elements in 5 groups, 43° picture angle, graduated in both metres and feet to 25 cm and 9 6/7 in, *f*/32 minimum aperture, fully automatic diaphragm, meter coupling prong for non-auto indexing cameras, M2, PK-3 or PK-13 extension ring extends close focusing from minimum 1:2 to 1:1 reproduction ration, 52 mm lens accessory size, dimensions 63.5 mm diameter × 70 mm length (2½ in × 2¾ in), weight 240 g (8.5 oz).

Macro lenses

55 mm *f*/3.5 or *f*/2.8 Micro-Nikkor:

1. Focusing ring
2. PK-3 tube reproduction ratio scale. PK-13 ring (above) gives AI metering with AI lenses and cameras
3. Distance indicator
4. Aperture index
5. Meter coupling pin
6. 1:1 tube coupling meter prong (on PK-3 tubes only)
7. Main lens reproduction ratio scale
8. Distance scales
9. Depth-of-field scale
10. Aperture scale
11. Meter coupling prong
12. Lens release button
13. Lens alignment mark
14. Camera body alignment mark
15. AI meter coupling ridge
16. ADR scale

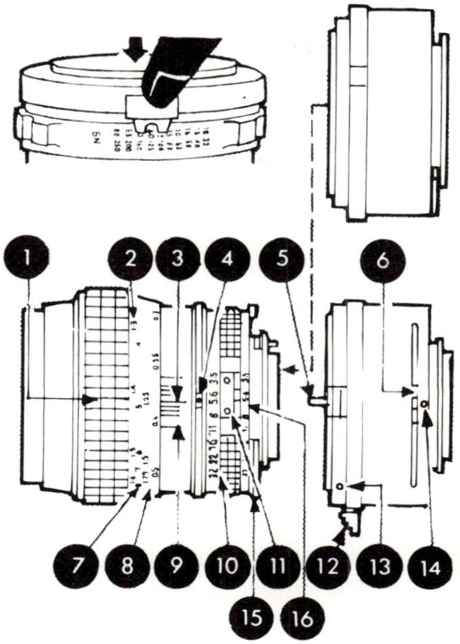

200 mm *f*/5.6 Medical Nikkor:

1. Auxiliary lenses
2. Focusing lamp switch
3. Sync socket
4. Flash ready-light
5. Window shows number or magnification to be printed on film
6. Film speed index dot
7. Film speed scale and magnification scale ring
8. Protecting ring with auxiliary lens selecting chart
9. Lens front ring (unscrew to remove ringlight)
10. Plastic cover
11. Ringlight flashtube
12. Focusing bulbs
13. Pilot lamp switch
14. 200 mm *f*/5.6 lens
15. Film speed lock
16. Aperture ring lock
17. Aperture scale ring

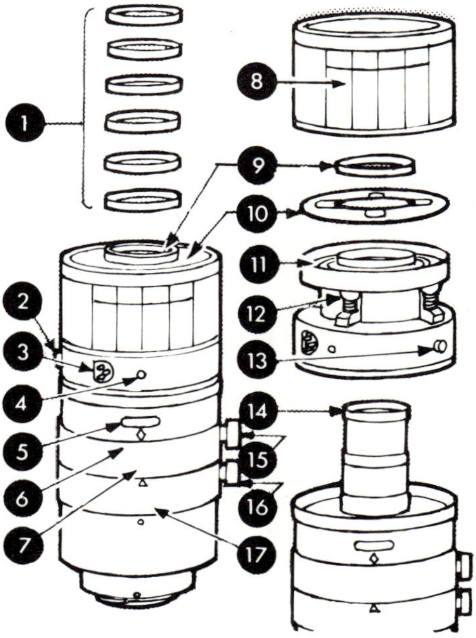

Although this lens performs best at a 1:10 reproduction ratio, its excellent resolving power changes little over its entire focusing range, making it fine for general photography as well as close work. It offer exceptional flatness of field, high colour correction, lack of linear distortion, and is equally good for photography of insects or flowers; or copying flat objects such as drawings, artwork, stamps or making slide duplicates. With the discontinued M2 ring, the automatic diaphragm coupling to the camera is retained for life-size copying although there is no meter coupling and the exposure readings must be made at the shooting aperture. The PK-3 ring provides full meter coupling for all Nikkors with prongs which do not have automatic maximum aperture indexing (AI). The PK-13 ring provides full meter coupling for all lenses with AI when fitted to the newer Nikons and Nikkormats which have automatic maximum aperture indexing built in. The lens barrel, besides having the standard meter and footage scales, also has reproduction ratios clearly marked in blue. The lens can also be used for even greater reproduction ratios with various accessories such as the bellows focusing attachments.

For best possible all-round focusing, a Type B screen is recommended, although I have had no problems with the Type K. The front lens element is considerably recessed, so you don't need a lens hood unless you have a filter at the front of the lens. A lens hood suitable for the 35 mm *f*/2.8 Nikkor-Auto lens can be fitted.

Besides the 55 mm *f*/2.8 Micro-Nikkor, Nikon also offers a longer focal length macro-focusing lens in a similar mount, the 105 mm *f*/4 Micro-Nikkor. This offers the convenience and compactness of a regular lens barrel, with automatic diaphragm and meter coupling for full aperture metering. This lens is preferable to the 55 mm Micro-Nikkor if you intend to shoot three-dimensional subject material, since the greater focal length allows you to maintain about twice the camera-to-subject distance of the 55 mm *f*/2.8 Micro-Nikkor, thus improving the reproduction of perspective. The greater working distance is also more convenient if photographing live subjects, such as insects. In terms of its ability to photograph flat work, it is about equal to the 55 mm *f*/2.8 Micro-Nikkor.

105 mm f/4 Micro-Nikkor 5 elements in 3 groups, 23° 20′ picture angle, graduated in both metres and feet to 0.45 m and 1.55 ft, *f*/32 minimum aperture, fully automatic diaphragm, meter coupling prong for non-auto indexing cameras, PN-1 extension ring (PN-11 for newer auto indexing cameras and lenses) extends close-focusing range from minimum 1:2 to 1:1 reproduction ratio, 52 mm lens accessory size, dimensions 68.5 mm diameter × 104 mm length (2 11/16 in × 4 3/32 in), weight 500 g (17.7 oz).

Another special-purpose Nikon lens triumph is the internally focusing 200 mm *f*/4 Micro-Nikkor IF, which provides almost double the film plane-to-subject working distance of the 105 mm *f*/4 Micro-Nikkor. It is especially useful for shy live insects and small animals, yet because of its length can be used also for superior results in photojournalism, landscapes, candids or wildlife photography. By adding a 2× Nikon teleconverter the lens can focus to a life-size 1:1 magnification while becoming a 400 mm *f*/8. Optically it offers unusual field flatness and sharpness to the picture corners. Its internal focusing makes it an easy lens to operate.

200 mm f/4 Micro-Nikkor IF 9 elements in 6 groups, 12° 20′ picture angle, graduated in metres and feet to 0.71 m and 2.34 ft, *f*/32 minimum aperture, fully automatic diaphragm, meter coupling prong for non-auto indexing cameras, tripod collar, TC-200 teleconverter extends close-focusing range from 1:2 to 1:1 reproduction ratio while increasing focal length to 400 mm and decreasing maximum aperture to *f*/8, 52 mm lens accessory size, dimensions 67 mm diameter × 180 mm length (2⅝ in × 7¼ in), weight 640 g (22.6 oz).

Medical-Nikkor lens

The 200 mm *f*/5.6 Medical-Nikkor Auto has far more uses than purely in medical photography, although it was originally designed for that. The 200 mm focal length is ideal for much close-up work. It lets you work at twice the distance you would use with the 105 mm *f*/4 Micro-Nikkor; with consequent advantages. While normally computed long-focus Nikkors can be used on bellows or extension tubes, they are not designed for close-up work. They provide optimum image quality at focusing distances between their normal marked close-focusing distance and infinity. Used closer, they give lower definition and less flat field. The decrease becomes more marked the closer these long lenses are required to focus. The 200 mm *f*/5.6 Medical-Nikkor has been optically designed to provide optimum sharpness from an image ratio of 1/15 at 3350 mm (11 ft) to 3× life size at 70 mm (2.76 in) from the front of the lens. The various magnifications are provided by threading specially computed close-up lenses over the master lens. This unique optic has a built-in electronic ringflash with a 6000 K colour temperature (for daylight films). It also has an identification number printing device so negatives can be easily marked in camera.

200 mm f/5.6 Medical-Nikkor Auto 4 elements in 4 groups, 12° 20′ picture angle, *f*/4.5 minimum aperture, fully automatic diaphragm, built-in electronic ringflash and negative identification system, auxiliary close-up lenses provide focusing from reproduction ratio of 1/15× to 3×, accepts 38 mm screw-in lens cap, dimensions 79 mm diameter × 177 mm length (3⅛ in × 6⅞ in), weight 700 g (24.6 oz).

The Medical-Nikkor can best be understood simply as a lens with a single fixed focus of 3359 mm (10 ft 11.89 in) which can focus closer through one or two of six close-up lenses. In picture taking, once the lens combination has been decided the photographer moves back and forth towards and away from the subject to obtain proper focus instead of the more conventional method of standing fast and moving the lens. The lens alone gives a 15× reproduction ratio. Each of the six accessory lenses is marked with its reproduction ratio, and are colour-coded for ease of identification. Four combinations of lens pairs are recommended to bring the number of reproduction ratios up to 11. The combinations are indicated on the front of the lens barrel. When you fit a combination of lenses, always put the more powerful one nearest the main lens.

The lens aperture is controlled through two rings. Once the film speed (in ASA units) on the front ring has been set against the diamond-shaped index, setting the rear ring to the magnification sets the lens aperture. That aperture is also marked on the back of the rear ring. Both rings can be locked with knurled screws. Of course, this limits the range of magnifications you can use with film of a particular speed. However, if you need to go a little closer, you can set the power pack to one-quarter power. Then set your ASA speed against the ¼ index mark.

Besides the built-in ringlight (which, incidentally, can be removed for servicing or to provide other lighting angles when the flat ringlight result is not wanted) there are four incandescent pilot lamps to provide easier focusing in poor light. The flash and the pilot bulbs are powered from a separate pack. You can choose between an AC unit and a DC unit (with eight 1.5 V D-cells). The flash operated at full power recycles in 8 seconds; decreased to ¼ power, recycling time drops to 5 seconds with the AC power source. The AC power unit can be set to voltages of 100, 117, 220 or 240 by turning a small slotted screwhead. When manganese alkaline cells are employed in the portable battery case approximately 600 flashes are available at full power or about 1400 at ¼ power.

The lens has a built-in ready lamp on the barrel and there is a three-pronged recessed connecting socket on the lens to attach it to the power source. A standard 3 mm (PC) socket for a sync cord connects to the camera's sync terminal.

To turn on the built-in pilot focusing lamps, push in the white button on the lens barrel. When you release it, the lights go out. To print an identification number on your negative or transparency, turn the knurled white ring on the lens barrel until the number from 1 to 38 appears in the small window opposite the white diamond. To print a reproduction ratio, turn the ring past 38 where the factors to 3× appear. If you wish nothing printed, set the black dot opposite the diamond.

The lens, of course, can be used without flash. In fact, you can take it off and leave it at home if you like. To do this, you unscrew the front chrome ring (the one you screw the accessory lenses into). The other disassembly you may need is to replace the pilot bulbs. To reach them, just unscrew the black cover round the flash. They are ordinary 2.5 V screw-cap bulbs.

120mm f/4 Medical-Nikkor

Here are its main features:

1. 3-pin sync cord SC-22
2. 2× close-up attachment lens
3. Focusing lamp
4. Power socket
5. Data button
6. Focusing ring
7. ASA/ISO ring locking screw
8. Reproduction ratio/distance index
9. 2-pin sync cord SC-20
10. Sync socket
11. Distance scale conversion sticker
12. Aperture scale
13. ASA/ISO ring
14. Reproduction-ratio scale (with prime lens)
15. Reproduction-ratio scale (with 2× close-up attachment lens)
16. Distance scale (with prime lens)
17. Distance scale (with 2× close-up attachment lens)

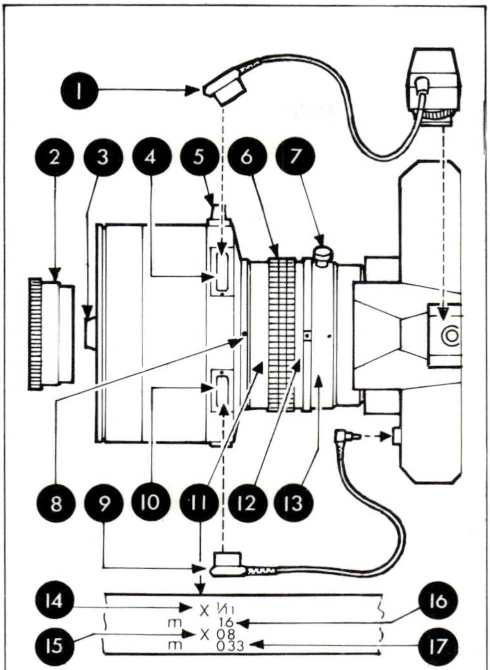

The flash and focusing lamp of the Medical-Nikkor are powered either by a variable voltage AC LA-2 Power Unit or an eight AA cell LD-2 DC Power Pack Unit.

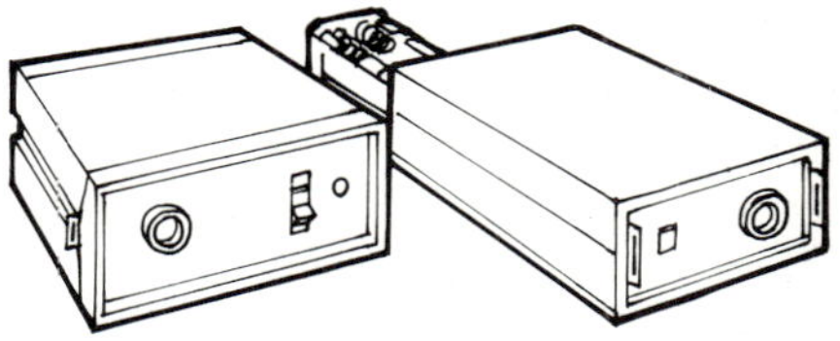

The lens can be focused either in the usual manner, by turning the focusing ring until the subject is sharp, or by setting the reproduction ratio and then moving back and forth until the subject is sharp in the viewfinder.

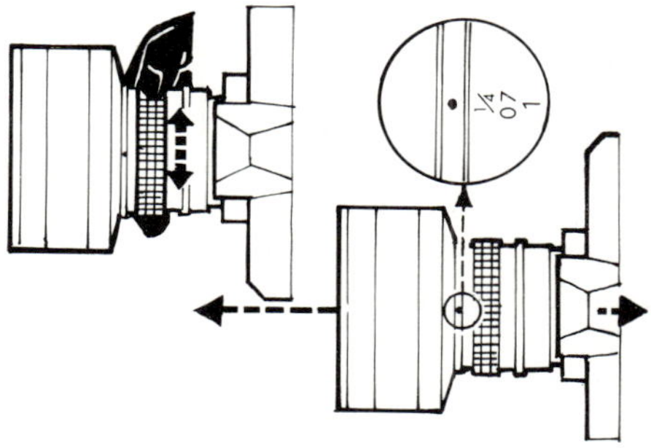

The lens comes with a distance scale in metres which can be converted to feet by attaching the self-sticking footage scale (supplied) directly over the metre scale.

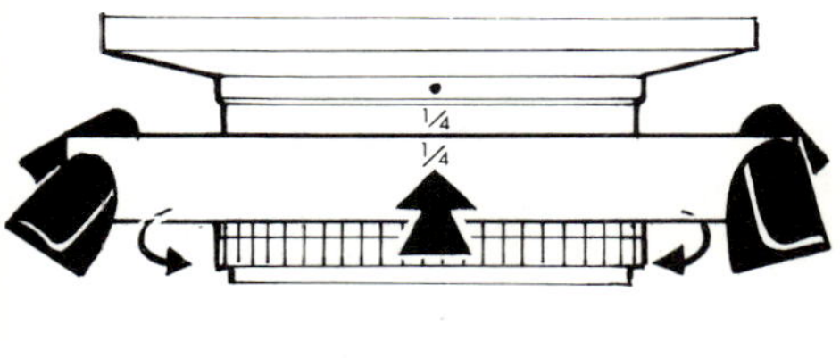

For flashless shooting, regular behind-lens meter readings can be made at shooting aperture since the lens does not have a coupling prong to the full aperture metering system. However, there is an automatic diaphragm, so once you have selected your exposure you can focus and view at full aperture and then press the shutter release when you want. A Type B focusing screen is recommended.

A few suggestions when using this lens with flash. When photographing a glossy surface, avoid direct head-on shots or you may produce an image of the flash-ring on the subject. Also, to avoid possible electric shock from the hot shoe of the Nikon F or F2, attach the safety cover provided on the shoe, or take the flash shoe off the camera. Full tables indicating the magnifications possible, exposure factors and subject field sizes at various magnifications appear in the 'Facts and figures' section at the back of this book.

The 120 mm *f*/4 IF Medical-Nikkor allows continuous variable focusing from a 1⁄11× magnification to 1× using internal focusing (instead of the less convenient set of close-up lenses employed by the 200 mm *f*/5.6 Medical Nikkor). Like the 200 mm version, it features a built-in flash ring and a continuous focusing light. Using a screw-in 2× close-up attachment, reproduction ratios from 0.8× to 2× are possible. Electronic flash exposure is automatic and the reproduction ratio in use can be printed directly on the film during the exposure. Two power sources are available: the LD-2 eight 1.5-volt AA Battery Pack and the LA-2 AC Mains Power Unit.

Mount the lens to your camera as you would any Nikkor. There is no meter-coupling prong to attach to older cameras. If the battery power pack is used, slide the battery-chamber lid aside, remove the battery clip, load with eight alkaline-energiser (preferably) cells and replace the clip. If using the AC power unit, set the correct voltage by turning the screw on the unit to the proper voltage with the edge of a coin.

Connect the battery pack or AC power unit to the lens by plugging the rectangular end of the SC-21 Power Cord (supplied with the lens) into the lens's power socket, and the round end into the battery power socket until it clicks into place. If you're using the AC power unit, plug the AC cord into a convenient wall outlet. The power-unit pilot lamp will go on immediately.

The lens's electronic flash and focusing system can be connected to your camera either by a 2-pin SC-20 Sync Cord which attaches to the lens sync socket and the X sync PC terminal of the camera body (except the Nikon EM and FG), or by the 3-pin SC-22 Sync Cord. The latter attaches to the lens in the same manner but the other end slides into any Nikon or Nikkormat accessory shoe having a sync contact. With the Nikon F, F2 or F3 cameras the proper flash-unit coupler is needed. With the SC-22 the flash ready light in the finder of any camera having such is operable.

Set the ASA/ISO film speed on the lens by loosening ASA/ISO ring-locking screw and turning it until the film speed is opposite the index mark. Dots on the scale represent intermediate setting. Tighten the locking screw.

The shutter speed to be used for flash depends on the type of sync cord in use, the film speed and the camera model. Consult the tables below for the correct settings.

With 2-Pin Sync Cord SC-20

Film speed	*F3*	*FE*	*FM*	*EM*	*Nikkormat cameras**	*F2*	*F**
ISO 100/21° to 800/30°	1/80 s (X) or slower	1/125 s or slower, M90	1/125 s or slower	Not usable	1/125 s or slower	1/60 s or slower	or slower
ISO 25/15° to 80/20°	1/60 s or slower	1/60 s or slower	1/60 s or slower	Not usable	1/60 s or slower	1/60 s or slower	1/30 s or slower

With 3-Pin Sync Cord SC-22

Film speed	*F3 (with AS-4)*	*FE*	*FM*	*EM*	*Nikkormat cameras**	*F2 (with AS-1)*	*F* (with AS-1)*
ISO 100/21° to 800/30°	A (AUTO), 1/2000 s or slower†, X, B	AUTO, M90, 1/125 s or slower	1/125 s or slower	AUTO, M90	1/125 s or slower	1/80 s or slower	1/60 s or slower
ISO 25/15° to80/20°	1/60 s or slower	1/60 s or slower	1/60 s or slower	B	1/60 s or slower	1/60 s or slower	1/30 s or slower

* When using a camera having a sync selector, such as the Nikon F or Nikkormat EL, set it to the electronic flash sync setting.
† At 1/2000 s, the shutter speed is automatically switched to 1/80 s for proper flash synchronisation.

Turn on the power supply. A red LED will light on top of the lens barrel when the flash is ready to fire. It will relight after each shot when the unit has recycled completely and is ready for another exposure (as will the ready light within the the camera finder if your camera has one and you're using the SX-22 sync cord).

You can focus either in the usual manner by turning the focusing ring until the subject is sharp, or you may set the focusing ring to the reproduction ratio you want and then approach the subject until the image is sharp in finder. If you find that the existing light is too dark to obtain accurate focusing, push the lamp button on the lens. The focusing lamp will stay on for 16 seconds after you remove your finger. To turn it off before 16s, switch off the power supply. To change bulbs if one burns out, unscrew the lamp cover counterclockwise and then do the same to the bulb. When placing the new bulb in the socket, align the bulb base protrusions with the notches in the lamp socket. Press the bulb into the socket and turn clockwise.

The distance scale on the lens is in metres. However, a footage distance scale sticker is provided with each lens, which can be put on the metre scale on the lens's focusing ring.

To mount the 2× close-up lens, set the aperture ring of the main lens to *f*/32, insert the 2× lens into the centre of the ringlight, apply slight pressure and screw the close-up lens in clockwise. While the 2× close-up lens is being used, the lens will operate at *f*/32 regardless of the actual aperture set on the scale.

To imprint the reproduction ratio onto the film, push the data button on the side of the lens barrel. The ratios will appear in the lower right-hand section of the picture only when the unit has recycled completely and is ready to fire. The focusing ring must be set at a click stop or the reproduction ratios will not be accurate. The reproduction ratios will appear correctly when the 2× close-up attachment is in place as well.

If you're shooting in colour and the lower right-hand background is green, the date may be difficult to read since it is imprinted in green. With black-and-white film it may not show up if the background is of a light tonal value.

When you are finished with the reproduction ratio imprinting, it can be turned off again with another press of the data button.

The Medical Nikkor can also be operated by existing light. However, exposure must be computed and made at stop-down aperture using the depth-of-field lever or button. If your camera does not have one, the lens cannot be so used.

120mm f/4 Medical-Nikkor 9 elements in 6 groups, 20° 30′ picture angle, *f*/32 minimum aperture, fully automatic diaphragm, built-in electronic ringflash and negative magnification system, reproduction ratios from 1⁄11× to 1× with lens alone, from 0.8× to 3× with furnished close-up lens, accepts 49mm accessories, dimensions 97mm diameter × 142mm length (3 13⁄16in × 5⅝in), weight 920g (32.5oz).

Fisheye lenses

There is one optical field in which Nikon is undoubtedly an originator, innovator and leader – fisheyes. Developed in the 1950s as a lens for a 2¼ non-SLR camera, Nikon adapted the fisheye concept for a 35mm rangefinder camera and finally to the Nikon F and Nikkormat cameras. The term 'fisheye' originated primarily because of the physical resemblance of the pronounced hemispherical front lens elements to the eye of a fish. The term now tends to mean the circular photos taken by such a lens, or the strong barrel distortion of full-film area fisheye lenses. While the original fisheye lens for the Nikon and Nikkormat cameras, the 8mm *f*/8, has now been discontinued, it has spawned five fisheye Nikkors all serving different purposes.

Basically, the fisheye lens may be defined as an extreme wide-angle lens covering a field angle of over 140° (usually 180° or more) featuring increasing barrel distortion towards the picture edges, culminating in the characteristic circular image. This linear distortion can be accepted for the technological applications for which these lenses were originally designed – meteorological and astronomical work, recording of cloud formations, surveillance, and examining the interiors of restricted places such as boilers and pipes. Their strange images are also used for effect, being seen in countless advertising and journalistic photos throughout the world. All the fisheye Nikkors are equipped with built-in filter turrets and all produce circular images on the film except the 16 mm *f*/3.5. Let's take a look at them one by one.

6mm f/2.8 Fisheye-Nikkor Auto 12 elements in 9 groups, 220° picture angle, graduated in both metres and feet to 0.3 m and 1 ft, *f*/22 minimum aperture, fully automatic diaphragm, meter coupling prong for non-auto indexing cameras, built-in filter turret with L1A, Y48, Y52, O56 and R60 filters, equi-distant image projection, 23 mm diameter image on film, dimensions 236 mm diameter × 171 mm length (9⁹⁄₃₂ in × 6²³⁄₃₂ in), weight 5.2 kg (11.5 lb).

This most incredible lens records not only everything in front, above, below and to the side, but also sees slightly behind itself while allowing the user to view, focus and make exposure readings at full aperture through the viewfinder. The large maximum aperture provides unusually good illumination in the finder and makes pinpoint focusing and selective picture control quite possible even in dim light. However, it is an enormous and costly piece of equipment. The 6 mm *f*/2.8 applies the equi-distant projection formulae (y = CO) in order to encompass the extreme picture angle within a finite field size. The zenith angle of any point in the image on film is proportional to its distance from the centre of the image. Because of this constant factor, the lens can be used for measuring the zenith or azimuth angles of astronomical bodies, surveying, recording cloud distribution patterns and, of course, for unusual photographic effects in standard photography.

To position the five built-in filters (Skylight L1A, medium yellow Y48, deep yellow Y52, orange O56 and red R60), turn the knurled filter selector dial on the side of the lens mount until the engraved marking of the filter you wish appears and clicks into place on the dial rim. Do not set the dial to a between filter. When shooting outdoors in sunlight, it's advisable to take several exposures at greater and lesser than the meter recommendations since direct sunlight falling on the fisheye may cause erroneous readings. Alternatively, determine the exposure you need by measuring from suitable parts of the subject with another lens.

8mm f/2.8 Fisheye-Nikkor 10 elements in 8 groups, 180° picture angle, graduated in both metres and feet to 0.3 m and 1 ft, *f*/22 minimum aperture, fully automatic diaphragm, meter coupling prong for non-auto indexing cameras, built-in filter turret with L1A, Y48, Y52, O56 and R60 filters, equi-distant image projection, 23mm diameter image on film, 120mm accessory size, dimensions 123mm diameter × 140mm length ($4^{27}/_{32}$ × $5\frac{1}{2}$in), weight 1kg (2.2lb).

This is probably the most useful of the fisheye lenses for the average photographer. While it does cover a slightly smaller maximum image angle, it's small, light, it allows through-lens viewing, focusing and metering. The range of filters and control is similar to that on the 6mm *f*/2.8 lens.

10mm f/5.6 OP Fisheye-Nikkor 9 elements in 6 groups, 180° picture angle, fixed focus, *f*/22 minimum aperture, manual diaphragm, viewing with accessory direct viewfinder only, built-in filter turret with L1A, Y48, O56, R60 and X0 filters, orthographic image projection, 20mm diameter image on film, 79mm accessory size, dimensions 84mm diameter × 105mm length ($3^{5}/_{16}$in × $4\frac{1}{8}$in), weight 400g (14.1oz).

While the other Nikon Fisheye lenses are more concerned with the placement of objects and their recording in a specified area, the OP fisheye is concerned with determining the exact luminance of objects. The lens provides equal illumination of all objects in the picture area so that the relative and actual brightness of such items as street lighting or sky luminance can be recorded and measured accurately. In order to accomplish this, the lens uses an orthographic projection formula, $y = \sin\theta$ rather than the equi-distant formula $y = C\,\theta$. To meet the needs of orthographic projection, the front lens surface is aspheric. When the area of a light source is measured in an OP photograph, it is proportional to the illumination on a plane parallel to the film surface. Obviously, this lens is even more a special scientific purpose optic than the other fisheyes, although it too can be used for creative photographic purposes. The lens must be used with the mirror locked upwards in the camera and so needs its accessory direct viewfinder. This lens cannot be used on any Nikon or Nikkormat camera without a mirror lockup. Exposure readings can be obtained either with a hand-held meter or by first taking a meter reading through the camera's normal lens. A filter wheel similar to that on the 6mm *f*/2.8 Fisheye is provided. Since illumination may vary in intensity to a considerable degree, it's advisable to take several readings of various parts of the subject and to average the results for your exposure.

16mm f/3.5 Fisheye Nikkor 8 elements in 5 groups, 170° picture angle, graduated in both metres and feet to 0.3m and 1ft, *f*/22 minimum aperture, fully automatic diaphragm, meter coupling prong for non-auto indexing cameras, built-in filter turret with L1BC, O56, and A2 filters, equi-distant image projection, fills entire picture area, dimensions 63.5mm diameter × 61mm length ($2\frac{1}{2}$in × $2\frac{3}{5}$in), weight 310g (10.9oz).

While the other Fisheye Nikkors have been designed primarily for scientific applications but can also be used for special dramatic creative effects, this Fisheye-Nikkor's primary purpose is for creative photography where the picture taker wishes to make use of the linear barrel distortion of the fisheye effect, yet fill the entire picture area. The lens does have some characteristics in addition which makes it most suitable for general-purpose photogaphic use. Flare has been kept to a minimum and, unlike the other fisheyes, even a bright light source directly in the picture area will only cause minimal amounts of ghost imaging on the film.

Because the lens couples directly to the camera's metering system and allows through-lens viewing, focusing and full aperture metering, it's a most convenient lens to use. Its effects can be seen easily on the focusing screen. Skylight, orange, light amber or a light blue filter can be selected by sliding the filter selector lever on the side of the lens mount until the white indicator dot clicks into place opposite the desired filter designation.

Shooting with fisheyes

We have now covered the various Nikon Fisheye lenses. However, some additional instruction is necessary for them.

Using a fisheye lens takes thought and preplanning. Images within the picture area will not appear in the shape or size that they actually are. Central objects come out larger and less distorted than those nearer to the edge of the picture area. Distances are all very much exaggerated. With all fisheyes, but particularly with the 6 mm fisheyes which cover 220°, you must be careful not to include yourself or part of your tripod in the picture unless you want them. Remember, when using a fisheye which requires a direct viewfinder, the viewfinder only shows 160° and therefore not the entire picture. Consequently, just because part of you or the tripod doesn't appear in the finder does not mean that it won't appear in the picture.

Try to prevent direct sunlight from striking the surface of the fisheye lens, since this can cause ghost images. One way to prevent (or at least minimise) this effect is to create an artificial eclipse of the sun by using a 3 in diameter cardboard sunshield held in the picture area by a wire. Hold the cardboard on the wire in front of the lens in such a manner as to black out the sun's rays from falling on the lens. The further away from the lens you can hold the cardboard circle and still provide the needed shade, the better, and the less chance there will be of the cardboard showing up in the picture.

Metering with the built-in exposure system can be a little tricky with fisheye lenses. When using the 16 mm *f*/2.8 which covers the entire picture format you can meter normally. However, with fisheye lenses having a full circular pattern it's advisable to bracket exposures with particular attention to decreasing exposure slightly by ⅓ to ⅔ of an *f*/stop.

I would suggest, however, that those wishing to make use of fisheyes primarily for dramatic effects will find the 8 mm *f*/2.8 and 16 mm *f*/3.5 Fisheye-Nikkor Auto lenses the most useful for the purpose.

Focusing screens

While we will deal further with the various Nikkor lenses in forthcoming chapters, one important aspect of their use should be discussed here – the choice of the proper focusing screen to suit the photographer and the lens.

Nikkormat cameras have a fixed screen. In later Nikkormats, this is in a split-image rangefinder, surrounded by a microprism collar in a 12 mm ground-glass circle outlining the 60 per cent major weighting of the meter. Surrounding this is a fresnel focusing field – quite similar to the K screen on Nikons. Earlier Nikkormats were fitted with either split-image or microprism rangefinders in the centre of the 12 mm circle of ground glass – similar to the standard Nikon A or J screens. Nikkormat screens are not interchangeable by the user.

The central microprism and split-image rangefinder works its best with lenses having apertures of *f*/4.5 or larger. The way a rangefinder works depends on the angle of the two prisms or of the tiny microprism pyramids. Unfortunately, it isn't possible to provide such focusing aids which will work equally with all lenses. When using lenses having smaller maximum apertures, such as teles – or in doing close-up work in which the aperture is effectively less than *f*/4.5 – you may have problems with the focusing aids. With split-image rangefinders, one or the other of the semi-circles goes dark, making it impossible to line up the image of one semi-circle with another. In a microprism grid spot, the tiny pyramid sides will darken, giving a coarse, sandy appearance to the circle, thus making focusing more difficult. At this point Nikkormat owners should switch to the outer fine-focusing areas for best and most accurate results. Unfortunately, there are some extreme picture-taking cases, such as under high magnification on a microscope, or using very long bellows or tube extensions, where low illumination levels make screen focusing well nigh impossible.

Nikon F, F2, F3, FE, FM2 interchangeable screens

The Nikon F, F2 and F3 accept a common grouping of 13 different interchangeable focusing screen types and a total of 19 different screens which not only cover almost any eventuality where a Nikon camera may be used, but generally give you a multiple choice of screens for each subject. Nikon F and F2 screens are interchangeable with each other but F3 screens have a different frame and cannot be used in an F or F2 camera and vice-versa. The Nikon FE and FM2 have a third set of physical dimensions for their screens. These cameras use common screens, but are limited to screens Type B, K and E described later. FE and FM2 screens will not fit other Nikon cameras. Screen choice depends on your preferences. However, with F and F2 cameras some of the specialised screens will need some amount of exposure meter adjustment when they are used with photomic

Nikon focusing screens

Focusing screen inserts for Nikon cameras are made up of a fresnel lens (1) to brighten viewing image to the corners, a condenser lens (2) also to enhance brightness, a matte surface upon which the image is focused (3) and a focusing aid if fitted, here (4) a split-image prism rangefinder as on Type A screen.

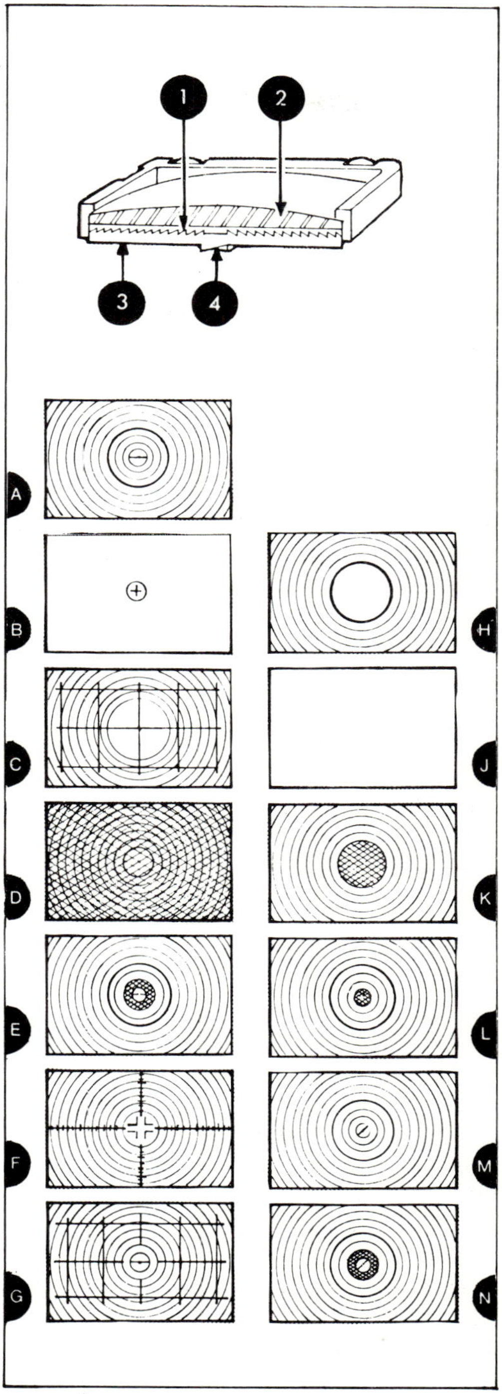

A. Type A screen: General usage with split image rangefinder, fine outer fresnel rings allow full focusing.

B. Type C screen: Central cross hair in clear field with fine matte surround for high magnification parallax focusing.

C. Type E screen: Similar to H but with etched lines for compositional, reproduction, or architectural work.

D. Type H screen: Full microprism for moving objects in poor light.

E. Type K screen: General use with split image rangefinder, microprism collar.

F. Type M screen: Double cross hair, reticle, scales, clear field with fresnel. Same use as C.

G. Type R screen: Similar to C but with split-image rangefinder.

H. Type B screen: Fine matte centre for focusing small aperture lenses.

J. Type D screen: Plain matte for closeup and tele work.

K. Type G screen: Microprism with clear outer area for low light focusing.

L. Type J screen: Microprism matte with fresnel. General usage.

M. Type L screen: Same as A but with rangefinder diagonally.

N. Type P screen: Same as Type K (E) but with rangefinder diagonally.

heads – an adjustment which we discuss and set forth in a table for you. Please bear in mind that Nikon is always improving and adding to this list, so it is advisable to consult your dealer for the latest complete listings.

Type A: The screen formerly supplied with each Nikon F or F2 has a 3 mm diameter circular split-image rangefinder spot and 12 mm diameter circle outlining the major weight of the exposure meter. This screen provides swift focusing with all Nikkor lenses having apertures of *f*/4.5 or larger. If there is no suitable straight edge, however, you have to focus on the fine focusing area. The split image is very effective when using extreme wide-angle lenses which are usually hard to focus because of their great depth of field. Many photographers who have eyeglass problems find this screen the easiest to use since the two split-image semi-circles provide a direct, clear infinity view instead of the standard eye-to-screen focusing distances (see discussion on focusing screen distances, page 127).

Type B: 12 mm fine-ground matte focusing and meter weighting spot, plus full area fresnel-screen focusing. With this screen, usable with every Nikkor and Nikon lens regardless of aperture, you need considerable experience in judging comparative sharpness. There is no yes-or-no rangefinder; you have to use your subjective opinion as to relative sharpness between one focus setting and another. You decide the exact point of utmost sharpness yourself. Many professionals prefer this screen because there are no central focusing aids to distract from the composition.

Type C: 4 mm clear spot and cross-hair with surrounding fine-ground matte field. Although many photographers avoid any screen with cross-hair central focusing aid, thinking it too complicated for them to use, it's actually quite simple. This screen has been created primarily for photomicrography, astrophotography and other high-magnification applications. If you want to use your Nikon on a high-magnification microscope or telescope with a fairly short focal length lens on a long bellows exterior, or other application where a focusing screen would normally get very dark, this screen may be the one you need. The central clear spot remains bright at quite low illumination. By shifting your eye slightly from side to side, you can compare cross-hair with the subject. When the subject is out of focus, the cross hair moves in relation to the subject. However, when the cross-hair and your subject both remain stationary as you shift your eye, the subject is in focus. This most precise type of focusing is called parallax focusing with aerial images. It can only be done with high-magnification subjects. The rest of the field tends, however, to have a rather dark image, especially toward the edges. The Type M screen (which we'll discuss in alphabetical order) with fresnel field is a brighter alternative.

Type D: Overall fine-ground matte field most suitable for 6 and 8 mm fisheyes, tele lenses of 600 mm and over, the 200–600 mm *f*/9.5 Zoom, the 105 mm Bellows Nikkor and the 200 mm *f*/11 Reflex telephoto. This screen type was the very first ever used on an eye-level single-lens reflex. While it delivers an adequate, very fine and usable image centrality, it has no fresnel screen to enhance brightness to the corners by redirecting corner light rays to the user's eye. As a result, the screen darkens considerably away from the centre. This darkening effect can give you a very wrong impression of the overall visual brightness of your picture area.

Type E: 12 mm fine-ground matte focusing and major meter weighting spot with etched horizontal and vertical lines. Same as Type B, but in addition has etched horizontal and vertical lines ideal for architectural or copying work where exact linear alignment is needed – the perfect screen for the PC (Perspective Control) Nikkors.

Type F: There was one, but it is now discontinued. It was quite similar to the J screen (which we'll discuss), but had a 12 mm diameter central microprism spot instead of the present 4 mm microprism spot of the J.

Type G: 12 mm microprism focusing and meter weighting spot with surrounding bright but non-focusing fresnel field. This screen allows you to focus precisely with the microprism and offers an extremely bright picture area to the screen corners even in dim light, but the outer screen area cannot be used for focusing. This screen type is most useful when shooting in very low-level illumination such as for flash photography at night. With the bright picture area you will be able to see all elements plus the framing of your picture. There are four different models of the G screen, marked G1, G2, G3 and G4. Choice depends on the focal length of the lens in use. Each screen has a fresnel screen of different construction to provide brightness to the screen corners just for that particular focal length. The focal lengths for each screen designation can be read from the Focusing Screen Selector Chart on page 427.

Type H: Microprism focusing pattern over entire picture area plus clear fresnel screen. Another series of screen (H1 through H4 depending on focal length of lens used) designed for low-illumination photography. Screen is brighter than a normal A or J to the corners, but not as bright as Type G. However, the entire picture area can be used for focusing, thanks to the overall microprism. The screen does, however, provide a rather unusual, unnatural moiré pattern effect in out-of-focus areas.

Type J: 4 mm central microprism focusing spot and 12 mm diameter circle outlining the major weighting of the exposure meter with full focusing fresnel field. The microprism area consists of tiny pyramid-shaped wedges similar to those employed in a split-image rangefinder, which have the effect of shattering out-of-focus images. When the image comes into focus, the picture seems to snap together. This screen is usable on almost every type of subject material and can indeed be employed to focus on a plain wall – and all other subjects which are difficult for a Type A screen rangefinder. However, some Nikon users do find it difficult to use a microprism instead of a split-image rangefinder. Try both before making a choice. Of course, you can use the outside picture area for fine focusing as you would the centre of a Type B screen.

Type K: Combination of Type A and J, having a 3 mm diameter split-image rangefinder surrounded by a 1 mm microprism collar and full focusing fresnel field. Screen is suitable for all subjects handlable by A and J. Really, it is more an improved A than a better J, since the 1 mm microprism collar is too narrow to substitute for the much more usable 4 mm diameter microprism spot of the J. This is the standard screen type on current Nikon cameras.

Type L: Same as Type A, but with a split-image rangefinder line at a 45° angle instead of a horizontal. This screen has been created for those rangefinder enthusiasts who find that they are encountering too many horizontal line subjects which don't lend themselves to easy focusing unless the camera is deliberately held vertically. The 45-degree split is equally suitable for horizontal or vertical subjects whether the camera is held horizontally or vertically.

Type M: 5.5 mm clear spot and double cross-hair with millimetre scale on full focusing fresnel field. Similar in use to Type C already described, but has brightness-enhancing fresnel to the screen corners, plus highly useful millimetre scale for calculation of object-image magnifications or measuring subjects. I prefer this to the C for microscope, telescope or other high-magnification work.

Type P: Same as Type K, but with split-image rangefinder at 45° as in Type L (see previous descriptions). This is my favourite split-image Nikon screen.

Type R: Same as Type A, but with rangefinder semi-circular prisms having sloping surfaces at a smaller angle, plus etched and vertical lines as in Type E screen (see previous descriptions). The angle of the prisms has been altered to provide brightness of both semi-circles when working with lenses at apertures between *f*/3.5 and *f*/5.6 where other split-image rangefinder screens might have one or the other semi-circles blacking out.

Type T (TV Format for F and F2): Same as Type A but with 12 mm reference circle, horizontal and vertical lines, dotted lines indicating TV-screen format. Solid line shows 'safe action' area and broken lines indicate 'safe title' area. Screen is primarily for preparing slides for TV broadcasts.

Which screen?

The chart on page 427 provides you with instant information on which screen can be used for what lens. However, Types C and M are only to be used with high-magnification work, and putting any lens on a long bellows draw or many extension tubes for close-ups will change the effective maximum aperture and therefore require a screen to fit the new effective maximum *f*/number. For instance, a 50 mm *f*/1.4 Nikkor when used on a long bellows may only give an effective *f*/number of *f*/3.5 or even smaller. A Type A or L split-image rangefinder won't work too well, but a Type R will, although normally suitable. When in doubt, try out a screen if possible at your Nikon dealer.

A brief hint to split-image rangefinder screen users. When you are using an effective aperture which is too small to allow both semi-circles of the split-image rangefinder to be adequately illuminated at once, there is a trick you can employ to make the rangefinder at least partially operable. If you move your eye slightly from one side of the image split to the other, you will notice that the darkening and lightening of the two semi-circles changes one to the other. Therefore, if you are attempting to align a subject during focusing, you may be able to get the bright parts of the two halves to coincide, or make some estimation, by shifting your eye continuously back and forth between the two semi-circles, brightening up one and then the other while aligning your subject.

While almost all the focusing screens available for the Nikon F and F2 cameras will operate properly with the through-lens metering system of the Photomic finders, there are a few screens, namely the C, D, G and H series, which with certain specific lenses do not transmit the required amount of illumination to the focusing screen for proper exposure meter readings. With these, a screen adjustment is needed. This requires the user to set the ASA index of the film in use to one of the dots or numerals on the rim of the ASA setting dial atop the shutter speed dial on the Photomic finder rather than using the red triangle indicator. The chart on page 428 indicates the setting you *must* use with these particular screen-lens combinations. Nikons do not require exposure adjustment when changing screens.

Motor drives and bulk film backs for F and F2

A high-speed motor drive has been available for Nikon cameras since the introduction of the Nikon S-2E motor drive rangefinder camera. Consequently, the Nikon F SLR was designed specifically to accept a motor drive as an accessory. The motors for the Nikon F2 are more refined, convenient, versatile and an integrated part of the camera system.

Why a motor? The first use it conjures up is sports photography. With a fast motor drive, no part of a broad jump, a dive, a motor race turn, a horse race finish need be missed. With the motorised camera, you can shoot single shots and have the motor advance film only; or set the motor to fire bursts so that it releases the shutter and advances film continuously up to 5 frames per second. For flexibility, various power supplies are available. And the system couples to bulk film backs allowing up to 250 pictures per loading, a great asset when using large quantities of film in motorised operation.

The field of sports, however, represents only one segment of the motor's possible uses. With timing devices it can record the opening of a rose, automatically exposing and winding film at set intervals; it can take pictures by remote control either with wires or by radio signal. It can monitor a rocket lift-off. And lastly, it can serve as an excellent aid for any Nikon owner who simply wants to be sure that he won't miss the important shot. With a motor drive you are always ready.

Perhaps one of the most desired characteristics of a motor is portability. This the Nikon motors have – designed for easy hand-holding as well as stationary use. We'll start with the motors for the Nikon F and then go on to the F2.

Nikon F motors

Although there are two officially designated motor drive systems for the Nikon F, the F-36 and the F-250, the basic motor drive is much the same for both. The major difference is that the F-36 makes use of the camera's regular 36-exposure film chambers while the F-250 provides the bulk film back,

Motor drive F-36 for Nikon F

Here are the controls:

1. Fire-rate adjusting knob
2. Release button and single or continuous firing ring
3. Exposure setting ring
4. Frame counter

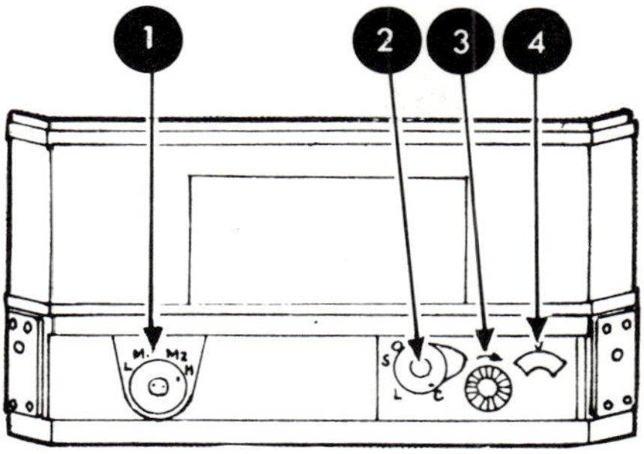

Motor is attached to camera in the same way as the regular camera back but each Nikon F camera must be factory modified to accept motor.

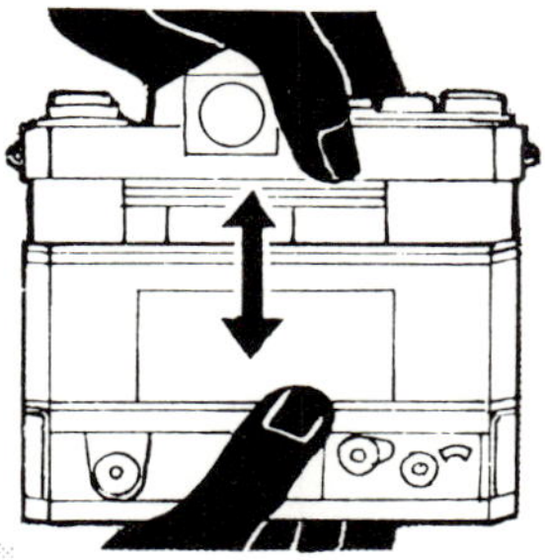

Cordless battery pack makes motor drive camera into single unit, houses 8 1.5 V AA cells.

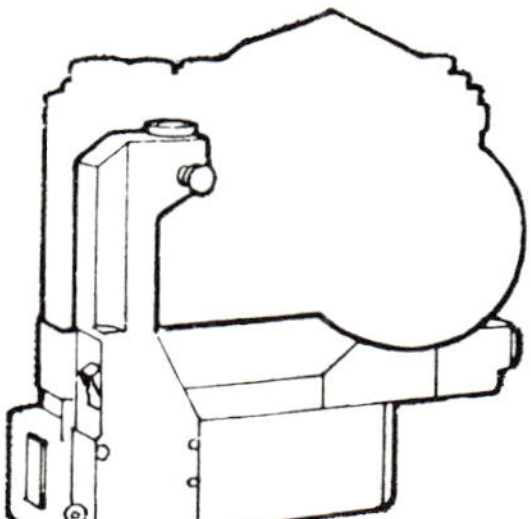

Standard battery pack takes same batteries but is supplied with shoulder strap, 1 metre connecting cord.

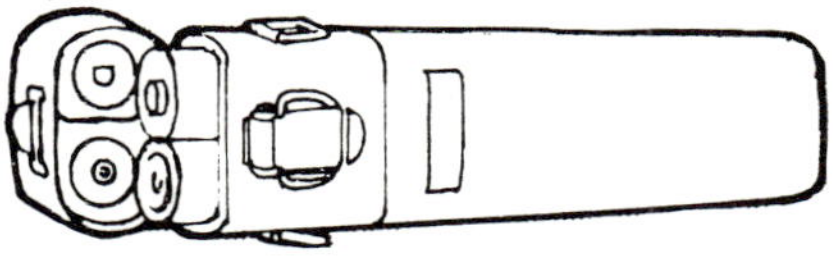

Standard battery pack attaches to camera via connecting cord plug which inserts into motor drive terminal. Other end plugs into battery pack top. Note pack has its own remote firing button for single shots, lock or continuous operation.

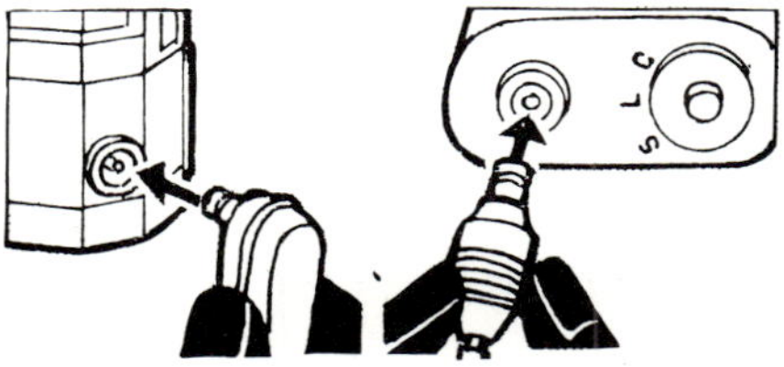

allowing up to 250 frames to be made. The motorised operations of both are similar, although you need more battery power to drive the 250 than the 36, due to the large roll film bulk. Both motors can be run off various power sources which include battery packs separate with shoulder strap, or from AC lines.

F-36 motor drive

The F-36 motor drive unit attaches to a Nikon F camera body in the same way as an ordinary camera back except that the Nikon F must be factory (or authorised factory repair shop) modified to accommodate it. Once modified, the camera still accepts the regular camera back instead of the motor drive back. Film is loaded in the standard manner, but you must make quite certain that both upper and lower film perforations are securely caught by the film drive sprockets before you put the motor drive back on. Nikon recommend that you use Nikon reloadable film cassettes. They cause less drag on the film because they don't need felt light traps, unlike regular cartridges. So you get longer battery life. However, few professional photographers who constantly use motors have the time or the inclination to switch over. They use the film manufacturer's standard film cassettes with no problem.

After you've finished the roll of film, you rewind it manually, using the top-of-camera controls as you would if the camera were motorless.

Controls for the motor drive are located at the bottom of the back of the motor drive, while the top part of the back carries a large, easy-to-read chart indicating the firing rates of various settings and shutter speeds. Controls from left to right are a *firing rate adjusting knob* which governs the number of frames per second that the motor drive will fire in continuous bursts; the *release button S-C ring* which has three click-stop positions for single shots (S), continuous bursts (C) or release lock (L); the *shutter release* for the motor drive is at the hub of the ring; adjacent to the ring is the exposure counter setting ring (by turning it with the ball of your finger you can set the frame counter at the far right of the camera back). Instead of indicating the number of pictures already made (as does the top-of-the-camera frame counter), the motor drive frame counter reveals the number of pictures you have left to take. When zero is reached, the frame counter locks and prevents any further firing or film advancing. Therefore, once the film is loaded and advanced to the first regular frame, the motor frame counter should be set carefully to precisely the number of frames of the roll (20 or 36). If you set the motor to more frames than there are remaining, the motor can pull the film right from the take-up spool. Then you're stuck until you get to a darkroom.

Your standard frame counter continues to count frames already taken.

Let's go back to the firing rate adjustment knob for a minute. There are four firing rates: L (for low speed), M1 (medium speed), M2 (medium speed

2) and H (high speed). L provides up to 2 frames per second; M1, 2.5 frames; M2, 3 frames; and H, 4 frames. However, you must be careful not to exceed certain shutter speed ranges with each different firing rate. Otherwise the motor will start to move the film before the shutter has closed. The table of speeds (which also appears on the back of the F-36 motor) can be found in the back of this book.

Battery packs

The standard battery pack is a separate unit to be carried over the shoulder. Besides the shoulder strap, it's provided with a metre-long (one yard) connecting cord. After you release the opening clip and open the battery case cover, you can insert the 8 C-cell batteries as shown inside the battery pack. Connect the battery pack to the motor drive by inserting the right-angle plug into the motor drive power socket and the straight plug into the terminal on the lid of the battery pack.

You'll note on the battery pack that it has its own release button and a duplicate group of settings to those on the motor drive proper: 'S', 'L' and 'C', so the motor can operated remotely. There is an alternate cordless battery pack, powered by 8 AA cells, which fastens directly to the bottom of the F-36 motor drive. To fit the cordless battery pack, insert the battery pack terminal adapter into the terminal of the motor drive, connect the main body to the terminal adapter and tighten the motor drive attaching screw to the tripod socket of the motor drive by turning the slotted base screw with the edge of a coin. Then depress and tighten the fastening knob on the front of the pack so that the battery pack is held firmly in position. You needn't remove the pack to load or unload film. All you need do is loosen the fastening knob and turn the lock on the camera baseplate to the open position. You can then slide the camera back free of the camera body.

The cordless battery pack has a release button and S-C switch, as does the standard battery pack, so that the motor can be controlled from battery pack position. There's also a release lock ring around the release button to prevent accidental firing. The cordless battery pack has a remote-control socket at the side for the connection of a remote-triggering circuit, intervalometer for time studies or release by wireless control.

One of the most important questions, of course, is: just how many rolls of film will a set of batteries power? You should be able to shoot about 100 rolls of 36 exposures on a fresh set of manganese alkaline batteries. Such batteries will function in temperatures as low as −4°F (or −20°C). If testing the batteries with a voltmeter, you should replace them when voltage drops approximately 20 per cent under load.

AC power supplies

The F-36 motor drive can alternatively be powered by an external AC or DC power supply; however, the power source must be a constant 0.4-amp 12V

DC source. Varying voltages may damage the motor or circuitry. Be very certain when connecting such an external power source that the positive and negative terminals in the connector of the connecting cord are correct. It's recommended that a Nikon Relay Box be used to connect any external power source to the motor drive. Attach the power source to the DC terminal on one side of the box. Then use the metre-long connecting cord supplied with the box to link the motor drive terminal of the relay box to the power terminal of the motor drive. Follow the positive and negative polarity indications on the relay box.

Single frame operation

For single shots with the motor drive (the motor advancing film automatically after every picture, to the next frame), turn the motor S-C ring until the black mark clicks in adjacent to the S setting. Set the firing rate adjusting knob to the H setting for minimum motor vibration. When shooting single shots you can select any shutter speed except T. However, if you do plan to use the B setting, you must lock up the mirror and reduce the external power supply voltage to 9 V. Now you can depress the release button on the motor drive and make your exposure. As soon as you release pressure on the button, the motor will automatically wind both film and shutter to the next exposure. At slow speeds below 1/60 second it is essential that you keep your finger on the release, holding it down until the exposure is actually completed. Failure to do so will result in shortened exposure times and a lock-up of the rapid return mirror. If desired, you can still operate your Nikon F manually by using the regular shutter release button and wind both film and shutter manually with the standard camera rapid wind lever.

Continuous firing

To shoot continuous bursts of pictures for sequence photography, turn the S-C ring until the C setting clicks opposite the black dot. In this position the motor drive releases the shuter, winds on, and releases again continuously as long as pressure is kept on the shutter release button. Of course, the limit depends on how many exposures you have on your 20- or 36-exposure roll. Before firing bursts, select the proper firing rate from the table on the back of your motor as previously described (or from the back of this book). Set the firing adjustment knob to the correct speed. On 'H' for high speed (4 frames per second), the camera mirror *must* be locked up. If you want to view, you must fit a separate finder. By checking the table you will note that the range of shutter speeds available at most firing rate settings can be extended by locking up the mirror. For instance, at the M1 (2.5 frames per second) setting, you can use any shutter speed from 1/60 s upwards, but with the mirror locked you can also use 1/30 second.

Nikon motor drive F-250

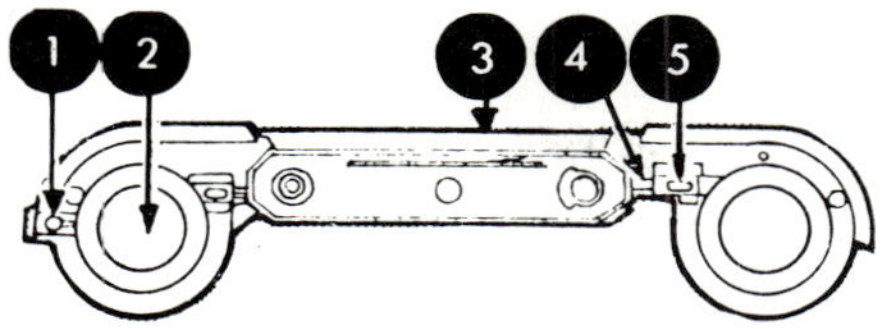

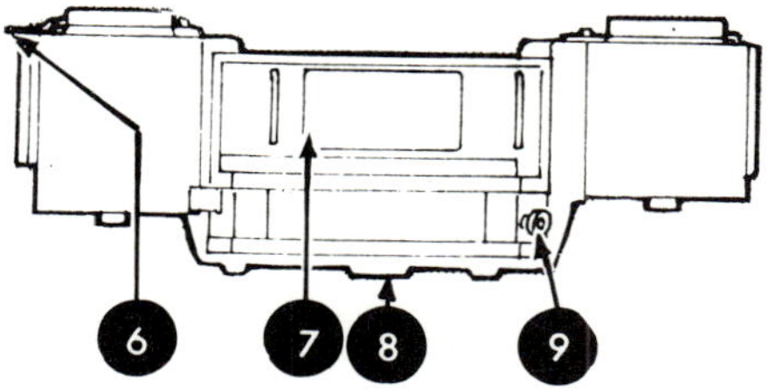

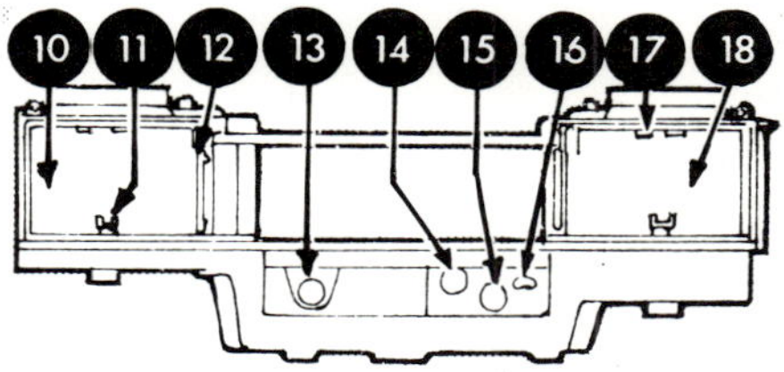

Here are the controls:

1. Back plate lock
2. Open-Close knob
3. Backplate
4. Eyelet guiding recess
5. Camera eyelet fastener
6. Back plate latch
7. Film pressure plate
8. Tripod socket
9. Power terminal
10. Film chamber
11. Cassette spindle
12. Film roller
13. Firing rate adjusting knob
14. Single shot-continuous firing selector knob
15. Frame counter setting knob
16. Frame counter
17. Position pin guiding recess
18. Film chamber

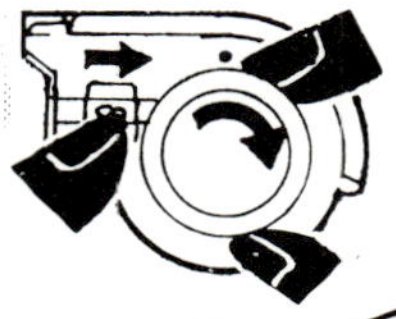

To attach F-250 motor drive to camera, twist knurled knobs on both film chambers in direction of arrows until they click into position. Pull both camera fasteners outwards.

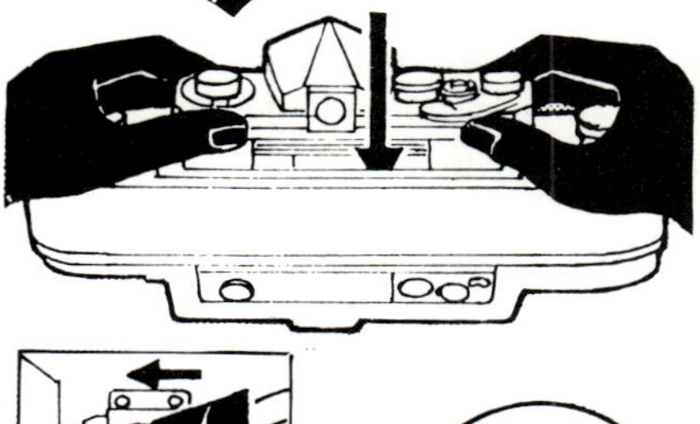

Slide backless Nikon F camera body into motor drive. Seat carefully.

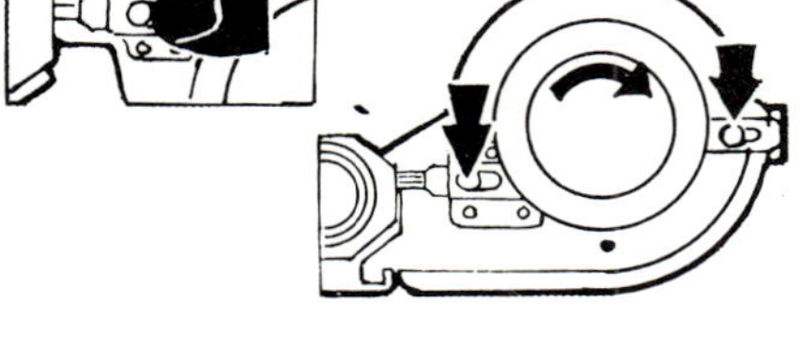

Move camera fasteners inwards on both film chambers.

After loading film, turn both knobs on film chambers to closed position. They automatically slide camera fasteners inwards. Right knob also locks back plate latch.

Do not, however, use speeds below 1/8 s at any time on continuous setting, or exposure will be incorrect and the mirror will stay up. As in single-shot setting, you can alternatively use the regular manual release and wind controls as well as the self-timer while the motor is on the C setting. If the motor drive is firing a burst, however, and at the same the self-timer sets off the shutter, you will lose one exposure, so this should be avoided. With some practice you can keep the motor drive on the C position and get single shots by removing your finger swiftly after the single exposure. There is no run-on with the Nikon Motor Drive, so the motor operation will stop instantly.

Dual controls

There is usually some confusion as to the dual controls on the camera motor drive and the battery pack, since each has a release button and S-C control ring. Each is separate from the other. The camera motor will operate in whatever mode the S-C control is set. In other words, should you set the camera motor ring to S or C or the locked position, but decide to operate from the battery pack controls, the motor drive will obey the battery pack setting.

Remote control

You can set off the motor drive at a distance by cable, timer or radio control. Using a long cable is, of course, the simplest method. A 10 m (33 ft) extension cord is available to connect to the standard 1 m battery pack cord. You can increase this distance by splicing an additional three-wire cable (following the colour coding of each wire). For best operation the total resistance of the conductor should not exceed 3 ohms.

If you have the cordless battery pack, you can operate the motor remotely by connecting a regular two-wire cable and male plug to the socket on the battery pack. A remote switch can then be attached to the other end of the cable.

The Nikon Relay Box (already discussed) is recommended for this purpose. You can control the motor drive from the relay box since the box has its own S-C switch. One end of the relay box has the connecting terminals to the motor drive, battery pack and DC power supply source. The opposite end has R1 and R2 terminals for connecting remote switches, timers and other triggering circuits. To use the relay box for a remote cable trigger, attach the box to the motor drive using the cables supplied with the box. Now attach a standard 2-wire cable to the R1 and R2 terminals with any ordinary switch at the opposite end. Closing the switch acts in the same way as pressing the release on the motor drive itself. While remote control by cable is possible up to a distance of two miles, using the relay box (provided the two-wire cable isn't exceptionally small in diameter), at long distances a radio control is far more convenient. The radio control receiver wires are simply connected to the R1 and R2 terminals.

For time-lapse studies, connect an intervalometer in place of the switch at the R1 and R2 terminals.

Using a relay box connection with each camera body, you can connect two or more relay boxes to a single operating switch for simultaneous release of more than one camera. Follow either circuit diagram given at the back of this book for a proper hook-up.

While the Nikon motor drive units are nearly instantaneous in operation, there is inevitably, in any electro-mechanical system, some amount of time delay between pressing the control and the actual ensuing operation. For instance, when a switch closes the R1 and R2 terminal connection on the relay box there will be a shutter release time delay of about 0.04 second with the mirror locked up or 0.07 s with the mirror operational. When using two or more relay boxes to fire more than one camera simultaneously, synchronisation error between cameras will be no more than 0.02 s. When using a timer or intervalometer and the relay box to set off the motor, there will be a delay of about 0.3 s before exposure with the mirror locked up, or about 0.4 s with the mirror operating.

F-250 motor drive

The Nikon F-250 motor drive is basically the same mechanism as the F-36 save for the enlarged film capacity to accept up to 10 m (33 ft) of bulk film for 250 exposures. The F-250 can also allow the camera to accept regular 35 mm cartridges for 20 or 36 exposures with the motor drive or with manual advance.

Since the motor controls and hook-ups are the same for the F-250 as the F-36, owners of the F-250 should consult the directions already given for motorised operation of the F-36 motor. Here we will first concentrate on the differences in the F-250, starting with the enlarged film capacity which does require a different method of attaching to the camera. Like the F-36, the camera itself must be specially adapted to work with the F-250 by an official Nikon dealer, distributor or by the manufacturer.

To attach the F-250 to the camera, you first turn the two film chamber knurled knobs in the direction indicated by the arrows. They will click into the proper open position with the 'open' marking opposite the white indicator dots. Now pull both camera fasteners outward and slide the camera body (without its regular back, of course) into the motor drive. You may have to use some pressure to seat the camera body properly, but don't force anything. Move the camera fasteners inwards, allowing them to pass over the camera body neckstrap eyelets. They should now hold the camera firmly.

Loading

The right and left film chambers of the F-250 motor drive contain two reloadable film cassettes, one for film supply and the other for take-up. Once film is shot, it is not rewound into the original chamber as in standard 20- or 36-exposure cartridges. Instead, it is wound completely onto the take-up spool, the chamber closed, and the take-up cassette removed. The supply spool can then be moved to the take-up cassette chamber and a new bulk-loaded supply cassette fitted.

Each film cassette has an inner spool, inner shell and outer shell. To open a cassette, hold the outer shell in your left hand with the 'Nikon' mark facing you. Press the release button and turn the inner shell until the opening of both outer and inner shells coincide. Pull gently on the inner shell and you can slide it from the outer.

In a suitably darkened room, open and unwrap your bulk film. Trim the end with scissors to form a tongue, about 3 cm (1.2 in) long and 2 cm (0.8 in) wide. Make a bend near the end. Insert the tongue with the emulsion side of the film downwards into one of the two slits in the spool and wind the film onto the spool. You need 10 m (33 ft) for a full 250 exposures, but up to this length you can load just what you want. Nikon offers a darkroom bulk film loader for this purpose. It can be preset to wind on any predetermined number of frames, after which it will lock automatically (see page 280).

Place the loaded spool in the inner shell of the cassette, allowing the end of the film to protrude from the opening. Now slide the outer cassette shell over the inner. Turn the inner shell clockwise until the catch falls into the deeper recess of the outer shell and you hear and feel two clicks. Then you can turn on the light.

To fasten the load into the F-250 back, place the camera itself, with motor and back already attached, face down on a flat surface. Pull upwards on the back plate latch. Lift and remove the back plate. Pull out the cassette spindle in the base of the left-hand film chamber. The open marking on the knurled knob must be opposite the white indicator dot on the film chamber. Insert the loaded cassette into this film chamber. Line up the red indicator dot on the side of the cassette with a white line marked on the floor of the film chamber. The small projection on the outside of the cassette should fit into the guide notch in the wall of the film chamber. Make sure that the positioning pin and the release button slide into the recess at the top of the film chamber. Push the cassette spindle back in to hold the loaded cassette in place.

Pull the film leader out from the loaded cassette. After opening the take-up cassette, thread the film leader tongue, emulsion side downwards, into one of the two slits in the take-up spool. Reassemble the cassette and insert it into the right-hand film chamber. Rotate the film supply cassette spindle counterclockwise until some tension can be felt. This takes up the film slack. The film perforations must mesh with the sprockets on the sprocket drive.

Replace the 250-exposure motor drive back plate by first inserting the left-hand end into the external groove. Press the right-hand end home until it snaps in place. Turn both knurled knobs on the film chambers until they click into place with the 'close' mark opposite the white indicator dots that open both the film cassettes. The knobs have an additional duty of sliding the camera fasteners inwards to hold the camera firmly in place. The right-hand knob also locks the back plate latch to prevent an accidental opening.

You can now remove any slack in the film by turning the A-R ring on the camera body to the 'R' position and again rotating the cassette spindle of the left-hand film chamber in a counterclockwise direction until you feel some tension. Be sure to turn the A-R ring back again to the 'A' position before shooting.

Shooting with the F-250

To wind on the exposed film leader, shoot off five blank exposures manually, using the camera's own advance lever and shutter release button. The frame counter on the camera itself should now read '3'. To be certain the film is advancing correctly in the back, check while winding the white dots on the left-hand chamber cassette spindle. If they rotate clockwise, film has been loaded correctly and it is advancing properly.

The motor drive is operated in the same manner as that of the F-36 save for the fact that the frame counter at the rear indicates up to 250 exposures remaining instead of just up to 36. Like the F-36 motor, the motor locks and ceases to operate when the counter reaches zero. To unload film, make five additional exposures, using the manual shutter advance lever and release button to wind on the last exposures made. Rotate both knurled knobs on the film chambers to the 'open' position. This closes the film cassettes, preventing any light from striking the film when it's removed from the back. It is most important, however, that you make certain to rotate *both* knobs fully by making complete turns.

You can now remove the backplate of the motor drive by pulling up the back plate latch. Pull out the cassette spindles of the right- and left-hand film chambers. Turn the motor drive downwards and the cassettes drop out.

While the F-250 motor drive has been designed to accommodate more pictures than possible with a standard 35-exposure load of film, there are times when you don't need or want to use that many frames. You can load the camera with a regular 36 mm cassette without the back just as you would with a Nikon F and a regular camera back (after removing the camera from the motor drive as already explained). The standard Nikon reloadable cassette cannot be used with the F-250 motor drive.

While holding the film cassette in the camera body with your left hand and grasping the take-up spool end of the camera with your right, slide the camera from above into the motor drive until it's in place. Replace the base plate, thus closing the motor drive. Turn the knurled knobs on the film chambers to the 'close' position. Advance film, using the rapid wind lever and shutter release, until you reach frame 1. Now set the frame counter on the motor drive and you're ready for the first exposure. In setting the frame counter, be sure not to overestimate the number of frames in the load. If anything, it's better to underestimate the number of frames if you have any doubts – set 35 for a 36-exposure roll, for instance. Remember the motor continues advancing film with full power until the motor drive counter indicates that the last frame has been taken. If your overestimate the amount of film, the motor can either tear the film perforations or even pull the film away from the cassette spool, making it impossible to rewind the film.

In normal operation, using either the motor drive or manual shutter wind and release with a 20- or 36-exposure cartridge, you will have to rewind film after the last exposure. You do this just as you would without a motor drive. Turn the A-R ring to the 'R' or rewind position and rewind with the unfolded rewind crank.

Retrieving a broken film

Should you pull the film from the cassette, take your camera into an absolutely light-tight room. If your film was in a cassette that you can open easily, you can put the film back into it. Otherwise you need a light-tight container for loose film. Remove the camera from the motor drive in the dark, turn the A-R ring to the rewind position. If you can take the cassette apart, tape the film to the central spool. Wind the film onto the spool and reassemble the cassette. If your cassette is crimped and impossible to open, wind the film off carefully into the fairly tight roll by hand. Be careful not to touch the film surface or allow the film to slide unduly against itself in the roll. Tape the end of the film to the roll with a small piece of masking tape to prevent the film from unrolling and put it into the light-tight container which you have brought with you. Don't open the container until you are again in a darkroom ready for film processing. If the film is to be processed by a commercial film processor, make sure the container is labelled sufficiently – particularly explain to the processor that it has raw film in it and must not be opened except in a darkroom.

Battery power

Unlike the F-36 motor drive, the F-250 is powered by eight C-cells in a separate over-the-shoulder pack with a 1-metre long connecting cord. However, all connections are carried out in the same manner as the separate battery pack for the F-36 already described. Remote-control power sources are likewise connected in the same manner.

Nikon MD-1 and MD-2 motor drives for Nikon F2 models

1. Single-continuous run knob
2. Trigger button
3. Locking screw
4. Drive shaft
5. Three-pin socket
6. Power socket
7. Tripod socket
8. Camera back open-close lever
9. Rewind lever lock release
10. Rewind lever
11. Rewind warning lamp (MD-2 only)
12. Frame counter
13. Camera open-close key storage socket
14. Firing speed selector
15. Shutter speed table
16. Rewind slide button
17. Frame number wheel
18. Rewind stop electrical contact points

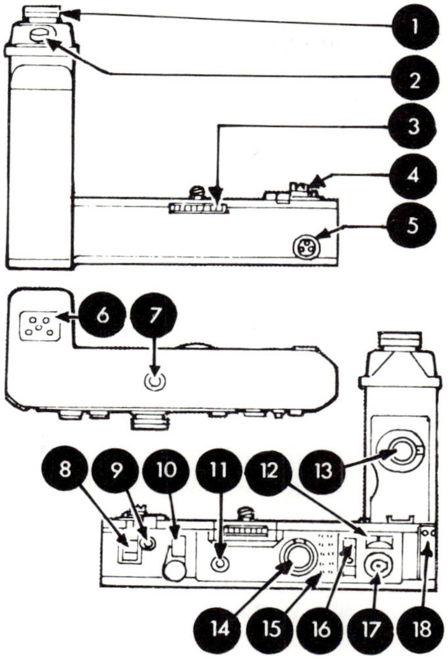

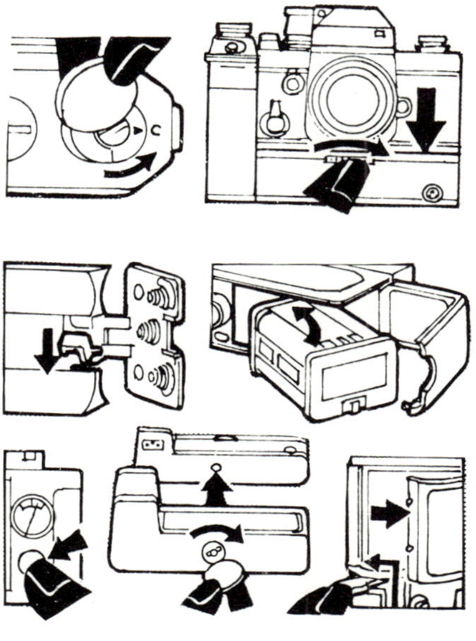

To attach motor drive to camera remove bottom open-close key by turning slotted screw counterclockwise with coin edge. Place camera and motor together and tighten knurled locking knob.

To install AA cells in battery units, release clip on cover. Place batteries in holders. Check holders for proper positioning of batteries. Slip two battery holders into pack and shut.

If batteries are all right, needle of battery checker will swing into green when button is pressed. Later battery checker has two diode lamps instead of needle. When both light, batteries are fully charged, one light indicates half charge. No light means exhausted batteries. Battery pack attaches to motor drive with locking screw. Use coin edge to tighten. To load camera with motor, fold out open-close lever and turn to left. Back will swing open.

Bulk loader

The Nikon bulk film loader is almost an essential piece of equipment for the F-250 motor drive. It allows you to wind onto the motor drive spool any number of frames from a standard 33 m (100 ft) bulk film length. First, before opening the bulk film spool. Pull up the exposure frame dial of the bulk film loader and turn it counterclockwise until the number of the frames you want to load is opposite the triangular mark. The 50, 100, 150, 200 and 250 frame markers are painted with fluorescent paint to make them easier to see in the dark. Each between-marking represents five frames, but these are not treated with fluorescent paint.

In the darkroom, unscrew the detachable flange from the film drum, open the package of bulk film. Trim the end of the film with a pair of scissors to form a tongue about 3 cm (1.2 in) long and 2 cm (0.8 in) wide. Make a bend near the end. Push the roll of bulk film onto the spool of the film drum. Replace the flange and tighten it. Push the loaded film drum onto the film drum spindle so that the end of the film can be pulled to the left with the film emulsion side down. Take a spool from a 250-exposure film cassette and slide it over the cassette spool spindle. Thread the tongue of the film leftward over the sprocket drive shaft. Now insert the tongue, emulsion-side downwards, into one of the two slots of the spool. Lower the film pressure lever so that the two film pressure shafts rest on the back of the film. Make certain that the sprocket teeth of the sprocket shaft engage the sprockets of the film.

When you rotate the winding handle clockwise, the loader winds film onto the cassette spindle. Continue winding gently with the same amount of pressure until the winder automatically stops at the final exposure. Cut the film half-way between the spools, remove the loaded cassette spool and place it in the cassette as already described. Be sure to shut the cassette, repackage and seal any film left over before turning on a light.

F2 motor drives

The motor system for the Nikon F2 was designed together with the camera body. The resultant MD-1, MD-2 and MD-3 motor drives (for standard 36-exposure cartridges) and the MF-1 250-exposure motor drive offer far greater convenience, speed and flexibility than the F-36 and F-250 for the Nikon F. In capsule form, the improvements of the MD-1 and MD-2 motor drives over the F-36 and F-250 (for the Nikon F) are that the new motor drives attach to the bottom of the camera with no need for adaptation, need not be removed for loading, become integral, locked-on parts of the camera module, allow up to 5 frames per second sequences, and have motorised rewind. In addition, the MD-1, MD-2 and MD-3 can be powered by interchangeable AA cells or rechargeable nickel cadmium batteries in a lock-on cordless battery pack as well as separate power sources. As we'll see, there is a vast simplification of a much improved motorised system.

MD-1 and MD-2 drives

Since the MD-1 and MD-2 motor drives are almost identical, we'll handle them together, describing their small differences when we reach the appropriate point. The MD motor drives are designed to fit and work perfectly with any Nikon F2 or F2 Photomic camera with no need for any factory adjustment.

To attach the motor drive, first unscrew the O/C (open/close) key on the camera bottom with the edge of a coin or similar object. This must not be done in the light if you have film in the camera. The removal of the O/C key opens up the film chamber to light from outside the camera, thus possibly fogging the film.

Thread the O/C key into the storage hole on the motor drive grip so that you don't lose it. Then set the camera on the motor drive and fasten them together by tightening the knurled locking knob. All drive shafts and couplings are now interlocked.

The simplest power source to use is the MB-1 battery pack. This just fits below the motor drive.

Operating MD motor drives

You can load your motorised F2 or F2 Photomic camera as you would a normal F2 or F2 Photomic. Pull up on the black O/C lever at the far left of the motor back and move it to the left to open the hinged camera back. You can now load the camera in the normal way.

After loading the camera, lock the back and return the O/C lever to the down position. Depress the small chrome locking button on the rewind slide, right of the firing speed selector knob, and push the slide upward until the frame counter returns to 'S'. Now advance and release the shutter and film wind with the rapid film wind lever and the manual shutter release button to wind on the exposed portion of the film leader. The camera body frame counter should now show frame 1, indicating that you are ready to take the first picture, while the frame counter on the back of the motor shows frame 36, indicating that you have 36 pictures to shoot. If you have loaded a 20-exposure roll or any number of frames less than 36, turn the frame counter preset wheel with the ball of the finger until it indicates exactly the number of frames of your film. This is quite important, since the motor drive stops automatically when the motor frame counter reaches zero. If you have preset more frames than you actually have loaded, the powerful motor drive may rip the perforations of your film or pull it right from the supply spool, making rewinding impossible. You will then have to resort to a darkroom to remove the film from the take-up chamber (see page 278).

The MD motor drives can be used either for single-frame shooting or continuous-sequence firing up to 5 frames per second. You can select either single shot or continuous bursts by setting the SC knob on top of the motor drive grip to 'S' for single shots, 'C' for continuous bursts (or to 'L', locking the trigger release against accidental firing). You can vary the firing speed of the motor on continuous run by setting the selector knob control. You can also determine the number of shots to be made on any sequence by presetting the motor drive frame counter to just that number of frames you want. You can only turn the frame number preset wheel downwards. Should you desire to reset it to a higher number, you have to depress the locking button on the rewind slide again and push the slide upward to return the frame counter to 'S'. Then reset it to the number of frames you want.

In single-frame operation, the motor drive automatically winds the film and shutter to the next exposure as soon as pressure is released from the trigger button on the hand grip. At speeds below 1/60 second, make sure you keep your finger on the button for a sufficient length of time to complete the exposure or the speed will be abbreviated, causing underexposure.

Continuous shooting

When you have the selector knob set for 'C' (continuous bursts), the motor drive continues to advance film and release the shutter as long as you keep the trigger depressed. When you do take your finger from the release button, the camera winds to the next exposure. While you are firing the camera, you can change the selector for another setting. By removing your finger quickly from the release button after firing a shot, you can make single shots as well as bursts. With practice this gives you slightly faster single shots than you can get on 'S'.

There are five settings of the firing speed selector knob on the back of the motor. The number of frames per second you get at each setting depends to a large extent on the power supply used. See facing page for a table showing just what rates these are.

The range of shutter speeds possible depends on the frames per second sequence selected. However, the minimum speed required is clearly delineated in green numbers around the firing speed selector knob. At the 'L' setting you must use speeds faster than 1/4 second; at 'M1', faster than 1/8 s; at 'M2', faster than 1/60 s; at 'M3', faster than 1/125 s, and at 'H', also faster than 1/125 s. However, on 'H', the mirror of the camera must be locked up; and a separate viewfinder used if viewing is needed during the sequence.

If you want, you can select an in-between setting number of frames per second. If you do, consult the range of usable shuter speeds and select the next highest shutter speed setting.

Unloading

After you have fired the last shot, the film must be rewound into its original cartridge before it can be removed from the camera. Whether you wish to

Nikon MD-1, MD-2 motor operation

After loading with film press R slide button and push slide upwards. Frame counter will return to S for start. Turn frame number preset wheel until number of frames you intend to shoot shows in frame counter.

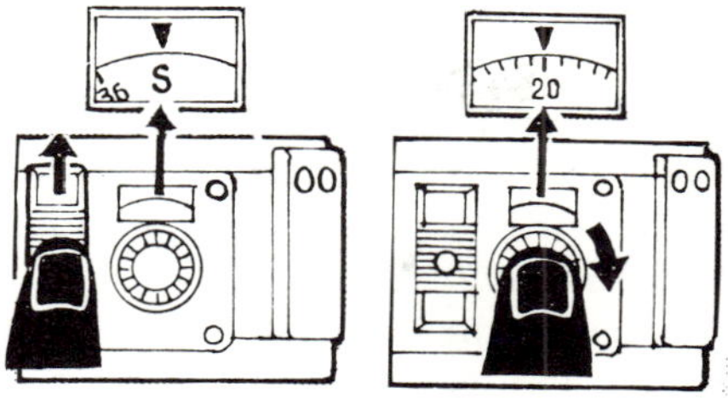

Set SC knob to single or continuous run (1), set shutter speed you intend to use (2), press trigger button (3) to make single or continuous exposures.

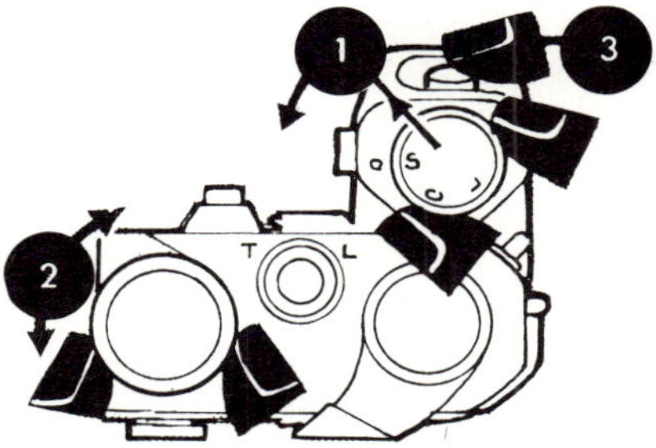

Firing speed selector knob controls number of frames per second motor will fire under continuous run. Knob dial indicates slowest shutter speed to be set for each firing rate. Table at right shows actual frames per second rate for each setting depending on power source.

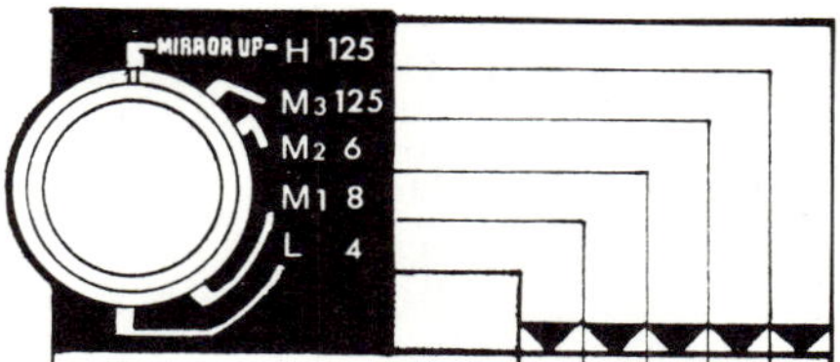

POWER SOURCE	Frames per Second (L)	(M1)	(M2)	(M3)	(H)
Alkaline-Manganese Penlight Batteries (15v) / Zinc-Carbon Penlight Batteries (15v)	1	2	3	3.5	4
NC Battery Unit MN-(15v)	1.3	2.5	3.8	4.3	5

To rewind film by motor, push R slide button and move slide upwards until S appears in frame counter. While pressing rewind lever lock-release, push rewind lever to right.

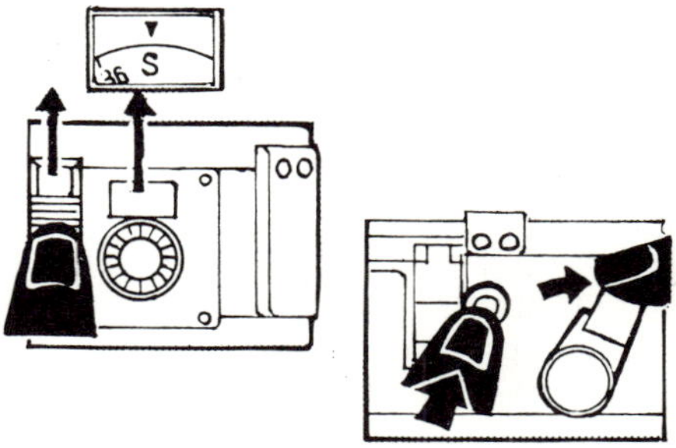

rewind the film manually using the rewinding crank or let the motor rewind the film automatically, the same initial steps must be taken. Press the locking button on the rewind slide and push the slide upwards as far as it can go. This releases the film drive (and returns the counter to 'S'). For motorised rewinding, press the locking button located to the left of the rewind lever and push the rewind lever to the right until it stops. With a 36-exposure roll this will take about 7 seconds.

It is here in the rewinding of the film that the primary difference between the MD-1 and the MD-2 motors can be appreciated. With the MD-1 motor, film is rewound completely into the original cartridge. You should move the rewind lever back to its original position when you hear the motor speed up, indicating that the film is no longer attached to the take-up spool. During rewinding, the rewind knob should turn if rewinding is occurring properly.

MD-2 motor drive

With the MD-2 motor *and* the special MF-3 camera back which can be fitted to it, the motor rewind stops automatically as soon as the film leader becomes disengaged from the take-up spool. A small lamp located between the speed selector knob and the rewind lever glows to indicate that rewinding is complete. The same lamp glows during normal motor operation when the camera is advancing film properly. Aside from this, the MD-1 and MD-2 motors are identical. However, the MF-3 camera back, which has a moulded finger grip for easier camera holding, cannot be fitted to the MD-1 motor drive.

The MD-2 motor drive does provide those who do not wish their film completely rewound into the cartridge with the alternate solution of leaving the leader protruding. Whether you want the film leader in or out is very much a matter of personal preference. I recommend rewinding it in, since a leaderless cartridge immediately indicates that the film has been shot and there is no danger of accidentally reloading an already-exposed film again into the camera. However, there is one situation in which you need the leader left out. Should you wish to change film in mid-roll and later place the half-used film back into the camera, it cannot be done if the film is wound in completely. If you do decide to use this option, make sure you mark the film carefully, indicating the number of frames already shot, so that when you do reload it you can advance the film beyond this point before starting to shoot again. Of course, in advancing the film over these preshot frames, make sure you do it in subdued light at a high speed and small aperture with a lens cap in place to prevent the already-exposed frames from being lightstruck during the film advance. It is always advisable to advance the film at least one exposure further along than you already shot, as a safety measure against accidental double exposures.

Film cassettes

The MD motor drives have been designed to accept as many brands of film cassette as possible; but there are so many variations throughout the world that you will find some whose central spindle will not mate properly with the motorised drive rewinding key. If this occurs, or you simply want to rewind the film manually in any event, you can do so by pressing inwards on the rewind slide button, pushing the slide upwards and rotating the unfolded rewind crank in the direction of the arrow, just as you would if you weren't using a motor drive at all.

If you wish to use a motorised rewind, you should check the film cassette spindle of the film before you buy it. Nikon makes a reloadable film cassette, the AM-1, which accepts full motorised operation loads up to 36 exposures.

Batteries

The standard power source for the MD motor drives is the cordless battery pack MB-1 which can hold either two NiCad (nickel cadmium) rechargable batteries or 10 penlight cells in two reloadable MS-1 cartridges of 5 cells each. If you're using penlight batteries, first release the end clip on the MS-1 battery holder and open the cover. Insert the 5 batteries with their positive (+) and negative (−) terminals facing as indicated in the battery holder. To insert the two loaded MS-1 cartridges into the battery pack, open the pack by turning the unfolded locking screw in the direction of the arrow. Insert the two battery holders with the connecting terminals toward the rear, facing centrally. Snap shut the two back covers of the battery pack. Fold down the key. The NiCad battery fits into the same MS-1 battery holder.

The exact number of rolls that it's possible to fire on one set of batteries or a single charge of NC batteries is difficult to determine with any certainty, since much depends on the rate of fire, age of the batteries and consistency of usage. If the motor is running virtually continuously, a much greater number of rolls can be fired than if the motor is used at intervals. For general guidance purposes, fresh manganese alkaline cells will drive through approximately 80 rolls of 36-exposure film continuously or 20 intermittently; NiCads, 60 rolls continuously or 50 intermittently. Regular batteries will handle about 50 rolls continuously or 10 rolls intermittently. More rolls can actually be shot, but the figures given indicate an estimation of the number of rolls that can be handled before the motor begins to slow down. Manganese alkaline batteries won't work at temperatures below −10°C. The NiCads should be replaced after they've been recharged for the 100th time.

You can check battery strength by pushing the check button on the lower right-hand side of the battery pack. If the adjacent needle indicator swings into the green region or beyond, the bateries are still OK. (Newer battery packs have two light diodes instead of a meter needle. One diode indicates half power; two, full power. No lights, batteries dead.) If the batteries are dead, replace them before doing any more shooting. Important: if manganese alkaline cells remain in the battery holder for any length of time, the terminals may oxidise slightly, producing a 'dead' reading even when they are still quite usable. If this occurs, remove all batteries, clean terminals with the eraser on the end of a pencil and replace them in the holders.

The cordless battery pack fits below the motor drive, becoming a single unit. Press the motor drive and pack together, joining the electric terminals, and tighten the locking screw on the bottom of the pack with a coin edge.

NiCad batteries

For constant and heavy motor drive use, you will find NiCad batteries more convenient and economical than using manganese alkaline cells. However, the NiCad batteries do require a separate recharging unit, the Nikon Quick Charger MH-1, and considerable care.

With an MF-1, the two NiCad units needed to drive the motor can be recharged from near complete exhaustion to near full capacity in 3 hours. Before using, make certain that the voltage selector on the back of the MH-1 has been set to the proper voltage, by turning the slotted selector with the edge of a coin or similar object until the red dot is opposite the proper voltage numeral. Then plug two NiCad battery units vertically into the two recessed bases at the front of the charger. Connect the charger to an AC power source. When you switch on with the rocker switch, a neon pilot light above the switch lights. Two neon charge-indicator lights at the bases of the NC units will glow, indicating that they are being charged. When the units reach 80 per cent of capacity, the two neon lights dim and go out. You can stop charging at this point and use the units, or you can continue charging for another three hours without the indicator lights to reach 100 per cent charge.

In using the MH-1 charger, a few safety precautions should be observed. Charging should be done at room temperature but not below 0°C (32°F). Outside these limits, the indicator lamps go out too soon – in about two hours instead of three, when the NiCad units have reached only 60 to 70 per cent of full charge. If the charge indicator lamps do not go out after 4½ hours of charging, there is either something wrong with the power source or a malfunction of the charger.

In order to keep the NiCad battery units fully charged, they must be recharged at least once a month even when not in use, since they tend to lose their charge gradually. However, additional steps must be taken if you haven't used NiCad units for six months or more. In this case, you must charge them for *five hours* more after the indicator lights go out. Then you may insert them into the motor drive and, by operating the camera and drive, discharge them completely. You should repeat this sequence at least twice more to restore the NC batteries to full capacity. If you do not, the NC

MD-1, MD-2 motor drive accessories

AC/DC Converter MA-2 provides power to drive motor from any 100–240V AC house current. Connects to motor drive with connecting cord MC-2.

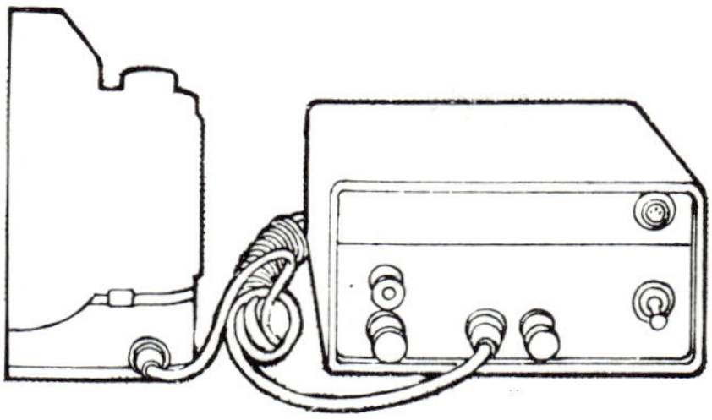

Motor can be operated by cord remote control. SC knob and trigger button can be removed from motor drive by pressing release buttons on side of grip head. Three metre (10ft) SC cord MC-1 connects grip head and motor drive socket.

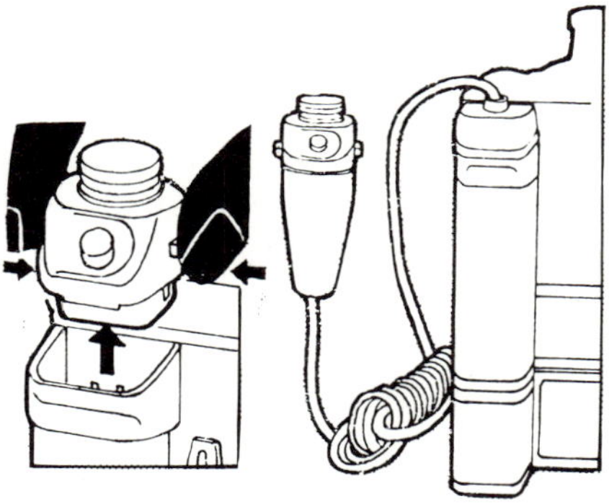

Camera back MF-3 has contoured hand grip, automatically halts film rewinding with film leader outside cartridge lip. Works with MD-2 Motor Drive only.

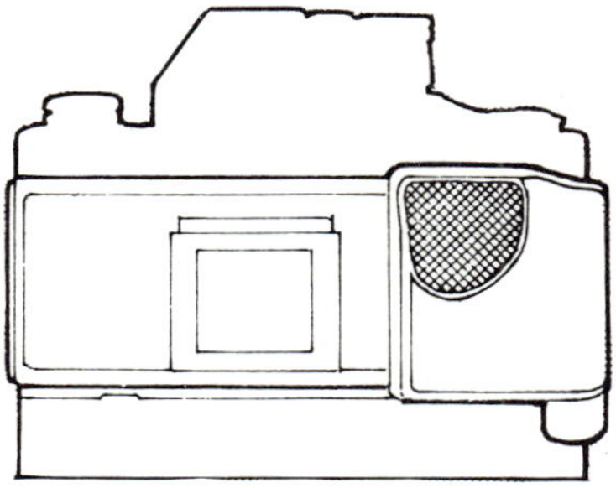

Nicad power source: Quick Charger MH-1 accepts two MN-1 nickel cadmium battery units, recharges in 3 hours. Has charging and full charge indicators. NC battery units fit cordless battery pack directly.

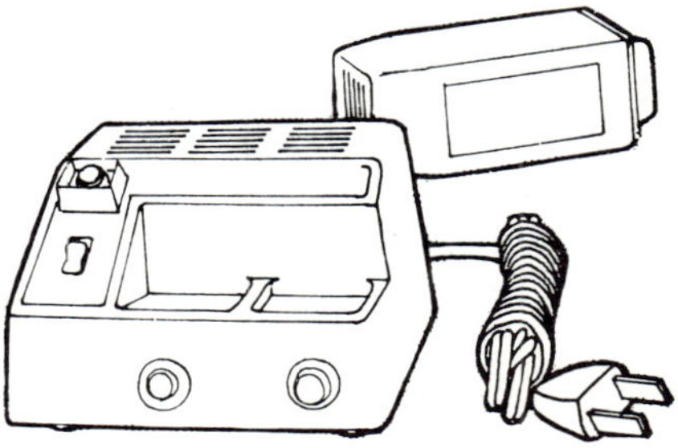

units will not hold a full charge and you will not be able to get the maximum number of rolls of film through the camera motor drive. Obviously, if your use of the motor drive is to be intermittent and you may not use it for extended periods of six months or more, you will be far better off loading up with the throw-away alkaline cells.

External power supplies

The MD motor drives can also be operated from external power sources instead of the cordless battery pack MB-1. However, the current supplied must be stable at 0.4 A and 15 V. Higher voltages can damage the motor's circuitry. There is a three-pin socket on the front of the MD motor drives to allow connection of a power source. Nikon supplies two suitable AC/DC Converter power sources, the MA-2 to power the motor drive only, and the MA-4 which powers the motor drive and the EE aperture control attachment DS-1 when in use. We will describe the MA-4 since the MA-2 is near identical, save for the absence of a connecting point for the EE control unit.

MA-4 power supply

The MA-4 allows both the MD motor drives and the EE control unit to be powered by any house current either separately or simultaneously. It has a release button to trigger the motor drive directly from the converter, and also has remote control terminals to create a circle for a remote release, switch or wireless control. The MA-4 has built-in voltage stabilisers to ensure a stable current and has automatic protection safeguards for the output circuits as well as a line fuse. Before using the MA-4, make certain that you are using the correct voltage. The voltage is factory-set for either 100–120 V or 200–240 V operation, and this is so indicated on the unit's rear plate.

Using the MC-2 accessory cord, connect the three-pin socket on the motor drive to the converter's output jack, marked MD. If you are using the EE Aperture Control unit, plug one end of the DM-1 accessory cord in the EE battery chamber and the other into the EE control attachment output jack on the converter marked EE. The attaching cords both have locking screws on their ends for secure fitting.

Connect the AC line plug at the back of the unit to a correct voltage source, and put on the power switch on the front of the MA-4. The pilot light at the top right front of the unit then lights.

The MA-4 has a fuse behind a prominently marked cap at the back. Twist off the cap (in the direction of the arrow). If necessary, replace with a 1 A 6.3 × 30 mm line fuse.

Earthing (or grounding)

In some operating areas it may be advisable to operate the AC power cord with an earthed or grounded three-core cable. First remove the tiny screw just behind the front collar on the power cord plug and the two screws securing the rear of the plug. Then unscrew the broad metal ring until the plug terminal is exposed. Unsolder the two ends of the cable from the pins and remove the cable. Replace the cable with three-core cable, passing it through the power cord plug and soldering the three ends to the terminal pins. The earth pin is numbered on the plug and should be soldered to the earth core of the cable. Reassemble the plug and connect as needed.

Firing

You can use the converter release button to fire the motor drive up to 10 feet away with the MC-2 cord. The firing speed and mode are, naturally, controlled by the setting of the MD motor drive itself. You can, however, set the motor drive to the 'L' position and still have the MA-4 release button trigger the motor for single-shot operation.

Remote control

If you wish to create a remote switch trigger circuit with the MA-4 or operate with radio control, connect the R1 and R2 terminals at the left front of the unit with a length of two-core cable and a switch. When you close the switch it will set off the motor just as the release button on the MA-4. You can use any length cable provided circuit resistance doesn't exceed 100 ohms. For long distances, however, it's preferable to use radio control.

If you wish to make time-lapse studies, you can replace the on/off switch in the trigger circuit with an electric timer or intervalometer. There will, however, be a delay between the closing of the remote-control circuit and the release of the shutter. With the mirror locked in the up position, the delay will be between 0.03 and 0.05 s, while the delay with the mirror in action will be somewhat longer, between 0.05 and 0.07 s. A longer delay will be experienced if an intervalometer or similar timing unit is connected. Then the delay with mirror up will be about 0.23 s, and 0.26 s with the mirror down.

The MD motor drives can also be controlled remotely by battery power. The grip head of the MD motor drives, containing the SC knob and trigger button, is removable. After pressing the release buttons on the sides of the grip head, you can lift and remove the head. Connect the 4-pin plug of the accessory 3 metre (10 ft) SC cord MC-1 to the motor drive socket in place of the grip head and fit the removed grip head to the other end of the cord.

The motor drive can now be controlled up to 3 metres from the camera, using the controls on the grip head.

Alternatively, you can trigger the motor remotely on battery with a MC-4 cord. One end of the MC-4 fits on the socket on the front of the motor drive. The other end of the cord has red and black plugs to which you can attach a switch or an intervalometer for time-lapse studies. You can increase cable length as long as desired provided again you do not exceed circuit resistance of more than 100 ohms. For long distances, again a radio control is preferable.

Flash

The Nikon SB-5 (and more recent SB-6) electronic flash units are intended to be used with motor drive. While the SB-5 and 6 are eminently suitable for standard single-frame picture-taking, and feature 28 mm lens coverage plus rechargeable NiCad bateries which allow the user to take up to 2.5 frames per second for motor-drive sequence shots, even with automatic exposure provision, a high-voltage power pack of two 240 V batteries can be substituted allowing up to 4 frames per second for high-speed sequence work.

Pistol grip

While the MD motor drives and cordless battery packs provide a very convenient, easy-to-handle hand-hold module, some photographers prefer to mount the camera motor and battery to a pistol grip with its own firing trigger. Such a method of operation is especially useful when the motors are to be used with long tele lenses. The Pistol Grip Model 2 fastens to the tripod socket of the camera, or to that of the long lens. The accessory coiled cord MC-3 connects the pistol grip trigger to the front motor drive connection plug. However, I did find that the F2 or F2S Nikons, MD motor drives and cordless battery packs make such well-integrated units that a pistol grip is really superfluous. Don't let me stop you trying it yourself, though.

Multiple cameras

Should you wish to fire two or more cameras together, either in single shots or continuous bursts, you can do it by connecting the MC-4 cord already described. Then connect the red and black cord plugs to a single switch.

Time lapse

For time-lapse or delayed-action pictures, the on/off switch in the trigger circuit can be replaced with a timer or intervalometer. However, this does introduce a slight delay between the moment that the circuit is closed and the shutter operates. With the mirror locked up, the delay is between 30 and 50 milliseconds; with the mirror operational, the delay extends from 50 to 70 milliseconds, depending to some extent on the power source and voltage.

For precise interval timing, the trigger circuit delay obviously must be taken into consideration. The interval of exposure for time-lapse work in the

MF-1 250 magazine

For use with the MD-1, MD-2 motor drives on all Nikon F2 models, the MF-1 allows up to 250 exposures without reloading. Here are the controls:

1. Fingerguard
2. Open-close knob
3. Frame number preset knob
4. Frame counter
5. Camera lock
6. Camera lock knob
7. Film advance safety catch
8. Cassette ejector knob
9. Cassette spindle knob
10. Film roller
11. Tripod socket
12. Film pressure plate
13. Lock for power plug
14. Mounting socket
15. Power plug for micro-motor

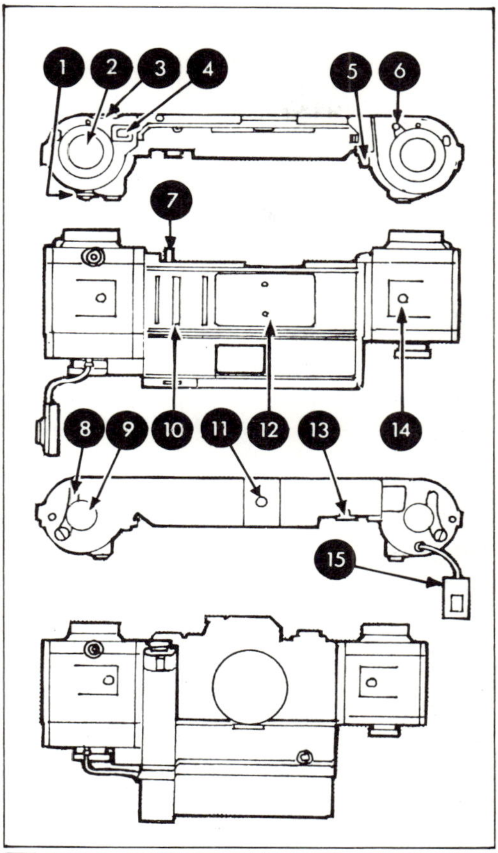

The 250-exposure magazine back has its own shutter release button. To use it for continuous firing, SC knob on motor must be in C position.

To unload film, turn knurled knobs atop film chambers to 'open'. Remove back plate, pull out cassette spindles, press lever next to spindles as shown and cassettes will pop out part way.

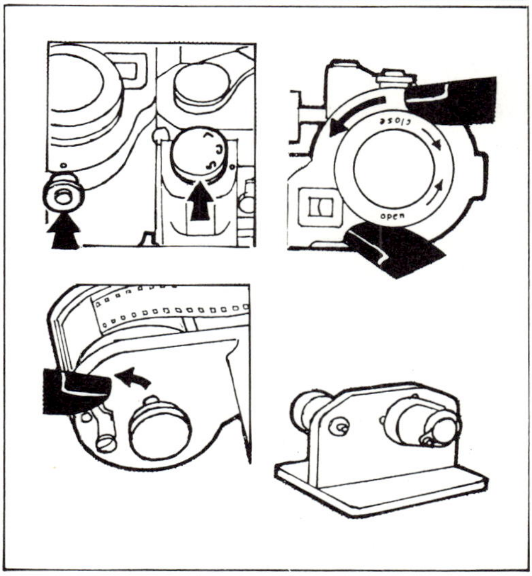

You can load up to 250 exposures in the dark from a 100-ft bulk film roll using the Nikon bulk film loader.

C setting depends on the time delay, the shutter speed selected and the minimum interval between the beginning of one exposure and the next. This minimum interval depends on the position of the firing speed selector. The table of intervals is given at the back of this volume.

When the SC knob is set at 'S', any shutter speed can be used. The minimum interval now depends upon the sum of the time for completion of the exposure plus the winding interval which at a minimum would be 0.25 second.

Remote control modulite ML-1

The Remote Control ML-1 is unique. It consists of a receiver unit which mounts in the accessory shoe of the camera plus a small transmitter to be held in the hand. Instead of a radio or infra-red signal, the ML-1 uses a double-pulse high-intensity light emitted by the transmitter to activate the receiver. The receiver has two channels, as does the transmitter, so two cameras can be controlled at the same time. The light beam can be transmitted directly or reflected from a ceiling or wall if this is more convenient. The four 1.5 V AA cells will make up to 750 transmissions at ranges up to 60 m (200 ft).

In addition to activating cameras, the ML-1 will also trigger the SB-5 and SB-6 electronic flash units. So it can be fired in place of a flash gun to trigger remote (slave) units. The ML-1 is equally effective in running a Nikon motion-picture camera by remote control. Transmitter and receiver both have neon signal lamps and channel selectors.

250-exposure back MF-1

The MF-1 250-exposure back for the Nikon F2 camera series replaces the regular hinged removable back, and is used in conjunction with the MD series motor drives. The MF-1 has its own micromotor to drive the film in the take-up magazine, its own shutter release button and two frame counters: one showing the number of frames shot and the other showing the number of frames yet to be shot. The film feeds from a loaded cassette into an empty one. No rewinding is necessary.

Before attaching the MF-1, place the camera body on the MD Motor Drive as already described. The rewind lever on the motor drive must be in the 'Up' position. Open the regular camera back and remove it by depressing the hinged locking catch.

When securing the camera body to the bulk film back it is essential first to press the camera lock lever outwards, locking the camera body, and then to turn the left-hand chamber knurled knob so that the close mark is opposite the white dot, thus locking the camera lock lever in place. You can't turn the knob first and then the lock lever. If you do, the lock won't work.

Setting up MF-1 250 magazine back for all Nikon F2 models

To attach camera to magazine back, press camera lock release lever on left hand film chamber. Insert right side of camera, then left. Return lock to original position.

Push locking catch pin backwards, insert power cord connector plug into motor drive power socket. Attach cordless battery pack to assembly or connect assembly to external power source.

To open 250-exposure cassette, press release pin, turn inner shell until openings coincide.

Slip film tongue into spool slit, emulsion down. Wind on film.

Place loaded spool in inner cassette shell with film end protruding.

Slide outer shell over inner shell, turn inner shell clockwise until catch falls into deeper recess of outer shell with two clicks.

Complete 250-exposure film cassette consists of three parts: (1) Outer shell. (2) Inner shell and (3) Spool.

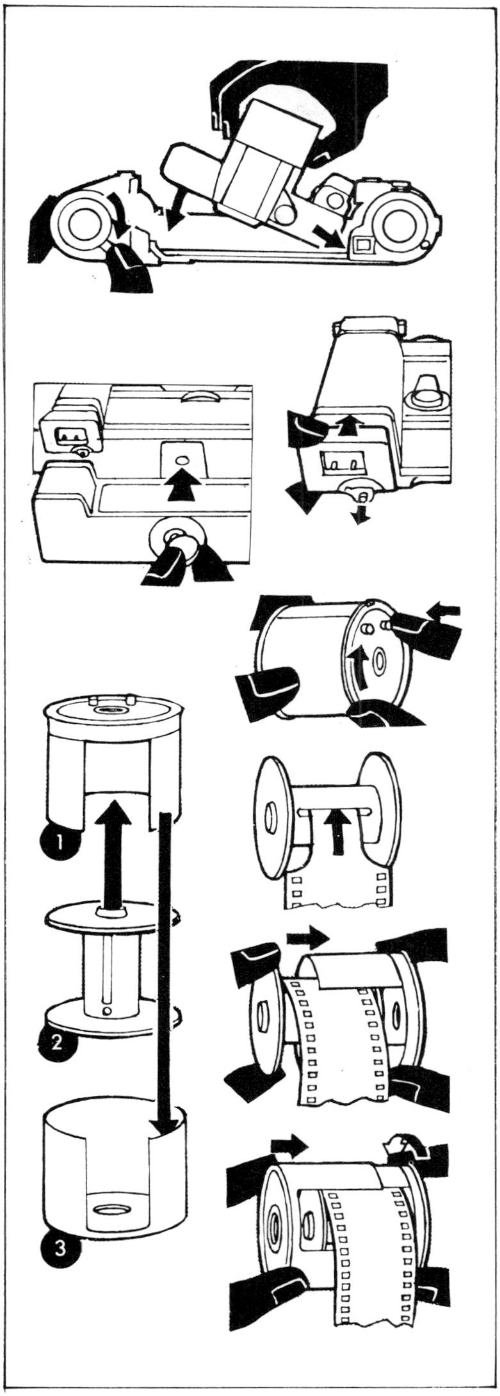

Turn the film chamber's knurled knobs in the direction of the arrows until they click into place with the open marks opposite the white dots.

By pressing the left-hand film chamber top inwards, toward the centre of the back, you release the magazine back camera lock allowing the camera body to be fastened within the MF-1. While holding the lever, place the camera body over the magazine back, secure the right-hand end of the camera in place and then the left-hand. Return the camera lock lever to the original position to lock the bulk film back and camera together.

Push the small pin on the locking catch beneath the magazine towards the rear of the back and insert the plug on the power cord connected to the magazine back into the power socket of the motor drive. This powers the bulk film back micromotor.

Attach the motor-drive magazine back assembly to the cordless battery pack or an external power source via the three-pin socket on the motor drive.

The MF-1 magazine back film cassette is loaded in the same manner as that for the F-250 motor drive for the Nikon F already described, together with the Nikon bulk loader. Once you have the cassette loaded you're ready to load the MF-1 magazine back. First lock both shutter release buttons to avoid accidental exposure. Turn the SC knob on the motor grip to the 'L' position and lift and turn the fingerguard collar around the shutter release button on the front of the right-hand film chamber clockwise until the 'L' points to the white dot.

Put the camera/motor-drive assembly face downwards on a clean surface. Turn the film chamber knobs to the open position. Open the hinged back plate by pulling up on the right-hand latch; hinge it back to about 45°. Pull the end of the film leader from the loaded cassette, open the supply cartridge as described in the F-250 motor drive for the Nikon F, and thread the end of the leader into one of the two slits in the spool, emulsion side down. Then reassemble the cassette.

Pull out the cassette spindles from the film chamber bases and insert the loaded cassette within the left-hand chamber and the take-up cassette within the right-hand chamber. Align the red dots on the sides of the cassettes with the white lines within the film chambers. The index and release pins on top of the cassettes must slide into recesses on each film chamber.

Push in the cassette spindles. Rotate the left-hand one counterclockwise until a slight resistance is felt. This removes any slack in the supply cassette. Make sure that the film perforations mesh correctly with the teeth of the sprocket wheel.

Replace the MF-1 back plate by inserting the left-hand end in the groove and pressing on the right-hand end until it snaps into position. Turn the knobs on the film chambers to the 'close' position. This opens the light traps, allowing the film virtually friction-free movement. It also locks the back plate latch to prevent accidental exposure. To release the lock, turn the finger-guard on the magazine back clockwise until the black dots point to the white

Loading MF-1 magazine back for all Nikon F2 models

With film chamber knobs in 'open' position, pull up back latch open and remove hinged back plate.

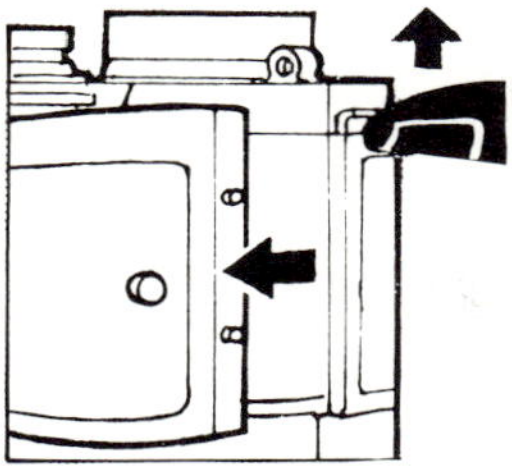

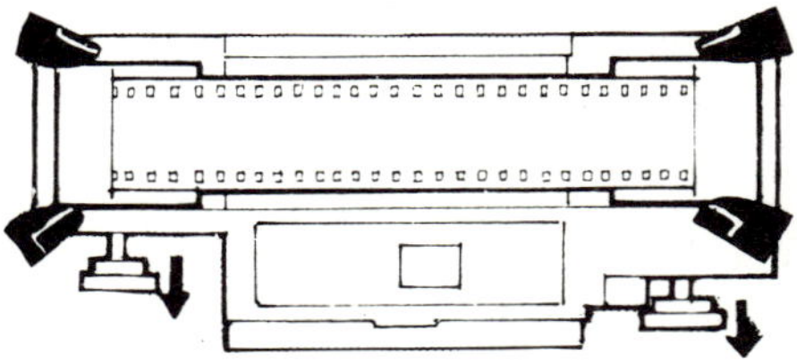

Pull film leader from cassette, thread into either slot of spool in other, opened cassette. Reassemble take-up cassette. Pull cassette spindles downwards (see arrows). Insert loaded cassette in left chamber, other cassette in right. Line up dots on cassettes sides with white lines inside film chambers. Make certain index and release pins slide into recesses in each film chamber (arrows). Push in cassette spindles, rotate left hand one to take out slack. Film perforations must mesh with sprockets.

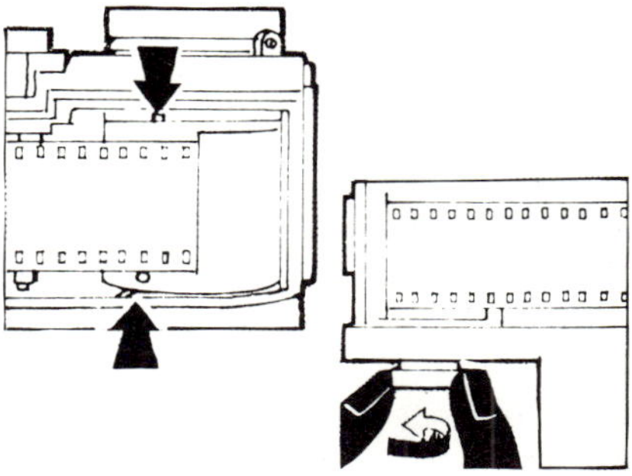

Replace plate back. Turn knobs atop film chambers to 'close'. Set subtractive frame counter to any number over 5. Press and release shutter for 5 exposures to dispose of exposed film leader.

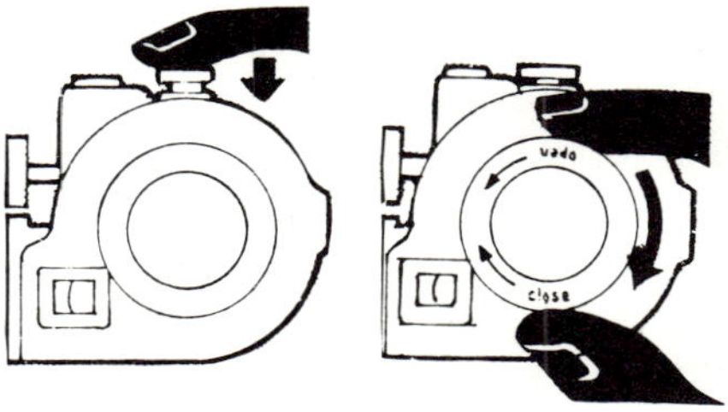

The magazine back has two frame counters. Left hand counter is subtractive showing number of frames yet to shoot in preset sequence. Motor will stop at 0 automatically. To set, turn knurled ring in direction of arrow. Additive counter, which sets itself, shows frames already shot.

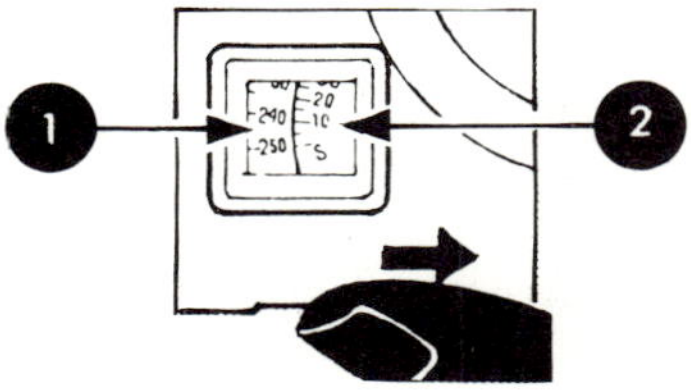

dot. Set the subtractive frame counter to any number over 5 and make 5 blank exposures by pressing the shutter release button. This winds on any exposed film leader and also takes up any possible slack in the take-up magazine. If you've loaded the film correctly and it's travelling through the back properly, the white dots on the left-hand cassette spindle should rotate clockwise during film advance.

A few words of warning. Be very careful of the magazine back plate since each is made specifically for one magazine back and no other. Also do not use the camera's manual film advance lever when you have the magazine back in place. It still must be used, however, as the exposure meter on/off switch if a Photomic finder is fitted to the camera.

Film counting

There are two frame counters on the top of the magazine back near the take-up spool knob. At the left is the subtractive counter indicating the number of frames yet to be shot. The one on the right is the additive counter indicating the number of exposures made.

When the subtractive counter reaches zero, the motor stops. You can therefore preset any number of exposures for burst firing or simply set the counter for the total number of frames loaded if you wish to shoot them all without interruption. The subtractive counter must be set manually by turning the knurled frame preset ring in the direction of the arrow until the number of frames to be preset is opposite the white dot. The scale lines each represent 5 frames and any number up to 250 frames can be set.

The additive counter showing the number of frames shot resets itself automatically to 'S' (start) when the knurled knob on the right-hand film chamber is turned to the open position. Neither counter works if there is no film in the back. When the back is fitted, the standard counter on the Nikon F2 body is inoperative.

The MF-1 has its own shutter release button located on the front of the right-hand film chamber. You can fire this button for single-frame shots even if the SC knob on the motor drive grip is set to 'L'. For continuous burst shooting, however, the grip knob must be turned to 'C'. Hold down the button for a sufficient length of time at shutter speeds below 1/60 second so the shutter can complete its action or underexposure will result.

If you wish, you can lock the release button on the MF-1 back as already described and then use the motor drive grip head control. Of course, when both the head and MF-1 release button are locked, you can still fire the motor drive remotely through the three-pin socket.

After all film has been exposed, set the subtractive film counter to any number greater than 5 and make 5 blank exposures. Turn both film chamber knobs to the 'open' position, thus closing the internal light traps to prevent film fogging. Remove the back plate by pulling up on the latch and pull out the cassette film spindles and the cassettes will pop out part way to make removal easier.

Nikon motor drive MD-3

The MD-3 is a more moderately-priced and featured motor drive for the F2 camera than the MD-1 or 2. It lacks the motorised rewind, firing speed selector, provision for bulk film back and remote firing via the head grip. It can be powered by the same MB-1 cordless battery pack with 10 AA cells or rechargeable NiCad batteries, but in addition can use its own MB-2 8 AA cell battery pack. With NiCad batteries or MA-4 AC/DC Converter, up to 4 fps are possible on the C (continuous setting), 3.5 fps with AA cells in Pack MB-1 and 2.5 fps with Pack MB-2. On C setting, speeds from 1/80 to 1/2000 second can be used. At slower speeds the S single shot setting must be used and the motor firing trigger button depressed until the exposure is complete. The MD-3 fits the F2 in the same manner as the MD-1 and MD-2 and accepts the same external firing mechanisms: MT-1 Intervalometer, ML-1 Modulite, etc.

Films

Until recently, it has been the fashion in the camera guides to discuss black-and-white film and black-and-white photography prior to colour work. However, in the past few years the use of colour film by both professional and amateur has increased to the point where 'photography' virtually means 'colour' in most people's minds.

This is not to denigrate black-and-white work. In many ways the technical and mental translation of a coloured world into the dramatic tones of black and white, plus the ensuing artistry of black-and-white printing, transcends what can be and is done in colour. Many of the world's greatest photographers hardly ever approach colour film. They feel that black and white is their one true artistic metier. Nevertheless, with a bow to today, we feel we should begin with colour.

In addition to its popularity, colour offers the speediest way to check out your new camera accurately and provide you with a fast visual reward. With the many very superior colour films we have today, a photographer can have a choice of truly brilliant prints or slides for projection even from commercial laboratories. More often, good black-and-white work must be done at home or by specialised laboratories. The latter are getting more and more expensive.

Film speed

Whether the film is black and white or colour, for making slides or prints, its most important practical characteristic is its sensitivity to light or film speed. Basically, a slow film is less sensitive to light and needs more exposure than a fast film to produce a satisfactory image on the negative or slide. Two systems for measuring film speed are used in the Western World today. ASA and DIN. ASA is the system described by the American National Standards Institute (formerly the American Standards Association). The use of the recommended ASA meter setting with any film leads generally to the minimum exposure needed to yield a good negative or transparency. ASA

Which film?

Colour films are either reversal (which produce a transparency when processed) or negative.

Reversal films provide transparencies; each is usually mounted for viewing and projection. Duplicate slides or prints can be made from slides.

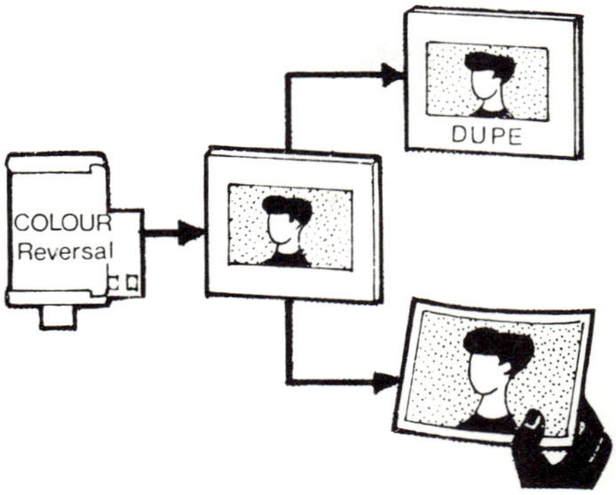

Colour negatives are a source of colour or black-and-white prints. Slides can also be made from them.

Colour reversal film is the obvious choice if you want slides for projection while colour negative film is best if your first choice is for colour prints.

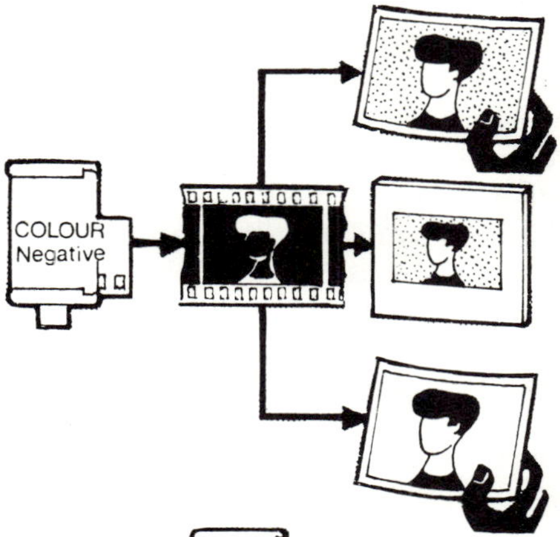

Film latitude

For best results, always expose properly, but films do vary in their ability to produce adequate results even if exposure is in error. Since films which produce negatives can be adjusted in printing, they do yield greater exposure latitude than reversal film. The diagram indicates just how much exposure latitude you can expect at a maximum from each film type.

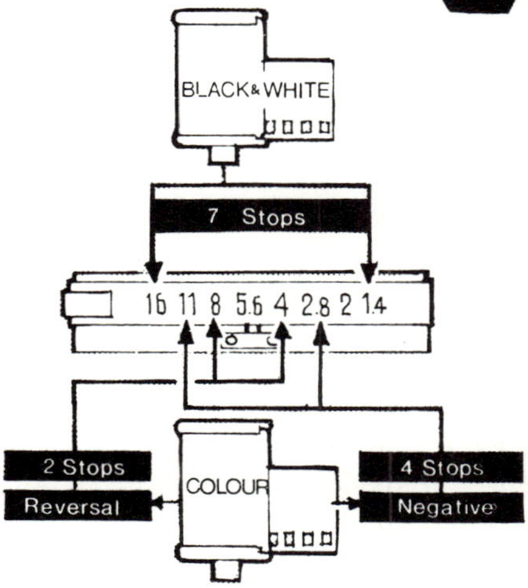

film speeds are on an arithmetical scale. Doubling the ASA number doubles the speed of the film. In other words, an ASA 200 film is twice as fast as an ASA 100 film. ASA 400 film is twice as fast as ASA 200 film, and so on. Since *f*/stops are doubling (or halving) of the exposure, each doubling of the ASA speed needs the equivalent one *f*/stop less of exposure. Therefore, if you need 1/125 at *f*/5.6 for accurate exposure with ASA 200 film, you need 1/125 at *f*/4 (or 1/60 at *f*/5.6, of course) under the same conditions with a 100 ASA type.

The DIN (Deutsche Industrie Norm) system devised by the German Standards Association (Deutsche Normenausschuss) uses a logarithmic scale. An increase of three represents an arithmetic doubling of the film speed. For instance, a 21 DIN film is twice as fast as an 18 DIN film.

Grain

Besides film speed, another important characteristic of all film, colour and black and white, is graininess. Almost all of today's 35 mm negative colour films have graininess very much the same and are suitable for making colour enlargements up to 275 × 350 mm (11 × 14 in) or so. If you have grain problems, shop around for the best combination of film and processor and stick to them.

Graininess in colour transparency film, I feel, is more important, since slides are often projected onto large screens. This gives far greater magnification than you would obtain in print. We'll discuss the grain on black-and-white films in somewhat more detail later.

Colour transparency film

Generally speaking, slower colour transparency films have finer grain and are able to be projected to a large size image without detail break-up because of graininess. They also tend to have somewhat more exposure latitude, so slight exposure errors don't affect them as much. Also, you can get more detail in both highlight and shadow details in brightly lit scenes. The slower films generally produce deeper, richer colours than the faster films. Some photographers find this preferable; but there are times when only a faster film can be used. No colour film reproduces all colours and tones with complete accuracy. Film manufacturers strive for pleasing colours rather than accurate ones. So you should select the film that most closely matches your own ideas of pleasing colour.

For your first films with a new camera – whether you are a beginner or an old hand – use a fairly slow daylight-type transparency film with very fine grain. Limited exposure latitude (compared with negative films) means that your meter must be accurate or your slides will be improperly exposed – a good test of metering. Fine grain shows up best a camera's ability to deliver sharp, crisp pictures. If your camera is operating properly and you have used your meter correctly, a glance at your slides will tell you immediately that all is well. You can then project the slides or, lacking a projector, examine with a hand glass or slide viewer to see if they are properly exposed and adequately sharp.

Colour negative film, designed for making prints, is more forgiving. It has greater exposure latitude, so small cameras or user errors can be compensated for in printing. The small snap-shot sized colour prints, no matter how charming and pocketable, are not sufficiently large to give you proper indication of picture quality from such an instrument as a Nikon or Nikkormat. Further, any unpleasant effects which may turn up on a colour print are more likely to be the fault of the processor than of the camera. So even if you don't intend to use transparency film again, shoot your first rolls with it to check out yourself and the camera. (If you have had limited experience in looking at colour slides, a knowledgeable friend or photo dealer should be able to analyse quality for you.) Try to avoid shooting your first roll on a brilliant sunlit day with much contrast. No colour film can encompass such a wide range of brightnesses, and you may blame the detail-less shadows or burned-out highlight areas on yourself or the camera. Instead, try a bright overcast day or, lacking that, bright shade.

It has been my experience that an entire roll which appears too light or too dark is usually caused either by an improper ASA film speed setting or by camera malfunction. On the other hand, if the exposures vary all over, throughout the roll, they were probably the result of mis-setting the camera controls.

Transparencies, in my opinion, are the most spectacular form of picture taking and viewing. If you are a good technician with sharp, colourful slides, you can fill a home screen with huge panoramas far more impressive (because they are bigger) and far more brilliant (because they are being viewed in the dark) than any print can deliver. The preference for a fine-grained colour transparency film differs from film choice in black and white. In the latter, apparent sharpness with a grainier film can be preferred to finer grain. In colour slides this is not the case unless you view well back from the screen, the grainier colour films may indeed *appear* sharper just as a mosaic might. However, I don't think it is ever wise to sacrifice fine graininess in a transparency for apparent sharpness at a distance.

For everyday use, you'll probably be happiest with a relatively slow film, say 25–100 ASA (15–21 DIN). Which brand and type you choose depends a great deal on your personal taste. When you've chosen a film, stick to it, and stick to one processing lab. It's not that it's necessarily the best, but if you keep changing, you'll change the characteristics of your transparencies. Also, be sure of your processor. Slides, if ruined, are seldom salvageable and you are likely to get no more redress than a replacement for your damaged roll of film.

If you are taking photographs in poor lighting conditions or wish to make use of the fast shutter speeds on your camera, you may need a film faster than 100 ASA. There are a number of these available. Generally speaking, their colours are not as deep and bright as those of the slower films and they tend to show graininess to a more pronounced degree. However, they do allow you to make pictures under lighting conditions that might be impossible without them; and you may prefer the paler colours. A number of the faster films can be used at even higher than rated ASA meter settings. They are put through special processing lines. These may be available through the film manufacturer's own laboratories or those of independent processors. Quality of the results can be poorer than when the film is exposed at the normal meter setting; however, I have seen some really remarkable results from such 'pushed' films.

The colour of light

Although you don't notice it directly, light is widely variable in colour. Daylight is white – almost bluish – and tungsten lamps give a yellow-orange colour. You can see the different colours if you look at a building at dusk. The colours don't really matter for your eyes, but they show in colour photographs. Take a picture by tungsten lighting on daylight film and you get an orange-coloured transparency. Conversely, a daylight scene comes out blue on film intended for tungsten lighting.

For photographic purposes, the colour of light is measured as colour temperature. This is, in fact, the temperature of a theoretically perfect radiator (a black body) heated up to emit light of the same colour. The temperature is measured on the absolute (kelvin) scale. A kelvin is exactly the same as a celsius (centigrade) degree. But the scale starts from absolute zero (the coldest possible) which is −273.15°C. So 100°C is the same temperature as 373.15 K.

Colour temperature

At round about 1000 K a reddish light is emitted. As the colour temperature rises, the light emitted changes from red, through orange, yellow and white, to blue. Perversely, the higher the colour temperature, the 'colder' the illumination looks. Basically, light sources with low specific outputs – matches, domestic lamps, and so on – tend to produce reddish, low-coloured temperature light (2000–3500 K). daylight has a much higher colour temperature (5000–6000 K), and artificial light sources can match this.

Daylight

The quality of daylight varies considerably from a bright sunlit day to a dark cloudy one. Since one particular type of daylight had to be selected as a

Matching colour film to the light

Although most white light looks about the same to our eyes, it doesn't to colour films. To distinguish the colour, we use the colour temperature. To achieve normal colour balance, reversal film must be balanced for approximately the Kelvin (K) colour temperature of the light source. Filters can compensate for colour temperature differences.

The outdoor scenics shown here with their colour temperatures from top to bottom are: blue north sky, overcast daylight, average daylight with sunlight, sunlight at noon, and English daylight standard.

Tungsten light sources, top to bottom are: blue flashbulb, electronic flash, 'daylight' fluorescent, clear flashbulb, warm white fluorescent, 3400 K floodlights, projector lamps, 100watt and similar general-purpose lamps, small lower wattage general-purpose lamps.

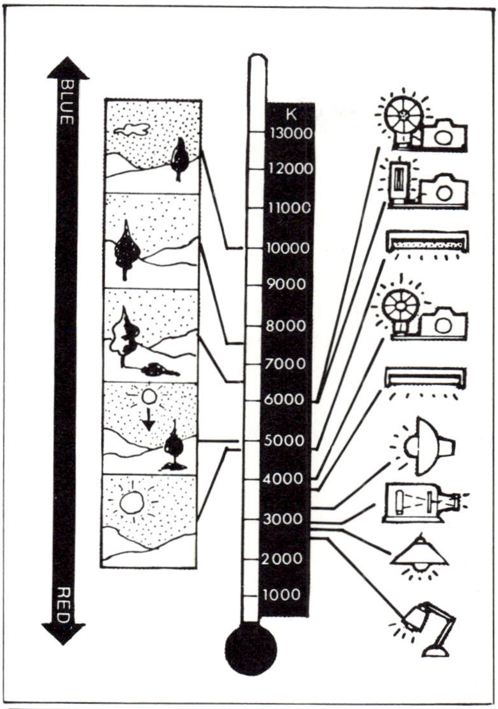

Which B & W film?

Choose your film to fit your subject. But remember the faster the ASA index, the more graininess, less resolution and, usually, less contrast.

For fine copying work or subjects to be made into giant enlargements.

For bright outdoor scenes, where sharpness and resolution are essential.

For action where fairly fast shutter to halt movement is needed.

For high-speed action or where poor lighting conditions would make it impossible to use slower film. Now often used for general-purpose photography.

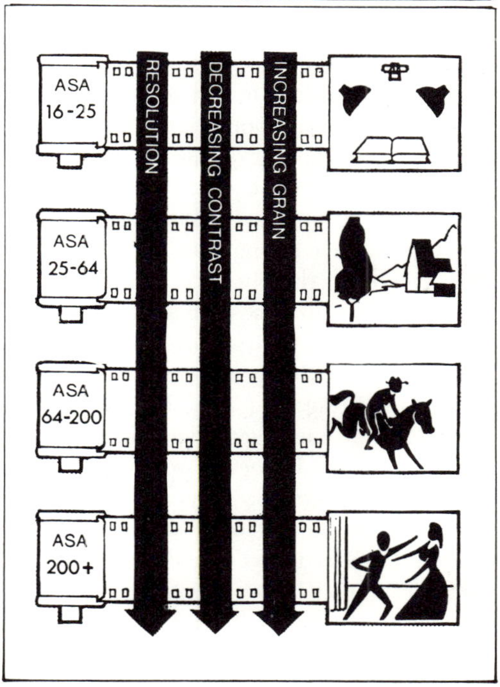

standard, photographic daylight in film terms is defined as a combination of direct sunlight and light reflected from a clear blue sky with a few white clouds during that time of the day when the sun is more than 20° from the horizon. This is between 5500 and 6000 K. Daylight-type colour films are balanced for such lighting.

What happens when a daylight film is used for daylight under other conditions, such as a heavily overcast sky which can have a colour temperature as high as 7500 K or late-afternoon sunlight which may go as low as 4000 K?

Your transparencies come out with a slightly bluish tinge in the former case and a golden glow in the latter. Your eyes compensate for the conditions when you're there, so the colour cast is almost invariably stronger than you noticed at the time. The bluish effect of an overcast day and the gold of a low sun can depict the time of the day well, even if slightly overdramatically. You can change the colours with filters on your camera (see page 198). This gives a neutral colour, but can lose the atmosphere of the scene.

You'll probably do most of your transparency work on daylight-type film. For unlit shots, you can use electronic flash or blue flashbulbs. These are made to give the right colour balance with daylight films.

Artificial light

Continuous artificial light sources and clear flashbulbs, however, are usually a much lower colour temperature. Whether you're trying to take pictures by the light of nothing more than a household table lamp, or carefully lighting a studio set with photographic floodlights, you don't really want a colour slide balanced for daylight. The colour temperature of such lighting, no matter how bright, is far lower. It contains more red and less blue. You can use filters to balance daylight-type film properly for such illumination (see page 199). However, the filter you need is a fairly deep blue and so cuts down the light considerably. So, with artificial illumination except for flash, tungsten-type colour slide film is more convenient.

Two slightly different sorts are made: Type A, balanced for photoflood (3400 K) lighting; and Type B, balanced for tungsten studio lamps (3200 K). Formerly, you could get Type F film, balanced for clear flashbulbs. This is no longer available. However, you need only pale filters to adjust between any of these light sources. So they don't cause much problem.

Home lighting is a lower colour temperature than any of these sources, so you need a filter to get true colour reproduction. However, for most existing light pictures at home, the higher-speed Type B films are quite suitable. I have achieved quite acceptable results with such films without filtration even from subjects lit with only a single 100-watt table lamp.

Viewing transparencies

There are three basic ways to enjoy transparencies. You can view them by hand, project the slides, or have prints made from them. Few hand viewers are really first class in construction or optics. For really critical examination of a slide by hand, we would recommend that the Nikon or Nikkormat owner obtain an inexpensive viewing box. This is simply a rectangular opal glass or plastic surface lit evenly from underneath. Slides may be sorted and viewed on the surface with the aid of a good magnifier of 5× to 10×. Magnifiers used by stamp collectors or the small folding linen testers with self-attached stands employed by cloth merchants are excellent and generally available at most optical shops. For critical slide examination, to check extreme detail, you may wish to own a small pocket microscope of 25× or so. I find this is ideal for sorting slides into shows quickly.

As we've said, nothing is as impressive in photography as the projection of really fine, brilliant, crisply sharp slides. To achieve this you need two basic elements: a fine slide projector with good lens, and a suitable projection surface. These are actually not as easy to acquire as they may sound. Most slide projectors do not hold the slide sufficiently parallel to the screen, and few slide projectors have optics to do justice to really good slides. Test out any machines carefully before you purchase them, particularly with respect to sharpness in the corners of the projected slide. Cardboard-mounted slides have unsupported film areas which do not remain completely flat. In fact, one manufacturer supplies lenses computed to take account of the expected bowing in cardboard-mounted slides. This is effective for some slides, but works adversely with others.

In addition, heat from the projector causes further buckling. For best possible flatness and overall screen sharpness, slides should be mounted in between glass. However, except for lecturers or those amateurs or pros who have set slide shows, few of us today mount slides in glass although we would get better results by doing it.

In testing out a slide projector for sharpness (unless you can use the special curved-field lens), mount one crisp slide in glass so that you are indeed giving the projector an objective test with flat film.

What do you wish to use as a screen? We have fortunately grown up and away from the old traditional bedsheet which really soaked up much illumination and gave us such poor results. There are today basically three screen surfaces – beaded, lenticular and matte. Both beaded and lenticular screens provide surfaces which can be used even if room illumination if fairly high; some are good for viewing in daylight if needed. They do have, however, somewhat restricted viewing angles. Those sitting to the sides of the screen see the picture, but it's nowhere near so bright. The biggest drawback, however, to the serious slide-maker is the beaded or lenticular surface which tends to break up the fine detail in the photograph. The third type of screen surface, matte, is harder to find, but well worth the effort. It doesn't provide the brilliance of the lenticular or beaded screen and should be used in a well-darkened room. Its fine surface reflects nearly every bit of detail in the slide. So if you pride yourself on fine detail in slides, you'll want to try a matte surface. Lacking a matte screen, I find a matte white wall a suitable substitute.

Making colour slides with transparency film does have one distinct drawback: you have only one original slide. You can, of course, make or have made slide duplicates. This can be somewhat expensive if you have them done commercially. However, with the proper slide-duplicating accessories, you can make your own duplicates easily and inexpensively. Admittedly, even the best duplicate can never match the original exactly, although it may come very close. Perhaps by better cropping and some filtration the duplicate can be made more acceptable than the original. However, we will analyse slide duplicating in the chapter on close-ups.

Colour negatives

Most colour film sold throughout the world is negative film. It is quite possible first to have such film developed and then examine the negative to see which, if any, are worth printing. However, it has become more and more the fashion to let the photo-finisher print up the whole roll immediately after developing it. Besides providing an easier way to get prints, negative films have other advantages. Exposure errors can usually be corrected in printing. I have seen excellent prints made from colour negatives under- or overexposed by as much as three *f*/stops.

Most negative colour films are balanced to provide correct results when used in daylight illumination. However, unlike transparencies, all is not lost if you expose them to other light sources. A good laboratory can make quite reasonable prints from negatives even exposed in house lighting. If you do your own colour work, you too can do such correction.

Negative colour films do have their limitations, however. While colour slides can be made from them, this is a relatively expensive process. Ordinary commercial laboratories usually produce somewhat harsh and contrasty results, grainier than slides made directly on transparency material. On the other hand, transparency films today can be made into prints every bit as good as those from negative films. If you wish to make colour prints yourself, there are more and more processes which allow you to make prints directly from transparencies, with no need to make a time-consuming inter-negative. Therefore, the advantage of the negative film as an easier-to-print colour material is fast fading. Lastly, the transparency material provides you with viewable slides at moderate processing cost as opposed to the higher cost of printing all the negatives colour. From the slides you can select just those which you want to have printed. It's a convenient and more

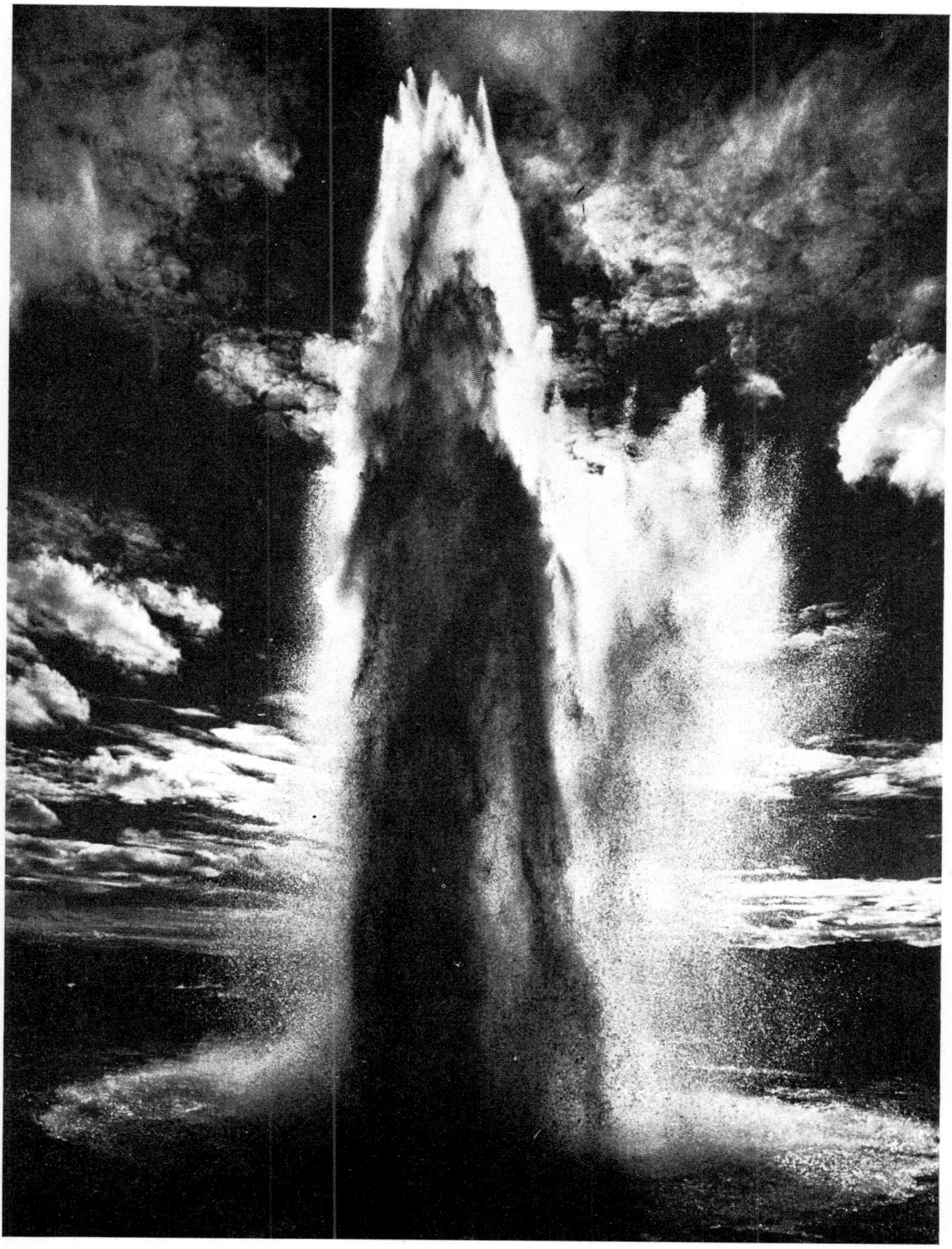

Dramatic nature

Shooting this Icelandic geyser against the sun heightens its impact. A high shutter speed on a 20 mm *f*/3.5 lens freezes the movement. *Walter Mayr.*

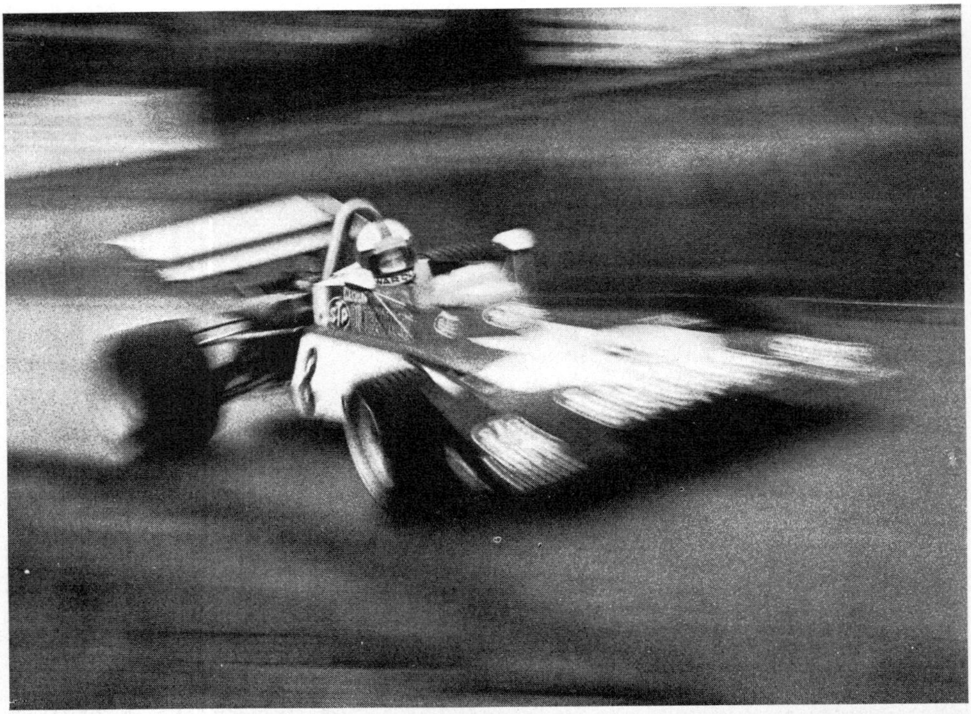

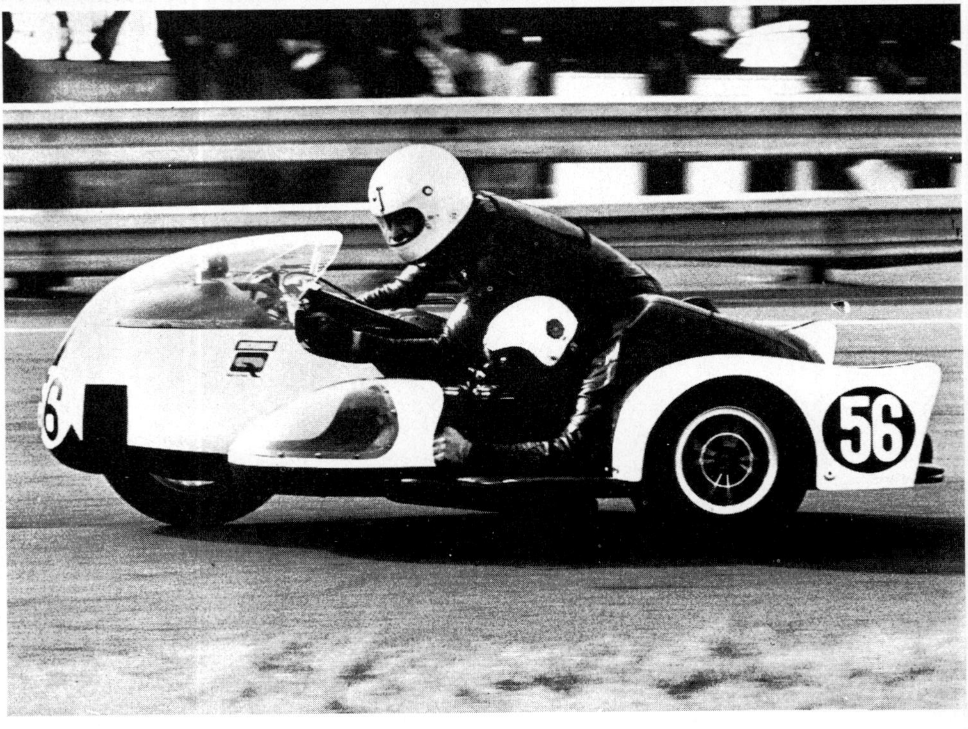
56

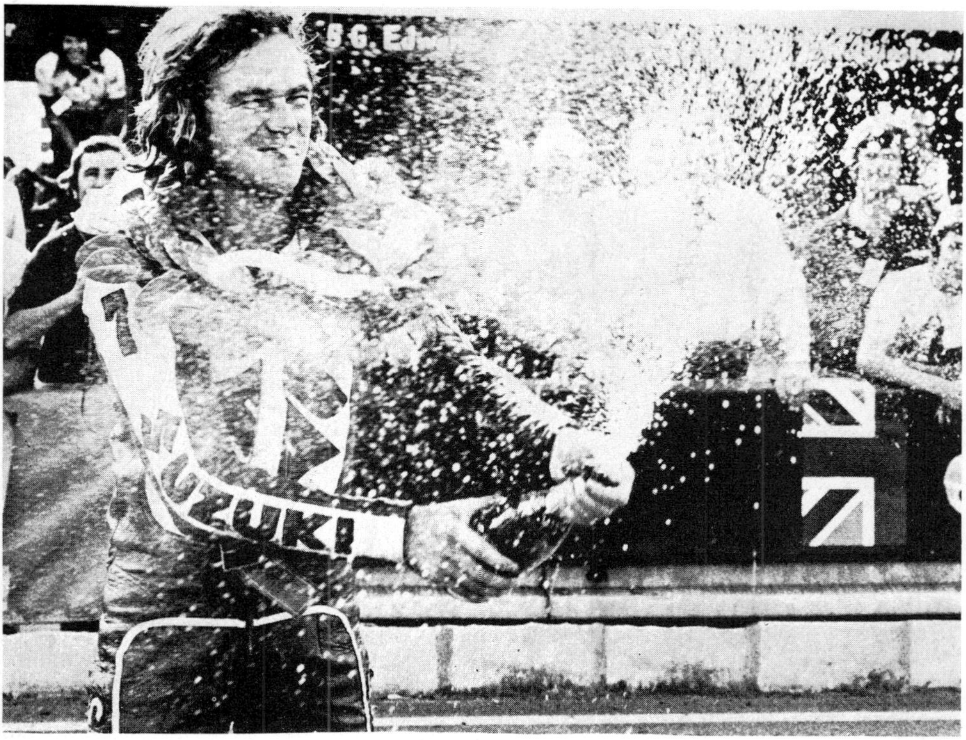

Movement

Opposite, top. Close-up with a relatively short focus lens, you can produce a 'zoom' effect as you pan with a moving subject. Here, the photographer used a 55 mm Micro-Nikkor at $\frac{1}{15}$ second. *Ed Buziak.*

Frozen

Opposite, bottom. Pan at a higher shutter speed, stand further back, and the whole subject comes out sharp. Here the photographer has produced an excellent record, but not so much impression of movement. *Ed Buziak.*

Champagne

Above. Barry Sheene, world motorcycle champion, celebrates another victory in the traditional way. The photographer had to brave the spray to get this tightly-cropped shot with his 55 mm Micro-Nikkor. *Ed Buziak.*

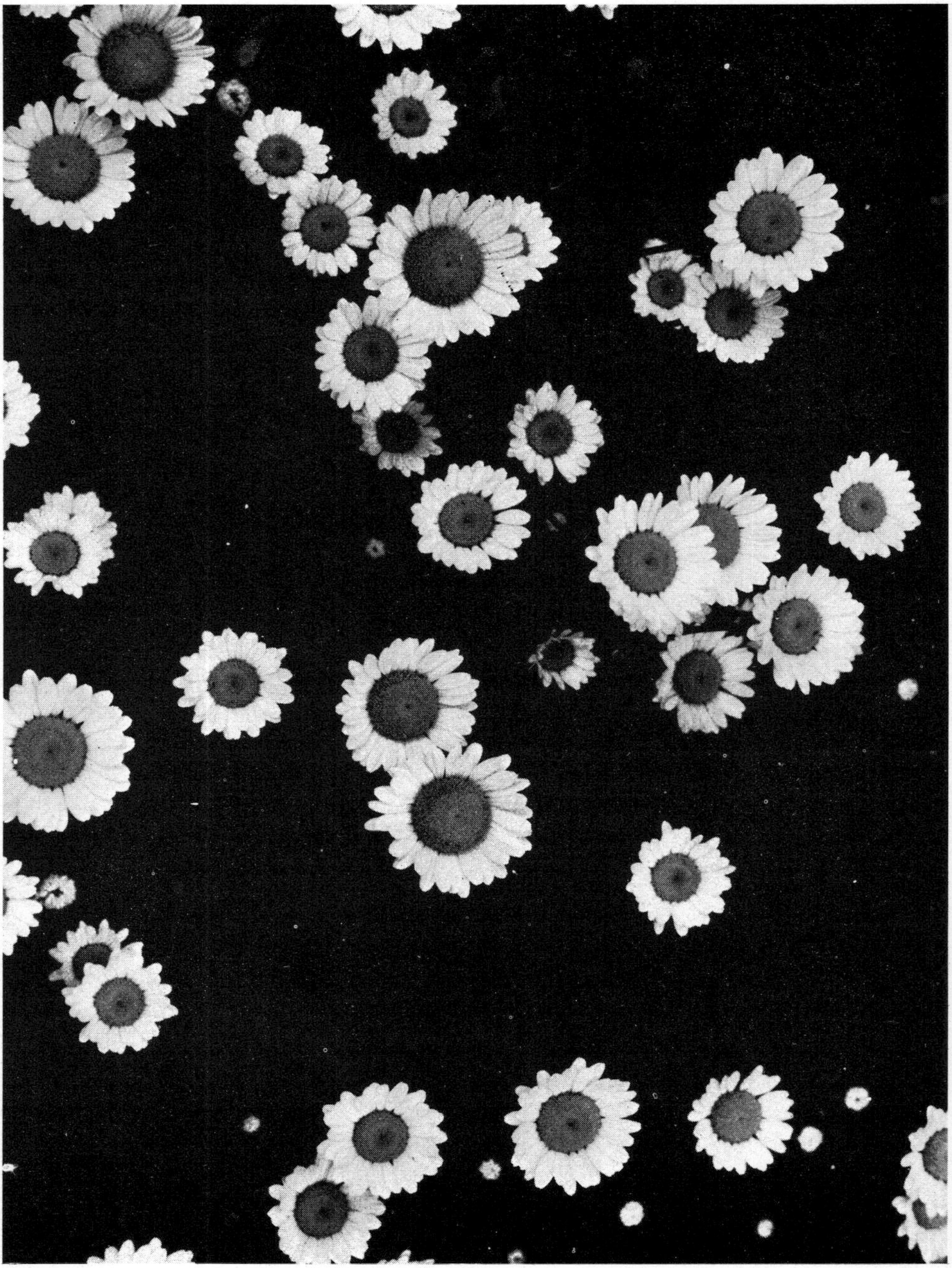

Daisies in summer

Exposure on medium-speed black-and-white film was calculated for flower heads, leaving ground level underexposed and dark. Still, potassium ferricyanide lightening of each flower was needed during processing. Nikon F, 58 mm *f*/1.4 Nikkor, about *f*/8, 1/125 second.

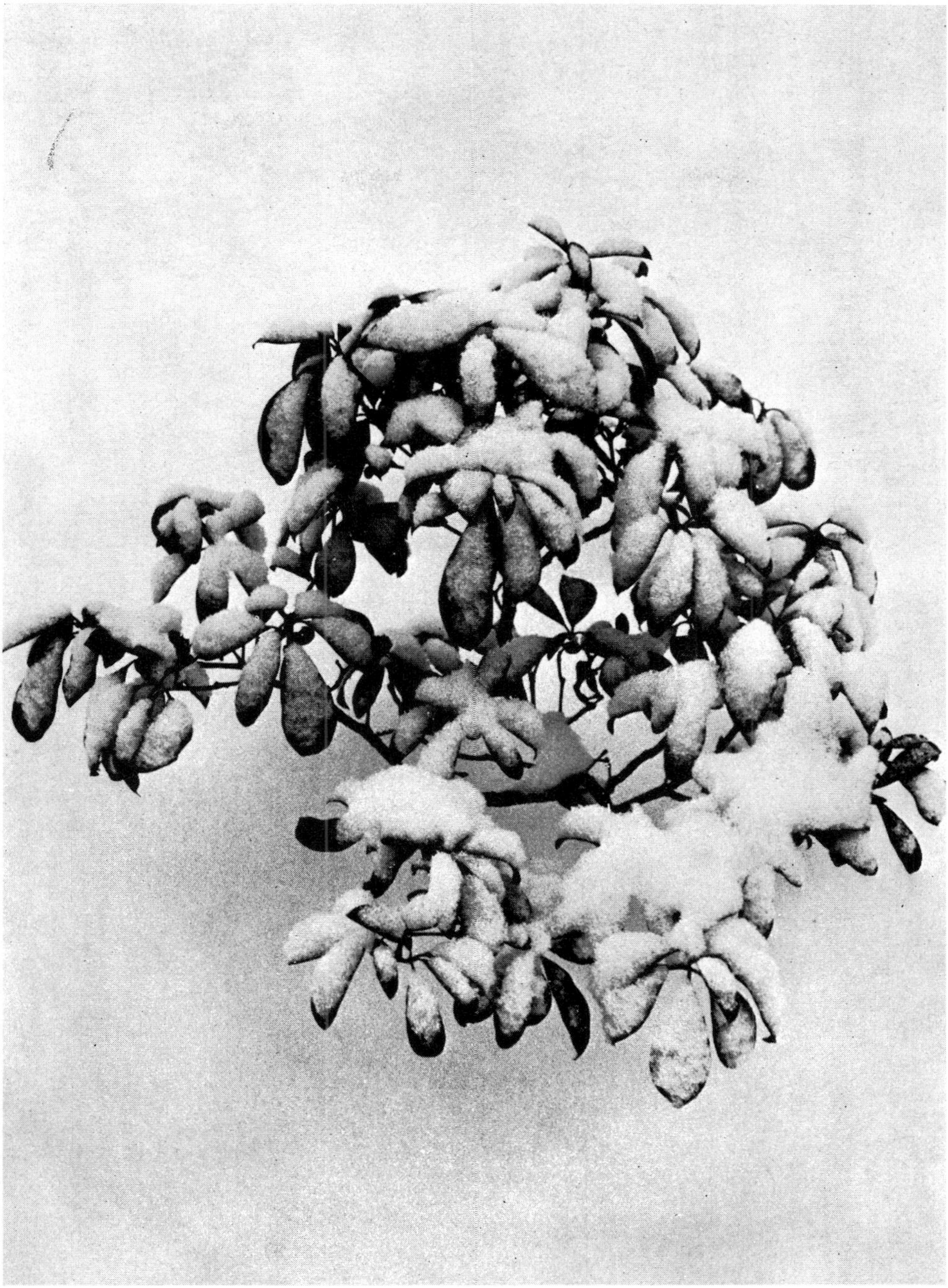

Bush in winter

Fresh fallen snow creates new shapes, textures, and patterns from familiar objects. This bush stuck through snow near my house. I used a 105 mm *f*/2.5 Nikkor, Nikkormat FT and high-speed film, 1/125 second, *f*/8.

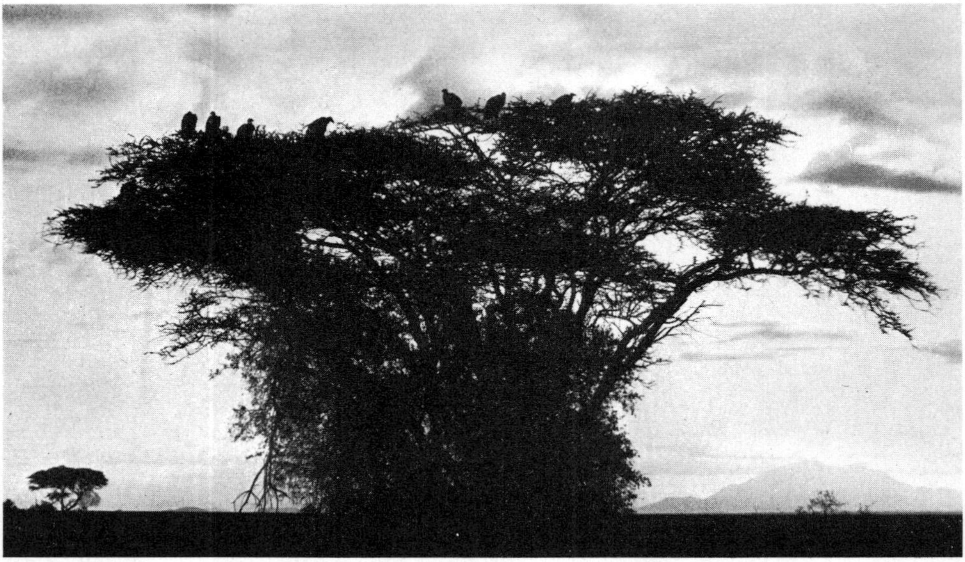

Scenic silhouette

Centre-weighted Nikkormat FTn, meter suggested 1/125 second at *f*/5.6 exposure on fast black-and-white film through 105 mm *f*/2.5 Nikkor for vultures poised in thorn tree on East African plain. To heighten silhouette I cut aperture to *f*/8.

Tree patterns

Pattern formed by fir tree trunks interrupted by bushy treetops in outskirts of Kyoto, Japan, were photographed on high-speed film with my Nikkormat FTN, 105 mm *f*/2.5 Nikkor, 1/125 second, *f*/8, overcast sky.

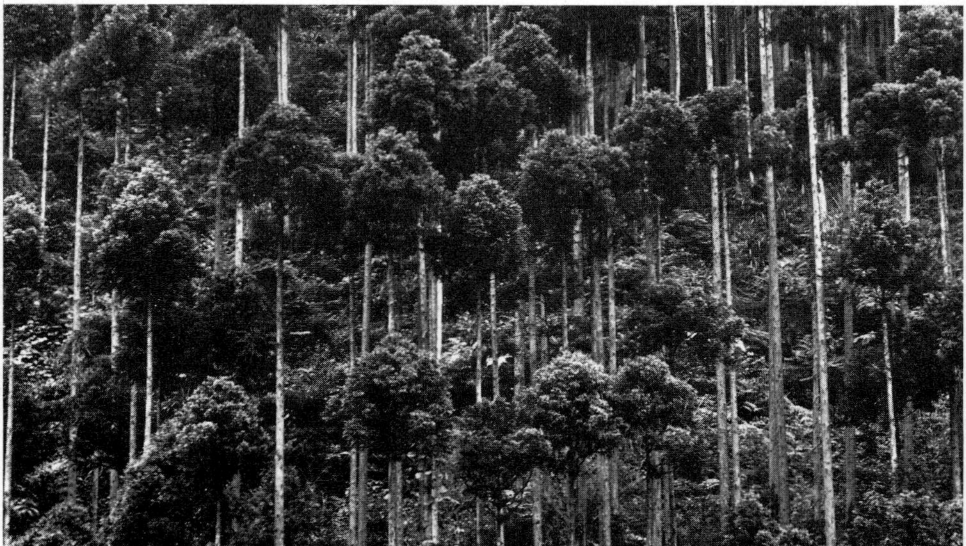

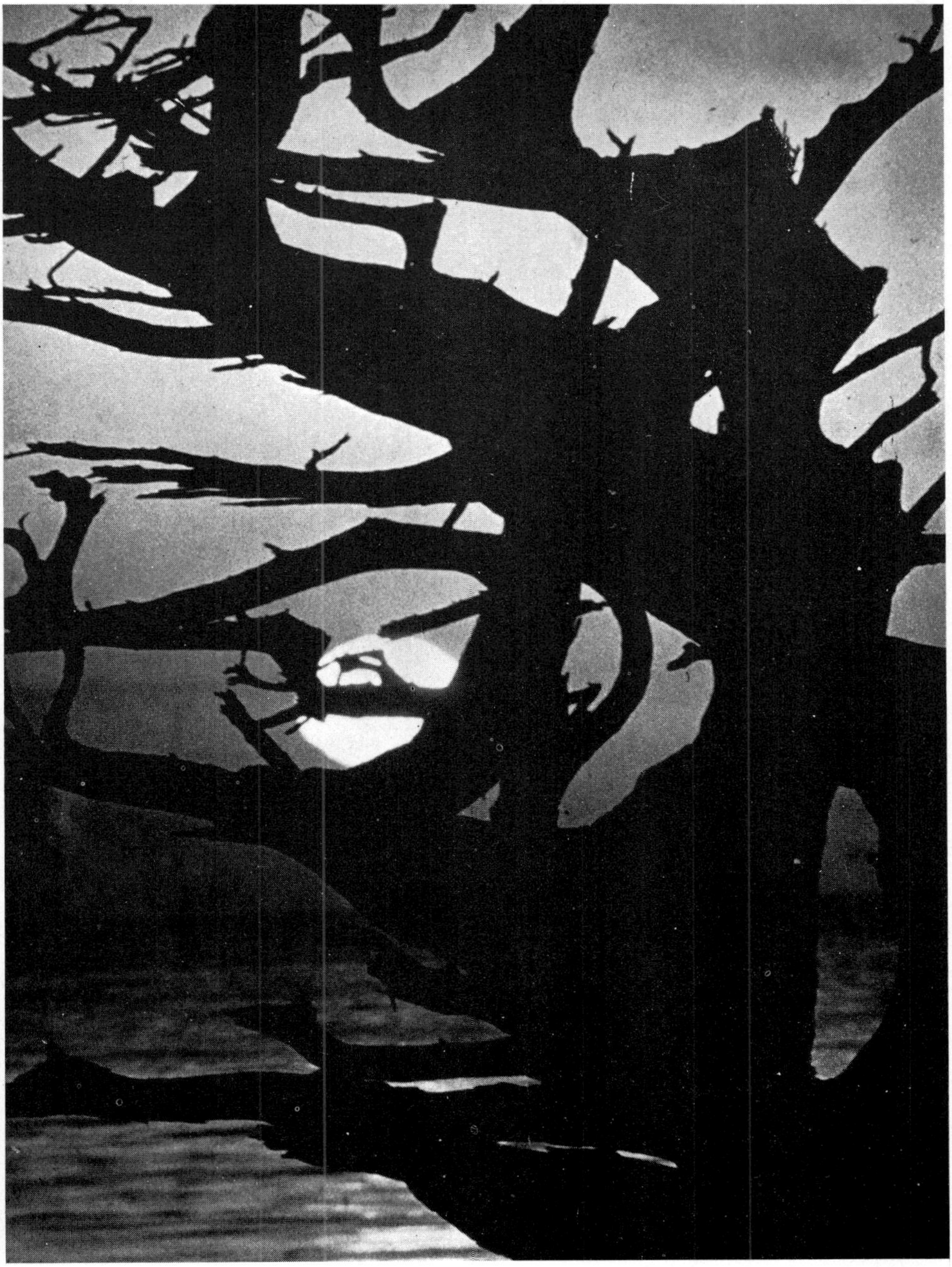

Sunset

I waited in front of fantastically shaped cypress tree on 17-mile drive near Monterey, California for the sun to drop to just the right place. Then I made the photograph with a 400 mm lens on Nikon F at *f*/f8 on high-speed film with lens resting on car for support.

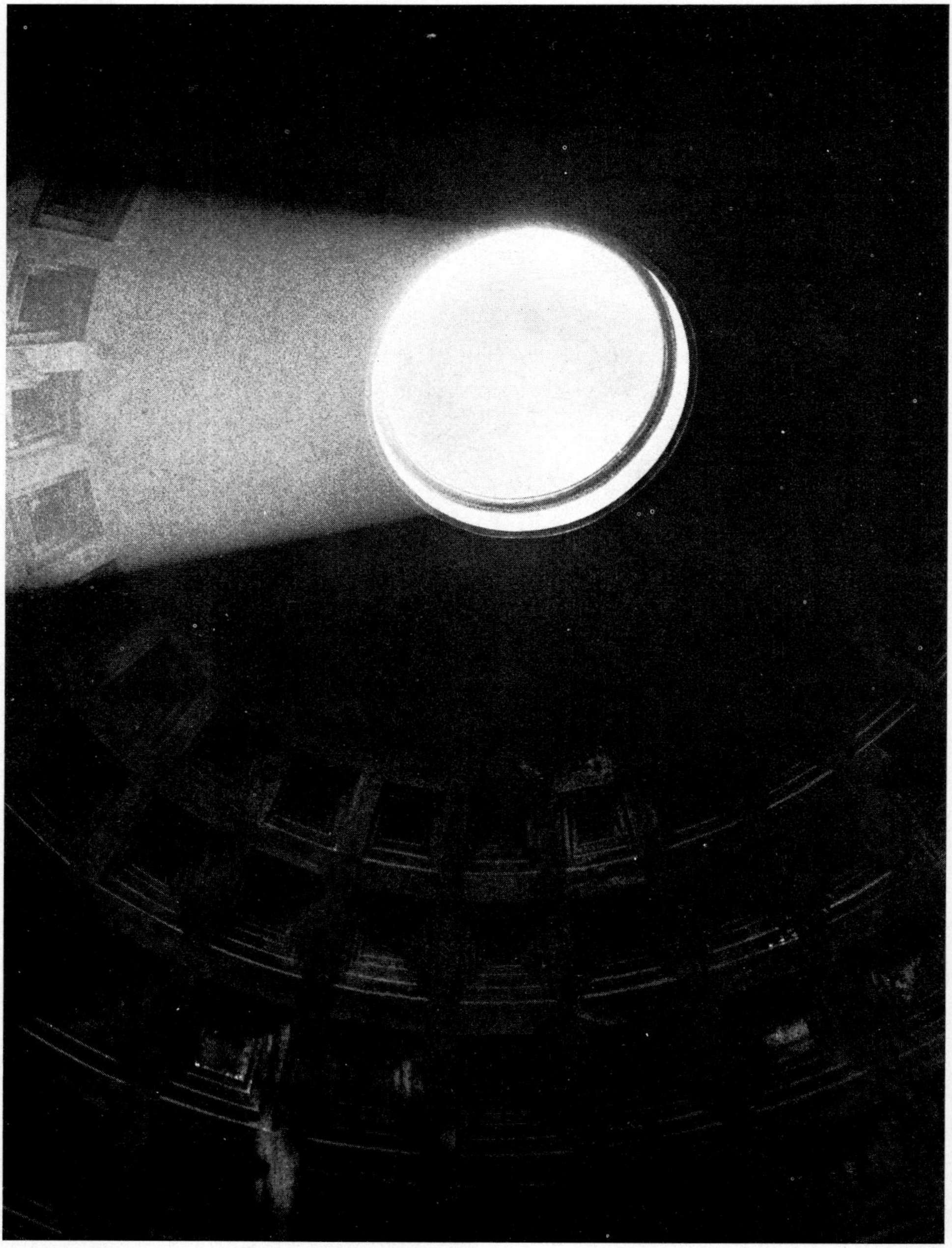

Pattern of light

The ceiling of the Pantheon in Rome catches late-afternoon shaft of sunlight through open central port. High-speed film, Nikon F, 58 mm *f*/1.4 lens, about 1/30 second at *f*/4.

economical system. However, I have seen excellent prints as large as 16 × 20 in from both slides and colour negatives.

I prefer transparency material except when forced by circumstances beyond my control, such as by relatives who want prints only at Christmas time. Then I use negative film.

Expiry (expiration) date

A few words of warning concerning the date printed on the film box. I have found that black-and-white films are fine well after the date suggests. The same is not true of colour film. The colour balance keeps shifting as the film grows older, even after exposure, until the film is processed. The manufacturers estimate the time it takes from manufacture of the film until you get it so that the film has the proper balance when you expose it. The end of the period when the manufacturer feels the film is longer accurate and usable is marked by the expiry date. Beyond this date the film may be just as sensitive, but pictures may come out with an overall colour cast. So, don't trust outdated colour films without first exposing an experimental roll from a specific emulsion batch and supplier. Almost all film manufacturers list the emulsion number of the film on the box.

When buying a number of rolls at one time, it's advisable to make sure they are all of the same emulsion number. Then if one has the right colour balance, they all should, and if one is wrong, you had best return the whole batch. This is particularly a sound practice when you intend to expose several rolls of colour film and cannot afford any poor results. You can buy rolls all from one batch, test one roll, have it processed before you leave, and then go quite secure in the knowledge that you have proper film with you.

You may find that you have a number of film rolls which you don't intend to use for a while, yet you don't wish them to go out of date. You can delay or prolong their life by placing the rolls in a deep-freeze. There is no definite rule as to how long film can be preserved in this manner, but black-and-white film frozen after exposure in the Arctic has been processed and found perfect after 75 years, and I have known professionals to keep colour-slide films for up to 10 years with no ill effects. Many photographers automatically load all newly purchased film into a freezer, withdrawing it only as needed. If you do freeze film, make sure the film remains in its airtight metal, plastic or foil container and that you do allow it sufficient time (5 hours) after removal from the freezer to warm to shooting temperature before using it. Otherwise you'll get water condensing on the surface.

Black-and-white films

Black-and-white photography is no longer the vastly dominating influence it once was. However, for the Nikon or Nikkormat photographer, amateur or professional, black and white is often still looked on as the bread and butter of picture making.

Over the past quarter-century there have been considerable advances in black-and-white films. Once, workers were forced to use extremely slow film and vastly toxic developing agents to coax fairly fine results from their tiny 1 × 1½in (24 × 36mm) negative. Today, even fast films can yield negatives capable of vast enlargement with surprisingly good quality. Producing crisp, sharp prints from 1 × 1½in negatives no longer is a feat of darkroom magic, but an everyday procedure which you can certainly master. A properly made 35mm negative should readily be enlargable to 200 × 250mm (8 × 10in) or more and your prints be indistinguishable from similar prints made with a 6 × 6cm (2¼ × 2¼in) or larger negative.

Just like colour films, black-and-white emulsions are given ASA and DIN ratings. Black-and-white films are suitable for any light source, so are divided into types solely on speed.

In 35mm photography, it has been customary to divide black-and-white films into four groups.

Group 1: Very slow (finest grain) ASA 25 (DIN 15) and below.

Group 2: General purpose (medium slow, very fine grain) ASA 32–64 (DIN 16–19).

Group 3: General purpose (medium fast, fine grain) ASA 80–200 (DIN 20–24).

Group 4: High speed (moderate grain) above ASA 200 (DIN 24).

Unfortunately, the name of the film seldom gives you much of an indication as to speed. However, you'll find the ASA and DIN ratings marked somewhere on the box. Most major film manufacturers produce films in each of the four groups. Film in Group 1, which is rather a specialised item, is made mainly for microfilming and similar applications; but there are one or two such films on the general market. The brand you choose is a matter of personal taste, but you should not assume that all films of the same speed by different manufacturers have the same characteristics – they do not. Different films may respond quite diversely to a particular processing procedure. One company's ASA 400 film may have far less graininess than another's. Experiment with a few in the speed range you will be using and select the one that you prefer. Stick to it, and to your developer (or laboratory). Shy away from unknown brands and special buys, however, since quality control of such films can be poor. In fact, you may be buying two or three different brands of film with the same label. One roll may give you excellent results, but you can never tell about the next.

Black-and-white film characteristics

Black-and-white films have several characteristics that can affect your choice. These are: colour sensitivity, graininess, resolving power and sharpness.

Colour sensitivity: Plain silver bromide, the major light-sensitive material in negative emulsions, is sensitive only to blue and ultra-violet radiations. By adding suitable dyes, it is possible to extend the sensitivity to green (which is called orthochromatic sensitisation), through the red (panchromatic sensitisation), into the (invisible) infra-red region of the spectrum. Virtually all normal photographic films now available are panchromatic. Specialised materials such as infra-red-sensitive and blue-sensitive copy films are indeed available, but are outside the scope of this volume.

Panchromatic film has a response to the visible spectrum similar to your eye, and it records colours in various tones of grey with about the same relative brightness as they appear to the observer. Even so, blue and violet parts of the screen tend to come out rather too pale. The relative brightness at which colours are reproduced in black and white can be changed with filters, as we'll see in the chapter on filters.

Graininess, resolving power and sharpness: I shall deal with these three generally misused terms together since they are very closely interrelated. Most photographers talk in terms of graininess implying that a lack of grain automatically means better results than you would get from a film with more grain. This is not always true. The silver grains in an emulsion are too small for anyone to see in a negative or print without a high-power microscope. What we think of as graininess is actually the clumping together of many grains.

Those films that have grain and small grain clumps were long thought to produce sharper prints. However, sensitometrists have discovered that sharpness and lack of graininess are not identical at all. The apparent sharpness of a picture depends partly on the fineness of the grain and partly on the sharpness of the grain-clump edges. If the grain clumps have soft, mushy edges, the pictures will never appear quite as sharp even if they can resolve very fine detail. The resolution of a film, however, which is often measured in its ability to reproduce very fine lines per millimetre on a test chart, is more a function of the fineness of the grain clumping than of sharpness. In other words, it is quite possible for a picture to *appear* sharper if you are using a film having sharper-edged, larger grain clumps than softer-edged small grain clumps.

This conclusion has in the past 20 years revolutionised the manufacture and choosing of films. It was once most fashionable to rely on the film with the fineest grain and then to expose and process it with special, often toxic developers to produce an extremely small grain clump, soft-edge negative which would resolve fine detail. However, when the same subject material was photographed with film having larger, sharper-edged grain clumps, the resulting negative when made into a print and viewed at a reasonable distance *looked* sharper and crisper. The trend, then, today is to choose a compromise film which has sharpness to produce snappy prints at normal viewing distances while still yielding sufficient detail.

A further influence has been the general adoption of high-acutance developers and films. These emphasise the edges between parts of a different density. So they further increase the sharpness of the grain clumps. This has resulted in photographers using faster and more 'grainy' film for general purposes than was preferred previously, since the faster films do have the larger, sharper-edged grain clumps. Admittedly, if you have specialised work – copying documents, paintings, or making murals – which will be viewed at far closer distances than the standard formula calls for, you will be more interested in detail and resolution than sharpness, and should choose your film accordingly.

Perhaps the best simile we can relate would be the difference between a finely detailed painting and a mosaic of the same subject. While the painting would have far greater actual detail when viewed close, the mosaic at a distance could well appear sharper because of its larger, sharp-edged pieces. Now let's see how one can compromise properly between the fine painting and the mosaic in terms of choosing a film from the four categories.

Choice of black-and-white film

The films in Group 1 need only be used when extreme fine detail is needed in giant enlargements such as murals. They generally have very small grain clumps with fairly soft edges and don't yield the crisp results available from faster films.

Group 2 are still listed as general purpose, although most photographers today have gone on to something faster (and apparently sharper). However, for anyone interested in making large salon enlargements which may be viewed very closely, films in this group are probably preferable.

Group 3 contains the emulsions in most general use today. When properly exposed and processed they will yield results amazingly close to those of Group 2 but admittedly with some loss of fine detail, possibly compensated by increased apparent sharpness. Enlargements to 11 × 14 in are possible which are almost identical in graininess to Group 2. However, in enlargements beyond that there will be a noticeable difference if viewed close. We would recommend that you choose your general-purpose film from this group.

The fast films from Group 4 are becoming more and more used. Photo-journalists shooting for magazine-page-size pictures sometimes now depend solely on films in the group (usually with a 200 or 400 ASA rating) for all black-and-white work. In my experience, excellent 11 × 14 in prints can indeed be made provided exposure and processing is correct and the *image is in sharp focus*. This latter point is most important. If the image on the print is crisp and in focus, graininess is not as apparent as when the image is not sharp – and this is most evident in films in this group. Because of the speed of these films, another limitation appears. In bright light, the films might even be too fast to achieve a proper exposure. In really light conditions, a fast film may need a shorter exposure than a 1/1000 second at *f*/16 outdoors on a bright sunny day. Even if the exposure is within your camera's ability, the setting of a small aperture and high shutter speed may not be what you wish. For instance, if you want to blur an action to make it more realistic with a slower shutter speed, or you wish to use a fairly large aperture to render an undesired background sharp, you may find that you cannot do it with a fast film and still get proper exposure unless you resort to a filter to cut the light suitably.

I mention these exposure limitations because I have seen many professional photographers armed only with fast black-and-white film being made utterly helpless outdoors in bright light. If you do indeed find that you are satisfied with print quality from a high-speed film, always carry some slower film for emergencies.

Before leaving film choice, it would be unfair not to mention the excellence of fast films under poor lighting conditions. With today's fast films you can take pictures literally anywhere you can see. Also these fast films make the small not-too-powerful electronic flash units far more usable.

Vario-speed black-and-white films

Both Agfa and Ilford have introduced new types of black-and-white negative materials called Agfa Vario-XL and Ilford XP1 400 which are capable of producing properly-exposed negatives over a wide range of ASA indexes on the same film. The Agfa film can be exposed at ASA indexes from 125 to 1600, and the Ilford from ASA 50 to 1600. The manufacturers claim that the films, when exposed for low ASA indexes, produce negatives which are equal to slow fine-grain regular black-and-white films, and superior to high-speed black-and-white films when exposed at high ASA indexes. Careful tests indicate that they do come remarkably close to their claims.

The two films are similar in concept, being multilayered 'chromogenic' films, similar in construction to negative colour materials and indeed processable only in chemistry similar to negative colour films. They are therefore more expensive to purchase than ordinary black-and-white films, and do require special processing. Certainly any photographer seriously concerned with black-and-white photography should look at them critically.

Developers

It is almost impossible to discuss films without also talking about developers. You will never go very far wrong by shooting your film as the manufacturer recommends, using the given ASA film speed and then developing the film in the developer he also suggests. When the manufacturer lists more than one developer, usually one will be a general all-purpose developer while the other, a 'fine-grain' developer, gives a slightly finer grain clump but may yield a softer, less crisp negative with less apparent sharpness. The listing may include times for the developers straight from the bottle or in various dilutions to minimise graininess. I prefer the results overall that can be obtained by using the general developer full strength.

Besides the developers recommended by the film manufacturers, there are many others, including those recommended as high-speed developers, which can produce usable negatives even if you underexpose your film. Of course, no one should deliberately go about underexposing; but in many instances there may not be sufficient light to allow you to set the shutter speed apertures as you wish. These special developers allow you to adopt a higher-than-normal film speed index and then compensate for the under-exposure with forced or 'pushed' development. Unhappily, many photographers are fooled into thinking they are getting extra film speed when they are not. The additional speed is often illusory, sometimes being only an overall fog adding density to the negative. If you are testing a special brew designed to give you extra speed, make certain you run the same test with a second roll of film using your regular developer. After both rolls have been processed, look for shadow detail in the 'pushed' film. If you don't get the same detail from the 'pushed' film you're not getting additional speed. It has been my experience that no more than about 1½ *f*/stops of true additional speed can be achieved with the best of such fast developers. In other words, an ASA 400 film speed could be shot at an index of 1000 with equal shadow detail. Generally, however, speed increase is accompanied by an increase in graininess.

Printing black and white

We shall discuss printing and enlarging here only briefly since they could easily fill a book themselves.

While commercial processors often do well in colour, not many do in black and white. If you shoot black and white, and let a commercial photo-finisher develop the film and make small prints for you by machine, you will never realise what your camera is capable of. Commercial photo-finishing using mass production-line machinery often first ruins the negatives and then produces poor greyed-out prints.

To exploit all the potential of your camera, you should learn to process your own film and do your own printing and enlarging. Your camera and film give you an objective observation of the scene. A straight print on a normal grade of paper may yield results very different from what you realised. Gone will be the rich blacks, the finely detailed highlights and the crispness. Only by making your own prints and learning how to get the most from the negative by print manipulation can you realise how exciting and fulfilling black and white can be. Many photographers who let themselves fall into the clutches of inexpensive mass processing simply attribute the lack of quality of the prints to the small negative size. Only with special hand work, preferably done by you, can you withdraw from the negative every bit of vital information – and many a print from 35 mm need bow to no other larger camera in terms of quality.

It may be, however, that you simply do not have the space, time or equipment to do black and white properly. Rather than resort to mass commercial printing, instead seek out a 'custom' laboratory, preferably one also used by professionals, who can develop your film properly and make the necessary enlargements. While the laboratory cannot interpret the printing of the picture as you could yourself, you will get results far superior to those from the commercial printers. Once you have seen the results from a good custom printer, perhaps it may inspire you to get into the act yourself.

Lighting

Although daylight outdoors certainly remains the prime consideration in photography, the availability of inexpensive and convenient alternatives for indoor use (or to be used outdoors in conjunction with daylight) is growing rapidly. While it was once imperative to start any discussion of artificial lighting with floodlight, today's ever-increasing use of electronic flash makes it the first alternative choice for illumination by both professionals and amateurs. The range of prices for units is incredible: from tiny compacts costing no more than two or three rolls of colour film to giant studio models costing far more than a Nikon outfit with an array of lenses. Almost all Nikon camera models have special coupled flash units available for them as accessories. These are discussed with the cameras in the appropriate chapters.

Electronic flash

The principle of all electronic flash units is simple. A high-voltage electric charge is stored in a capacitor or condenser. This is discharged very quickly through a tube filled with gas, causing the gas to produce a brilliant but extremely brief light. The electronic flash has many advantages over other sources of illumination. Once the unit itself is purchased, its upkeep cost is negligible (compared with flashbulbs) since the total cost is the small amount of electricity used to recharge the nickel cadmium batteries if they are used, or the cost of new throw-away batteries after many flashes.

Compared with flashbulbs, the very short flash duration is a great advantage for stopping action. With bulbs, the action stopping is limited by the shutter speed you select. This can be fairly restricted with the generally available bulbs. With electronic flash, however, the flash duration is about 1/1000 second, and in many cases much shorter. Therefore, subject blur, particularly for action, can be virtually eliminated.

More and more modern flash units, including those made by Nikon, are offering rather versatile systems of automatic exposure making it unnecessary for you to calculate your lens opening. Instead, a photo cell on the front of the unit (or on a separate sensor) or a cell within the camera body itself, behind the lens, measures the amount of illumination reflecting back from the subject during the exposure and switches off the flash during exposure to restrict it to the correct amount of light. This can't be done with flashbulbs.

Lastly, electronic flash is self-contained (except for a charger or AC cord if they are needed). There is no need to carry around a quantity of extra bulbs and no problem of trying to dispose of their remains.

There are three main disadvantages with electronic flash. Few small compact ones favoured by many photographers are anywhere as powerful as even the smallest flashbulbs: a tiny AG-3b bulb may give three times the light of a small electronic flash.

Secondly, because of the instantaneous nature of electronic flash units with their very short flash duration, the flash itself must be used only at shutter speeds when the whole film is uncovered at once for part of the time. If, at the necessary aperture to produce a properly exposed electronic flash picture, there is sufficient existing light present to form an image, you may get a secondary or ghost image on the same picture frame. Therefore, you must make certain the existing light is considerably lower than you would need for the exposure setting.

Thirdly, with most electronic flash units there is a recycling time between flashes as the battery refills the capacitor before the next discharge. This may vary from only a split second in certain units to as long as 30 seconds with units running on partially exhausted batteries. With flashbulbs you can shoot as fast as you can change bulbs.

Choice of unit

Every modern Nikon camera has one or more Nikon accessory electronic flash unit which automatically couples to the camera's electronic system. These are recommended over all others and are described and explained in the chapters devoted to the specific camera models. The following discussion is for older Nikons and Nikkormats, or for those who for their own reasons do not wish to take advantage of the Nikon Speedlight units made specifically for their cameras. However, following the choice of a flash unit, information on flash-unit use is equally applicable in most cases to all electronic flash units.

Once you decide that you want an electronic flash unit, how do you decide on which one? While there is a regrettable tendency on some photographer's parts to choose one for compactness alone, this is wrong. The two main considerations must be power needed and type of power source. Let's take up power needed first, since many flash manufacturers provide units very near alike with alternative or multiple power sources.

Guide numbers

If you are buying a manual exposure electronic flash unit, check the guide numbers as given by the manufacturers of the flash unit. These are generally a pair of numbers for various film speeds. You can find the proper exposure by dividing the guide number by the distance from the flash to the subject. One of the numbers is for the distance in metres, the other (smaller) number for the distance in feet, although some manufacturers quote only one or the other figure.

For instance, if the guide number given for ASA 100 film is 17 m, you would set your camera to *f*/5.6 if you were to shoot at 3 m (17 ÷ 3 = 5.6). Now if you have a 50 mm *f*/1.4 lens, you can alternatively divide 17 m by 1.4 to find the maximum number of metres you could shoot flash. This is 12 m, probably sufficient for most of us. (You can do this just as well in feet if the guide number is imperial and you measure your camera-to-subject distance in feet). However, you may wish to use a telephoto lens, perhaps a 135 mm *f*/3.5 or a 35 mm *f*/2.8 wide-angle. What then? With the 135 mm, your maximum shooting distance now would be 5 m and with the 35 mm lens it would be 6 m (17 ÷ 3.5 and 17 ÷ 2.8). Perhaps this would be sufficient, and then again maybe it would not; you must decide. Perhaps you might be willing to use a faster film with flash rather than go to a more powerful unit. But in any case, decide just how powerful a unit you will need based on your maximum shooting distances, the speed of the lenses you intend to use and the speed of your film.

Power sources

There are three possible power sources: AC house lines, rechargeable batteries, and throw-away manganese alkaline batteries (in an emergency you can use throw-away carbon zinc batteries usually used for flashlights, but they give a very limited number of flashes and so are not recommended for general electronic flash use). Rechargeable batteries have the advantage of not having to be replaced often (but eventually even they will give out). Battery for battery, they usually give you about a third the number of flashes per charge as a set of throw-away alkaline batteries. They must be recharged according to the manufacturer's instructions even when not in use or they lose their ability to hold a charge.

Flash units with built-in rechargeable batteries are initially more expensive than units using throw-away batteries.

While most rechargeable electronic flash units used to take 24 hours to recharge fully, many today recharge in a few hours or even less. If you are a careful worker and take care of your rechargeable unit, keeping it topped up even when not in use, it will serve you well provided the number of flashes available per charge is sufficient for your needs. For instance, many such

Older flash units

Flash Unit BC-7 has tilting fan reflector for bounce flash, accepts bayonet, miniature or AG-1 bulbs, fits Nikon accessory shoe directly or Nikkormat EL and FT2 with proper coupler.

Nikon Speedlight Units SB-2, SB-3 fits Nikon accessory shoe, has energy-saving circuit, works on 4 AA cells.

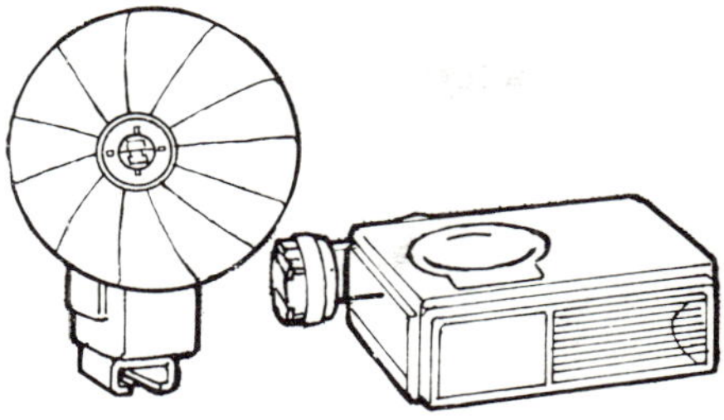

Flash Unit Coupler AS-1 provides direct sync mounting of any hot foot accessory on Nikon.

Flash Unit Coupler AS-2 allows Flash Unit BC-7 or Speedlight SB-2 to connect to hot shoes of Nikkormat EL and FT2.

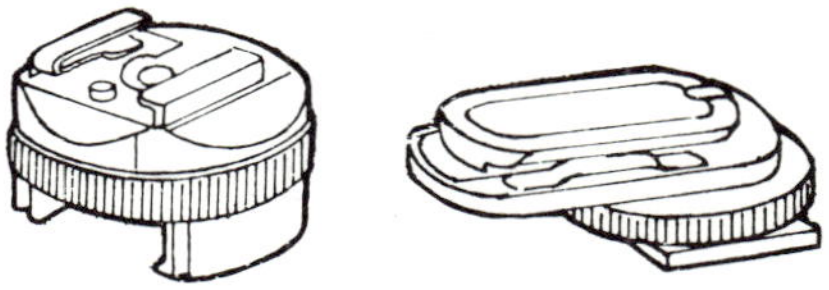

Nikon SB-5 Speedlight system covers angle of 28mm lens, syncs with motor drives, uses rechargeable nicads, high-voltage pack or house mains, has provision for auto flash control.

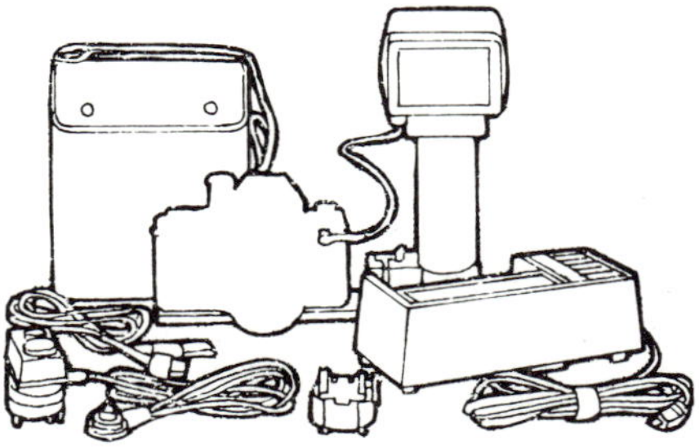

How autoflash works

Autoflash units often provide choice of two or three distance and aperture ranges. Calculator dials are colour-coded. This dial set for ASA 25 provides three ranges: 10m to 1m at *f*/2; from 6m at *f*/4; from 2.6m at *f*/8. Units can also be used on manual exposure.

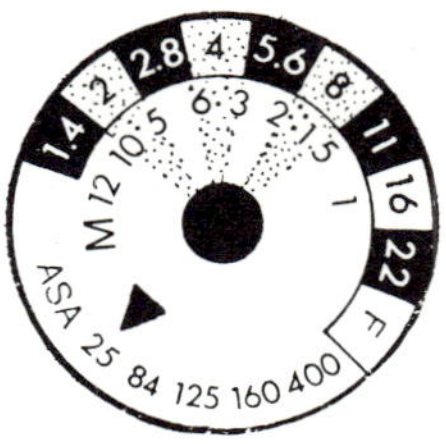

Energy-saving electronic flash units can save time and power e.g.: Unit at 0.6m from subject (1) gives 500 flashes, almost instant recycle; at 3m (2) 150 flashes ½s recycle and at 6m (3), 40 flashes with 6s recycle.

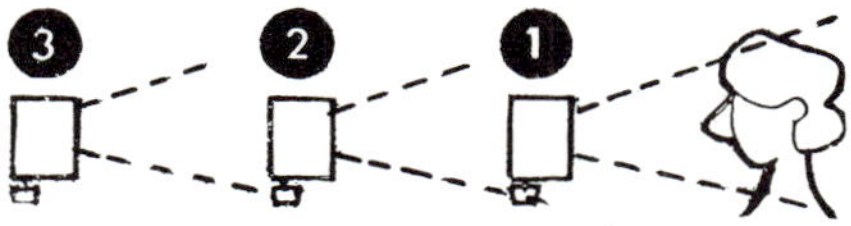

Automatic bounce flash: Some electronic flash units have tilting head for bounce light but auto sensor reads light right from subject for proper exposure.

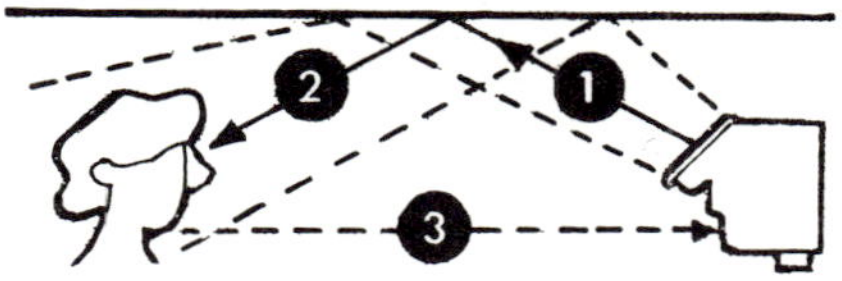

units provide only 40 or so flashes per recharge. If you plan to shoot two rolls of 36 exposures, such a unit will not be sufficient. However, some have interchangeable rechargeable batteries and you can carry spares. The same size units with throw-away manganese batteries may give you between 300 and 500 flashes. The expense, of course, is the throw-away batteries. However, if the unit is left dormant for long periods, you can reactivate it with no difficulty in seconds with a new set of batteries.

One additional problem with rechargeable units is the need to carry a charger if you are travelling, and to find a suitable current. Many chargers have provision for switching to a number of different voltages. Some do not.

Of course, the units which allow a choice of either nickel cadmium batteries or manganese alkaline offer the best of both worlds. If, as most people do, you use your flash mainly indoors, you could consider an AC power unit. You just plug the lead into any suitable house socket, and there you are. The lead is a bit of a nuisance, but you can get used to it. Most AC-powered units allow you to fit batteries as an alternative when there is no power supply, or you don't want to bother with the leads.

Covering power

Covering power is another important consideration in choosing an electronic flash unit, particularly if you intend to use a wide-angle lens. Many units are designed to cover the angle of a 45 mm or longer lens of a 35 mm camera. For normal or longer lenses, therefore, there will be no trouble. However, with 35 mm and wider lenses, units which do not cover will produce darkened corners and edges. If you do intend to use a wide-angle lens, check the flash unit manufacturer's specifications for the diagonal angle of the lens covered (alas, many makers give horizontal or vertical angles) and make sure it at least matches the wide-angle lens you intend to use. Today there is a tendency among the better small electronic flash manufacturers to produce flash units covering greater angles. An often-available alternative is a wide-angle adapter which fits over the electronic flash faceplate and widens the angle (although, of course, lowering the overall guide number somewhat because it spreads the same light over a wider area). Tele adapters to match telephoto lenses are also available.

Automatic flash

When choosing an automatic electronic flash unit, it is important to check the range of distances. This is usually given at a specific aperture and a range of flash-to-subject metres. For instance, a small unit might provide a range of between 0.6 and 5 m (2 and 15 ft) at *f*/5.6 with an ASA 100 film. If you use faster film the aperture may become smaller but the automatic range remains the same. The larger and more expensive units may provide more than one range, perhaps three or more. In other words, you may be able to shoot between 0.6 and 8 m (2 and 25 ft) at *f*/4, or 1 and 5 m (3 and 15 ft) at *f*/8, and 1.3 and 4 m (4 and 12 ft) at *f*/11 – all with a single-speed film. This is an advantage since it allows you to use a smaller lens opening such as *f*/8 at close distances if you wish. A single-aperture-only unit forces you to use the same lens opening throughout. You can still switch to manual-flash guide numbers for maximum distances, or tiny apertures for close-up. Again you should choose a unit based on your maximum distances, lens apertures and film speed needs.

To use an automatic electronic flash unit intelligently, you should know how they work. The photo cell which we have already mentioned usually reads a central area of the subject, between 12 and 20 degrees. So you must make sure there is a central subject to bounce the light back from the sensor. If not, switch to manual control.

Remember the photo cell of an automatic electronic flash unit acts just like a regular exposure meter cell in determining the correct exposure for the tones it is reading. If the subject is very dark, less light will be reflected, leading to increased exposure to lighten the subject. If the subject is very light, much light will be reflected back and the unit will cut the illumination, possibly producing underexposure. However, these are extremes. In most instances the automatic control yields surprisingly even results.

Energy conservation

To make the most of your automatic electronic flash unit, it's important that you know just where the energy that's not used goes. Let's say you are shooting at short distances. The sensor tells the electronic flash to cut the flash duration. What happens to the rest of the light that's cut? In many of the smaller, less-expensive or older automatics, this light is simply dumped in a quench tube.

However, in the better units, called energy-saving units or thyristorised (which is incorrect, since many non-energy-saving units use thyristors for other purposes), the flash not used isn't lost. It is returned to the flash circuit, where it is stored again in the capacitor ready for the next flash. Shooting close to the subject, such energy-saving units provide a greater number of flashes and faster recycling times.

Size and weight

Unfortunately, the more powerful the unit, the larger and heavier it will probably be. Most small units are designed with accessory feet to slip into an accessory shoe on a camera. They can be mounted on the accessory shoe of any camera, but take care if your flashgun does *not* have a hot shoe contact. It may short out the connection, causing the flash to fire as soon as it charges up. If this happens, you can make a temporary cure with plastic tape. For permanent operation, get a separate accessory shoe on a bracket. Older Nikkormats can be fitted with accessory shoes to accept such units, while the Nikon F, F2 and F3 need flash coupler units which fit and lock over the rewind knobs of the camera where the accessory shoe flash contact is located. This is necessitated by the interchangeable nature of the F, F2 and F3 finders. You can change finders and keep the flash unit in place. However, you do have to remove it to rewind film.

The accessory shoes for older Nikkormats do not have built-in flash contacts, so the units will have to be connected with 3 mm (PC) cords to the correct contact of the camera. The flash couplers for the F, F2 and F3 have central flash contacts so that cordless electronic flash units can be used. The other Nikons, Nikkormats FT2, FT3 and EL have a built-on permanent hot shoe which accepts cordless electronic flash units. If desired, however, all the Nikkormats or Nikons can be used with standard PC cords as well as the hot shoes. Additionally, both Nikon and other flash manufacturers make special electronic flash units with built-in connecting shoes for the Nikon rewind knob shoe.

An interesting feature built into the finders of most current Nikons is the ready light. With many flashguns specially designed for these cameras, the light indicating flash-ready actually can be seen in the finder, so you needn't take your eye away from the picture to check whether the flash unit is ready for the next shot.

Flash mounting

While it has been the fashion to offer larger and larger (and heavier and heavier) electronic flash units for shoe mounting on cameras, I would not recommend using any except the smaller, lighter guns on the accessory shoes. Heavier ones can easily damage the prism housing. The flash couplers for the F, F2 and F3 can carry them, however.

For the large single-piece units, even if provided with accessory feet for hot shoe attaching, it is best to use an accessory flash bracket. These usually fit beneath the camera and attach by means of the tripod screw socket. The flash unit, often in the shape of a handle with a flash-head, sits to the side of the camera. Such units usually have some sort of quick-release bracket so you can immediately detach the handle and head from the bracket for off-camera flash or aim it upwards or at a wall for bounce flash. However, a growing number of smaller accessory shoe-mounted electronic flash units also provide bounce flash capability in the form of a swivelling or hinged flash-head.

The most powerful portable electronic flash units in general are two pieces having a head and handle for attaching to the camera (or hand-holding) plus a battery case which you carry on a strap over your shoulder. These, too, are available as fully automatic as well as manual, with throw-away batteries or with rechargeable cells.

Flash lighting

Most experienced photographers prefer to use the flash slightly off camera instead of on camera position. While keeping the flash unit attached to the camera is undeniably more convenient, lighting is somewhat flat, less interesting and does not reveal detail and surface texture. Light directed to the subject from slightly off-camera generally reduces these deficiencies. Most new Nikon flash units do have accessory off-camera flash-connecting cords. The simplest approach is just to hold the flash above the camera and to the side with the flash-head directed towards the subject. For shots over 3m (10ft), arm's length at about 30 degrees from directly overhead is just about right. This may be too high for closer subjects, where no more than 0.6m (2ft) away from the camera can be sufficient.

Using flash off-camera also minimises the possibility of causing red-eye, a common subject disease with on-camera flash. If the subject is looking at the camera, flash close to the lens produces a bright red dot in the pupil of each eye. The lower the light level in the room and the correspondingly larger the subject's pupil, the larger the dot may appear. In black-and-white photographs it appears as a white dot, sometimes actually adding a sparkling highlight to the eyes. In colour, however, it is never an advantage except when photographing animals such as lions or tigers where red eyes, although completely false, make the animals appear more dangerous and sinister.

Red-eye is caused by the light from the flash being reflected directly back to the camera from the retina of the eye. By increasing the distance between the flash and the camera lens, the angle formed at the eye between flash and camera can be increased sufficiently so the reflection will not be seen by the camera lens.

Bounced flash

An alternative to pointing flash directly at the subject is to reflect the light from a nearby surface onto the subject. This softens the light considerably, eliminating harsh shadows, and is generally a far more flattering light for human subjects. Light 'bounced' from a ceiling or wall tends to be more evenly distributed. The result is a far more natural photograph. If there is no suitable white wall, you take your own. The best answer is to bounce electronic flash directly from the inside of the white or silver umbrellas to produce an overall soft studio light without unsightly facial wrinkles, or eye-socket shadows often caused by bouncing the light from a ceiling.

There are three major problems in using bounce flash. First, a great deal of light is lost since the light must, instead of travelling directly to the subject, travel at an angle to the ceiling, wall or other flat surface and then travel back down again to the subject, again at an angle. A certain amount of additional illumination is lost as light is absorbed by the reflecting surface.

Secondly, because of the variables of ceiling height and reflective surface absorption, the problem of calculating the proper exposure is that much more difficult.

Thirdly, if you are shooting colour, any colouration of the reflecting surface changes the colour of your slides.

Let's take the problems one at a time. Do you have enough light for bounce flash? You can figure this out swiftly. Make a small drawing of your bounce needs around your home. Measure the distances, put them on the drawing, find your total flash-to-subject distance and add approximately two *f*/stops additional light for absorption. If you are bouncing the light from the ceiling, a bit of maths gives the distance easily. If you are, say, 3 m away from your subject and you have a 3 m ceiling, you can quickly calculate the approximate distance to the ceiling from floor level by squaring the height of the ceiling (9), adding the square of half the distance to the subject (2.25) and taking the square root of the sum (3.36). Double this amount for the distance to the ceiling and back down again to the subject (6.72 m). Calculate your aperture from the guide number and add the two *f*/stops for light absorption.

Bouncing computer flash

If you have an automatic electronic flash unit which does not have a bounce flash provision, you must set it to manual. Otherwise, the sensor measures the light from the bounce surface, not the subject. If you have an automatic electronic flash unit which does have a special auto bounce provision for tilting the flash-head only, it doesn't necessarily follow that it will work properly. There may not be enough illumination to stay within the automatic exposure range confines. Only those units offering an exposure check light can guarantee proper exposure, so letting you use them without a trial. Once bounce flash is mastered, however, you will find the very natural results well worth the trouble.

A special advantage is that the flash covers a much wider area than normal. I have had amazing results with extreme wide-angle lenses – even 20 mm – by bouncing the flash from the ceiling in a large low-ceilinged banquet room. While there was admittedly some illumination fall-off, by using a 400 ASA black-and-white film I was able to capture every one in the room thanks to the bounce spreading the light.

Multiple flash

A single flash on the camera is not an ideal light source. Although bouncing it helps, you may well feel you want extra units to give you exact control over your lighting. Excellent studio electronic flash units are available which provide direct hook-ups for your camera to two or more flash-heads. Such

Artificial lighting techniques

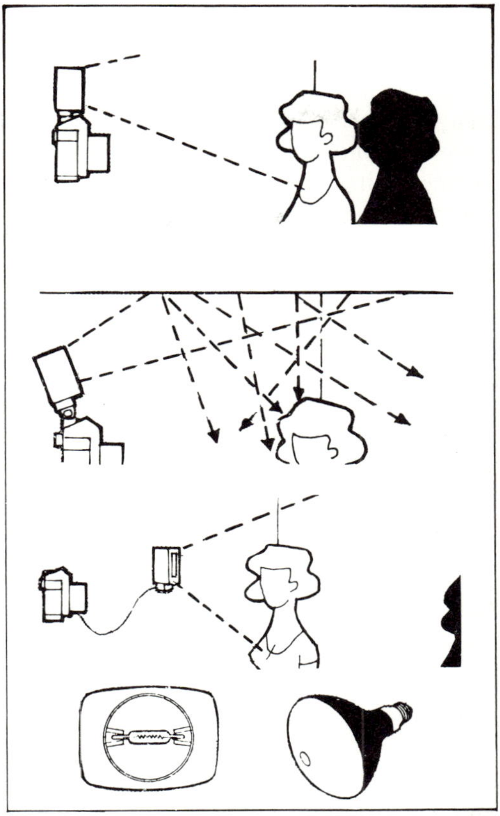

On-camera lighting is convenient but provides rather flat illumination with shadow on background.

Off-camera lighting gives subject more roundness, can eliminate shadow by moving it off to one side.

Bounce lighting from ceiling provides excellent overall illumination but with flash may be hard to calculate for proper exposure.

For continuous light sources, quartz halogen lamps, left, provide constant brightness and colour temperature.

Floods, either plain or with built-in reflectors (right) are inexpensive but lose power and shift in colour temperature as they age.

Electronic flash fill-in outdoors

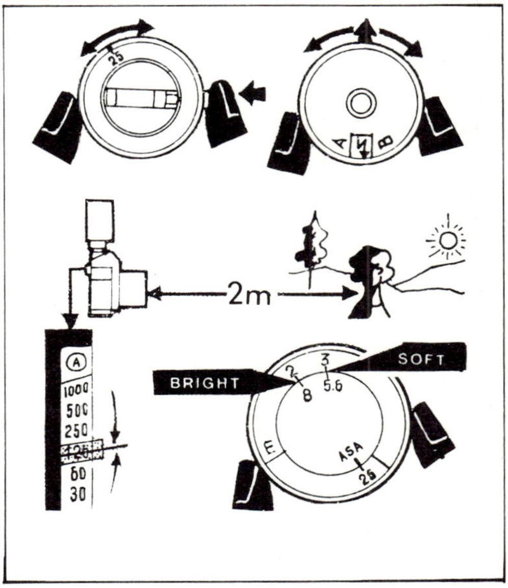

First set meter in camera to ASA of your film.

Set camera sync for electronic flash, and select correct shutter speed.

Set aperture to give correct daylight exposure. Note the aperture. On flash unit calculator dial, find this aperture and note suggested footage (here 2m). Shoot the picture at this footage from subject. For slightly less bright fill-in (softer results) move equivalent of 1 *f*-stop further away (3m in this example).

units may have built-in continuous tungsten illumination modelling lights. These mimic the direction and spread of the electronic flash, so that you can see the results of the light prior to shooting. For proper exposure determination with studio lighting, it's advisable to make use of a good electronic flash meter. If you do plan on shooting much bounce electronic flash even with smaller units, and are having difficulty determining proper exposure, a good electronic flash meter might be a very wise purchase. These meters may need either reflected or incident light. Many have flash firing circuits. You connect the meter to all your flash equipment through a normal sync cord. Then, when you press the meter switch, you fire all the flashguns.

It is also possible to add additional electronic flash units to portable on-camera flash. Direct wiring is possible in some instances, but you can run into some technical problems. Two different guns wired together may fire each other, or fail to fire at all. Two the same may overload your camera contacts and reduce their life. The resulting mess of wires can also be a nuisance.

However, small photo sensors (called slave units) can be plugged into most flash units. The slave fires the units when the main flash (connected to the camera) is fired. The Nikon Modulite Remote Control SU-1 sensor can be used, provided a Nikon SB-5 Speedlight Unit is mounted at camera as the transmitting light.

Fill-in flash

Instead of forming the principal light source, electronic flash can serve as an excellent fill-in or secondary light outdoors. It can eliminate harsh shadows on a bright sunny day, or provide adequate foreground illumination against a bright sky, such as at sunset. The problem is simply one of balancing the exposure of the electronic flash with the existing illumination. Here's how you go about it.

1. Set the meter of your Nikon or Nikkormat and the calculator dial of your electronic flash unit to the proper ASA – for the film you are using.
2. Set your camera for X-synchronisation. If you have an automatic electronic flash unit, switch it to manual operation.
3. Using the regular, built-in metering system (or an accessory hand-held meter if you prefer), set your aperture for proper exposure in the existing light. You may, however, find that there doesn't appear to be enough light for a proper exposure. If so, use a slower shutter speed than X-sync. (You can go down to 1/15 s or even slower if you have a tripod and a stationary subject.)
4. Check your flash unit calculator dial and read the distance opposite the aperture you have set on the camera. This is the flash-to-subject distance for illumination, being just about equal to the existing illumination on

your main subject. For a more natural effect when lighting in shadows of a high-contrast scene, you need less flash. Use the distance appropriate to about two stops smaller aperture.

If you take the electronic flash unit off the camera position and use a fairly long connection cord, you need not keep the camera at the same distance as the flash. In such a case you can change camera-to-subject distance for best framing, but the flash-to-subject distance must remain constant for proper fill-in. A zoom lens is also a splendid tool to frame your subject as you wish, without changing flash distance.

Bulb flash

The ability of various models to synchronise properly with flashbulbs varies with model and shutter speed as well as bulb sync. Check the flash sync tables in the chapter 'Facts and figures' for your own needs. (Using flashbulbs with the Nikon EM is not to be recommended.)

With the use of flashbulbs for fill or main lighting, we have a somewhat complex situation. However, with bulbs, you can often choose from your entire range of shutter speeds, thus minimising secondary or ghost images. Additionally, flashbulbs provide far greater illumination than do most small electronic flash units.

A flashbulb (or flashcube) resembles a tiny lightbulb in construction. It is filled with highly inflammable metal wire or foil in an oxygen atmosphere. Various other gases may be added to heighten the brightness or hasten the burning. In most flashbulbs, an electrical current gives lighter paste to light the wire. (In magicubes, however, no current is needed to set off the bulb. Instead, it is set off mechanically with the aid of a tiny amount of impact explosive as a primer. However, this has limited application for users of Nikons or Nikkormats, since magicubes are designed to be used on cameras with built-in mechanical synchronisers.) Virtually all commonly available bulbs are blue-lacquered to provide light suitable for daylight colour film.

Flashbulbs take time to produce their light. The bulb ignites, burns to a bright peak and then loses brightness until it is quenched completely. There are basically two types of flashbulbs. The long peak type, usually FP (for focal plane), are designed to burn with a fairly even illumination for a long time. They provide sufficiently even illumination during the focal plane shutter travel to expose the entire picture evenly. Class M and MS bulbs have shorter, sharper peaks. In order to use such bulbs perfectly, the shutter must be completely open for virtually the whole peak.

However, many flashbulbs synchronise successfully at high speeds on many Nikon and Nikkormat cameras. Almost all bulbs can be used at all speeds with Nikkormat cameras except the FT2 and FT3, which cannot use bulbs at 1/60 or 1/125 second, or over 1/30 s with MF-class bulbs. The F3, FE,

FG, FM and FM2 cannot use bulbs at all over 1/30 s. Class M bulbs can be used up to 1/125 s with Nikon F cameras, and MF bulbs to 1/30 s. With the Nikon F2 camera, class M and MF bulbs work up to 1/30 s, M bulbs only at 1/125 s, although some class M bulbs can be used at all speeds except 1/60 s and the X setting of 1/80 s. If you wish to use an untried bulb at fast speeds, it's advisable to make a trial before risking important pictures.

You must make sure that your camera gives you the synchronisation you need. The Nikkormats, Nikon EL2 and Nikon F2 have just two flash settings – one for electronic, the other for bulb. The way it is selected differs with camera.

On the Nikkormat EL and ELW, you lift the milled ring around the shutter dial, and turn it to the bulb (B) symbol. On the Nikkormats FT and FTn, you choose the correct 3 mm (PC) socket. On the F2, EL2, FT2 and 3, the synchronisation is set as you choose the shutter speed. The Nikon FE, FG, F3, FM and FM2 are X-synchronised only.

With the Nikon F, on the other hand, you switch the synchronisation manually depending on bulb type and shutter speed to be used. A complete switching table for the Nikon F as well as full tables showing usable speeds for all Nikons and Nikkormats are in the Facts and Figures section.

When determining the proper settings for flashbulb pictures, consult the directions from the bulb manufacturer which are printed on the carton of the flashbulb pack.

The guide number given depends not only on the speed of film (ASA or DIN) and the aperture of the lens as in electronic flash, but also on the shutter speed to be set.

In use, flashbulbs are quite similar to electronic flash. On-camera flash tends to produce flat pictures with undesirable shadows and possibilities of red-eye. The Nikon BC-7 folding fan flash is made to slide either into the camera accessory shoe or over the rewind knob of the Nikon F and F2 for cordless flash contact into the accessory shoe of other Nikkormats with regular 3 mm cord connection.

Several flashbulbs can be fired together for better coverage of large areas or filling-in light. This can be done by direct wiring or using flash slaves to fire off the extra flash units.

Tungsten illumination

Continuous light sources hold out advantages over electronic flash, the principal one being that you can see the effects precisely on the subject, which you cannot normally do in electronic flash. They do, however, create a great deal of heat; the tangle of wiring is discouraging, and most are limited to areas where you can plug into house or studio mains.

Despite this, for careful portraiture, copying, attempting to photograph through glass or at glass, continuous illumination is obviously superior because you can see what you're doing.

For occasional use, the relatively inexpensive No. 1 and 2 Photoflood bulbs which can be fitted into moderately priced aluminium reflectors on clamps or stands are fine. There are also reflector spots and floods which have their own built-in reflectors. Most such floods or spots have a rather limited life span, but the hours they will burn are generally marked on the carton. It's always advisable to keep a few spares around.

For more sophisticated equipment, you have the choice of lights with ordinary tungsten-type bulbs, or the newer tungsten halogen lamps. The halogen encourages the tungsten to recycle back to the filament in a continuous cycle. This allows the filament to run at a much higher temperature without burning out; and reduces black deposits on the glass envelope always produced in ordinary floods or spot bulbs. This is a great advantage, since the bulb neither grows dim with age nor changes illumination colour. Tungsten halogen lamps are available in a range of sizes, usually in specially-designed reflectors. They have much greater (up to 4×) specific light output than normal tungsten lighting.

Using tungsten illumination (of either type) alone or combined with daylight presents no problems for the black-and-white photographer, but does for the colour worker. There are some blue 'daylight' bulbs manufactured, but many photographers find this unsatisfactory. Small photofloods are made for Type A film, while most regular floods (including tungsten halogen units) are balanced for Type B colour film. But a glance at the shelves in even a large camera store will reveal very few colour films balanced for tungsten illumination. However, you will find some labelled either as Type A or Type B. Type A is balanced at 3400 K and Type B at 3200 K. However it's a simple matter to use either film type with the opposite type of bulb by fitting a filter over your lens. The nomograph in the 'Facts and figures' section at the back of this book will give you the right filter for crossing over.

Is it possible to filter either the illumination or the camera lens so tungsten light can be used with daylight film? The answer is yes, but you will lose about ¾ the speed of the film. An 80B filter allows you to use daylight film with 3400 K lamps, while an 80A with do the same for 3200 K lamps. The daylight-type filters you can use over tungsten illumination sources tend to be quite expensive if of good even quality; and, of course, they cut down the light measurably.

How many lamps?

An ideal small flood set-up which can handle most home situations would consist of three lights – two floods and a spot. One flood can used fairly close to the main subject, the second at a distance to lighten the shadows, while the spot can brighten the background or furnish a toplight. Use upon built-in meter or a good hand-held accessory meter to determine the right exposure.

While living and working with the brightness and heat of flood is not particularly pleasant, it can be stood at average photographic distances. However, when shooting small objects such as plants or small insects or copying stamps, the intense brightness and heat of close lighting can be dangerous. I have found that the small high-intensity lamps incorporating 6V bulbs which have become rather popular are balanced just about properly for Type B films when they are set to their high-intensity level of brightness. These work quite well if you can pick one whose reflector will give you good overall even illumination. Two make a good working team.

Close-ups and copying

Before the advent of the SLR camera, making close-ups in 35mm was a time-consuming, painstaking procedure. A built-in rangefinder wouldn't focus closer than 1 m or so; and the viewfinder could not accurately delineate the field of the lens because it was placed above the camera where it showed a slightly different area. Through-the-lens (SLR) cameras make both viewing and focusing close-ups easy and convenient; and, further, through-the-lens meterings systems eliminate the rather complicated calculations once necessary to achieve proper close-work exposures.

In photography, over the usual standard distance from 0.6 m to infinity, we think of the size of the image on film in terms of the focusing distance. For instance, we talk of close-ups at 0.6 m to 1 m. This, however, is a very inexact way of knowing just how big an image we're getting on the film. For instance, while a normal 50mm lens of any aperture lens used at 0.6 m will give you a good-sized close image, a 20mm wide angle at 0.6 m will give you a much smaller, almost distant image on the negative. So in close-up photography, image sizes are generally discussed in terms of magnification. There are two different ways that this is done: as a ratio, or as a magnifying factor. For instance, a 1:2 image magnification means that the image on the film is half the size of the object photographed; this is also called 0.5× magnification. If you see the ratio 3:1 it means that the image on film is three times as big as the subject, that is a magnification of 3×. In close-up photography we'll be discussing all magnifications in this manner. Camera-to-subject distance (and sometimes lens-to-subject distance) is only relevant to convenience in taking the picture or in apparent perspective sense.

Close-up range

Before we go further, we need to define a few terms in the way we'll use them:

Close-ups: Photographs of subjects which are too close to the camera to be focused by the normal camera focusing mechanism. In other words, any picture which is taken closer than the closest point at which you normally can focus your lens is a close-up.

Macrophotography: Pictures larger than 1:1 or 1× life-size made with ordinary camera lenses up to 10:1 or 10×.

Photomicrography: Pictures of minute objects made with a camera and a microscope greater in magnification than 10:1 or 10× magnification. Don't confuse this term with microphotography, which is the process of making tiny pictures from large objects. We won't be dealing with microphotography at all.

While the terms are explicit and appear to have definite boundaries, in actual practice the limits can be somewhat diffuse. For instance, it is quite possible in extreme cases to get more than 10× magnification with ordinary camera lenses without a microscope. Is the result still a photomicrograph? In order to prevent such linguistic confusion we will define any photomicrograph as being an image greater than 10× no matter how it is made, but we will state the technique used. Therefore, image magnification tells us how large the image is on the film in relationship to the original object, close-ups cover all pictures made at distances closer than the normal focusing of our camera lenses, macrophotography refers to close-ups from 1× to 10×, and photomicrography delineates close-ups at more than 10×.

Close-ups

The easiest way to make close-ups is with accessory lenses over the main camera lens. This, in effect, shortens the focal length of the lens while maintaining the same lens-to-camera distance. That allows closer focusing and hence increases magnification. The second method is to move the camera lens further away from the film plane, again allowing closer focusing, and so producing a large image on film. This can be done by removing the lens and placing either fixed extension tubes or an extension bellows between the lens and camera body.

Close-up lenses

Photo stores can supply you with close-up lenses at all sorts of prices and magnifying powers. Unhappily, they are not all equally good. Any close-up lens tends to degrade the optical ability of your normal camera lens. They can introduce linear distortion, flare, field curvature, secondary colour, and other aberrations. The more powerful the close-up lens and the longer the focal length of the camera lens on which it is used, the greater the increase in the lens faults listed. However, by using *f*/8 or smaller apertures for picture taking, these faults can be minimised (except for linear distortion, which is not a function of aperture).

Close-up magnification

The close-up ability of equipment is generally considered in terms of magnification. The stamp you see complete at top is actual size of the subject itself. At 1×, the negative shows the subject exactly the same as the original. This is often expressed as 1:1 also. At 2×, the image is twice the linear size of the original subject and so on.

When the close-up picture is less than 1×, the magnification is expressed as a fraction or a ratio. Note that when the subject on the negative is but ⅓ the size of the original, it can be expressed as 1:3 (1 being the size of negative image and the 3 indicating that the actual subject is 3× the negative image). 1:10 is similarly shown.

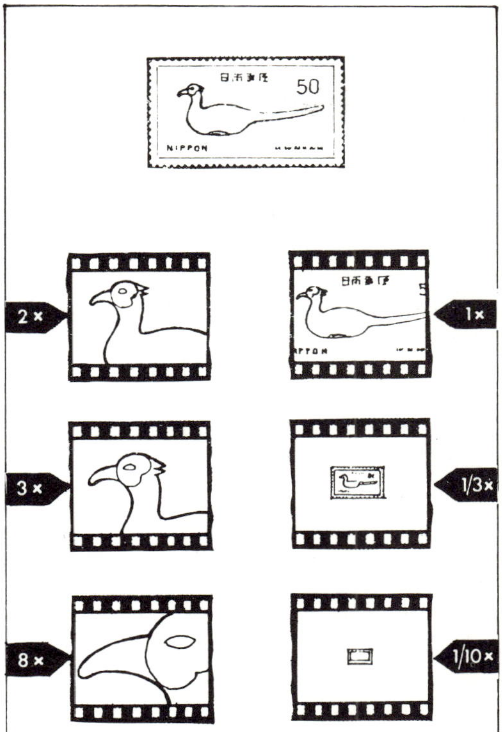

The chart at right shows you the magnification ranges covered by some of the more popular focal length lenses when fitted with close-up accessories.

A. Close-up lenses attached to the camera lens.

B. Extension Ring Set K attached to camera lens.

C. Lens on Bellows PB-4 or 5.

D. Lens reversed front to rear on Bellows PB-4 or 5.

The dotted area at the lower edge of the chart indicates the focusing range of the lens alone.

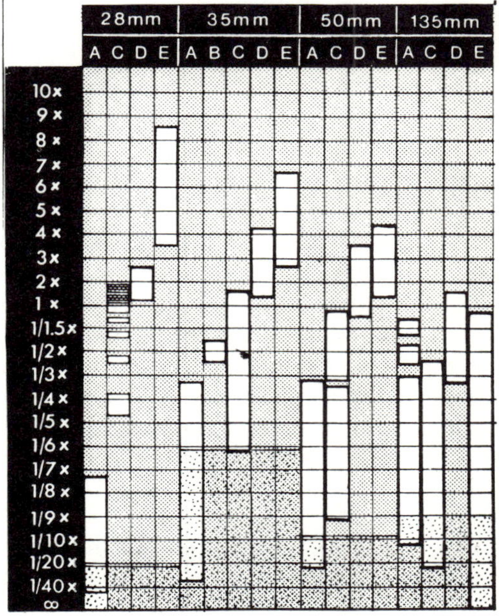

The Nikon Close-up Attachment lenses have been designed specifically to give best possible definition with the Nikkor lenses (specifically those accepting 52 mm lens accessories). At one time I thought this was merely rhetoric. However, the Nikkor attachments appear to be made of thicker glass, so I tested them. They provided superior close-ups in terms of definition than did the independent manufacturers's close-up lenses I had to hand. With a standard 50 mm lens, I have achieved results with the Nikon attachments equal to that which I would expect with a macro-focusing lens made just for that purpose.

The three Nikon Close-up Lenses, while numbered as 0, 1 and 2, are actually 0.7, 1.5 and 2 diopter power, respectively. (Most manufacturers list close-up lenses directly in diopters, usually making them in whole numbers: 1, 2, 3, etc.)

The diopter is simply the reciprocal of the close-up lens's focal length expressed in metres or as a formula,

$$d = \frac{1}{\text{focal length (metres)}}$$

The larger the diopter number, the more powerful the close-up lenses and the closer the focusing with any given focal length lens.

In fact, when set to infinity on its focusing scale, a lens combination focuses on an object exactly the focal length of the close-up lens away. So, on any lens at infinity focus, a 2-diopter lens focuses 50 cm from the front of the lens. Of course, as you turn the focusing ring, the combination focuses even closer.

Nikon has provided the in-between diopter numbers so that users can have a continuous, somewhat overlapping magnification with lenses up to 50 mm. The optical engineers have restricted the greatest power to 2 diopters, but have suggested this close-up lens can be used with the 1.5-diopter lens together for great magnification. The Nikkor designers feel that higher-strength lenses would measurably reduce image quality.

The No. 0 Close-Up lens has been designed primarily for the 43 to 86 mm *f*/3.5 Zoom Nikkor (now discontinued), although it can be used with any of the other 52 mm diameter lenses as well. When the No. 1 and 2 Close-Up lenses are used in combination, No. 2 should be closest to the camera lens. The combination should not be used with the 43 to 86 mm *f*/3.5 zoom lens, since the two together will cause vignetting at the picture edge. It's also unwise to use the combination with the 200 mm *f*/4 Nikkor, since it results in too much image deterioration to make the use worthwhile.

Magnifications

While there are full tables in the back of this book giving you the magnifications, working distances and areas covered with these close-up lenses when they are used with prime lens focal lengths from 50 mm through 200 mm, let's take a quick look at some of the possibilities. With your 50 mm lens, a combination of the No. 1 and 2 lenses can get you an image size ratio up to 1:3 with the prime lens focused as close as it will go. However, a No. 2 alone on a 135 mm can produce an even larger image of 1:1.8. By using your regular lens focusing mount, the magnification ratio can be altered. You'll see just how much by examining the tables.

We have mentioned that close-up lenses work by shortening the actual supplementary-lens-plus-camera-lens total focal length. The question may arise as to how much, since changing the focal length can have a marked effect on apparent perspective distortion if you have to alter your camera-to-subject distance measurably to compensate for the change in focal length. The 50 mm lens when fitted with a No. 2 Nikkor Close-up attachment becomes 42.9 mm.

Here is the formula if you wish to work out the total focal length with other prime and close-up lenses:

$$\text{Combination Focal Length} = \frac{D \times f}{D + f}$$

D = the distance from the front of the lens to the subject, f = the focal length of the camera lens itself. This lessening of focal length explains why close-ups with close-up lenses are always made at a shorter camera-to-subject distance than close-ups of the same magnification with the same camera lens if bellows or extension tubes are used.

Close-up lenses are severely limited in terms of their magnification power before image deterioration sets in, and they must be used at fairly small apertures for best results. But, they are far more convenient to use than other close-up devices. In addition, they do not disturb your regular automatic diaphragm mechanism or your through-the-lens metering. However, do not use the central split-image rangefinder if fitted to your camera. With most close-up lens and camera lens combinations, the split-image rangefinder point of exact focus and that of the surrounding fine-focusing collar will not agree. This disparity occurs because the split-image rangefinder uses the maximum diameter of the lens aperture as a base for the two images within the circle. At full aperture at which focusing is done even in close-ups, the amount of field curvature present (which we've mentioned) throws off the split-image rangefinder. However, the fine-focusing collar is accurate.

Extension devices

The alternative method of shooting close-ups with your Nikon or Nikkormat camera is to extend the lens further from the camera body by inserting either tubes or a bellows between camera body and lens. Nikon offers a number of different accessories for doing this.

Extension Ring Set K is a five-tube set totalling 46.6mm when attached together. The individual tubes are K1 (5.8mm), K2 (5mm), K3 (5.8mm), K4 (10mm), and K5 (20mm). There are nine possible combinations of these rings, which allow you to take close-up shots at reproduction ratios from 1:8.9 to 1:1. K1 has a bayonet mount on either side for mounting directly between camera and lens. K2 has a bayonet on the camera end and a screw thread at the other. K3 has a bayonet mount on the lens end and a screw thread at the other end. K4 and K5 are threaded at both ends for mounting between various other tubes having bayonet mountings to attach to camera and body. A full set of charts giving possible combinations and their effects plus a nomograph giving you the right extension length for any desired magnification can be found at the back of this book. The tubes can be used with virtually all interchangeable Nikkor lenses and in combination with all other close-up accessories. The lens diaphragm must be opened and closed manually and meter readings made as you would with any manual diaphragm lens. While even the narrowest of tubes, the K1, do not provide you with continuous close-up focusing from the closest normal focusing distance of a 50mm lens onwards (as do the close-up lenses), the tubes do provide a greater maximum magnification with all lenses up to and including the 85mm Nikkor lenses. After that point the close-up lenses again provide stronger magnification, although admittedly at the price of less sharpness and definition.

While the other rings will unthread, thread and bayonet into place quite normally, the K2 ring has three possible orientations on the camera via three holes instead of one at the rear to accept the camera mount locking pin. This allows you to position the lens so you can see the aperture scale. When using any sort of extension between your camera lens and the body, you must allow additional exposure if you do not make your readings directly through the lens.

Extension ring set PK

Besides the set of K Ring tubes, Nikon provides Set PK, three individual rings to be used singly or combined, which have internal fully-automatic diaphragm and metering coupling capabilities. With these tubes you can view and meter at full aperture. When the shutter is released, the lens attached closes down to the proper aperture just as it does when mounted directly on the camera. The PK-1 tube increases the lens-to-film distance by 8mm, PK-2 by 14mm and PK-3 by 27.5. For cameras and lenses with automatic maximum aperture indexing the corresponding tubes are PK-11, PK-12, PK-13. Full details of possible magnifications appear at the back of this volume. While they do not offer the variations and flexibility in terms of possible magnifications that the K rings do, the PK set provide greater magnification in total and the convenience of through-the-lens metering at full aperture plus auto-diaphragm operation.

Extension bellows

While rings are compact, they restrict you to a minimum ratio because of their short length. A bellows extension is far more flexible. Unfortunately, any bellows take up a substantial amount of space even when compressed. So, with a normal lens you are restricted to making quite large close-ups. You have not got the moderate close-focusing capability that you would get with the slimmer extension tube or a close-up lens.

There are two Nikon Bellows Focusing attachments, the PB-4 (now discontinued) and the PB-6. The PB-4 provides continuously variable extension from 43 to 185 mm, producing reproduction ratios ranging from 1.2× to 3.6× with a 50 mm Nikkor, and up to 4.4× with the lens reversed using the necessary BR-2 Macro Adapter. The lens and camera panels can be moved independently, while a dual twin track allows the entire unit to move back and forth without altering the position of the two panels. This provides an easy method of focusing when the magnification has been set on the bellows scale. The lens panel may be swung or shifted for moving the depth-of-field plane, or maintaining perspective. The camera body can be rotated 90 degrees on the camera mount for either vertical or horizontal picture formats without disturbing the unit. We retain this unit in our listing because it has unique features, and can still sometimes be found in stores.

The tripod head has eight holes spaced around the tripod socket, so the whole assembly can be mounted at any 90-degree angle or obliquely in any direction on the Nikon Repro-Copy Outfit PF-4.

The PB-6, while not having the swing and shift lens panel of the PB-4, offers a more comprehensive modular bellows system, including a macro copy stand, extension bellows increasing maximum extension from 208 mm to 438 mm; and both camera and lens standards plus tripod rack are all attached to a single double dovetail rail. The lens is automatically held open at full aperture during viewing and focusing, the front panel incorporates a built-in semi-automatic diaphragm control socket and is reversible with no need of the BR-2 ring. Because of its modular construction, the unit can be dismantled and stored easily. Unless you have specific need of the PB-4's swing and tilt controls, this bellows is preferable. It has all the same movements as the PB-4 and can be fitted with a slide-copying adapter. Reproduction ratios from 1:1.1 to 4:1 are possible with a 50 mm lens mounted normally.

Camera mounting

To mount any Nikon or Nikkormat camera body on a bellows, loosen the locking knob on the camera panel of the bellows, slide the panel backwards as far as it will go and attach the camera body and lens panel as you would attach any lens to your camera. To change the camera body position from horizontal to vertical or vice versa on the bellows, depress the spring catch on the left side of the camera body panel and twist the camera body to the new position. Camera lenses can be attached to the other end of the bellows as you would normally attach a camera lens to your camera body. Removing is also done normally.

While the bellows units can be used with any Nikon or Nikkor lenses from 24 mm to 300 mm, you will get the best results from the 50 mm *f*/2 or *f*/1.8 camera lenses, the 105 mm *f*/4 Micro-Nikkor, or the 55 mm *f*/2.8 or *f*/3.5 Micro-Nikkor. For magnifications greater than 1:1 (1×), it's best to reverse your lens (by means of the BR-2 ring with the PB-4) so that the front faces the bellows and the rear of the lens is forward. Thread the front of the Nikkor Macro-Adapter Ring BR-2 into the front 52 mm threads of your camera lens. The BR-2 can then be bayoneted into the bellows as you would a regular camera lens.

To reverse the lens on the PB-6 bellows, you reverse the lens panel on the rail. Unscrew the bellows retaining screw on the side of the lens panel and detach the bellows from the panel. Now unscrew the front end-stop from the rail and remove it. Unclamp the lens panel and rack it out to the rail end. Slip it off the front. Reverse the panel and replace it on the rail with the front of the lens facing the bellows. As gently as possible, clamp the end of the bellows to the front rim of the lens by turning the bellows-retaining screw. Screw the front end-stop back onto the rail.

This allows that part of the lens closest to an image-forming plane to be closest to the subject, while the front of the lens, usually further away, will again be further away, but this time from the film. Optically, this give you better overall definition.

At any given bellows extension, a short focal length lens provides greater magnification than will a longer one. At any set magnification, a longer focal length lens provides greater lens-to-subject distance than does a shorter one. Therefore, if you need maximum magnification, choose a shorter focal length lens; but if you wish to work at a longer distance from your subject you need a longer focal length lens. While short lenses can and should be used in reverse for even higher magnification, reversing a long lens does *not* increase the magnification; instead, magnification is decreased. So you get a larger image with any lens longer than 55 mm in the forward position.

Apertures

While maximum aperture of a lens may cause some slight loss of overall picture quality over its normal focus range, the amount of image deterioration becomes much greater in close-up work. However, the smallest aperture available may be equally harmful. With the 50 mm *f*/2 or *f*/1.8 Nikkor you can use apertures to the smallest. This is true also of most lenses 85 mm and longer. With most shorter lenses, *f*/8 is the best aperture. The deterioration at

The PB-4 bellows

Here are the controls:

1. Lens alignment mark
2. Lens release button
3. Top rails
4. Camera mount flange
5. Camera panel spring catch
6. Camera panel
7. Lens panel sliding knob
8. Bellows
9. Tripod head sliding knob
10. Camera panel sliding knob
11. Lens panel
12. Shift lock
13. Red indicator dot
14. Camera panel locking knob
15. Bottom rails
16. Tripod head locking knob
17. Tripod head
18. Lens panel base
19. Lens panel locking knob
20. Slide copying adapter knob
21. Swing lock
22. Control knobs
23. Locking knobs
24. Slide copying adapter socket
25. Lever movement to shift panel
26. Lever movement to swing panel

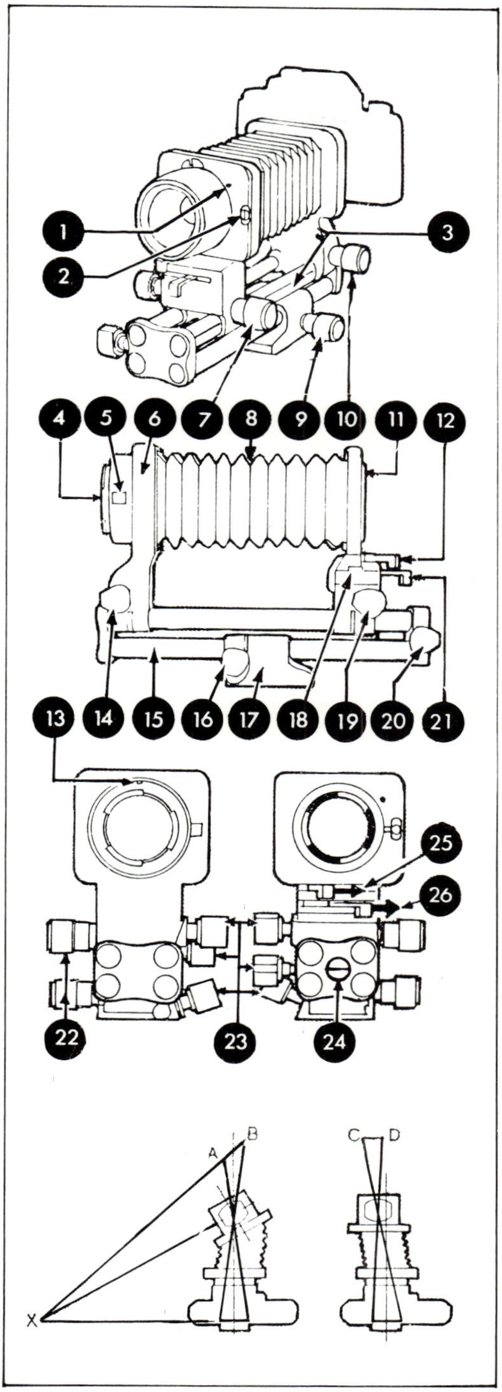

To render a slanted subject completely sharp, such as between A and B, we can use bellows swing and tilt so lines of subject film plane and lens intersect at single point X. Depth of field is also increased.

Shift movement only (far right) can be used to correct apparent perspective distortion as with perspective control lens or control coverage of subject without tilting lens.

the smallest and largest apertures is not nearly so great with lenses computed specially for close-up work, such as the 105 mm *f*/4 or the 55 mm *f*/3.5 or *f*/2.8 Micro-Nikkor.

Whenever a bellows unit is mounted between the camera body and a lens, both the coupled metering and the automatic diaphragm connections between lens and camera body are severed. For maximum brightness and convenience in viewing and focusing, turn the lens diaphragm to maximum aperture. Of course the lens must be closed to the taking aperture before making the exposure. On the PB-6 bellows there is a handy control lever on each side of the lens panel. The lever allows you to hold the lens open at full aperture for focusing and viewing. Depressing the lever closes the lens automatically to the preselected aperture or to check depth of field. By pushing the lever inwards, the lens can be locked at the shooting aperture. When the lever is pulled outwards, the lens will automatically reopen to full aperture. With a lens in reverse on the PB-4 for greater magnification or superior definition, it is advisable to use a Double Cable Release AR-4 and Auto Ring PW-1. PW-1 fits the rear of your lens on bellows or tubes. AR-4 attaches to the camera cable release socket and a socket on the PW-1. The PB-6's lens panel has a built-in socket to accept the cable release which works equally well whether the lens panel is used in the forward position or reversed so no Auto Ring PW-1 is needed. Whichever bellows you use, pressure on the double cable closes the lens down to your preset aperture and then releases the shutter itself. For easiest focusing, use Type B, E or M screens for Nikon cameras.

Focusing

The PB-4 and PB-6 have three focusing controls. These are the knurled knobs governing the front panel, the rear panel and tripod head rail.

One method of operation is to lock the camera panel in place at the extreme end and focus using the knob for the lens panel. This has one main disadvantage, I've found. In close work, the protruding rail or rails reach far forward of the lens itself and may interfere with the subject.

I find it is far better to lock the lens panel as far forward as it will go and govern bellows extension with the rearward movement of the camera panel. Try locking the lens panel forward, extending the camera panel sufficiently to set the amount of actual magnification desired and then move the two fixed panels back and forward with the knob on the bottom to achieve proper focus.

Reproduction ratios

The reproduction ratio is determined by the extension and the lens. Read off the extension from the millimetre scale markings which appear on the

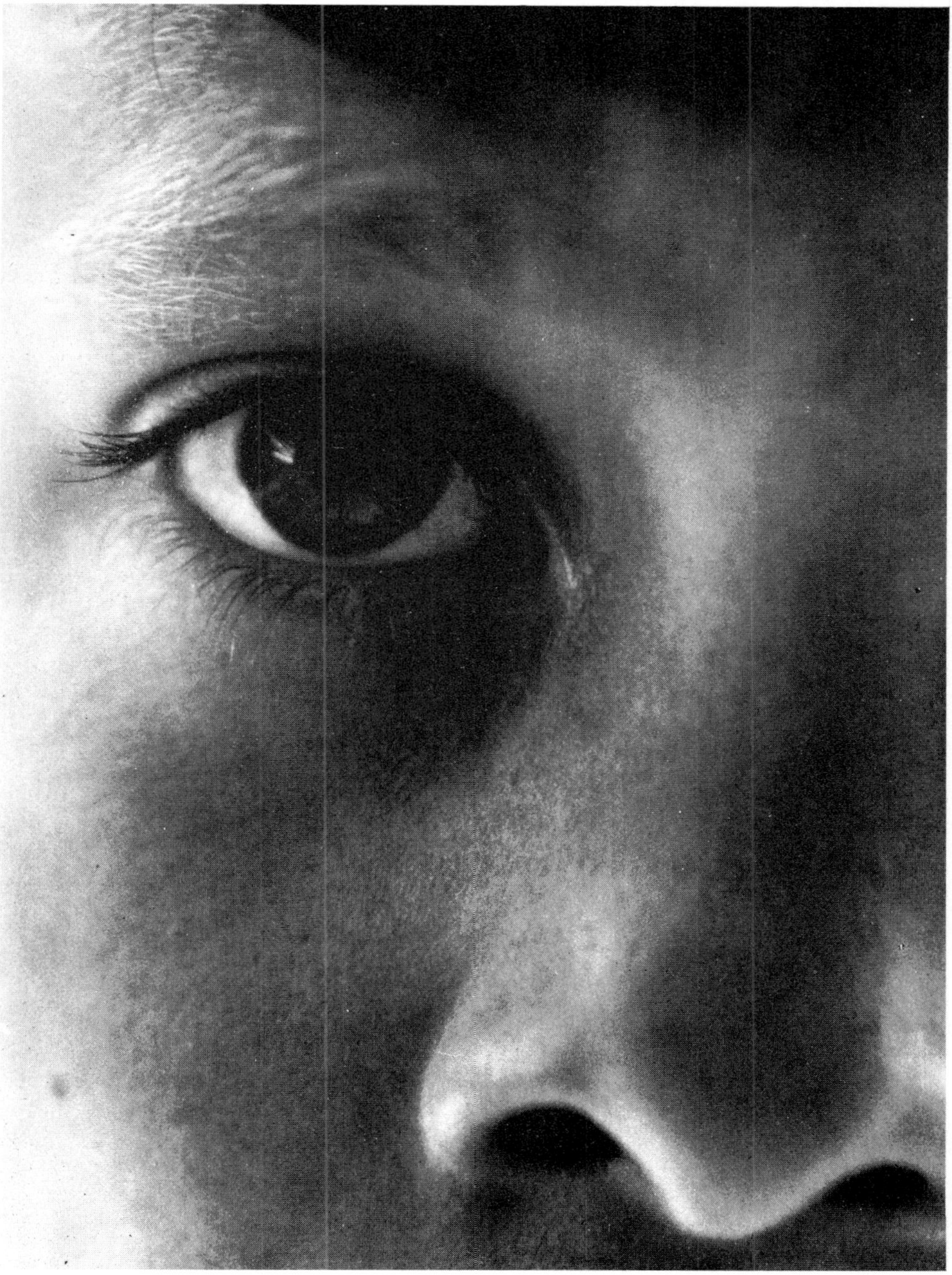

Always the eyes

While testing another lens, I also used my 105 mm *f*/2.5 Nikkor, full aperture at 1/125 second slow-speed film with extension tube. Note how sharp focus on eye virtually negates unsharp nose. Imagine sharp nose, unsharp eye! Conclusion: always focus on the eye(s).

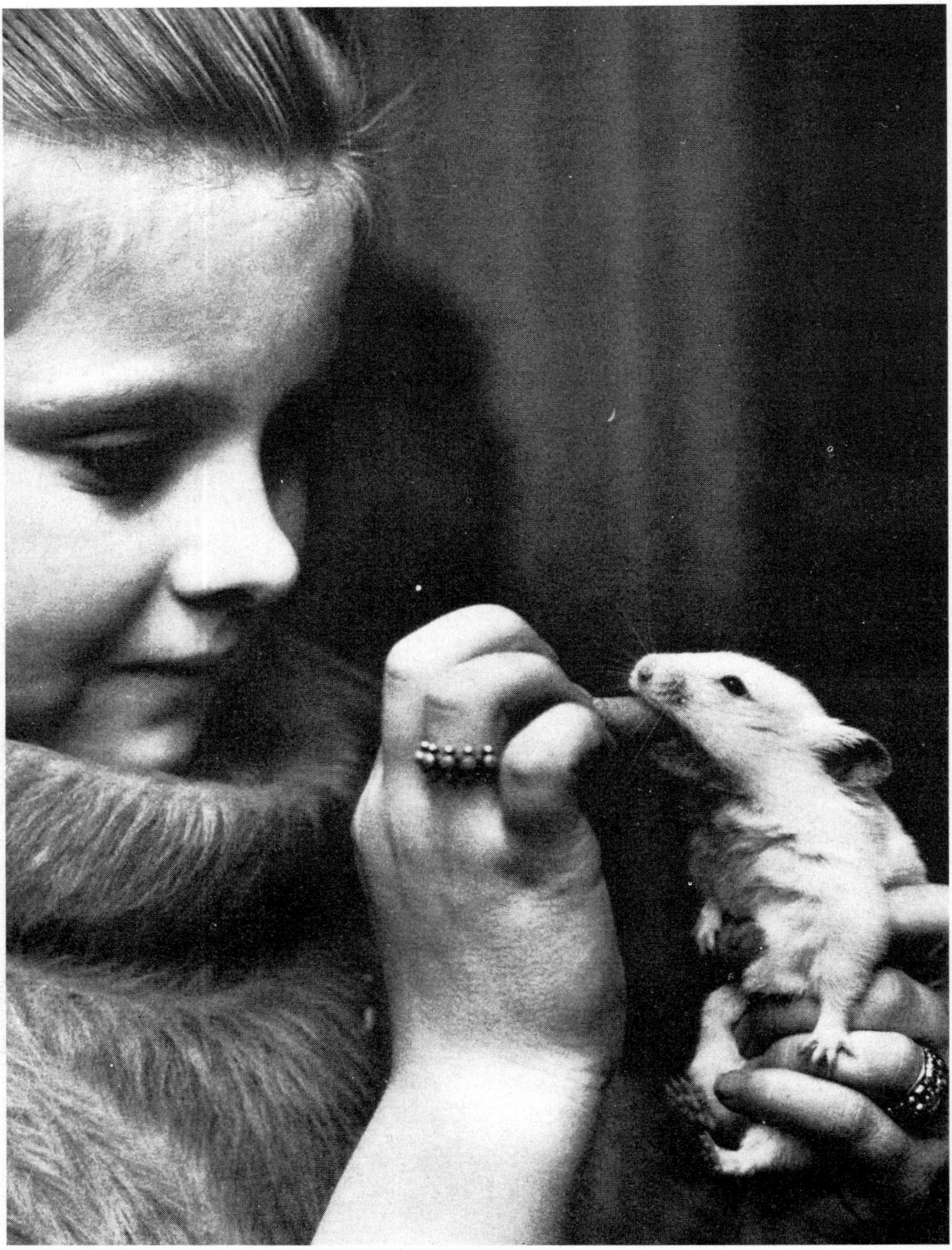

Roomlight is most natural

While flash of floods might guarantee a sharper, easier-to-make photograph, the roomlight as you find it will often best preserve the true picture. Nikkormat FT, high-speed film, 1/30 second with 105 mm *f*/2.5 Nikkor at full aperture even captures whiskers of hamster if you look closely. Prime focus is on hamster's head where viewers' eye falls first.

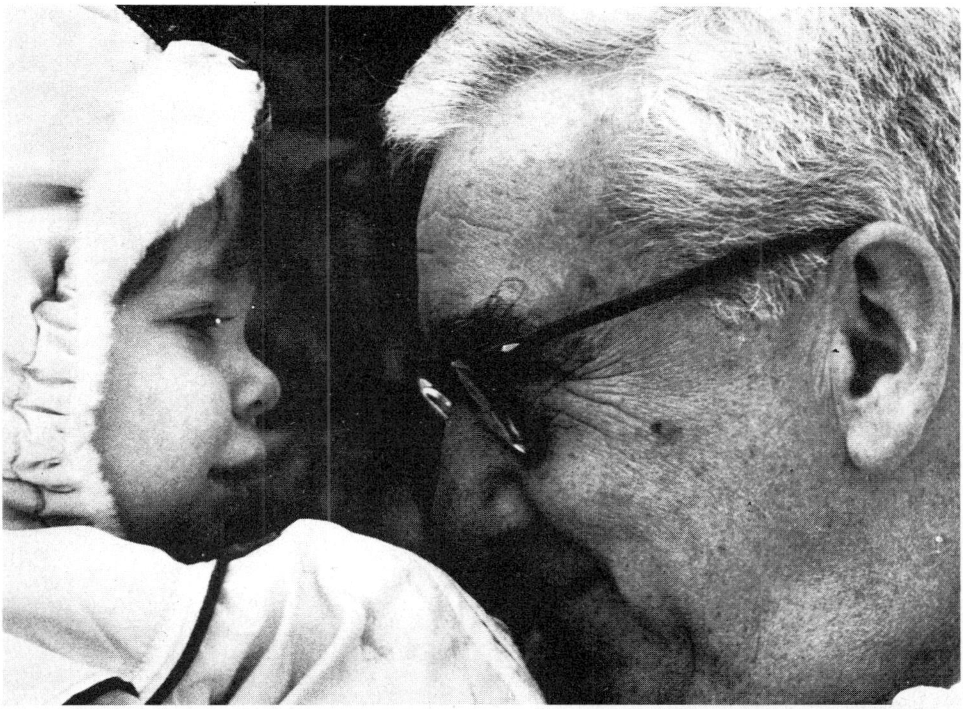

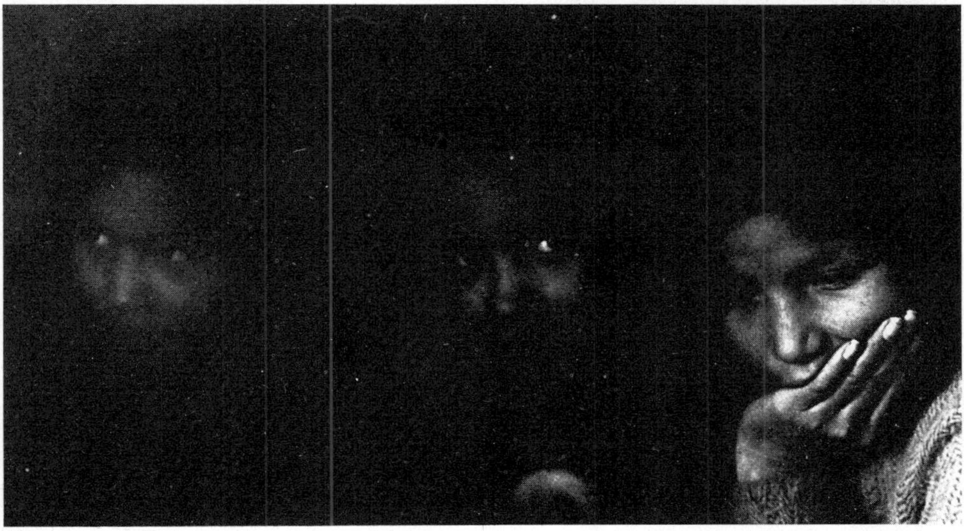

Skipping a generation

Grandfather/grandmother-child pictures often make a more efective adult-child comparison than mother/father child. Here the size and age is nicely caught by my 135 mm *f*/3.5 Nikkor, 1/125 second at *f*/5.6.

Low-key existing light

A dark room, three dusky Indian children's faces in low key with bright sparkling eyes. Exposure of 1/60 second at *f*/2.8 on high-speed film made for highlights only.

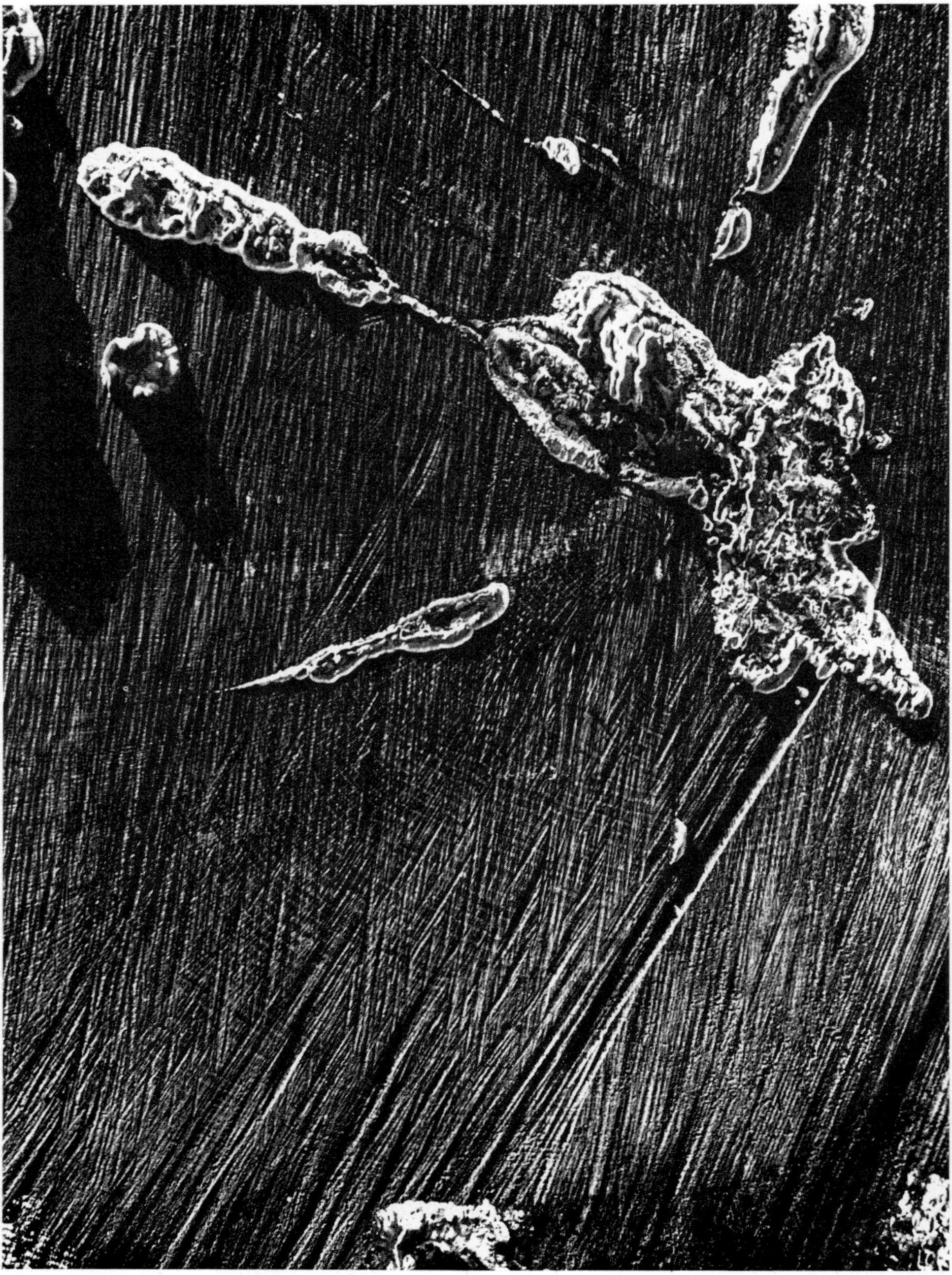

Cut wood

Go in close to a natural object – and you can create a picture. An 85 mm lens lets you crop without getting too close. *Neville Newman.*

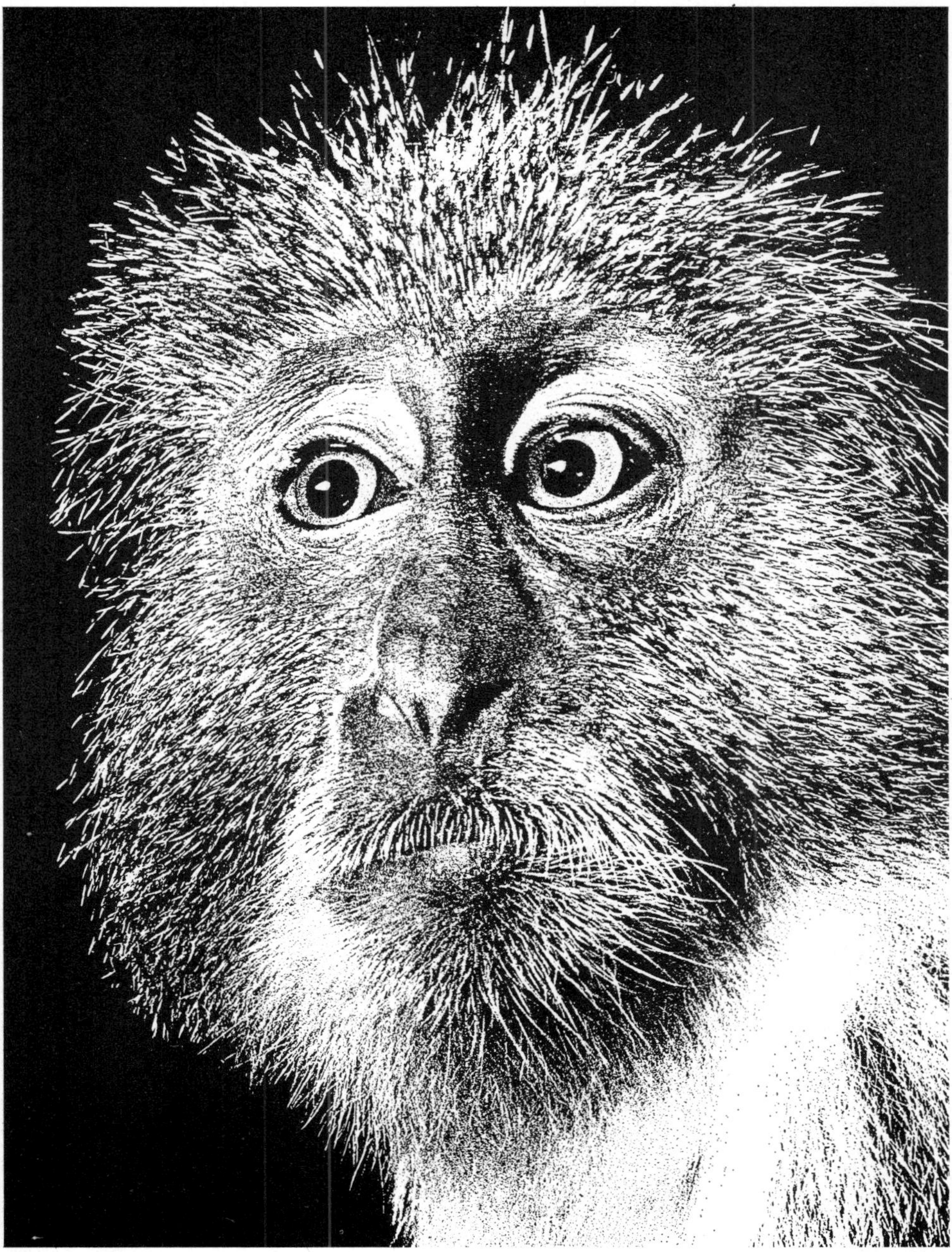

Ape

Sometimes you can improve your pictures with after-work. This striking picture has been given greater impact by reducing its tones to pure black and white. *H. Landold.*

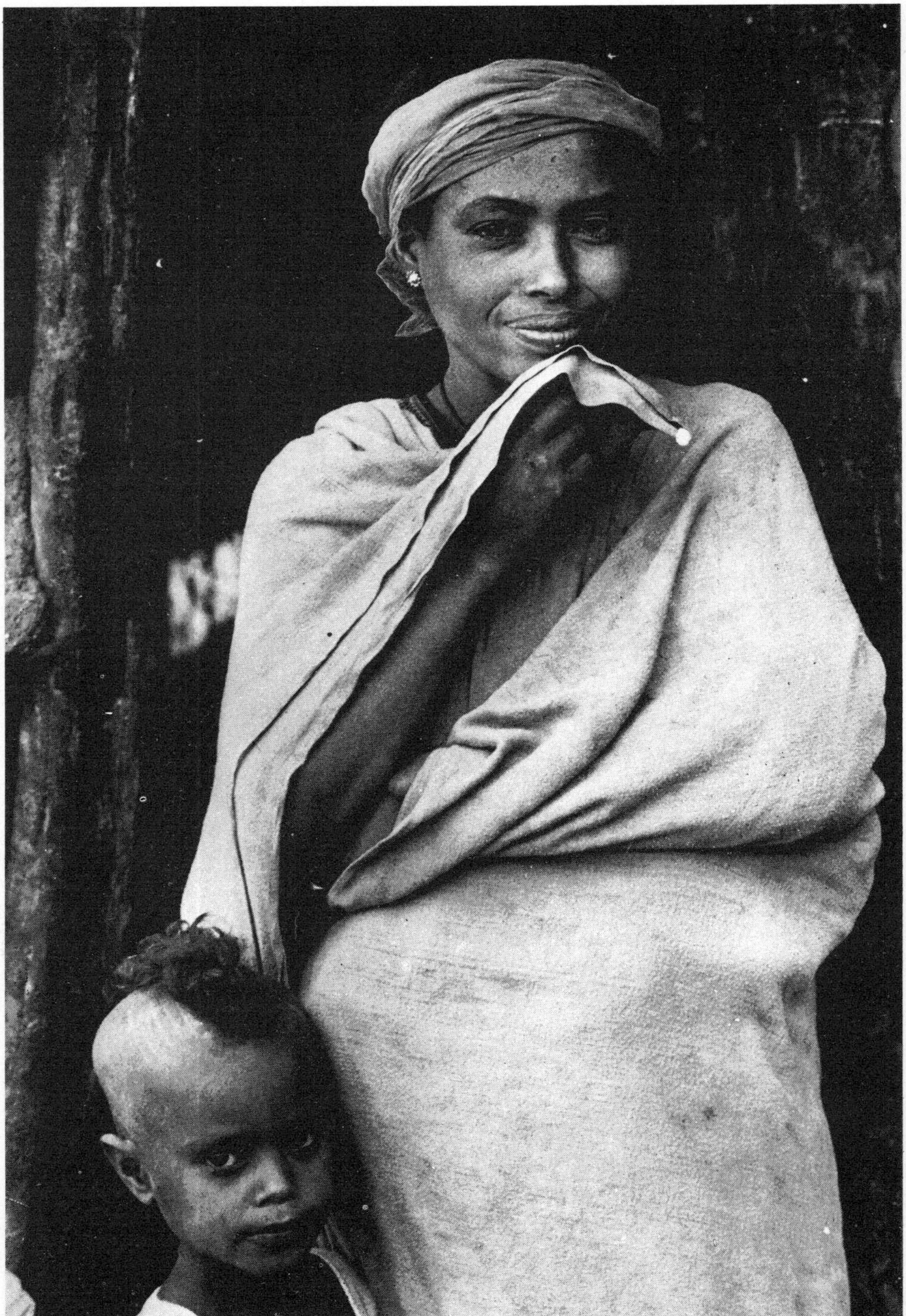

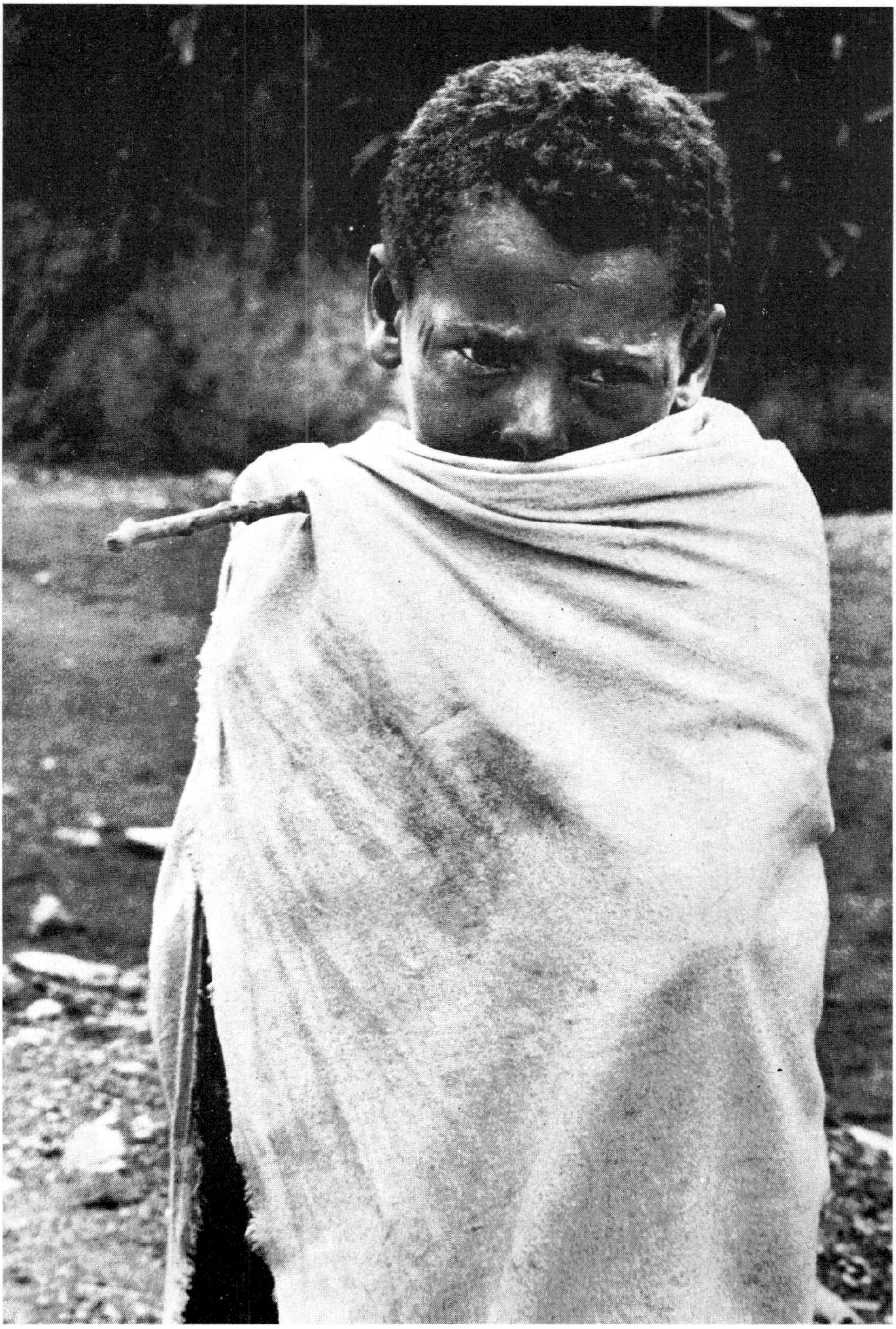

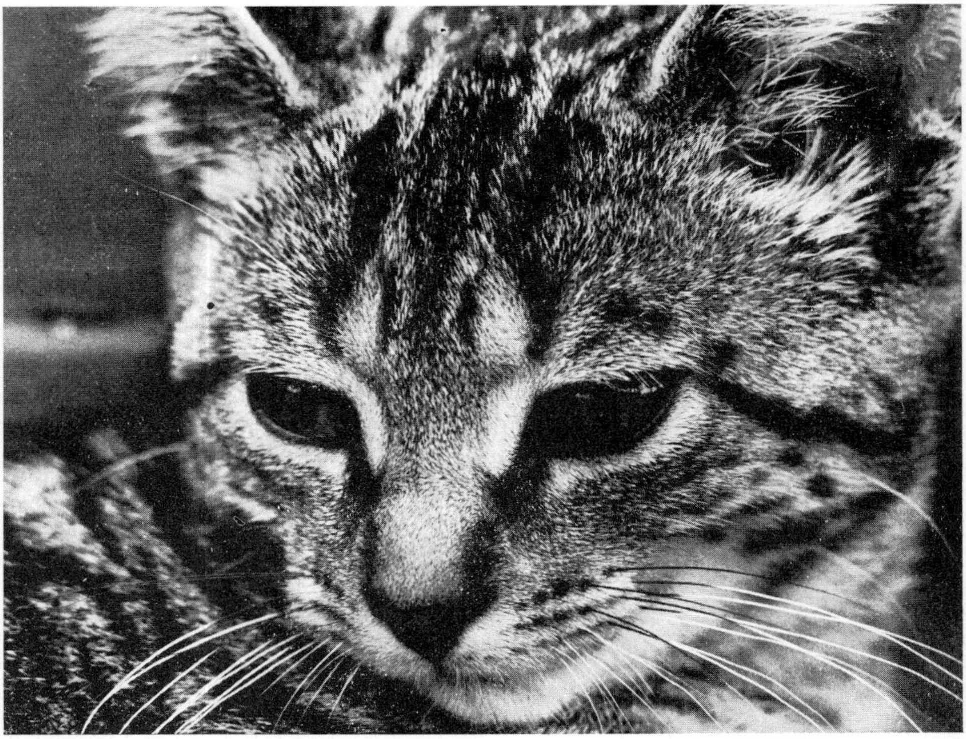

Using textures

Previous spread, left. The varying textures in the scene outside this Ethiopian house were important. With 105 mm *f*/2.5 Nikkor on Nikkormat FT, I approached close and closer until I had this tight composition. High-speed film, 1/125 second, *f*/8.

Photographing strangers

Previous spread, right. Strangers may be suspicious tht you are photographing them because they are peculiar or poor or simply different from you. Patience, smiles and explanations are your best counterweapons. Nikkormat FT, 105 mm *f*/3.5 Nikkor, *f*/8, 1/125 second, high-speed film.

Pet portraits

Natural light is best since it isn't disturbing your cat, dog or what have you. Also you can see effect of light on fur or skin textures. My cat Tiger was photographed with 50 mm *f*/1.4 Nikkor at *f*/8, 1/60 second high-speed film.

outside edges of the camera and lens panels where they join the bellows rails. Now consult the extension table in the back of this book to determine just what magnification the extension represents with your particular lens. If you know what reproduction ratio you want, you can find out from the table just how much bellows extension will be needed to get that particular magnification ratio. For all table use, your camera lens should be set to infinity.

Meter reading

As with the uncoupled extension tubes, all meter readings should be made at shooting aperture with your camera set as if you were making a reading with a manual lens. If you are not using a through-the-lens meter, increase your normal exposure using this formula: Exposure Increase Factor = $(1 + \text{Reproduction Ratio})^2$. The tables at the back of this book give you the reproduction ratios.

Swing and shift

The front lens panel of the PB-4 can be swung in an arc through 25 degrees, making it possible to swing the plane of sharp focus from one side of the picture to the other. It can also be shifted 10 mm to either side to bring a subject not quite directly in front of the camera lens into position without swinging or tilting the camera. Quite often these two movements can be used in conjunction with one another. A typical use of this lens would involve a close subject at an angle to the lens. Even if you stopped down your lens to *f*/16, the depth of field might be enough just to render part of the subject sharp but not the entire subject. However, by swinging the lens so that it is parallel to the subject and then using the shift mechanism to bring the subject back centrally in the finder, you can render the entire subject sharply – and probably at a large lens opening than *f*/16. Unfortunately, since the problem and the possibility of solution depend so much on the subject, the distance, the angle from the camera, and the lens you are using, no absolute rules or directions can be given, save to use your depth-of-field preview button to check how much additional depth you are achieving in your specific.

The swing and shift movements are controlled by two locking levers, one above the other, which protrude from the bottom of the bellows lens panel. To swing the lens panel, press the bottom lever to the right. While looking through the finder, turn the lens panel in the direction the subject is slanted and adjust for maximum sharpness edge to edge of the picture. You'll find the 6× Focusing Finder on a Nikon most helpful for this critical work. When you find the point of best overall sharpness, push the lock back to central locking position.

You can shift the lens panel sideways by pressing the top lever to the right. Look through your finder while sliding the panel until you get the picture framed as you want it. Then relock the panel by returning the lever to central position.

PB-6 bellows focusing accessories

The PB-6 Bellows has two unique accessories: the extension bellows, which provides a total of 438 mm of bellows extension when attached, and the Macro Copy Stand PB-6M.

To attach the PB-6E Extension Bellows, remove the lens panel of the PB-6 as you would if you were going to reverse it. Unscrew the end stops from the PB-6E, loosen the locking knobs on the tripod/rail connector and slide it halfway off the extension rail end. Slip the PB-6's front end rail into the head/rail connector until the rails meet and the millimetre scales are continuous. Tighten the locking knobs. Connect the PB-6 Bellows front to the back of the PB-6E mounting panel. Replace the PB-6 lens panel on the front end of the PB-6E extension rail and tighten the locking knob. Connect the PB-6E Extension Bellows to the lens panel. Connect the bellows to the front rim of the lens. Screw the end-stops into the front of the PB-6E extension rail. The combination unit can now be used.

The Macro Copy Stand PB-6M can be attached to the PB-6 by removing the PB-6's front end rail stop and then threading the PB-6M's locking screw to the front of the rail. The stand can be used horizontally or vertically.

Lighting for close-ups

Lighting close-up subjects is a science all its own. Large floods and spotlights employed for standard work are too big and clumsy, hard to get close enough to the subject, and, worse, at such distances will heat up the subject and might even damage it. Certainly if you are photographing living subjects, large, powerful lights must be avoided.

Separate electronic flash

Today's small electronic flash units attached to your camera can provide suitable illumination. However, you should make a series of test shots at the magnifications you intend to use to arrive at the proper exposure. Some of the small units have automatic exposure provision workable as close as 30 cm (1½ ft) from the subject. These are quite handy provided you are using close-up lenses or an extension which is not sufficiently great to require additional exposure compensation. If, according to your bellows scales, your additional exposure factor should be 2×, you can open up your lens by one *f*/stop more than your auto-flash demands. Unfortunately, most of the

The PB-6 bellows

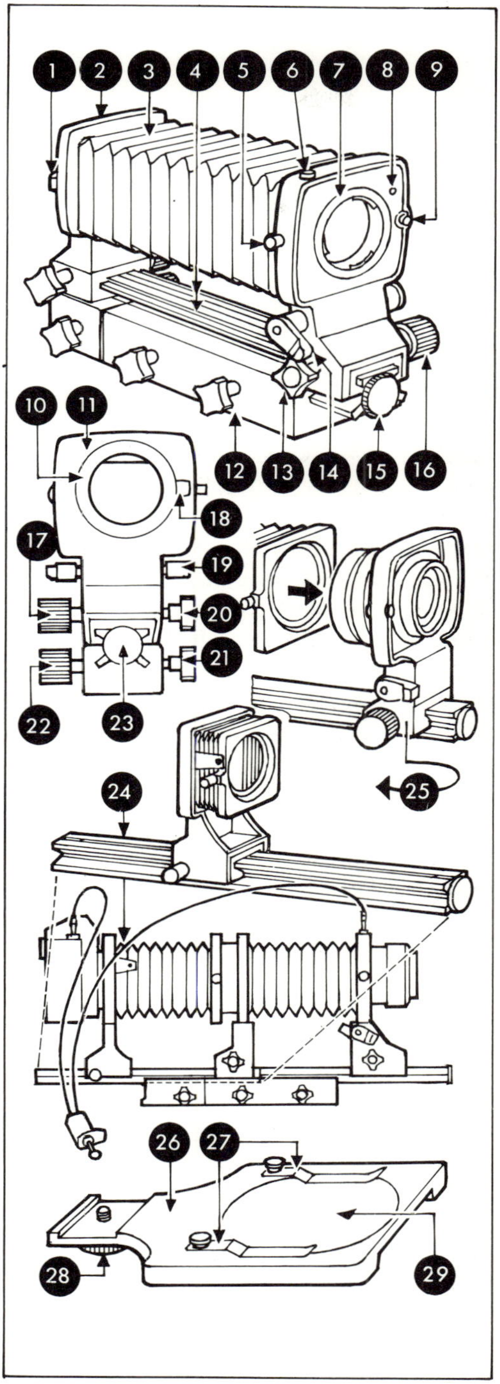

Here are the controls:

1. Horizontal-vertical format catch
2. Back panel
3. Bellows
4. Rail
5. Bellows retaining screw
6. Cable release attachment
7. Lens panel
8. Lens mounting index
9. Lens release button
10. Camera mounting ring
11. Camera panel
12. Extension bellows carriage
13. Lens panel locking knob
14. Aperture control lever
15. Front end stop
16. Lens panel traversing knob
17. Camera panel traversing knob
18. Camera rotation clamp
19. Alternate aperture control lever
20. Camera panel locking knob
21. Tripod head locking knob
22. Tripod head traversing knob
23. Rear end stop
24. PB-6E Bellows extension rail
25. Reversed lens panel

PB-6 Bellows correctly coupled to PB-6E Extension bellows with AR-4 Double Cable Release attached for automatic diaphragm control.

PB-6M Macro Copy Stand features

26. Copy stand base
27. Spring subject holding clips
28. Attaching thread head
29. 18% grey reflective subject support

automatic exposure electronic flash units have little choice of apertures at which they work. The smallest ones may demand apertures too large for best results in close-up photography. Some of the newest units do provide three or more automatic exposure apertures and a minimum aperture of *f*/16 with an ASA 100 film. This type is usable. However, if you need to use smaller apertures, you had best switch to manual flash operation. Calculate the increase exposure factor from your bellows or tube tables and open up your aperture accordingly. At such short distances your flash may be too powerful to reach a proper minimum exposure. In this case use a layer of handkerchief over the flash or, for more precise control, a neutral density filter.

A number of the new Nikon cameras, including the F3 and FG, are provided with electronic-flash auto-exposure systems in which the proper amount of flash illumination is determined from a cell-reading directly off the film during the exposure. With the proper electronic flash units for these cameras, there is no need to make special exposure calculations. They will determine correct exposure through the bellows or extension tubes at the actual shooting aperture, and will warn you if the illumination is insufficient by the flash confirmation light within the camera viewfinder.

I have found that a small electronic flash unit attached to the accessory shoe on a Nikon or Nikkormat provides very satisfactory close-up illumination if you insert a simple swivel or ball head bracket between flash and camera. Then you can angle the light downwards toward the subject. Lacking that, a regular right-angle flash bracket which attaches to the bottom tripod socket and brings your flash up at the side of the camera is a good substitute, provided it too can be swivelled toward your subject. Alternatively, you may like to use a bracket which mounts one (or two) small flashguns on the front of your lens.

I prefer directional flash of this nature, rather than ringlight, for living close-ups, since a ringlight provides shadowless illumination which tends to flatten out the subject. Directional light produces natural shadows behind the subject as the sun would, and creates planes in depth.

Ringlight

For copying work or photographing the intricate parts of machinery, such as inside a watch movement, you may not wish shadows and so prefer a ringlight. There are many excellent ringlights available, including Nikon ringlights. The ringlight is simply an electronic flashtube in the shape of a ring which is fastened to the front of your lens, generally by the front lens screw thread. Directions for determining exposure accompany the units.

Continuous light sources

While electronic flash has the advantage of providing a burst of energy so short that there is virtually no chance of either camera or subject movement blurring the picture, it is almost impossible to determine exactly the lighting effect with close-ups. A continuous light source, be it sunlight or an incandescent source such as a flood, allows you to see readily on the focusing screen just how the subject is lit. In addition, exposure is very much simplified, since you can use your behind-the-lens metering system as you would with any subject.

A 35 mm slide projector with no slide makes a good light source. The beam can be aimed just where it's needed. If you wish to cut down the area of coverage further, merely make a mask which can be fitted into the slide holder of the projector. Microscope lamps provide an alternative source. I have also found that the small high-intensity lamps now readily available provide an excellent small and easy-to-manoeuvre source of illumination which is not too hot or bright for tiny subjects. Most of these, like the projector illumination, have colour temperatures of about 3200 K, ideal for Type B colour films or even usable with daylight films and an 80A (or Nikon B12) filter. While two such lights might give you additional brightness, a single light source plus a small white card (an index file card does nicely) can be used at the opposite side of the subject to reflect light for fill in.

Lighting direction

The direction of the lighting is quite important in close-up photography. Front lighting, as with a ringlight, is even but rather characterless. It picks up very little of the surface detail in three-dimensional subjects, although it's fine for non-textured things such as printed pages or stamps.

For best three-dimensional effects, cross-lighting provides good highlights and shadows – as it does in standard distance photography. However, if two lights are used, double shadows can be confusing. It's best to allow one light to predominate or (as we've suggested) use one light and a white reflector. For such subjects as embossings, engravings or basreliefs, a rimlight at almost 90 degrees from camera position, skimming the surface of the subject, is quite effective for picking up the fine lines and reproducing them with necessary contrast.

When photographing two-dimensional subjects, lighting should be frontal and as even as possible. There should be no more than a 25 per cent light fall-off between any areas in the picture or the darkening may show up in the negative or the transparency.

Glossy and semi-glossy surfaces are difficult to photograph, and a subject behind glass even more so. Lighting and camera must be manoeuvred so that no glare or hot spots or reflections are visible through the camera's finder. If they appear in the finder, they will appear on film. With glass-covered surfaces, try directing the light onto large white cardboard reflectors and thence to the surface – or cover both the light sources and camera with polarising materials, as suggested in the chapter on filters.

Filters

While we have discussed filters for general use, they do play a slightly different but important role in close-up work. In tungsten illumination, which is often used for copying, red tones are produced on panchromatic film much lighter than we normally see them, while blue tones tend to come out darker than we would wish. A pale blue filter (Nikon B2) can offset this tendency and produce a more normal visual effect.

If you're using daylight as a source to copy onto black-and-white pan film, blues may tend to be too light. In such cases a pale green or pale yellow will negate the blue sensitivity of the film. Of course, if you're photographing a plain black-and-white subject, you won't need any such filtration.

Thus far we've been discussing filtration in terms of producing a result precisely (or as near precisely as possible) as you see it. However, there are many times when you will wish either to enhance a colour or to eliminate it completely. Suppose you wish to copy a picture on which blue ink has been spilled. You can either partially or completely eliminate it (depending on how deep the stain is) by using a blue filter. Blue filters are also excellent for copying partially faded photos, while yellow filters 'absorb' the yellowish overall hue in old photographs.

Such filtration, of course, is for black-and-white only. In colour photography, simply follow the directions we have already given in our filters chapter.

Slide copiers

There are two slide-copying units fitting the PB-4 bellows unit, one of which can be considered de luxe while the other, with fewer features, is an economy model. Since both are constructed with equal care and rigidity, those photographers not needing the additional features will do just as well with the less-expensive unit. Both PS-4 and PS-5 Slide Copying adapters can be fitted to either PB-4 or the discontinued PB-5 Bellows Attachments. The PB-6 Bellows accepts the PS-6 Slide Copying Adapter. The PS-4 and PB-6 allow the original to be moved up, down or sideways for cropping while copying, and these units also have found trays to support rolls of unmounted rolls of film to be copied. The PS-5 allows direct central copying only and doesn't have the supporting trays, although it will accept uncut film strips for copying.

To fasten slide copiers to the PB-4 or PB-5 Bellows, unscrew the locking knob at the very front of the bellows and slide the copying attachment rod into the front central hole. Then retighten the knob temporarily. Now bring the lens panel with lens to the front of the bellows, lock it in place and connect the rear of the slide copier bellows to the interior thread of the lens by pressing the buttons on either side of the slide copier's clip ring – much like you would fasten a lens cap over your lens. The clip will attach to any

PS-4 and PS-6 slide copying adapter

Here are the controls:

1. Mounting rod
2. Roll-film holder
3. Snap-on button
4. Rear plate
5. Bellows
6. Slide mount slot
7. Film carrier
8. Hinged diffuser plate holder
9. Opal diffuser plate

10. Lens panel grip
11. Magnetic holder
12. Snap-on lens mount

13. BR-3 adapter ring
14. Normal lens mounted in reverse for best quality close-up
15. BR-2 Macro Adapter ring

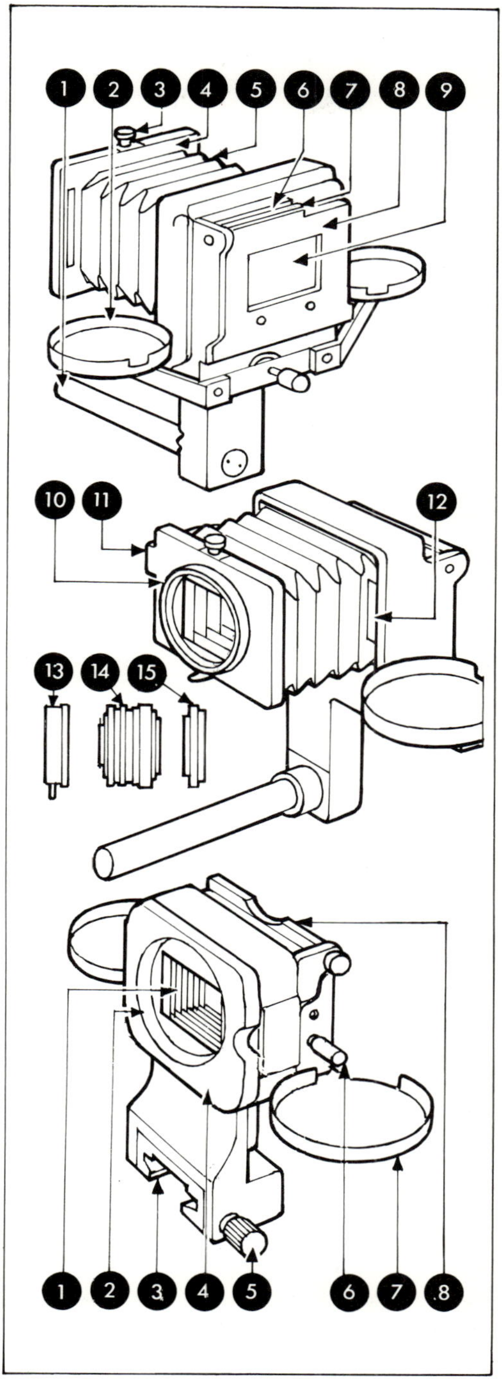

PS-6 slide copying adapter

1. Light shielding bellows
2. Lens connecting tim
3. Mounting foot
4. Front plate
5. Clamping knob
6. Film tray clamping screw
7. Film tray
8. Front plate

52 mm threaded lens and can also be attached to any reversed lens by using a BR-3 adapter ring.

The PB-6 Bellows accepts only its own PS-6 Slide Copying Adapter. To attach it, first loosen the clamping knob on the PS-6's mounting foot. Unthread the front end stop on the PB-6 Bellows Focusing Attachment and remove it. Slide the PS-6 onto the PB-6's rail; and replace the front end stop. Tighten it. Slide the PS-6 to the rail's front end until it touches the front end stop. Tighten the clamping knob.

Pull out the front plate of the PS-6 and slide it over the front rim of the lens. Using the clamping screw, attach the lens and front plate.

If you mount the lens in reverse, attach the front plate to the raised ring of the inside of the lens barrel.

The slide to be copied fits into the slot on the slide carrier, with the subject material upside down. You can quickly check to see whether the slide is orientated properly right to left by viewing it directly through your finder once you get in focus. If it's wrong, simply remove the slide and place it back correctly. However, with most films you will be able to locate the dull side easily and make sure it is facing forwards towards the front optical glass of the slide copier itself. Any slide to 4 mm thick can be fitted.

If you are copying a picture from an uncut strip or roll of film, pull the opal glass plate forward and slip the film into the channel, making sure that the dull film side faces the opal glass. Now snap the plate shut again. Position the proper picture centrally before shutting the plate.

Lenses

Not all lenses can be used for making slide duplicates. You must choose only a lens which will reproduce the duplicate with the ratio you want. For instance, all Nikkors from 24 mm to 85 mm can be fitted and used for various magnifications, but only the 50 mm *f*/1.8 or *f*/2, the 55 mm *f*/3.5 or *f*/2.8 Micro-Nikkor and the 85 mm Nikkors (in reverse) will give you a same size (1:1) duplicate. The 50 mm *f*/1.4 and *f*/1.2 are physically capable of being mounted in forward position for 1:1 slides, but optically they are not suitable. A complete listing of all lenses and their magnification ranges in forward and reverse mountings is at the back of this book.

Best lenses are the 50 mm *f*/2 or *f*/1.8 and the 55 mm *f*/3.5 or *f*/2.8 Micro-Nikkors.

Duplicating slides

If you plan on making duplicate colour slides, certainly the easiest film to use and the most readily available is a fine-grained colour transparency film. However, regular transparency film gives an increased contrast in the duplicate slide when compared to the original, which means that either some highlight or shadow detail will be eliminated and some colours will be washed out or become too deep. If the original contrast of the slide is not too great and the brightness range is fairly limited, you can get quite a good duplicate or ordinary colour film with not too objectionable an increase in contrast.

To decrease the contrast while using regular colour transparency film as the duplicating film, you can preflash the film by exposing it to a uniform amount of the same light you will use to make the slide duplicate for 1/100 the duplicating time exposure. This will require, of course, that you make two exposures on the same film, an easy matter for the Nikon F2 but also possible with the Nikkormat cameras if you take the slack from the film by winding and holding the rewind knob, pushing in the rewind button and rewinding the shutter for the second exposure using the rapid rewind lever. The easier method of making a 1/100 exposure is to buy a 2.0 neutral density filter. Use the same exposure through it that you do without it when duplicating the slide.

Films

Certainly the best slide duplicates can be obtained by using the special slide-duplicating films produced by the film makers themselves especially for duplicating. However, these films are primarily manufactured for the use of professional laboratories and sometimes are not listed in the regular amateur film catalogues. It may be necessary for you to buy the film in bulk and load it into cartridges yourself, or you may have to purchase a specific minimum number of duplicating film cartridges at one time. If you have friends or members of your club also interested in duplicating, perhaps they can join you in sharing the cost. Unused film can always be stored indefinitely in a freezer, or the life at least prolonged considerably in a refrigerator.

No precise information on the use of these special duplicating films can be given here since the brands from each company differ greatly. However, nearly all are designed for tungsten or electronic flash illumination and a filter pack of colour-compensating filters which you can purchase in gelatin form and place in front of the opal glass of your duplicator. Most of these duplicating films have very low exposure indexes, perhaps even lower than the ASA indexes available on your camera. In this case you have to adjust your shutter speed and aperture accordingly. For instance, if your Nikkormat has a minimum ASA index of 25 but the duplicating film speed is 12, you would make your meter readings through your lens at ASA 25 but then give double the exposure to correct for the ASA 12 speed of the film. While this does seem like considerable trouble, the duplicates you can achieve are far superior even to those usually available commercially. I have made many which are virtually impossible to tell from the original transparency. Do not be confused, however, into considering colour film designed for photomicrography. This has a much higher contrast than normal films, with enhanced colour saturation and (sometimes) an odd colour balance.

Magnification

You can make a duplicate at any specific magnification ratio that you wish. First set the lens's own focusing ring to the infinity mark. Then consult the reproduction ratio scale for your bellows unit in the back of this book and adjust the camera and lens panels of the attachment to give the magnification ratio by using the suggested millimetre extension for the bellows.

To focus the slide, loosen the locking knob at the front of the bellows and, while looking through the viewfinder, move the copier rod in and out until the subject is sharp. Use the full aperture of your lens. If you have a 6× focusing magnifier or eyepiece magnifier, use it to determine precise focus. While you can also control focus by slight movements of the camera or lens panels of the bellows, or by turning the focusing ring of the lens itself, doing so changes the magnification ratio. Keep in mind that the Nikon F, F2 and F3 cameras show exactly in the finder what will appear on the film, while other Nikons and Nikkormats show about 9× in the finder. If you are copying a cardboard-mounted slide which usually has 1/10th of its outer area hidden underneath the carboard mask, the Nikon may show you part of the cardboard in the finder and it will be reproduced on film if seen. You may wish to make a small adjustment for a slightly greater magnification to eliminate the cardboard mount.

With other Nikons and Nikkormats, adjust the magnification carefully just so that no cardboard mount is seen at all through the finder. Actually, of course, the edge of the carboard will be duplicated on the film but will be hidden underneath the duplicate cardboard mount. These instructions are quite important if you wish to preserve in the duplicate every bit of the picture area you have in the original.

Cropping

With either the PS-4 or PS-5 you can crop the slide and enlarge the central image only by increasing the magnification beyond the same size 1:1 duplicating ratio. However, with the PS-5 you can also crop selectively up or down, to the right or left of the original slide. After achieving the approximate magnification you wish and getting accurate focus, loosen the locking screw on the film carrier and move it up or down (to 6 mm) or sideways (to 9 mm) or a combination of both movements to obtain the cropping you wish. Tighten the screw when you reach the required cropping. After duplicating, you can return the carrier to central position and it will click into place.

Other copies

While making duplicate colour slides is probably the principal use of the slide copiers, they can also be used for producing black-and-white slides from either colour or black-and-white negatives, colour negatives from colour transparencies or black-and-white negatives from colour or black-and-white transparencies. Consult the table in the back of this book for film choice.

Lighting

Having chosen the film type you intend to use for making your duplicates, it remains to select the proper lighting source, determine exposure and shoot the duplicate.

Quite often natural daylight coming through a north window, or electronic flash for daylight-balanced colour film, are recommended light sources. I find that the first varies too much in colour quality to be reliable for good colour balance, while electronic flash requires the use of various test exposures beforehand or making a large number of shots at various exposures to make certain that at least one is correct. A continuous light source, such as a 3200 K flood is far more controllable and allows you to make very exact exposure readings with the use of your through-the-lens Nikon or Nikkormat metering system. If you wish to use a daylight-balanced colour film with the 3200 K floods, you'll need a Nikon B12 or an 80A filter over your camera lens. Alternatively, you can use an equivalent, but inexpensive, gelatin or acetate filter in front of the opal glass of the copier. While the distance you place the lamp from the opal glass is not critical, obviously it should not be close enough to create undue heat on the slide nor be so far that the exposure time becomes lengthy.

Exposure

Generally a straight through-the-lens meter exposure leads to a correctly exposed duplicate. With an auto-exposure camera, you can simply allow it to select the proper shutter speed with no correction. However, if you wish to lighten or darken a slide, you may want to allow slightly less exposure (darken) or more (to lighten). Also, some slides with pronounced shadow areas in which you want to hold detail will require an additional half stop of exposure. High key photographs will do best with about ½ *f*/stop of additional exposure.

For best possible duplicate sharpness, lenses should be used at *f*/8 for slide duplication. Smaller apertures can cause deterioration of sharpness.

Flat copy

The most convenient method of copying flat materials such as pages from books, stamps, artwork, maps and similar subjects, is to mount your camera on a suitable copying stand such as the Nikon Repro-Copy Outfit Model PF-4. The PF-4 features a vertical column and movable camera support system to ensure precise alignment of the camera and lens during focusing and framing on the baseboard. A spring counterbalance for the camera support plus both coarse- and fine-focusing systems provide convenient and precise operation. The camera, with or without motor winders or bellows, can focus directly on the baseboard, at an angle, or on the floor or wall for large subjects. The PF-4 provides a rigidity seldom found on copy units made to accommodate many different brands of cameras.

To use the PF-4, attach film-loaded camera as described. Position subject on baseboard. Squeeze coarse-focusing handles together. Move camera up or down until subject is framed correctly. Focus the image with camera lens. Use fine-focusing knob on the saddle for pinpoint, precise focus. Lock after use. Use a small lens aperture for increased depth of field and lens sharpness.

For lighting, Nikon manufactures a PL-3 Lighting Unit which is not available in all countries due to local electrical codes. However, whether bulbs in reflectors or reflector bulbs are used, one should each be placed right and left at about 45 degrees above the baseboard. Bulbs with the proper colour balance for tungsten-type films should be mounted if you are making copies in colour.

Use a cable release for exposures, with all controls firmly locked to minimise vibrations. The camera's self-timer can be used to make the exposure if you don't have a cable release.

The 55 mm *f*/2.8 Micro-Nikkor is probably the finest all-round lens for copying. The 105 mm *f*/4 Micro-Nikkor is also suitable but requires nearly twice the camera-to-subject distance for the same subject image size on film. Of all the general photography Nikkor lenses, the 50 mm *f*/1.8 is the best for copying.

For exposure, use the directions for through-the-lens metering and follow them – except when copying black-and-white subjects such as a page from a book. In this case, substitute an 18 per cent reflectable grey card and make your exposure reading from it.

While the PF-4 can provide a reproduction ratio from ½ to ¼× on the baseboard with a 55 mm Micro-Nikkor lens, you may find with large subjects that the total height of the copy stand with the camera at top position is insufficient to encompass the entire subject area. You can increase the covering area as follows.

Position the rear of the baseboard at the edge of a table. Reverse the column in the column-attachment bracket so the camera is pointing at the floor. Place the subject on the floor or, if necessary, on a slightly nearer support.

The Nikon Repro-Copy Outfit PF-3 weighs 9.1 kg (19 lb 13 oz), and is a sturdy and versatile copying system. It features a rectangular cross-section vertical column with a maximum useful height of 888 mm (34⅞ in). The

Repro-copy outfit PF-4

The Repro-Copy PF-4 is the basic unit of Nikon's comprehensive close-up system.

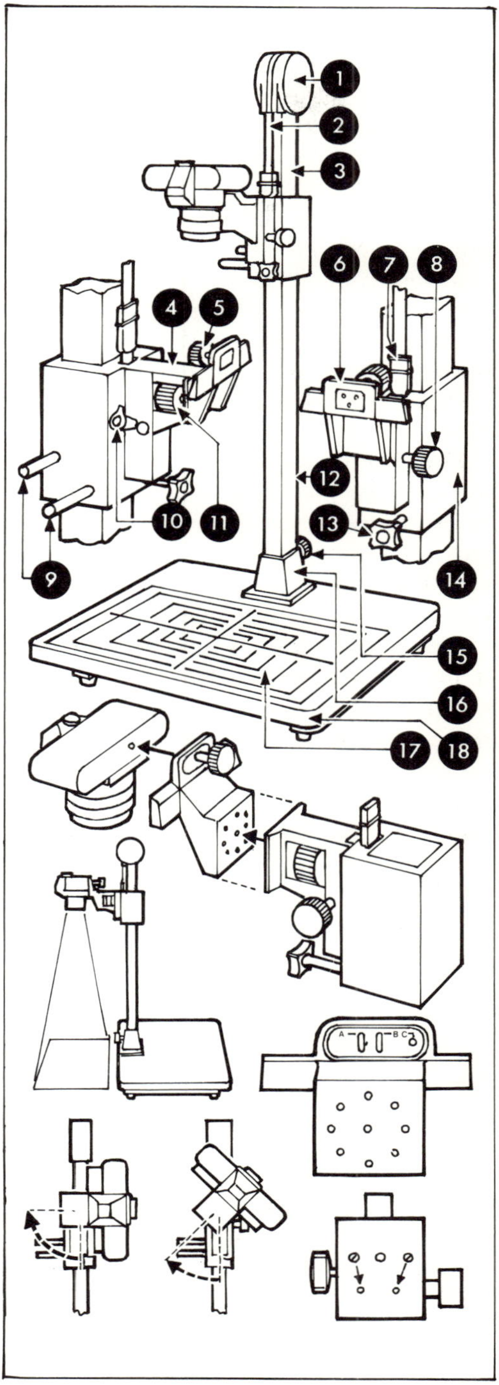

Here are the controls:

1. Spring counterbalance
2. Spring counterbalance tape
3. Reproduction ratio scale
4. Saddle arm
5. Attachment screw
6. Camera cradle PH-4
7. Tape attachment clip
8. Fine-focus clip
9. Coarse-focus handles
10. Fine-focus clamping knob
11. Camera cradle attachment knob
12. Column
13. Saddle-clamping knob
14. Saddle
15. Column-clamping knob
16. Column-attachment bracket
17. Grey card
18. Baseboard

Nikon camera body attaches to camera cradle which is then connected to saddle arm. Bellows units or cameras with motor drives attach directly to the saddle.

Column should be reversed in bracket to accommodate larger subjects which can then be placed on floor.

Appropriate attachment screw-mounting hole should be used depending on camera body model. Table furnished with outfit indicates A, B or C mounting.

By loosening camera cradle attachment screw, camera can be remounted for angle or horizontal shooting.

For cordless battery pack motor-driven Nikons, unscrew alignment pins and transfer them to bottom holes as per arrows.

baseboard's usable area is 475 × 335 mm (18 11/16 × 13 3/16 in). The camera cradle's saddle support is counterbalanced by coiled spring. The column can be reversed 180° for copying large areas from the floor. Additionally, the camera cradle can be swung and locked in 45° angle increments for angle shooting of three-dimensional objects, attaching a camera to an angled eyepiece microscope or for horizontal copying from a wall. With and without the camera cradle and an optional PH-3 MD holder, the Repro-Copy Outfit can accommodate all Nikons and Nikkormats, with and without motors, auto winders, cordless battery packs, magazine backs and bellows units. The unit has both coarse-focusing handles and a fine-focusing knob with lock. The column is marked with a reproduction-ratio scale. With a 50 mm lens, the maximum reproduction ratio is 1:15, covering a subject field of 35 × 52.6 cm (13¾ × 20¾ in). The accessory PL-3 Lighting Unit clamps to the column above or below the cradle saddle and provides two movable lamp holders, without reflectors, which can accommodate lamps up to 500 W.

To set up the stand, first place the baseboard on a firm, level surface. Insert the lower end of the column with the two dovetail cut-outs and tapped holes into the column attachment bracket. Make certain that the reproduction ratio scale is correctly positioned. Now insert the column-clamping screw into the bracket hole and tighten it.

Thread the coarse-focusing handles into the tapped holes in the side of the saddle. Loosen the saddle clamping knob, squeeze the coarse-focusing handles together and lower the saddle down over the column. You can stop the saddle movement by releasing the coarse-focusing handles. The spring counterbalance should be attached to the column top by slipping the square end of the housing into the open end of the column. Move the saddle upwards to the top of the column and connect the spring counterbalance tape to the clip on the saddle arm top.

Place the camera cradle on the saddle and tighten the attachment knob, You can then mount the camera with lens on the cradle using the proper mounting holes for that specific camera model. When the camera is seated correctly in the cradle, the camera front should rest on the supporting arms and be parallel with the baseboard.

Hole A is for Nikons F3, F2, FM, FE, EL2, Nikkormats, EM, F+ 250 exposure back and F3 + MD-4 motor (the latter requiring an AH-2 tripod adapter). Hole B is for Nikon F, F2 + MD-2 or 3 motors and battery packs, FM and FE + MD-11 and 12 motors (with adapter AH-2), EL2 and AW-1 motor, EM + MD-E, F2 + MF-1 + MD-2. Hole C is for Nikon F + F-36. When mounted correctly, the front of the camera rests on the support arms securely and is absolutely parallel to the baseboard. If you are mounting the camera and bellows, the bellows itself should be attached to the PF-4, directly to the saddle.

If you're using a Nikon F2 with motor drive, you'll need the accessory PH-3 MD Holder. For Nikon F cameras with motor drives and cordless battery packs, remove the cradle and attach the camera directly to the saddle arm. You must unscrew the alignment pins and transfer them to the lower holes. The pins are slotted for a screwdriver blade.

Nikon bellows units also are to be fitted directly to the saddle, thus reducing the possibility of camera vibration.

To use the PF-3, place the subject to be copied on the baseboard, loosen the saddle-clamping knob and while squeezing the coarse-focusing handles together, raise or lower the camera until the subject is framed properly. Focus the camera. Using the fine-focusing knob, make the fine adjustments in framing and focusing. You'll find it most convenient to focus with the aid of the DW-2 6× Focusing Finder or the Eyepiece Magnifier. At high column operation, the DR-2 Right Angle Viewing Attachment is most useful.

For high-magnification work, a small lens aperture is suggested. Focusing screens with split-image rangefinders are sometimes difficult to use, and if your Nikon has interchangeable screens, a matte screen of the C,D or E type is preferable. However, if your screen is not interchangeable, focus using the outer fine-focusing area. Exposures should be made with a cable release.

If you wish to photograph a greater area than is possible with the camera at the top of the column, there are two ways to go about it.

Place the rear of the baseboard at the table edge. Reverse the column in the attachment bracket so the camera is now pointing to the floor. You now have the additional table height plus the column height with which to work.

Alternatively, the camera can be used horizontally with the subject attached to a wall or other vertical support. To swing the camera horizontally, loosen the camera cradle attachment screw and remount the cradle with the camera facing the required direction. Since the cradle base has 8 equidistantly-spaced holes, the camera can be positioned at 8 different angles at 45° intervals. The 45° inclined position is good for photographing small three-dimensional objects, or to align the camera with a microscope eyepiece.

As with the Nikon bellows units, the 50 mm *f*/2 or 1.8 lens or the 55 mm *f*/3.5 or *f*/2.8 Micro-Nikkor lenses are most suitable for close-up work using the stand. When the coarse- and fine-focusing adjustments are set level with the top of the saddle, the scales on the side of the column give the reproduction ratio as well as the diagonal length of the subject as it would be recorded using the 55 mm *f*/3.5 or *f*/2.8 Micro-Nikkor.

Photography through the microscope

Nikon has made provision for taking microphotographs through a microscope with two different systems. The Nikon Microscope Camera Adapter Model 2B allows viewing the image on the camera's viewing and focusing screen. The exposure can be made with the camera's focal plane shutter. It is quite suitable for low-magnification work where the microscope objective is not more than 20×. For greater magnification, a photomicroscopist should use one of four available models of the Microflex which has its own leaf shutter to minimise vibration and its own viewing system with ocular. The Standard Model PFX has a mechanical leaf shutter, while other Microflex models provide automatic exposure control. However, the Microflex models form only part of a most comprehensive system of Nikon Micrographic equipment which is really outside the scope of this book. Consult your dealer or Nikon importer about these units.

Microscope adapter

The Nikon Microscope Camera Adapter 2B allows the Nikon or Nikkormat camera body to be fitted to a Nikon or similar microscope eyepiece tube. The adapter has its own projection lens which produces a real image of half the magnification of the microscope itself. (The microscope magnification is the product of multiplying the magnification of the eyepiece by the magnification of the objective.) In other words, if the eyepiece magnification was 5× and the objective 10×, the total magnification of the microscope would be 50× and the Adapter would provide on film a 25× magnification.

The adapter consists of a connecting tube and an eyepiece collar. The collar itself comprises three parts which are only used together for a high eyepoint type of eyepiece. If you're using an ordinary Huygenian or compensation-type eyepiece, you remove the middle piece of the collar.

First bayonet the camera body to the top of the adapter tube. Now pull out the eyepiece from the microscope and insert it from above into the eyepiece adapter collar. Fasten it by means of the eyepiece adapter lockscrew so that the top end of the eyepiece is about 1 mm lower than the top edge of the eyepiece adapter. Insert the eyepiece adapter tube into the eyepiece adapter collar and fasten the adapter lock screw.

With Nikon cameras having interchangeable screens, the Type C screen with matte surface and cross hairs or a totally transparent screen with double cross hairs (Type M) should be used. To focus using the cross hairs, just compare the cross hair position with that of the subject seen through the finder. Move your eye slightly from side to side. If the subject is out of focus, the image will appear to move in relationship to the cross hairs. Focus the microscope until the cross hairs and the subject remain stationary in relationship to each other as you shift your eye. The subject is now properly focused.

Even if a waist-level or critical focusing magnifier is most convenient for viewing and focusing through a microscope, the Photomic metering head of the Nikon or the built-in metering system of a Nikkormat is by far the simplest method of determining a possible exposure. Lacking any means of making a reading directly through the microscope, you would have to rely on test exposures given a specific light source and subject. Then, based on your test shots, you could determine proper exposure for other magnifications

Microscope adapter

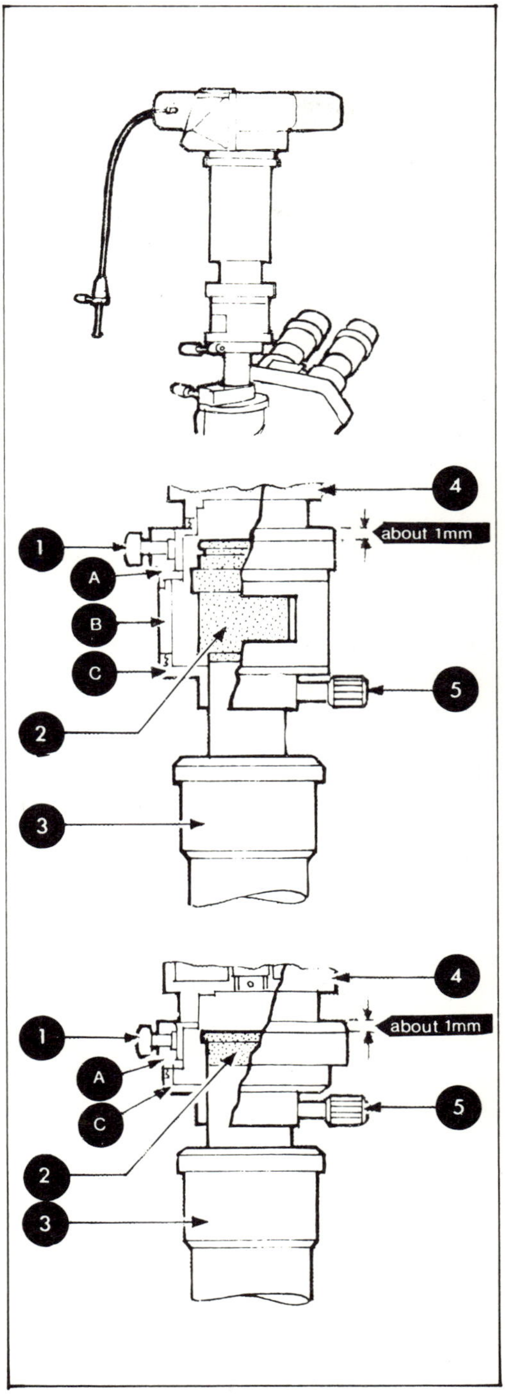

Here's the Adapter Model 2 set up to accommodate a high eyepoint type eyepiece:

1. Locking knob
2. High eyepoint eyepiece
3. Eyepiece tube
4. Microscope-camera adapter
5. Eyepiece adapter lock screw

A. Top of adapter collar
B. Middle adapter collar
C. Bottom adapter collar

Note that in this technique, top end of eyepiece is about 1 mm lower than top edge of eyepiece adapter.

Here's the adapter with intermediate collar piece B removed for an ordinary Huygenian or compensation type eyepiece. Note that top end of eyepiece is about 1 mm lower than top of eyepiece adapter.

provided your light source and subject did not change. Certainly no field was ever better served with a through-the-lens metering system.

To make a reading with Nikon or Nikkormat, set the camera's metering system as if you were using a preset lens or you were working with a Bellows Attachment. For non-auto indexing cameras, the Photomic prong should be pushed upwards at the *f*/5.6 position or the Nikkormat coupling pin should be pushed as far right as it will go. Obtaining proper exposure by centering the meter needle or causing the proper diodes to light can only be accomplished by changing shutter speed or illumination level. The Nikkormat EL, ELW and Nikon EL2, F3, FE, EM and FG can provide automatic exposure through the microscope. However, no matter what camera you are using, it's advisable to overexpose slightly to increase contrast. One way to accomplish this is to set only half the ASA index on the camera. In other words, if you are using an ASA 100 film, set the camera to 50. However, additional exposure compensation may be needed depending on the nature of the subject.

A green filter is supplied with the adapter and it should be used when photographing yellowish or pinkish stained specimens with black-and-white film. In colour, if you are working with a daylight-type film, a proper colour-compensation filter is essential. Increase transformer voltage, if you're using one, to 7.5 V and photograph through a Nikon colour-compensating filter CD 165 or its equivalent.

Photographing people

Photographs of people range from a simple family snapshot through stage and sports photography, news events, and street candids to formal portraiture. Many photographers handle all of this with just a Nikon or Nikkormat plus their standard lens; but several accessories increase your versatility.

Informal pictures

At home or among friends is by far the best locale to begin learning how to handle people before your camera.

No matter how dreadful a family picture may be photographically, it has the inherent advantage of revealing a likeness which will be treasured by the family. Shooting such photos with a Nikon or Nikkormat does not, contrary to many camera owners' thinking, improve the picture one jot. By using proper techniques on the very same subject matter, you can take a picture that has artistic as well as family appeal. Indeed the subjects appear better to family viewers if the relatives look natural, rather than stiff and squinting.

First, let's recognise the fact that the average person who is not a professional model does not know how to pose and the average photographer does not know how to pose a subject.

Outdoors, first get the subject out of the sunlight. No one, not even a professional model, can look directly into the sun. Sunlight, as you've seen in the chapter on exposure, is difficult to handle, producing unflattering shadows around the nose and under the eyes. It also makes your subject squint.

Search for a proper area to take the picture where the subject is relaxed or can relax. Bright shade under a tree or beside a building is good. An overcast day is excellent almost anywhere. If there is no shade, reversing roles so that the subject has his or her back to the sunlight may be better than having the sun behind the photographer with the subject having to squint uncomfortably into the sun.

Posing

Few people just left standing know what to do with their hands, arms or legs. It is an awkward situation. Encourage your subject to sit in a chair, on a bench, on the ground, lean in a doorway or take up any suitably natural position.

Avoid photographing from head on. The subject can turn his or her head towards you if you want a straight-on expression. When shooting from the same level, arrange for a sitting subject to lean forward slightly. If you are picturing someone on the ground, perhaps he or she can lean backwards on hands or arms and look up at you for a more natural shot. Whatever the pose, it must be comfortable for the subject and should be in a position that he or she would most likely assume naturally.

Watch out for your background. Many photographers are so concerned over the subject that they forget what lies behind. If the background displeases you, you have many alternatives – move; shoot from another direction; change your height, angle; use a larger lens aperture to throw the background out of focus; or change focal length lenses to make the background objects appear bigger (longer lenses) or smaller (shorter lenses) while keeping the subject the same size by shifting camera-to-subject distances.

Expressions

If you have everything so far under control, your subject in place, your camera up to your eye and are just waiting for a good expression, the chances are that you will never get just the look you want. There are a number of tricks that will help out. Have the subject look elsewhere and then call him (or her) to look directly at you just before you take the picture. Talk constantly to the subject to keep a two-way conversation on matters of interest until he or she relaxes. Keep studying the expression changes through your viewfinder. Another way is to have a friend keep the subject in conversation while standing behind you. Again, watch for the proper moment to shoot.

A few words of warning. Check the subject carefully through the viewfinder. Is there a lock of hair out of place that you can see? Is there a wrinkle in a dress, a button that has come open, any small blemish?

Backgrounds

Backgrounds which have a definite relationship to the subject can add considerably to the appeal of the picture. A person photographed in his own home, for instance, would be better placed than the same person photographed in a strange house. An artist in his studio or a man fond of his books in his library provide additional interest in the picture and insight into the subject. Incongruous backgrounds which conflict should be avoided. A brick wall, for instance, would probably be rather inappropriate except if photographing a bricklayer.

A subject actively engaged in an activity is an easier one to photograph than a static person. For instance, someone lighting a pipe or a cigarette makes a good picture. A person reading a book and suddenly looking up at you is another possibility. Children need toys, a book, a ball, an ice cream cone to engross them. When photographing children, by the way, try to keep to their level. Too many grownups are always shooting down at them, making them look like little dwarfs (the same is true of animals). Being on the subject's level is always safer than not.

Focus

Where do you focus? In portraits, always on the eyes. It is the first place that a viewer looks – as he would if he were present in the actual scene. If you have a split-image finder screen you may not find it easy to bisect an eye and bring it together for accurate focus. Instead, use the outer fine-focusing or microprism area (if your screen has it). Eye focusing is particularly important since if you are shooting a portrait you'll be fairly close with little depth of field – even if you have a fairly small lens aperture. An ear or nose out of focus will not be noticeable. But an eye out of focus is immediately seen. And if you are photographing someone whose head is not looking directly at you, the near eye is the one on which you'd better concentrate.

Distance

How far away from a person should you be to get a good picture? As close as possible. Simply look through your viewfinder and advance forwards until you feel that some essential part of the picture may be eliminated if you take another step. Now stop and shoot. In all photography, far more pictures are ruined by being taken from too far a distance than from too near. Close in until you can't close in any more.

In giving you advice to get close to your subject, we are presuming you have the appropriate focal length lens – a longer-than-normal for tight head-and-shoulder portraits, for instance. With a normal lens or – even more so – a wide-angle, there is a grave danger of apparent perspective distortion. Because you are so close to your subject with a short lens, the nearest part of the subject – an arm or even a nose – may appear overly large. The longer focal length lenses will allow you to capture the same size image at a greater camera-to-subject distance, thus preventing the apparent distortion.

Lenses

In lens choice, favourite focal lengths vary from 85 mm all the way to 180 or 200 mm. The 105 mm lens is particularly popular. This allows you to remain about twice as far from the subject as a normal 50 mm lens. Added camera-to-subject distance helps the subject relax and also provides you with less apparent perspective distortion – noses or hands are less likely to appear overly large in the photos. An 85 or 105 mm lens is quite handlable. Longer lenses are generally used for portraits when the photographer cannot approach the subject sufficiently close for a good portrait – such as when photographing prominent people during news events.

When photographing people, don't forget that your camera has both a horizontal and vertical position. It should be quite obvious that if you were photographing a person standing or sitting, the camera should be used in the vertical for most shots, to make utmost of the film format. But never be too rigid in this respect. Make the format fit the subject at hand.

Groups

If one person is difficult to photograph, more than one can be even more complicated. Most photographers tend to allow the subjects to look directly and stiffly into the camera. This is a very awkward pose and should be avoided. Try to arrange your subjects, whether two or two dozen, in more relaxed poses. They can sit or stand, but should preferably be engaged in conversation with each other if you are dealing with a group of four people or more. If you do want head-on photos, call to them all at the last moment and shoot quickly when they look up – before they have time to freeze. Use your entire picture frame to arrange the subjects. Don't jam them in the middle.

Some photographers, when shooting groups, in error select a wide angle lens automatically for the photograph. In many instances it is no more advisable to use a wide angle lens for a group than a wide angle lens for an individual. If you do have the room, a normal or longer lens will be preferable for just the same reasons that it's best for single portraits – lack of apparent perspective distortion, as we've discussed. However, if space is a problem and you must resort to a wide angle lens, be careful of close objects which may appear overly large and also watch out for subject matter at mid or close distances at the picture edges – particularly with lenses of 28 mm or shorter. At the edges they tend to look spread out – most unflattering for human beings.

Indoor portraits

While it was once the fashion – almost an imperative – to make all photos of people outdoors or risk overlong exposures or very hot floodlighting, today's fast films and high speed lenses allow a photographer to operate very well indoors often with no more light than is actually existing in the house. In many instances the most interesting portraits and group shots can be undertaken indoors. By using the existing available light in your house, these pictures can be made to look very informal and real.

Houselamps often yield enough light not just for black-and-white photography using high speed films, but for colour as well. As we've seen in the chapter on colour film, houselamps with white shades are often sufficient for photographs with Type B colour films and need no filtration. Daylight from windows can also be employed to good advantage indoors. In any of these cases, the very atmosphere of the house and the subject's ability to relax in a living-room chair or lean against a window frame will go far in helping you get a very natural photograph. I often check the illumination around my house in terms of needed exposure so that when picture opportunities do occur, I am able to shoot quickly with assurance that I do have enough light. In areas where I feel I am lacking illumination, I either bring in another lamp or raise the wattage in the lamps that are available.

Portraits using window light can be very effective. However, you should avoid harsh direct sunlight. A bright overcast day outdoors yields good results indoors – or use windows away from the sun.

As the subject moves away from the window, the light diminishes. The best compromise is usually with your subjects virtually standing at the window and your camera placed close to the window wall. You can take effective silhouettes quite easily by keeping the subject between your and the window. Make your exposure for the windowlight.

'Candids'

Readiness is not carrying your camera in your gadget bag or snapped up in your ever-ready case. You will never be able to haul the camera out and get it set in time for a real candid, although you might be able to capture a building or some other non-moving stationary object. So the first rule to be learned is to keep your camera at the ready. Either remove it from its case completely or keep it in the camera body part of the case. Hang it around your neck at high chest position where it can be brought to your eye swiftly. Alternatively, carry it in your hand, with the strap wrapped round your wrist.

Willingness is a word seldom used in candid photography as far as the photographer himself is concerned, yet in many ways I do find that it indeed may be the major key. Willingness means the photographer's willingness to take the picture. Now this might seem strange, but the biggest obstacle often to be overcome in picture-taking is timidity. The photographer is simply afraid to take a picture of a person he or she does not know. I can only say from experience that 'he who hesitates is lost'. Once anyone before a camera has an intimation that you are unsure of yourself, there is a chance you may indeed have a problem and you may simply miss the picture completely. I have found that a positive approach of immediate action is best. That's what professionals use. But it does require a bit of nerve. I know of some professionals who go out on the street in their spare time and practise taking pictures of strangers, just to overcome their own doubts.

There is, of course, the other side of the coin. Owning a Nikon or Nikkormat which can so capably capture a slice of someone else's life does not give a photographer license to invade the privacy of others. Pictures which might hold a subject up to ridicule, poses that might embarrass a subject, pictures of people living in poverty, should be avoided. Put yourself in the position of the subject. Would you mind having your picture taken under the same circumstances? If the answer is no, go ahead and shoot.

I have found in travelling all over the world that many countries do have various laws and customs governing photography. In some, it is illegal to take a picture of a stranger unless you obtain permission. It is always wise to check regulations, although any rule requiring that a photographer always obtain permission before shooting tends to wreck naturalness.

Ability

We now come to ability. This means that you are physically able to take the picture. You must be able to judge the exact instant that the action, expression or composition is at its peak and snap the shutter then. You must be able to hold the camera rock-steady and press the shutter release without jarring the camera. Don't expect to be an expert at both immediately. Working swiftly but still holding a camera steady and not jarring it when pressing the shutter release takes practice.

What is needed for success here, I find, is the word 'freeze'. Try to keep relaxed and loose until that instant when you have the camera at eye level, it is set properly and you are ready to take the picture. Then freeze. Your stance must be solid, both feet placed slightly apart, flat on the ground, your left arm dug into your side but your left palm supporting the camera or lens (if you are using a long lens) and your right hand aiming the camera. Your first finger should be pressing smoothly but firmly on the shutter release. At the instant of picture-taking, hold your breath. I have found that it is quite possible to walk down a street, see a subject, interrupt my walk for only a split second to freeze and then continue walking while my subject wasn't even aware that I had stopped or taken his or her picture.

Travel and scenics

Taking photographs while travelling, whether only a few miles from home, or on a trip half way around the world, is highly enjoyable.

Equipment

Choosing the type of film to purchase and just what accessories to take can be bewildering; but there are certain specific items that you should always carry in your gadget bag: a lens brush for removing dust; lens tissue (not silicon-impregnated eyeglass tissue!) for cleaning off more recalcitrant dirt from the lens or finder, and a small bottle of lens cleaner to make removal of the inevitable fingerprint on lens or finder easy and certain. Carry the camera instructions (you'll be surprised how often even experienced photographers misuse cameras because they have forgotten some simple operating procedure).

Carry a small pocket flashlight for setting the camera under adverse lighting conditions. A miniature screwdriver can come in handy in case any camera or lens screw start to work themselves loose. (Note: later cameras use screws with cross heads. Buy the proper screwdriver for these.) By all means make certain that you have fresh batteries in your camera to operate the metering or electronically timed shutter. And even if you have fresh batteries, carry spares in case you inadvertently drain the battery in the camera. Carry small plain gummed labels on which you can write such useful information as where you shot what film plus special instructions for processing.

If you own but one camera body, I would recommend the purchase of a back-up hand-held meter, preferably a selenium cell instrument which requires no batteries. Check your behind-the-lens meter, if you have one, against your spare hand-held meter once a day when taking pictures to make sure they read within ½ stop of one another. Of course, if you have two camera bodies, both with meters, a hand-held meter (unless a highly specialised one) is somewhat superfluous.

Small clear plastic bags are very handy. They fold into almost nothing until needed and then can hold all your exposed film, protecting it from moisture, if you close the bag with a rubber band or metal wire twist. These basics, by the way, I always keep in my carrying case.

Carrying cases

If you have a single camera and lens, it is quite sensible to carry it in its ever-ready case while travelling. Your other essentials can be slipped into a second, over-the-shoulder carrying bag of modest dimensions. However, as soon as you become the owner of a second lens and then more, the ever-ready camera case must give way to a compartmented gadget bag which can hold camera and lenses. It's almost impossible to operate with a camera plus ever-ready case and a second lens with its case. Instead leave your ever-ready case at home. Choose a compartmented case (Nikon has splendid ones) in which you will have separate compartments for each lens and major accessory (so you can grab them easily and they can't knock together causing damage or paint nicks). There should be a compartment for fresh film and one for used film so you won't get them mixed up. The compartments should not be so small and the fitting so precise that it requires much time and dexterity to load the case.

Film

If you have but one camera and are only interested in shooting colour or black and white, you can make a fairly simple choice as to your medium. On the other hand, if you wish both colour and black and white, choices must be made at the outset. If you need just prints, black and white or colour, it's best to settle for a negative colour film since it can yield both colour and black-and-white prints (although admittedly the graininess of colour negative material will not allow the same size black-and-white enlargements with the same quality as you would get from a fine-grained black-and-white film). However, it is a compromise that can be lived with.

If you wish to shoot colour transparencies and also black and white, use a fine-grained colour slide film and make black-and-white negatives for black-and-white prints directly from the colour transparencies using a slide duplicator. Again the black-and-white prints will not always equal the best from black-and-white film, but results will generally be satisfactory.

The best of all worlds if you wish to shoot black and white and colour is to have two camera bodies. If you have a choice, buy one chrome body (for colour film) and one black body (for black-and-white work). In this manner you can avoid any mistakes as to which camera has what film. The two cameras should have sturdy neckstraps of such length that when both cameras hang from your neck, one camera will hang just under the other without touching. This will allow you to bring either camera to your eye without difficulty.

What type of film? Slow, finer-grained films are to be preferred and can make up the bulk of your film purchases – if you are to be primarily outdoors when taking pictures. However, even so, it's advisable to take some rolls of high speed film for those times when you find yourself indoors. Colour or black-and-white films which can be force-processed for higher film speed are useful (but remember to use those blank labels to mark any film needing special processing). If you are to be equally busy shooting outdoors in very bright light and indoors under low light, there is no way but to carry equal amounts of both films. Compromise speed film quite often won't cover either end of the picture-taking spectrum.

How much film should you take? Estimate your needs and double it if you think you will be unable to replenish film during your trip. Nothing is worse than running out of film. Any film that remains can be placed in a refrigerator to prolong its life considerably or into a freezer to prolong life indefinitely.

With colour slide film, it is advisable that you try out a roll of film from any emulsion number you intend to use in quantity before you go on any long unrepeatable trip. Colour film does vary and it's heartbreaking to come back from a trip to find all your transparencies off colour. Don't take chances on processing by using a cut-rate service. Send your film to a well recognised laboratory.

Handling film

Before going on a trip, I remove the outer boxes and direction sheets but don't break open the hermetically sealed containers, if any. Outer boxes and directions slow up camera loading when in a hurry and create a waste problem. Keep one set of instructions for each type of film, though. If the inner package has no identification as to film type or speed, label each container clearly.

Once you expose the film, have it processed as quickly as possible. Colour film, especially, deteriorates or shifts in colour far more after exposure than before. It is humidity which causes the greatest damage, and before exposure the film was sealed against humidity. During and after exposure the film is exposed to varying humidity conditions. If travelling in a relatively humid climate, use plastic bags with a sealing wire or rubber band to seal the package for film storage. If possible, obtain packages of dessicant (drying agent) such as silica gel to absorb moisture in the bag. Previous to your trip, bake the silica gel in an oven at 300°F (150°C) for 30 minutes to remove all moisture, then seal it in a plastic bag. After shooting in a hot and/or humid climate, await the cool of evening or find an air-conditioned room or room with a dehumidifier before transferring exposed, loose film into the plastic package with the silica gel. Before each trip, recondition the silica gel by baking it again. However, even if you do not have silica gel, storing transferred exposed film to a sealed plastic bag in a relatively dry area is advisable. If you have film which is supplied in self-sealing plastic or metal, you can, of course, return the exposed film to these under relatively dry conditions instead of using a single communal plastic bag.

Should you have your film processed while travelling? Only if you know the work of the laboratory. Never trust precious film to the unknown. It is far safer to carry your film back home with you and then give it to a reliable processor. Should you mail the film back home for processing? It depends on your opinion of the reliability of the postal service as against the reliability of bringing the film back yourself.

X-rays

A great deal has been said and written about the X-raying of film at airports during security checks as you board a plane. While much hue and cry has been raised concerning the possibility of X-ray fogging of the film, there has been little positive identification of fogged film caused by X-ray to any airline passenger during routine hand luggage inspection when X-ray machines were labelled as being 'film-safe'. If they are *not* so labelled, demand hand-inspection. Contrary to popular belief, checked luggage is seldom X-rayed and it is almost always safe to carry your film there – except for a few rolls which you will need during the plane trip. It is true, however, that X-ray is cumulative. What will not harm film when passed through once, may indeed harm it if film is exposed again and again to X-ray. Therefore, if you intend to change planes many times during your trip and feel you might be subject to a long series of X-rays, be careful that the same rolls of film are not continually inspected.

Have there been instances of X-ray damage to film? Yes, but not in routine inspection. During various bomb scares, the police have brought in some highly-specialised powerful X-ray units which have been known to fog film. Film kept in the hold of the plane in close proximity to radioactive materials being shipped has also known to have become affected. However, these two happenings are most unlikely. With medical experts becoming more and more concerned about the effect of X-rays even on the airport personnel in charge of operating the units, it does seem as if this danger to film or anything else will be minimised even further in the future.

Filters

How about filters for travel photography? A green filter to enhance foliage and darken the sky is handy for black and white. For colour a skylight filter to warm up pictures in the shade or on dull days is quite useful. If you wish to simplify the types of colour films you carry, you might decide to use just a tungsten-balanced film, with conversion daylight filter over your lens for non-tungsten shots. This combination of tungsten film and conversion filter has proved quite satisfactory for many discerning photographers, although purists may still wish to shoot daylight film outdoors for the very best results.

Close-ups

Besides filters, it's always advisable to travel with the necessary equipment to make close-ups. If you don't own a macro focusing lens such as the 55 mm *f*/2.8 Micro-Nikkor, the Plus 1 and 2 Nikon close-up lenses are good travelling companions, taking up little room and fitting most general-use Nikkor lenses having the standard 52 mm front accessory thread.

Tripods

If you intend to shoot any photographs indoors where a small electronic flash unit is not powerful enough, it is advisable to carry along a small folding tripod. This is particularly necessary if you wish to photograph interiors such as churches where exposures beyond the hand-held range are necessary. There are many excellent small tripods, but do avoid the real flimsies with the thin telescoping legs. The best ones are those with centre bracing and outer flip locks to hold the legs secure in place once the tripod is open.

When buying a tripod, take your camera and longest lens along. Place the camera with lens on tripod. Fasten a small mirror to camera with tape. Shine light from a small flash-light off the mirror so it reflects on to a wall. Fire the camera. Does the light on wall jiggle or move? If so, the tripod isn't sturdy enough. Get one that lets you fire the shutter without any perceptible movement.

Lenses

What are the best lenses for travelling? A good range would be a 28 or 35 mm, your 50 mm, an 85, 105 or 135 mm. The latter three lenses can be replaced with the 80 to 200 mm *f*/4 zoom lens. A wide to moderate tele zoom is another excellent travelling lens. If you intend to do much interior photography, you might require something wider – a 24 mm or even a 20 mm lens, although the latter does tend to exaggerate width and depth. Still, the lens lets you encompass incredible interior areas.

If most of your picture taking is outdoors, the slower, more compact and lighter lenses will do. If you intend to shoot indoor colour by existing light, the high speed, large aperture Nikkors can prove invaluable.

Flash

We have mentioned that you should carry a small electronic flash unit. One which is powered by disposable batteries is best, since manganese alkaline batteries provide a greater number of flashes than rechareable nicads and you will not have the possible difficulties of trying to match a battery charger to the line current available.

Pictures

Having now settled what hardware and film materials should go with you while travelling, let's see how best to improve travel pictures.

When travelling, do not attempt to produce scenes as they appear in postcards. They seldom turn out as well since the postcard photographers can wait for the perfect weather, have all annoying cars removed from the streets and finally call on the services of a retoucher to make the view look perfect. Rather than attempting to imitate this rather sterile perfection, try to get more personal travel pictures by including someone in your travel party. No, don't have them stand in front of monuments staring into the camera. Make sure your subjects stay animated. They should appear to be ignoring the camera completely: looking at the scenery or statuary, conversing among themselves, pointing to some interesting area within the picture. If you are travelling with your family, coax them into wearing clothes which will add extra colour to your scenes, so that they become your very own photographs, duplicatable in no postcard. If you're travelling alone, include yourself in the picture, either with the aid of the self-timer (that's what it's for) or by getting someone to take the picture for you.

Scenics

Photographing scenery properly takes the most skill and practice. Luckily the scene stays put, so that you can analyse and find the best angle, height, composition and framing somewhat at your leisure.

What's a scenic? Any photograph in which the setting itself dominates the picture – this may be a cityscape, landscape, seascape. Although the main theme is the scene, don't automatically exclude people. Most scenes benefit from figures in just the right spot. They lend proportion to pictures, increase interest and colour – the right seasoning to make a scenic come alive.

But how should a scenic be composed? Where should the people be placed? What should be in or out of focus? How far away should the scene be? Perhaps more rules have been made for scenic photography than for any other kind. These rules, based on general rules of thumb for classic landscape painters, are difficult to follow in a photograph, and any rigid application is likely to reduce your creative ability.

However, some guidelines are in order. Every scenic ought to have a focal point of interest to which your eye will be drawn. It may be a human figure, animal, tree, or distant mountain. It may be small or large, but it ought to be there. If there is no such point of interest, the viewer's eye wanders round until it gets tired and the picture thus defeats itself in its inability to hold the viewer's attention.

While the size of the main point of interest is not too important, it obviously must be of such a stature as to be clearly recognisable. A tiny figure which the viewer cannot truly identify will prove a bother, not a focal point. For instance, if you are trying to capture the majesty and immenseness of mountains, the mountains must look big and the human figures small. How can you control this? By moving backwards and forwards towards or away from your subject or having your human figures move. Obviously as they increase their distance from the camera, they soon become minute compared to the mountains. You can also control the mountains by using an interchangeable lens. For example, longer focal length enlarges the distant mountains.

We've just discussed a situation where your main focal point – a person or persons – appears quite small so as to emphasise the mountains. You will find an equal number of cases where the main subject ought to be treated large. A train racing through a valley might be treated as a dynamic focal point with your camera up close. To emphasise it, you might even wish to switch to a wide angle lens, approach closer to the train to maintain large image size, which will also tend to make the distant mountains or surrounding landscape smaller in dimension by comparison. By playing the camera-to-subject distance against the focal length choice, you can achieve many varied effects even with the same subject material.

Where should your focal point be placed? It's seldom desirable to place it directly in the centre unless it is a static subject such as a mountain whose vast size is overpowering. Usually the focal point is best when placed off centre, but not too far into the picture edges or corners.

Of course a landscape can have two focal points of interest, although it's best if one remains primary and one secondary so the viewer's eye will naturally travel from the main focal point to the secondary one. For instance, there might be some small human figures with mountains. The eye should travel to the people and then to the mountains. If you are shooting in colour, brightly coloured attire will cause your human figures to stand out and automatically attract the viewer's eye.

Frames

Dynamic central images often don't require any framing at all. A huge central mountain, or a train photographed head on as it faces the viewer are subjects quite sufficient in themselves. Some scenes, though, appear lost in the picture area without some additional subject-framing to enclose it. Foliage is probably the most popular framing material for the top and sides. Some photographers actually carry a few tree branches with them to hold in the picture area if there is no foliage available. It's also possible to print in foliage from another negative if you are making black-and-white enlargements. A doorway or archway makes a complete frame. A fence or gate is good for foreground framing. The purpose of all framing is simply to channel the viewing eye to the main subject.

Depth of field

Most scenics benefit from complete sharpness from foreground to background. An out-of-focus foreground or background can be tremendously disturbing since the viewer's eye lights on it and tries to bring it into focus. To avoid this, use your depth-of-field scale as a guide in obtaining maximum sharpness in depth (see chapter on exposure and depth of field).

Distance

Only stereo photographs show a scene in true depth, so we must use the two dimensions we have to create an illusion of depth. This is best done by attempting to include as many different planes of reference as possible. For instance, top foliage framing close, fence in the foreground, person in middle ground, buildings beyond and distant mountains beyond the buildings.

Filters

Whether you're working in colour or black and white, filters can enhance scenics probably more than any other type of subject. For black-and-white work, the sky is usually far too light when shot with today's panchromatic emulsions. If there are clouds, they do not stand out sufficiently. A medium yellow filter darkens the sky to a natural degree while maintaining the clouds as being light, a deeper yellow increases the contrast, while a red filter can produce stark dramatic results of billowy white clouds (if they're there) against a near-black sky. Many landscape photographers use a green filter rather than a yellow since a green filter not only darkens the sky in a similar manner to yellow, but also lightens green foliage to a more realistic tone.

In colour, distant shots can generally be aided with a Skylight or UV filter which helps cut the bluish cast that you may otherwise get. For dramatic results with increased colour saturation and contrast there's nothing like a polarising filter. Make certain the lighting conditions are such that you can make use of the polariser. For instance, it will not operate unless the sun is shining, and the sun must be in the proper position. This is all explained on page 200. However, with a polariser you can achieve colour pictures that simply cannot be got without it.

Keep level

In photographing scenics, your camera should be kept as level as possible with the plane of your subject parallel to the film plane of your camera. If you do point the camera upwards to include a certain tree or the top of a mountain or building, the resulting apparent perspective distortion can make all subjects appear as if they are falling over backwards. There are three possible remedies. Increase your camera-to-subject distance, change to a wider angle focal length lens (or a shorter focal length setting if you have a zoom), or use a Nikkor 28 mm or 35 mm perspective control lens as explained on pages 245–246.

If you do manage to produce a photograph in which the perspective appears awry because you have pointed the camera upwards, you may still be able to rescue the photograph by tilting the easel when making the enlargement. Unfortunately there is little you can do to alter a colour transparency.

Architecture, distortion and other subjects

For many years architectural photography was the exclusive province of the view camera with its correcting swings and tilts. Now, more and more photographers make use of the convenience of the Nikon and Nikkormat cameras and accessories in this most demanding of fields.

While it is true that many limitations (not having swinging and tilting movements) cannot be overcome completely, much can be accomplished by the knowledgeable photographer.

Converging lines caused by not keeping the back of the camera parallel to the subject (as when pointing the camera upwards to photograph a building) can often be minimised or entirely eliminated by the use of the 28 or 35 mm Nikkor perspective control lenses, tilting the negative carrier or baseboard during enlarging, or both, as explained in the previous chapter in the section headed 'scenics'.

Lenses

The normal 50 mm lens does produce in most architectural photography a close approximation of the perspective that one actually sees. However, often this lens's angle of view is simply insufficient to cover the needed picture area. But when a wide angle lens is used, there is the inherent danger of apparent perspective distortion. The apparent depth between objects appears greater than actuality, making objects in depth appear larger. A room interior, for instance, would look much deeper. The shorter the lens, the larger the room will appear. However, such wide angle lenses as 24 mm, 20 mm, 18 mm and even the 15 mm and 13 mm are available when needed. Obviously one should choose the longest focal length that will do the job in order to cut down on apparent depth distortion.

Wide-angle lenses do produce another phenomenon which can be particularly undesirable in architectural photography. This is called marginal distortion. The images of solid objects at the edges of the picture appear progressively more distorted and drawn out. This is caused by the fact that the image projected off-centre meets the film at a greater oblique angle. Unlike the retina of the eye which is curved and thus will record these angles in the same way they are formed, film is flat and therefore distorts the image. The result is quite familiar to those accustomed to viewing wide angle picture. The images at the edges tend to flatten out considerably unless viewed from impossibly close up.

It is the viewing distance which provides the key to correcting apparent perspective distortion. Technically, if images are to appear in the perspective relationship you saw them, you must view them from a distance equal to the product of the focal length of the lens multiplied by the magnification of the image. So you should look at a 10× enlargement from a 20 mm lens at 10 × 20 mm or 200 mm (just under 8 inches). By viewing the print further away you can create the apparent perspective distortion. The same rule holds true for long-focus lenses. A 500 mm shot in a 10× enlargement should be viewed at 5000 mm if seen in a 10× enlargement; then the compression of depth vanishes.

Another type of distortion, linear, is caused by magnification not being the same over the entire field covered by the lens. As a result, straight lines parallel to the edges of the picture curve so that lines either bulge outwards (barrel distortion) or inwards (pin-cushion distortion). While most subjects will tend to hide these distortions, architectural subjects such as buildings with many straight lines both horizontally and vertically reveal such distortion. Linear distortion is particularly noticeable in zoom lenses at the extreme focal lengths and with very wide angle lenses.

Linear distortion cannot be minimised by stopping down the lens; it is the same at all apertures. While there is some measure or trace of linear distortion in almost every lens, the Micro Nikkors in particular have been corrected for this to a great degree, as have the 28 and 35 mm perspective control Nikkors. These obviously should be the choice optics for architectural photographers. In addition, the two perspective control lenses provide correction for converging parallel lines in the form of a shifting movement (see pages 245–250) and can also be used for continuous panoramic pictures as also described on those pages.

The amount of linear distortion is measurable optically, but you can quickly check it yourself by observing any straight horizontal line through your viewfinder with the camera body parallel to the subject. Compare the line with the edge of the finder. The amount of curve will become quite clear.

Regrettably, if you do produce images with linear distortion, there is no way of correcting it.

While on the subject of lens choice, you will find the wide angle lenses particularly useful when photographing miniature models of interiors or exteriors. The added apparent depth does much in providing a very realistic perspective to models.

Filters

When you are photographing architectural subjects outdoors, the use of filters can produce good delineation between light-coloured buildings and the sky. A green or yellow filter darkens the sky while retaining the same relative hue of the building in black-and-white photography, thereby producing a needed separation of contrast.

Interiors

Interiors are not too difficult to photograph provided they have sufficient illumination and you are working in black and white. A careful meter reading and rock-steady camera mounting should yield a photo very close to the actual scene. However, you may wish to show the entire interior in bright light. Interiors may also be far too large for the use of the floods or flash that you may have at hand. If the interior isn't too large, you can place your camera on the tripod, open up the shutter, use B with a locking cable release on the Nikkormats, or on T or B on the Nikons. Then 'paint' the room with light by moving a floodlight on an extension cord around in the picture area during a long exposure at a small aperture. However, this need considerable experience to achieve even lighting and correct exposure.

Balancing an interior for colour pictures is quite difficult. If you do not have the proper amount of photographic illumination you must rely on taking a picture with available daylight on daylight-balanced colour film or using available tungsten illumination with type B film. Often such illumination is of an unknown colour and can very well lead to off-colour photographs. This is particularly true when shooting under fluorescent lights, some of which come out better on daylight film. One check is to make test shots on instant colour film. By shooting first with various corrective filters you can decide which filters you need.

Night photography

Pictures of road traffic at night, particularly on a two-way thoroughfare, can be made to show bright headlight streaks approaching and red tail lights receding. The more traffic, the more streaks. For such pictures, place your camera on a tripod, focus on the main stream of traffic and leave the camera shutter open on B or T as long as you wish. Try several different lengths of time. Set an aperture which would provide proper exposure for a tail light close-up at 1/30 second. You may see such photos apparently taken at twilight. They are usually double exposures. First you photograph the overall scene in late afternoon, perhaps with slight underexposure to simulate twilight. Then cap the lens (or if your Nikon or Nikkormat has provision for making double exposures, you can close the shutter). Your second exposure by uncapping the lens (or reopening the shutter of your camera can make double exposures) is made at night with all the traffic and street lights.

Pictures of the moon and by moonlight can be delightful. To get a good-sized image of the disc itself, you need a long tele lens – 200 mm or more. The moon is much brighter than you think. You can easily make a behind-the-lens meter reading of the moon with your Nikon or Nikkormat. It's advisable, however, to cut the suggested exposure in half if you want any moon detail, or else you will only get a silvery undetailed disc (or part of a disc). Exposures of 1/30 s or less are very possible. Longer exposures should be avoided, since the moon actually moves at a fairly good clip and you will blur it through a long lens.

Scenic pictures by moonlight require fairly long exposures which will probably be outside the range of your meter. A meter reading will suggest about 90 seconds at *f*/2 with 400 ASA film. However, this can produce an unreal daylit effect, so try about 15 seconds (at *f*/2).

Fireworks

Fireworks can be photographed in almost the same way as moving traffic lights – by keeping your camera on a tripod and using the B or T shutter setting during the path of the rocket or time of display. Usually one rocket is insufficient for a good photograph, and the tracing of several rockets superimposed is more interesting if not documentarily accurate. Don't put too many into one picture, though, otherwise you'll just get a jumble. Use a fairly large aperture, *f*/2 or *f*/2.8 with a colour film of 50 ASA or more.

Theatres

You may wish to photograph theatricals from the audience. However, at any play, musical, circus or sporting event, you must check with the management first. In many places regulations strictly forbid photography from the audience during a performance.

In circuses and other entertainments where spotlights follow the performers, arc lamps are generally employed. These are balanced closely to daylight-type colour film. Therefore that's the film you should use. For most stage plays, general illumination by regular spots and floods which are best captured on tungsten-type film. In black and white, of course, you don't have such a problem of film choice. However, in all cases you will want to use a high ASA speed film.

With arc lamps, a behind-the-lens reading if used directly may produce slight overexposure. We would advise exposing for about ½ *f*/stop less than the meter recommends. Where there is no brilliant spotlight, you can follow your behind-the-lens meter. However, if you are a considerable distance from the stage and there is but one distant spotlight, you may have to compensate by allowing one *f*/stop additional exposure. If possible, try to position yourself close to the stage for shots of individual faces and subjects or within the first rows of the first balcony to cover more of the entire stage presentation.

Amateur plays and shows offer the average photographers a far better opportunity of obtaining successful pictures, since the camera owner can get to the stage during dress rehearsal to make some accurate close-up readings right from the subjects.

Most of the interesting circus acts are performed in a blacked-out arena with a spotlight on the subject. Generally these are arclights so you can use daylight film. Surprisingly the amount of lighting is very intense, usually sufficient for exposures of around 1/60 s at *f*/2.8 with high speed colour films. With extremely bright spots or arcs it's advisable to cut exposure by about 1/2 *f*/stop to prevent overexposure. Very good photos can be made from an audience seat. A zoom lens, such as the 80 to 200 mm *f*/4 Nikkor is useful. At full focal length you can single out individual high-wire performers, while the shorter focal lengths allow you to capture group actions of acrobats, horses, elephants, clowns. Even if you shoot with a shorter focal length, you will find the longer focal length lenses convenient for making close-up meter readings of performers, thus giving you more exposure information. If you are using an automatic exposure Nikkormat or Nikon, remember to take it off the automatic exposure mode – or make the necessary compensation after you have made your initial close-up reading with the long focal length and have returned to the shorter length for actual picture taking. Since you are limited by the lighting to a moderately slow speed, try to capture all actions at their peaks where subject movement is less of a problem.

Movies

Don't expect to make still photographs of motion picture images which are the equivalent in quality to your regular pictures. When you watch a movie you are seeing many images one right after the other – from 16 frames per second in amateur movies to 24 in professional films. You do not see the graininess and possible unsharpness of individual movie frames. Copy a single frame with your still camera, though, and then you see all the blemishes.

To obtain best possible quality still photos from motion pictures, work with the original film. Photograph it as you would when duplicating a transparency – with additional magnification, of course, to enlarge the 8, 16, or single frame 25 mm frame to 24 × 36 mm. This can be done using such a lens as the 55 mm *f*/3.5 or *f*/2.8 Micro-Nikkor reversed on bellows. One of the Nikon slide duplicators can be used as an improvised holder for the film.

Such a method of duplication is quite possible if you own the film or can borrow it. However, with most professional films, you will not be able to get the original footage and will have to shoot directly from the screen.

Any black-and-white film with a speed of around ASA 400 will do nicely. Colour films are slower and must match the colour temperature of the projected image. Most professional projectors in movie houses use arc lamp illumination and are therefore best balanced for daylight-type colour films. Amateur, industrial and school projectors usually have standard 3200 K lamps suitable for Type B colour films. If higher speed processing is available for the film you are using it would be advisable to use it. For instance, with some high speed colour films, processing to 2½ times greater exposure speed is available from the manufacturer's or independent labs.

Do not use shutter speeds faster than 1/20 s. Better still, try to remain at 1/15 s and select instants in the movie when action is virtually non-existent. The reason for such slow speeds is that the movie projector shutter is constantly opening and closing. At faster speeds than 1/30 s (and perhaps even then) you might shoot when the projector shutter is closing or partially closed. At 1/15 s you can be assured of an image. Your through-the-lens meter should be sufficiently adequate for obtaining an accurate reading to set the correct aperture. With all cameras which automatically set the shutter speed in the automatic exposure mode, use manual operation to prevent the shutter speed from accidentally rising too high.

You get the best results by projecting on a plain white surface rather than a lenticular grid or beaded screen. These tend to make images appear less sharp to the camera if not to the naked eye.

TV pictures

Pictures made directly from your TV set are also possible. However, here the production of the image is quite different than in motion pictures. In movies, complete images are projected intermittently. The TV image is produced by a single luminescent spot within the picture tube which travels back and forth across the face of the tube at phenomenal speed. Because the tube glows after the spot passes and your eye tends to retain the image after the spot begins to change or fade, the TV screen appears to form a complete picture made up of many horizontal lines. These lines are interlaced with the spot covering the whole picture tube in about 1/50 s. But in this time, the spot has only traced every other line. Now it goes back and fills in the missing lines. The complete picture is thus filled in about 1/25 s. These are the figures for the British 50 Hz system. In the US 60 Hz system, the picture is complete in 1/30 s. However, because a focal plane shutter is actually a travelling slit, taking much longer than 1/25 or 1/30 s for its total travel time, do not use shutter speeds higher than 1/8 s. For black-and-white pictures try a fast film of ASA 400 or so. For proper colour choose a fairly high speed colour film balanced for daylight. A CC40R filter is advisable to bring out the reds properly. Follow your behind-the-lens meter suggestions for exposure. For best quality, adjust the TV set so that the contrast is slightly less than normal (copying any picture increases contrast). Adjust the brightness control so that both highlight and shadow areas of the TV image show detail. Using a colour film with an ASA of about 160, your exposure should be in the neighbourhood of 1/8 s at *f*/4 to *f*/5.6.

Action and underwater photography

For many years it has been standard practice to analyse action subjects by their speed and the angle at which they are moving in relation to the camera. From this you can establish some sort of table to predict the shutter speeds needed, to 'freeze' the movement. Such frozen action can be very useful from an analytical point of view, but hardly looks natural.

The main problem, though, is that the tables apply only to the fastest moving *part* of the subject. You only have to analyse a man running to see the problem. While his whole body may be moving at a rate of so many miles per hour, his legs and arms are not moving at this rate – they are going faster in some instances and slower in others. The shutter speed that is sufficient to 'stop' the forward body motion may not stop the arms and legs. Similarly, the speed needed just to 'halt' a locomotive is not enough to stop its wheels and piston rods. An aeroplane 'frozen' in mid-air will still have blurred propellers and so on.

Stopping action

If the action must be stopped completely for analytical purposes, using an electronic flash unit with its very short flash duration is probably the best method if its use is feasible. If not, a speed of 1/250 s should stop a runner at right angles to the camera. 1/125 s is often enough to halt children at play. If action is coming at the camera or at a 45 degree angle to it, speeds of the camera need not be as high to halt the action.

When action is travelling at right angles to the camera, panning with the action can yield a more natural result as the eye actually sees the action. The main subject will be adequately sharp at speeds of 1/125 s or so with background blurred, producing a visual indication of motion. In recent years, though, photographers have made more use of movement to picture very blurred subjects.

How to depict action

It is not always wise to use the fastest shutter speed to 'freeze' all action; it may look stationary. By creative use of a slight blur we can produce an image which looks much closer to what our eyes actually see. For a person running at about 15–25 miles per hour:

1/8 s: too much blur, no subject visible.
1/30 s: good resemblance of motion but no subject sharpness.
1/250 s: slight rear edge blur on leg but not enough to suggest action.
1/1000 s: completely frozen.
1/30 s and pan: by swinging camera with subject, background blurs, heightening sense of motion.
1/15 s and flash: Existing light creates one blurred image, flash creates second, double image.

Direction of movement also affects sharpness; as here at 1/60 s.
At right angles: partially blurred.
At 45° angle: less blur.
Head on: virtually no blur.

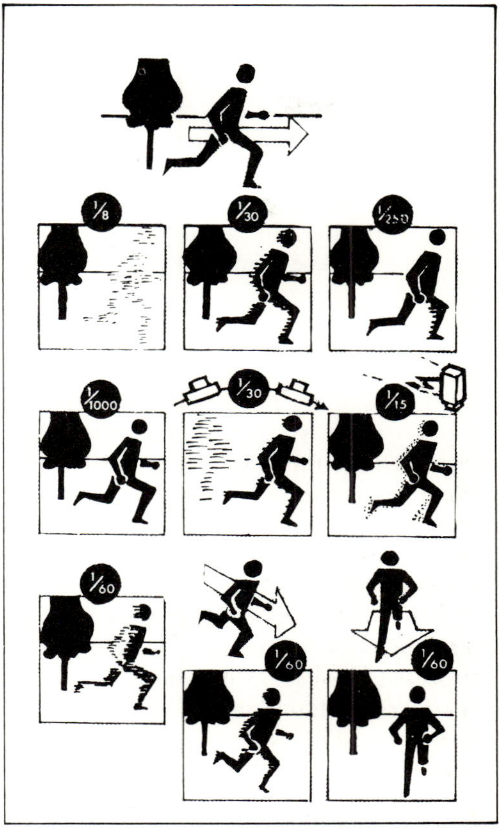

Underwater photography

Nikon and Nikkormat cameras can be operated at depths to about 11 m using flexible plastic bag camera housings.

The best underwater housings are of metal or clear plastic like this one which allows you to set and check controls. Flash is off to side to avoid scatter from murky water.

All objects below the surface appear 1/3 larger and closer than they really are.

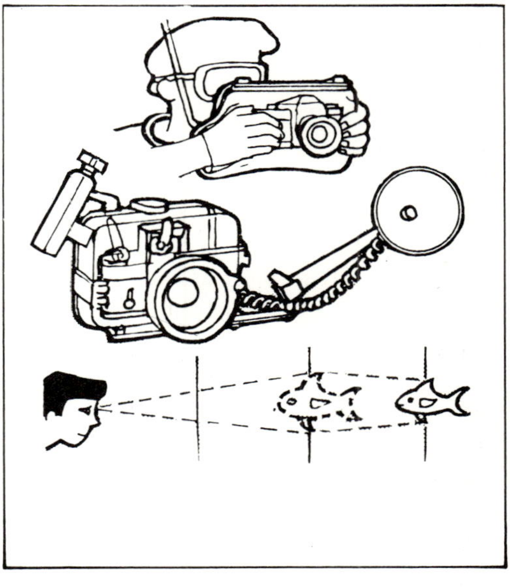

Image size

The blur at any shutter speed is proportional to the relative movement of the image. So the smaller the reproduction, the less the blur, whether the small image is produced by subject distance or by a short focus lens. However, if you enlarge wide-angle or distant images to the same size as long-focus or close shots, you find exactly the same amount of motion blur. Only two factors can alter the amount of blur in motion: the shutter speed, and whether you have panned with the action.

Look for peaks

While many action subjects such as a runner or a train travelling are continuous, there are many other action subjects which reach a specific peak – a pole vaulter is a human example, a ball tossed in the air is another. At the very height of the vault, when all the movement has stopped and just an instant before the downward motion begins, a speed of even 1/30 s is enough to produce a sharp picture. Being able to press the shutter release just a split instant before a peak occurs is one of the necessary skills of a master sports photographer. To a certain point it can be sensed. But the perfection of this technique of stopping action requires much practice and experience. However, unlike the constant action halted by a very fast speed, a frozen action at the peak does seem natural because it is just as the eye sees it with almost all motion stopped.

Lenses

For any type of sports or action photos, zoom lenses are excellent, since you can continue to maintain exact framing of your subject while it moves. The zoom lens choice depends to a great extent on the type of event to be covered and the distance you will be from the subject. A spectator seated in an arena at a distance will need a far longer tele zoom than will a news photographer right at the point of action. A good all-round zoom is the 80–200 mm *f*/4 Zoom Nikkor.

If you do not own a zoom lens, a moderate to long tele is a fine choice if you are a spectator. News photographers often opt for shorter lenses, even wide-angle, when they are allowed right down on the field of action. Incidentally, a small but solid tripod is really useful in the stalls. You can often set it up right in front of you. If this is impossible, a monopod (single pole of a tripod) serves as a good support.

Underwater

Nikon does make a specialised compact underwater camera, the Nikonos, which requires no additional protective housing. But there are advantages using a Nikon or Nikkormat instead. The reflex cameras are easily adaptable to close focusing for small marine life with no need for additional accessories. Also, you already own a Nikon or Nikkormat and therefore do not have to purchase a special additional camera for underwater work (although, of course, you must get the underwater housing).

While Nippon Kogaku itself makes no underwater housings for its camera, there are many specialised manufacturers who do. These are made of either transparent plastic material or metal (except for the lens port which must be glass for best-quality light transmission). Metal housings have the advantage of being sturdier, and often stand greater pressure and thus greater depth. They are usually more expensive than plastic housings. Plastic housings, however, do allow you to see aperture, distance and shutter speed settings more easily. Most important, the clear plastic lets you see any small leaks immediately so that you can prevent damage to the camera.

Unfortunately, while the joys of underwater photography are great, the dangers to photo equipment are also great. Any defect in the housing or its water-tight seals, or human error in closing the housing, can quickly lead to total destruction of the camera within. A Nikon or Nikkormat immersed in water – particularly salt water – can almost always be written off as a total loss. By the time the camera can be rushed to a qualified repairman, corrosion will have done its work and usually complete disassembly, cleaning and replacement of damaged parts plus reassembly works out more costly than buying a new camera. The greatest care must be taken by the underwater photographer to make certain that his equipment has been pretested for leakage and is in proper working order, and that the housing has been sealed securely.

Nature photography

The world of nature photography ranges from the infinitesimally small creatures, visible only through microscopes, to the infinitely large world of scenics. The art and practice of photomicroscopy are quite specialised, depending largely on the aim of the study and the microscopic equipment available, and are beyond the scope of this book other than the information previously supplied on the Nikon equipment specially designed for connecting camera to microscope. The other end of the nature spectrum, the scenic, we have already covered. Between, however, we have a vast array of subjects from insect photography through flowers, plants, birds and animals – wild and domesticated.

Insects

Close examination of tiny creatures, be they mosquito wrigglers, beetles, spiders or ants, reveals a fascinating miniature world, often brilliant and jewel-like.

Normal 50 mm lenses on a Nikon or Nikkormat are not the best optics for picturing them. At their closest focusing distances, normal lenses do not provide a sufficiently large image. The use of close-up lenses or bellows, of course, rectifies this, but the front of lens-to-subject distance with a normal lens is perilously short.

Small creatures do not react well to photographers and lenses which might be construed as endangering them. Also, the close focus distance produces unpleasant perspective. Most photographers prefer to work with lenses or at least double normal focal length when photographing insects. The Medical Nikkor lenses (see page 253) are great favourites with insect photographers since they allow greater distance from the subject at the same image size magnification as a normal lens; and are equipped with built-in focusing and light sources. However, the average Nikon or Nikkormat owner will probably wish to adapt his own daily equipment to take insect pictures.

Probably the handiest Nikkor lens for insect photography is the 105 mm or 200 mm *f*/4 Micro-Nikkor since each provides far more film-to-subject distance than does the 55 mm *f*/3.5 or *f*/2.8 Micro-Nikkor. A standard 105 mm *f*/2.5 Nikkor can also be used with extension tubes or close-up lenses, but your working ability is not continuous in distance. You have to change extension tubes or close-up lenses as you shift magnifications and focusing distances. Also, non-micro lenses were computed for normal ranges of operation from their marked closest focusing ranges to infinity. At extreme close-focusing ranges, using either close-up lenses or extension tubes, they do not deliver as good definition as the Micro Nikkors. Still, for the occasional insect photographer either a 105 or 135 mm lens plus tubes or close-up lenses can be employed successfully. Zoom lenses should usually be avoided for such close work with or without extension tubes or close-up lenses, since their definition at such close distances is often inferior to single focal length lenses.

Lighting

The easiest way of photographing insects is with natural lighting since your through-the-lens meter can be used without any special treatment. However, existing light, except extremely bright daylight (in which you are probably not going to encounter insects), is generally insufficient illumination. To bring out the most detail and texture in insects (and to stop action!) you need artificial lighting. Continuous illumination such as floodlighting is inadvisable as no sensible insect will stand for it for very long. Some photographers do capture insects, place them in refrigerators for varying lengths of time to slow them down or immobilise them completely. This would allow the use of floods, but other biologists claim that a frozen or immobile insect is no more natural than a frozen or immobile person. The answer, of course, is electronic flash, but its use for extreme close-up work is, to say the least, tricky, because of the necessary exposure compensations needed when focusing at very close distances, except with those Nikon cameras having TTL auto-flash measuring capabilities.

Ringlights

Many photographers use Nikon ringlights – electronic flash tubes in the form of a ring that fits in front of your lens. Instructions for computing proper exposure usually accompany each unit. No general instructions for all such units can be given since the distribution of the light changes the closer you approach the subject, and this differs from unit to unit. For many years ringlights were the principal type of illumination employed by insect photographers. However, ringlights have some distinct liabilities. They deliver an even overall illumination with no shadow detail. Consequently the subject is apt to appear two-dimensional and without surface detail or texture. Some ringlight owners overcome this by masking off parts of the ring with black tape, thereby providing the ring with a semblance of directional lighting.

A now popular alternative is to use a small standard electronic flash head mounted on the camera but angled downwards toward the subject; or even multiple flash heads attached to rings at the front of the lens. These heads can be angled as needed and different effects produced depending on the varying flash-to-subject distances and angles of the flash to the subject. Basically what such photographers are doing is to use the same lighting techniques with tiny subjects as insects as they would with full sized subjects at standard photographing distances. One lamp can be a main light source and the other lamp a fill-in, if desired. However, since electronic flash is instantaneous and these small lamp heads don't have built-in modelling lights, the photographer must have considerable experience in lighting insects to predict just how the light from two lampheads will affect the subject.

Exposure

Exposure calculation with electronic flash is complicated because of the many variables of increased exposure needed depending on the magnification required plus the actual pattern delivered by the flash-head when used at such close distances. Most insect photographers devise some specific setups at various magnifications and distances, arrive at the proper exposure for these through trial and error at a preliminary shooting and then use this knowledge and specific setup when actually taking pictures.

However, this is a rather lengthy and rigid technique which requires a good memory for just what exposure was required previously. Fortunately almost all of the auto-exposure electronic flash units today can operate at film-to-subject distances down to 0.6 m or so, quite adequate for close nature work, particularly if you are using a 100 mm lens or longer which increases film-to-subject distance. With the Nikon F3 and FG, the proper electronic flash exposure will automatically be computed and set. With other Nikons and Nikkormats, auto flash units with separate on-flash sensors will usually produce proper exposure if aimed directly at the subject. However, in very close work where the lens indicates additional exposure is needed, simply use a larger-than-suggested lens aperture to compensate for the subject magnification. For instance, if the lens you're using suggests a 2× exposure increase and your auto flash aperture is *f*/8, just open the diaphragm to *f*/5.6.

Flora

Flowers and plants provide other sources of subject material for close-up photography. They are best photographed by existing light. Relatively long

Close-up work outdoors

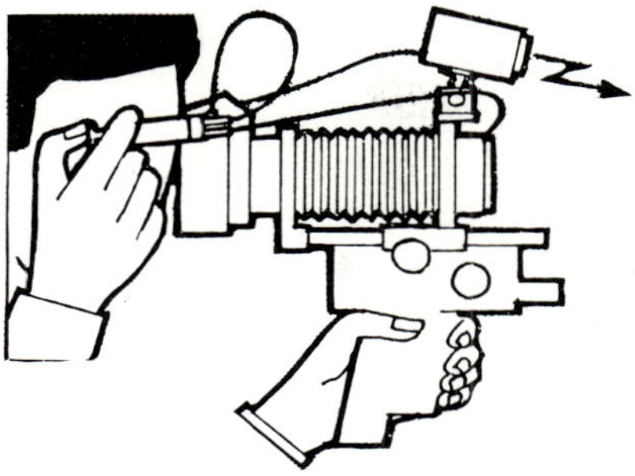

For sharpest, best-lit outdoor nature close-ups you need electronic flash.

With bellows, double cable release allows you to focus at full aperture and close down lens to shooting aperture before shutter is released. Flash unit at lens position provides constant exposure from 0.8 m to 1:1 image ratio. Note pistol grip focusing.

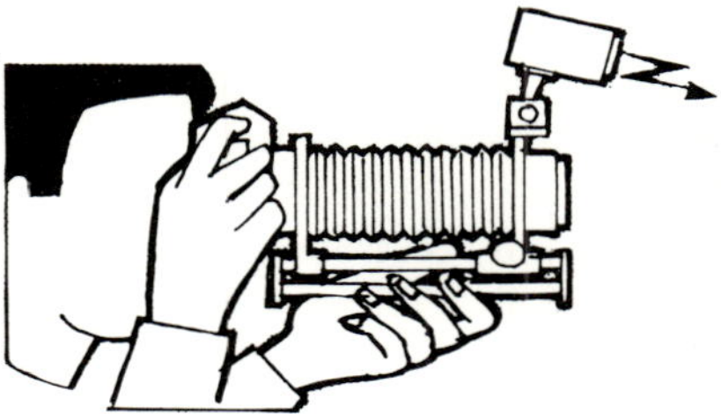

Alternative set-up with regular bellows such as Nikon can be used with manual closing down of lens. Flash can be mounted and used in same way however.

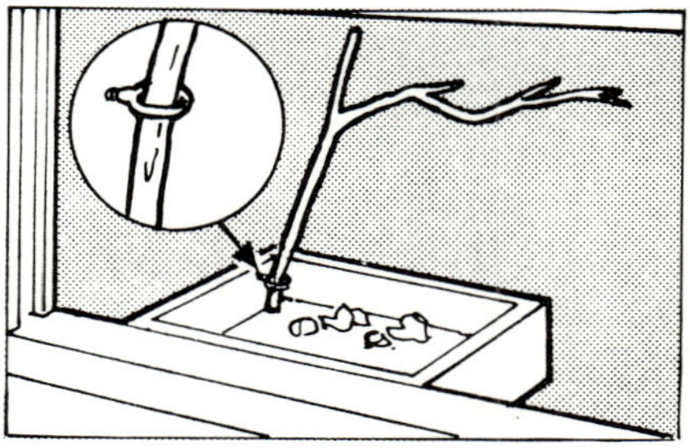

By attaching twig to windowsill bird feeder, you can give your winged subject a natural perch. No one will know shot was made at a feeder.

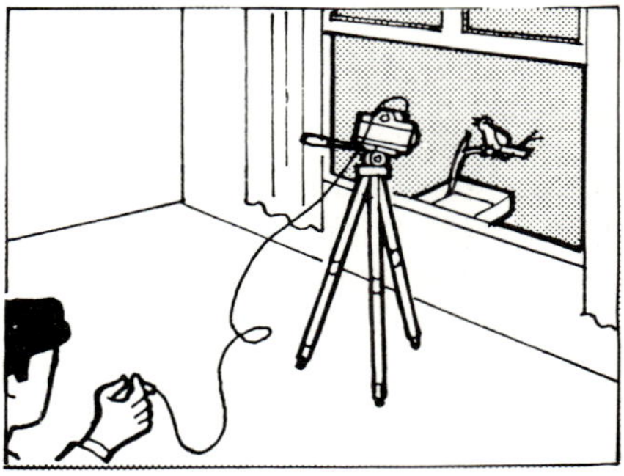

To avoid scaring birds, set up camera and tripod near open window with focus and framing on twig perch. Wait for bird and proper pose. Release shutter with long cable or air release.

exposures are sometimes possible with these inanimate objects, but wind can be a major problem. Where you might wish to photograph individual flowers or blossoms, a cardboard cylinder can sometimes be dropped over the plant or flower to prevent movement. You then shoot down through the open cylinder end, but this can create a background problem. The colour of the cylinder can be of green or brown for a most natural appearance.

Wild flowers

Perhaps wild flower photography holds the most fascination. The spring and summer months in most climes offer a constantly changing landscape of wildflowers which must first be found, identified, inspected for the best specimens and photographed before they fade from view until next year. A knowledgeable friend is the best wildflower identification aid, but a small pocket guide is also helpful.

You must spend much time flat on your stomach peering across if not upwards at tiny blossoms. If you don't get down to flower level you will not get very good pictures. Don't inadvertently crush some other valuable wildflowers with your feet or body. Your elbows resting on the ground make excellent camera supports when not working with a pocket tripod. If you find lowering yourself to ground level difficult, a waist-level viewfinder can be of help. As in sports photography where there is a specific peak to the action when you should shoot – in flower photography it's when the breeze dies for an instant. At most times flower photographs can be made a 1/125 s (even at 1/30 s on a breezeless day). Experiment with different apertures. Shoot at a small aperture and at a large one to see which type of flower or plant picture appeals to you most. I find nothing more satisfying on a spring or summer day than to wander alone through a field of wildflowers with a Nikon or Nikkormat!

For the most scientifically-minded Nikon or Nikkormat photographer there is the excitement of examining an opening bud or flower in a series of timed lapse sequence photographs using motor drive and an intervalometer to make the exposure at set intervals.

Birds

There are two ways of photographing birds: make them come to you or go out after them. Since the techniques are quite dissimilar, we'll discuss the simple one first, attracting and then photographing birds at home.

To photograph birds successfully at home, all you need is a bird feeder fastened to a window and some bird seed. Surprisingly this often works even in a city apartment many floors up, although your visitors will be fewer and perhaps not of too great assortment. Again some identification aid – a friend or good guide book – is most useful.

To photograph birds, set your Nikon or Nikkormat on a tripod, position it near the open window where the bird-feeder is located and then just wait. Inevitably the birds will come and you'll be able to capture them even with a 50 mm lens. If you remain fairly still and make no swift movements, the birds will ignore you after a few minutes so you can click and wind film with no problems. If your presence seems to annoy the birds, focus on the feeder, attach a long cable release to your camera and fire from a way back. A longer focal length lens – 105 or 135 mm – is also an asset, while a good zoom such as the 80–200 mm *f*/4 Nikkor allows you to remain fairly far back from the window but provide different compositions with no need to move the camera forward or backward. If your lens does not provide as large an image on the film as you would wish, even at its closest focusing, a short extension tube in the case of single focal length lenses or a mild close-up lens such as the No. 0 or 1 in the case of a single focal length or a zoom might be needed – particularly with small birds.

Try to position the feeder in a window where you will get more than just heavy backlight. Backlight only will produce silhouettes or near-silhouettes. Sidelighting is preferable. You may wish to place your feeder a couple of metres or so away from your window for better lighting.

A feeder by itself, however, does not guarantee the best bird photos. You certainly can photograph the birds, but the feeder will always be in the picture as well. This can easily be corrected. Attach two eyelet screws vertically to an end of the feeder so that they can hold a small branch or twig. Then select an appropriate branch and insert it through the two eyelets. The birds will soon learn to light on the branch or twig before or after eating. You can frame your photos on the twig. For variety, keep a number of different branches or twigs with buds, blossoms or leaves. No one will be able to tell that you were not actually photographing the birds in the trees. Birds establish a specific pattern of eating. They may fly first to a nearby bush or tree, then take off for the branch and then land on the feeder perch. After eating, they may reverse the procedure. By learning their travel plans, you can anticipate actions and get some interesting taking off and landing photos. I found that if I snapped the shutter just after a specific bird left the feeder perch, I would automatically have a picture of the bird landing on the attached branch. To stop all bird wing action, you may have to use electronic flash, but at 1/125 s or so you can retain a certain amount of blur which does appear natural. With the bird perched on the branch, you can get a very sharp photo at 1/30 or 1/60 s.

Besides the birds which eat from your feeder, you will soon discover other birds which are attracted and will eat the excess from the ground. Good pictures can be made of them, particularly in the winter when they contrast with fallen snow.

If there is not sufficient light for adequate exposure or you need additional action-stopping speed, try using electronic flash. While the birds may at first flinch, they quickly come to accept the short bursts. If you are using a longish lens and are somewhat back in the room, use your flash off-camera, closer to the feeder. Even at 1/1000 s, about the speed of many smal manual electronic flash units, the complete movement of the bird – his wings for instance – may not be stilled. However, by using a small automatic exposure electronic flash, you can achieve far higher speed bursts for better action-stopping. However, with an automatic electronic flash unit, make certain there is an object close by the bird which will guarantee you the needed reflection for the automatic sensor of the flash.

While flash is useful for stopping the action of the birds, it may create a disparity with a brightly illuminated bird against an underexposed or black background.

If you do feed the birds, you can keep them nearby both summer and winter. Once you start feeding birds in late fall or early winter, you should continue to do so or they will starve. If you go on vacation or holiday, make certain some friend will continue to bird-feed in your absence.

Birds in natural surroundings

Stalking birds, whether around your home, in forest or bird sanctuary, is far more difficult than shooting pictures near your window next to a bird feeder. Professional bird photographers often go to great lengths and spend much time tracking down birds and then build elaborate hides in which to remain concealed. While some photographers carry tripods around to support the long lenses almost essential for field photography, most tend to rely on hand-holding the lens or steadying it, if possible, by using a monopod, handy fence or other support.

Lenses of 400 mm and upwards are needed, since a close approach to wild birds is not usually possible. There is a great controversy among bird photographers concerning the use of the all-glass tele lenses such as the 400 mm *f*/5.6 Auto Nikkor, which is bulky and heavy, and the 500 mm *f*/8 Reflex Nikkor which is lighter and relatively compact. The all-glass lens focuses as close as 5 m, and provides a variable aperture for sharpness and exposure control. The Reflex Nikkor gives a 25 per cent larger image, provides focusing to 4 m, but has only a single (*f*/8) aperture.

Out-of-focus highlights, instead of being plain discs, become reproductions of the mirror lens design itself, forming rings. This disturbs some photographers.

The 400 mm *f*/5.6 Auto Nikkor transmits about as much light as its *f*/5.6 aperture implies. The Reflex Nikkor, like all mirror lenses, is actually closer to *f*/9.5, making quite a disparity in light transmission between the two lenses.

The best time for bird photography is in the spring when the birds have returned from the south (if you are living in northern climes) and the leaves

Getting sharp pictures with tele lenses

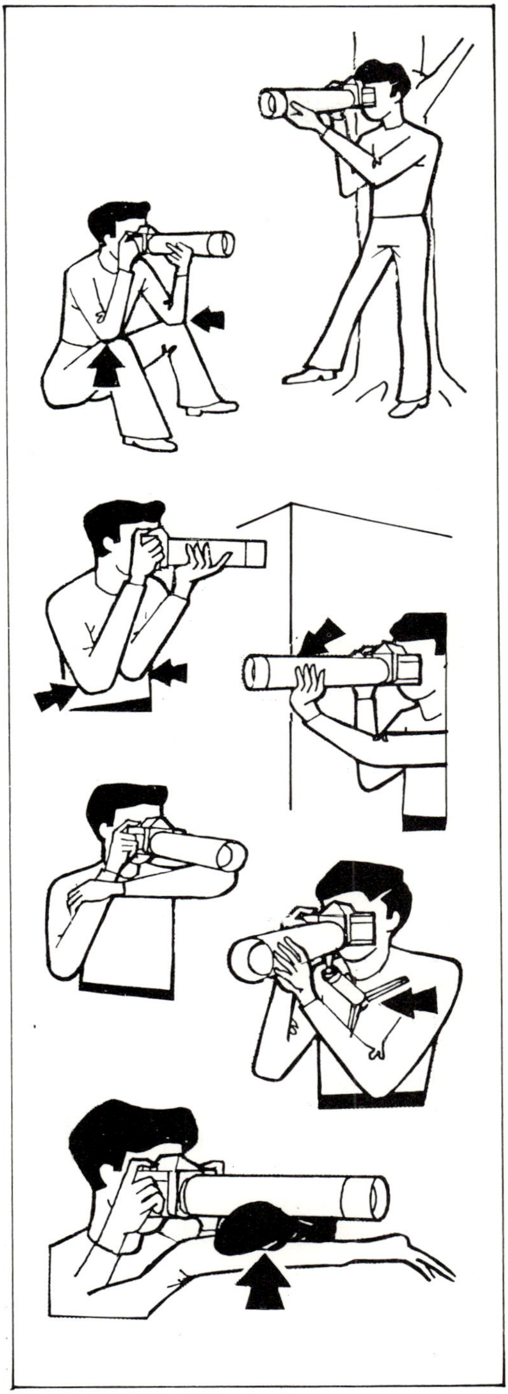

Most telephoto lens pictures are unsharp, not because of subject movement, but from the photographer's inability to hold the lens steady. Here are some helpful hints:

Sit with the knees drawn up. Rest elbows in soft depression inside of knee area.

To prevent swaying, lean against any convenient object.

If you must hand-hold with no outside support, cradle lens in left hand, control camera with right, dig elbows into body for as much support as possible.

If there's a vertical support handy, such as a building corner, hold lens against it tightly.

Alternative to stance directly above, preferred by some professionals.

Small table top tripod attached to lens or camera, resting on your chest, makes good additional support.

Famous African safari support has wide application. Make small beanbag to use as camera rest on any surface.

of the trees are still buds or at least small so the birds can be indeed seen. Heavy foliage in late spring and summer has the further disadvantage of cutting down illumination, forcing you to longer exposures, a difficult situation with tele lenses that are hard to hand-hold and by nature have small apertures to begin with.

Electronic flash in field work has generally been considered impractical. However, if you are shooting from a hide, you can buy or build a 'tele-flash' unit. The flash units mount directly on the camera. These units are especially useful where the birds are in darkish places, such as a nest under the eaves of a roof. The stopping ability of electronic flash is an additional aid.

The bird photographer doing field work must learn to hold the camera and lens rock-steady. This takes practice. Hold the right side of the camera body and operate rapid wind, shutter release and, in the case of Nikons, speed changes with your right hand. With your left hand, support the long lens at its centre of balance, if possible. However, the focusing ring should fall naturally in the left hand grasp so you can focus continually. Draw your elbows into your body as closely as possible with the left elbow actually digging in if practicable. Many photographers find various shoulder stock and pistol support grips useful, but these are very much a personal matter.

Other animals

Because they are often much larger than birds, you can often get good pictures of wild mammals with moderate telephoto lenses. If you are able to photograph big game from a vehicle, zoom lenses are very handy for composing the picture precisely – a most useful feature in areas where it is often difficult to move your vehicle exactly as you want. I have found a far simpler solution for shooting from vehicles. Make a small bag from about 55 cm square of old denim or similar material. It should have a zip-fastener one side. Then you can carry it empty, and fill it up when you get to your destination. Fill it about two thirds full with small dried pulse such as lentils or peas. When available, small plastic beads make an excellent filling while even sand or sawdust can be pressed into service in an emergency. You then rest the camera and lens with the bean bag on any suitable part of the vehicle. Hold the lens down onto the bag with your left hand. The bean bag becomes the camera and lens support. It has the advantage of being easily portable and, positionable just about anywhere, and cushions the lens against minor shocks. Using a bean bag, I have successfully held lenses of up to 600 mm focal length at speeds as low as 1/30 s. The bean bag tends to absorb shutter vibration as well.

Equipment care and storage

Camera equipment can only be counted on to work properly if it is properly cared for. A Nikon, Nikkormat, Nikkor lens or related piece of equipment must be handled as the fine instrument which it is. While the manufacturer has made each unit sufficiently rugged to withstand hard use, they are not intended to survive abuse or gross mishandling.

Proper maintenance of equipment should be divided into three areas: correct procedures in use; storage; and when cleaning and preparing the equipment for operation. Let's start out with the first, the camera in use.

Carrying cases

The best method of preserving the finish of your camera is to carry it and all equipment in individual leather cases. Many amateurs do just this, opening the case only when necessary to make a photograph. However, as pointed out earlier in this book, it is most inconvenient and time-wasting to carry a camera in its ever-ready case (often dubbed the never-ready case). It simply takes too long to unsnap the front, get it out of the way and go into action.

If you are also carrying individual accessory lenses and other items, the beautifully made, very well-cushioned lens and other cases are really too bulky. Such cases also require too much time to open for convenient use in the field. Professionals usually adopt equipment-carrying styles that are really horrendous – often dumping bare cameras and lenses into compartmentless carrying cases so they can grab the camera, lens or accessory immediately and use it. The equipment is usually jostled together, paint chips off showing the brass underneath, lens rims and camera edges get bent, everything becomes scratched and the equipment, even if working perfectly well inwardly, has a most unhappy outward appearance, often thought of as 'looking professional'.

However, even for professionals such treatment is not advisable or necessary. A dented camera part may result in improper film plane registration, a bent lens lip may make the threading of accessories impossible. Certainly the proper compromise between such no-protection and the overprotection of individual cases must be found. This secret is in the judicious choice of a properly compartmented gadget bag. Like the three chairs in the story of the three bears, it should not be too large or too small, but just right. An investigation into the many camera cases made available by Nikon is first called for since the compartments have been specifically designed with the size of Nikon equipment in mind. Only if you cannot find precisely what you need should you look elsewhere.

For general photography, if you do intend to carry only one camera and lens, just unsnap and remove the front of your ever-ready case and carry your camera by the neckstrap with the camera-body half of the case in place. The neckstrap should be sufficiently short to allow you to sling it over your shoulder but have the camera itself protected under your arm close to your elbow. There is a disadvantage to such a system. The case must be removed for camera loading.

When not in use, keep a lens cap over the lens. While the Nikkor lens caps are convenient and can be replaced or removed almost instantly, they do have a habit of catching on things and springing off. I have found that threaded metal caps are an excellent alternative. They fasten securely, are handy to carry in the pocket, and when threaded in place give excellent protection to those delicate front lens threads. If you have Nikkor lenses from 20 mm upwards to 200 mm, all you may need are 52 mm thread-in caps. They will be interchangeable on all or nearly all of your lenses.

The neckstrap itself should have some sort of shoulder pad with a coarse or rubberised gripping undersurface to prevent the strap from slipping from your shoulders. It should also distribute the camera weight more evenly when you're carrying the camera, or when the camera is around your neck. Neckstraps should be kept as short as possible to prevent the camera from swinging out of centrifugal force when you turn around.

As soon as you carry an additional lens or other somewhat bulky accessory, you will need the aforementioned carrying case. The case should hold your camera and either lens and provide a separate compartment or a separator for the lens accessory you are not using. And don't forget that every lens needs a front and back lens cap. Do not accept non-Nikkor back caps. While many companies make back lens caps which supposedly fit all Nikkors, I have found that they do not: they fit some lenses and not others. While the Nikon back lens covers are of a fairly brittle plastic material and are liable to split or break if fastened with too much enthusiasm, they are still the best and, luckily, relatively inexpensive.

If you have but one compartment, some protection will be needed to prevent the equipment from knocking together. I have found that soft flannel pouches, the same type often used by jewellers to store silverware or other precious items, offer good protection. Such pouches are usually in the form of deep envelopes with flaps. You place the lens or accessory within, and wrap the remaining material around the item a few times before placing it in the case. The item can be removed swiftly and taken from the pouch. With interchangeable lenses, you can remove one lens, slip another in the empty pouch and drop it back into your camera case. Commercial lens pouches, often with cute little drawstrings, are most unhandy. Either you must try extracting the lens by gripping its front edge between thumb and first finger, or you must turn the pouch upside down and shake – a most dangerous procedure. The flannel pouch need only be unrolled and the lens removed. If you can't find such flannel pouches, I would recommend that you have a good seamstress make them for you out of old flannel garments.

Should your carrying bag be hard or soft? Many photographers feel that only a hard-sided bag offers proper protection; but I have found hard bags too bulky and limiting, yet have never had trouble with items being damaged in soft-sided bags provided I protect individual items as already explained.

While one camera and two lenses can safely be carried together in a soft case with no compartmentation (if each item is wrapped), the addition of more equipment demands compartments. They also assist you in remembering the location of each lens or accessory without rummaging around. Each item should be reachable and replaceable with no need for you to look into the bag. You should be able to keep on the move, watching your subjects, while easily interchanging equipment safely as you go. That's the goal, anyway. Camera bags with specific compartments for many items are indeed handy, but beware of bags with only clips to hold lenses. Consider what might happen if a lens becomes unclipped. Compartments are much better. If you do find a bag you like but it does not have sufficient compartments, take it to a good leather shop or shoemaker. A leather worker can sew in dividers or compartments for you.

Does the camera bag need to be of leather? Certainly not. Today's substitutes are excellent, longer lasting, do not spot with rain and are much cheaper. However, most do have a tendency to tear, particularly if you overload a bag and put stress on it. Tearing usually occurs right where the carrying strap is fastened to the bag. The best ones have carrying straps which go all around the bag, thus supporting the weight at the bottom as well as the bag itself at the sides. How efficient is your camera bag? Check it. Load up equipment and see how quickly you can locate items, exchange them and put them safely back into the bag.

If you find yourself at a complete loss as to the size of bag you need, since sometimes you take a little equipment and sometimes much, you may need two bags. But photographers, whether amateurs and professionals, do have a tendency to carry more equipment than they need and can comfortably carry. Keep your load down as small as possible.

Now a word about those very handsome and somewhat expensive cast aluminium or sheet-metal cases with foam-lined interiors that many professionals use. They are truly excellent for transporting large amounts of equipment when you are travelling. I have even travelled half-way around the world with large quantities of delicate underwater housings, flash units, lenses and cameras, using such cases. However, these cases are primarily for transporting equipment. Once you arrive at your destination and are ready to take pictures, you will find them heavy, bulky and inconvenient for use as gadget bags, which they are not.

Adverse conditions

So far we have been speaking of standard operating procedures. However, obviously adverse weather conditions will cause you to make some essential changes or alterations.

If it is raining or you think you will encounter much dust, dirt, salt spray and the like, each piece of equipment should be wrapped in a plastic bag such as is used in the kitchen for keeping foods in the refrigerator. The bags should be fairly deep so you can wrap the excess plastic around the equipment as added protection. While it might even seem sensible to use fasteners or rubber bands to seal the bags, I have found in practice that you also seal in some air which makes the bags rather bulky. Carry extra plastic bags with you. They take little room and you may need them if you rip those you have in use.

Care

Advice on proper use of equipment is almost always obvious. Don't force any controls, don't be rough, and keep all equipment protected against dust and dirt. Do your best to keep your fingers away from all glass to prevent fingermarks.

While we will examine the methods of cleaning cameras and lenses later, suffice to say now that only a soft brush, chamois skin or lens tissue should be used to clean lenses. Don't weaken and use your handkerchief or the silicon-impregnated cloth which often comes with cameras or lenses (we'll see why later) or the end of your tie, even if made of silk (it probably has surface grit on it). The item which will probably need cleaning most in the field is your eyepiece. Not only is it subject to fingerprints, but the oil on your eyelashes can also make it grimy. Many photographers, unaware of this, are quite mystified when the view through the prism suddenly appears misty, lacking contrast and is hard to focus. Usually this indicates that the eyepiece needs cleaning. Useful oddments for maintenance that you should carry, besides lens tissue, are: small bottle of lens cleaning fluid, soft lens brush, some painter's black masking tape, and a small set of jeweller's screwdrivers.

The black tape is quite useful for all sorts of immediate repairs. It can block light leaks almost anywhere (such as if you lose a small camera screw), and can repair damaged camera cases temporarily. The screwdriver set can help you keep all camera and lens screws tight. Make certain they are of the proper size. Nikon in recent years has favoured cross-head screws instead of single-slotted ones, so do get the right screwdrivers. Never use screwdrivers that are too large or too small, as these will not only scratch the screwhead, but also damage the slot.

Storage

So much for in-use protection. Many problems occur from non-use. The camera and lenses are simply ignored until they are again needed – be it in a day or a year. They are then hauled out and expected to function perfectly.

If you are going to use the camera again within the next few days, you need to do more than store the camera properly – in a cool, dry place out of direct sunlight. However, if you are working or living in a tropical climate where fungus is known to be a hazard for optics, precautions must be taken, even for a few days. Alas, quite often, once fungus starts, it cannot be overcome. In such climes, the purchase of silica gel or other dessicants is most advisable. The equipment should be placed in airtight plastic bags along with the silica gel, properly dried out (baked at over 350°F for 30 minutes). The silica gel should be re-treated whenever camera equipment is removed and put back – unless the gell has a colour-warning system which indicates when it is exhausted and needs baking. In such cases, of course, just follow the colour warning.

If you intend to leave the camera for more than a few days, you should remove all batteries from the equipment. If you keep them in the refrigerator (within a plastic bag to prevent them from getting too much moisture), they will last longer. Batteries left in cameras or other equipment tend to corrode or at least build up a thin layer of corrosion which can possibly interfere with proper electrical connection. Perhaps nothing may happen in a week or so of non-use. But why take chances? After being left for weeks at a time, the camera equipment, just like an inactive person, needs exercise. While I have not personally noticed any difference between storing a Nikon with shutter wound or not wound, it does seem sensible that the camera should be stored with the shutter release and the spring tension removed. However, I wouldn't deliberately waste a picture frame just to release the tension of the shutter. On the other hand, film shouldn't be left in the camera for weeks – particularly colour film – since more damage can be caused to the film's balance than can be caused to the shutter by being tensioned.

Exercising the camera is simple. Use it at least five times at each shutter speed with the lens set at *f*/16 or *f*/22 to move its automatic diaphragm the most. Attach the accessory lenses and give them a workout of at least five times at smallest aperture and high shutter speed. Store cameras in their cases. If you must put a bare camera in a drawer with other items, put it in a plastic bag to prevent dust, fluff or other airborne material from getting to it. All lenses should be capped. If you have a camera body alone, it should have a body cap.

Cleaning

We now come to the cleaning of the equipment. Like a good watch, your Nikon or Nikkormat camera and normal lens should be cleaned, lubricated and adjusted about every three years under ordinary use, or even little or no use. If you are a professional with the camera operating nearly every day, it should have the treatment about once a year. The lubricants in cameras become gummy or tend to break down. Shutter speeds can slip from best possible speed adjustment. The needle galvanometer (if pressed) may need zeroing correctly. I have found that lenses need attention much less often than cameras. (I have some Nikkors going back as far as 15 years. I am ashamed to say they have never been cleaned, lubricated or adjusted and they're working just fine.)

What can you, the owner, do for your equipment? First, let's start with the Nikon or Nikkormat camera body itself. It should be kept as clean as possible. The many nooks and crannies on the outside, particularly on top near the controls, collect dust. I use a small finely-tipped paint brush rather than the usual lens brush, since the paint brush can get into smaller areas. You can dust off the whole body with one of those blue silicon-impregnated cloths often packed with Nikon equipment – but don't use it on the lens; it is only meant for the body. Silicon, when in contact with optical coatings of lenses, tends to build up an additional chemical coating. So keep the cloths away from the lens itself.

Very little need be done inside the camera body unless you have managed to get a film chip lodged there. If you know where it is, you can take it out with tweezers. Keep your hands off the shutter blinds.

Viewfinder systems

Inevitably, dust, dirt or tiny bits of lint will wedge themselves into the optical system of your viewfinder. While they will not show up on film, and you may not even notice them when actually taking pictures, they are nonetheless annoying and you will wish to get rid of them.

With a Nikkormat camera, any sharply delineated piece of dust or lint which appears in the finder is most probably actually on the underside of your focusing screen. Remove the lens, hold your camera near your eye and very carefully insert a small thin-handled paint brush, absolutely clean, up to the focusing screen through the lens mount opening. Since you will be able to see just where the tip of the paint brush makes contact with the focusing screen, you should have little trouble in reaching the extraneous material.

Sometimes you will succeed only in moving it from one place to another, but eventually you will succeed. You can remove the material from the brush by slapping the brush handle smartly in the palm of your hand. Do not succumb to the temptation of pulling the brush hairs through your fingers to clean them. Fingers, unless very freshly washed, deposit an oil film on the brush. Never touch the brush hairs. (It's not a bad idea to wear white cotton laboratory gloves when carrying out cleaning operations.)

The same technique can also be used for cleaning the mirror. Be very careful of the mirror. Its surface must never be touched. Single lens reflex mirrors, unlike the mirrors that you have in your home, are coated on the front surface, where the coating is completely unprotected. (This is made necessary because a coating under the mirror would result in double image reflections from the top glass and the coating.) Once you have a fingerprint or smudge on the mirror, it is virtually impossible to remove. While such a smudge or small print really has little or no effect on the viewing image, it is, nevertheless, annoying to have one there. The only way such a smudge can usually be removed is by replacing the mirror.

In recent years the availability of compressed air in pressurised spray cans, usually available from photo or art stores, has made it possible for amateurs to clean camera equipment as professionals do – by using a stream of compressed air to drive off dust or lint or dirt. However, remember that if you do use such a technique, you are only dislodging the dust. It will go somewhere else and it may very well simply lodge there. Hold your camera in such a manner that the dust, once dislodged, can fall, by gravity, out of the camera instead of back into it again.

If you see dust or lint just slightly out of focus in your Nikkormat, it means that it has somehow managed to lodge on the top side of the Fresnel condensing lens or right beneath the prism. This is a rare occurrence. Only a competent repairman can remove this, since the camera has to be disassembled. Unless there is a great deal of foreign material, it may be best to leave it alone.

Nikon screens

Some Nikons are more prone than Nikkormats to foreign matter in the viewing system because they have interchangeable finders and screens. The items can be taken apart and cleaned, either with a small brush or with compressed air (I have also used a small, low-powered suction cleaner with good results). You can quickly locate the source of the foreign matter if you remember that a sharp image on the focusing screen indicates the material is directly in the screen bottom, whereas unsharp matter means it is either on top of the screen or on the bottom of the prism finder. Dust or material on the rapid return mirror won't show up in the focusing path, but it can easily become transferred to the screen bottom when the mirror moves upwards during exposure.

When taking the screen from a Nikon camera, do so over a clean, pre-washed lintless cloth which will not add additional foreign material to the screen. Never put the prism down with its exposed surface resting on another surface. While cleaning the prism bottom and screen, you may experience difficulty because of static electricity which causes the dust or lint to cling to the optics. You can treat the glass or plastic screen with an antistatic fluid or brush without doing any harm.

Don't be alarmed if you reassemble the Nikon viewing system only to find that you still have some foreign matter within the finder system and must disassemble it again. It happens to all photographers and is the small price you must pay for having the convenience and flexibility of interchangeable finders and/or screens.

Lenses

Dust, lint and similar materials that can be swept away with a brush, blown off with air or sucked out by a vacuum cleaner are the easiest matters to attend to. Removing fingerprints are the most difficult. There is scarcely a photographer, professional or amateur, who does not sooner or later get a fingerprint on the front of the lens, the rear of the lens (when changing lenses) or on the eyepiece of the camera. Often a photographer doesn't notice it until after he has already taken photographs and found them soft, hazy and full of flare (if the mark is on the front or rear of the lens). A constant watch should be undertaken for inadvertent fingerprints.

Some photographers always place a skylight filter or even a plain optical glass flat over their lenses as preventative maintenance. If a fingerprint does appear at the front, it is on the filter. The filter can quickly be removed if you must take the picture immediately. The filter can be cleaned with no worry concerning the actual lens surface.

In order to remove the oil film of a fingerprint or similar smudge, you will need more than a lens brush. Lens tissue is best, but make sure that it is indeed pure lens tissue and not a silicon-impregnated tissue manufactured for cleaning eyeglasses. Most people do not know how to use a lens tissue, and use it to rub the surface of the lens as if they were cleaning a window. The less pressure you place on optical glass (which tends to be soft) the better. I have found a rather simple and convenient way of using lens tissue which I can recommend. Remove one sheet from the pack. Roll it into a tight tube. Tear the tube in half. Use the two torn ends against the lens surface while holding onto the tubes together. In this way the springiness of the rolled lens tissue will act as a buffer against the glass.

For many years photographers have breathed on the surface of lenses to provide the tiny bit of moisture needed to clean lenses with tissue. I have found nothing wrong with this. Breathe lightly on the lens's surface and immediately begin to clean before the moisture evaporates from the glass surface. Operate in a circular manner but not from the centre to the outside, as many people do. This just drives the smudge deposit into the edge of the lens-retaining rim, where it is most difficult to remove. Instead, start from the outside and work inwards.

Don't expect to be completely successful the first time around. Cleaning a fingerprinted lens completely takes patience. Use as little pressure as possible. Don't re-use the same piece of lens tissue, since the lens tissue will be picking up the oil and you don't want to deposit it back down again. Removing the image of the fingerprint itself is not sufficient. Look at the lens surface by reflected light to see whether the oil film itself has been completely removed.

Stubborn fingerprints and smudges may need something more than a light breath. There are a number of excellent lens cleaning fluids available. Use them sparingly. Don't pour any on the lens surface. Dip the rolled-up, frayed edges of the lens tissue into the fluid. Read the directions carefully. If you get fingerprints or smudges on the focusing screens or prism surfaces, you can use the same cleaning methods as already discussed.

Screws

Virtually all cameras and lenses, including Nikons, Nikkormats and Nikkors, are fastened together with tiny screws. In older Nikons and Nikkormats, all were single-slotted. Today more and more use the cross-head screws as already mentioned. Many screws are prevented from loosening with paint or a tiny touch of lacquer, particularly on the newer equipment. However, many screws are still in rather exposed positions where they might loosen. By carefully applying the correct jeweller's screwdriver to the head, you can check tightness. I would advise you not to do this on those screws which are threaded into black metal and are painted black themselves. They seldom loosen in my experience, and any attempt to check for tightness may chip the paint in the screw head slots.

Black finish

One of the annoyances unique to those who own cameras with black finishes is the possible chipping or wearing-away of the blacking. Since this finish is factory-applied and baked, once painted it is most difficult for even an experienced camera repairman to refinish. However, if you are very handy and are accustomed to painting small objects, you can do a creditable job of touch-up. Proceed as follows:

1. Clean the areas to be refinished with a solvent such as alcohol. A cotton swab can be used.

2. Apply glossy black enamel touch-up paint available from auto supply stores. It should be applied thin with a fine, well-tipped brush in long strokes. Gouged areas may take several coats to build up the enamel to the original level of the old paint.

3. Bake the paint with a 60 or 75 watt lamp held about 15 cm from the area for about 30 minutes. If the paint shrinks, you may have to apply a coat or two more.

4. Smooth the dried paint and blend with surrounding areas by applying regular household scouring-powder dry with a finger. If you overdo it, you may have to apply additional paint.

5. Polish the area with a polishing rag or buffing bit on a small power tool. If the finish is too bright and glossy, use a bit more scouring-powder to dull it down.

Engraved indexes

If your camera or lens has long rugged use, the coloured material in the numeral engravings may begin to disappear. A china marking pencil or a child's crayon can be used to renew the lettering and numerals.

Batteries

We have suggested that you remove all batteries from your camera and equipment when storing for any length of time to prevent corrosion. If you fail to do this and then find that you are not getting electrical contact, remove the battery and rub the contacts in the camera with a pencil eraser. Clean all corrosion from the battery with a dry cloth (but preferably replace the battery) and re-insert the battery. If corrosion is heavy (usually leaving a greenish or whitish chemical deposit), you may have to scrape the contacts clean with the end of a jeweller's screwdriver blade or knife point. Be gentle. In some instances the spring holding the battery into contact may not have sufficient tension. It can be raised or stretched slightly to remedy the matter.

Accuracy of exposure mechanisms

While metering systems are best checked for accuracy using film, you can run a quick check by comparing meter readings of your camera with another camera belonging to a friend, or trying one at a store. Make certain the target to be read is illuminated evenly. I have always found it advisable to own a small selenium-celled meter to use as a check. Meter readings should be within 1 *f*/stop of each other throughout the meter coupling range.

Shutter speed accuracy is best checked by a competent camera technician. To do it yourself, a film test is almost essential. A high-contrast colour-slide film should be used and the ensuing transparencies examined carefully for accurate exposure. You can check exposure consistency by running the following test: make a reading from an evenly-lit uniform test subject, such as a wall. Then expose at each possible shutter speed with the correct matching aperture. All resulting transparencies should be near identical in density.

Needless to say, if a camera malfunctions, shutter speeds or meter indications appear to be in error, controls work with difficulty, lenses focus heavily or sound as if some grit or sand is wedged within the focusing mount, a qualified technician should be consulted.

Water

While we have warned Nikon and Nikkormat owners against the danger of water immersion, the number of such occurrences yearly indicates that some suggestions as to possible action in such as event is not out of place. While we naturally cannot guarantee any of the following will indeed save your camera, these suggestions have been given us by an American Nikon repairman.

1. Whether immersed in fresh or salt water, wash thoroughly in fresh water, place in a food freezer bag and place in freezer or freezing section of a refrigerator until frozen solid. Get frozen camera to a repairman quickly using a thermal container or other carrier, possibly packed with dry ice or ice and salt. Make certain camera does not come into contact with ice or salt, however.
2. If immersed only in fresh water, place in oven at very low temperature for two to three hours. If it has been in salt water, rinse in fresh before placing in oven. When dry, get camera to repairman quickly.
3. If there is no freezer or oven, but there is a compressed air supply, use compressed air to blow out all water possible (after the camera has been rinsed in fresh water). Then dry under a portable hair dryer for 10 to 15 minutes. And again, get it to a repairman swiftly.

Any of the preceding emergency measures must be followed by an immediate disassembly, cleaning and lubrication. Word of warning: such an undertaking is definitely expensive, but often less so than buying a new camera and lens.

Temperature

If you are headed into northern or extreme southern regions of the globe – or anywhere else where temperatures are liable to reach the freezing point and beyond, you can run into camera- and lens-operating difficulties. Today's Nikon and Nikkormat cameras do operate at far lower temperatures without problems than did equipment made years ago. Metering systems are most immediately affected by cold weather since the mercury or silver oxide batteries are not able to deliver efficiently at temperature below the freezing mark. Either use a separate hand-held meter which can be kept inside your clothing until needed, or remove the batteries on your photo equipment, keep them warm next to your body and only insert them into the camera at the last moment before actually shooting.

For photographers operating in cold climes who wish to keep their operating batteries warm outside the camera, thus allowing the cameras to operate properly, Nikon makes an Anti-Cold Battery Pack DB-2 specially for the F3, FM, EM, FG and FM2 cameras. The battery holder can be kept near your body for warmth. It connects to the camera via a cable and threaded male connection which replaces the battery cover and clip in the camera.

For prolonged cold use, most professionals used to 'winterise' their cameras. This involved removing virtually all lubricants from the camera and lenses, since it is the lubricants which become sludgy and stiff in cold weather first. However, factory-authorised technicians tell us that today's Nikon factory lubricants do operate over a far greater temperature range and no special precautions are generally needed down to −29°C (−20°F). Beyond this, professionals still winterise cameras – or more correctly have technicians winterise them. To do so, all factory lubricants throughout the camera and lenses are replaced with aviation and dry lubricants. These tend to make the camera operation less smooth, but these cold weather lubricants need not be removed for regular weather use. Formerly, when it was the practice to remove all lubricants, you ran the risk of increasing camera wear immeasurably, thus shortening the life of the camera and equipment.

When taking pictures, however, a few precautions should be taken (besides making every attempt to keep your equipment as warm as possible). Use shutter speeds slower than 1/500 s and wind and rewind film slowly to avoid tearing brittle film.

Temporary problems can occur when a photographer goes swiftly from a relatively cool, dry climate to a moist, hot one. For instances, if you have your equipment in an air-conditioned area and suddenly step out under a hot tropical sun, moisture will condense on all elements – glass and metal – until the metal and glass become the same temperature as the surroundings. If this is a consistent problems, various anti-fog solutions and salves are available at opticians' stores, which can prevent fogging on the exterior glass surfaces. If you experience temporary interior fog, there is little you can do about it except wait.

Facts and Figures

Lens Modification

In 1977 Nikon announced a change in its lens mounting system and introduced a new series of lenses featuring Automatic Maximum Aperture Indexing as well as Direct Aperture reading through the finder for many of the new Nikon and Nikkormat Cameras. Older, non-auto indexing lenses can only be used with the metering systems of the new auto indexing cameras by making meter readings at stop down aperture. However many of the older, non-auto indexing lenses can be converted to the new mount at moderate cost through Nikon dealers throughout the world. Here is a listing of those older lenses which can be so converted:

The following lenses can be accepted for AI modification.

Lens	*Serial No.*
6mm f/2.8 Fisheye	628001 and higher
8mm f/2.8 Fisheye	230011 ,, ,,
16mm f/3.5 Fisheye	272281 ,, ,,
13mm f/5.6	175021 ,, ,
15mm f/5.6	321001 ,,
18mm f/4	173111 ,, ,,
20mm f/3.5	421241 ,, ,
20mm f/4	103001 ,, ,
24mm f/2.8	242821 ,, ,,
28mm f/2	280001 ,, ,,
28mm f/2.8	382011 ,, ,,
28mm f/3.5	195531-301010; 625611 and higher
35mm f/1 4	350001 and higher
35mm f/2	717011 ,, ,,
35mm f/2.8	255311 ,, ,,
50mmf/1.4	532011 ,, ,,
50mm f/2	742111 ,, ,,
55mm f/1.2	184711 ,, ,,
85mm f/1.8	219901 ,, ,
105mm f/2.5	234011 ,, ,,
135mm f/2	175011 ,, ,,
135mm f/2.8	189311 ,, ,,
135mm f/3.5	111111-720100; 831211 and higher
180mm f/2.8	312011 and higher
200mm f/4	304411 ,, ,,
300mm f/4.5	326511 ,, ,,
300mm f/4.5 ED	173101 ,, ,,
400mm f/5.6	256031 ,, ,,
400mm f/5.6 ED	260001 ,, ,,
28-45 mm f/4.5 Zoom	174011 ,, ,,
43-86mm f/3.5 Zoom	438611 ,, ,,
50-300mm f/4.5 Zoom	740101 ,, ,,
80-200mm f/4.5 Zoom	101911 ,, ,,
85-250mm f/4 Zoom	184771 ,, ,,
45mm f/2.8 GN	238011 ,, ,,
55mm f/3.5 Micro	238011 ,, ,,
	740101 ,, ,,
	238011 ,, ,, (Combined use with PK-13 required after modification)
105mm f/4 Micro	174011 and higher (Combined use with PN-11 required after modification)

CLOSE-UPS WITH EXTENSION TUBES

These tables are mathematically calculated and are intended for guidance only. Each individual lens may give fractionally different results when working at such close range. In many cases the figures have been rounded off. The metric figures are the more accurate. In practical work, further rounding off is possible, especially when the exposure factors are applied to black-and-white work. In such circumstances, there is no practical difference for example, between 1.8 and 2.0. Measurements are given in feet and inches with metric figures in brackets, i.e. 1-6 denotes 1ft 6in.

DATA WITH EXTENSION RING SET PK-1, 2, 3 and PK-11, 12, 13

(While these tables list the PK-1, 2 and 3 rings, the PK-11, 12 and 13 are used in the same manner. PK-1 = PK-11, PK-2 = PK-12, PK-3 = PK-13)

Left figures: Lens set at ∞
Right figures: Lens set at the closest focusing distance

Nikkor 20mm f/3.5

Extension Ring	*Reproduction ratio*	*Subject area* (in./cm)	*Subject distance* (in./cm)	*Exposure factor*
None	1/∞–1/10.5X	∞ × ∞–9.9 × 14.8	∞–11.8	1–1.1
		∞ × ∞–25.1 × 37.7	∞–30.0	
PK-1	1/2.6–1/2.1	2.4 × 3.6–1.9 × 2.9	5.7–5.4	1.2–1.3
		6.1 × 9.2–4.9 × 7.4	14.5–13.7	
PK-2	1/1.5–1/1.3	1.4 × 2.1–1.2 × 1.8	5.1–5.0	1.4–1.5
		3.5 × 5.2–3.1 × 4.6	12.9–12.7	

New Nikkor 20mm f/4

Extension Ring	*Reproduction ratio*	*Subject area* (in./cm)	*Subject distance* (in./cm)	*Exposure factor*
None	1/∞–1/11.0X	∞ × ∞–10.4–15.5	∞–11.8	1–1.1
		∞ × ∞–26.3 × 39.5	∞–29.9	
PK-1	1/2.6–1/2.1	2.4 × 3.6–2.0 × 2.9	5.3–5.0	1.4–1.4
		6.1 × 9.2–5.0 × 7.4	13.4–12.6	
PK-2	1/1.5–1/1.3	1.4 × 2.1–1.2 × 1.8	4.6–4.6	1.7–1.8
		3.5 × 5.2–3.1 × 4.6	11.7–11.6	
PK-1 + PK-2	1.1–1.2	0.88 × 1.3–0.81 × 1.2	4.5–4.5	2.1–2.2
		2.2 × 3.3–2.1 × 3.1	11.5–11.5	
PK-3	1.4–1.4	0.10 × 1.1–0.66 × 0.98	4.6–4.6	2.5–2.6
		1.8 × 2.7–1.7 × 2.5	11.6–11.7	
PK-1 + PK-3	1.7–1.8	0.54 × 0.81–0.52 × 0.77	4.8–4.8	3.0–3.1
		1.4 × 2.1–1.3 × 2.0	12.1–12.2	
PK-2 + PK-3	2.0–2.1	0.46 × 0.70–0.44 × 0.67	4.9–5.0	3.4–3.6
		1.2 × 1.8–1.1 × 1.7	12.5–12.7	

Nikkor 24mm f/2.8

Extension Ring	*Reproduction ratio*	*Subject area* (in./cm)	*Subject distance* (in./cm)	*Exposure factor*
None	1/∞–1/9.1X	∞ × ∞–8.6 × 12.8	∞–11.8	1–1.1
		∞ × ∞–21.7 × 32.6	∞–30.0	
PK-1	1/3.0–1/2.3	2.8 × 4.3–2.1 × 3.2	6.3–5.7	1.3–1.4
		7.2 × 10.8–5.4 × 8.1	16.0–14.5	
PK-2	1/1.7–1/1.4	1.6 × 2.4–1.4 × 2.0	5.3–5.2	1.5–1.6
		4.1 × 6.2–3.5 × 5.2	13.5–13.1	
PK-1 + PK-2	1/1.1–1.0	1.0 × 1.6–0.92 × 1.4	5.1–5.0	1.8–1.9
		2.6 × 3.9–2.3 × 3.5	12.8 × 12.8	
PK-3	1.2–1.3	0.82 × 1.2–0.75 × 1.1	5.1–5.1	2.1–2.2
		2.1 × 3.1–1.9 × 2.9	12.8–12.9	
PK-1 + PK-3	1.5–1.6	0.64 × 0.96–0.59 × 0.89	5.2–5.3	2.4–2.6
		1.6 × 2.4–1.5 × 2.3	13.2–13.3	

Nikkor 28mm f/2

Extension Ring	*Reproduction ratio*	*Subject area* (in./cm)	*Subject distance* (in./cm)	*Exposure factor*
None	1/∞–1/7.2X	∞ × ∞–6.8 × 10.1	∞–11.8	1–1.1
		∞ × ∞–17.2 × 25.7	∞–30.0	
PK-1	1/3.6–1/2.4	3.4 × 5.1–2.3 × 3.4	8.0–6.8	1.2–1.4
		8.6 × 12.9–5.7 × 8.6	20.2–17.2	
PK-2	1/2.0–1/1.6	1.9 × 2.9–1.5 × 2.3	6.5–6.1	1.5–1.6
		4.9 × 7.4–3.8 × 5.7	16.4–15.5	
PK-1 + PK-2	1/1.3–1/1.1	1.2 × 1.8–1.0 × 1.6	5.9–5.9	1.8–1.9
		3.1 × 4.7–2.6 × 4.0	15.1–14.9	
PK-3	1.0–1.1	0.98 × 1.5–0.86 × 1.3	5.9–5.9	2.0–2.1
		2.5 × 3.7–2.2 × 3.3	14.9–14.9	
PK-1 + PK-3	1.2–1.4	0.76 × 1.1–0.68 × 1.0	5.9–6.0	2.3–2.5
		1.9 × 2.9–1.7 × 2.6	15.0–15.2	
PK-2 + PK-3	1.5–1.6	0.65 × 0.98–0.59 × 0.89	6.0–6.1	2.6–2.8
		1.7 × 2.5–1.5 × 2.3	15.3–15.5	
PK-1 + PK-2 + PK-3	1.7–1.9	0.55 × 0.82–0.51 × 0.76	6.2–6.3	3.0–3.2
		1.4 × 2.1–1.3 × 1.9	15.8–16.0	

New Nikkor 28mm f/2.8

Extension Ring	*Reproduction ratio*	*Subject area* (in./cm)	*Subject distance* (in./cm)	*Exposure factor*
None	1/∞–1/7.5X	∞ × ∞–7.1 × 10.7	∞–11.8	1–1.1
		∞ × ∞–18.1 × 27.1	∞–30.1	
PK-1	1/3.6–1/2.4	3.4 × 5.1–2.3 × 3.4	7.6–6.4	1.3–1.5
		8.6 × 12.9–5.8 × 8.7	19.2–16.3	
PK-2	1/2–1/1.6	1.9 × 2.9–1.5 × 2.3	6.1–5.7	1.6–1.8
		4.9 × 7.4–3.9 × 5.8	15.4–14.5	
PK-1 + PK-2	1/1.3–1/1.1	1.2 × 1.8–1.1 × 1.6	5.6–5.5	2.0–2.2
		3.1 × 4.7–2.7 × 4.0	14.1–13.9	
PK-3	1.0–1.1	0.98 × 1.5–0.86 × 1.3	5.5–5.5	2.3–2.5
		2.5 × 3.7–2.2 × 3.3	13.9–13.9	
PK-1 + PK-3	1.2–1.4	0.76 × 1.1–0.69 × 1.0	5.5–5.6	2.7–3.0
		1.9 × 2.9–1.7 × 2.6	14.0–14.2	
PK-2 + PK-3	1.5–1.6	0.65 × 0.98–0.60 × 0.89	5.6–5.7	3.1–3.4
		1.7 × 2.5–1.5 × 2.3	14.3–14.5	
PK-1 + PK-2 + PK-3	1.7–1.9	0.55 × 0.82–0.51 × 0.76	5.8–5.9	3.7–4.0
		1.4 × 2.1–1.3 × 1.9	14.8–15.0	

Nikkor 28mm f/3.5

Extension Ring	*Reproduction ratio*	*Subject area* (in./cm)	*Subject distance* (in./cm)	*Exposure factor*
None	1/∞–1/7.5X	∞ × ∞–7.1 × 10.7	∞–11.7	1–1.2
		∞ × ∞–18.1 × 27.1	∞–29.7	
PK-1	1/3.6–1/2.4	3.4 × 5.1–2.3 × 3.4	7.4–6.3	1.4–1.6
		8.6 × 12.9–5.8 × 8.7	18.9–15.9	
PK-2	1/2.0–1/1.6	1.9 × 2.9–1.5 × 2.3	5.9–5.6	1.7–1.9
		4.9 × 7.4–3.9 × 5.8	15.1–14.2	
PK-1 + PK-2	1/1.3–1/1.1	1.2 × 1.8–1 1 × 1.6	5.4–5.4	2.2–2.4
		3.1 × 4.7–2.7 × 4.0	13.7–13.6	
PK-3	1.0–1.1	0.98 × 1.5–0.86 × 1.3	5.3–5.3	2.5–2.8
		2.5 × 3.7–2.2 × 3.3	13.6–13.6	
PK-1 + PK-3	1.2–1.4	0.76 × 1.1–0.69 × 1.0	5.4–5.5	3.1–3.4
		1.9 × 2.9–1.7 × 2.6	13.7–13.8	
PK-2 + PK-3	1.5–1.6	0.65 × 0.98–0.60 × 0.89	5.5–5.6	3.6–3.9
		1.7 × 2.5–1.5 × 2.3	14.0–14.2	
PK-1 + PK-2 + PK-3	1.7–1.9	0.55 × 0.82–0.51 × 0.76	5.7–5.8	4.2–4.6
		1.4 × 2.1–1.3 × 1.9	14.4–14.7	

New PC Nikkor 28mm f/4

Extension Ring	*Reproduction ratio*	*Subject area (in./cm)*	*Subject distance (in./cm)*	*Exposure factor*
None	1/∞–1/7X	∞×∞–6.6×9.9	∞–11.9	1–1.1
		∞×∞–16.8×25.2	∞–30.1	
PK-1	1/3.6–1/2.4	3.4×5.1–2.2×3.4	8.2–7.0	1.2–1.4
		8.6×12.9–5.7×8.5	20.7–17.7	
PK-2	1/2.1–1/1.6	1.9×2.9–1.5×2.3	6.7–6.3	1.5–1.6
		4.9×7.4–3.8×5.7	16.9–16.0	
PK-1+PK-2	1/1.3–1/1.1	1.2×1.9–1.0×1.6	6.1–6.1	1.7–1.9
		3.1×4.7–2.6×4.0	15.6–15.4	
PK-2	1.0–1.1	0.99×1.5–0.86×1.3	6.1–6.1	2.0–2.1
		2.5×3.8–2.2×3.3	15.4–15.4	
PK-1+PK-3	1.2–1.4	0.76×1.2–0.68×1.0	6.1–6.2	2.3–2.5
		1.9×2.9–1.7×2.6	15.5–15.7	
PK-2+PK-3	1.5–1.6	0.65×0.98–0.59×0.89	6.2–6.3	2.6–2.8
		1.7×2.5–1.5×2.3	15.8–16.0	
PK-1+PK-2+PK-3	1.7–1.9	0.55×0.82–0.51×0.76	6.4–6.5	3.0–3.2
		1.4×2.1–1.3×1.9	16.3–16.5	

Nikkor 35mm f/1.4

Extension Ring	*Reproduction ratio*	*Subject area (in./cm)*	*Subject distance (in./cm)*	*Exposure factor*
None	1/∞–1/5.4X	∞×∞–5.1×7.6	∞–11.7	1–1.1
		∞×∞–12.9×19.3	∞–29.7	
PK-1	1/4.5–1/2.4	4.3×6.4–2.3×3.5	10.5–7.9	1.2–1.3
		10.8×16.2–58.8×88.2	26.7–20.0	
PK-2	1/2.6–1/1.7	2.4×3.6–1.6×2.5	8.0–7.1	1.3–1.4
		6.2×9.3–4.2×6.3	20.3–18.0	
PK-1+PK-2	1/1.6–1/1.3	1.6×2.3–1.2×1.8	7.0–6.7	1.5–1.6
		3.9×5.9–3.0×4.5	17.8–17.1	
PK-3	1/1.3–1/1.1	1.2×1.9–0.99×1.5	6.8–6.7	1.6–1.8
		3.1×4.7–2.5×3.8	17.1–16.9	
PK-1+PK-3	1.0–1.2	0.96×1.4–0.81×1.2	6.6–6.7	1.8–2.0
		2.4×3.7–2.0×3.1	16.9–17.0	
PK-2+PK-3	1.2–1.3	0.82×1.2–0.71×1.1	6.7–6.8	1.9–2.1
		2.1×3.1–1.8×2.7	16.9–17.2	
PK-1+PK-2+PK-3	1.4–1.6	0.69×1.0–0.61×0.91	6.8–6.9	2.2–2.3
		1.7×2.6–1.5×2.3	17.2–17.6	

Nikkor 35mm f/2

Extension ring	*Reproduction ratio*	*Subject area (in./cm)*	*Subject distance (in./cm)*	*Exposure factor*
None	1/∞–1/5.5X	∞×∞–5.2×7.9	∞–11.6	1–1.2
		∞×∞–13.3×19.9	∞–29.5	
PK-1	1/4.5–1/2.5	4.3×6.4–2.4×3.5	10.2–7.6	1.3–1.5
		10.8×16.2–6.0×8.9	26.0–19.3	
PK-2	1/2.6–1/1.8	2.4×3.6–1.7×2.5	7.7–6.8	1.5–1.8
		6.2×9.3–4.2×6.3	19.6–17.3	
PK-1+PK-2	1/1.6–1/1.3	1.6×2.3–1.2×1.8	6.7–6.4	1.9–2.2
		3.9×5.9–3 0×4.5	17.1–16.4	
PK-3	1/1.3–1/1.1	1.2×1.9–1.0×1.5	6.5–6.4	2.1–2.5
		3.1×4.7–2.5×3.8	16.4–16.2	
PK-1+PK-3	1.0–1.2	0.96×1.4–0.81×1.2	6.4–6.4	2.5–2.9
		2.4×3.7–2.1×3.1	16.2–16.2	
PK-2+PK-3	1.2–1.3	0.82×1.2–0.71×1.1	6.4–6.5	2.9–3.2
		2.1×3.1–1.8×2.7	16.2–16.5	
PK-1+PK-2+PK-3	1.4–1.6	0.69×1.0–0.61×0.91	6.5–6.6	3.3–3.7
		1.7×2.6–1.5×2.3	16.5–16.9	

Nikkor 35mm f/2.8

Extension Ring	*Reproduction ratio*	*Subject area* (in./cm)	*Subject distance* (in./cm)	*Exposure factor*
None	1/∞–1/5.8X	∞ × ∞–5.5 × 8.2	∞–11.8	1–1.3
		∞ × ∞–13.9 × 20.9	∞–30.0	
PK-1	1/4.5–1/2.5	4.3 × 6.4–2.4 × 3.6	10.0–7.5	1 3–1.6
		10.8 × 16.2–6.1 × 9.1	25.5–19.0	
PK-2	1/2.6–1/1.8	2.4 × 3.6–1.7 × 2.5	7.5–6.7	1.6–2.0
		6.2 × 9.3–4.3 × 6.4	19–2.16.9	
PK-1 + PK-2	1/1.6–1/1.3	1.6 × 2.3–1.2 × 1.8	6.5–6.3	2.1–2.4
		3.9 × 5.9–3.1 × 4.6	16.6–15.9	
PK-3	1/1.3–1/1.1	1.2 × 1.9–1.0 × 1.5	6.3–6.2	2.4–2.8
		3.1 × 4.7–2.6 × 3.8	16.0–15.7	
PK-1 + PK-3	1.0–1.2	0.96 × 1.4–0.82 × 1.2	6.2–6.2	2.9–3.3
		2.4 × 3.7–2.1 × 3.1	15.7–15.8	
PK-2 + PK-3	1.2–1.3	0.82 × 1.2–0.71 × 1.1	6.2–6.3	3.3–3.8
		2.1 × 3.1–1.8 × 2.7	15.8–16.0	
PK-1 + PK-2 + PK-3	1.4–1.6	0.69 × 1.0–0.61 × 0.92	6.3–6.5	3.9–4.4
		1.7 × 2.6–1.6 × 2.3	16.1–16.4	

New Nikkor 35mm f/2.8

Extension Ring	*Reproduction ratio*	*Subject area* (in./cm)	*Subject distance* (in./cm)	*Exposure factor*
None	1/∞–1/5.5X	∞ × ∞–5.2 × 7.9	∞–11.8	1–1.3
		∞ × ∞–13.3 × 19.9	∞–29.9	
PK-1	1/4.5–1/2.5	4.3 × 6.4–2.4 × 3.5	10.4–7.8	1.3–1.7
		10.8 × 16.2–6.0 × 8.9	26.3–19.7	
PK-2	1/2.6–1/1.8	2.4 × 3.6–1.7 × 2.5	7.9–7.0	1.6–2.0
		6.2 × 9.3–4.2 × 6.3	20.0–17.7	
PK-1 + PK-2	1/1.6–1/1.3	1.6 × 2.3–1.2 × 1.8	6.9–6.6	2.1–2.4
		3.9 × 5.9–3.0 × 4.5	17.4–16.7	
PK-3	1/1.3–1/1.1	1.2 × 1.9–1.0 × 1.5	6.6–6.5	2.4–2.8
		3.1 × 4.7–2.5 × 3.8	16.8–16.5	
PK-1 + PK-3	1.0–1.2	0.96 × 1.4–0.81 × 1.2	6.5–6.5	2.9–3.3
		2.4 × 3.7–2.1 × 3.1	16.5–16.6	
PK-2 + PK-3	1.2–1.3	0.82 × 1.2–0.71 × 1.1	6.5–6.6	3.3–3.8
		2.1 × 3.1–1.8 × 2.7	16.6–16.8	
PK-1 + PK-2 + PK-3	1.4–1.6	0.69 × 1.0–0.61 × 0.91	6.7–6.8	3.9–4.4
		1.7 × 2.6–1.5 × 2.3	16 9–17.2	

PC Nikkor 35mm f/2.8

Extension Ring	*Reproduction ratio*	*Subject area* (in./cm)	*Subject distance* (in./cm)	*Exposure factor*
None	1/∞–1/5.4X	∞ × ∞–5.1 × 7.7	∞–12.0	1–1.2
		∞ × ∞–13.0 × 19.5	∞–30.5	
PK-1	1/4.5–1/2.5	4.3 × 6.4–2.3 × 3.5	10.8–8.2	1.3–1.5
		10.9 × 16.3–5.9 × 8.9	27.5–20.7	
PK-2	1/2.6–1/1.7	2.4 × 3.7–1.7 × 2.5	8.3–7.4	1.5–1.7
		6.2 × 9.3–4.2 × 6.3	21.1–18.7	
PK-1 + PK-2	1/1.6–1/1.3	1.6 × 2.3–1.2 × 1.8	7.3–7.0	1.8–2.1
		3.9 × 5.9–3.0 × 4.5	18.5–17.7	
PK-3	1/1.3–1/1.1	1.2 × 1.9–1.0 × 1.5	7.0–6.9	2.0–2.3
		3.2 × 4.7–2.5 × 3.8	17.8–17.6	
PK-1 + PK-3	1.0–1.2	0.96 × 1.5–0.81 × 1.2	6.9–6.9	2.4–2.7
		2.4 × 3.7–2.1 × 3.1	17.6–17.6	
PK-2 + PK-3	1.2–1.3	0.82 × 1.2–0.71 × 1.1	6.9–7.0	2.7–3.0
		2.1 × 3.1–1.8 × 2.7	17.6–17.8	
PK-1 + PK-2 + PK-3	1.4–1.6	0.69 × 1.0–0.61 × 0.91	7.1–7.2	3.1–3.5
		1.8 × 2.6–1.5 × 2.3	17.9–18.3	

GN Nikkor 45mm f/2.8

Extension Ring	*Reproduction ratio*	*Subject area* (in./cm)	*Subject distance* (in./cm)	*Exposure factor*
None	1/∞–1/15X	∞ × ∞–14.2 × 21.3	∞–31.3	1–1.1
		∞ × ∞–36.0 × 54.0	∞–79.5	
PK-1	1/5.8–1/4.2	5.5 × 8.2–4.0 × 5.9	14.7–11.8	1.4–1.5
		14.0 × 20.9–10.1 × 15.1	37.2–30.0	
PK-2	1/3.3–1/2.7	3.1 × 4.7–2.6 × 3.9	10.3–9.4	1.7–1.9
		8.0 × 12.0–6.5 × 9.8	26.3–23.8	
PK-1 + PK-2	1/2.1–1/1.9	2.0 × 3.0–1.8 × 2.6	8.4–8.1	2.2–2.4
		5.1 × 7.6–4.4 × 6.7	21.4–20.5	
PK-3	1/1.7–1/1.5	1.6 × 2.4–1.4 × 2.2	7.9–7.7	2.5–2.7
		4.1 × 6.1–3.6 × 5.5	20.0–19.5	
PK-1 + PK-3	1/1.3–1/1.2	1.2 × 1.9–1.1 × 1.7	7.5–7.4	3.1–3.3
		3.1 × 4.7–2.9 × 4.3	19.0–18.9	
PK-2 + PK-3	1/1.1–1.0	1.1 × 1.6–0.99 × 1.5	7.4–7.4	3.6–3.8
		2.7 × 4.0–2.5 × 3.8	18.8–18.7	
PK-1 + PK-2 + PK-3	1.1–1.1	0.89 × 1.3–0.84 × 1.3	7.4–7.4	4.3–4.5
		2.3 × 3.4–2.1 × 3.2	18.7–18.8	

Nikkor 50mm f/1.4

Extension Ring	*Reproduction ratio*	*Subject area* (in./cm)	*Subject distance* (in./cm)	*Exposure factor*
None	1/∞–1/9.8X	∞ × ∞–9.3 × 13.9	∞–23.7	1–1.1
		∞ × ∞–23.5 × 35.3	∞–60.1	
PK-1	1/6.5–1/3.9	6.1 × 9.1–3.7 × 5.5	16.9–12.0	1.2–1.3
		15.5 × 23.2–9.3 × 14.0	43.0–30.3	
PK-2	1/3.7–1/2.7	3.5 × 5.2–2.5 × 3.8	11.6–9.7	1.3–1.5
		8.8 × 13.3–6.4 × 9.6	29.4–24.7	
PK-1 + PK-2	1/2.3–1/1.9	2.2 × 3.3–1.8 × 2.7	9.2–8.4	1.5–1.7
		5.6 × 8.4–4.5 × 6.8	23.2–21.4	
PK-3	1/1.9–1/1.6	1.8 × 2.7–1.5 × 2.2	8.4–8.0	1.7–1.9
		4.5 × 6.8–3.8 × 5.7	21.4–20.3	
PK-1 + PK-3	1/1.5–1/1.3	1.4 × 2.1–1.2 × 1.8	7.9–7.7	1.9–2.1
		3.5 × 5.2–3.0 × 4.6	20.0–19.5	
PK-2 + PK-3	1/1.2–1/1.1	1.2 × 1.8–1.0 × 1.6	7.7–7.6	2.1–2.3
		3.0 × 4.5–2.6 × 4.0	19.5–19.3	
PK-1 + PK-2 + PK-3	1.0–1.1	0.98 × 1.5–0.89 × 1.3	7.6–7.6	2.4–2.6
		2.5 × 3.8–2.3 × 3.4	19.3–19.3	

New Nikkor 50mm f/1.4

Extension Ring	*Reproduction ratio*	*Subject area* (in./cm)	*Subject distance* (in./cm)	*Exposure factor*
None	1/∞–1/6.9X	∞ × ∞–6.5 × 9.8	∞–17 8	1–1.2
		∞ × ∞–16.5 × 24.8	∞–45.2	
PK-1	1/6.5–1/3.3	6.1 × 9.1–3.2 × 4.7	16.9–10.9	1.2–1.4
		15.5 × 23.2–8.0 × 12.0	43.0–27.7	
PK-2	1/3.7–1/2.4	3.5 × 5.2–2.3 × 3.4	11.6–9.2	1.3–1.5
		8.8 × 13.3–5.8 × 8.6	29.4–23.5	
PK-1 + PK-2	1/2.3–1/1.7	2.2 × 3.3–1.7 × 2.5	9.2–8.2	1.5–1.8
		5.6 × 8.4–4.2 × 6.3	23.2–20.9	
PK-3	1/1.9–1/1.5	1.5 × 2.7–1.4 × 2.1	8.4–7.9	1.7–1.9
		4.5 × 6.8–3.5 × 5.3	21.4–20.0	
PK-1 + PK-3	1/1.5–1/1.2	1.4 × 2.1–1.1 × 0.21	7.9–7.7	1.9–2.2
		3.5 × 5.2–2.9 × 4.3	20.0–19.4	
PK-2 + PK-3	1/1.2–1/1.1	1.2 × 1.8–1.0 × 1.5	7.7–7.6	2.1–2.4
		3.0 × 4.5–2.5 × 3.8	19.5–19.3	
PK-1 + PK-2 + PK-3	1.0–1.1	0.98 × 1.5–0.86 × 1.3	7.6–7.6	2.4–2.7
		2.5 × 3.8–2.2 × 3.3	19.3–19.3	

Nikkor 50mm f/2

Extension Ring	*Reproduction ratio*	*Subject area* (*in./cm*)	*Subject distance* (*in./cm*)	*Exposure factor*
None	1/∞–1/9.7X	∞ × ∞–9.2 × 13.7	∞–23.7	1–1.2
		∞ × ∞–23.2 × 34.9	∞–60.1	
PK-1	1/6.5–1/3.9	6.1 × 9.1–3.7 × 5.5	17.2–12.2	1.3–1.5
		15.5 × 23.2–9.3 × 13.9	43.7–30.9	
PK-2	1/3.7–1/2.7	3.5 × 5.2–2.5 × 3.8	11.8–10.0	1.5–1.7
		8.8 × 13.3–6.4 × 9.6	30.0–25.3	
PK-1 + PK-2	1/2.3–1/1.9	2.2 × 3.3–1.8 × 2.7	9.4–8.7	1.9–2.1
		5.6 × 8.4–4.5 × 6.8	23.9–22.1	
PK-3	1/1.9–1/1.6	1.8 × 2.7–1.5 × 2.2	8.7–8.3	2.1–2.4
		4.5 × 6.8–3.8 × 5.7	22.0–21.0	
PK-1 + PK-3	1/1.5–1/1.3	1.4 × 2.1–1.2 × 1.8	8.1–8.0	2.5–2.8
		3.5 × 5.2–3.0 × 4.5	20.7–20.2	
PK-2 + PK-3	1/1.2–1/1.1	1.2 × 1.8–1.0 × 1.6	7.9–7.9	2.9–3.2
		3.0 × 4.5–2.6 × 4.0	20.2–20.0	
PK-1 + PK-2 + PK-3	1.0–1.1	0.98 × 1.5–0.89 × 1.3	7.9–7.9	
		2.5 × 3.8–2.3 × 3.4	19.9–19.9	3.3–3.7

New Nikkor 50mm f/2

Extension Ring	*Reproduction ratio*	*Subject area* (*in./cm*)	*Subject distance* (*in./cm*)	*Exposure factor*
None	1/∞–1/6.7X	∞ × ∞–6.3 × 9.5	∞–17.7	1–1.3
		∞ × ∞–16.1 × 24.1	∞–44.9	
PK-1	1/6.5–1/3.3	6.1 × 9.1–3.1 × 4.7	17.2–11.1	1.3–1.6
		15.5 × 23.2–78.9 × 11.8	43.7–28.1	
PK-2	1.3.7–1/2.4	3.5 × 5.2–2.3 × 3.4	11.8–9.5	1.5–1.9
		8.8 × 13.3–5.7 × 8.6	30.0–24.0	
PK-1 + PK-2	1/2.3–1/1.7	2.2 × 3.3–1.6 × 2.5	9.4–8.5	1.9–2.2
		5.6 × 8.4–4.2 × 6.3	23.9–21.5	
PK-3	1/1.9–1/1.5	1.8 × 2.7–1.4 × 2.1	8.7–8.1	2.1–2.5
		4.5 × 6.8–3.5 × 5.3	22.0–20.7	
PK-1 + PK-3	1/1.5–1/1.2	1.4 × 2.1–1.1 × 1.7	8.1–7.9	2.5–3.0
		3.5 × 5.2–2.9 × 4.3	20.7–20.1	
PK-2 + PK-3	1/1.2–1.0	1.2 × 1.8–0.99 × 1.5	7.9–7.9	2.9–3.3
		3.0 × 4.5–2.5 × 3.8	20.2–19.9	
PK-1 + PK-2 + PK-3	1.0–1.1	0.98 × 1.5–0.85 × 1.3	7.9–7.9	3.3–3.8
		2.5 × 3.8–2.2 × 3.2	19.9–20.0	

Nikkor 55mm f/1.2

Extension Ring	*Reproduction ratio*	*Subject area* (*in./cm*)	*Subject distance* (*in./cm*)	*Exposure factor*
None	1/∞–1/9.2X	∞ × ∞–8.7 × 13.0	∞–23.7	1–1.1
		∞ × ∞–22.0 × 32.9	∞–60.1	1.2–1.3
PK-1	1/6.9–1/3.9	6.5 × 9.7–3.7 × 5.6	18.8–12.7	
		16.5 × 24.8–9.4 × 14.1	47.8–32.2	
PK-2	1/3.9–1/2.7	3.7 × 5.6–2.6 × 3.9	12.7–10.4	1.3–1.5
		9.4 × 14.1–6.6 × 9.9	32.2–26.3	
PK-1 + PK-2	1/2.5–1/2.0	2.4 × 3.5–1.9 × 2.8	9.9–9.0	1.5–1.7
		6.0 × 9.0–4.7 × 7.1	25.2–22.8	
PK-3	1/2.0–1/1.6	1.9 × 2.8–1.6 × 2.3	9.0–8.5	1.7–1.9
		4.8 × 7.2–3.9 × 5.9	23.0–21.6	
PK-1 + PK-3	1/1.5–1/1.3	1.5 × 2.2–1.3 × 1.9	8.4–8.1	1.9–2.1
		3.7 × 5.6–3.2 × 4.8	21.3–20.6	
PK-2 + PK-3	1/1.3–1/1.2	1.3 × 1.9–1.1 × 1.6	8.1–8.0	2.1–2.3
		3.2 × 4.8–2.8 × 4.2	20.6–20.3	
PK-1 + PK-2 + PK-3	1/1.1–1.0	1.1 × 1.6–0.94 × 1.4	8.0–8.0	2.4–2.6
		2.7 × 4.0–2.4 × 3.6	20.3–20.2	

New Nikkor 55mm f/1.2

Extension Ring	*Reproduction ratio*	*Subject area* (in./cm)	*Subject distance* (in./cm)	*Exposure factor*
None	1/∞–1/7.2X	∞ × ∞–6.8 × 10.3	∞–19.6	1–1.2
		∞ × ∞–17.4 × 26.1	∞–49.8	
PK-1	1/6.9–1/3.5	6.5 × 9.7–3.3 × 5.0	18.8–11.9	1.2–1.4
		16.5 × 24.8–8.5 × 12.7	47.8–30.2	
PK-2	1/3.9–1/2.5	3.7 × 5.6–2.4 × 3.6	12.7–10.0	1.3–1.5
		9.4 × 14.1–6.1 × 9.2	32.2–25.4	
PK-1+PK-2	1/2.5–1/1.9	2.4 × 3.5–1.8 × 2.6	9.9–8.8	1.5–1.8
		6.0 × 9.0–4.5 × 6.7	25.2–22.4	
PK-3	1/2.0–1/1.6	1.9 × 2.8–1.5 × 2.2	9.0–8.4	1.7–1.9
		4.8 × 7.2–3.8 × 5.6	23.0–21.3	
PK-1+PK-3	1/1.5–1/1.3	1.5 × 2.2–1.2 × 1.8	8.4–8.1	1.9–2.2
		3.7 × 5.6–3.1 × 4.6	21.3–20.5	
PK-2+PK-3	1/1.3–1/1.1	1.3 × 1.9–1.1 × 1.6	8.1–8.0	2.1–2.4
		3.2 × 4.8–2.7 × 4.0	20.6–20.3	
PK-1+PK-2+PK-3	1/1.1–1.0	1.1 × 1.6–0.91 × 1.4	8.0–8.0	2.4–2.6
		2.7 × 4.0–2.3 × 3.5	20.3–20.2	

Micro-Nikkor 55mm f/3.5

Extension Ring	*Reproduction ratio*	*Subject area* (in./cm)	*Subject distance* (in./cm)	*Exposure factor*
None	1/∞–1/2X	∞ × ∞–1.9 × 2.8	∞–9.5	1–2.3
		∞ × ∞–4.8 × 7.2	∞–24.1	
PK-1	1/6.9–1/1.5	6.5 × 9.7–1.5 × 2.2	19.3–8.8	1.3–2.7
		16.5 × 24.8–37.2 × 55.8	49.0–22.4	
PK-2	1/3.9–1/1.3	3.7 × 5.6–1.3 × 1.9	13.1–8.6	1.6–3.1
		9.4 × 14.1–3.2 × 4.8	33.4–21.8	
PK-1+PK-2	1/2.5–1/1.1	2.4 × 3.5–1.1 × 1.6	10.4–8.4	2.0–3.6
		6.0 × 9.0–2.7 × 4.0	26.3–21.4	
PK-3	1/2–1.0	1.9 × 2.8–0.94 × 1.4	9.5–8.4	2.3–4.0
		4.8 × 7.2–2.4 × 3.6	24.1–21.4	
PK-1+PK-3	1/1.5–1.2	1.5 × 2.2–0.82 × 1.2	8.8–8.5	2.7–4.6
		3.7 × 5.6–2.1 × 3.1	22.4–21.5	
PK-2+PK-3	1/1.3–1.3	1.3 × 1.9–0.75 × 1.1	8.6–8.5	3.1–5.1
		3.2 × 4.8–1.9 × 2.9	21.8–21.6	
PK-1+PK-2+PK-3	1/1.1–1.4	1.1 × 1.6–0.67 × 1.0	8.4–8.7	3.6–5.8
		2.7 × 4.0–1.7 × 2.6	21.4–22.0	

Nikkor 85mm f/1.8

Extension Ring	*Reproduction ratio*	*Subject area* (in./cm)	*Subject distance* (in./cm)	*Exposure factor*
None	1/∞–1/9.8X	∞ × ∞–9.3 × 13.9	∞–39.4	1–1.3
		∞ × ∞–23.5 × 35.3	∞–100	
PK-1	1/10.6–1/5.1	10.0 × 15.1–4.8 × 7.2	42.1–24.0	1.2–1.5
		25.5 × 38.3–12.2 × 18.3	107–60.9	
PK-2	1/6.1–1/3.7	5.7 × 8.6–3.5 × 5.3	27.1–19.7	1.4–1.8
		14.6 × 21.9–9.0 × 13.5	68.9–50.0	
PK-1+PK-2	1/3.9–1/2.8	3.7 × 5.5–2.6 × 3.9	20.1–16.8	1.7–2.1
		9.3 × 13.9–6.6 × 10.0	51.0–42 5	
PK-3	1/3.1–1/2.3	2.9 × 4.4–2.2 × 3.3	17.7–15.6	2.0–2.3
		7.4 × 11.1–5.6 × 8.5	44.9–39.5	
PK-1+PK-3	1/2.4–1/1.9	2.3 × 3.4–1.8 × 2.7	15.7–14.5	2.3–2.7
		5.7 × 8.6–4.6 × 6.9	39.8–36.7	
PK-2+PK-3	1/2.0–1/1.7	1.9 × 2.9–1.6 × 2.4	14.8–13.9	2.6–3.0
		4.9 × 7.4–4.1 × 6.1	37.5–35.3	
PK-1+PK-2+PK-3	1/1.7–1/1.5	1.6 × 2.4–1.4 × 2.1	14.0–13.5	2.9–3.4
		4.1 × 6.2–3.5 × 5.3	35.5–34.2	

New Nikkor 85mm f/1.8

Extension Ring	*Reproduction ratio*	*Subject area* (in./cm)	*Subject distance* (in./cm)	*Exposure factor*
None	1/∞–1/8.0X	∞ × ∞–7.6 × 11.4	∞–33.5	1–1.3
		∞ × ∞–19.2 × 28.9	∞–85.1	
PK-1	1/10.6–1/4.6	10.0 × 15.1–4.3 × 6.5	42.1–22.3	1.2–1.6
		25.5 × 38.3–11.0 × 16.5	107.0–56.6	
PK-2	1/6.1–1/3.5	5.7 × 8.6–3.3 × 4.9	27.1–18.8	1.4–1.8
		14.6 × 21.9–8.3 × 12.4	68.9–47.7	
PK-1 + PK-2	1/3.9–1/2.6	3.7 × 5.5–2.5 × 3.7	20.1–16.3	1.7–2.2
		9.3 × 13.9–6.3 × 9.4	51.0–41.3	
PK-3	1/3.1–1/2.2	2.9 × 4.4–2.1 × 3.2	17.7–15.2	2.0–2.4
		7.4 × 11.1–5.4 × 8.0	45.0–38.7	
PK-1 + PK-3	1/2.4–1/1.8	2.3 × 3.4–1.7 × 2.6	15.7–14.3	2.3–2.8
		5.7 × 8.6–4.4 × 6.6	39.8–36.2	
PK-2 + PK-3	1/2.0–1/1.6	1.9 × 2.9–1.5 × 2.3	14.8–13.8	2.6–3.1
		4.9 × 7.4–3.9 × 5.9	37.5–35.0	
PK-1 + PK-2 + PK-3	1/1.7–1/1.4	1.6 × 2.4–1.3 × 2.0	14.0–13.4	2.9–3.5
		4.1 × 6.2–3.4 × 5.1	35.5–34.0	

New Nikkor 105mm f/2.5

Extension Ring	*Reproduction ratio*	*Subject area* (in./cm)	*Subject distance* (in./cm)	*Exposure factor*
None	1/∞–1/8.3X	∞ × ∞–7.9 × 11.9	∞–42	1–1.3
		∞ × ∞–20.0 × 30.0	∞–107	
PK-1	1/13.1–1/5.1	12.4 × 18.6–4.8 × 7.2	61.6–28.9	1.2–1.5
		31.5 × 47.3–12.2 × 18.3	157–73.5	
PK-2	1/7.5–1/3.9	7.1 × 10.6–3.7 × 5.6	38.6–24.4	1.3–1.6
		18.0 × 27.0–9.5 × 14.2	98.1–62.0	
PK-1 + PK-2	1/4.8–1/3.0	4.5 × 6.8–2.9 × 4.3	27.7–21.0	1.5–1.8
		11.5 × 17.2–7.3 × 10.9	70.2–53.2	
PK-3	1/3.8–1/2.6	3.6 × 5.4–2.5 × 3.7	23.9–19.5	1.6–2.0
		9.2 × 13.7–6.3 × 9.4	60.8–49.4	
PK-1 + PK-3	1/3.0–1/2.2	2.8 × 4.2–2.1 × 3.1	20.1–18.0	1.8–2.2
		7.1 × 10.6–5.2 × 7.9	52.5–45.6	
PK-2 + PK-3	1/2.5–1/1.9	2.4 × 3.6–1.8 × 2.8	19.1–17.2	2.0–2.4
		6.1 × 9.1–4.7 × 7.0	48.6–43.7	
PK-1 + PK-2 + PK-3	1/2.1–1/1.7	2.0 × 3.0–1.6 × 2.4	17.8–16.5	2.2–2.6
		5.1 × 7.6–4.1 × 6.1	45.1–41.9	

New Micro-Nikkor 105mm f/4

Extension Ring	*Reproduction ratio*	*Subject area* (in./cm)	*Subject distance* (in./cm)	*Exposure factor*
None	1/∞–1/2X	∞ × ∞–1.9 × 2.8	∞–18.6	1–2.1
		∞ × ∞–4.8 × 7.2	∞–47.1	
PK-1	1/13.1–1/1.7	12.4 × 18.6–1.6 × 2.5	62.8–17.8	1.1–2.3
		31.5 × 47.3–4.2 × 6.2	159–45.2	
PK-2	1/7.5–1/1.6	7.1 × 10.6–1.5 × 2.2	39.8–17.4	1.3–2.5
		18.0 × 27.0–3.8 × 5.7	101–44.1	
PK-1 + PK-2	1/4.8–1/1.4	4.5 × 6.8–1.3 × 2.0	28.8–17.0	1.4–2.7
		11.5 × 17.2–3.4 × 5.1	73.2–43.1	
PK-3	1/3.8–1/1.3	3.6 × 5.4–1.2 × 1.9	25.1–16.8	1.5–2.8
		9.2 × 13.7–3.2 × 4.7	63.7–42.7	
PK-1 + PK-3	1/3.0–1/1.2	2.8 × 4.2–1.1 × 1.7	21.8–16.6	1.7–3.1
		7.1 × 10.6–2.9 × 4.3	55.5–42.2	
PK-2 + PK-3	1/2.5–1/1.1	2.4 × 3.6–1.1 × 1.6	20.3–16.5	1.8–3.3
		6.1 × 9.1–2.7 × 4.0	51.6–42.0	
PK-1 + PK-2 + PK-3	1/2.1–1/1.0	2.0 × 3.0–0.97 × 1.5	18.9–16.5	2.0–3.5
		5.1 × 7.6–2.5 × 3.7	48.1–41.9	

Nikkor 135mm f/2.8

Extension Ring	*Reproduction ratio*	*Subject area (in./cm)*	*Subject distance (in./cm)*	*Exposure factor*
None	1/∞–1/9X	∞ × ∞–8.5 × 12.8	∞–58.9	1–1.4
		∞ × ∞–21.6 × 32.4	∞–150	
PK-1	1/16.9–1/5.9	15.9 × 23.9–5.6 × 8.3	100–42.6	1.2–1.6
		40.5 × 60 8–14.1 × 21.1	255–108	
PK-2	1/9.6–1/4.7	9.1 × 13.7–4.4 × 6.6	62.3–36.4	1.3–1.7
		23.1 × 34.7–11.2 × 16.8	158–92.3	
PK-1 + PK-2	1/6.1–1/3.6	5.8 × 8.7–3.5 × 5.2	44.0–31.3	1.5–2.0
		14.7 × 22.1–8.8 × 13.1	112–79.5	
PK-3	1/4.9–1/3.2	4.6 × 7.0–3.0 × 4.5	37.6–29.0	1.7–2.1
		11.8 × 17.7–7.6 × 11.4	95.6–73.7	
PK-1 + PK-3	1/3.8–1/2.7	3.6 × 5.4–2.5 × 3.8	32.1–26.7	1.9–2.4
		9.1 × 13.7–6.4 × 9.6	81.5–67.7	
PK-2 + PK-3	1/3.3–1/2.4	3.1 × 4.6–2.3 × 3.4	29.4–25.4	2.1–2.6
		7.8 × 11.7–5.7 × 8.6	74.7–64.5	
PK-1 + PK-2 + PK-3	1/2.7–1/2.1	2.6 × 3.9–2.0 × 3.0	26.9–24.1	2.4–2.9
		6.5 × 9.8–5.0 × 7.5	68.4–61.3	

Nikkor 135mm f/3.5

Extension Ring	*Reproduction ratio*	*Subject area (in./cm)*	*Subject distance (in./cm)*	*Exposure factor*
None	1/∞–1/8.9X	∞ × ∞–8.5 × 12.7	∞–59	1–1.4
		∞ × ∞–21.5 × 32.2	∞–150	
PK-1	1/16.9–1/5.8	15.9 × 23.9–5.5 × 8.3	101–43.0	1.2–1.6
		40.5 × 60.8–14.0 × 21.0	257–109	
PK-2	1/9.6–1/4.6	9.1 × 13.7–4.4 × 6.6	62.8–36.8	1.4–1.8
		23.1 × 34.7–11.1 × 16.7	160–93.5	
PK-1 + PK-2	1.6.1–1/3.6	5.8 × 8.7–3.4 × 5.2	44.5–31.8	1.6–2.1
		14.7 × 22.1–8.7 × 13.1	113–80.8	
PK-3	1/4.9–1/3.2	4.6 × 7.0–3.0 × 4.5	38.2–29.5	1.8–2.3
		11.8 × 17.7–7.6 × 11.4	97.0–75.0	
PK-1 + PK-3	1/3.8–1/2.7	3.6 × 5.4–2.5 × 3.8	32.6–27.2	2.0–2.6
		9.1 × 13.7–6.4 × 9.6	82.9–69.1	
PK-2 + PK-3	1/3.3–1/2 4	3.1 × 4.6–2.3 × 3.4	29.9–25.9	2.2–2.8
		7.8 × 11.7–5.7 × 8.6	76.0–65.8	
PK-1 + PK-2 + PK-3	1/2.7–1/2.1	2.6 × 3.9–2.0 × 3.0	27.5–24.7	2 5–3.1
		6.5 × 9.8–5.0 × 7.5	69.7–62.7	

Nikkor 180mm f/2.8

Extension Ring	*Reproduction ratio*	*Subject area (in./cm)*	*Subject distance (in./cm)*	*Exposure factor*
None	1/∞–1/8.2X	∞ × ∞–7.8 × 11.7	∞–72.1	1–1.4
		∞ × ∞–19.7 × 29.6	∞–183	
PK-1	1/22.5–1/6.0	21.3 × 31.9–5.7 × 8.5	173–56.9	1.1–1.6
		54.0 × 81.0–14.4 × 21.7	439–144	
PK-2	1/12.9–1/5.0	12.2 × 18.2–4.7 × 7.1	105–50.0	1.3–1.7
		30.9 × 46.3–12.0 × 18.1	266–127	
PK-1 + PK-2	1/8.2–1/4.1	7.7 × 11.6–3.9 × 5.8	71.9–43.8	1.4–1.9
		19.6 × 29.5–9.8 × 14.8	183–111	
PK-3	1.6.5–1/3.6	6.2 × 9.3–3.4 × 5.2	60.5–40.8	1.6–2.1
		15.7 × 23.6–8.7 × 13.1	154–104	
PK-1 + PK-3	1/5.1–1/3.1	4.8 × 7.2–3.0 × 4.4	50.3–37.5	1.7–2.3
		12.2 × 18.3–7.5 × 11.3	128–95.2	
PK-2 + PK-3	1/4.3–1/2.8	4.1 × 6.2–2.7 × 4.0	45.4–35.6	1.9–2.5
		10.4 × 15.6–6.8 × 10.2	115–90.5	
PK-1 + PK-2 + PK-3	1/3.6–1/2.5	3.4 × 5.2–2.4 × 3.6	40.7–33.7	2.1–2.7
		8.7 × 13.1–6.1 × 9.1	103–85.6	

Nikkor 200mm f/4

Extension Ring	*Reproduction ratio*	*Subject area* (in./cm)	*Subject distance* (in./cm)	*Exposure factor*
None	1/∞–1/7.1X	∞ × ∞–6.8 × 10.1	∞–78.7	1–1.8
		∞ × ∞–17.1 × 25.7	∞–200	
PK-1	1/25–1/5.6	23.6 × 35.4–5.3 × 7.9	219–66.5	1.2–2.0
		60.0 × 90.0–13.3 × 20.0	555–169	
PK-2	1/14–1/4.8	13.5 × 20.3–4.5 × 6.8	134–60.5	1.4–2.2
		34.3 × 51.4–11.4 × 17.1	341–154	
PK-1 + PK-2	1/9.1–1/4.0	8.6 × 12.9–3.8 × 5.7	93.8–54.8	1.6–2.5
		21.8 × 32.7–9.6 × 14.4	238–139	
PK-3	1/7.3–1/3.6	6.9 × 10.3–3.4 × 5.1	79.7–51.9	1.7–2.7
		17.5 × 26.2–8.6 × 13.0	202–132	
PK-1 + PK-3	1/5.6–1/3.1	5.3 × 8.0–3.0 × 4.5	67.1–48.6	2.0–3.0
		13.5 × 20.3–7.6 × 11.3	170–124	
PK-2 + PK-3	1/4.8–1/2.9	4.6 × 6.8–2.7 × 4.1	60.9–46.7	22.–3.3
		11.6 × 17.3–6.9 × 10.4	155–119	
PK-1 + PK-2 + PK-3	1/4.0–1/2.6	3.8 × 5.7–2.4 × 3.7	55.1–44.7	2.5–3.6
		9.7 × 14.5–6.2 × 9.3	140–114	

Nikkor 300mm f/4.5

Extension Ring	*Reproduction ratio*	*Subject area* (in./cm)	*Subject distance* (in./cm)	*Exposure factor*
None	1/∞–1/10.5X	∞ × ∞–9.9 × 14.8	∞–155	1.1.6
		∞ × ∞ × 25.1 × 37.6	∞–394	
PK-1	1/37.5–1/8.2	35.4 × 53.2–7.7 × 11.6	474–128	1.2–1.8
		90.0 × 135–19.6 × 29.4	1200–326	
PK-2	1/2.1–1/7.0	20.3 × 30.4–6.6 × 10.0	284–115	1.3–2.0
		51.4 × 77.1–16.9 × 25.3	722–293	
PK-1 + PK-2	1/13.6–1/5.9	12.9 × 19.3–5.6 × 8.4	192–102	1.5–2.2
		32.7 × 49.1–14.2 × 21.3	489–260	
PK-3	1/10.9–1/5.3	10.3 × 15.5–5.0 × 7.6	160–95.8	1.6–2.3
		26.2 × 39.3–12.8 × 19.2	407–243	
PK-1 + PK-3	1/8.5–1/4.7	8.0 × 12.0–4.4 × 6.6	132–88.2	1.8–2.6
		20.3 × 30.4–11.2 × 16.8	335–224	
PK-2 + PK-3	1/7.2–1/4.3	6.8 × 10.3–4.0 × 6.1	118–83.7	1.9–2.8
		17.3 × 26.0–10.3 × 15.4	298–213	
PK-1 + PK-2 + PK-3	1/6.1–1/3.8	5.7 × 8.6–3.6 × 5.4	104–78.9	2.1–3.0
		14.5 × 21.8–9.2 × 13.8	264–200	

Nikkor ED 300mm f/4.5

Extension Ring	*Reproduction ratio*	*Subject area* (in./cm)	*Subject distance* (in./cm)	*Exposure factor*
None	1/–∞1/10.3X	∞ × ∞–9.8 × 14.7	∞–156	1–1.5
		∞ × ∞–24.8 × 37.2	∞–396	
PK-1	1/37.5–1/8.1	35.4 × 53.2–7.7 × 11.5	476–130	1.1–1.7
		90.0 × 135–19.5 × 29.2	1210–330	
PK-2	1/21.4–1/7.0	20.3 × 30.4–6.6 × 9.9	286–117	1.2–1.8
		51.4 × 77.1–16.7 × 25.1	727–297	
PK-1 + PK-2	1/13.6–1/5.9	12.9 × 19.3–5.6 × 8.3	195–104	1.4–2.0
		32.7 × 49.1–14.1 × 21.2	494–265	
PK-3	1/10.9–1/5.3	10.3 × 15.5–5.0 × 7.5	163–97.7	1.5–2.1
		26.2 × 39.3–12.7 × 19.1	413–248	
PK-1 + PK-3	1/8.5–1/4.7	8.0 × 12.0–4.4 × 6.6	134–90.2	1.7–2.3
		20.3 × 30.4–11.2 × 16.7	340–229	
PK-2 + PK-3	1/7.2–1/4.3	6.8 × 10.3–4.0 × 6.0	120–85.8	1.8–2.5
		17.3 × 26.0–10.2 × 15.3	304–218	
PK-1 + PK-2 + PK-3	1/6.1–1/3.8	5.7 × 8.6–3.6 × 5.4	106–80.9	2.0–2.7
		14.5 × 21.8–9.2 × 13.8	270–206	

DATA WITH EXTENSION RING SET K

Lens	*Combination*	*Focused Distance* (cm/in.)	*Magnification*	*Subject Area* (cm/in.)	*Exposure Factor*
	K1	18.5~15.7 7.3~ 6.2	1/4.1~1/2.8	9.9×14.9~ 6.8×10.2 3.9× 5.9~ 2.7× 4.0	1.2~1.3
	K3+K2	14.4~13.6 5.7~ 5.3	1/2.2~1/1.8	5.3× 8 0~ 4.3× 6.4 2.1× 3.1~ 1.7× 2.5	1.4~1.5
	K3+K2+K1	13.1~12.9 5.2~ 5.1	1/1.5~1/1.3	3.5× 5.2~ 3.0× 4.5 1.4× 2.0~ 1.2× 1.8	1.6~1.7
	K3+K4+K2	12.9~12.8 5.1~ 5.1	1/1.2~1.0	2.8× 4.2~ 2.5× 3.7 1.1× 1.7~0.98× 1.5	1.8~1.9
24mm f/2.8	K3+K4+K2+K1	12.8~12.9 5.1~ 5.1	1.1~1.2	2.2× 3.2~ 2.0× 3.0 0.87× 1.3~0.79× 1.2	2.0~2.1
	K3+K5+K2	13.0~13.1 5.1~ 5.2	1.3~1.4	1.9× 2.8~ 1.7× 2.6 0.75× 1.1~0.67× 1.0	2.2~2.3
	K3+K5+K2+K1	13.2~13.3 5.2~ 5.2	1.5~1.6	1.6× 2.4~ 1.5× 2.2 0.63×0.94~0.59×0.87	2.5~2.6
	K3+K5+K4+K2	13.5~13.7 3.3~ 5.4	1.7~1.8	1.4× 2.1~ 1.3× 2.0 0.55×0.83~0.51×0.79	2.7~2.9
	K3+K5+K4+ K2+K1	13.8~14.2 5.4~ 5.6	1.9~2.1	1.2× 1.9~ 1.2× 1.8 0.47×0.75~0.47×0.71	3.0~3.1
	K1	23.8~18.1 9.4~ 7.1	1/4.9~1/2.9	11.8×17.8~ 7.0×10.5 4.7× 7.0~ 2.8× 4.1	1.2~1.3
	K3+K2	17.8~15.8 7.0~ 6.2	1/2.7~1/1.9	6.4× 9.5~ 4.7× 7.0 2.5× 3.8~ 1.8× 2.7	1.3~1.5
	K3+K2+K1	15.8~14.8 6.2~ 5.8	1/1.7~1/1.4	4.1× 6.2~ 3.3× 5.0 1.6× 2.4~ 1.3× 2.0	1.6~1.7
	K3+K4+K2	15.2~14.5 6.0~ 5.7	1/1.4~1/1.2	3.3× 5.0~ 2.8× 4.2 1.3× 1.9~ 1.1× 1.6	1.7~1.9
	K3+K4+K2+K1	14.9~14.5 5.9~ 5.7	1/1.4~1.1	2.6× 3.9~ 2.2× 3.4 1.0× 1.5~0.88× 1.3	1.9~2.1
28mm f/2	K3+K5+K2	14.8~14.6 5.9~ 5.7	1.1~1.2	2.2× 3.3~ 2.0× 3.0 0.87× 1.3~0.77× 1.2	2.1~2.3
	K3+K5+K2+K1	15.1~14.8 5.9~ 5.8	1.3~1.4	1.9× 2.8~ 1 7× 2.5 0.74× 1.1~0.66×0.99	2.4~2.6
	K3+K5+K4+K2	15.2~15.1 6.0~ 5.9	1 4~1.6	1.7× 2.5~ 1.5× 2.3 0.66×0.99~0.60×0.90	2.6~2 7
	K3+K5+K4+ K2+K1	15.6~15.4 6.1~ 6.1	1.6~1.8	1.5× 2.2~ 1.4× 2.0 0.57×0 87~0.53×0.79	2.8~3.0
	K1	22.5~19.7 8.9~ 7.8	1/4.9~1/3.9	11.8×17.8~ 9.3×14 0 4.7× 7.0~ 3.7× 5.5	1.3~1 3
	K3+K2	16.5~15.7 6.5~ 6.2	1/2.7~1/2.3	6.4× 9.5~ 5.5× 8.3 2.5× 3.7~ 2.2× 3.3	1.5~1.6
	K3+K2+K1	14.4~14.1 5.7~ 5.6	1/1.7~1/1.6	4.2× 6.2~ 3.8× 5.7 1.7× 2.4~ 1.5× 2.4	1.8~1.9
	K3+K4+K2	13.8~13.7 5.5~ 5.4	1/1.4~1/1.3	3.3× 4.0~ 3.1× 4.6 1.3× 1.6~ 1.2× 1.8	2.1~2.2
28mm f/3.5	K3+K4+K2+K1	13.6~13.5 5.4~ 5.3	1/1.1~1.0	2.6× 3.9~ 2.4× 3.0 1.0× 1.5~0.95× 1.5	2.5~2.6
	K3+K5+K2	13.6~13.6 5.4~ 5 4	1.1~1.1	2.2× 3.3~ 2.1× 3.2 0.87× 1.3~0.83× 1.3	2.8~2.9
	K3+K5+K2+K1	13.7~13.8 5.4~ 5.4	1.3~1.3	1 9× 2.8~ 1.8× 2.7 0.75× 1.1~0.71× 1.1	3.2~3 3
	K3+K5+K4+K2	13.9~14.0 5.5~ 5.5	1.4~1.5	1.7× 2.5~ 1 6× 2.4 0.67×0.98~0.63×0.85	3.5~3.6
	K3+K5+K4+ K2+K1	14.2~14.3 5.6~ 5.6	1.6~1.7	1.5× 2.2~ 1.4× 2.1 0 59×0.87~0.55×0.83	4.0~4.1

Lens	Combination	Focused Distance (cm/in.)	Magnification	Subject Area (cm/in.)	Exposure Factor
	K1	32.6~20.4	1/6.2~1/2.9	14.8×21.9~ 7.0×10.4	1.1~1.2
		12.8~ 8.0		5.8× 8.6~ 2.8× 4.1	
	K3+K2	22.7~17 9	1/3.3~1/2.1	8.0×11.7~ 5.0× 7.4	1.2~1.4
		8.9~ 7.0		3.1× 4.6~ 2.0× 2.9	
	K3+K2+K1	19 1~16.7	1/2.2~1/1.5	5.2× 7.7~ 3.7× 5.5	1.3~1.5
		7.5~ 6.6		2.0× 3.0~ 1.5× 2.2	
	K3+K4+K2	17.9~16.7	1/1.7~1/1.3	4.2× 6.1~ 3.1× 4.7	1.4~1.6
		7.0~ 6.4		1.6× 2.4~ 1.2× 1.8	
	K3+K4+K2+K1	17.2~16.0	1/1.4~1/1.1	3.2× 4.8~ 2.6× 3.9	1.6~1.7
35mm f/1.4		6.8~ 6.3		1.3× 1.9~ 1.0× 1.5	
	K3+K5+K2	16.9~16.1	1/1.2~1.1	2.8× 4.1~ 2.3× 3.4	1 7~1.8
		6.7~ 6.3		1.1× 1.6~0.90× 1.4	
	K3+K5+K2+K1	16.8~16.2	1.0~1.2	2.4× 3.5~ 2.0× 3.0	1.8~2.0
		6.6~ 6.3		0.93× 1.4~0.78× 1.2	
	K3+K5+K4+K2	16 9~16.3	1.1~1.3	2.1× 3.1~ 1.8× 2.7	1.9~2.1
		6.7~ 6.4		0.83× 1.2~0.71× 1.1	
	K3+K5+K4+	17.1~16.6	1.3~1.5	1.9× 2.7~ 1.6× 2.4	2.1~2.3
	K2+K1	6.7~ 6.5		0.72× 1.1~0.63×0.94	
	K1	31.9~20.8	1/6.2~1.3	14.9×22.3~ 7.1×10.7	1.2~1.4
		12.5~ 8.5		5.9× 8.8~ 2.8× 4.2	
	K3+K2	22.0~18.2	1/3.3~1/2.1	8.0×12.0~ 5.0× 7.6	1.4~1.7
		8.7~ 7.2		3.1× 4.7~ 2.0× 3.0	
	K3+K2+K1	18.4~16.9	1/2.2~1/1.6	5.2× 7.8~ 3.8× 5.6	1.6~1.9
		7.3~ 6.7		2.0× 3.1~ 1.5× 2.2	
	K3+K4+K2	17.3~16.5	1/1.7~1/1.3	4.2× 6.2~ 3.2× 4.8	1.8~2.1
		6.8~ 6.5		1.7× 2.4~ 1.3× 1.9	
35mm f/2	K3+K4+K2+K1	16.5~16.2	1/1.4~1/1.1	3.2× 4.9~ 2.6× 3.9	2 1~2.4
		6.5~ 6.4		1.3× 1.9~ 1 0× 1.5	
35mm f/2.8	K3+K5+K2	16.3~16.2	1/1.2~1.0	2.8× 4.2~ 2.3× 3.5	2.3~2.6
		6.4~ 6.4		1.1× 1.7~0.91× 1.4	
	K3+K5+K2+K1	16 2~16.3	1.0~1.2	2.4× 3.5~ 2.0× 3.0	2.6~2.9
		6.4~ 6.4		0.94× 1.4~0.83× 1.2	
	K3+K5+K4+K2	16.2~16.4	1.1~1.3	2.1× 3.2~ 1.8× 2.7	2.8~3.2
		6.4~ 6.5		0.83× 1.3~0.71× 1.1	
	K3+K5+K4+	16.4~16.7	1.3~1.5	1.9× 2.8~ 1.6× 2 4	3.2~3.5
	K2+K1	6.5~ 6.6		1.75× 1.1~0 63×0.95	
	K1	47.3~34.4	1/8.0~1/5.2	19.2×28.8~12.5×18.8	1.3~1.4
		18.7~13 6		7.6×11.4~ 4.9× 7.4	
	K3+K2	30.5~26.0	1/4.3~1/3.4	10.3×15.5~ 8.0×12.0	1.5~1.7
		12.0~10.3		4.1× 6 1~ 3.2× 4.7	
	K3+K2+K1	24.0~22.0	1/2.8~1/2.4	6.7×10.0~ 5.6× 8.5	1.8~2.0
		9.5~ 8.7		2.6× 4.0~ 2.2× 3.4	
	K3+K4+K2	21.9~20.5	1/2.2~1/1.9	5.3× 8.0~ 4.7× 7.0	2.1~2.3
		8.6~ 8.1		2.1× 3.2~ 1.9× 2.8	
GN 45mm f/2.8	K3+K4+K2+K1	20.1~19.3	1/1.7~1/1 6	4.2× 6.3~ 3.8× 5.6	2.5~2.7
		7.9~ 7.6		1.7× 2.5~ 1 5× 2.2	
	K3+K5+K2	19.5~18.9	1/1.5~1/1.4	3.6× 5 4~ 3.3× 4.9	2.8~3.0
		7.7~ 7.5		1.4× 2.1~ 1.3× 1.9	
	K3+K5+K2+K1	18.9~18.5	1/1.3~1/1.2	3.0× 4.5~ 2.8× 4.2	3.2~3 4
		7.5~ 7.3		1.2× 1.8~ 1.1× 1.7	
	K3+K5+K4+K2	18.7~18.4	1/1.1~1/1.1	2.7× 4.1~ 2.5× 3.8	3.5~3 8
		7.4~ 7.3		1.1× 1.6~0.99× 1.5	
	K3+K5+K4+	18.7~18 4	1 0~1.1	2.4× 3.6~ 2.2× 3.4	4 0~4.3
	K2+K1	7.4~ 7.3		0.95× 1.4~0.87× 1.3	

Lens	Combination	Focused Distance (cm/in)	Magnification	Subject Area (cm/in.)	Factor
	K1	55.4~34.1	1/8.9~1/4.7	21.3×32.0~11.2×16.8	1.1~1.3
		21.8~13.4		8.4×12.6~ 4.4× 6.6	
	K3+K2	34.7~27.1	1/4.8~1/3.2	11.5×17.2~ 7.7×11.6	1.3~1.4
		13.7~10.7		4.5× 6.8~ 3.0× 4.6	
	K3+K2+K1	26.6~23.3	1/3.1~1/2.4	7.5×11.2~ 5.7× 8.5	1.4~1.5
		10.5~ 9.2		3.0× 4.4~ 2.2× 3 3	
	K3+K4+K2	23.8~21.8	1/2.5~1.2	6.0× 8.9~ 4.8× 7.1	1.5~1.7
		9.4~ 8.6		2.4× 3.5~ 1.9× 2.8	
50mm f/1.4	K3+K4+K2+K1	21.6~20.5	1/2~1/1.6	4.7× 7.0~ 3.9× 5.8	1.7~1.8
		8.5~ 8.0		1.9× 2.8~ 1.5× 2.3	
	K3+K5+K2	20.7~19.9	1/1.7~1/1.4	4.0× 6.0~ 3.4× 5.2	1.8~2.0
		8.2~ 7.9		1.6× 2.4~ 1.3× 2.0	
	K3+K5+K2+K1	19.9~19.5	1/1.4~1/1.2	3.4× 5.1~ 3.0× 4.4	2.0~2.1
		7.9~ 7.7		1.3× 2.0~ 1.2× 1.7	
	K3+K5+K4+K2	19.5~19.3	1/1.3~1/1.1	3.0× 4.6~ 2.7× 4.0	2.1~2.3
		7.7~7.6		1.2× 1.8~ 1.1× 1.6	
	K3+K5+K4+	19.3~19.3	1/1.1~1.0	2.7× 4.0~ 2.4× 3.6	2.3~2.5
	K2+K1	7.6~ 7.6		1.1× 1.6~0.95× 1.4	
	K1	56.1~34.6	1/8.9~1/4.6	21.4×32.0~11.1×16.7	1.2~1.4
		22.0~13.6		8.4×12.6~ 4.4× 6.6	
	K3+K2	35.3~27.7	1/4.8~1/3.2	11.5×17.2~ 7.7×11.5	1.4~1.6
		13.9~10.9		4.5× 6.8~ 3.0× 4.5	
	K3+K2+K1	27.3~23.9	1/3.1~1/2.4	7.5×11.2~ 5.6× 8.5	1.6~1.9
		10.7~ 9.4		3.0× 4.4~ 2.4× 3.3	
	K3+K4+K2	24.5~22.4	1/2.5~1.2	6.0× 8.9~ 4.7× 7.1	1.9~2.1
		9.7~ 8.8		2.4× 3.5~ 1.9× 2.9	
50mm f/2	K3+K4+K2+K1	22.3~21.1	1/1.9~1/1.6	4.7× 7.0~ 3.9× 5.8	2.1~2.3
		8.8~ 8.3		1.9× 2.8~ 1.5× 2.3	
	K3+K5+K2	21.3~20.6	1/1.7~1/1.4	4.0× 6.0~ 3.4× 5.1	2.3~2.6
		8.4~ 8.1		1.6× 2.4~ 1.3× 2.0	
	K3+K5+K2+K1	20.5~20.1	1/1.4~1/1.2	3.4× 5.1~ 3.0× 4 4	2.6~2.9
		8.6~ 7.9		1.3× 2.0~ 1.3× 1.7	
	K3+K5+K4+K2	20.2~20.0	1/1.3~1/1.1	3.0× 4.6~ 2.7× 4.0	2.8~3.1
		8.0~ 7.9		1.2× 1.8~ 1.1× 1.6	
	K3+K5+K4+	20.0~19.9	1/1.1~1.0	2.7× 4.0~ 2.4× 3.6	3.2~3.5
	K2+K1	7.9~ 7.8		1.1× 1.6~0.95× 1.4	
	K1	63.0~36.3	1/9.6~1/4.6	23.0×34.4~11.1×16.7	1.1~1.3
		24.8~14.3		9.1×13.5~ 4.3× 6.6	
	K3+K2	38.9~29.2	1/5.1~1/3.3	12.3×18.5~ 7.9×11.8	1.3~1.4
		15.3~11.5		4.9× 7.3~ 3.1× 4.7	
	K3+K2+K1	29.6~25.2	1/3.3~1/2.4	8.0×12.0~ 5.9× 8.8	1.4~1.6
		11.7~ 9.9		3.1× 4.7~ 2.3× 3.5	
55mm f/1.2	K3+K4+K2	26.2~23.5	1/2.7~1/2.1	6.4× 9.6~ 4.9× 7.4	1.5~1.7
		10.3~ 9.3		2.5× 3.8~ 1.9× 2.9	
	K3+K4+K2+K1	23.6~22.0	1/2.1~1/1.7	5.0× 7.5~ 4.1× 6.1	1.7~1.9
		9.3~ 8.7		2.0× 3.0~ 1.6× 2.4	
	K3+K5+K2	22.4~21.4	1/1.8~1/1.5	4.3× 6.5~ 3.6× 5.4	1.8~2.0
		8.8~ 8.4		1.7× 2.6~ 1.4× 2.1	
	K3+K5+K2+K1	21.4~20.8	1/1.5~1/1.3	3.6× 5.5~ 3.1× 4.7	2.0~2.3
		8.4~ 8.2		1.4× 2.2~ 1.2× 1.9	
	K3+K5+K4+K2	21.0~20.6	1/1.4~1/1.2	3.3× 4.9~ 2.8× 4.3	2.2~2.4
		8.3~ 8.1		1.3× 1.9~ 1.1× 1.7	
	K3+K5+K4+	20.6~20.5	1/1.2~1/1.1	2.9× 4.3~ 2.5× 3.8	2.4~2.6
	K2+K1	8.1~ 8.1		1.1× 1.7~0.98× 1.5	

Lens	Combination	Focused Distance (cm/in.)	Magnification	Subject Area (cm/in.)	Exposure Factor
	K1	141~67.3	1/14.7~1/5.9	35.2×52.8~14.1×21.1	1.2~1.5
		55.6~26.5		13.9×20.8~5.6×8.3	
	K3+K2	83.9~55.0	1/7.9~1/4.4	18.9×28.3~10.4×15 7	1.3~1.6
		33.0~21.6		7.5×11.1~4.1×6.2	
	K3+K2+K1	61.1~47.0	1/5.1~1/3.4	12.3×18.4~8.1×12.1	1.5~1.9
		24.1~18.5		4.8×7.3~3.2×4.8	
	K3+K4+K2	52.7~43.4	1/4.1~1/2.9	9.8×14.7~6.9×10.4	1.7~2
		20.7~17.1		3.9×5.8~2.7×4.1	
	K3+K4+K2+K1	45.7~39.9	1/3.2~1/2.4	7.7×11.5~5.8×8.7	1.9~2.3
		18.0~15.7		3.0×4.5~2.3×3.4	
85mm f/1.8	K3+K5+K2	42.5~38.2	1/2.8~1/2.2	6.6×9.9~5.2×7.8	2.1~2.5
		16.7~15.0		2.6×3.9~2.0×3.1	
	K3+K5+K2+K1	39.3~36.4	1/2.3~1/1.9	5.6×8.4~4.5×6.8	2.3~2.8
		15.5~14.4		2.2×3.3~1.8×2.7	
	K3+K5+K4+K2	37.7~35.5	1/2 1~1/1.7	5.0×7.5~4.1×6.2	2.6~3
		14.8~14.0		2.0×3.0~1.6×2.4	
	K3+K5+K4+ K2+K1	36.0~34.5	1/1.8~1/1.5	4.4×6.6~3.6×5.5	2.8~3.2
		14.2~13.6		1.7×2.6~1.4×2.2	
	K1	208~83.3	1/18.1~1/6.1	43.4×65.2~14.7×22.0	1.2~1.6
		82.0~32.8		17.1×25.7~5.9×8.7	
	K3+K2	121~69.3	1/9.7~1/4.7	23.3×35.0~11.4×17.1	1.4~1.8
		47.7~27.3		9.2×13.8~4.5×6.7	
	K3+K2+K1	85.4~59.5	1/6.3~1/3.8	15.2×22.8~9.0×13.5	1 6~2.2
		32.6~23.4		6.0×9.0~3.5×5.3	
	K3+K4+K2	72.3~54.8	1/5 ~1/3.3	12.1×18.1~7.8×11.7	1.8~2 3
		28.5~21.6		4.8×7.1~3.1×4.6	
105mm f/2.5	K3+K4+K2+K5	61.4~50.1	1/4 ~1/2.8	9.5×14.2~6.6×9.9	2.0~2.6
		24.2~19.7		3.7×5.6~2.6×4.0	
	K3+K5+K2	56.1~47.7	1/3.4~1/2.5	8.2×12.2~6.0×9.0	2.2~2.8
		21.7~18.8		3.2×4.8~2.4×3.5	
	K3+K5+K2+K1	51.0~45.1	1/2.9~1/2.2	6.9×10.3~5.3×7.9	2.5~3.[illegible]
		20.0~17 8		2.7×4.1~2.1×3.1	
	K3+K5+K4+K2	48.4~43.7	1/2.6~1.2	6.2×9.3~4.8×7.2	2.7~3.3
		19.1~17.2		2.4×3.7~1.9×2.8	
	K3+K5+K4+ K2+K1	45.6~42.1	1/2.3~1/1.8	5.4×8.1~4.3×6.5	3.0~3.6
		18.0~16.6		2.1×3.2~1.7×2.6	
	K1	341~116	1/23.3~1.6.5	55.8×83.8~15.6×23.4	1.1~1.5
		134~45.8		22.0×33.0~6.2×9.2	
	K3+K2	195~99.9	1/12.5~1/5.2	30.0×45.0~12.6×18.9	1.3~1.6
		77.0~39.3		11.8×17.7~5.0×7.5	
	K3+K2+K1	138~87.4	1/8 1~1/4.3	19.5×29.3~10.2×15.4	1.4~1.8
		54.5~34.4		7.7×11.5~4.0×6.1	
135mm f/2.8	K3+K4+K2	116~81.1	1/6.5~1/3.8	15.6×23.4~9.0×13.6	1.5~1.9
		45.8~32.0		6.2×9.2~3.5×5.4	
135mm f/3.5	K3+K4+K2+K1	97.7~74.5	1/5.1~1/3.2	12.2×18.3~7.8×11.7	1.7~2.1
		38.5~29.4		4.8×7.2~3.1×4.6	
	K3+K5+K2	88.8~71.0	1/4.4~1.3	10.5×15.8~7.1×10.6	1.8~2.3
		35.0~28.0		4.1×6.2~3.0×4.2	
	K3+K5+K2+K1	79.9~67.0	1/3.7~1/2.6	8.8×13.2~6.3×9.4	2.0~2.5
		31.5~26.4		3.5×5.2~2.5×3.7	
	K3+K5+K4+K2	75.2~64.8	1/3.3~1/2.4	7.9×11.9~5.8×8.7	2.1~2.6
		29.5~25.5		3.1×4.7~2.3×3.4	
	K3+K5+K4+ K2+K1	70.3~62.3	1/2.9~1/2.2	6.9×10.4~5.3×7.9	2.3~2.8
		27.7~24.5		2.7×4.1~2.1×3.1	

Lens	Combination	Focused Distance (cm/in.)	Magnification	Subject Area (cm/in.)	Exposure Factor
	K1	592~151	1/31~1/6.5	74.4×112 ~15.5×23.3	1.1~1.6
		233~59.2		29.3×43.9~ 6.1× 9.2	
	K3+K2	334~133	1/17~1/5.5	40.0×60.0~13.2×19.8	1.2~1.7
		132~52.4		15.7×23.6~ 5.2× 7.8	
	K3+K2+K1	230~119	1/11~1/4.7	26.0×39.0~11.2×16.8	1.3~1.8
		90.5~46.7		10.5×15.4~ 4.4× 6.6	
	K3+K4+K2	191~111	1/8.7~1/4.2	20.7×31.1~10.1×15.1	1.4~1 9
		75.1~43.7		8.1×12.2~ 4.0× 5.9	
180mm f/2.8	K3+K4+K2+K1	158~103	1/6.8~1/3.7	16.2×24.3~ 8.9×13.3	1.5~2.1
		62.0~40.3		6.4× 9.6~ 3.5× 5.2	
	K3+K5+K2	141~97.6	1/5.8~1/3.4	14.0× 1.0~ 8.2×12.2	1.6~2.2
		57.6~38.4		5.5× 8.3~ 3.2× 4.8	
	K3+K5+K2+K1	125~92.1	1/4.9~1/3.1	11.8×17.7~ 7.4×11.1	1.8~2.3
		49.3~36.3		4.7× 7.0~ 2.9× 4.4	
	K3+K5+K4+K2	117~88.8	1/4.4~1/2.9	10.5×15.8~ 6.9×10.3	1.9~2.4
		45.8~34.9		4.1× 6.2~ 2.7× 4.1	
	K3+K5+K4+	107~85.0	1/3.9~1/2.6	9.3×13.9~ 6.3× 9.5	2~2.6
	K2+K1	42.2~33.5		3.6× 5.5~ 2.5× 3.7	
	K1	745~237	1/34.5~1.9	82.8×124.1~21.6×32.4	1.1~1.7
		294~93.4		32.6×48.9~ 8.5×12.8	
	K3+K2	426~204	1/18.5~1/7.4	44.4×66.6~17.6×26.5	1.3~1.8
		168~80.4		17.5×26.2~ 6.9×10.4	
	K3+K2+K1	297~179	1/12~1/6.1	28.9×43.3~14.5×21.8	1.5~2.1
		117~70.5		11.4×17.0~ 5.7× 8.6	
	K3+K4+K2	249~166	1/9.6~1/5.4	23.1×34.6~12.9×19.3	1.6~2.2
		98.1~65.4		9.1×13.6~ 5.1× 7.6	
200mm f/4	K3+K4+K2+K1	207~152	1/7.5~1/4.7	18.0×27.0~11.2×16.7	1.8~2.5
		81.6~60.0		7.1×10.6~ 4.4× 6.6	
	K3+K5+K2	187~144	1/6.5~1/4.2	15.6×23.4~10.2×15.2	2.0~2.7
		73.7~56.7		6.1× 9.2~ 4.0× 6.0	
	K3+K5+K2+K1	167~135	1/5.5~1/3.8	13.1×19.7~ 9.0×13.6	2.2~2.9
		65.8~53.2		5.2× 7.8~ 3.5× 5.4	
	K3+K5+K4+K2	157~130	1/4.9~1/3.5	11.8×17.6~ 8.4×12.6	2.4~3.1
		61.9~51.2		4.6× 6.9~ 3.3× 5.0	
	K3+K5+K4+	145~124	1/4.3~1/3.2	10.3×15.4~ 7.6×11.4	2.6~3.4
	K2+K1	57.1~48.9		4.0× 6.0~ 3.0× 4.5	
	K1	1630~342	1/51.7~1/8.7	124×186 ~20.9×31.3	1.1~1.7
		642~135		48.7×73.1~ 8.2×12.3	
	K3+K2	912~310	1/27.8~1/7.6	66.6×100 ~18.2×27.4	1.2~1.9
		359~122		26.2×39.4~ 7.2×10.8	
	K3+K2+K1	622~281	1/18.1~1/6.6	43.4×65.1~15.9×23.8	1.3~2.0
		245~111		17.1×25.6~ 6.3× 9.4	
	K3+K4+K2	513~265	1/14.4~1/6.1	34.6×51.9~14.5×21.8	1.4~2.2
		202~104		13.6×20.5~ 5.7× 8.6	
300mm f/4.5	K3+K4+K2+K1	419~246	1/11.3~1/5.4	27.0×40.6~13.0×19.5	1.6~2.3
		165~96.9		10.6×16.0~ 5.1× 7.7	
	K3+K5+K2	373~235	1/9.7~1/5	23.4×35.1~12.1×18.1	1.7~2.4
		147~92.6		9.2×13.9~ 4.8× 7.1	
	K3+K5+K2+K1	327~222	1/8.2~1/4.6	19.7×29.5~11.0×16.5	1.8~2.6
		129~87.5		7.8×11.6~ 4.3× 6.5	
	K3+K5+K4+K2	302~214	1/7.4~1/4.3	17.6×26.5~10.3×15.5	1.9~2.7
		119~84.3		6.9×10.5~ 4.1× 6.1	
	K3+K5+K4+	275~205	1/6.4~1/4	15.4×23.1~ 9.6×14.3	2.1~2.9
	K2+K1	108~80.8		6.1× 9.1~ 3.8× 5.6	

DATA WITH EXTENSION RING E2

Lens	*Focused Distance* (cm/in.)	*Magnification*	*Subject Area* (cm/in.)	*Exposure Factor*
24mm f/2.8	13.5 ~ 13.1	1/1.7 ~ 1/1.4	4.1 × 6.2 ~ 3.5 × 5.2	1.5 ~ 1.6
	5.3 ~ 5.2		1.6 × 2.4 ~ 1.4 × 2.1	
28mm f/2	16.4 ~ 15.1	1/2.0 ~ 1/1.6	4.9 × 7.4 ~ 3.8 × 5.7	1.5 ~ 1.6
	6.5 ~ 5.9		1.9 × 2.9 ~ 1.5 × 2.3	
28mm f/3.5	15.1 ~ 14.6	1/2 ~ 1/1.8	4.9 × 7.4 ~ 4.4 × 6.6	1.7 ~ 1.8
	6.0 ~ 5.8		1.9 × 2.9 ~ 1.7 × 2.6	
35mm f/1.4	20.3 ~ 17.1	1/2.6 ~ 1/1.7	6.2 × 9.1 ~ 4.7 × 6.3	1.3 ~ 1.4
	8.0 ~ 6.7		2.4 × 3.6 ~ 1.8 × 2.5	
35mm f/2	19.6 ~ 17.4	1/2.6 ~ 1/1.8	6.2 × 9.3 ~ 4.2 × 6.4	1.5 ~ 1.8
	7.7 ~ 6.9		2.4 × 3.7 ~ 1.7 × 2.5	
35mm f/2.8	19.2 ~ 16.9	1/2.6 ~ 1/1.8	6.2 × 9.3 ~ 4.3 × 6.4	1.6 ~ 2.0
	7.6 ~ 6.7		2.4 × 3.7 ~ 1.7 × 2.5	
GN 45mm f/2.8	26.3 ~ 23.5	1/3.3 ~ 1/2.7	8.0 × 12.0 ~ 6.5 × 9.8	1.7 ~ 1.9
	10.4 ~ 9.3		3.1 × 4.7 ~ 2.6 × 3.8	
50mm f/1.4	29.4 ~ 24.7	1/3.7 ~ 1/2.7	8.8 × 13.3 ~ 6.4 × 9.6	1.3 ~ 1.5
	11.6 ~ 9.8		3.5 × 5.2 ~ 2.5 × 3.8	
50mm f/2	30.0 ~ 25.3	1/3.7 ~ 1/2.7	8.8 × 13.3 ~ 6.4 × 9.6	1.5 ~ 1.8
	11.8 ~ 10.0		3.5 × 5.3 ~ 2.5 × 3.8	
55mm f/1.2	32.7 ~ 26.6	1/4 ~ 1/2.8	9.5 × 14.3 ~ 6.6 × 9.9	1.4 ~ 1.5
	12.9 ~ 10.5		3.7 × 5.6 ~ 2.7 × 3.9	
85mm f/1.8	68.9 ~ 50.0	1/6.1 ~ 1/3.7	14.6 × 21.9 ~ 9.0 × 13.5	1.5 ~ 1.8
	27.1 × 19.6		5.7 × 8.6 ~ 3.5 × 5.3	
105mm f/2.5	97.5 ~ 63.3	1/7.5 ~ 1/4.1	18.0 × 27.0 ~ 9.9 × 14.9	1.5 ~ 2
	38.4 ~ 25.0		7.1 × 11 ~ 3.9 × 5.9	
135mm f/2.8	158 ~ 92.4	1/9.6 ~ 1/4.7	23.1 × 34.7 ~ 11.2 × 16.8	1.3 ~ 1.7
	62.2 ~ 36.5		9.1 × 13.6 ~ 4.4 × 6.6	
180mm f/2.8	266 ~ 125	1/12.9 ~ 1/5.0	30.8 × 46.2 ~ 12.0 × 18.0	1.3 ~ 1.8
	105 ~ 49.0		12.1 × 18.2 ~ 4.7 × 7.1	
200mm f/4	341 ~ 189	1/14 ~ 1/6.6	34.3 × 51.4 ~ 15.8 × 23.7	1.4 ~ 2
	134 ~ 74.4		13.5 × 20.2 ~ 6.2 × 9.3	

REPRODUCTION RATIOS OBTAINABLE WITH SLIDE COPYING ADAPTER

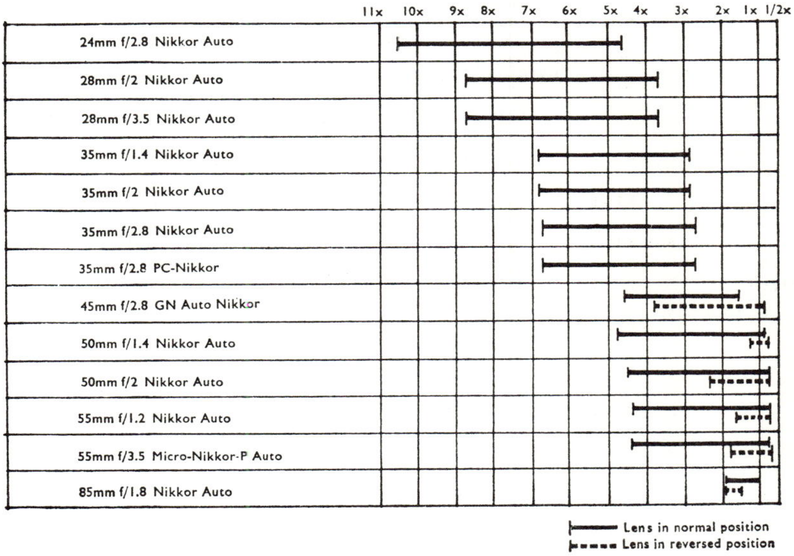

REPRODUCTION RATIOS AND BELLOWS EXTENSIONS **Note: Lens set at infinity**

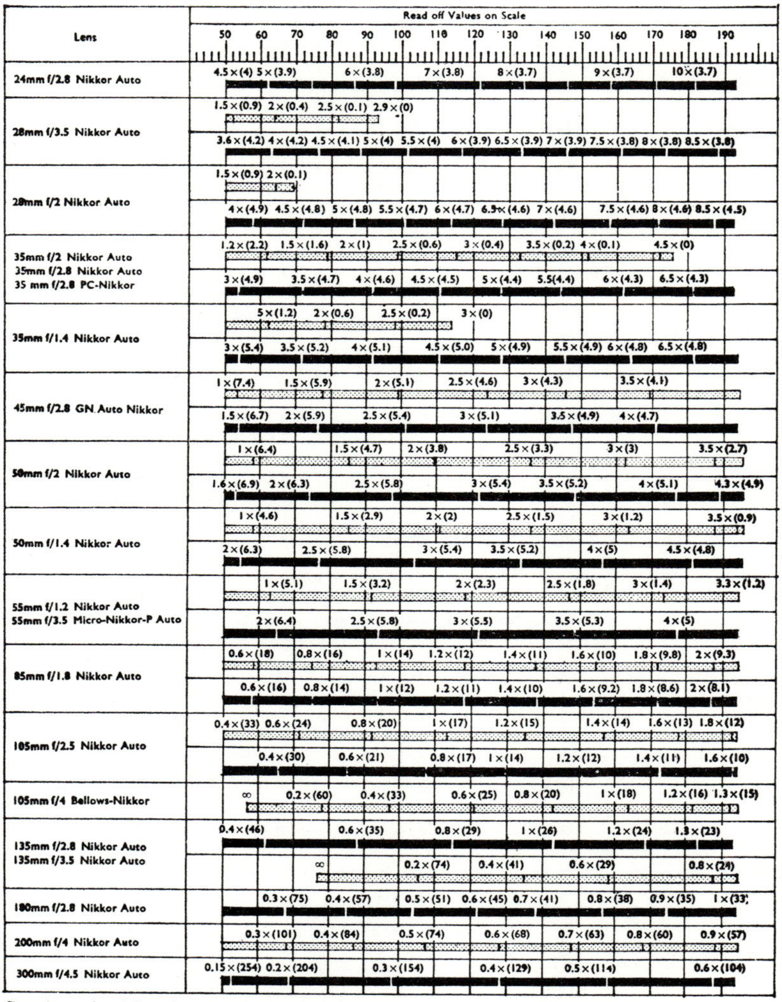

Figures in parentheses indicate distance from the subject plane in focus to the lens barrel edge in cm.

Lens in normal position (dotted bar)
Lens in reversed position (solid bar)

CLOSE-UP ATTACHMENT LENSES

Lens	*Close-up Attachment*	*Focused Distance* (cm/in.)	*Magnification*	*Subject Area* (cm/in.)
	No. 0	148~55.5	1/30~1/10	72.9×109~24.0×36.0
		58.3~21.9		28.4×42.6~ 9.5×14.2
GN 45mm f/2.8	No. 1	75.1~42.9	1/14~1/7.3	34.7×52.1~17.6×26.3
		29.6~16.9		13.2×19.9~ 6.9×10.3
	No. 2	41.5~31.0	1/7.3~1/4.8	17.5×26.2~11.6×17.4
		16.4~12.2		6.9×10.3~4.5 ×6.84
	No. 0	46~147	1/27~1/7.1	26×17 ~97 ×65
		17.9~58.0		10.1×6.7 ~38.3×25.5
	No. 1	40~78	1/13~1/5.7	20×14 ~47 ×31
50mm f/1.4		15.5~30.6		8.1×5.4~18.4×12.3
	No. 2	31~44	1/6.5~1/4.0	14×9 ~23 ×16
		12.2~17.4		5.7×3.8~ 9.2×6.1
	No. 1+No. 2	27~34	1/4.4~1/3.1	11×7.5~16 ×11
		10.6~13.2		4.4×2.9~ 6.2×4.2
	No. 0	47~150	1/27~1/7.1	26×17 ~97 ×65
		18.5~59.2		10.1×6.7~38.3×25.5
	No. 1	40~78	1/13~1/5.5	20×14 ~47 ×31
		15.3~30.2		7.8×5.2~18.4×12.3
50mm f/2	No. 2	30~43	1/6.5~1/3.8	14×9 ~23 ×16
		11.9~17.0		5.4×3.6~ 9.2×6.1
	No. 1+No. 2	26~33	1/4.4~1/3.0	11×7.5~16 ×11
		10.2~12.8		4.3×2.8~ 6.2×4.2
	No. 0	48~151	1/25~1/6.7	24×16 ~91 ×61
		18.7~59.7		9.5×6.3 ~36.0×24.0
	No. 1	40~78	1/12~1/5.2	19×13 ~44 ×29
		15.7~30.7		7.4×5.0~17.1×11.4
55mm f/1.2	No. 2	31~44	1/6.1~1/3.7	13×8.8~22 ×15
		12.3~17.5		5.2×3.5~ 8.6×5.8
	No. 1+No. 2	27~34	1/4.1~1/2.9	10×6.9~15 ×9.8
		10.7~13.3		4.1×2.7~ 5.8×3.9
	No. 0	67~154	1/17~1/6.1	22×15 ~60 ×40
		26.4~60.6		8.7×5.9~23.6×15.7
85mm f/1.8	No. 1	52~80	1/7.9~1/4.3	15×10 ~28 ×19
		20.5~31.5		5.9×3.9~11.0×7.5
	No. 2	38~47	1/4.0~1/2.8	10×7 ~14 ×10
		15.0~18.5		3.9×2.8~ 5.5×3.9
	No. 0	70~153	1/13~1/5.0	18×12 ~48 ×32
		27.4~60.3		7.1×4.7~19.1×12.7
105mm f/2.5	No. 1	53~80	1/6.4~1/3.5	13×8.4~23 ×15
		20.9~31.5		5.0×3.3~ 9.1×6.1
	No. 2	39~46	1/3.2~1/2.2	8.0×5.3~12 ×8
		15.2~18.3		3.2×2.1~ 4.6×3.0
	No. 0	85~156	1/10~1/4.6	17×11 ~38 ×25
		33.6~61.5		6.6×4.5~14.8×9.9
135mm f/2.8	No. 1	62~82	1/5.0~1/3.0	11×7.3~18 ×12
		24.3~32.5		4.3×2.9~ 7.0×4.7
	No. 2	44~49	1/2.5~1/1.8	6.6×4.4~ 9 ×6
		17.2~19.3		2.6×1.7~ 3.5×2.4
	No. 0	85~155	1/10~1/4.6	17×11 ~36 ×24
		33.2~61.0		6.5×4.3~14.2×9.5
135mm f/3.5	No. 1	61~81	1/5.0~1/3.0	11×7.2~18 ×12
		23.9~32.0		4.3×2.8~ 7.1×4.7
	No. 2	43~48	1/2.5~1/1.8	6.5×4.3~ 9 ×6
		16.8~18.8		2.6×1.7~ 3.5×2.4
200mm f/4	No. 0	102~162	1/7.1~1/3.2	11.4×7.6~25.4×16.9
		43.6~63.7		4.5×3.0~10.0×6.7

200 mm *f*5.6 MEDICAL NIKKOR

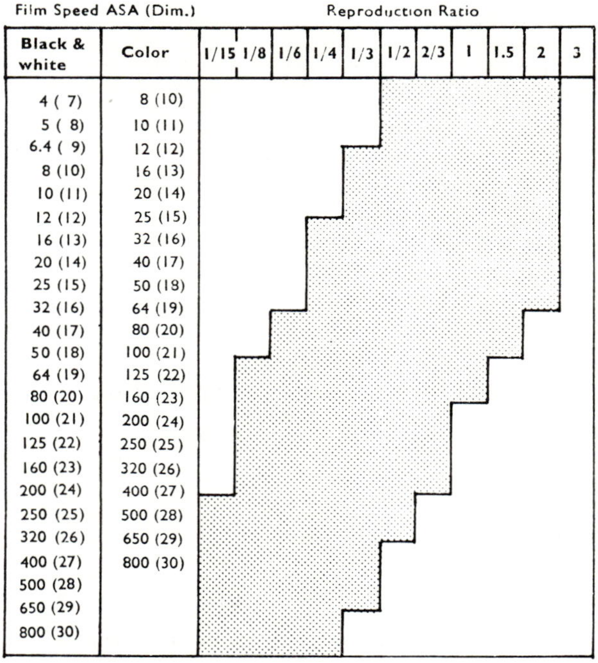

The range of film speed that can be used with the chosen magnification ratio. Shaded area indicates possible magnification—film speed combinations

Reproduction ratio	Combination of lenses	Distance of subject from front surface of lens (inch)	(mm)	Subject field (inch × inch)	(mm × mm)
1/15X	Master lens	10′ 11.89″	3,350	14.17 × 21.26	360 × 540
1/8X	1/8X + Master lens	5′ 10.08″	1,780	7.56 × 11.34	192 × 288
1/6X	1/6X + Master lens	4′ 4.64″	1,337	5.67 × 8.50	144 × 216
1/4X	1/4X + Master lens	2′ 11.04″	890	3.78 × 5.677	96 × 144
1/3X	1/4X + 1/6X + Master lens	2′ 1.0″	635	2.72 × 4.06	69 × 103
1/2X	1/2X + Master lens	1′ 5.32″	440	1.89 × 2.83	48 × 12
2/3X	1/2X + 1/4X + Master lens	1′ 0.72″	323	1.38 × 2.09	35 × 53
1X	1X + Master lens	8.66″	220	0.94 × 1.42	24 × 36
1.5X	1X + 1/2X + Master lens	5.98″	152	0.67 × 0.98	17 × 25
2X	2X + Master lens	4.17″	106	0.47 × 0.71	12 × 18
3X	2X + 1X + Master lens	2.76″	70	0.33 × 0.50	8.4 × 12.6

Caution: The camera is provided with a body earth. To avoid receiving an electric shock when using the Nikon F, attach the safety cover on the camera accessory shoe so that the photographer's hand will not touch synch contact near the rewind crank.

MD-2 MOTOR DRIVE COUPLING RANGE

Setting at	Number of exposures per sec.	Range of shutter speed to be used	Electronic flash	Reflex Mirror in camera
L	2 approx.	1/1000–1/8	Can be used at X contact	Flips up each time exposure is made
M 1	2.5 approx.	1/1000–1/60	Can be used at X contact	Flips up each time exposure is made
M 2	3 approx.	1/1000–1/125	Cannot be used	Flips up each time exposure is made
H	4 approx.	1/1000–1/125	Cannot be used	Must be held in up position

—TABLE 1. FIRING SPEEDS (FRAMES PER SECOND)

Firing Speed Setting (Power Source: 15V)	H (Mirror locked up)	M3	M2	M1	L	Approx. Number of 36 ex. Roll		Lowest Usable Temperature
Slowest Usable Shutter Speed (sec.)	1/125	1/125	1/60	1/8	1/4	A	B	
NC Battery Unit MN-1	5	4.3	3.8	2.5	1.3	60	50	−20°C
Alkaline-Manganese Batteries	4	3.5	3	2	1	80	20	−10°C
Zinc-Carbon Batteries	4	3.5	3	2	1	50	10	0°C
AC/DC Converter MA-2	5	4.3	3.8	2.5	1.3	—	—	

Remarks: A. Approximate number of film per set of fresh batteries.
B. Approximate number of film within which the rated firing speed is assured.

Meter coupling limits

These charts indicate the ranges for most Nikon and Nikkormat models. The diagonal lines indicate the shutter speed coupling limits for various film speed and aperture combinations. For instance on the Nikkormat FT3, FT2 or FTN, an ASA 25 film with an *f*16 aperture measures shutter speeds from 2 sec (bulb) at the top, to 1/125 sec. An ASA 400 film used at *f*1.4 indicates shutter speeds of 1/15 sec and faster. Any line such as the ASA100 *f*5.6 which extends completely from top to bottom indicates complete coupling at all shutter speeds. For between ASA listed numbers, read the nearest printed. For apertures not listed, find the closest one and extend the range one f-stop for each aperture. For instance, for ASA 25 at *f*11, use the ASA 25 at *f*16. This line indicates a limit of 1/125 sec. At *f*11 the limit would extend to 1/250 sec.

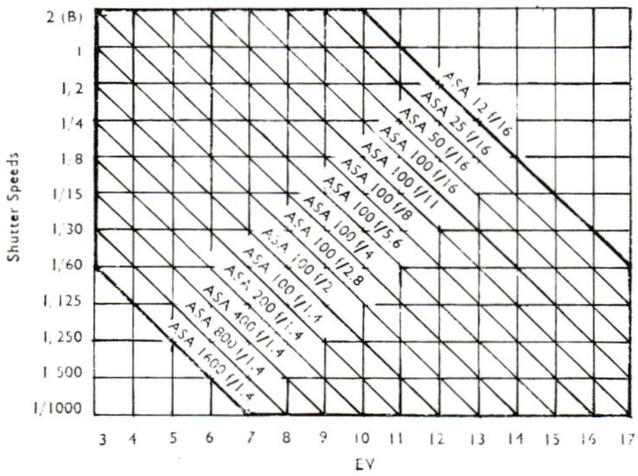

Exposure Coupling Range: Nikkormat FT3, FT2 or FTN with 50mm *f*1.4 lens.

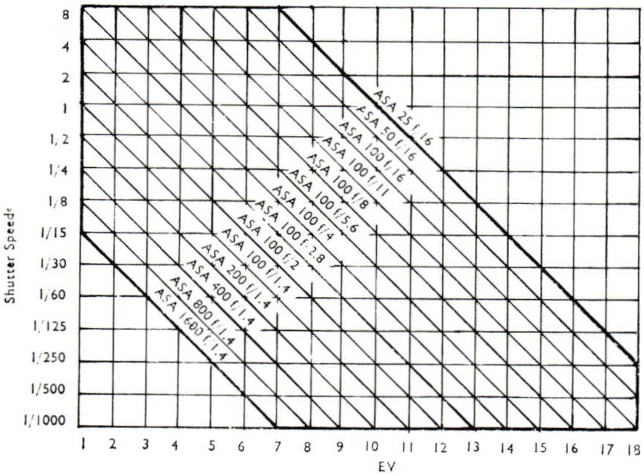

Exposure Coupling Range: Nikon EL2 with 50mm *f*1.4; Nikkormat EL(W) has same range but only to 4 sec. maximum exposure.

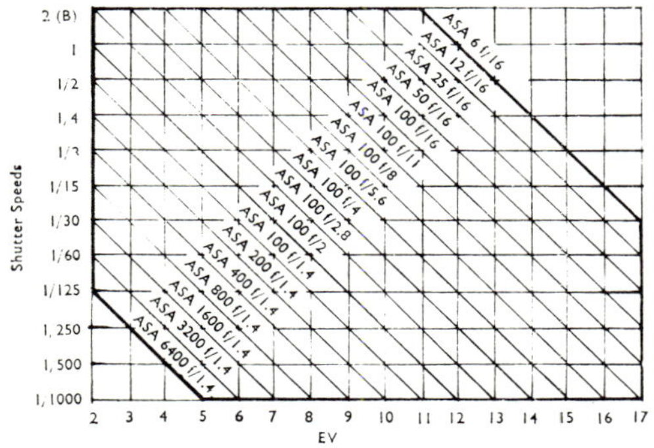

Exposure Coupling Range: Nikon Photomic FTn with with 50mm *f*1.4 lens.

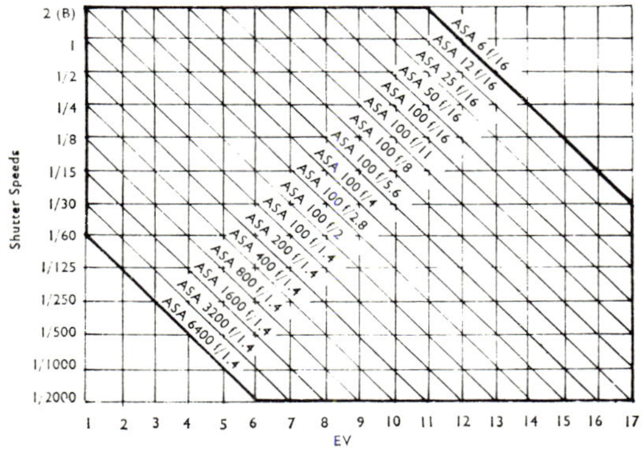

Exposure Coupling Range: Nikon F2 and F2A Photomic with 50mm *f*1.4 lens.

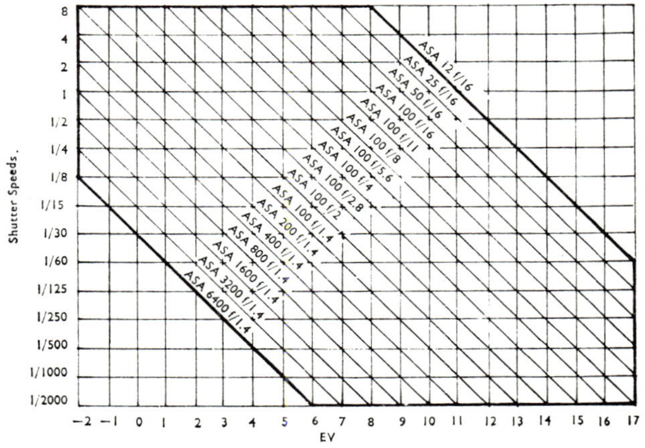

Exposure Coupling Range: Nikon F2S, F2Sb and F2AS Photomic with 50mm *f*1.4 lens.

FLASH SYNCHRONISATION ○ = synchronised ● = cannot be used

NIKON F

Select the colour of the synchro-selector marking that matches the corresponding coloured numbers on the shutter-speed dial. FX is electronic flash.

	1/1000	1/500	1/250	1/125	1/60	1/30	1/15	1/8	1/4	1/2	1	B
Electronic	–	–	–	–	FX	FX	FX	FX	FX	FX	FX	FX
FP	G	G	G	G	R	○F	○F	○F	○F	○F	○F	○F
M	–	–	–	G	R	○F	○F	○F	○F	○F	○F	○F
MF	–	–	–	–	–	○F	○F	○F	○F	○F	○F	○F

NIKON F2, F2S, F2Sb, F2A, F2AS

All F2 models are designed to synchronise with various types of flashbulbs at almost all shutter speeds and with electronic flash at speeds up to 1/80.

	1/2000	1/1000	1/500	1/250	1/125	X(1/80)	1/60	1/30	1/15	1/8	1/4	1/2	1
Electronic	●	●	●	●	●	○	○	○	○	○	○	○	○
FP	○	○	○	○	○	●	●	○	○	○	○	○	○
M	●	●	●	●	○	●	●	○	○	○	○	○	○
MF	●	●	●	●	●	●	●	○	○	○	○	○	○

NIKON FE & FM

The FM is designed to synchronise with electronic flash at speeds to 1/125 second. However, note that no flashbulbs can be used at speeds over 1/30 second.

	1/1000	1/500	1/250	1/125	1/60	1/30	1/15	1/8	1/4	1/2	1	B
Electronic	●	●	●	○	○	○	○	○	○	○	○	○
Flashbulb	●	●	●	●	●	○	○	○	○	○	○	○

NIKON FM2

The FM2 is primarily intended for electronic flash at all speeds up to 1/125 and X200 (1/200) second.

	1/4000	1/2000	1/1000	1/500	1/250	X200	1/125	1/60	1/30	1/15	1/8	1/4	1/2	1	B
Electronic	○	○	○	○	○	●	●	●	●	●	●	●	●	●	●
Flashbulb	○	○	○	○	○	○	○	○	●	●	●	●	●	●	●

NIKON F3

This camera is designed primarily to be used with electronic flash to which it can be synchronised at all speeds up to X which is 1/80 second. However, it can be used with flashbulbs as well as speeds up to and including 1/30 second.

	1/2000	1/1000	1/500	1/250	1/125	X(1/80)	1/60	1/30	1/15	1/8	1/4	1/2	1	2	4	8	B
Electronic	●	●	●	●	●	○	○	○	○	○	○	○	○	○	○	○	○
Flashbulb	●	●	●	●	●	●	●	○	○	○	○	○	○	○	○	○	○

NIKON FG, EM

Primarily intended for electronic flash, at 1/90 second. Set either to M90 or use 'dedicated' flash. FG can be used also at slower manual settings.

	1/1000	1/500	1/250	1/125	1/90	1/60	1/30	1/15	1/8	1/4	1/2	1	B
Electronic	●	●	●	●	○	○	○	○	○	○	○	○	○
Flashbulb	●	●	●	●	●	●	○	○	○	○	○	○	○

NIKKORMAT FTN

The 'M' terminal is for use with flashbulbs types, M, FP and MF. The 'X' terminal accepts electronic flash having a standard PC synchro cord.

	1/1000	1/500	1/250	1/125	1/60	1/30	1/15	1/8	1/4	1/2	1	B
Electronic	●	●	●	○	○	○	○	○	○	○	○	○
FP	○	○	○	○	○	○	○	○	○	○	○	○
M	○	○	○	○	○	○	○	○	○	○	○	○
MF	●	●	●	●	○	○	○	○	○	○	○	○

NIKON EL2, NIKKORMATS FT2, FT3

These cameras feature an accessory shoe with built-in hot-shoe contact and automatic MX switch-over via shutter-speed selection.

	1/1000	1/500	1/250	1/125	1/60	1/30	1/15	1/8	1/4	1/2	1	B
Electronic	●	●	●	○	○	○	○	○	○	○	○	○
FP	○	○	○	●	●	○	○	○	○	○	○	○
M	○	○	○	●	●	○	○	○	○	○	○	○
MF	●	●	●	●	●	○	○	○	○	○	○	○

NIKKORMAT EL & ELW

To set the camera for flashbulb, lift up the milled synch selector ring around the shutter-speed dial and turn it until the bulb symbol appears in the selector window. For speedlight, follow the same procedure until the lightning-bolt symbol appears.

	1/1000	1/500	1/250	1/125	1/60	1/30	1/15	1/8	1/4	1/2	1	2	4	B
Electronic	●	●	●	○	○	○	○	○	○	○	○	○	○	○
Flashbulb	○	○	○	○	○	○	○	○	○	○	○	○	○	○

Lens	Screen	A/L	B	C	D	E	G1	G2	G3	G4	H1	H2	H3	H4	J	K/P	M	R
Fisheye	6mm f2.8	A	A	B	A	A	A	A			A	A			A	A		D
	8mm f/2.8	A	A	B	A	A	A	A			A	A	A		A	A		D
	16mm f/3.5	A	A			A	A				A				A	A		A
Wideangle	15mm f/5.6	B	A			A		C				A			A	B		A
	20mm f/3.5	A	A			A	A				A				A	A		A
	24mm f/2.8	A	A			A		A			A	A			A	A		D
	28mm f/3.5	A	A			A	A				A				A	A		A
	28mm f/2	A	A			A	A	A			B	A			A	A		D
	35mm f/2.8	A	A			A	A				A	B			A	A		D
	35mm f/2	A	A			A	C	A			B	A			A	A		D
	35mm f/1.4	A	A			A		A			B	A			A	A		D
Normal	50mm f/2	A	A			A	A	A			A	A			A	A		D
	50mm f/1.4	A	A			A		A				A			A	A		D
	55mm f/1.2	A	A			A		A				A			A	A		D
Telephoto	85mm f/1.8	A	A			A		A			B	A			A	A		D
	105mm f/2.5	A	A			A		A			B	A			A	A		D
	135mm f/3.5	A	A	C	C	A		A				A			A	A		A
	135mm f/2.8	A	A	C	C	A		A	C			A			A	A		D
	180mm f/2.8	A	A	C	C	A			A			C	C	C	A	A		D
	200mm f/4	A	A	C	C	A		A				A			A	A		A
	300mm f/4.5	A	A	C	C	A			A			C	A	C	A	A		A
	400mm f/5.6	B	A	C	C	A			A	C			A	C	A	B		A
	400mm f/4.5	A	A	C	C	A			A	C			A	C	A	A		A
	600mm f/5.6	B	A	B	A	A			A	A			C	A	A	B		A
	800mm f/8	B	A	B	A	A			A	A			C	A	B	B		B
	1200mm f/11	B	A	B	A	A				C			C	A	B	B		B
Zoom	43~86mm f/3.5	A	A			A		C				A			A	A		A
	50~300mm f/4.5	A	A			A			A	A			C	A	A	A		A
	80~200mm f/4.5	A	A			A			C			A	A		A	A		A
	200~600mm f/9.5	B	A	B	A	A			C	A			C	A	B	B		B
GN	45mm f/2.8	A	A			A	A				A				A	A		D
Micro-P	55mm f/3.5	B	A			A		C				C			B	B		B
PC	35mm f/2.8	B	A			A									B	B		D
Bellows	105mm f/4	B	A	C	A	A			C					C	B	B	A	B
Medical	200mm f/5.6	B	A			A						A	C		B	B		B
Reflex Telephoto	500mm f/8	B	A	C	C	A									B	B		B
	1000mm f/11	B	A	C	C	A							C	C	B	B		B
	2000mm f/11	B	A	B	A	A			C	A				A	B	B		B

A B C D

Focusing Screen Selector Chart

For best possible focusing and viewing results, the screen of your Nikon camera should be the proper one for the lens you are using. Often more than one screen is useable. Sometimes two screens can be used but one is preferable. There are some screen-lens combinations which should not be used at all.

A = Excellent.

B = Acceptable (the image is bright, edge to edge but the central rangefinder, microprism or cross hair area is dim. Focus on the surrounding matte area.

C = Acceptable (Slight darkening of corners and/or edges or moire pattern with microprisms affects the viewing image.)

D = Acceptable (But inadvisable with lenses having larger apertures than *f*2.8 because of possible inaccuracy of screen rangefinder.)

Blank spaces = Do not use these combinations.

Lens	Screen	A·L	B	C	D	E	G1	G2	G3	G4	H1	H2	H3	H4	J	K·P	M	R
Fisheye	6mm f/2.8			−1/2	−1/2													
	8mm f/2.8			−1/2	−1/2													
	16mm f/3.5						−1/2											
Wideangle	15mm f/5.6							−1-1/2				−1/2						
	20mm f/3.5						−1/2											
	24mm f/2.8										+1/2							
	28mm f/3.5						−1/2											
	28mm f/2						+1/2	+1/2			+1/2	+1/2						
	35mm f/2.8						−1/2											
	35mm f/2						+1/2				+1/2							
	35mm f/1.4							+1/2			+1/2	+1/2						
Normal	50mm f/2						+1/2	+1/2			+1/2	+1/2						
	50mm f/1.4							+1/2				+1/2						
	55mm f/1.2																	
Telephoto	85mm f/1.8							+1/2			+1/2	+1/2						
	105mm f/2.5										+1/2	+1/2						
	135mm f/2.8							−1										
	135mm f/3.5											+1/2						
	180mm f/2.8																	
	200mm f/4							−1-1/2				−1						
	300mm f/4.5								−1-1/2			−1-1/2	−1	−1-1/2				
	400mm f/5.6								(C)	(C)			(C)	(C)				
	400mm f/4.5	(B)	(B)	(B)	(B)	(B)			(C)	(C)			(C)	(C)	(B)	(B)		(B)
	600mm f/5.6	(B)	(B)	(B)	(B)	(B)			(C)	(C)			(C)	(C)	(B)	(B)		(B)
	800mm f/8	(B)	(B)	(B)	(B)	(B)			(C)	(C)			(C)	(C)	(B)	(B)		(B)
	1200mm f/11	(B)	(B)	(B)	(B)	(B)				(C)			(C)	(C)	(B)	(B)		(B)
Zoom	43 ~ 86mm f/3.5											−1/2						
	50 ~ 300mm f/4.5									(C)			−1-1/2	(C)				
	80 ~ 200mm f/4.5						−1/2					−1-1/2	−1/2					
	200 ~ 600mm f/9.5	(B)	(B)	(B)	(B)	(B)		−2	(C)	(C)			(C)	(C)	(B)	(B)		(B)
GN	45mm f/2.8							−1										
Micro-P	55mm f/3.5							(C)				(C)						
PC	35mm f/2.8	(B)	(B)			(B)									(B)	(B)		(B)
Bellows	105mm f/4	(B)	(B)	(B)	(B)	(B)			(C)					(C)	(B)	(B)	(C)	(B)
Medical	200mm f/5.6	(B)	(B)			(B)						(C)	(C)		(B)	(B)		(B)
Reflex Telephoto	500mm f/8	(B)	(B)	(B)	(B)	(B)									(B)	(B)		(B)
	1000mm f/11	(B)	(B)	(B)	(B)	(B)							(C)	(C)	(B)	(B)		(B)
	2000mm f/11	(B)	(B)	(B)	(B)	(B)			(C)	(C)				(C)	(B)	(B)		(B)

☐ A ▨ B ■ C

Exposure Corrections

Various focusing screen-lens combinations require exposure adjustments of the Photomic metering systems in order to provide accurate exposure meter readings for Nikon cameras. The table opposite, provides you with the amount of adjustment needed in full or partial f-stops. In addition the variation in the cross hatching or stipling within each box indicates how the exposure meter reading should be made:

A = Measure exposure by regular full aperture reading.

B = Measure exposure at shooting aperture.

C = Accurate metering cannot be accomplished through lens.

Blank spaces = Unuseable combinations.

Which Filter For Which Job

Use this chart to select the right filter with black-and-white panchromatic film.

Subject	If you want this effect	use this filter
clouds against clear blue sky or as a background	natural sky	medium yellow or light green
	darker than normal sky	dark yellow or orange
	very dark sky	red
	almost black	dark red
fabric—including draperies, upholstery, clothing, etc.	to darken	one of complementary color to the subject
	to lighten	one of the same color as the subject
flowers	lighten green foliage to make dark flowers stand out	light green
	lighten flowers to make them stand out against darker leaves	one as close as possible to the color of the flowers
glass objects, china, pottery, etc.	reduce unwanted reflections	polarizing
	darken to increase contrast and show up pattern, design, details, etc.	one of complementary color to the subject
landscapes	natural	medium yellow or light green
	increased contrast and haze reduction	dark yellow or orange
	greater contrast and haze reduction	red
marine scenes and subjects	natural rendition of water	medium yellow or light green
	darkened water	orange or dark yellow
outdoor portraits with sky showing	natural skin tones and natural sky	light green
polished surfaces—waxed floors, tiles, Formica, etc.	reduce reflections to show better detail	polarizing
portraiture	reduce contrast between blemishes and skin tones	medium yellow or dark yellow
	darken skin tones to emphasize tan or bring out rugged, masculine quality of male subject	light green
sand and snow, lighted by sun with blue sky	natural	medium yellow or light green
	increased contrast to emphasize texture	dark yellow, orange, or red
wood	emphasize grain of dark wood such as mahogany	red
	emphasize grain of yellowish woods such as maple, oak, walnut	dark yellow or orange
	emphasize grain of light, blond-finished woods	medium yellow

Index